The World's Armies

The World's ARMIES

General Editor **Chris Chant**

David & Charles   Newton Abbot   London

©Talos Publishing Ltd 1979
4 Chillingworth Road, London, N7 8QJ

British Library Cataloguing in Publication Data

The world's armies.
   1. Armies – Dictionaries
   355'.003   UA15

   ISBN 0–7153–7688–8

Typeset and printed in Great Britain
by Redwood Burn Limited, Trowbridge and Esher
for David & Charles (Publishers) Limited
Brunel House   Newton Abbot   Devon

Contents

Introduction

The World's Armies is intended as a manageable but nonetheless comprehensive guide to the armies of the world at the beginning of 1979, and it is hoped that periodic editions of the book will enable the information to be updated in the light of developments. Unfortunately, it is in the very nature of such works that they are inherently 'out-of-date', perhaps by only a few months, as continued procurement of new equipment, the phasing out of older equipment, and attrition in accidents and combat alter the situation. At the same time political and economic fluctuations alter the number of items on order (a case in point being Iran in the aftermath of the Shah's downfall at the beginning of 1979: the interim government of Mr Bakhtiar cut foreign orders considerably, and the current Islamic government, beset by internal problems with left-wing guerrillas, and determined to move out of the free West's sphere of interest, is likely to cut the remaining orders still further). More changes in army strengths have resulted from the clashes between Tanzania and Uganda, the struggle between the Ethiopians and their Eritrean separatists, the overrunning of Kampuchea by Vietnam, and the 'punitive' campaign launched by China against Vietnam. Of a lesser compass are the civil war in Chad and a number of other limited engagements. In general, however, the army strengths and equipment types are up-to-date as far as the beginning of 1979.

For a variety of reasons it has been impossible to cover every type of weapon currently operated by the world's armies, and an editorial selection of the types covered has therefore been inevitable. The types covered, accordingly, are basically the following:

    (i) armoured fighting vehicles (main battle tanks, light tanks, scout vehicles, armoured personnel carriers, mechanised infantry combat vehicles and self-propelled artillery)
    (ii) battlefield support artillery missiles
    (iii) anti-tank/assault missiles
    (iv) mobile AA missile systems
    (v) mobile AA gun systems
    (vi) portable AA missiles
    (vii) artillery (conventional and AA)
    (viii) portable anti-tank weapons
    (ix) mortars
    (x) flame-throwers
    (xi) machine-guns and cannon
    (xii) rifles and carbines

Large numbers of aircraft and helicopters are operated by modern armies, and although the armies' air resources are listed in the tabular sections, the details of the aircraft and helicopters themselves will be found in the companion volume

The World's Air Forces, in which reference to the index will allow the reader quickly to find the right entry in the technical section.

The volume is arranged alphabetically by country, and consists of two main 'strands':

(a) the tabular sections detailing the numbers and equipment operated by each country's army, together with an organisational break-down of the more important armies
(b) the technical sections giving details of the armies' equipment

A third, occasional strand is provided by brief examinations of the nature and capabilities of the world's most important (not necessarily largest) armies.

Rather than locate the armies' equipment by country of origin, which would have led to a considerable imbalance in the book, most equipment being produced by only a few countries, it has been decided to arrange the equipment by type within the sections dealing with one of the user countries: for example, though the M41 tank is of American design and manufacture, it is listed under Argentina. The reader may find each type that has an entry by recourse to the index, which gives the location of all entries. A further rationale for this editorial decision is that in many instances the equipment is no longer used by the country of origin or was produced solely for the export market.

Each technical entry has been designed to provide an easily assimilable, but relatively complete, quantity of data, to allow the reader to assess the capabilities of the weapon, together with brief notes intended to elucidate the weapon's history, design and variants. Where there are variants, the notes indicate to which of the variants the technical specification applies, unless the variants differ so little that the same basic technical specification is applicable to all.

Most of the sub-headings for the various categories of weapon are self-explanatory, but some may need a little additional explanation. For the AFVs, for example:

(i) *Weights*: Empty refers to the vehicle without fuel, ammunition, crew and other movable equipment, while *Weight*: Loaded refers to the vehicle with all these items
(ii) *Performance*: vertical obstacle refers to the vehicle's ability to cross a vertical 'step', trench refers to the ability to cross a gap and wading refers to the vehicle's ability to move through water barriers (with and without preparation)
(iii) *Armament* – a coaxial machine-gun is one aligned to fire along the same axis as the main armament.

For missiles and rockets:

(i) *Booster* indicates the method by which the missile or rocket is accelerated from stationary towards cruising speed
(ii) *Sustainer* indicates the method by which the missile is accelerated to maximum speed.

For artillery:

(i) *Barrel length* is normally measured in terms of the number of calibres (bore diameters) long it is.

All measurements are in Imperial units, with metric equivalents, calculated at the following conversion factors:

inch to millimetre: multiply by 25.4
inch to centimetre: multiply by 2.54
foot to metre: divide by 3.2808
mile (and mph) to kilometre (and kph): multiply by 1.6094
inch² to centimetre²: multiply by 6.4516
lb/in² to kg/cm²: divide by 14.22
pound to kilogramme: divide by 2.2046
ton to tonne: multiply by 1.016

Where the compiler of the technical sections has been unable to find an exact figure, or where the sources conflict, he has left the sub-heading blank, so that the reader may fill in the space for himself should he be able to find a figure which satisfies him. In this context, the publishers would be most grateful for any comments on the book and for any further information readers may be able to supply.

Afghanistan

100,000 men and 150,000 reservists.

3 armd divs.
10 inf divs.
3 mountain inf bdes.
1 arty bde, 3 arty regts.
2 cdo regts.
200 T-34, 500 T-54/-55, T-62 med, 40 PT-76 lt tks; BMP MICV; 400 BTR-40/-50/-60/-152 APC; 900 76mm, 10mm, 122mm and 152mm guns/how; 100 120mm mor; 50 132mm multiple RL; 350 37mm, 85mm, 100mm towed, 20 ZSU-23-4 SP AA guns; 'Sagger', 'Snapper' ATGW; SA-7 SAM.

T-34/85

Type: medium tank
Crew: five
Weights: Empty
　　Loaded 70,547 lb (32,000 kg)
Dimensions: Length (gun forward) 24 ft 7 in (7.5 m); (hull) 19 ft 8½ in (6.0 m)
　　Width 9 ft 7 in (2.92 m)
　　Height 7 ft 10 in (2.39 m)
Ground pressure: 11.2 lb/in² (0.8 kg/cm²)
Performance: road speed 31 mph (50 kph); range 186 miles (300 km); vertical obstacle 33 in (79.0 cm); trench 8 ft 2 in (2.49 m); gradient 30°; ground clearance 1 ft 4 in (40.6 cm); wading 4 ft 4 in (1.32 m) without preparation
Engine: one 500-hp V-2-34 inline diesel engine
Armament: one 85-mm Model 1944 ZIS S53 L/51 gun with 55 rounds, plus one

7.62-mm DT machine-gun co-axial with the main armament, and one 7.62-mm DT machine-gun in the bow. Some 2,394 rounds of 7.62-mm ammunition are carried
Armour: $\frac{7}{10}$ in (18 mm) minimum; 3 in (75 mm) maximum
Used also by: Albania, Angola, Bulgaria, China, Cuba, Cyprus, East Germany, Ethiopia, Guinea-Bissau, Iraq, Mali, Mongolia, Mozambique, North Korea, North Yemen, Poland, Romania, Somali Republic, South Yemen, Syria, Uganda, Vietnam, Yugoslavia
Notes: Derived in 1943 from the earlier T-34/76B, the T-34/85 differed from its predecessor principally in having as main armament a high-velocity 85-mm gun. The type entered service with the Russian Army in December 1943, and was built up into the 1950s. Many are still in service with smaller countries today.

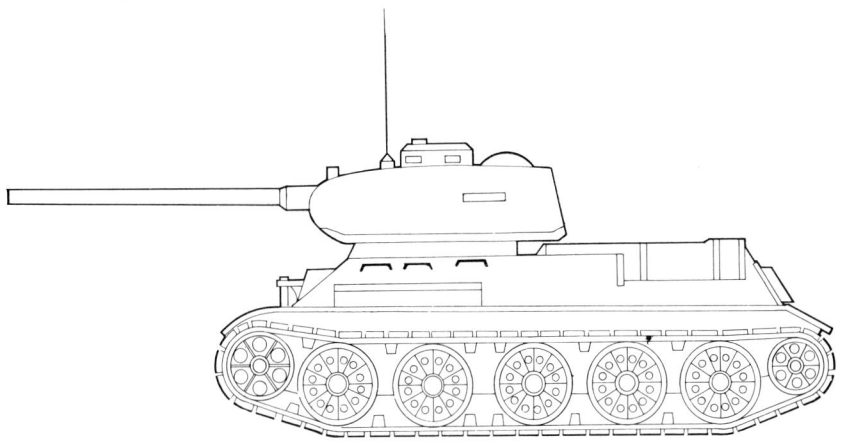

SPG-82 launcher

Type: anti-tank rocket launcher
Calibre: 82 mm
Barrel length:
Muzzle velocity:
Ranges: Maximum 301 yards (275 m)
　　Minimum
Elevation:
Traverse:
Rate of fire:

Weights: For travel 83.8 lb (38 kg)
　　In firing position 94.8 lb (43 kg)
Dimensions: Length 7 ft 0⅔ in (2.15 m)
　　Width
　　Height
Ammunition: HE or HEAT warhead
Crew: two
Used also by: Syria
Notes: The Russian SPG-82 was introduced before the Korean War, but is now mostly obsolete. The missile weighs 11 lb (5 kg), and can penetrate 9.06 in (230 mm) of armour.

Albania

30,000 (20,000 conscripts) and 60,000 reservists.

1 tk bde.
8 inf bdes.
2 tk bns.
1 arty regt.
2 AD regts.
8 lt coastal arty bns.
70 T-34, 15 T-54, 15 T-59 med tks; BRDM-1 scout cars; 20 BA-64, BTR-40/-50/-152, K-63 APC; 76mm, 85mm, 122mm, 152mm guns/how; SU-76, SU-100 SP guns; 120mm mor; 107mm RCL; 45mm, 57mm, 85mm ATK guns; 37mm, 57mm, 85mm, 100mm AA guns; SA-2 SAM.

T-54/T-55

Type: main battle tank
Crew: four
Weights: Empty
　　Loaded 80,468 lb (36,500 kg)
Dimensions: Length (overall) 29 ft 7 in (9.02 m); (hull) 21 ft 2 in (6.45 m)
　　Width 10 ft 8¾ in (3.27 m)
　　Height (to top of cupola) 7 ft 10½ in (2.4 m)
Ground pressure: 11.38 lb/in² (0.8 kg/cm²)
Performance: road speed 30 mph (48 kph); range 391 miles (630 km) using optional long-range tanks on rear of hull; vertical obstacle 31½ in (80.0cm); trench 9 ft (2.84 m); gradient 60%; ground clearance 17 in (43.0 cm); wading 4 ft 11 in (1.5 m) without preparation, and 17 ft 8⅝ in (5.4 m) with the aid of a schnorkel

Engine: (T-54) one 520-hp V-2-54 inline diesel engine; (T-55) one 580-hp V-2-55 inline diesel engine
Armament: one 100-mm D-10 gun with 34 (T-54) or 43 (T-55) rounds of AP, APC, HE, HEAT and HVAP ammunition, plus one 7.62-mm SGMT machine-gun co-axial with the main armament, one 7.62-mm SGMT machine-gun in the hull bow, and one 12.7-mm DShK AA machine-gun on the turret roof. Some 3,000 rounds of 7.62-mm and 500 of 12.7-mm ammunition are carried
Armour: 6¾ in (170 mm) maximum
Used also by: Albania, Afghanistan, Algeria, Angola, Bangladesh, Bulgaria, Cuba, Czechoslovakia, East Germany, Egypt, Ethiopia, Finland, Guinea-Bissau, Hungary, India, Iraq, Israel, Libya, Mongolia, Moroc-

co, Mozambique, North Korea, North Yemen, Pakistan, Peru, Poland, Romania, Somali Republic, South Yemen, Sudan, Syria, Uganda, USSR, Vietnam, Yugoslavia, Zambia

Notes: The T-54/T-55 family of MBTs has been produced in greater numbers than any other AFV, and entered service in the late 1940s. Although a relatively unsophisticated design, the type has a good gun, first-class cross-country performance and long range. Generally, the finish of the vehicles is poor, and the fighting compartment cramped enough to reduce the crew's efficiency seriously in any prolonged action. Tactically, the T-54/T-55 is hampered by the fact that its gun can be depressed only to −4°, making it all but impossible for the vehicle to adopt a hull-down defensive position. Night vision equipment has been introduced, and an NBC system can be fitted. There are many versions and derivatives of the basic type:

1. T-54 with no muzzle bore evacuator, T-44 road wheel pattern and a bulge at the rear of the turret
2. T-54A, introduced in 1956, with a hemispherical turret, a bore evacuator, the main armament stabilised in elevation, and new road wheels
3. T-54B, introduced in 1959, with improved sights and rangefinder
4. T-55, without an AA machine-gun on the loader's hatch, a more powerful engine, and improved schnorkel capability
5. T-54T armoured recovery vehicle, equipped with a powerful winch and a wide-diameter schnorkel so that the crew can climb out of the tank during river crossings
6. T-54BTU (*Buldosernoje Tankowoje Ustrojstwo*), a standard T-54 fitted with a dozer blade to dig defensive positions and prepare river crossing points
7. T-54MTU (*Mostoukkladtschik Tankowoje Ustrojstwo*) armoured vehicle-launched bridge, capable of bridging a 39 ft 4½ in (12 m) gap with a single-span structure capable of taking 50-ton vehicles
8. T-54 mine-roller vehicle
9. T-54 engineer vehicle
10. ZSU-57-2 (*Zenitny Samokhodnaya Ustanovka*) self-propelled twin 57-mm AA mounting.

The guns used in the various models are the D-10T in the T-54, the D-10TG in the T-54A, the D-10T2S in the T-54B and the D-10T2S again in the T-55. Ranging is optical, and the maximum rate of fire is some five rounds per minute.

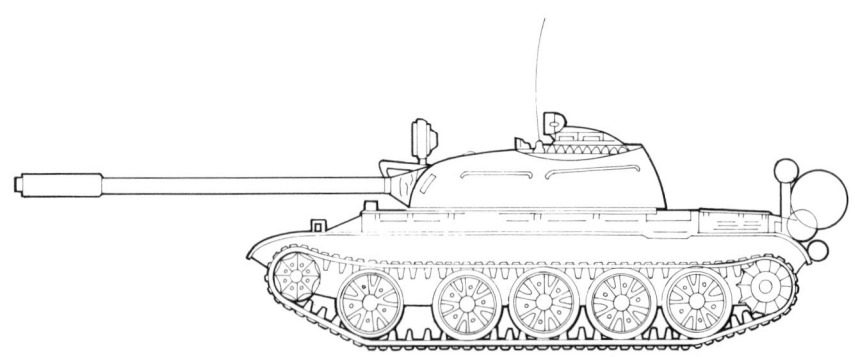

K-63

Type: armoured personnel carrier
Crew: one, plus nine infantrymen
Weights: Empty
          Loaded 22,046 lb (10,000 kg)
Dimensions: Length
            Width
            Height
Ground pressure:
Performance:
Engine:
Armament: one 12.7-mm machine-gun
Armour:
Used also by: China, Tanzania
Notes: The K-63 is an armoured personnel carrier of Chinese design and manufacture,

possibly based on the hull of the T-60 light tank, itself a development of the Russian PT-76 light tank. The running gear of the K-63 resembles that of the T-60.

SU-76

Type: self-propelled gun
Crew: four
Weights: Empty
Loaded 24,692 lb (11.200 kg)
Dimensions: Length (including gun) 16 ft 5 in
(5.0 m)
Width 8 ft 11 in (2.74 m)
Height 7 ft 3 in (2.2 m)

Ground pressure: 8.09 lb/in² (0.57 kg/cm²)
Performance: road speed 28 mph (44 kph);
range 166 miles (265 km); vertical obstacle 23¾ in (60.0 cm); trench 6 ft 7 in (2.0
m); gradient 47%; ground clearance 12½ in
(31.75 cm); wading 35 in (90.0 cm)
Engine: two 85-hp GAZ-202 inline petrol engines

Armament: one 76.2-mm Model 1942 (215-
3) L/41.5 gun with 62 rounds of AP and HE
Armour: ⅖ in (10 mm) minimum; 1⅜ in (35
mm) maximum
Used also by: China, Vietnam, Yugoslavia
Notes: The SU-76 was introduced into Red
Army service in 1943, and combines the
high-velocity Model 215-3 anti-tank gun
and the chassis of the T70 light tank.

M-1931/1937 (A-19) gun

Type: field gun
Calibre: 122 mm
Barrel length: 46.27 cal
Muzzle velocity: 2,625 ft (800 m) per second
Ranges: Maximum 22,747 yards (20,800 m)
with HE; 984 yards (900 m) with
APHE
Minimum
Elevation: −2° to +65°
Traverse: 58° total
Rate of fire: five to six rounds per minute
Weights: For travel 17,432 lb (7,907 kg)
In firing position 15,690 lb (7,117
kg)
Dimensions: Length 25 ft 9¾ in (7.87 m)
Width 8 ft 0¾ in (2.46 m)
Height 7 ft 5⅝ in (2.27 m)
Ammunition: APHE and HE
Crew: eight
Used also by: Algeria, Bulgaria, China, Cuba,
Czechoslovakia, East Germany, Egypt,
Guinea-Bissau, Hungary, Kampuchea, North
Korea, North Yemen, Poland, Romania,
Somali Republic, Syria, Tanzania, Yugoslavia
Notes: The HE round weighs 56.2 lb (25.5
kg), and the slightly lighter APHE round will
penetrate 7½ in (190 mm) of armour at
1,094 yards (1,000 m).

M-1942 gun

Type: anti-tank gun
Calibre: 45 mm
Barrel length: 68.6 cal
Muzzle velocity: 3,510 ft (1,070 m) per
second with HVAP
Ranges: Maximum 4,812 yards (4,400 m)
with HE
Minimum
Elevation: −8° to +25°
Traverse: 30° left and right
Rate of fire: 25 rounds per minute
Weights: For travel
In firing position 1,257 lb (570 kg)
Dimensions: Length 16 ft (4.885 m)
Width 5 ft 4⅓ in (1.63 m)
Height 3 ft 11¼ in (1.2 m)
Ammunition: APHE, HE and HVAP
Crew: six
Used also by: North Korea
Notes: The M-1942 gun is similar to the earlier M-1937, but is longer, and has disc
wheels rather than spoked units. The
weapon is all but obsolete, and the 2-lb
(0.9-kg) HVAP round will penetrate only
2.6 in (66 mm) of armour at 547 yards
(500 m).

M-1938/1939 gun

Type: anti-aircraft gun
Calibre: 37 mm
Barrel length: 69.6 cal
Muzzle velocity: 3,150 ft (960 m) per second
with HVAP
Ranges: Maximum (horizontal) 8,749 yards
(8,000 m); (vertical) 19,685 ft (6,000
m)
Minimum
Elevation: −5° to +85°
Traverse: 360°
Rate of fire: 80 rounds per minute
Weights: For travel
In firing position 4,409 lb (2,000
kg)
Dimensions: Length 20 ft 2½ in (6.16 m)
Width 5 ft 7⅓ in (1.71 m)
Height 8 ft 10¼ in (2.7 m)
Ammunition: AP, HE and HVAP
Crew: eight
Used also by: Bulgaria, China, Cuba, East
Germany, Egypt, Mongolia, North Korea,
North Yemen, Romania, Syria, Tanzania,
Vietnam and Yugoslavia
Notes: The M-1938 was closely modelled on
the Swedish Bofors gun, and the M-1939
has only slight alterations from the M-
1938. Feed is by five-round clips, and the
effective ceiling is 4,593 ft (1,400 m). The
AP round will penetrate 1.8 in (46 mm) of
armour at 547 yards (500 m).

Algeria

70,000 men and up to 100,000
reservists.

1 armd bde.
4 mot inf bdes.
3 indep tk bns.
50 indep inf bns.
1 para bn.
12 coys desert troops.
10 indep arty bns.
7 AA arty bns.
3 engr bns.
350 T-54/-55/-62 med tks; AML armd
cars; 440 BTR-40/-50/-60/-152,
Walid APC; 600 85mm, 122mm,
152mm guns and how; 85 SU-100,
JSU-122/-152 SP guns; 80 120mm,
160mm mor; 20 140mm, 30 240mm
RL; 'Sagger' ATGW; 57mm, 85mm,
100mm AA guns.

Walid

Type: armoured personnel carrier
Crew: two, plus possibly eight infantrymen
Weights: Empty
Loaded 13,000 lb (5,900 kg)
Dimensions: Length
Width
Height
Ground pressure:
Performance:
Engine: Deutz diesel
Armament: possibly one 12.7-mm machine-gun
Armour:
Used also by: Egypt, North Yemen, Palestinian Liberation Army and South Yemen
Notes: Little is known of the *Walid* APC,
which is a 4 × 4 vehicle designed and built
in Egypt.

JSU-122/155

Type: self-propelled assault gun
Crew: five
Weights: Empty
Loaded between 90,830 and
92,152 lb (41,200 and 41,800 kg)
depending on the gun fitted
Dimensions: Length (overall) between 29 ft 4
in (8.93 m) and 36 ft 10 in
(11.23 m) depending on gun
Width 11 ft (3.36 m)
Height 8 ft 10 in (2.68 m)
Ground pressure: between 11.6 lb/in² (0.82
kg/cm²) and 11.8 lb/in² (0.83 kg/cm²)
Performance: road speed 23 mph (37 kph);
range 150 miles (240 km); vertical obstacle 3 ft 5 in (1.03 m); trench 8 ft 10 in (2.7
m); gradient 36°; ground clearance 17¾ in
(45.0 cm); wading 4 ft 3 in (1.3 m) without
preparation
Engine: one 520-hp Model V2 JS inline
diesel engine
Armament: one 122-mm D-25S or A-19S
gun with 40 rounds, or one 152-mm
M1937/43 or ML-20S gun/howitzer with
20 rounds, plus one 12.7-mm DShK-38
machine-gun with 450 (JSU-122) or 1,000
rounds (JSU-152)

Armour: ⅘ in (20 mm) minimum; 4⅓ in (110 mm) maximum

Used also by: China, Iraq, Syria, Vietnam

Notes: The JSU-122 and 152 could become each other by the change of main armament, and entered Russian service in 1943 as heavy assault and anti-tank weapons. The gun is mounted in an ungainly and vulnerable high sided barbette built up on the chassis of the KV-1S heavy tank. The JSU-122BM and JSU-152BM, introduced in 1944, use the more powerful BL series of guns.

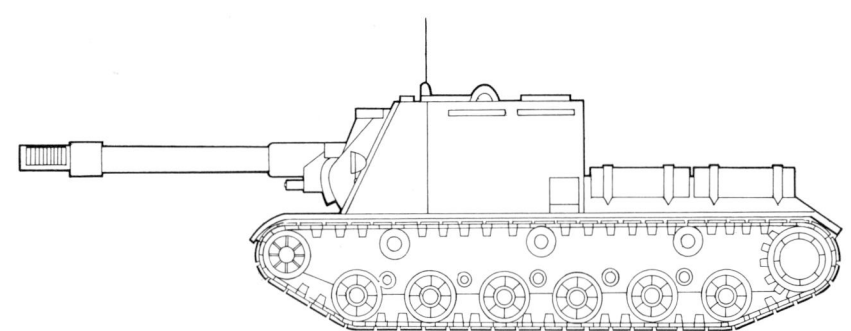

Angola

30,000 men.

1 armd regt.
9 inf regts.
1 cdo regt.
1 AD regt.
85 T-34, 75 T-54 med, some 50 PT-76 lt tks; 200 BRDM-2 armd cars; 150 BTR-50/-60/-152, OT-62 APC; 120 guns, incl 76mm, 105mm, 122mm; 500 82mm, 120mm mor; 110 BM21 122mm multiple RL; ZIS-3 76mm ATK guns; 75mm, 82mm, 107mm RCL; 'Sagger' ATGW; 23mm, 37mm AA guns; SA-7 SAM.*

*Eqpt totals uncertain. Some 23–25,000 Cubans serve with the Angolan forces and operate ac and hy eqpt. Some Portuguese also serve; several hundred Soviet advisers and technicians are reported in Angola.

BTR-50

Type: armoured personnel carrier
Crew: three, plus up to 12 infantrymen
Weights: Empty
Loaded 30,864 lb (14,000 kg)
Dimensions: Length 22 ft 7⅔ in (6.9 m)
Width 10 ft 5⅛ in (3.18 m)
Height 6 ft 6¾ in (2.0 m)
Ground pressure: 8.96 lb/in² (0.63 kg/cm²)
Performance: road speed 27 mph (43 kph); water speed 6.2 mph (10 kph); range 155 miles (250 km); vertical obstacle 41¾ in (1.06 m); trench 9 ft 2¼ in (2.8 m); gradient 30°; ground clearance 13¾ in (35.0 cm); the BTR-50 is fully amphibious, being driven in the water by waterjets
Engine: one 240-bhp inline diesel engine
Armament: up to four machine-guns of 7.62-, 12.7- or 14.5-mm calibre
Armour: ⅖ in (10 mm) maximum
Used also by: Afghanistan, Albania, Algeria, Cyprus, East Germany, Egypt, Finland, India, Iran, Iraq, Israel, Romania, Somali Republic, Sudan, Syria, USSR, Vietnam, Yugoslavia

Notes: The BTR-50 is the armoured personnel carrier member of the AFV family centred on the PT-76 light tank. There are several models:
1. BTR-50P initial production variant, which is open topped (it can carry a 57-, 76- or 85-mm anti-tank gun) and was introduced in 1955
2. BTR-50PK, which has an armoured roof and appeared in 1960
3. BTR-50PA with a 14.5-mm KVPT or ZPU-1 machine-gun
4. BTR-50PU command vehicle with extra radio equipment and special navigation facilities, which appeared in 1962
5. BTR-50 (ECM) electronic counter-measures vehicle.
The BTR-50P has no night vision equipment or NBC system, but all later vehicles have had these added. The Czech OT-62 (TOPAS) is derived from the BTR-50 series.

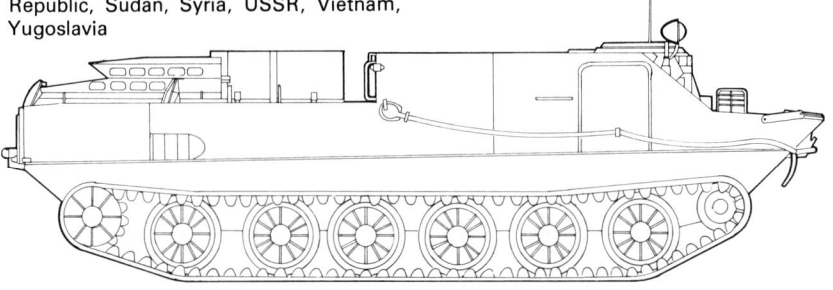

MG34 machine-gun

Type: general-purpose machine-gun
Calibre: 7.92 mm
System of operation: short recoil
Muzzle velocity: 2,480 ft (755 m) per second
Range: 1,968 yards (1,800 m) with a tripod; 601 yards (550 m) with a bipod
Rate of fire: 900 rounds per minute (cyclic)
Cooling system: air
Feed system: 50-round metal-link belt, or 75-round saddle drum magazine
Dimensions: Barrel length 24.76 in (629 mm)

Overall length 48.2 in (1.224 mm)
Width
Height
Weights: 26.7 lb (11.5 kg) with bipod; 42.3 lb (19.2 kg) for tripod
Sights: blade (fore) and leaf notch (rear)
Ammunition: 7.92 mm × 19
Used also by: Vietnam and possibly others
Notes: The MG34 was the main machine-gun of the German Army at the beginning of World War II, and marked a highpoint in the design of general-purpose machine-guns, being very versatile, reliable and with a high rate of fire.

MG42 machine-gun

Type: general-purpose machine-gun
Calibre: 7.92 mm
System of operation: gas-assisted recoil
Muzzle velocity: 2,480 ft (755 m) per second
Range: effective 875 yards (800 m) with a bipod

Rate of fire: 1,100 to 1,200 rounds per minute (cyclic)
Cooling system. air
Feed system: 50-round metal-link belt
Dimensions: Barrel length 21 in (533 mm)
Overall length 48.23 in (1,230 mm)
Width
Height

Weights: 25.6 lb (11.6 kg) with bipod; 42.3 lb (19.2 kg) for tripod
Sights: folding blade (front) and V notch with tangent (rear)
Ammunition: 7.92 mm × 19
Used also by: various African, Asian and South American countries
Notes: The MG42 is a classic general-purpose machine-gun, and marked the general arrival of pressings and stampings in machine-guns to replace many of the costly machined parts used in earlier guns. The MG42 was in its time notable for its high rate of fire, reliability and accuracy.

Argentina

80,000 men and 250,000 reservists (200,000 National Guard; 50,000 Territorial Guard).

2 armd bdes.
4 inf bdes.
2 mountain bdes.
1 airmobile bde.
5 AD bns.
1 aviation bn.
100 M-4 Sherman med, 80 AMX-13 lt tks; Shorland armd cars; 140 M-113, 60 MOWAG, AMX-VCI, M-3 APC; 155mm towed, M-7 155mm SP guns; 105mm (incl pack), 155mm towed, 24 Mk F3 155mm SP how; 81mm, 120mm mor; 75mm, 90mm, 105mm RCL; SS-11/-12, Bantam, Cobra ATGW; 30mm, 35mm, 40mm, 90mm AA guns; Tigercat SAM; 5 Turbo Commander 690A, 2 DHC-6, 3 G-222, 4 Swearingen Metro IIIA, 4 Queen Air, 1 Sabreliner, 5 Cessna 207, 15 Cessna 182, 20 U-17A/B, 5 T-41 ac; 7 Bell 206, 4 FH-1100, 20 UH-IH, 4 Bell 47G, 2 Bell 212 helicopters (5 Turbo Commander ac; 3 CH-47C helicopters on order.)

Para-Military Forces: 42,000. Gendarmerie: 11,000; M-113 APC, 20 lt ac, 10 helicopters under Army command, mainly for frontier duties. National Maritime Prefecture: 9,000. Policía Federal: 22,000; APC, 4 BO-105 helicopters.

TAM

Type: medium tank
Crew: four
Weights: Empty
Loaded 65,036 lb (29,500 kg)
Dimensions: Length (including gun) 26 ft 7¾ in (8.12 m); (hull) 21 ft 6¾ in (6.57 m)
Width 10 ft 2⅘ in (3.12 m)
Height 7 ft 10½ in (2.4 m)
Ground pressure: 11.23 lb/in² (0.79 kg/cm²)
Performance: road speed 47 mph (75 kph); range 373 miles (600 km), or 621 miles (1,000 km) with auxiliary fuel tanks; vertical obstacle 39⅖ in (1.0 m); trench 8 ft 2½ in (2.5 m); gradient 60%, ground clearance 17⅓ in (44.0 cm); wading 4 ft 11 in (1.5 m)

without preparation, and 13 ft 1½ in (4.0 m) with a schnorkel
Engine: one 740-hp inline diesel engine
Armament: one 105-mm L7A3 gun with 50 rounds, plus one 7.62-mm machine-gun co-axial with the main armament, and one 7.62-mm machine-gun for AA defence on the turret roof
Armour: classified
Used only by: Argentina
Notes: The TAM has been developed by Thyssen Henschel to an Argentinian requirement, and is based on the chassis of the *Marder* MICV, with a fully powered turret at the rear. The TAM is designed to co-operate with the VCI version of the *Marder* MICV as the armoured element of the Argentinian Army.

AMX-VCI

Type: armoured personnel carrier
Crew: one, plus up to 12 infantrymen
Weights: Empty
Loaded 30,865 lb (14,000 kg)
Dimensions: Length 18 ft 2 in (5.54 m)
Width 8 ft 3 in (2.51 m)
Height 7 ft 7 in (2.32 m)

Ground pressure: 9.9 lb/in² (0.7 kg/cm²)
Performance: road speed 40 mph (65 kph); range 249 miles (400 km); vertical obstacle 25⅜ in (65.0 cm); trench 5 ft 3 in (1.6 m); gradient 60%
Engine: one 250-hp SOFAM 8 GXb inline petrol engine
Armament: one 7.5- or 12.7-mm machine-gun

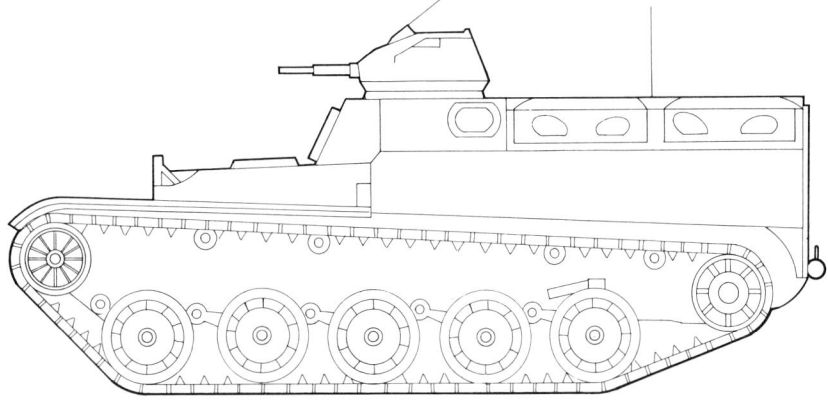

Armour: $\frac{2}{5}$ in (10 mm) minimum; $1\frac{1}{5}$ in (30 mm) maximum

Used also by: Belgium, Ecuador, France, Netherlands, United Arab Emirates, Venezuela

Notes: The *Véhicule de Combat d'Infanterie* (VCI) was developed from the chassis of the AMX-13, and adopted in French service in 1956. Vehicles in French service have been retrofitted with an NBC system and night vision equipment, but the type is hampered tactically by the fact that it is not amphibious. There are many variants:

1. 81-mm mortar carrier with a crew of six and 128 mortar bombs
2. 120-mm mortar carrier with a crew of five and 60 mortar bombs
3. battery command post to operate with self-propelled guns. This can also tow an ammunition trailer
4. command vehicle with extra radio equipment
5. ambulance vehicle with a crew of four and accommodation for three stretcher and four sitting patients
6. AMX-VCA support vehicle for the AMX-155 Mk F3 SP howitzer

7. AMX TOW anti-tank vehicles used by the Dutch Army
8. AMX *Entac*, with two launchers and 26 *Entac* anti-tank missiles
9. AMX *Véhicule de Combat de Genie* or armoured engineer vehicle with a crew of 11, an 'A' frame, winch and a dozer blade.

Model 68 recoilless rifle

Type: recoilless rifle
Calibre: 105 mm
Barrel length: 9 ft 10 in (3.0 m)
Muzzle velocity: 1,329 ft (405 m) per second with HEAT ammunition
Ranges: Maximum 10,061 yards (9,200 m)
Minimum 1,094 yards (1,000 m)

Elevation: −7° to +40.5°
Traverse: 360°
Rate of fire: about 10 rounds per minute
Weights: For travel 1,014 lb (460 kg)
In firing position
Dimensions: Length 13 ft 2$\frac{1}{4}$ in (4.02 m)
Width 3 ft 11$\frac{1}{2}$ in (1.205 m)
Height 3 ft 6 in (1.07 m)

Ammunition: HE and HEAT
Crew: two or three
Used only by: Argentina
Notes: The HEAT round will penetrate 15$\frac{3}{4}$ in (400 mm) of armour, and weighs 24$\frac{1}{2}$ lb (11.1 kg).

Oerlikon Type GDF-001

Type: AA gun mounting
Calibre: 35 mm
Barrel length:
Muzzle velocity: 3,855 ft (1,175 m) per second
Ranges: Maximum 4,374 yards (4,000 m)
Minimum
Elevation: −5° to +85°
Traverse: 360°
Rate of fire: 55 rounds per minute (cyclic) per barrel

Weights: For travel 13,889 lb (6,300 lb)
In firing position 14,771 lb (6,700 kg)
Dimensions: Length 25 ft 9$\frac{3}{4}$ in (7.87 m)
Width 7 ft 5 in (2.26 m)
Height 8 ft 6$\frac{1}{3}$ in (2.6 m)
Ammunition: HEI, HEI-T, SAPHEI and SAPHEI-T
Crew: three
Used also by: Austria, Finland, Japan, South Africa, Spain, Switzerland

Notes: The GDF-001 is a versatile and hard-hitting twin 35-mm AA mounting, capable of defeating the armour of light AFVs in the ground-to-ground role. Each barrel has a magazine holding 56 rounds, and 63 extra rounds per barrel are carried. The projectiles weigh 1.2 lb (0.55 kg), and the SAPHEI round can penetrate 1$\frac{3}{4}$ in (44 mm) of armour at 1,094 yards (1,000 m). For AA fire the weapon is usually operated in conjunction with a radar fire-control system.

PA3-DM sub-machine gun

Type: sub-machine gun
Calibre: 9 mm
System of operation: blowback
Muzzle velocity: 1,312 ft (400 m) per second
Range: effective 219 yards (200 m)
Rate of fire: 650 rounds per minute (cyclic)
Cooling system: air

Feed system: 25-round box magazine
Dimensions: Barrel length 11.4 in (290 mm)
Overall length 27.56 in (700 mm) with solid butt; 20.59 in (523 mm) with sliding butt retracted
Width
Height

Weights: 7.5 lb (3.4 kg) with solid stock; 7.6 lb (3.45 kg) with sliding stock (both without magazine)
Sights: pillar (fore) and flip aperture (rear)
Ammunition: 9 mm × 19 Parabellum
Used only by: Argentina
Notes: The PA3-DM is made by the Fabrica Militar de Armas Portatiles at Rosario, and is a modern weapon capable of single-shot or automatic fire, and grenade-launching.

Australia

32,084 men and 22,900 reservists.

1 inf div HQ and 3 task force HQ.
1 armd regt.
1 recce regt.
1 APC regt.
6 inf bns.
1 Special Air Service regt.
4 arty regts (1 med, 2 fd, 1 lt AA).
1 aviation regt.
3 fd engr, 1 fd survey regt.
2 sigs regts.
87 Leopard med tks; 778 M-113 APC; 34 5.5-in guns; 254 105mm how; 72 M-40 106mm RCL; Redeye SAM; 17 Pilatus Porter, 9 Nomad ac; 50 Bell 206B-1 helicopters; 32 watercraft. (16 Leopard med tks, 13 M-113 APC, 20 Rapier SAM, 10 Blindfire AD radar on order.)

Deployment: Egypt (UNEF/UNTSO): 10.

M113

Type: armoured personnel carrier
Crew: two, plus up to 11 infantrymen
Weights: Empty 21,390 lb (9,702 kg)
Loaded 24,595 lb (11,156 kg)
Dimensions: Length 15 ft 11½ in (4.86 m)
Width 8 ft 9¾ in (2.69 m)
Height (overall) 8 ft 2¼ in (2.5 m)
Ground pressure: 7.68 lb/in² (0.54 kg/cm²)
Performance: road speed 42.5 mph (68.4 kph); water speed 3.6 mph (5.8 kph); range 305 miles (491 km); vertical obstacle 24 in (61.0 cm); trench 5 ft 6 in (1.68 m); gradient 60%
Engine: one 215-bhp General Motors Corporation Model 6V53 inline diesel engine
Armament: one 0.5-in (12.7-mm) Browning M2 machine-gun with 2,000 rounds on the commander's cupola
Armour: aluminium, ½ in (12 mm) minimum; 1½ in (38 mm) maximum

Used also by: Argentina, Bolivia, Brazil, Canada, Chile, Denmark, Ecuador, Egypt, Ethiopia, Greece, Guatemala, Haiti, Iran, Israel, Italy, Jordan, Kampuchea, Laos, Lebanon, Libya, Morocco, Netherlands, New Zealand, Norway, Pakistan, Peru, Philippines, Portugal, Saudi Arabia, Singapore, South Korea, Spain, Switzerland, Taiwan, Thailand, Turkey, Upper Volta, USA, West Germany, Zaire

Notes: The M113 was developed in the mid-1950s to replace the M59 APC, and was designed by the FMC Corporation. The M113 is the world's first AFV made of aluminium armour, which helps to make the vehicle an inherent amphibian. There have been two basic marks of the APC:

1. M113, with a 209-bhp Chrysler 75 M inline petrol engine, a weight of 23,523 lb (10,670 kg), a speed of 40 mph (64 kph), and a range of 200 miles (322 km)

2. M113A1, to which the technical specification above applies, with a diesel engine and improved performance as well as less tendency to catch fire when hit in combat

The M113/M113A1 also forms the basis for a large number of other vehicles, some of the more important of which are:

1. two versions mounting anti-tank guided missiles, one carrying the SS.11, and the other TOW
2. two versions carrying battlefield radar, one carrying AN/TPS-25, and the other AN/PPS-4
3. Improved TOW vehicle
4. M106 and M106A1 107-mm mortar carriers, with a crew of six, a weight of 26,449 lb (11,997 kg) for the M106A, and an ammunition capacity of 88 rounds
5. M125 and M125A1 81-mm mortar carriers, with a crew of six, a weight of 24,824 lb (11,260 kg) for the M125A1, and stowage for 114 mortar rounds. Like the M106 and M106A1, the M125 and M125A1 are armed with a single 0.5-in (12.7-mm) defensive machine-gun
6. M132 and M132A1 flamethrower vehicles, with crews of two, a weight of 23,810 lb (10,800 kg), and an armament of one turret-mounted M108 flame gun. This has a range of 164 yards (150 m) and a sustained fire duration of 32 seconds
7. M163 20-mm Vulcan Air Defense System Vehicle

8. M577 and M577A1 command post vehicles, which have crews of five, a weight of 25,382 lb (11,513 kg), a height of 8 ft 9½ in (2.68 m), and extra radio equipment, mapboards and the like
9. Ambulance vehicle
10. Recovery and repair vehicle
11. Cargo carrier
12. Lance missile launch vehicle
13. Chaparral AA missile launch vehicle
14. HAWK missile launch vehicle.

5.5-in gun

Type: field gun
Calibre: 5.5 in (139.7 mm)
Barrel length: 31 cal
Muzzle velocity: 1,950 ft (594 m) per second
Ranges: Maximum 18,050 yards (16,505 m)
Minimum
Elevation: −5° to +45°
Traverse: 60° total
Rate of fire: two rounds per minute
Weights: For travel 13,633 lb (6,184 kg)
In firing position 12,900 lb (5,851 kg)
Dimensions: Length 24 ft 8 in (7.52 m)
Width 8 ft 4 in (2.54 m)
Height 8 ft 7 in (2.62 m)
Ammunition: separate loading, HE, Illuminating and Smoke
Crew: 10
Used also by: Burma, India, Malaysia, New Zealand, Oman, Pakistan, Portugal, South Africa
Notes: Despite its age, the 5.5-in gun is still an accurate and effective weapon, although somewhat heavy and limited in

ammunition types by modern standards. The maximum range of 18,050 ft (16,505 m) is attained with the 80-lb (36.3-kg) shell, maximum range with the 100-lb (45.35-kg) shell being 16,185 yards (14,800 m). The 100-lb shell was in fact superseded by the 80-lb shell, which has less metal but more explosive, and is far more effective.

Owen sub-machine gun

Type: sub-machine gun
Calibre: 9 mm
System of operation: blowback
Muzzle velocity: 1,200 ft (366 m) per second
Range: effective 219 yards (200 m)
Rate of fire: 700 rounds per minute (cyclic)
Cooling system: air
Feed system: 33-round box magazine
Dimensions: Barrel length 9.85 in (250 mm)
Overall length 32 in (813 mm)
Width
Height

Weights: 10.7 lb (4.86 kg) loaded; 9.33 lb (4.23 kg) unloaded
Sights: offset blade (fore) and offset aperture (rear)
Ammunition: 9 mm × 19 Parabellum
Used also by: various countries in south-east Asia
Notes: The Owen sub-machine gun was accepted for Australian service in November 1941. The weapon has the unusual distinguishing feature of a for-ward-sloping magazine on top of the receiver. There were several models before production ceased in 1944:

1. Mark I/42 initial production model
2. Mark I/43, to which the specification above applies, with an unfinned barrel and lightening holes in the frame
3. Mark I/44 with a bayonet
4. Mark II/43 of which only a very few were made for trials purposes only.

F1 sub-machine gun

Type: sub-machine gun
Calibre: 9 mm
System of operation: blowback
Muzzle velocity: 1,200 ft (366 m) per second
Range: effective 219 yards (200 m)
Rate of fire: 600 to 640 rounds per minute (cyclic)
Cooling system: air
Feed system: 34-round box magazine
Dimensions: Barrel length 8.39 in (213 mm)
Overall length 28 in (714 mm)
Width
Height

Weights: 7.2 lb (3.27 kg) unloaded; 9.48 lb (4.3 kg) loaded, with bayonet
Sights: offset blade (fore) and offset aperture (rear)
Ammunition: 9 mm × 19 Parabellum
Used only by: Australia
Notes: Like the Owen, the Australian F1 sub-machine gun is notable for the fact that the magazine is located above the receiver. The weapon is also notable for its straight-through design and the incorporation of a number of components from the L1A1 rifle.

L2A1 rifle

Type: heavy-barrelled support rifle
Calibre: 7.62 mm
System of operation: gas
Muzzle velocity: 2,750 ft (838 m) per second
Range: effective 875 yards (800 m)
Rate of fire: 675 to 750 rounds per minute (cyclic); about 75 rounds per minute (bursts)

Cooling system: air
Feed system: 30-round box magazine
Dimensions: Barrel length 21 in (533 mm)
Overall length 44.75 in (1.137 m)
Width
Height
Weights: 15.2 lb (6.9 kg)

Sights: blade (fore) and aperture (rear)
Ammunition: 7.62 mm × 51
Used only by: Australia
Notes: The L2A1 was produced in Australia to enable units other than infantry to be provided with light support fire. The rifle is based on the L1A1 rifle, itself a licence-built version of the British L1A1 rifle.

Austria

33,000 men (18,000 conscripts) and 113,000 reservists (another 800,000 have reserve commitments).

1 mech div of 3 mech bdes, each with 1 tk, 2 mech inf (1 trg), 1 armd arty and/or 1 armd ATK bns.
3 inf bdes, each with 3 inf, 1 arty bns.
4 inf regts (to form 4 inf bdes on mobilization).
3 arty bns.
1 cdo bn.
3 engr, 5 sigs bns.
150 M-47, 120 M-60 med tks; 460 Saurer 4K4F APC; 22 SFKM2 155mm guns; 108 M-2 105mm, 24 M-1 155mm how, 38 M-109 155mm SP how; 300 81mm, 100 M-2 107mm, 82 M-30 120mm mor; 18 Steyr 680 M3 130mm multiple RL; 240 M52/M55 85mm towed, 150 *Kürassier* SP ATK guns; 400 M-40 106mm RCL.

Deployment: Cyprus (UNFICYP): 1 inf bn (332); Syria (UNDOF): 1 bn (523); other Middle East (UNTSO): 12.

Reserves: 113,000; 4 reserve bdes (each of 3 inf, 1 arty bns), 16 regts and 4 bns *Landwehr* distributed among 8 regional military comds. 800,000 have a reserve commitment.

M47

Type: main battle tank
Crew: five
Weights: Empty
Loaded 98,560 lb (44,707 kg)
Dimensions: Length (hull) 20 ft 9 in (6.33 m)
Width 11 ft 6 in (3.505 m)
Height 9 ft 8½ in (2.96 m)
Ground pressure: 13.37 lb/in² (0.94 kg/cm²)
Performance: road speed 25 mph (40 kph); range 80 miles (128 km); vertical obstacle 36 in (91.4 cm); trench 8 ft 6 in (2.59 m); gradient 60%; ground clearance 18 in (45.7 cm); wading 4 ft (1.22 m) without preparation
Engine: one 810-bhp Continental AB-1790-5B inline petrol engine
Armament: one 90-mm M36 gun with 70 rounds of HE and HVAP, plus one 0.3-in (7.62-mm) machine-gun co-axial with the

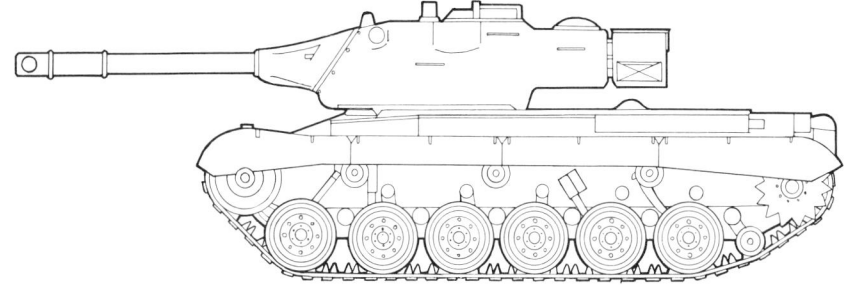

main armament, one 0.3-in (7.62-mm) machine-gun in the hull bow, and one 0.5-in (12.7-mm) machine-gun on the turret roof for AA defence

Armour: $\frac{1}{2}$ in (12 mm) minimum; $4\frac{1}{2}$ in (115 mm) maximum

Used also by: Belgium, Ethiopia, Greece, Iran, Italy, Jordan, Pakistan, Portugal, South Korea, Spain, Taiwan, Turkey

Notes: The M47 is basically the M46 Patton, itself an improved M26 Pershing, with the same hull and track system, but with a more powerful engine and ballistically improved turret. The Spanish Army is currently improving its M47s by increasing fuel capacity, fitting the AVDS-1790-2A engine, adding a new exhaust system and transmission, and incorporating other detail improvements. Among the variants of the M47 are an armoured recovery vehicle, an armoured engineer vehicle, and an armoured vehicle-launched bridge.

4KH7FA-B *Greif*

Type: armoured recovery vehicle
Crew: four
Weights: Empty
       Loaded 43,651 lb (19,800 kg)
Dimensions: Length 20 ft 7 in (6.275 m)
       Width 8 ft 2$\frac{2}{5}$ in (2.5 m)
       Height 7 ft 6$\frac{1}{2}$ in (2.3 m)
Ground pressure: 10.52 lb/in² (0.74 kg/cm²)
Performance: road speed 40 mph (65 kph); vertical obstacle 31$\frac{1}{2}$ in (80.0 cm); trench 7 ft 10$\frac{1}{2}$ in (2.4 m); gradient 70%; ground clearance 15$\frac{3}{4}$ in (40.0 cm); wading 39$\frac{2}{5}$ in (1.0 m) without preparation
Engine: one 320-hp Steyr Type 7FA inline diesel engine
Armament: one 0.5-in (12.7-mm) AA machine-gun
Armour: $\frac{1}{3}$ in (8 mm) minimum; $\frac{1}{2}$ in (12 mm) maximum

Used only by: Austria

Notes: The *Greif* is derived from the *Panzerjäger* 'K', but with a new superstructure and a front-mounted dozer blade. The *Greif* has two winches, one with a capacity of 44,092 lb (20,000 kg) and the other of 13,228 lb (6,000 kg). The *Greif* also has an extendable crane, operated hydraulically.

Saurer *Schützenpanzer* 4K4FA

Type: armoured personnel carrier
Crew: driver and eight infantrymen
Weights: Empty 24,471 lb (11,000 kg)
       Loaded 33,069 lb (15,000 kg)
Dimensions: Length 17 ft 8$\frac{2}{3}$ in (5.4 m)
       Width 8 ft 2$\frac{1}{2}$ in (2.5 m)
       Height 5 ft 5 in (1.65 m) excluding MG etc
Ground pressure: 7.25 lb/in² (0.51 kg/cm²)
Performance: road speed 40 mph (65 kph); road range 186 miles (300 km); step 2 ft 7$\frac{1}{2}$ in (0.8 m); trench 6 ft 10$\frac{3}{5}$ in (2.1 m); unprepared wading 3 ft 3$\frac{2}{5}$ in (1.0 m); ground clearance 1 ft 4 in (0.42 m); gradient 75%
Engine: one 200-bhp Saurer 3F, 250-bhp Saurer 4F or 250-bhp Steyr 4FA 6-cylinder diesel
Armament: one 20-mm Oerlikon 204 GK cannon with 425 rounds (early models had a 12.7-mm Browning machine-gun)
Armour: $\frac{1}{3}$ in (8 mm) minimum; $\frac{1}{2}$ in (12 mm) maximum

Used only by: Austria

Notes: Variants include: SPz-FüA 1 and 4 artillery control vehicles, SPz-FüFla AA control vehicle, SPz-GrW 1 and 2 mortar carriers, SPz Fü 1 and 2 radio vehicles, SPz-FS teleprinter vehicle, and SPz-San ambulance.

M42

Type: self-propelled AA mounting
Crew: six
Weights: Empty
      Loaded 49,500 lb (22,453 kg)
Dimensions: Length 20 ft 10 in (6.35 m)
         Width 10 ft 6 in (3.2 m)
         Height 9 ft 4 in (2.84 m)
Ground pressure: 9.24 lb/in² (0.65 kg/cm²)
Performance: road speed 45 mph (72 kph); range 100 miles (160 km); vertical obstacle 28 in (71.1 cm); trench 6 ft 4 in (1.93 m); gradient 60%
Engine: one 500-bhp Continental or Lycoming inline petrol engine
Armament: two 40-mm Bofors L/60 guns with 480 rounds, plus one 7.62-mm 1760 machine-gun with 1,750 rounds for local defence
Armour: ⅓ in (9 mm) minimum; 1 in (25 mm) maximum
Used also by: Japan, Jordan, Lebanon, Saudi Arabia, USA, West Germany
Notes: The M42 self-propelled AA mounting is based on the chassis of the M41 Walker Bulldog light tank, with the guns on an open-topped cylindrical turret traversed manually through 360°. The guns elevate from −5° to +87°, and the cyclic rate of fire is 120 rounds per gun per minute. Effective ceiling is 26,900 ft (8,200 m), but lack of any adequate fire-control system, and the slow traverse of the guns, makes the M42 an ineffective weapon in modern conditions. The type entered service in 1953–4.

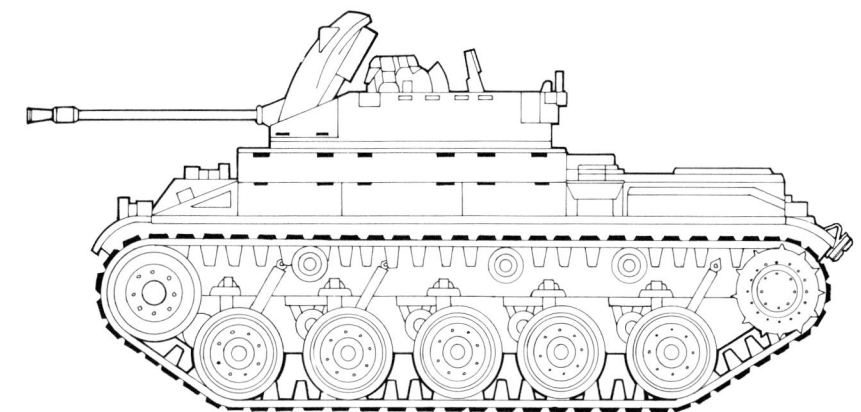

Steyr-Daimler-Puch MPi 69 sub-machine gun

Type: sub-machine gun
Calibre: 9 mm
System of operation: blowback
Muzzle velocity: 1,250 ft (381 m) per second
Range: effective 219 yards (200 m)
Rate of fire: 550 rounds per minute (cyclic); 100 rounds per minute (automatic)
Cooling system: air
Feed system: 25- or 32-round box magazine
Dimensions: Barrel length 10.24 in (260 mm)

Overall length 26.5 in (673 mm) with butt extended; 18.5 in (470 mm) with butt retracted
Width
Height
Weights: 6.5 lb (2.95 kg) without magazine; 7.76 lb (3.52 kg) with loaded magazine
Sights: post (fore) and aperture (rear), or Singlepoint
Ammunition: 9 mm × 19 Parabellum
Used only by: Austria
Notes: The MPi 69 is a simple but effective sub-machine gun with strong similarities to the Israeli UZI. The gun makes extensive use of pressings.

Oerlikon Type GAI-BO1 cannon

Type: AA cannon mounting
Calibre: 20 mm
System of operation: recoil
Muzzle velocity: 3,609 to 3,937 ft (1,100 to 1,200 m) per second
Range: tactical 2,187 yards (2,000 m)
Rate of fire: 1,000 rounds per minute (cyclic)
Cooling system: air
Feed system: 8-round box or 50-round drum
Dimensions: Barrel length 117.7 in (2.99 m) including muzzle brake
      Overall length 14 ft 5¼ in (4.4 m) travelling
      Width 5 ft 1 in (1.55 m) in firing position
      Height 11 ft 10¾ in (3.625 m) at maximum elevation
Weights: travelling 1,199 lb (544 kg); in firing position 844 lb (383 kg)
Sights: optical graticule
Ammunition: HE and AP
Used only by: Austria

Notes: The GAI-BO1 was formerly known as the 10 La/57G, and is a useful piece of dual-purpose equipment for AA and ground defence. The gun can be elevated from −5° to +85°, and traverse is 360°. For transport the weapon is towed on a two-wheeled carriage, though each component of the system can be carried over short distances by two men. The weapon is notable for its high rate of fire. The system can also be mounted on a vehicle.

SSG 69 rifle

Type: sniping rifle
Calibre: 7.62 mm
System of operation: manually-operated rotating bolt
Muzzle velocity: 2,821 ft (860 m) per second
Range: effective 875 yards (800 m)
Rate of fire:
Cooling system: air
Feed system: 5-round rotary magazine, or 10-round box
Dimensions: Barrel length 25.6 in (650 mm)
Overall length 44.49 in (1.13 m)
Width
Height
Weights: 8.45 lb (3.84 kg) without magazine; 8.88 lb (4.03 kg) with loaded magazine
Sights: blade (fore) and V (rear), or × 4 telescopic sight
Ammunition: 7.62 mm × 51
Used only by: Austria
Notes: The SSG (*Scharfschützen-Gewehr*) is made by Steyr-Daimler-Puch, though it is a Steyr-Mannlicher design. The weapon is the standard sniping rifle of the Austrian Army.

Bahrain

2,300 men.

1 inf bn.
1 armd car sqn.
8 Saladin armd cars; 8 Ferret scout cars; 6 81mm mor; 6 120mm RCL.

Daimler Ferret

Type: scout car
Crew: two
Weights: Empty
Loaded 7,680 lb (4,395 kg)
Dimensions: Length 11 ft 1 in (3.385 m)
Width 6 ft 3 in (1,905 m)
Height 6 ft 2 in (1.88 m)
Ground pressure:
Performance: road speed 58 mph (93 kph); range 186 miles (300 km); vertical obstacle 1 ft 4 in (40.6 cm); gradient 60%
Engine: one 129-bhp Rolls-Royce B.60 Mark 6A inline petrol engine
Armament: one 0.3-in (7.62-mm) machine-gun
Armour: ⅝ in (16 mm)
Used also by: Burma, Cameroon, Canada, Central African Empire, France, Ghana, Indonesia, Iran, Iraq, Jordan, Kenya, Kuwait, Libya, Malagasy Republic, Malawi, Malaysia, New Zealand, Nigeria, North Yemen, Qatar, Rhodesia, Saudi Arabia, South Africa, South Yemen, Sri Lanka, Sudan, Uganda, United Arab Emirates, UK, Zambia
Notes: The Ferret scout car was introduced into British service in 1953, and has since served in a variety of marks:

1. Mark 1/1 with a Bren or 0.3-in (7.82-mm) machine-gun on a pintle mount in an open top, with 450 rounds
2. Mark 1/2 with a small flat turret armed with a 0.3-in (7.62-mm) machine-gun on top
3. Mark 2/3 is similar to the Mark 1 but with a turret-mounted 0.3-in (7.62-mm) machine-gun and 2,500 rounds. The technical specification above applies to this mark
4. Mark 2/6 is the Mark 2/3 fitted with a BAC Vigilant wire-guided anti-tank missile on each side of the turret. Two spare missiles are carried
5. Mark 3 is a Mark 1/1 with larger wheels, improved suspension and a flotation screen
6. Mark 4 is a Mark 2/3 with larger wheels, improved suspension and a flotation screen
7. Mark 5 or FV712 has larger wheels, improved suspension, a turret of aluminium alloy, and an armament of two BAC Swingfire anti-tank missiles on each side of the turret, which is armed with a 7.62-mm machine-gun. Two spare missiles are carried.

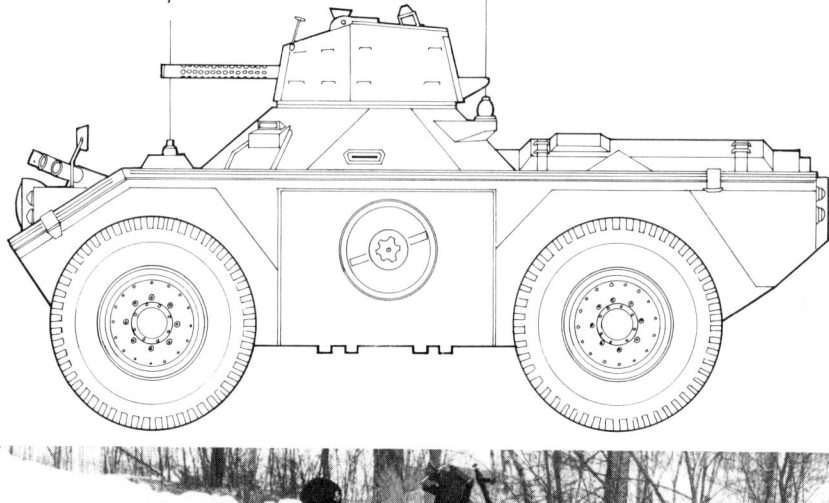

Bangladesh

65,000 men.

5 inf div HQ.
11 inf bdes (33 inf bns).
1 tk regt.
7 arty regts.
3 engr bns.
30 T-54 med tks; 30 105mm, 5 25-pdr guns/how; 81mm, 50 120mm mor; 106mm RCL.

Para-Military Forces: 20,000 Bangladesh Rifles, 36,000 Armed Police Reserve.

25-pounder gun

Type: gun/howitzer
Calibre: 88 mm
Barrel length: 26 cal
Muzzle velocity: 1,750 ft (533 m) per second
Ranges: Maximum 13,400 yards (12,253 m) Minimum
Elevation: −5° to +40°
Traverse: 4° left and right, and 360° on the turntable
Rate of fire: five rounds per minute
Weights: For travel 3,968 lb (1,800 kg) In firing position

Dimensions: Length 26 ft (7.924 m)
Width 6 ft 11½ in (2.12 m)
Height 5 ft 5 in (1.65 m)
Ammunition: APDS, Chemical, HE, Illuminating, Smoke and Target Indicating
Crew: six
Used also by: Burma, Cyprus, Egypt, Eire, Ghana, India, Indonesia, Israel, Jordan, Kuwait, Malaysia, Netherlands, New Zealand, Nigeria, Oman, Pakistan, Portugal, Qatar, Rhodesia, Singapore, South Africa, South Yemen, Sri Lanka, Sudan, United Arab Emirates
Notes: The 25-pounder was one of the most important artillery weapons of World War II, and is still a useful piece of ordnance. All projectiles weigh 25 lb (11.34 kg).

Belgium

63,400 men (incl Medical Service), (22,600 conscripts) and 50,000 reservists (10,000 train every year, 1 mech, 1 mot inf bde train every three years).

1 armd bde.
3 mech inf bdes.
3 recce bns.
2 mot inf bns.
1 para-cdo regt.
3 arty bns.
1 SSM bn with 4 Lance.
2 SAM bns with 24 HAWK.
5 engr bns (3 fd, 1 bridge, 1 eqpt).
4 aviation sqns.
334 Leopard, 52 M-47 med, 136 Scorpion lt tks; 154 Scimitar AFV; 1,229 M-75 and AMX-VCI, 174 Spartan APC; 22 105mm, 15 203mm how; 96 M-108 105mm, 25 M-44, 41 M-109 155mm, 11 M-110 203mm SP how; 5 Lance SSM; 80 Jpk C-90 SP ATK guns; *Entac, Milan* ATGW; 41 Striker AFV with Swingfire ATGW; 114 20mm, 40mm, 57mm AA guns; 60 HAWK SAM; 6 Piper Super Cub, 12 BN Islander ac, 74 *Alouette* II helicopters; 31 *Epervier* RPV. (90 Spartan APC, 55 *Gepard* SP AA guns, Swingfire ATGW on order.)

Deployment: Germany: 27,000; 1 corps HQ, 2 div HQ, 1 armd bde, 2 mech inf bdes.

Alvis FV101 Scorpion

Type: light reconnaissance tank
Crew: three
Weights: Empty
Loaded 17,548 lb (7,960 kg)
Dimensions: Length 14 ft 5 in (4.39 m)
Width 7 ft 2 in (2.18 m)
Height 6 ft 10 in (2.1 m)
Ground pressure: 4.9 lb/in² (0.345 kg/cm²)
Performance: road speed 54 mph (87 kph); water speed 4 mph (6.5 kph); range 400 miles (644 km); verticle obstacle 20 in (50.8 cm); trench 6 ft 9 in (2.06 m); gradient 70%; ground clearance 13¾ in (35.0 cm); wading 3 ft 6 in (1.07 m) without preparation
Engine: one 195-bhp Jaguar XK inline petrol engine
Armament: one 76-mm gun with 40 rounds of HE and HESH, plus one 7.62-mm machine-gun with 3,000 rounds, co-axial with the main armament
Armour: classified

Used also by: Brunei, Eire, Honduras, Iran, Kuwait, Nigeria, Philippines, Thailand, United Arab Emirates, UK
Notes: The Scorpion light tank is designed specifically for reconnaissance work, special attention having been paid to making the vehicle as quiet as possible. Performance and agility are exceptional for a tracked vehicle, and the aluminium armour and hard-hitting 76-mm gun will enable the type to give a good account of itself in combat. Although the range of the main armament is 5,470 yards (5,000 m), effective range is lower, as the ranging method is optical estimating or machine-gun ranging. There are several derivatives:
1. Combat Vehicle Reconnaissance (Tracked) or CVR(T) FV101 Scorpion light reconnaissance tank, to which the specification above applies
2. CVR(T) FV102 Striker anti-tank vehicle, with an armament of five BAC Swingfire AT missile launchers
3. CVR(T) FV103 Spartan armoured per-

sonnel carrier, capable of transporting four infantrymen. The FV103 clearly does not have the capacity to become an effective infantry APC, but will instead be used for the carriage of special teams

4. CVR(T) FV104 Samaritan armoured ambulance vehicle, which can carry four stretchers
5. CVR(T) FV105 Sultan command vehicle with mapboards and a collapsible penthouse at the rear of the vehicle
6. CVR(T) FV106 Samson armoured recovery vehicle with a winch capable of pulling 12 tons (12,193 kg)
7. CVR(T) FV107 Scimitar anti-reconnaissance vehicle system, armed with a 30-mm Rarden cannon capable of penetrating the armour of reconnaissance vehicles and APCs.

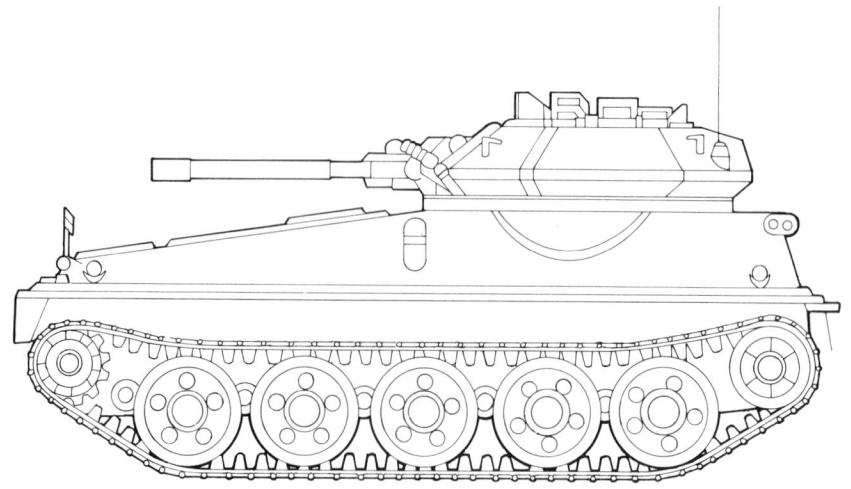

Flakpanzer 1 Gepard

Type: self-propelled AA gun
Crew: three
Weights: Empty
Loaded 99,208 lb (45,000 kg)
Dimensions: Length (guns forward) 25 ft 3 in (7.7 m)
Width 10 ft 8 in (3.25 m)
Height (with radar retracted) 10 ft 1 in (3.07 m)
Ground pressure: 13.5 lb/in² (0.95 kg/cm²)
Performance: road speed 40 mph (65 kph); range 373 miles (600 km); vertical obstacle 3 ft 9$\frac{1}{4}$ in (1.15 m); trench 9 ft 10 in (3.0 m); gradient 60%; ground clearance 17$\frac{3}{4}$ in (45.0 cm); wading 3 ft 11$\frac{1}{4}$ in (1.2 m) without preparation and 7 ft 4$\frac{1}{2}$ in (2.25 m) with preparation
Engine: one 830-hp MTU MB 835 Ca.500 inline multi-fuel engine
Armament: two 35-mm Oerlikon KDA cannon with 640 rounds of AA and 40 rounds of AT ammunition
Armour: $\frac{2}{5}$ in (10 mm) minimum; 2$\frac{3}{4}$ in (70 mm) maximum
Used also by: Netherlands and West Germany
Notes: The *Gepard* AA vehicle is based on the chassis of the Leopard 1 MBT, the only major difference being the addition of a 90-hp diesel engine and generators to supply extra electrical power. The turret houses the two 35-mm cannon, the radar and electronic equipment. The cannon have an effective AA range of 13,123 ft (4,000 m), and their accuracy is enhanced by equipment which measures the rounds' individual muzzle velocity and feeds the data to the fire-control computer, which acts on this information and data on the target supplied by the Siemens (on German and Belgian vehicles) and Hollandse Signaalapparaten (on Dutch vehicles) search (on turret rear) and tracking (on turret front) radars.

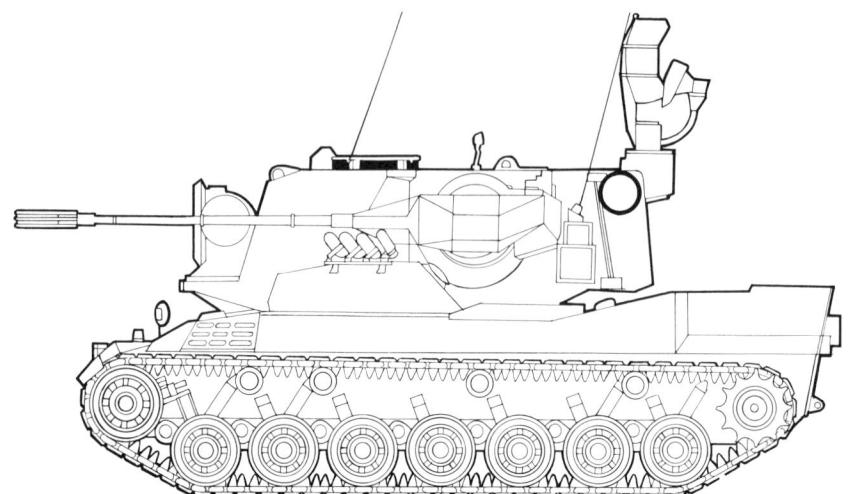

CVR(T) Spartan

Type: armoured personnel carrier
Crew: three, plus four infantrymen
Weights: Empty
Loaded 18,015 lb (8,172 kg)
Dimensions: Length 15 ft 10$\frac{1}{2}$ in (4.84 m)
Width 7 ft 2 in (2.18 m)
Height 7 ft 4$\frac{3}{8}$ in (2.25 m)
Ground pressure: about 4.9 lb/in² (0.345 kg/cm²)
Performance: road speed 54 mph (87 kph); water speed 4 mph (6.5 kph); range 400

miles (644 km); vertical obstacle 20 in (50.8 cm); trench 6 ft 9 in (2.06 m); gradient 70%; ground clearance 13¾ in (35.0 cm); the Spartan is fully amphibious
Engine: one 195-bhp Jaguar XK inline petrol engine
Armament: one 7.62-mm (0.3 in) machine-gun with 2,000 rounds of ammunition
Armour: classified
Used also by: UK
Notes: The Spartan (FV103) is the APC member of the CVR(T) family whose best known member is the Scorpion (FV101) reconnaissance vehicle.

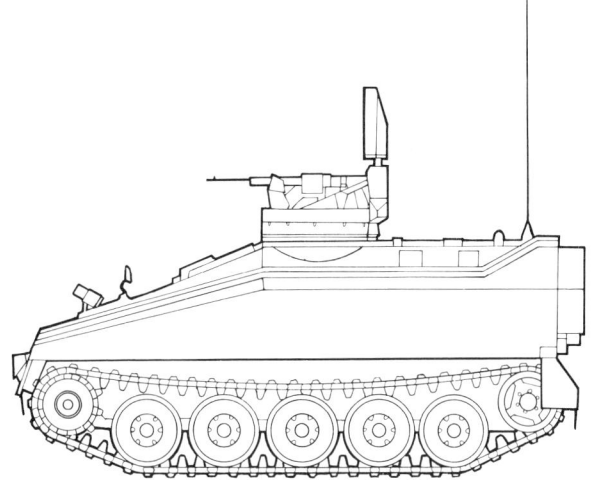

CVR(T) Scimitar

Type: anti-AFV vehicle
Crew: three
Weights: Empty
    Loaded 17,196 lb (7,800 kg)
Dimensions: Length 14 ft 5 in (4.39 m)
    Width 7 ft 2 in (2.18 m)
    Height
Ground pressure: 4.9 lb/in² (0.345 kg/cm²)

Performance: road speed 54 mph (87 kph); water speed 4 mph (6.5 kph); range 400 miles (644 km); vertical obstacle 20 in (50.8 cm); trench 6 ft 9 in (2.057 m); gradient 70%; ground clearance 13¾ in (35.0 cm); the Scimitar is fully amphibious
Engine: one 195-bhp Jaguar XK inline petrol engine
Armament: one 30-mm Rarden cannon with 165 rounds, and one 7.62-mm machine-gun co-axial with the main armament and provided with 3,000 rounds of ammunition
Armour: classified
Used also by: UK
Notes: The Scimitar (FV107) is the last member of the CVR(T) family, and is intended to meet enemy APCs and the like, whose relatively thin armour can be penetrated by the Rarden cannon, which is provided with a range of ammunition including HE, AP, APDS, and Armour Piercing Special Explosive Tracer.

M75

Type: armoured personnel carrier
Crew: two, plus up to 10 infantrymen
Weights: Empty 36,666 lb (16,632 kg)
    Loaded 41,500 lb (18,828 kg)
Dimensions: Length 17 ft (5.193 m)
    Width 9 ft 4 in (2.844 m)
    Height (overall) 10 ft (3.041 m)

Ground pressure: 8.1 lb/in² (0.57 kg/cm²)
Performance: road speed 44 mph (71 kph); range 115 miles (185 km); vertical obstacle 18 in (45.7 cm); trench 5 ft 6 in (1.68 m); gradient 60%; wading 48 in (1.22 m) without preparation, and 6 ft 8 in (2.03 m) with preparation
Engine: one 295-bhp Continental AO-895-4 petrol engine

Armament: one 0.5-in (12.7-mm) Browning M2 machine-gun on the commander's cupola with 1,800 rounds
Armour: ⅜in (9.5 mm) minimum; 1 in (25.4 mm) maximum
Used only by: Belgium
Notes: The M75 entered US service in 1952.

Messerschmitt-Bölkow-Blohm/ Aérospatiale *Milan*

Type: anti-tank missile, man-portable and tube-launched
Guidance: semi-automatic command to line-of-sight by means of wires
Dimensions: Span 10¾ in (27.0 cm)
    Body diameter 3½ in (9.0 cm)
    Length 2 ft 6⅓ in (77.0 cm)
Booster: solid-propellant ejector in launch tube
Sustainer: two-stage solid-propellant rocket
Warhead: hollow-charge high explosive, capable of penetrating 13.86 in (352 mm) of NATO armour plate at 65°
Weights: Launch 50.8 lb (23.05 kg) for missile and launch/guidance unit
    Burnt out
Performance: range 27 yards to 2,187 yards (25–2,000 m); speed 447 mph (720 kph)
Used also by: Egypt, France, Greece, Somali Republic, Syria, Turkey, UK, West Germany
Notes: Developed jointly by France and West Germany, the *Milan* (*Missile d'Infanterie Léger Antichar* or infantry light anti-tank missile) is a 2nd-generation AT missile.

After the missile is ejected from the tube, its wings spring open, and the missile is then gathered automatically onto the user's line-of-sight, which remains on the target.

RL-100 launcher

Type: portable anti-tank rocket launcher
Calibre: 101 mm
Barrel length: 18.66 cal
Muzzle velocity: 640 ft (195 m) per second
Ranges: Maximum effective 437 yards (400 m)
    Minimum

Elevation:
Traverse:
Rate of fire:
Weights: For travel
    In firing position 34.5 lb (15.65 kg)
Dimensions: Length 6 ft 2⅕ in (1.885 m)
    Width
    Height
Ammunition: HEAT warhead

Crew: one
Used also by: other nations
Notes: The Belgian RL-100 is a powerful anti-tank weapon, capable of penetrating 15¾ in (400 mm) of armour with its 6.06-lb (2.75-kg) projectile. To help aiming, the launch tube has a bipod at its front end.

RL-83 launcher

Type: man-portable anti-tank rocket launcher
Calibre: 83 mm
Barrel length: 20.48 cal
Muzzle velocity: 328 ft (100 m) per second
Ranges: Maximum 984 yards (900 m)
Minimum

Elevation:
Traverse:
Rate of fire:
Weights: For travel
In firing position 18.5 lb (8.4 kg)
Dimensions: Length 5 ft 7 in (1.77 m)
Width
Height

Ammunition: HEAT warhead
Crew: two
Used also by: other nations
Notes: The RL-83 is an obsolescent Belgian weapon, but still useful for light AFV opposition. The rocket can carry other types of warhead. Penetration is 11.8 in (300 mm) of armour.

MPA 75 launcher

Type: man-portable bi-tube anti-tank rocket launcher
Calibre: 75 mm
Barrel length:
Muzzle velocity: 197 ft (60 m) per second
Ranges: Maximum (AT) 109 yards (100 m); (anti-personnel) 328 yards (300 m)
Minimum

Elevation:
Traverse:
Rate of fire:
Weights: For travel
In firing position 5.73 lb (2.6 kg)
Dimensions: Length 20 in (51.0 cm)
Width
Height
Ammunition: HE or HEAT warhead

Crew: one
Used only by: Belgium
Notes: The MPA 75 is a versatile and powerful anti-personnel and anti-tank weapon. The missile, which weighs 2.09 lb (0.95 kg), can penetrate 10.63 in (270 mm) of armour. Once both missiles have been discharged, the launcher is discarded.

Fabrique Nationale MAG machine-gun

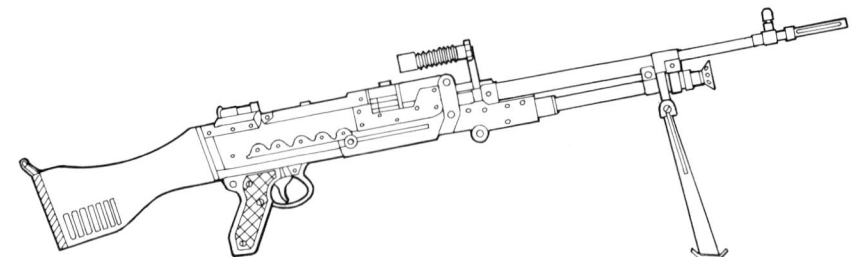

Type: general-purpose machine-gun
Calibre: 7.62 mm
System of operation: gas
Muzzle velocity: 2,756 ft (840 m) per second
Range: effective 1,312 yards (1,200 m)
Rate of fire: 600 to 1,000 rounds per minute (cyclic); 250 rounds per minute (automatic)
Cooling system: air
Feed system: metal-link belt
Dimensions: Barrel length 21.46 in (545 mm)
Overall length 49.41 in (1.255 m) with flash suppressor
Width
Height
Weights: 23.9 lb (10.85 kg) with butt and bipod; 23.15 lb (10.5 kg) for tripod
Sights: blade (fore) and aperture or U notch (rear)
Ammunition: 7.62 mm × 51
Used also by: Argentina, Cuba, Ecuador, India, Israel, Kuwait, Libya, Netherlands, New Zealand, Peru, Qatar, Rhodesia, Sierra Leone, South Africa, Sweden, Tanzania, Uganda, UK, Venezuela and other nations
Notes: The MAG (*Mitrailleuse à Gaz*) is one of the most successful machine-guns to be developed since World War II. It is accurate, manoeuvrable, and fitted with a gas regulator allowing the weapon to be used in difficult conditions. The weapon has also been produced in Sweden as the M58 general-purpose machine-gun in 6.5-mm calibre.

Fabrique Nationale Minimi machine-gun

Type: light machine-gun
Calibre: 5.56 mm
System of operation: gas
Muzzle velocity: 2,936 ft (895 m) per second with S101 ball
Range:
Rate of fire: 750 to 1,250 rounds per minute
Cooling system: air

Feed system: 100- or 200-round metal-link belts
Dimensions: Barrel length 18.43 in (468 mm)
Overall length 39.37 in (1.0 m) with fixed stock; 32.09 in (815 mm) with folding metal stock
Width
Height
Weights: 14.33 lb (6.5 kg) with bipod; 19.4 lb (8.8 kg) with 200 rounds

Sights: blade (fore) and aperture (rear)
Ammunition: 5.56 mm × 45, or S101
Used by:
Notes: The Minimi is the partner of the CAL rifle in the FN 5.56-mm small arms family, designed with a view to the standardisation of the 5.56 × 45 round in NATO service. The muzzle velocity of the weapon with this round is 2,559 ft (780 m) per second. This round's bullet weighs 3.5 grammes, compared with the more powerful S101 round's 4 gramme bullet.

Vigneron M2 sub-machine gun

Type: sub-machine gun
Calibre: 9 mm
System of operation: blowback
Muzzle velocity: 1,250 ft (381 m) per second
Range: effective 219 yards (200 m)
Rate of fire: 620 rounds per minute (cyclic); 120 rounds per minute (automatic)

Cooling system: air
Feed system: 32-round box
Dimensions: Barrel length 12 in (305 mm) with compensator
Overall length 34.88 in (886 mm) with butt extended; 27.8 in (706 mm) with butt retracted
Width
Height

Weights: 7.25 lb (3.29 kg) unloaded; 8.13 lb (3.69 kg) loaded
Sights: blade (fore) and aperture (rear)
Ammunition: 9mm × 19 Parabellum
Used by: Belgium, Congo, Zaire
Notes: The Vigneron was adopted by the Belgian Army in 1953, and makes wide use of metal stampings. The design is notable for the length of the barrel.

Fabrique Nationale FAL rifle

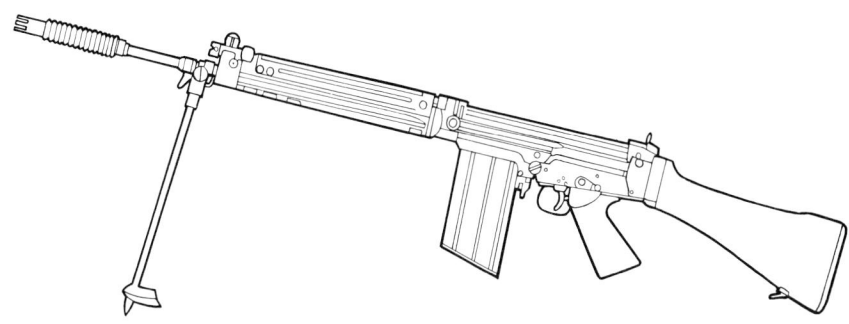

Type: automatic or self-loading rifle
Calibre: 7.62 mm
System of operation: gas
Muzzle velocity: 2,756 ft (840 m) per second
Range: effective 711 yards (650 m)
Rate of fire: 650 to 700 rounds per minute (cyclic); 120 rounds per minute (automatic); 60 rounds per minute (single shots)
Cooling system: air
Feed system: 20-round box magazine
Dimensions: Barrel length 20.98 in (533 mm)
Overall length 42.9 in (1.09 m); 49.6 in (1.26 m) with bayonet
Width
Height
Weights: 9.37 lb (4.25 kg) without bayonet and magazine; 11.47 lb (5.2 kg) with bayonet and magazine
Sights: post (fore) and aperture (rear)
Ammunition: 7.62 mm × 51
Used also by: Argentina, Australia, Austria, Brazil, Burundi, Chile, Cuba, Dominican Republic, Ecuador, Eire, India, Indonesia, Israel, Kuwait, Liberia, Libya, Luxembourg, Morocco, Mozambique, New Zealand, Paraguay, Peru, Portugal, South Africa, Singapore, UK
Notes: The FAL (*Fusil Automatique Légère*) is a versatile and very successful rifle using the NATO 7.62-mm round. There are two basic variants, one with a shorter barrel and a folding stock, and the other with a heavy barrel and bipod for use as a light machine-

gun. Some users, it should be noted, use only the self-loading rather than the full selective fire version of the rifle.

Benin

2,100 men and 1,000 para-military forces.

2 inf bns.
1 engr bn.
1 para/cdo coy.
1 arty bty.
7 M-8 armd cars; 105mm how; 60mm, 81mm mor.

M8

Type: light armoured car
Crew: four
Weights: Empty
Loaded 17,000 lb (7,711 kg)
Dimensions: Length 16 ft 5 in (5.0 m)
Width 8 ft 4 in (2.54 m)
Height 7 ft 4 in (2.23 m)
Ground pressure: 13.6 lb/in² (0.96 kg/cm²)
Performance: road speed 55 mph (88 kph); range 350 miles (560 km); vertical obstacle 12 in (30.0 cm); trench negligible; gradient 60%; wading 24 in (61.0 cm)
Engine: one 110-hp Hercules JXD inline petrol engine

Armament: one 37-mm M6 gun, plus one 0.3-in (7.62-mm) Browning M1919A4 machine-gun co-axial with the main armament, and one 0.5-in (12.7-mm) Browning M2 AA machine-gun on the turret roof
Armour: $\frac{1}{8}$ in (3.17 mm) minimum; $\frac{3}{4}$ in (19 mm) maximum
Used also by: Brazil, Cameroon, Colombia, Greece, Guatemala, Malagasy Republic, Mexico, Morocco, Niger, Peru, Toga, Venezuela
Notes: The M8 is a 6 × 6 vehicle, and entered US service in 1943.

Bolivia

17,000 men.

4 cav regts.
1 mech regt.
1 mot regt.
13 inf regts (1 Palace Guard).
2 ranger regts.
1 para bn.
3 arty regts.
6 engr bns.
some M3 lt tnks, 18 M-113, 10 V-200 Commando, 20 MOWAG APC; 6 75mm guns; 25 75mm pack, 20 FH-18, 25 M-101 105mm how.

M3 Stuart

Type: light tank
Crew: four

Weights: Empty
Loaded 27,400 lb (12,428 kg)
Dimensions: Length 14 ft 10½ in (4.53 m)
Width 7 ft 4 in (2.23 m)
Height 8 ft 3 in (2.51 m)

Ground pressure: 10.5 lb/in² (0.74 kg/cm²)
Performance: road speed 36 mph (58 kph); range 70 miles (112 km); vertical obstacle 24 in (60.0 cm); trench 6 ft (1.8 m); gradient 60%; wading 3 ft (91.4 cm) without preparation
Engine: one 250-hp Continental W-670 radial petrol engine

Armament: one 37-mm M5 or M6 gun, plus one 0.3-in (7.62-mm) Browning M1919A4 machine-gun co-axial with the main armament, two 0.3-in (7.62-mm) machine-guns in the hull sponsons, and one 0.3-in (7.62-mm) machine-gun on the turret roof
Armour:: ⅜ in (10 mm) minimum ⅝ in (16 mm) mm) maximum

Used also by: Brazil, Chile, Colombia, Ecuador, El Salvador, Mexico, Paraguay, Upper Volta
Notes: The M3 light tank entered service in 1940, and although undergunned by the standards of World War II, served with distinction as a reconnaissance vehicle. It is still encountered occasionally in remoter areas of the world.

Brazil

182,000 men (110,000 conscripts) and para-military forces 200,000 (State Militias in addition).

8 divs: each up to 4 armd, mech or mot inf bdes.
2 indep inf bdes.
1 indep para bde.
5 lt 'jungle' inf bns.
60 M-4 med, 220 M-3A1, 250 M-41, 25 X-1 lt tks; 120 *Cascavel*, M-8 armd cars; *Urutu*, M-59, 600 M-113 APC; 500 75mm pack, 450 105mm (some M-7, M-108 SP), 90 155mm how; 81mm mor; 108-R, 114mm RL; 106mm RCL; Cobra ATGW; 40mm, 90mm AA guns; 20 Roland SAM; 40 L-42 Regente, O-1E lt ac; 10 AB-206A helicopters.

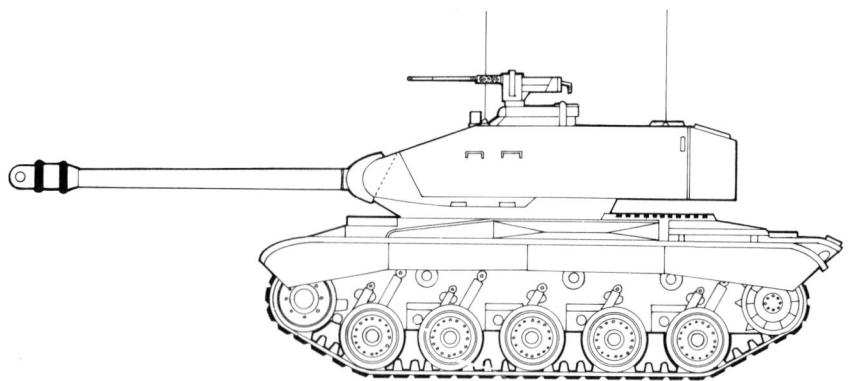

M41 Walker Bulldog

Type: light tank
Crew: four
Weights: Empty
　　　Loaded 51,800 lb (23,496 kg)
Dimensions: Length (with gun forward) 26 ft 11½ in (8.22 m); (hull) 19 ft 1¼ in (5.82 m)
　　　Width 10 ft 5¾ in (3.19 m)
　　　Height (overall) 10 ft 1¾ in (3.09 m)
Ground pressure: 10.2 lb/in² (0.72 kg/cm²)
Performance: road speed 45 mph (72 kph); range 200 miles (322 km); vertical obstacle 28 in (71.1 cm); trench 6 ft (1.83 m); gradient 60%; ground clearance 17¾ in (45.0 cm); wading 40 in (1.02 m) without preparation
Engine: one 500-hp Continental or Lycoming AOS 895-3 boxer petrol engine
Armament: one 76-mm M32 gun with 57 rounds of AP-T, HE, HVAP-DS-T, White Phosphorus and Canister, plus one 0.3-in (7.62-mm) Browning machine-gun with 5,000 rounds, co-axial with the main armament, and one 0.5-in (12.7-mm) Browning M2 machine-gun with 630 rounds on the turret roof
Armour: ⅘ in (20 mm) minimum; 1⅝ in (40 mm) maximum
Used also by: Austria, Belgium, Brazil, Denmark, France, Greece, Italy, Japan, Lebanon, Pakistan, Philippines, Saudi Arabia, Spain, Taiwan, Thailand, Tunisia, Vietnam, West Germany
Notes: The M41 light tank was the US successor to the M24 Chaffee light tank, and proved very successful. The M41 chassis was also widely used as the basis of other vehicles, including:
　1. M44 and M44A1 self-propelled 155-mm howitzer
　2. M52 and M52A1 self-propelled 105-mm howitzer
　3. M55 and M55A1 self-propelled 8-in (203-mm) howitzer
　4. M53 self-propelled 155-mm gun.

EE-17 *Sucuri*

Type: tank destroyer
Crew: four
Weights: Empty 39,021 lb (17,700 kg)
　　　Loaded 40,785 lb (18,500 kg)
Dimensions: Length 20 ft 10 in (6.35 m)
　　　Width 8 ft 6⅖ in (2.6 m)
　　　Height 9 ft 2¼ in (2.8 m) to top of turret
Ground pressure:
Performance: road speed 59 mph (95 kph); road range 373 miles (600 km); step 1 ft 11½ in (0.6 m); unprepared wading 3 feet 11¼ in (1.2 m); ground clearance 1 ft 3 in (0.38 m); gradient 65%
Engine: one 300-hp Detroit Diesel Model 6V53T 6-cylinder diesel
Armament: one French D 1504 105-mm QF gun with HEAT, HE and smoke rounds; one co-axial 7.62-mm machine-gun
Armour:
Used only by: Brazil

Notes: Designed by Engesa of Sao Paulo to be capable of taking on MBTs, despite weighing only half as much. The turret is the well proved French FL-12 oscillating unit. Many components of the EE-9 armoured car are used.

Cutia-Vete T1A1

Type: armoured personnel carrier and reconnaissance vehicle
Crew: four
Weights: Empty
　　　Loaded 5,997 lb (2,720 kg)
Dimensions: Length 12 ft 0 in (3.66 m)
　　　Width 6 ft 0 in (1.83 m)
　　　Height 3 ft 3$\frac{2}{5}$ in (1.0 m)

Ground pressure:
Performance: road speed 50 mph (80 kph); road range 230 miles (370 km);
Engine: one 4-cylinder petrol unit
Armament: one 7.62-mm machine-gun
Armour:
Used only by: Brazil
Notes:

EE-11 *Urutu*

Type: armoured personnel carrier
Crew: driver and 14 infantrymen
Weights: Empty 23,259 lb (10,550 kg)
　　　Loaded 26,014 lb (11,800 kg)
Dimensions: Length 19 ft 8$\frac{1}{4}$ in (6.0 m)
　　　Width 8 ft 2$\frac{2}{5}$ in (2.5 m)
　　　Height 7 ft 2$\frac{3}{8}$ in (2.2 m) without armament
Ground pressure:
Performance: road speed 59 mph (95 kph); road range 435 miles (700 km); step 1 ft 11$\frac{5}{8}$ in (0.6 m); ground clearance 19$\frac{7}{10}$ in (50.0 cm); gradient 65%
Engine: one 174-hp Mercedes Benz (Brazil) Model OM 352 6-cylinder diesel
Armament: various alternatives are possible, including:
　(a) ring-mounted 7.62-mm machine-gun
　(b) ring-mounted 12.7-mm machine-gun
　(c) turret-mounted 7.62-mm machine-gun
　(d) turret-mounted 12.7-mm machine-gun
　(e) turret-mounted 20-mm cannon or 60-mm mortar
　(f) turret-mounted 76- or 90-mm gun
Armour: estimated $\frac{1}{4}$ in (6 mm) minimum; $\frac{1}{2}$ in (12 mm) maximum
Used only by: Brazil
Notes: Basically amphibious, the EE-11 is propelled in water by the wheels. An alternative arrangement features twin propellers, twin rudders, trim vane, schnorkel and manual bilge pump for heavy sea operation. Built by Engesa.

M59

Type: armoured personnel carrier
Crew: two, plus up to 10 infantrymen
Weights: Empty 39,500 lb (17,917 kg)
　　　Loaded 42,600 lb (19,320 kg)
Dimensions: Length 18 ft 5 in (5.16 m)
　　　Width 10 ft 8$\frac{1}{2}$ in (3.26 m)
　　　Height 7 ft 10 in (2.39 m)

Ground pressure: 7.25 lb/in² (0.51 kg/cm²)
Performance: road speed 32 mph (51 kph); water speed 4.3 mph (6.9 kph); range 120 miles (193 km); vertical obstacle 18 in (45.7 cm); trench 5 ft 6 in (1.68 m); gradient 60%; the M59 is amphibious
Engine: two 127-bhp General Motors Corporation Model 302 petrol engines
Armament: one 0.5-in (12.7-mm) Browning

M2 machine-gun
Armour: $\frac{2}{5}$ in (10 mm) minimum; $\frac{3}{5}$ in (16 mm) maximum
Used also by: Greece, Turkey, and possibly Vietnam
Notes: The M59 has limited night-vision equipment, and can also be used as an ambulance and cargo carrier. There is also the M84 mortar-carrying version, armed with a 107-mm mortar.

M108

Type: self-propelled howitzer
Crew: seven
Weights: Empty
Loaded 49,500 lb (22,453 kg)
Dimensions: Length 20 ft (6.09 m)
Width 10 ft 3$\frac{1}{2}$ in (3.14 m)
Height 10 ft (3.04 m)
Ground pressure:
Performance: road speed 35 mph (56 kph); range 220 miles (354 km); vertical obstacle 21 in (53.3 cm); trench 6 ft (1.83 m); gradient 60%; wading 5 ft (1.524 m)
Engine: one 405-hp Detroit Diesel Model 8V71T turbo-charged inline diesel engine
Armament: one 105-mm L/22 howitzer with 89 rounds of Chemical and HE ammunition, plus one 0.5-in (12.7-mm) Browning M2 machine-gun for AA defence with 500 rounds
Armour: aluminium, $\frac{4}{5}$ in (20 mm) maximum

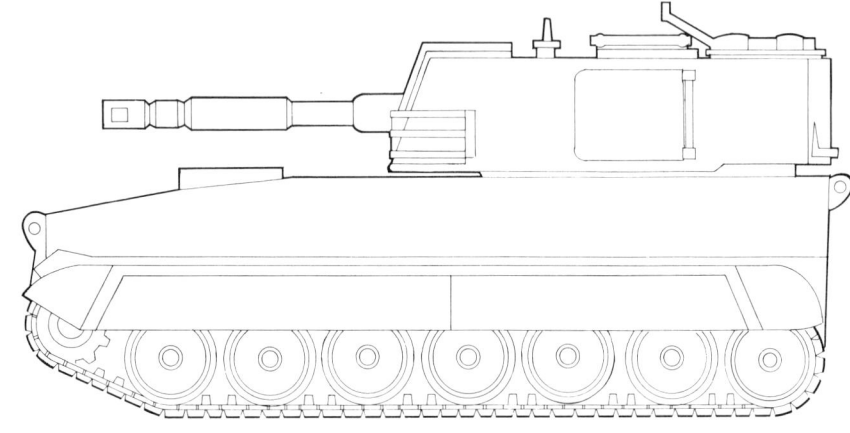

Used also by: Belgium, Spain
Notes: The M108 has the same hull as the M109, and has been in service since 1967 as a replacement for the M52. The turret traverses through 360°, and the howitzer has a range of 13,125 yards (12,000 m). The M108 is amphibious with the aid of flotation bags, being driven in the water by its tracks.

108R artillery rocket

Type: artillery rocket
Calibre: 80 mm
Barrel length:
Muzzle velocity:
Ranges: Maximum 8,202 yards (7,500 m)
Minimum
Elevation:
Traverse:
Rate of fire:
Weights: For travel
In firing position 37 lb (16.8 kg)
Dimensions: Length 3 ft 0$\frac{3}{4}$ in (0.93 m)
Width 4$\frac{1}{4}$ in (108 mm)
Height
Ammunition: HE warhead
Crew:
Used only by: Brazil
Notes: The 108R rocket is fired from the X2 16-tube launcher, which weighs 1,477 lb (670 kg) empty, and 2,028 lb (920 kg) loaded. The HE warhead of the rocket weighs 6.6 lb (3 kg).

X20 artillery rocket

Type: artillery rocket
Calibre:
Barrel length:
Muzzle velocity:
Ranges: Maximum 38,276 yards (35,000 m)
Minimum
Elevation:
Traverse:
Rate of fire:
Weights: For travel 255.7 lb (116 kg)
In firing position 255.7 lb (116 kg)
Dimensions: Length 9 ft 6 in (2.9 m)
Width 7 in (180 mm)
Height
Ammunition: HE warhead
Crew:
Used only by: Brazil
Notes: The X20 rocket being developed for the Brazilian Army is fired from a triple launcher by its solid-propellant motor, which develops a thrust of 4,850 lb (2,200 kg). The HE warhead weighs 77 lb (35 kg).

X40 artillery rocket

Type: artillery rocket
Calibre:
Barrel length:
Muzzle velocity:
Ranges: Maximum 74,365 yards (68,000 m)
Minimum
Elevation:
Traverse:
Rate of fire:
Weights: For travel
In firing position 330.7 lb (150 kg)
Dimensions: Length 15 ft 9 in (4.8 m)
Width 11.8 in (300 mm)
Height
Ammunition: HE warhead
Crew:
Used only by: Brazil
Notes: The X40 artillery rocket is under final development for the Brazilian Army. The rocket is fired from a single launcher, propulsion being by the solid-propellant rocket, which develops 15,653 lb (7,100 kg) of thrust. The warhead weighs 330.7 lb (150 kg).

INA MB50 and Model 953 sub-machine guns

Type: sub-machine gun
Calibre: 0.45 in (11.43 mm)
System of operation: blowback
Muzzle velocity: 920 ft (280 m) per second
Range: effective 219 yards (200 m)
Rate of fire: 650 rounds per minute (cyclic); 120 rounds per minute (automatic)
Cooling system: air
Feed system: 30-round box
Dimensions: Barrel length 8.39 in (213 mm) Overall length 31.26 in (794 mm) with stock extended; 21.5 in (546 mm) with stock retracted
Width
Height
Weights: 7.5 lb (3.4 kg) unloaded; 9.52 lb (4.32 kg) loaded
Sights: blade (fore) and aperture (rear)
Ammunition: 0.45 in ACP
Used only by: Brazil
Notes: The Brazilian MB50 is a copy of the Danish Madsen M-1946, identical in every respect with the Danish weapon. Model 953 has an enlarged magazine housing, and the cocking handle moved from the top to the right of the receiver.

Brunei

2,750 men.

2 inf bns.
1 armd recce sqn.
16 Scorpion lt tks; 24 Sankey APC, 16 81mm mor.

GKN Sankey AT 104

Type: armoured personnel carrier
Crew: two, plus up to nine infantrymen
Weights: Empty 17,635 lb (7,999 kg) Loaded 19,621 lb (8,900 kg)
Dimensions: Length 18 ft (5.486 m) Width 8 ft (2.438 m) Height 8 ft 2 in (2.489 m)
Ground pressure:
Performance: road speed 50 mph (80 kph)
Engine: one 146-bhp General Motors Bedford inline diesel engine
Armament: a wide variety of armament installations is possible to the user's requirements, but is usually a turret-mounted 7.62-mm machine-gun
Armour: $\frac{1}{4}$ in (6 mm) minimum, $\frac{1}{2}$ in (12.5 mm) maximum
Used only by: Brunei
Notes: The AT 104 is a simple APC intended basically for internal security duties. It is a 4×4 vehicle with adequate cross-country performance. Among the optional equipment fits are a barricade-remover, and a winch with a capacity of 26,455 lb (12,000 kg).

Bulgaria

115,000 men (75,000 conscripts) and 200,000 reservists.

8 mot rifle divs.
5 tk bdes.
1 AB regt.
3 SSM bdes with 'Scud'.
4 arty regts.
3 AA arty regts.
1 mountain bn.
2 recce bns.
125 T-34, 1,800 T-54/-55 med tks; 290 BRDM-1/-2 scout cars; 1,500 BTR-60, 35 OT-62 APC; 200 85mm, 400 122mm, 95 152mm guns/how; 82mm, 350 120mm, 160mm mor; BM-21 122mm RL; 36 FROG-7, 20 'Scud' SSM; 76mm ATK guns; 130 82mm RCL; 'Sagger', 'Snapper' ATGW; 57mm, 85mm AA guns; SA-6/-7 SAM.

Para-Military Forces: 15,000 border guards with AFV; 12,000 construction troops; 12,000 security police; 150,000 volunteer People's Militia.

BRDM-1 (or BTR-40P)

Type: reconnaissance car
Crew: five
Weights: Empty Loaded 12,346 lb (5,600 kg)
Dimensions: Length 18 ft 8$\frac{2}{3}$ in (5.7 m) Width 7 ft 4$\frac{3}{4}$ in (2.25 m) Height 6 ft 2$\frac{4}{5}$ in (1.9 m)
Ground pressure:
Performance: road speed 50 mph (80 kph); water speed 5.6 mph (9 kph); range 311 miles (500 km): The BRDM-1 is fully amphibious, being driven in the water by a single waterjet
Engine: one 90-bhp GAZ-40P inline petrol engine
Armament: one 7.62-mm SGMB machine-gun with 1,250 rounds on a pintle mount for the commander, though some vehicles have a second 7.62-mm SGMB machine-gun on a mounting at the rear of the hull
Armour: $\frac{2}{5}$ in (10 mm)

Used also by: Albania, Congo, Cuba, Czechoslovakia, East Germany, Egypt, Israel,
Poland, Syria, Uganda, USSR
Notes: The BRDM-1, or BTR-40P, was developed from the GAZ-63A lorry, and is a 4×4
vehicle with an extra four belly wheels that
can be lowered to improve traction in poor
going. This BRDM-1 was in itself derived
from the BTR-40, which had been introduced in 1951. The difference between the
BTR-40 and the BTR-40P lies in the addition of the four belly wheels and a central
tyre-pressure control system. The type has
also been developed as a command vehicle, NBC monitoring vehicle, and as a
launch vehicle for the AT-1 'Snapper', AT-2
'Swatter' and AT-3 'Sagger' AT missiles.

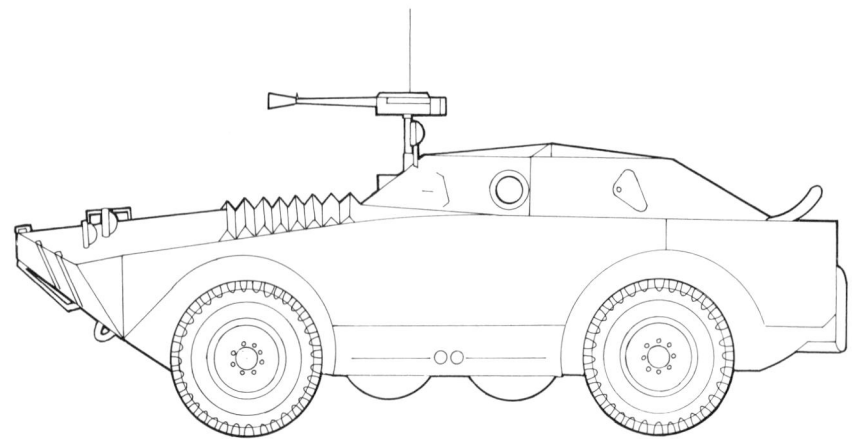

MT-LB

Type: multi-purpose military vehicle
Crew: three, plus up to 10 infantrymen
Weights: Empty 22,046 lb (10,000 kg)
Loaded 26,455 lb (12,000 kg)
Dimensions: Length 20 ft 10 in (6.35 m)
Width 9 ft 2¼ in (2.8 m)
Height 7 ft 5¾ in (2.28 m)
Ground pressure:
Performance: road speed 34 mph (55 kph);
water speed 3.1 mph (5 kph); range 249
miles (400 km); vertical obstacle 43⅓ in
(1.1 m), trench 39⅖ in (1.0 m); gradient
60%; ground clearance 13¾ in (35.0 cm);
the MT-LB is fully amphibious, being driven
in the water by its tracks
Engine: one 200-hp Model IZ-6 inline diesel
engine

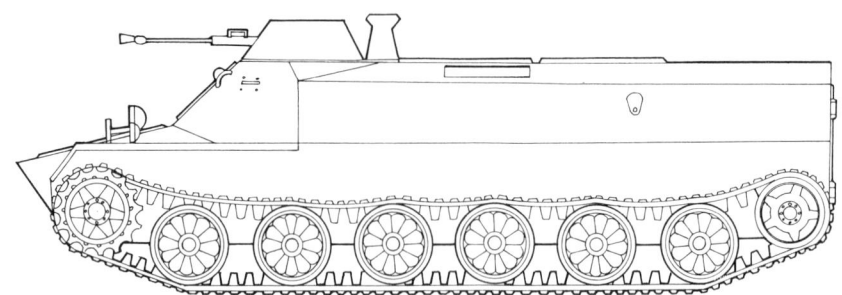

Armament: one turret-mounted 7.62-mm
PKT machine-gun
Armour:
Used also by: East Germany, USSR, and
other members of the Warsaw Pact
Notes: The MT-LB was known as the M1970
or GT-T when it first appeared in 1970, but

its true designation has since become
known. The type is very versatile, and can
be used as an APC, cargo vehicle, command vehicle, ambulance, fire-direction
vehicle and tractor for 85- and 100-mm AT
guns and 122-mm howitzers.

Burma

153,000 men.

3 inf divs, each with 10 bns.
2 armd bns.
84 indep inf bns (in regional comds).
5 arty bns.
Comet med tks; 40 Humber armd cars;
45 Ferret scout cars; 50 25-pdr, 5.5-
in guns/how; 120 76mm, 80 105mm
how; 120mm mor; 50 6-pdr and 17-
pdr ATK guns; 10 40mm, 3.7-in AA
guns.

Comet

Type: medium tank (originally cruiser tank)
Crew: five
Weights: Empty
Loaded 78,800 lb (35,696 kg)
Dimensions: Length 25 ft 1½ in (7.66 m)
Width 10 ft (3.04 m)
Height 8 ft 9½ in (2.98 m)
Ground pressure: 13.85 lb/in² (0.88 kg/cm²)
Performance: road speed 32 mph (51 kph);
range 123 miles (196 km); vertical obsta-
cle 3 ft (92.0 cm); trench 8 ft (2.43 m); gra-
dient 35%
Engine: one 600-bhp Rolls-Royce Meteor
Mark 3 inline petrol engine

Armament: one 77-mm gun with 61 rounds,
plus one 7.92-mm BESA machine-gun co-
axial with the main armament, one 7.92-
mm BESA machine-gun in the hull front
(with 5,175 rounds), and one 0.303-in
(7.7-mm) Bren gun with 600 rounds on the
turret roof for AA defence
Armour: ⅜ in (14 mm) minimum; 4 in (102
mm) maximum
Used also by: South Africa
Notes: The Comet entered British service in
1944, and remained in service until 1958.
It is still in service with some countries
despite its total obsolescence.

Humber Mark 1

Type: armoured car
Crew: three
Weights: Empty
Loaded 15,094 lb (6,846 kg)
Dimensions: Length 15 ft (4.57 m)
Width 7 ft 2 in (2.18 m)
Height 7 ft 10 in (2.39 m)

Ground pressure:
Performance: road speed 45 mph (72.5 kph); range 250 miles (402 km)
Engine: one 90-hp Rootes inline petrol engine
Armament: one 15-mm BESA machine-gun, and one 7.92-mm BESA machine-gun co-axial with the main armament

Armour: $\frac{3}{8}$ in (15 mm) maximum
Used also by: Cyprus, India, Mexico, Sri Lanka
Notes: The Humber armoured car dates from the early stages of World War II, but is still in limited service as a wheeled reconnaissance vehicle.

17-pounder gun

Type: anti-tank gun
Calibre: 76.2 mm
Barrel length: 55.1 cal
Muzzle velocity: 2,900 ft (950 m) per second
Ranges: Maximum 11,500 yards (10,516 m)
Minimum
Elevation: −6° to +16.5°
Traverse: 90° total
Rate of fire: 10 rounds per minute
Weights: For travel 6,700 lb (3,040 kg)
In firing position 6,445 lb (2,923 kg)
Dimensions: Length 24 ft 9 in (7.54 m)
Width 7 ft 2$\frac{1}{2}$ in (2.225 m)
Height 5 ft 6 in (1.68 m)
Ammunition: AP or HE

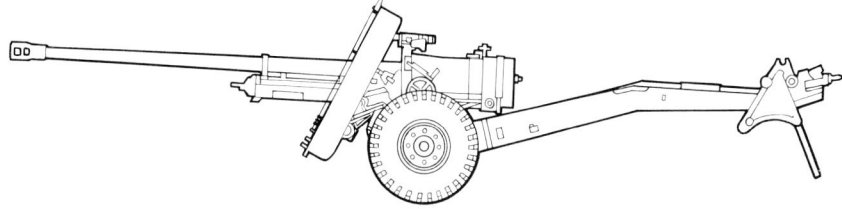

Crew: five
Used also by: Egypt, Israel, Pakistan, South Africa
Notes: The 17-pounder was introduced in 1942 and proved an effective tank-killer during World War II. As indicated by the designation, the piece fires a 17-lb (7.7-kg) AP shot.

BA52 sub-machine gun

Type: sub-machine gun
Calibre: 9 mm
System of operation: blowback
Muzzle velocity:
Range: effective 109 yards (100 m)
Rate of fire: 100 to 120 rounds per minute (automatic)

Cooling system: air
Feed system: 40-round box
Dimensions: Barrel length
Overall length 31.89 in (810 mm) with stock extended; 22.05 in (560 mm) with stock retracted
Width
Height

Weights: 8.27 lb (3.75 kg) loaded
Sights: blade (fore) and aperture (rear)
Ammunition: 9 mm × 19 Parabellum
Used only by: Burma
Notes: The Burmese BA52 is a copy of the Italian TZ45. It is an extremely simple weapon.

Burundi

4,500 total armed forces.

3 inf bns.
1 'para' bn.
1 'cdo' bn..
1 armd car coy.
AML armd cars.

Panhard AML-245

Type: light armoured car
Crew: three
Weights: Empty
Loaded 12,125 lb (5,500 kg)
Dimensions: Length (gun forward) 16 ft 9 in (5.11 m); (hull) 12 ft 5 in (3.79 m)
Width 6 ft 6 in (1.97 m)
Height (over machine-gun) 6 ft 10 in (2.07 m)
Ground pressure:
Performance: road speed 62 mph (100 kph); range 372 miles (600 km); vertical obstacle 12 in (30.0 cm); trench 2 ft 7$\frac{1}{2}$ in (80.0

cm) with one channel; gradient 60%; wading 3 ft 7 in (1.1 m) without preparation
Engine: one 90-hp Panhard Model 4 HD inline petrol engine
Armament: one 90-mm gun with 20 rounds of HE and HEAT, plus one 7.62-mm machine-gun co-axial with the main armament, and one 7.62-mm machine-gun on the turret roof. Some 2,400 rounds of 7.62-mm ammunition are carried
Armour: $\frac{1}{3}$ in (8 mm) minimum; $\frac{1}{2}$ in (12 mm) maximum
Used also by: Algeria, Angola, Chad, Congo, Ecuador, Eire, Ethiopia, France, Iraq, Israel, Ivory Coast, Kampuchea, Kenya, Libya,

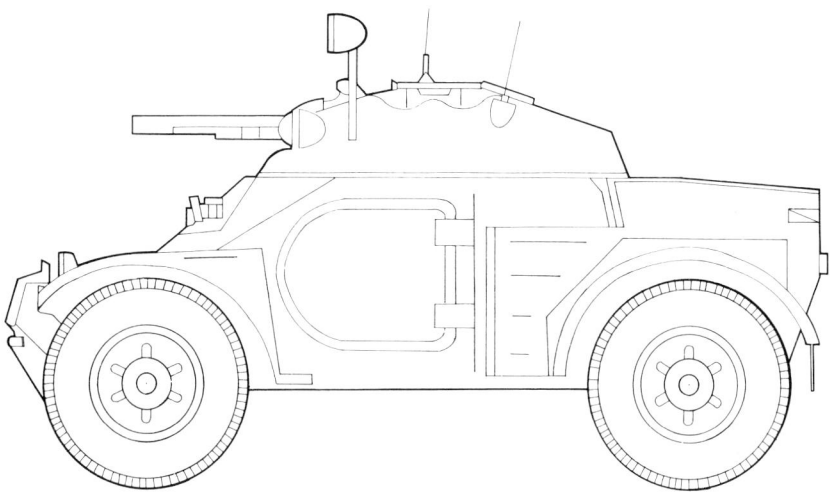

Malaysia, Mauritania, Morocco, Nigeria, Portugal, Rhodesia, Rwanda, Saudi Arabia, Senegal, South Africa, Spain, Tunisia, United Arab Emirates, Venezuela, Volta, Zaire

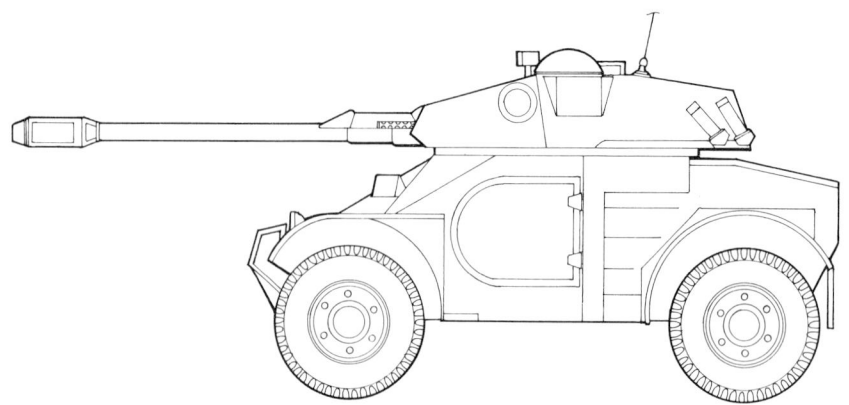

Notes: This *Automitrailleuse Légère* (AML) was adopted for French service in 1961, and has proved an outstandingly successful type, especially when armed with the 90-mm gun, whose HEAT rounds can penetrate $12\frac{3}{4}$ in (320 mm) of armour at 0°, or $5\frac{1}{2}$ in (140 mm) at 60°. In Israeli and South African hands the AML has proved more than adequate to the task of defeating Russian T-54 main battle tanks. The AML carries its own bridging equipment, in the form of two channels bolted to the hull front. The basic AML-245 can be fitted with a wide variety of turrets:

1. H90 F1-7, fitted with a 90-mm D921 gun and two 7.62-mm machine-guns. The technical specification above applies to the AML-245 fitted with this turret

2. HE 60-7, fitted with a 60-mm mortar and two 7.62-mm machine-guns, with 53 and 3,800 rounds respectively

3. HE 60-12, fitted with a 60-mm mortar and one 12.7-mm machine-gun, with 53 and 1,300 rounds respectively

4. HE 60-20, fitted with a 60-mm mortar and a 20-mm cannon, with 53 and 300 rounds respectively. A 7.62-mm machine-gun, for which 1,000 rounds are provided, can be mounted on the roof

5. HS-30, fitted with a 30-mm Hispano-Suiza 831 SL cannon and a 7.62-mm co-axial machine-gun, with 200 and 2,200 rounds respectively

6. S 530, with two 20-mm AME 621 cannon with 600 rounds

7. HE 60 (Brandt), fitted with a breech-loading Brandt 60-mm mortar and two 7.62-mm machine-guns, with 53 and 3,800 rounds respectively.

Cameroon

5,500 men.

4 inf bns.
1 armd car sqn.
1 para coy.
engr/spt units.

M-8 armd, Ferret scout cars; 18 Commando, M-3 APC; 75mm, 105mm how; 57mm ATK guns; 60mm, 81mm mor; 106mm RCL

M40A2 recoilless rifle

Type: anti-tank recoilless rifle
Calibre: 106 mm
Barrel length: 26.8 cal
Muzzle velocity: 1,650 ft (308 m) per second with HEAT
Ranges: Maximum 3,000 yards (2,745 m) with HEAT
Minimum
Elevation: −17° to +65°
Traverse: 360°
Rate of fire: one round per minute
Weights: For travel 485 lb (220 kg)
In firing position 520 lb (236 kg) loaded

Dimensions: Length 11 ft 1¾ in (3.4 m)
Width
Height
Ammunition: HEAT and HEP-T
Crew: two/four
Used also by: Australia, Austria, Brazil, Canada, Chile, Denmark, France, Greece, India, Iran, Israel, Italy, Japan, Luxembourg, Netherlands, New Zealand, Norway, Pakistan, Philippines, Singapore, South Korea, Spain, Switzerland, Taiwan, Thailand, Turkey, West Germany, USA
Notes: The M40 was standardised in 1953 as the basic US anti-tank weapon. Spotting is effected by a 0.5-in (12.7-mm) spotting rifle attached to the tube. Effective range is 1,200 yards (1,097 m).

M-1897 gun

Type: field gun
Calibre: 75 mm
Barrel length: 36.3 cal
Muzzle velocity: 1,886 ft (575 m) per second
Ranges: Maximum 12,140 yards (11,100 m)
Minimum
Elevation: −11° to +18°
Traverse: 6° total
Rate of fire: 12 rounds per minute
Weights: For travel 4,344 lb (1,970 kg)
In firing position 2,514 lb (1,140 kg)
Dimensions: Length 18 ft 3½ in (5.58 m)
Width 6 ft 7¼ in (2.01 m)
Height 4 ft 7¼ in (1.4 m)
Ammunition: HE and Shrapnel
Crew: four
Used also by: Greece, Kampuchea, Laos, Mexico, Morocco, Upper Volta
Notes: This is the celebrated 'French 75' of World Wars I and II, the gun which ushered in a new age in artillery. The shell weighs 13.66 lb (6.195 kg).

Canada

The Canadian Army

Properly speaking, there is no such thing as the 'Canadian Army', but rather the Land Forces of the Canadian Armed Forces, the unified armed service established in 1968 to replace the former Canadian Army, Royal Candian Navy and Royal Canadian Air Force. Service in the Canadian Armed Forces is entirely voluntary, and it is this factor that explains the relatively small size but technical expertise and excellent training of the Canadian Armed Forces. The Land Forces control all former army forces, and total manpower strength is 29,300, about 36.6 per cent of the Canadian Armed Forces, whose budget is some 1.84 per cent of the gross national product.

Within the Land Forces, it is the Mobile Command which controls Canada's land combat forces, numbering some 17,700 men of the land units and their supporting air units. The main strength of the Mobile Command is made up of two brigade groups and one special service force. The brigade groups each comprise one armoured regiment, three battalions of infantry, one light artillery regiment (made up of two close support and one air defence battery), one engineer regiment and various support units. These are well balanced units, but of limited size and capabilities in modern war. One of these mechanised brigade groups is based in Europe, and the other in Canada. The European brigade has some 2,800 men, all of Canada's 32 Leopard tanks, 375 M113 APCs, and 24 of the 50 M109 SP 155-mm howitzers. At the moment the Land Forces have a somewhat obsolescent *matériel* backing, but this will be redressed when the 114 Leopard MBTs on order are delivered, as well as the 177 MOWAG armoured cars and 241 MOWAG APCs. Air defence by means of missiles is adequate, as is air defence by guns, but serious thought must be taken in the near future to the upgrading of these units. Anti-tank capability is ensured by Carl Gustaf launchers and TOW missiles, and will be further strengthened by the delivery of more TOW missiles.

Apart from the mechanised brigade group deployed in Europe as part of NATO's defence of the theatre, Canada has deployed fairly substantial forces with various United Nations' peace-keeping groups: 515 with UNFICYP in Cyprus, 855 with UNEF in Egypt, 99 with UNIFIL in Lebanon, 161 with UNDOF in Syria, and 333 with other UN forces.

This leaves in Canada the following Mobile Forces combat units: one brigade group, one special service force, and one signal regiment. Also in Canada are various other Land Forces units attached to the Communications Command and Canadian Forces Training System. Also attached to the Mobile Command are Canada's reserve forces.

29,300 men and 15,200 reserves (99 combat arms units plus support units).

Mobile Command (about 17,700 land and air):
2 bde gps each comprising:
3 inf bns.
1 armd regt.
1 lt arty regt of 2 close support, 1 AD btys.
1 engr regt.
support units.
1 special service force comprising:
1 armd regt.
1 inf bn.
1 AB regt.
1 arty regt of 2 close support btys.
support units.
1 sigs regt.
32 Leopard A2 med tks:* 121 Ferret scout cars, 174 Lynx AFV; 827 M-113 APC; 58 105mm pack, 159 105mm how, 50 M-109 155mm SP how; 810 Carl Gustav 84mm RCL; 150 TOW ATGW; CL-89 drones; 57 40mm AA guns; 103 Blowpipe SAM. (114 Leopard med tks, 177 MOWAG Cougar armd cars, 241 MOWAG APC, TOW ATGW on order.)

Deployment:
Europe: One mech bde gp of 2,800 with 32 Leopard med tks, 375 M-113 APC/recce, 24 M-109 155mm SP how.
Cyprus (UNFICYP): 515.
Egypt (UNEF): 855.
Syria (UNDOF): 161.
Lebanon (UNIFIL): 99.
Other UN: 333.

Reserves: about 15,200 Militia; 99 combat arms units plus support units.

* (Leased until vehicles on order are delivered.)

Leopard 1

Type: main battle tank
Crew: four
Weights: Empty 89,066 lb (40,400 kg)
Loaded 93,475 lb (42,200 kg)
Dimensions: Length (including main armament) 31 ft 4 in (9.54 m); (hull) 22 ft 9¼ in (6.94 m)
Width 10 ft 8 in (3.25 m)
Height 8 ft 7 in (2.62 m)
Ground pressure: 12.8 lb/in² (0.9 kg/cm²)
Performance: road speed 40 mph (65 kph); range 373 miles (600 km); vertical obstacle 3 ft 9¼ in (1.15 m); trench 9 ft 10 in (3.0 m); gradient 60%; ground clearance 17¾ in (45.0 cm); wading 3 ft 11¼ in (1.2 m) without preparation, 7 ft 4⅝ in (2.25 m) with preparation, and 13 ft 1½ in (4.0 m) with a schnorkel
Engine: one 830-hp Daimler-Benz MTU MB 838 Ca.M500 supercharged multi-fuel inline engine
Armament: one 105-mm L7A3 gun with 60 rounds of APDS, HEAT, HESH and Smoke, plus one 7.62-mm machine-gun co-axial with the main armament, and one 7.62-mm machine-gun on the turret roof. Some 5,500 rounds of 7.62-mm ammunition are carried
Armour: ⅜ in (10 mm) minimum; 2¾ in (70 mm) maximum
Used also by: Australia, Belgium, Denmark, Italy, Netherlands, Norway, Turkey, West Germany
Notes: Built by Kraus-Maffei, the Leopard 1 MBT entered service in 1965. Night vision equipment and an NBC system are standard. The Leopard 1 is an outstanding vehicle of its kind, with excellent firepower, adequate protection and first-class mobility. There are several versions and derivatives of the Leopard 1:

1. Leopard 1 original production MBT, with a combat weight of 88,184 lb (40,000 kg)
2. Leopard 1 A1, the original version redesignated after the retrofitting of a Cadillac-Gage main armament stabilisation system, a thermal sleeve for the main armament, suspension skirts and deep-wading equipment, raising combat weight to 91,491 lb (41,500 kg)
2. Leopard 1 A2, some 232 A1s also fitted with ballistically improved turrets and image-intensifying night vision equipment, raising combat weight to 93,475 lb (42,400 kg)
3. Leopard 1 A3, with turrets welded from spaced armour
4. Leopard 1 A4, with turrets welded from spaced armour, and an integrated fire-control system combining the commander's stabilised panoramic telescope, the computer-controlled stereoscopic or coincidence rangefinder, the stabil-

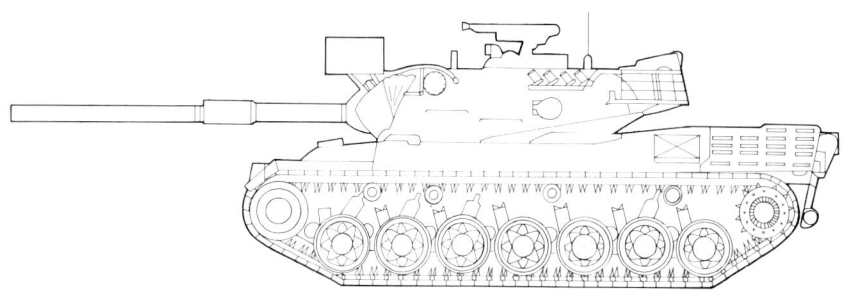

ised main armament and the ballistic computer

5. Leopard 1 armoured recovery vehicle, with a crane capable of lifting 44,092 lb (20,000 kg) and a winch with a capacity of 154,322 lb (70,000 kg) on double pull
6. Leopard 1 Armoured Engineer Vehicle with a dozer blade and earth-boring equipment
7. Leopard 1 *Biber* armoured vehicle-launched bridge, capable of spanning gaps of 65 ft 8 in (20.0 m)
8. *Flakpanzer* 1 *Gepard*, with twin 35-mm cannon and radar.

Various other derivatives have been developed up to prototype form, and some may yet be put into production. The designation Leopard 1, it should be noted, is one of convenience rather than of proper nomenclature, to distinguish this vehicle from the later Leopard 2.

Cougar

Type: armoured car
Crew: 12
Weights: Empty
    Loaded 21,164 lb (9,600 kg)
Dimensions: Length 19 ft 2 in (5.84 m)
    Width 8 ft 2⅖ in (2.5 m)
    Height 6 ft 0⅘ in (1.85 m)
Ground pressure:
Performance: road speed 62 mph (100 kph); water speed 6.2 mph (10 kph); range 621 miles (1,000 km); gradient 70%; ground clearance 19¾ in (50.0 cm); the Cougar is fully amphibious, being driven in the water by two propellers
Engine: one 300-hp inline diesel engine
Armament: one 76-mm L23 gun, plus one co-axial 7.62-mm machine-gun, or a turret-mounted cannon
Armour:
Used by: under construction for Canada
Notes: The Cougar is the name given to the 6 × 6 MOWAG Piranha built under licence in Canada. Some 350 examples are to be built, about 150 of them with the turret of the British Scorpion light tank. This

amalgamation has been successfully proved by the installation of such a turret on Australian M113 armoured personnel carriers.

FMC Corporation M113CR Lynx

Type: command and reconnaissance vehicle
Crew: three
Weights: Empty
    Loaded 19,667 lb (9,820 kg)
Dimensions: Length 15 ft (4.57 m)
    Width 7 ft 11½ in (2.41 m)
    Height 7 ft 2 in (2.18 m)
Ground pressure: 6.54 lb/in² (0.46 kg/cm²)
Performance: road speed 42 mph (68 kph); water speed 3.5 mph (5.6 kph); range 313 miles (504 km); vertical obstacle 2 ft (61.0 cm); trench 5 ft (1.52 m); gradient 60%; ground clearance 16 in (40.6 cm); the Lynx is inherently amphibious, being driven in the water by its tracks
Engine: one 215-bhp Detroit Diesel 6V53 inline diesel engine
Armament: one 0.5-in (12.7-mm) Browning machine-gun on the commander's cupola with 1,100 rounds, plus one 0.3-in (7.62-mm) Browning machine-gun on a pivot mount with 2,000 rounds for the observer
Armour: aluminium

Used only by: Canada
Notes: The Lynx, otherwise known as the M113CR or M113R, was developed as a private venture by FMC, on the basis of the M113 armoured personnel carrier, though smaller in size and with the engine and

transmission at the rear of the hull. As alternative armament installations, a turret-mounted 20-mm cannon, a recoilless rifle or an anti-tank guided weapon are available.

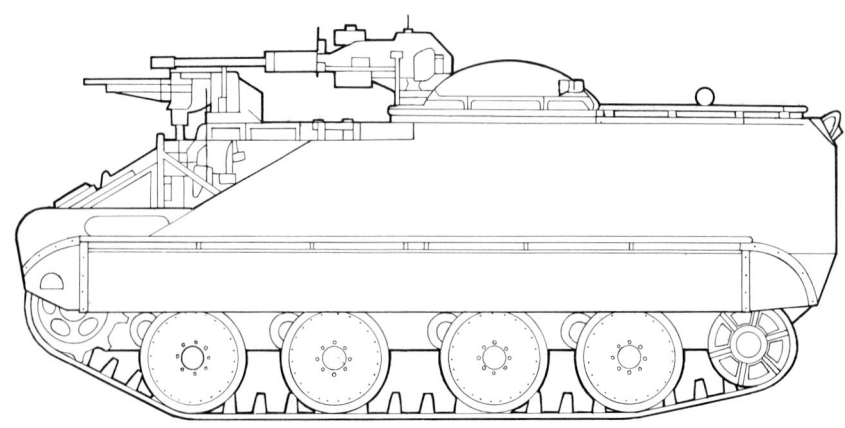

C1 sub-machine gun

Type: sub-machine gun
Calibre: 9 mm
System of operation: blowback
Muzzle velocity: 1,200 ft (366 m) per second
Range: effective 219 yards (200 m)
Rate of fire: 550 rounds per minute (cyclic); 120 rounds per minute (automatic)

Cooling system: air
Feed system: 30-round box
Dimensions: Barrel length 7.8 in (198 mm)
Overall length 27 in (686 in) with stock extended; 19.4 in (493 mm) with stock folded
Width
Height
Weights: 6.5 lb (2.95 kg) unloaded; 7.63 lb (3.46 kg) loaded

Sights: blade (fore) and aperture (rear)
Ammunition: 9 mm × 19 Parabellum
Used only by: Canada
Notes: The Canadian C1 is closely modelled on the British L2A1, the main differences between the two types being the smaller magazine of the Canadian weapon, which also uses the FAL rifle bayonet rather than the British No 5 bayonet.

C1 rifle

Type: self-loading rifle
Calibre: 7.62 mm
System of operation: gas
Muzzle velocity: 2,755 ft (840 m) per second
Range: effective 440 yards (402 m)
Rate of fire: 35 rounds per minute
Cooling system: air
Feed system: 20-round box
Dimensions: Barrel length 20.98 in (533 mm)
Overall length 44.72 in (1.136 m)
Width
Height
Weights: 9.37 lb (4.25 kg)
Sights: post (fore) and aperture (rear)
Ammunition: 7.62 mm × 51
Used only by: Canada
Notes: The Canadian C1 rifle is very similar to the British L1A1, the only major differences being the two-part firing pin and the ability to recharge the magazine of the Canadian rifle. The latter is achieved by means of

chargers and guides through an opening in the feed cover. The model with the two-part firing pin is designated C1A1. Canada, it should be noted, also uses a version of the FN heavy-barrel automatic rifle as a

squad automatic weapon, under the designations C2 and C2A1, the latter having a two-part firing pin and a plastic rather than wood carrying handle.

C2 rifle

Type: automatic rifle
Calibre: 7.62 mm
System of operation: gas
Muzzle velocity: 2,800 ft (854 m) per second
Range: effective 655 yards (600 m)
Rate of fire: 710 rounds per minute (cyclic); 60 rounds per minute (automatic); 35 rounds per minute (single shot)

Cooling system: air
Feed system: 20- or 30-round box
Dimensions: Barrel length 20.98 in (533 mm)
Overall length 44.72 in (1.136 m)
Width
Height
Weights: 15.28 lb (6.93 kg)
Sights: post (fore) and tangent, aperture (rear)

Ammunition: 7.62 mm × 51
Used only by: Canada
Notes: The C2 is the Canadian version of the FN heavy-barrel automatic rifle, and is used as a squad automatic weapon. The weapon may be distinguished from the C1 by the uncovered gas cylinder. The C2A1 has a two-part firing pin (to avoid premature firing as a result of a bent firing pin), and a plastic carrying handle.

Central African Empire

1,100 men.

1 inf bn.
1 engr coy.
1 sigs coy.
Ferret scout cars; 81mm mor; 106mm RCL.

Chad

5,000 men.

3 inf/para bns.
AML armd cars; 81mm, 120mm mor.

Chile

50,000 (20,000 conscripts) and 160,000 reservists.

6 divs, incl 7 cav regts (3 armd, 3 horsed, 1 helicopter-borne), 20 inf regts (incl 9 mot, 3 mountain), 6 arty groups, some AA arty spt dets.
M-4 med, 10 M-3, 60 M-41, 47 AMX-13 lt tks; M-113, MOWAG MR-8 APC; 105mm, M-56 105mm pack how; Mk F3 155mm SP how; 81mm, 120mm mor; 106mm RCL; 20mm, 40mm AA guns; 4 O-1, 5 T-25 trg ac, 9 Puma, 3 UH-1H, 2 AB-206 helicopters.

M101 howitzer

Type: field howitzer
Calibre: 105 mm
Barrel length: 24.7 cal
Muzzle velocity: 1,550 ft (473 m) per second
Ranges: Maximum 12,500 yards (11,438 m)
Minimum
Elevation: −5° to +65°
Traverse: 46° total
Rate of fire: four rounds per minute
Weights: For travel 4,978 lb (2,258 kg)
In firing position 4,899 lb (2,222 kg)
Dimensions: Length 19 ft 8 in (5.99 m)
Width 7 ft 1 in (2.16 m)
Height 12 ft (3.66 m)

Ammunition: HE, HEAT, HEAT-T, HEP-T, Chemical, Illuminating, Gas, and others
Crew: eight
Used also by: Argentina, Australia, Austria, Bangladesh, Belgium, Bolivia, Brazil, Colombia, Denmark, Dominican Republic, France, Greece, Guatemala, Haiti, Indonesia, Iran, Israel, Italy, Japan, Jordan, Kampuchea, Laos, Liberia, Libya, Mexico, Morocco, Netherlands, Norway, Pakistan, Peru, Philippines, Portugal, South Korea, Spain, Taiwan, Thailand, Uruguay, Venezuela, Vietnam, West Germany
Notes: The M101 is basically the pre-World War II M2A1 105-mm howitzer on the M2A2 carriage. The HE shell weighs 33 lb (14.98 kg), and the HEAT round will penetrate 4 in (102 mm) of armour at 1,640 yards (1,500 m).

le FH 18

Type: light field howitzer
Calibre: 105 mm
Barrel length: 25.77 cal
Muzzle velocity: 1,542 ft (470 m) per second
Ranges: Maximum 11,678 yards (10,675 m)
Minimum
Elevation: −6° 30' to +40° 30'

Traverse: 56° total
Rate of fire: six to eight rounds per minute
Weights: For travel 5,589 lb (2,535 kg)
In firing position 4,377 lb (1,985 kg)
Dimensions: Length 18 ft 4 in (5.59 m)
Width 6 ft 7 in (2.01 m)
Height 5 ft 10¾ in (1.8 m)
Ammunition: AP, HE, Smoke and others

Crew: six to ten
Used also by: Argentina, Austria, Bolivia, Czechoslovakia, Portugal, Sweden, Yugoslavia
Notes: This German field howitzer was introduced in 1935, and has one variant, the le FH 18(M) or 18(40), with a muzzle brake, spoked wheels and solid tyres. The HE projectile weighs 32.65 lb (14.81 kg).

Star Model Z45 sub-machine gun

Type: sub-machine gun
Calibre: 9 mm
System of operation: blowback
Muzzle velocity: 1,250 ft (381 m) per second
Range: effective 219 yards (200 m)
Rate of fire: 450 rounds per minute (cyclic); 120 rounds per minute (automatic)
Cooling system: air
Feed system: 30-round box

Dimensions: Barrel length 7.8 in (198 mm)
Overall length 33 in (838 mm) with stock extended; 22.8 in (579 mm) with stock folded
Width
Height
Weights: 8.5 lb (3.86 kg) unloaded; 10 lb (4.54 kg) loaded
Sights: blade (fore) and flip, notch (rear)
Ammunition: 9 mm Bergmann Bayard (Largo)

Used also by: Cuba, Portugal, Saudi Arabia, Spain
Notes: The Star Z45 is a Spanish weapon, closely modelled on the German MP40 of World War II, the principal difference being the relocation of the cocking handle on the right of the receiver. The weapon also has a compensator and a perforated barrel jacket. The weapon was initially made for sale to Germany, but by the time production got under way in 1944, lines of communication to Germany had been cut.

China

The Chinese Army

The army deployed by Communist China is known as the People's Liberation Army, and is the largest army in the world by a factor of about two. It numbers some 3,625,000 regular forces, about 83.3 per cent of China's total armed forces. These forces enjoy an annual budget of about 10 per cent of China's gross national product according to most western estimates, although this total may well rise in the next few years as the PLA was one of the major forces behind the elevation to the party chairmanship of Hua Kuo-feng after the death of Mao Tse-tung.

China is divided into 11 Military Regions, which serve primarily an administrative rather than a command function. Each of these districts is subdivided into Military Districts, there being about two or three districts to a region on average. Within the administrative area of each Military Region are a number of armies of the Main Forces, and various Local Forces. In the event of hostilities, the Military Region commands only its own Local Forces, command of the Main Forces being exercised both in peace and war by the Ministry of National Defence, controlled effectively by Teng Hsiao-ping, the Chief-of-Staff of the PLA General Staff, a key figure behind the strength of Chairman Hua's position.

It seems likely that each Military District has stationed in it an army, usually made up of the following Main Forces units: three infantry divisions, three artillery regiments, and in some cases three armoured regiments. In all, the Main Forces consist of 12 armoured divisions, 121 infantry divisions, three airborne divisions, 40 artillery divisions, 15 engineer (railway and construction) divisions, and 150 independent regiments. These Main Forces are intended for service anywhere in China, and are at a higher equipment and training level than any Local Force units.

Controlled by their parent Military Regions both administratively and tactically, the Local Forces are intended mainly for local defence and internal security, and are thus at a lower level of equipment and training. These forces comprise some 70 infantry divisions and 130 independent regiments, which are frequently used as border troops to leave the formations of the Main Forces free for major military activities.

Deployment of the PLA is basically as follows: in west and south-west China (Chengtu and Kunming Military Regions) 18 Main Force and 8 Local Force divisions; in central China (Wuhan Military Region) 15 Main Force (including the three airborne) divisions, and seven Local Force divisions; in east and south-east China (Tsinan, Nanking, Foochow and Canton Military Regions) 32 Main Force and 22 Local Force divisions; in north and north-west China (Lanchow and Sinkiang Military Regions) 15 Main Force and eight Local Force divisions; and in north and north-east China (Shenyang and Peking Military Regions) 55 Main Force and 25 Local Force divisions. This deployment, with the main strength in north, north-east and north-west China, clearly indicates the threat that Russia is considered to be by the Chinese high command. Other major forces are deployed fairly evenly throughout China, with slight emphasis on the industrial regions. Included in the totals for Chengtu, Kunming, Shenyang and Peking Military Regions, it should be noted, are the equivalent of eight to 12 divisions of border troops.

It is currently difficult to assess the combat worth of the PLA as a radical change in policy seems to be under way. Before the death of Chairman Mao, it was a long-established tenet of Chinese Communist military thought that the 'people's war' was not only historically inevitable but politically and militarily desirable. Hence the PLA, with its sheer bulk, and without significant numbers of modern weapons, must necessarily prevail, even at great cost in human lives. However, the accession of Chairman Hua and the reinstatement of Teng Hsiao-ping are bringing about a change not only in the overall importance of the PLA, but also in basic strategic policy. There are clear signs that the PLA command has decided on a complete modernisation of its Main Forces, even if this means a reduction in their numbers. Long reliant on Russian sources of supply for *matériel*, the closure of this source in the early 1960s meant relatively little to a force committed to the concept of the 'people's war'. Russian designs were copied, but little was done to develop new weapons and the tactics to accompany them. This is now changing, as is clear from Chinese efforts to purchase western technology if not weapons, and it is to be anticipated that in the mid-1980s there will begin to appear important numbers of new Chinese weapons.

For the time being, though, the PLA is geared to fight only a defensive war in China herself, or perhaps limited offensive wars in south-east Asia, though this latter seems a remote possibility. At present China lacks the strategic desire for large-scale offensive operations, and has consequently never built up the logistic apparatus for such operations. In general, therefore, the Chinese army cannot be regarded as a force of world importance, large and formidable though that army is.

3,625,000 men.

Main Forces:
11 armd divs.
121 inf divs.
3 AB divs.
40 arty divs (incl AA divs).
15 railway and construction engr divs.
150 indep regts.

Local Forces:
70 inf divs.
130 indep regts.
10,000 Soviet JS-2 hy, T-34 and Chinese-produced Type-59/-63 med, Type-60 (PT-76) amph and Type-62 lt tks; 3,500 M-1967, K-63 APC; 18,000 122mm, 130mm, 152mm guns/how, incl SU-76, SU-85, SU-100 and JSU-122 SP arty; 20,000 82mm, 90mm, 120mm, 160mm mor; 132mm, 140mm RL; 57mm, 75mm, 82mm RCL; 57mm, 85mm, 100mm ATK guns; 37mm, 57mm, 85mm, 100mm AA guns.

Deployment:
China is divided into 11 Military Regions (MR), in turn divided into Military Districts (MD), with usually two or three Districts to a Region. Divs are grouped into some 40 armies, generally of 3 inf divs, 3 arty regts and, in some cases, 3 armd regts. Main Force (MF) divs are administered by Regions but are under central comd.
The distribution of divs, excluding arty and engrs, is believed to be:
North and North-East China (Shenyang and Peking MR): 55 MF, 25 LF divs.
North and North-West China (Lanchow and Sinkiang MR): 15 MF, 8 LF divs.

East and South-East China (Tsinan, Nanking, Foochow and Canton MR): 32 MF, 22 LF divs.
Central China (Wuhan MR); 15 MF (incl 3 AB), 7 LF divs.
West and South-West China (Chengtu and Kunming MR): 18 MF, 8 LF divs.

Para-Military Forces: Public security force and a civilian militia with various elements: the Armed Militia, up to 7 million, organized into about 75 divs and an unknown number of regts; the Urban Militia, of several million; the Civilian Production and Construction Corps, about 4 million; and the Ordinary and Basic Militia, 75–100 million, who receive some basic training but are generally unarmed.

T-62

Type: light reconnaissance tank
Crew:
Weights: Empty
   Loaded about 46,297 lb (21,000 kg)
Dimensions: Length
   Width
   Height
Ground pressure:
Performance:
Engine:
Armament: one 85-mm gun, plus a 7.62-mm machine-gun co-axial with the main armament, and a 12.7-mm DShK machine-gun on the turret roof for AA defence
Armour:
Used also by: North Korea, Sudan
Notes: The T-62 appears to be a scaled down T-59.

T-60

Type: light tank
Crew: three
Weights: Empty
   Loaded
Dimensions: Length
   Width
   Height
Ground pressure:
Performance:
Engine:
Armament: one 85-mm gun, plus one 7.62-mm machine-gun co-axial with the main armament, and one 7.62-mm machine-gun on the turret roof for AA defence
Armour:
Used also by: Pakistan, Tanzania, Vietnam
Notes: The T-60 is the Chinese development of the Russian PT-76, and has a turret similar to that of the T-59, armed with an 85-mm gun and co-axial machine-gun.

Type 56

Type: armoured personnel carrier
Crew:
Weights: Empty
   Loaded
Dimensions: Length
   Width
   Height

Ground pressure:
Performance:
Engine:
Armament:
Armour:
Used by: China and some of her clients
Notes: The Type 56 is the Russian BTR-152 built in China. For details see the BTR-152 entry.

Type 55

Type: armoured personnel carrier
Crew:
Weights: Empty
Loaded
Dimensions: Length
Width
Height
Ground pressure:
Performance:
Engine:
Armament:
Armour:
Used by: China and some of her clients
Notes: The Type 55 is the Russian BTR-40 built in China. For details see the BTR-40 entry.

130-mm gun

Type: field gun
Calibre: 130 mm
Barrel length: 58.48 cal (with muzzle brake)
Muzzle velocity: 3,051 ft (930 m) per second with APHE and HE
Ranges: Maximum 33,902 yards (31,000 m) with HE; 1,280 yards (1,170 m) with APHE
Minimum
Elevation: −2.5° to +45°
Traverse: 50° total
Rate of fire: six to seven rounds per minute
Weights: For travel 18,629 lb (8,450 kg)
In firing position 16,975 lb (7,700 kg)
Dimensions: Length 34 ft 5¾ in (11.73 m)
Width 8 ft 0½ in (2.45 m)
Height 8 ft 4⅖ in (2.55 m)
Ammunition: APHE and HE
Crew: nine

Used also by: Bulgaria, East Germany, Egypt, Finland, India, Iraq, Mongolia, Nigeria, North Korea, Pakistan, Poland, Syria, USSR, Vietnam, Yugoslavia
Notes: The Chinese-built 130-mm gun is a copy of the Russian M-1946 130-mm field gun, to which the data and users above apply. The APHE round weighs 74 lb (33.6 kg), and can penetrate 9.85 mm of armour at 1,094 yards (1,000 m). Chinese-built guns are used by China and Pakistan.

Type 94 gun

Type: mountain gun
Calibre: 75 mm
Barrel length: 20.8 cal
Muzzle velocity: 1,263 ft (385 m) per second
Ranges: Maximum 9,099 yards (8,320 m)
Minimum
Elevation: −10° to +45°
Traverse: 40° on its carriage
Rate of fire:
Weights: For travel 1,199 lb (544 kg)
In firing position
Dimensions: Length 13 ft 1 in (3.99 m)
Width 4 ft 4 in (1.32 m)
Height
Ammunition: APHE, HE, HEAT, Shrapnel and Smoke WP
Crew: three
Used also by: Vietnam
Notes: This is the Japanese Type 94 (1934) gun, and breaks down into eight loads for pack transport. The complete semi-fixed QF round weighs 15.9 lb (7.2 kg).

M-1943 (ZIS-2) gun

Type: anti-tank gun
Calibre: 57 mm
Barrel length: 73 cal
Muzzle velocity: 4,167 ft (1,270 m) per second with HVAP
Ranges: Maximum 9,186 yards (8,400 m) with HE
Minimum
Elevation: −5° to +25°
Traverse: 56° total
Rate of fire: 20 to 25 rounds per minute
Weights: For travel
In firing position 2,535 lb (1,150 kg)
Dimensions: Length 22 ft 3½ in (6,795 m)
Width 5 ft 7 in (1.7 m)
Height 4 ft 6 in (1.37 m)
Ammunition: APHE, HE and HVAP
Crew: five to seven
Used also by: Albania, Bulgaria, Cuba, Czechoslovakia, East Germany, Egypt, Hungary, North Korea, Poland, Romania, Yugoslavia

Notes: The M-1943 is a Russian AT gun, and was developed from the M-1941. The type can be towed or air-lifted, and is still a moderately useful weapon, especially for night operations, in which an infra-red sight is usually fitted. The APHE round weighs 6.83 lb (3.1 kg), and will penetrate 4.17 in (106 mm) of armour at 547 yards (500 m); the HVAP round weighs 3.97 lb (1.8 kg), and will penetrate 5½ in (140 mm) of armour at the same distance.

ZPU-4 mounting

Type: quadruple AA gun mounting
Calibre: 14.5 mm
Barrel length: 93.7 cal
Muzzle velocity: 3,280 ft (1,000 m) per second
Ranges: Maximum (horizontal) 7,655 yards (7,000 m); (vertical) 16,404 ft (5,000 m)
Minimum
Elevation: −10° to +90°
Traverse: 360°
Rate of fire: 600 rounds per minute (cyclic) per barrel
Weights: For travel
In firing position 4,409 lb (2,000 kg)
Dimensions: Length 16 ft 4 in (4.98 m)
Width 5 ft 6 in (1.68 m)
Height 6 ft 10⅔ in (2.1 m)
Ammunition: API, API-T and IT
Crew: five
Used also by: Egypt, Vietnam
Notes: The ZPU-4 is a quadruple KPV mounting, designed principally for AA use, in which it has an effective ceiling of 4,593 ft (1,400 m). Each barrel has a 150-round ammunition drum. The API round can penetrate 1.26 in (32 mm) of armour at 547 yards (500 m).

Type 63 artillery rocket

Type: artillery rocket
Calibre: 107 mm
Barrel length:
Muzzle velocity: 1,263 ft (385 m) per second
Ranges: Maximum 8,803 yards (8,050 m)
Minimum
Elevation:
Traverse:
Rate of fire:
Weights: For travel
In firing position 41.9 lb (19 kg)
Dimensions: Length 2 ft 9 in (0.837 m)
Width 4⅙ in (106.7 mm)
Height
Ammunition: HE warhead
Crew:
Used also by: Albania, Vietnam
Notes: The Type 63 rocket is fired from a 12-barrel launcher weighing 1,327 lb (602 kg), which can be elevated from −3° to +57°, and traversed 32°.

Type 51 launcher

Type: man-portable anti-tank rocket launcher
Calibre: 90 mm
Barrel length:
Muzzle velocity: 325 ft (99 m) per second
Ranges: Maximum effective 1,300 yards (1,188 m)
Minimum
Elevation:
Traverse:
Rate of fire:
Weights: For travel 12 lb (5.45 kg)
In firing position
Dimensions: Length 5 ft 0¼ in (1.53 m)
Width
Height
Ammunition: HEAT warhead
Crew: two
Used only by: China
Notes: The Chinese Type 51 is a copy of the US 3.5-in (90-mm) rocket launcher. The rocket will penetrate 10½ in (267 mm) of armour.

Type 97 mortar

Type: medium mortar
Calibre: 90 mm
Barrel length: 13.33 cal
Muzzle velocity:
Ranges: Maximum 3,991 yards (3,650 m)
　　　　　Minimum

Elevation:
Traverse:
Rate of fire: about 15 rounds per minute
Weights: For travel 232 lb (105 kg)
　　　　　In firing position as above
Dimensions: Length
　　　　　　　Width
　　　　　　　Height

Ammunition: HE and Incendiary
Crew: three
Used also by: Algeria, Kampuchea, Laos, Vietnam
Notes: The Chinese Type 57 mortar is based on the obsolete Japanese Type 94 (1934) 90-mm mortar.

Type 63 mortar

Type: light mortar
Calibre: 60 mm
Barrel length: 10.16 cal
Muzzle velocity: 518 ft (158 m) per second
Ranges: Maximum 1,673 yards (1,530 m)
　　　　　Minimum

Elevation:
Traverse:
Rate of fire: 15 to 20 rounds per minute
Weights: For travel
　　　　　In firing position 27.3 lb (12.39 kg)
Dimensions: Length
　　　　　　　Width
　　　　　　　Height
Ammunition: HE

Crew: three
Used also by: Albania, Vietnam and various African 'freedom' fighters
Notes: Type 63 is an updated version of the Type 31, itself a copy of the US M2. The main difference between Types 63 and 31 is the former's rectangular rather than square baseplate. Type 63 also has only a single recoil cylinder.

Type 67 machine-gun

Type: light machine-gun
Calibre: 7.62 mm
System of operation: gas
Muzzle velocity: 2,739 ft (835 m) per second
Range: effective 875 yards (800 m)
Rate of fire: 650 rounds per minute (cyclic); 150 rounds per minute (automatic)
Cooling system: air

Feed system: 100-round metal belt
Dimensions: Barrel length 23.5 in (597 mm)
　　　　　　　Overall length 45 in (1.143 m)
　　　　　　　Width
　　　　　　　Height
Weights: 21.83 lb (9.9 kg)
Sights: pillar (fore) and leaf notch (rear)
Ammunition: 7.62 mm × 54R
Used by: China, and possibly other nations in South-East Asia and Africa

Notes: Type 59 is an indigenously produced Chinese weapon that has replaced Types 53 (Russian DPM light machine-gun) and 58 (Russian RP-46 company machine-gun). The design has drawn heavily on other similar weapons, the most notable features being the feed (Maxim), trigger (DPM), gas regulator (RPD) and bolt mechanism (Zb26). The weapon can be used on a bipod or a tripod.

Type 64 sub-machine gun

Type: silenced sub-machine gun
Calibre: 7.62 mm
System of operation: blowback
Muzzle velocity: 1,683 ft (513 m) per second
Range: effective 148 yards (135 m)
Rate of fire: 1,315 rounds per minute (cyclic)

Cooling system: air
Feed system: 30-round box
Dimensions: Barrel length 9.6 in (244 mm)
　　　　　　　Overall length 33.19 in (843 mm) with stock open; 25 in (635 mm) with stock closed
　　　　　　　Width
　　　　　　　Height

Weights: 7.5 lb (3.4 kg) empty
Sights:
Ammunition: 7.62 mm × 25 Pistol 'P'
Used also by: Vietnam
Notes: Type 64 uses a number of features derived from European sub-machine guns, but is an indigenously designed and produced Chinese weapon.

PPS-42 sub-machine gun

Type: sub-machine gun
Calibre: 7.62 mm
System of operation: blowback
Muzzle velocity: 1,640 ft (500 m) per second
Range: effective 219 yards (200 m)
Rate of fire: 700 rounds per minute (cyclic); 100 rounds per minute (automatic)
Cooling system: air
Feed system: 35-round box
Dimensions: Barrel length 10.75 in (273 mm)
　　　　　　　Overall length 35.63 in (905 mm) with stock extended; 25.2

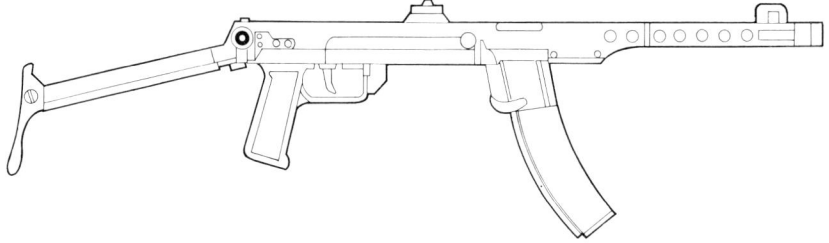

in (640 mm) with stock retracted
　　　　　　　Width
　　　　　　　Height
Weights: 6.5 lb (2.95 kg) unloaded; 8.05 lb (3.65 kg) loaded
Sights: post (fore) and L (rear)

Ammunition: 7.62 mm × Pistol 'P', or 7.63 mm Mauser
Used also by: Vietnam
Notes: The Russian PPS-42 is of World War II design, and makes considerable use of heavy gauge stampings, riveted and welded. The weapon is extremely basic.

Type 68 rifle

Type: selective fire automatic rifle
Calibre: 7.62 mm
System of operation: gas
Muzzle velocity: 2,395 ft (730 m) per second
Range: effective 219 yards (200 m) automatic; 437 yards (400 m) single shots
Rate of fire: 750 rounds per minute (cyclic); 85 rounds per minute (automatic); 40 rounds per minute (single shot)
Cooling system: air
Feed system: 15-round box (30-round AK box can be used with small modification)
Dimensions: Barrel length 20.5 in (521 mm)
　　　　　　　Overall length 40.5 in (1.029 m)
　　　　　　　Width
　　　　　　　Height
Weights: 7.7 lb (3.49 kg)

Sights: pillar (fore) and tangent notch (rear)
Ammunition: 7.62 mm × 39
Used by: China, and possibly other nations
Notes: Type 68 is a Chinese-designed weapon, but bears strong resemblances to the Type 56 (Russian SKS). There are two versions, the first having a machined receiver and the second a receiver of pressed and riveted steel sheet.

Colombia

60,000 men and 425,000 reservists.

11 inf bdes ('Regional Bdes').
1 Presidential Guard.
1 ranger bn.
4 AB bns.
1 AA arty bn.
7 mech cav, 25 inf, 7 arty, 7 engr units.
M-4A3 med, M-3A1 lt tks; M-8, M-20 armd cars; M-101 105mm how; mor; 40mm AA guns.

Para-Military Forces: 50,000 National Police Force.

M20

Type: utility armoured car
Crew: six
Weights: Empty
Loaded 15,650 lb (7,099 kg)
Dimensions: Length 16 ft 5 in (5.0 m)
Width 8 ft 4 in (2.54 m)
Height 7 ft 7 in (2.31 m)
Ground pressure:
Performance: road speed 56 mph (90 kph); range 250 miles (402 km); vertical obstacle 12 in (30.5 cm); gradient 30°; ground clearance $11\frac{1}{2}$ in (29.2 cm); wading 32 in (81.3 cm) without preparation
Engine: one 110-hp Hercules Model JXD inline petrol engine
Armament: one 0.5-in (12.7-mm) Browning M2 machine-gun with 1,050 rounds, plus one 2.36-in (60-mm) M9A1 or M18 rocket-launcher with 10 rounds
Armour: $\frac{4}{6}$ in (9.5 mm) minimum; $\frac{3}{5}$ in (15.9 mm) maximum
Used also by: Niger
Notes: The M20 was introduced into US service in 1943, and is basically an M8 armoured car with its turret removed and an M66 ring mount installed in its place. The primary role of the M20 is as a command vehicle.

SAFN M49 rifle

Type: self-loading rifle
Calibre: 7.92 mm
System of operation: gas
Muzzle velocity: 2,395 ft (730 m) per second
Range: effective 766 yards (700 m)
Rate of fire:
Cooling system: air
Feed system: 10-round magazine
Dimensions: Barrel length 23.19 in (589 mm)
Overall length 47.28 in (1.201 m)
Width
Height
Weights: 9.92 lb (4.5 kg)
Sights: shielded post (fore) and tangent aperture (rear)
Ammunition: 7.92 mm × 57 Mauser
Used also by: Argentina, Brazil, Egypt, Indonesia, Luxembourg, Turkey, Venezuela, Zaire
Notes: The Belgian *Arme Belgique Légère* or Saive *Automatique* FN (SAFN), has its origins in a Saive design of the late 1930s, perfected in the UK during World War II and produced by FN after that war in a variety of calibres.

Congo

6,500 men.

1 armd bn (5 sqns).
1 inf bn.
1 para-cdo bn.
1 arty gp.
1 engr bn.
T-59 med, 14 Chinese T-62, 3 PT-76 lt tks; 10 BRDM-1 scout cars; 44 BTR-152 APC; 6 75mm, 10 100mm guns; 8 122mm how; 82mm, 10 120mm mor; 57mm, 76mm ATK guns; 10 14.5mm, 37mm, 57mm AA guns.

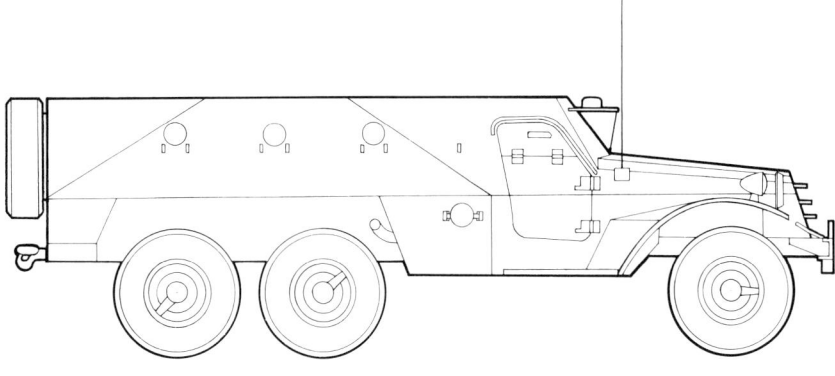

BTR-152

Type: armoured personnel carrier
Crew: two, plus up to 17 infantrymen
Weights: Empty
Loaded 19,731 lb (8,950 kg)
Dimensions: Length 22 ft 5 in (6.83 m)
Width 7 ft $7\frac{1}{3}$ in (2.32 m)
Height 6 ft $8\frac{3}{4}$ in (2.05 m)
Ground pressure:
Performance: road speed 47 mph (75 kph); range 404 miles (650 km); vertical obstacle $23\frac{2}{3}$ in (60.0 cm); trench $27\frac{1}{8}$ in (69.0 cm); gradient 30°; ground clearance $11\frac{3}{8}$ in (29.5 cm); wading $31\frac{1}{2}$ in (80.0 cm)
Engine: one 110-bhp ZIL-123 inline petrol engine
Armament: usually one 7.62-mm SGMB machine-gun with 1,250 rounds, but occasionally a 12.7-mm machine-gun
Armour: $\frac{1}{4}$ in (6 mm) minimum; $\frac{1}{2}$ in (13.5 mm) maximum
Used also by: Afghanistan, Albania, Algeria, Angola, China, Cuba, East Germany, Egypt, Ethiopia, Guinea-Bissau, India, Indonesia, Iran, Iraq, Israel, Kampuchea, Mali, Mongo-

lia, Mozambique, North Korea, North Yemen, Palestinian Liberation Army, Shri Lanka, Sudan, Syria, Tanzania, Uganda, Yugoslavia
Notes: The BTR-152 is a 6 × 6 vehicle, and entered service in 1950. The design is based on the ZIL-151, but later models use the ZIL-157 lorry chassis, with a central tyre pressure regulation system (BTR-152V). There are several variants:
1. BTR-152 basic model
2. BTR-152V1 with a front-mounted winch and a tyre pressure regulation system with external lines
3. BTR-152V2, as above, but with internal lines and no winch
4. BTR-152V3, as above but with a winch
5. BTR-152K, as above but with overhead armour
6. BTR-152AA with twin 14.5-mm rear-mounted KPV AA machine-guns (some Egyptian vehicles have four 12.7-mm MG53 machine-guns)
7. BTR-152 ATGW with 'Sagger' ATGW mounted over the rear compartment

8. BTR-152U with a higher roof, overhead armour and extra radio equipment for the command role.

Cuba

130,000 men and 90,000 reservists.

15 inf 'divs' (bdes).
3 armd regts.
Some indep 'regts' (bn gps).
Over 600 tks, incl 60 JS-2 hy, T-34/-54/
-55, 50 T-62 med, PT-76 lt; BRDM-
1 armd cars; 400 BTR-40/-60/-152
APC; 75mm pack, 122mm, 130mm,
152mm guns/how; 100 SU-100 SP
guns; 45 FROG-4 SSM; 57mm,
76mm, 85mm ATK guns; 57mm RCL;
'Snapper' ATGW; ZU-23, 37mm,
57mm, 85mm, 100mm, ZSU-23-4 SP
AA guns; SA-7 SAM

Deployment: Angola: 23–25,000;
Ethiopia: 16–17,000.*

* Cuban advisers and technicians are also reported in Algeria, Benin, Congo, Guinea Bissau, Libya, Mozambique, Sierra Leone, Tanzania, Uganda, South Yemen, Zambia.

JS-2

Type: heavy tank
Crew: four
Weights: Empty
    Loaded 101,963 lb (45,250 kg)
Dimensions: Length (with gun) 32 ft 9 in
    (10.74 m)
    Width 10 ft 6 in (3.44 m)
    Height 8 ft 11 in (2.93 m)
Ground pressure: 11.25 lb/in² (0.79 kg/cm²)
Performance: road speed 23 mph (37 kph);
range 94 miles (150 km); vertical obstacle
3 ft 3¾ in (1.0 m); trench 8 ft 2 in (2.86 m);
gradient 36°; ground clearance 13¾ in
(35.0 cm); wading 4 ft 3 in (1.3 m) without
preparation
Engine: one 520-hp Model V-2 JS inline
diesel engine
Armament: one 122-mm M1943 (D-25)

L/43 gun with 28 rounds, plus one 7.62-mm
DT or DTM machine-gun with 3,024
rounds co-axial with the main armament,
and one 12.7-mm DShK machine-gun with
350 rounds on the turret roof for AA
defence
Armour: ¾ in (19 mm) minimum; 4⅓ in
(110 mm) maximum
Used also by: China, USSR
Notes: The JS-2 appeared in 1943 as the
heavier element in Russian tank divisions,
and has remained in service with several
countries since that date.

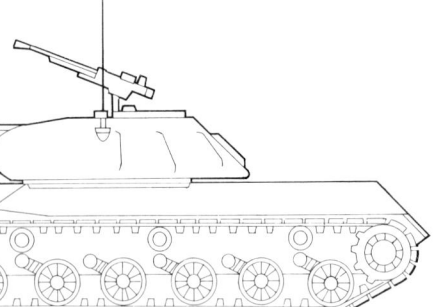

T17 Staghound

Type: armoured car
Crew: three
Weights: Empty
    Loaded 30,464 lb (13,818 kg)
Dimensions: Length 17 ft 7 in (5.36 m)
    Width 8 ft 10 in (2.7 m)
    Height 7 ft 8 in (2.34 m)
Ground pressure:

Performance: road speed 55 mph (88.5 kph);
range 450 miles (724 km); vertical obstacle 20 in (50.8 cm); gradient 57°; ground
clearance 13¼ in (33.66 cm); wading 32 in
(81.3 cm) without preparation
Engine: two 88-hp Chevrolet inline petrol engines
Armament: one 75-mm gun, plus one 7.92-
mm BESA machine-gun co-axial with the
main armament

Armour: ½ in (12 mm) minimum; 1¼ in (32
mm) maximum
Used also by: Nicaragua
Notes: The T17 Staghound was designed to a
British requirement, and entered service in
1943, in its Mark 1 version with a crew of
four, and armament of one 37-mm gun
plus two 0.3-in (7.62-mm) Browning
machine-guns. The Mark 2 mounted a 3-in
(76-mm) howitzer as main armament. The
Staghound is a 4 × 4 vehicle.

M-1963 (D-30) howitzer

Type: field gun/howitzer
Calibre: 122 mm
Barrel length: 39.2 cal with muzzle brake
Muzzle velocity: 2,428 ft (740 m) per second
    with HEAT

Ranges: Maximum 17,498 yards (16,000 m)
    with HE; 1,094 yards (1,000 m) with
    HEAT
    Minimum
Elevation: −7° to +70°
Traverse: 360°
Rate of fire: seven to eight rounds per
    minute

Weights: For travel
     In firing position 6,944 lb (3,150 kg)
Dimensions: Length 17 ft 8¾ in (5.4 m)
     Width 6 ft 3⅘ in (1.95 m)
     Height 5 ft 5¼ in (1.66 m)
Ammunition: HE and HEAT
Crew: seven
Used also by: Bulgaria, China, Czecho-slovakia, East Germany, Egypt, Finland, Hungary, Poland, Syria, USSR, Vietnam
Notes: The D-30 is the replacement weapon for the M-1938 (M-30), and was developed from the M-1946 (D-13) and M-1949 (D-24). The HE round weighs 48 lb (21.8 kg), and the HEAT round 31 lb (14.1 kg). The HEAT round will penetrate 18 in (460 mm) of armour. The D-30 is similar, but superior, to the M-1955 D-74 howitzer, which is used by Bulgaria, China, Cuba, East Germany, Egypt, Hungary, Nigeria, Poland, Romania, USSR, Vietnam.

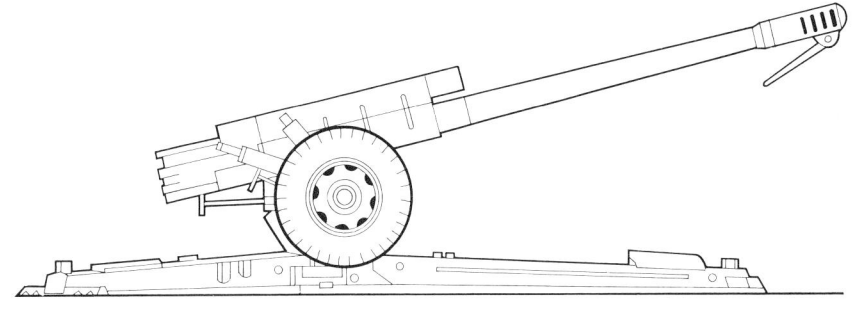

MG53 mounting

Type: quadruple AA gun mounting
Calibre: 12.7 mm
Barrel length: 84.2 cal
Muzzle velocity: 2,756 ft (840 m) per second with API
Ranges: Maximum (horizontal) 7,108 yards (7,000 m); (vertical) 18,044 ft (5,500 m)
    Minimum

Elevation: −7° to +90°
Traverse: 360°
Rate of fire: 600 rounds per minute (cyclic) per barrel
Weights: For travel 1,411 lb (640 kg)
    In firing position 1,384 lb (628 kg)
Dimensions: Length 9 ft 6⅛ in (2.9 m)
    Width 5 ft 3 in (1.6 m)
    Height 5 ft 10 in (1.78 m)

Ammunition: API
Crew: six
Used also by: Egypt, Vietnam
Notes: The MG53 is a Czech quadruple mounting for the Russian M-1938/1946 DShK heavy machine-gun. Each barrel is belt-fed from a 50-round drum, and the API round will penetrate ⅘ in (20 mm) of armour at 547 yards (500 m).

Cyprus

10,000 men and 20,000 reservists.

Greek-Cypriot Force:
1 armd bn.
2 recce/mech inf bns.
20 inf bns (under strength).
15 arty and support units.
25 T-34 med tks and BTR-50 APC; 30 Marmon-Herrington armd cars; 120

100mm, 105mm and 25-pdr guns and 75mm how; 40mm, 3.7-in AA guns.

Turkish-Cypriot Security Force:
About 5,000 men, organized in a number of inf bns.
Some T-34 med tks.

Czechoslovakia

140,000 men (95,000 conscripts) and 300,000 reservists.

5 tk divs.
5 motor rifle divs.
1 AB regt.
3 SSM bdes with 'Scud'.
2 ATK regts.
2 arty, 2 AA arty bdes.
3,400 T-54/-55 med tks; 680 OT-65, BRDM scout cars; 200 BMP MICV; 2,000 OT-62/-64/-810 APC; 300 100mm, 600 122mm, 50 130mm, 120 152mm guns/how; 122mm SP guns; 81mm, 120mm mor; 250 RM-70 122mm, M-51 130mm RL; 40 FROG, 27 'Scud' SSM; 125 82mm RCL; 125 'Sagger' ATGW; 200 57mm towed, M53/59 30mm SP AA guns; SA-4/-6/-7 SAM.

Para-Military Forces: 10,000 border guards, some APC, 82mm RCL; about 120,000 part-time People's Militia, 2,500 Civil Defence Troops.

OT-64 (SKOT)

Type: armoured personnel carrier
Crew: two, plus up to 18 infantrymen
Weights: Empty
  Loaded 31,967 lb (14,500 kg)
Dimensions: Length 24 ft 5 in (7.44 m)
  Width 8 ft 2 in (2.5 m)
  Height 8 ft 10 in (2.68 m)
Ground pressure:
Performance: road speed 59 mph (95 kph); water speed 5.6 mph (9 kph); range 442 miles (710 km); vertical obstacle $19\frac{3}{4}$ in (50.0 cm); trench 6 ft 7 in (2.0 m); gradient 60%; ground clearance $15\frac{3}{4}$ in (40.0 cm)
Engine: one 180-hp Tatra T-928-14 inline petrol engine
Armament: see notes below
Armour: $\frac{2}{5}$ in (10 mm) maximum
Used also by: Egypt, Hungary, India, Libya, Morocco, Poland, Sudan, Syria, Uganda
Notes: The OT-64 APC is based on the Tatra 813 lorry, and has 8 × 8 drive, with steering on the front four. The vehicle is fully amphibious, being driven in the water by two rear-mounted propellers. There are several versions of the OT-64:
1. OT-64 Model 1 with or without a lone 7.62-mm machine-gun
2. OT-64 Model 2 with a 7.62- or 12.7-mm machine-gun behind a curved shield
3. OT-64 Model 3 (SKOT-2A), fitted with the turret of the BTR-60PB, armed with a 14.5-mm KPVT machine-gun and a co-axial 7.62-mm PKT machine-gun. Some 500 rounds of 14.5-mm and 2,000 rounds of 7.62-mm ammunition are carried.
4. OT-64 Model 4 (SKOT-2AP), with a higher turret than the Model 3, but fitted with the same machine-guns
5. OT-64 Model 5, armed with a pair of 'Sagger' anti-tank missiles towards the rear of the vehicle
6. OT-64 Model 6 command vehicle, of which there are two submodels, the R2 and R3.

The OT-64 or SKOT entered service in 1963.

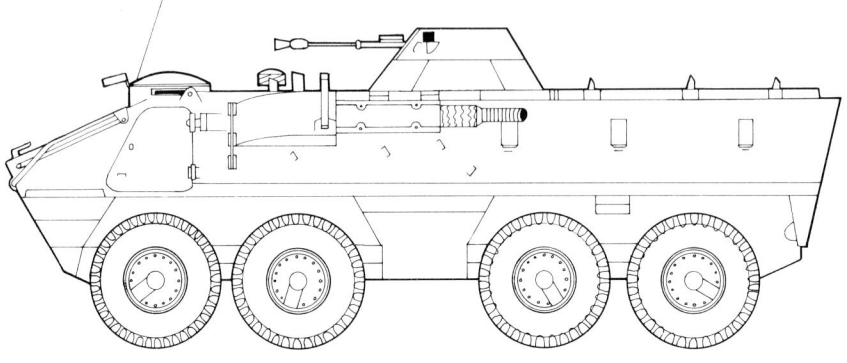

OT-62 (TOPAS)

Type: armoured personnel carrier
Crew: commander, driver and 12 infantrymen
Weights: Empty
  Loaded 36,133 lb (16,390 kg)
Dimensions: Length 23 ft $2\frac{3}{4}$ in (7.08 m)
  Width 10 ft 7 in (3.225 m)
  Height 8 ft $11\frac{1}{4}$ in (2.725 m) with turret
Ground pressure: 21.76 lbs/in² (1.53 kg/cm²)
Performance: road speed $38\frac{1}{2}$ mph (62 kph); water speed $6\frac{3}{4}$ mph (11 kph); road range 280 miles (450 km); step 3 ft $7\frac{1}{3}$ in (1.1 m); trench 9 ft $2\frac{1}{4}$ in (2.8 m); ground clearance $16\frac{3}{4}$ in (42.5 cm); gradient 70%
Engine: one 300-hp PV-6 6-cylinder diesel
Armament by model:
  Model 1: usually none
  Model 2: right-hand projecting bay has a turret with a 7.62-mm machine-gun and a T-21 recoilless rifle
  Model 3: large turret with a 7.62- and a 14.5-mm machine-gun
  Model 4: turret between and behind two projecting bays
Armour: $\frac{3}{5}$ in (14 mm) maximum
Used also by: Angola, Bulgaria, Egypt, Hungary, India, Iraq, Israel, Libya, Morocco, Poland, Romania
Notes: Czech-built version of the Russian BTR-50PK, better than the original, with superior performance. An NBC system is fitted. Fully amphibious, driven in water by waterjets.

OT-810

Type: armoured personnel carrier
Crew: two, plus up to 10 infantrymen
Weights: Empty
  Loaded 18,740 lb (8,500 kg)
Dimensions: Length 19 ft (5.8 m)
  Width 6 ft 11 in (2.1 m)
  Height (hull) 5 ft 9 in (1.75 m)
Ground pressure: 11.94 lb/in² (0.84 kg/cm²)
Performance: road speed 31 mph (50 kph); range 186 miles (300 km); trench 6 ft 6 in (1.98 m); gradient 24°; wading 24 in (61.0 cm) without preparation; vertical obstacle 10 in (22.5 cm); ground clearance $11\frac{4}{5}$ in (30.0 cm)
Engine: one 110-hp Tatra 912-2 inline diesel engine
Armament: one 7.62-mm machine-gun
Armour: $\frac{1}{4}$ in (6 mm) minimum; $\frac{1}{2}$ in (12 mm) maximum
Used also by: Romania
Notes: The OT-810 is the Czech-built version of the German *Sonderkraftwagen* (SdKfz) 251/1 half-track armoured personnel carrier and light prime mover of World War II.

M-18/46 howitzer

Type: howitzer
Calibre: 152 mm
Barrel length: 32 cal
Muzzle velocity: 1,667 ft (508 m) per second with HE
Ranges: Maximum 13,560 yards (12,400 m) with HE
    Minimum

Elevation: 0° to +45°
Traverse: 60° total
Rate of fire:
Weights: For travel
    In firing position 12,152 lb (5,512 kg)
Dimensions: Length 27 ft 2 in (8.284 m)
    Width 7 ft 4¾ in (2.255 m)
    Height 5 ft 7 in (1.707 m)
Ammunition: separate-loading HE and SAP
Crew: seven

Used only by: Czechoslovakia
Notes: The howitzer is a reworking of the German 150-mm medium howitzer of World War II. The barrel has been rebored to take the Russian 152-mm round, a double-baffle muzzle brake has been added, and a new shield is provided. The Semi-Armour Piercing (SAP) round will penetrate 3¼ in (82 mm) of armour at 1,094 yards (1 km).

M-55 gun

Type: anti-tank gun
Calibre: 100 mm
Barrel length: 64.3 cal
Muzzle velocity: 3,280 ft (1,000 m) per second with APHE
Ranges: Maximum 22,966 yards (21,000 m) with HE
    Minimum
Elevation: −5° to +40°
Traverse: 60° total
Rate of fire: eight rounds per minute
Weights: For travel
    In firing position 7,496 lb (3,400 kg)

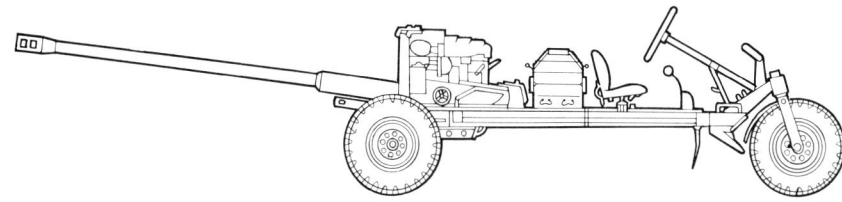

Dimensions: Length 28 ft (8.534 m)
    Width 7 ft 1¾ in (2.18 m)
    Height 8 ft 6½ in (2.606 m)
Ammunition: APHE, HE and HEAT
Crew: eight
Used also by: Austria
Notes: The Czech M-55 100-mm field anti-tank gun is also known as the M-53 field gun. It is very similar to the Russian 100-mm field gun, firing the same ammunition and having similar performance. The APHE round weighs 35 lb (15.9 kg) and will penetrate 7³⁄₁₀ in (185 mm) of armour at 1,094 yards (1 km).

M-52 gun

Type: field gun
Calibre: 85 mm
Barrel length: 59.65 cal
Muzzle velocity: 3,510 ft (1,070 m) per second with HVAP
Ranges: Maximum 17,673 yards (16,160 m)
    Minimum

Elevation: −6° to +38°
Traverse: 60° total
Rate of fire: 20 rounds per minute
Weights: For travel
    In firing position 4,619 lb (2,095 kg)
Dimensions: Length 24 ft 8 in (7.52 m)
    Width 6 ft 6 in (1.98 m)
    Height 5 ft (1.515 m)

Ammunition: APHE, HE and HVAP
Crew: seven
Used also by: Austria, East Germany
Notes: This is the Czech equivalent of the Russian D-44 gun, and is similar to it in appearance.

M-59A recoilless rifle

Type: anti-tank recoilless rifle
Calibre: 82 mm
Barrel length:
Muzzle velocity: 2,444 ft (745 m) per second with HEAT
Ranges: Maximum 8,366 yards (7,560 m)
    Minimum
Elevation: −13° to +25°
Traverse: 360° at 0° elevation; 60° at 25° elevation
Rate of fire: six rounds per minute

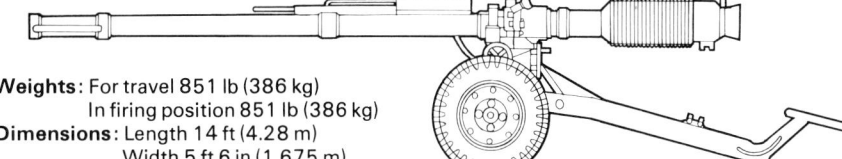

Weights: For travel 851 lb (386 kg)
    In firing position 851 lb (386 kg)
Dimensions: Length 14 ft (4.28 m)
    Width 5 ft 6 in (1.675 m)
    Height 3 ft 3⅔ in (1.0 m)
Ammunition: HE and HEAT
Crew: five
Used also by: Egypt
Notes: The M-59 and slightly modified M-59A are used for anti-tank and support fire by infantry units. The two rounds weigh 13.2 lb (6 kg), and the HEAT round will penetrate 9.85 in (250 mm) of armour. A 12.7-mm machine-gun mounted over the barrel is used for spotting.

M-53 gun mounting

Type: AA gun mounting
Calibre: 30 mm
Barrel length: 80.96 cal
Muzzle velocity: 3,280 ft (1,000 m) per second
Ranges: Maximum (horizontal) 10,936 yards (10,000 m); (vertical) 22,966 ft (7,000 m)
    Minimum
Elevation: −10° to +90°
Traverse: 360°
Rate of fire: 500 rounds per minute (cyclic) per barrel
Weights: For travel 4,630 lb (2,100 kg)
    In firing position 4,409 lb (2,000 kg)
Dimensions: Length 24 ft 10⅘ in (7.59 m)
    Width 5 ft 9 in (1.75 m)
    Height 5 ft 9 in (1.75 m)
Ammunition: HE and API
Crew: four
Used only by: Czechoslovakia
Notes: This twin AA mounting has hydraulic elevation and traverse, and feed from 50-round clips. The projectile weighs 1 lb (0.45 kg), and the maximum effective vertical range is 6,562 ft (2,000 m). When mounted on the Praga V3S lorry, the weapon system is known as the M-53/59.

RM-130 artillery rocket

Type: artillery rocket
Calibre: 128 mm
Barrel length:
Burnt-out velocity: 1,345 ft (410 m) per second
Ranges: Maximum 8,968 yards (8,200 m)
    Minimum
Elevation:
Traverse:
Rate of fire:
Weights: For travel
    In firing position 57.3 lb (26 kg)
Dimensions: Length 2 ft 7½ in (0.8 m)
    Width 5.04 in (128 mm)
    Height
Ammunition: HE warhead
Crew: six to eight
Used also by: Austria, Bulgaria, China, Egypt, Romania, Yugoslavia
Notes: The RM-130 system was introduced in 1951. The launcher is a 32-tube unit, which can be elevated to 45° and traversed 360°. The weight of the system, with the truck on which the launcher is mounted, is 26,455 lb (12,000 kg). The 32 tubes can be reloaded in two minutes.

P-27 grenade launcher

Type: anti-tank grenade launcher
Calibre: 45 mm (launcher); 120 mm (grenade)
Barrel length:
Muzzle velocity:
Ranges: Maximum effective 109 yards (100 m)
    Minimum
Elevation:
Traverse:
Rate of fire: three or four rounds per minute
Weights: For travel
    In firing position
Dimensions: Length 3 ft 11 in (1.092 m)
    Width
    Height
Ammunition: HEAT warhead
Crew:
Used also by: various Asian countries
Notes: The Skoda P-27 is the Czech version of the Russian RPG-2, and fires a grenade weighing 7.28 lb (3.3 kg).

M-1948 mortar

Type: light mortar
Calibre: 81 mm
Barrel length: 16.66 cal
Muzzle velocity:
Ranges: Maximum 4,046 yards (3,700 m)
    Minimum
Elevation:
Traverse:
Rate of fire: eight to ten rounds per minute
Weights: For travel 140 lb (63.5 kg)
    In firing position
Dimensions: Length
    Width
    Height
Ammunition: HE
Crew: three
Used only by: Czechoslovakia
Notes: The Skoda-built M-1948 mortar is designed for operations in difficult terrain, where the weapon's portability and good performance would be invaluable. There is also believed to be an improved version designated M-1952. The M-1948 has two baseplates, one a small unit attached to the barrel and used for hard-ground operations, the other a larger unit for operations in softer ground. The small baseplate slots into the larger one. Ammunition is the same as that for the Russian M-1937 mortar.

VZ59 machine-gun

Type: general-purpose machine-gun
Calibre: 7.62 mm
System of operation: gas
Muzzle velocity: 2,723 ft (830 m) per second with light bullet; 2,592 ft (790 m) per second with heavy bullet
Range: effective 1,640 yards (1,500 m) with a tripod; 1,094 yards (1,000 m) with a bipod
Rate of fire: 800 rounds per minute (cyclic) against ground targets; 1,000+ rounds per minute (cyclic) against aerial targets; 150/350 rounds per minute with light/heavy barrel (practical rate of fire)
Cooling system: air
Feed system: metal-link belt
Dimensions: Barrel length 27.28/23.35 in (693/593 mm) with heavy/light barrels (including flash hiders)
    Overall length 47.83/43.94 in (1.215/1.116 m) with heavy/light barrels
    Width
    Height
Weights: 19.11 lb (8.67 kg) empty with bipod; 42.4 lb (19.24 kg) with tripod; heavy barrel 8.36 lb (3.79 kg)
Sights: pillar (fore) and V notch (rear)
Ammunition: 7.62 mm × 54R, or 7.62 mm × 51
Used only by: Czechoslovakia
Notes: The Czech VZ59 is the successor to the VZ52, and is an effective weapon, as well as being cheaper and lighter than its predecessor. Used as a squad automatic weapon, with a bipod and light barrel, it is known as the VZ59L. The same designation is applied when the weapon is used as a light machine-gun on a bipod with the heavy barrel; but with a tripod and the heavy barrel, (medium machine-gun), it is designated VZ59. As a tank gun, fitted with a firing solenoid, it is known as the VZ59T.

VZ52 machine-gun

Type: light machine-gun
Calibre: 7.62 mm
System of operation: gas
Muzzle velocity: 2,477 ft (755 m) per second
Range:
Rate of fire: 1,200 rounds per minute (cyclic) belt-fed; 900 rounds per minute (cyclic) magazine-fed
Cooling system: air
Feed system: 100-round metal-link belt or 25-round box magazine
Dimensions: Barrel length 22.87 in (581 mm)
    Overall length 40.98 in (1.041 m)
    Width
    Height
Weights: 17.64 lb (8 kg)
Sights: blade (fore) and tangent with U (rear)
Ammunition: 7.62 mm M52, or 7.62 mm M52/57
Used only by: Czechoslovakia
Notes: The VZ52 is the last of a great family of Czech light machine-guns, including the Bren gun. Special attention was paid in design to the reduction of the mass of moving parts, thus allowing them a high acceleration and giving the gun a high rate of fire. For reasons of Warsaw Pact standardisation, the gun can fire the Czech M52 and the Russian M43 cartridges.

VZ24 sub-machine gun

Type: sub-machine gun
Calibre: 7.62 mm
System of operation: blowback
Muzzle velocity: 1,804 ft (550 m) per second
Range: effective 219 yards (200 m)
Rate of fire: 650 rounds per minute (cyclic)
Cooling system: air
Feed system: 32-round box
Dimensions: Barrel length 11.18 in (284 mm)
Overall length 27 in (686 mm)
Width
Height
Weights: 7.5 lb (3.41 kg)
Sights: hooded blade (fore) and square notch (rear)
Ammunition: 7.62 mm × 25 Pistol 'P'
Used only by: Czechoslovakia
Notes: The VZ24 is one of a family of sub-machine guns designed in Czechoslovakia and produced from 1949 onwards. The VZ23 fires the 9-mm Parabellum round, the VZ24 the 7.62-mm × 25 Pistol 'P' round, the VZ25 the 9-mm Parabellum round (this weapon differs from the VZ23 in having a folding metal stock in place of a fixed wooden stock), and the VZ26 the 7.62-mm × 25 Pistol 'P' round. The VZ26 has the same relationship to the VZ24 as the VZ25 to the VZ23.

VZ58 rifle

Type: assault rifle
Calibre: 7.62 mm
System of operation: gas
Muzzle velocity: 2,329 ft (710 m) per second
Range: effective 437 yards (400 m)
Rate of fire: 800 rounds per minute (cyclic); 90 rounds per minute (automatic)
Cooling system: air
Feed system: 30-round box
Dimensions: Barrel length 15.79 in (401 mm)
Overall length 32.28 in (820 mm) with stock extended; 24.6 in (635 mm) with stock folded
Width
Height
Weights: 6.92 lb (3.14 kg) empty; 8.42 lb (3.82 kg) loaded
Sights: post (fore) and tangent with V (rear)
Ammunition: 7.62 mm × 39
Used by: Czechoslovakia and various 'freedom fighter' groups
Notes: The Czech Army is the only army in the Warsaw Pact forces to be equipped with an assault rifle of local design, rather than the Russian AK47 or AKM. Early examples of the VZ58 have a fixed wooden stock, but later models have a folding metal unit.

Denmark

21,000 men (9,000 conscripts) and 74,500 reservists.

3 mech inf bdes, each with 1 tk, 2 mech, 1 arty bn, 1 recce sqn, 1 engr coy, spt units.
2 mech inf bdes, each with 1 tk, 2 mech, 1 arty bn, 1 engr coy, spt units.
1 indep recce bn.
Some indep mot inf bns.
120 leopard 1, 200 Centurion med, 48 M-41 lt tks; 630 M-113, 68 M-106 mortar-armed APC; 24 155mm guns; 144 105mm, 96 155mm, 12 203mm* how; 72 M-109 155mm SP how; 120mm mor; 252 106mm RCL; TOW ATGW; 224 L/60 and L/70 40mm AA guns; Hamlet (Redeye) SAM; 9 Saab T-17 lt ac; 12 Hughes OH-6A helicopters.

Deployment: Cyprus (UNFICYP): 360.

* (No nuclear ammunition for dual-capable 203-mm howitzers in Denmark.)

Reserves: 4,500 Augmentation Force, subject to immediate recall; 41,000 Field Army Reserve, comprising 12,000 Covering Force Reserve (to bring units to war strength and add 1 mech bn to each bde) and 29,000 other reserve units to provide combat and log support; 24,000 Regional Defence Force, with 21 inf, 7 arty bns, ATK sqns, support units; 56,100

Army Home Guard.

M106

Type: mortar carrier
Crew: two, plus six mortarmen
Weights: Empty
Loaded about 24,600 lb (11,156 kg)
Dimensions: Length 15 ft 11 in (4.86 m)
Width 8 ft 10 in (2.69 m)
Height 8 ft 2 in (2.5 m)
Ground pressure: 7.82 lb/in² (0.55 kg/cm²)
Performance: road speed 42 mph (67.6 kph); water speed 3.6 mph (5.8 kph); range 300 miles (483 km); vertical obstacle 24 in (61.0 cm); trench 5 ft 6 in (1.68 m); gradient 60%
Engine: 215-bhp General Motors Corporation Model 6V53 diesel engine
Armament: one 107-mm (4.2-in) mortar with 88 bombs
Armour: ½ in (12 mm) minimum; 1½ in (38 mm) maximum
Used by: Denmark and other NATO countries
Notes: The M106 is the M113 APC fitted with the US 4.2-in mortar, redesignated 107-mm Mortar M30.

M114A1 howitzer

Type: field howitzer
Calibre: 155 mm
Barrel length: 24.45 cal
Muzzle velocity: 1,850 ft (564 m) per second
Ranges: Maximum 18,150 yards (16,597 m)
Minimum

Elevation: −2° to +63°
Traverse: 25° left and 24° right
Rate of fire: about two rounds per minute
Weights: For travel 12,785 lb (5,799 kg)
In firing position 12,700 lb (5,761 kg)
Dimensions: Length 24 ft (7.32 m)
Width 8 ft (2.44 m)
Height 5 ft 11 in (1.8 m)
Ammunition: Chemical, Gas, HE, Illuminating, Nuclear and Smoke

Crew: 11
Used also by: Argentina, Austria, Belgium, Brazil, Ethiopia, Greece, Iran, Israel, Italy, Japan, Kampuchea, Laos, Libya, Netherlands, Pakistan, Peru, Philippines, Portugal, South Korea, Spain, Taiwan, Thailand, Turkey, West Germany, Yugoslavia
Notes: M114 is the designation adopted after World War II for the US M1 or M1A1

howitzer with the M1A1 or M1A2 carriage. Despite its age, the M114 offers good performance and great reliability. The HE shell weighs 95 lb (43 kg). The US Army uses a version of the weapon with auxiliary propulsion under the designation M123A1, and West Germany has produced the FH 155(L) improved model with a muzzle brake.

Hovea M49 sub-machine gun

Type: sub-machine gun
Calibre: 9 mm
System of operation: blowback
Muzzle velocity: 1,247 ft (380 m) per second
Range: effective 164 yards (150 m)
Rate of fire: 600 rounds per minute (cyclic)
Cooling system: air
Feed system: 36-round box

Dimensions: Barrel length 8.46 in (215 mm)
Overall length 31.89 in (810 mm) with stock extended; 21.65 in (550 mm) with stock retracted
Width
Height
Weights: 7.5 lb (3.4 kg) empty; 8.8 lb (4 kg) loaded

Sights: blade (fore) and V notch (rear)
Ammunition: 9 mm × 19 Parabellum
Used only by: Denmark
Notes: The M49 was designed by the Swedish firm Husqvarna, and was adopted when the Swedish Army preferred the Carl Gustav sub-machine gun. The weapon was originally intended for use with a Finnish 50-round magazine.

Dominican Republic

11,000 men.

3 inf bdes.
1 mixed armd bn.
1 mountain inf bn.
1 para 'bn'.
1 Presidential Guard bn.
1 arty regt.
1 AA arty regt.
1 engr bn.
1 armd recce sqn.
20 AMX-13 lt tks; AML armd cars; M-3 APC; 105mm how.

Christobal M2 rifle

Type: selective fire rifle
Calibre: 0.3 in (7.62 mm)
System of operation: delayed blowback
Muzzle velocity: 1,877 ft (572 m) per second
Range: effective 328 yards (300 m)
Rate of fire: 580 rounds per minute (cyclic); 120 rounds per minute (automatic); 40 rounds per minute (single shot)
Cooling system: air
Feed system: 25- or 30-round box
Dimensions: Barrel length 16.1 in (409 mm)
Overall length 37.2 in (945 mm)
Width
Height

Weights: 7.76 lb (3.52 kg)
Sights: blade (fore) and notch (rear)
Ammunition: 0.3 in M1
Used also by: Cuba
Notes: The Dominican Republic manufactures its own arms as a result of the Hungarian designer Pal Kiraly, who moved to that country after the Russian occupation of Hungary at the end of World War II. Not unnaturally, the M2 has many features in common with Hungarian sub-machine guns of Kiraly design.

East Germany

105,000 men (67,000 conscripts) and 250,000 reservists.

2 tk divs.
4 motor rifle divs.
2 SSM bdes with 'Scud'.
2 arty regts.
2 AB arty regts.
1 AB bn.
2 ATK bns.
About 2,500 T-54/-55 med tks (600 T-34 in storage); about 120 PT-76 lt tks; 880 BRDM-1/-2, FUG-66 scout cars; 1,500 BMP MICV, BTR-50P/-60P/-152 APC; 335 122mm, 100 130mm, 72 152mm guns/how; 250 120mm mor; 108 BM-21 122mm, RM-70 122mm RL; 24 FROG-7, 16 'Scud-B' SSM; 100mm ATK guns; 'Sagger', 'Snapper' ATGW; 130 57mm, 65 100mm towed, 105 ZSU-23-4 SP AA guns; SA-4/-7 SAM.

Para-Military Forces: 71,500. 46,500 border guards, some tks, AFV, 24 coastal craft; 25,000 security troops, 500,000 Workers' Militia.

FUG-70

Type: scout car
Crew: three, plus up to six infantrymen
Weights: Empty
Loaded 15,432 lb (7,000 kg)
Dimensions: Length 19 ft (5.79 m)
Width 7 ft 9 in (2.36 m)
Height 8 ft 3 in (2.52 m)
Ground pressure:
Performance: road speed 62 mph (100 kph); water speed 6.2 mph (10 kph); range 311 miles (500 km); vertical obstacle 15¾ in

(40.0 cm); trench 23⅜ in (60.0 cm); gradient 60%; ground clearance 12 in (30.5 cm); the FUG-70 is an inherent amphibian, driven in the water by waterjets
Engine: one Raba-Man diesel engine
Armament: one 14.5-mm KPVT machine-gun, plus one 7.62-mm machine-gun coaxial with the main armament
Armour:
Used also by: Hungary
Notes: The FUG-70 was derived from the FUG M-1963, but has a hull of different shape without belly wheels.

ASU-85

Type: assault gun
Crew: four

Weights: Empty
Loaded 30,864 lb (14,000 kg)
Dimensions: Length (with gun) 28 ft (8.54 m);
(hull) 20 ft (6.1 m)
Width 9 ft 2 in (2.8 m)
Height 6 ft 10⅔ in (2.1 m)

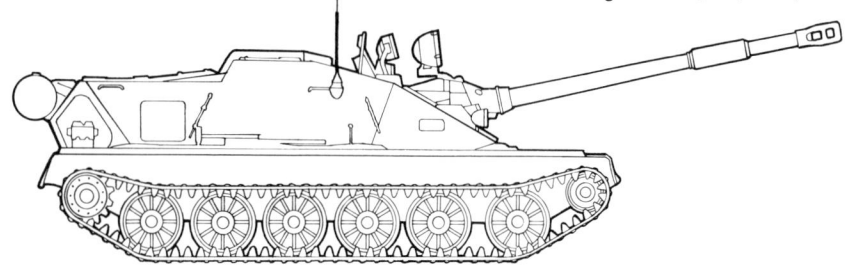

Ground pressure: 6.83 lb/in² (0.48 kg/cm²)

Performance: road speed 27 mph (44 kph); range 155 miles (250 km); vertical obstacle 43 in (1.1 m); trench 9 ft 2¼ in (2.8 m); gradient 70%; ground clearance 15¾ in (40.0 cm); wading 43 $\frac{3}{10}$ in (1.1 m) without preparation

Engine: one 240-hp inline diesel engine

Armament: one 85-mm SD-44 (Improved) gun with 40 rounds of APHE, HE and HVAP ammunition, plus one 7.62-mm PKT machine-gun co-axial with the main armament, and one 7.62-mm PKT AA machine-gun on the commander's hatch on some vehicles

Armour: 1 $\frac{7}{10}$ in (40 mm) maximum

Used also by: Poland, USSR

Notes: The ASU-85 assault gun is used by the airborne forces of the Warsaw Pact, and is air transportable. The chassis is derived from that of the PT-76, but is not amphibious. Night vision equipment and an NBC system are fitted as standard. The ASU-85 was brought into service in 1962.

ASU-57

Type: assault gun
Crew: three, plus up to six infantrymen
Weights: Empty
    Loaded 11,905 lb (5,400 kg)
Dimensions: Length (with gun) 16 ft 4⅔ in
    (4.995 m); (hull) 12 ft 2⅘ in
    (3.73 m)
    Width 7 ft 3 in (2.21 m)
    Height 5 ft 5 in (1.65 m)

Ground pressure:
Performance: road speed 28 mph (45 kph);
    range 155 miles (250 km)
Engine: one 55-hp M-20E inline petrol en-
    gine
Armament: one 57-mm Ch-51M gun with
    30 rounds, plus one optional 7.62-mm AA
    machine-gun
Armour: ¼ in (6 mm)
Used also by: Bulgaria, Czechoslovakia,
    Egypt, Hungary, Poland, Romania, USSR,
    Yugoslavia

Notes: The ASU-57 is intended to provide airborne troops with light anti-tank capacity,
and has been in service since 1957. Light
alloys are extensively used to keep down
weight, and the armour is very thin. Two
guns are used: the Ch-51 with a 34-slot
muzzle brake on the ASU-57A, and the Ch-
51 with a double-baffle muzzle brake on
the ASU-57B. The type is being superseded in Russian service by the BMD.

Model 41 flamethrower

Type: portable flamethrower
Notes: The Model 41 is the standard flamethrower of the East German Army, but few
details of the equipment are known. The

weapon consists of two cylinders carried
on the firer's back. One cylinder contains
fuel, and the other pressurised propellant.
Range is believed to be about 22 yards (20
m).

Ecuador

17,500 men.

11 inf bns (2 mot).
1 para bn.
3 recce, 4 horsed cav sqns.
1 Presidential Guard sqn.
10 indep inf coys.
3 arty gps, 1 AA arty bn.
2 engr bns.

30 M-3, 80 AMX-13 lt tks; 27 AML-60/
-90 armd cars; M-113, AMX-VCI
APC; 105mm, 6 Mk F3 155mm SP
how; 40mm AA guns; 1 Skyvan, 6
Arava, 3 Porter transports, 7 lt ac, 2
helicopters
(VAB APC on order.)

Para-Military Forces: 5,800.

Egypt

The Egyptian Army

The Egyptian Army numbers some
275,000 men in the army proper, and
another 75,000 in the Air Defence
Command. This total of 350,000 men
constitutes some 88.8 per cent of the
whole Egyptian armed forces, a
remarkably high percentage in what is
basically a sophisticated military
establishment. The armed forces have
an annual budget equivalent to 21.13
per cent of Egypt's gross national
product.

The main combat strength of the
Egyptian Army lies in its two armoured
divisions (each with one armoured and
two mechanised brigades), three
mechanised infantry divisions, and five

infantry divisions (each comprising two
infantry brigades). There is also the
Republican Guard Brigade, which is of
divisional strength. Apart from these
formations, Egypt also possesses a large
number of independent and special
service units: three independent
armoured brigades, seven independent
infantry brigades, two air-mobile
brigades, two paratroop brigades, six
artillery brigades, two heavy mortar
brigades, one anti-tank missile brigade,
two surface to surface missile regiments
(with up to 24 'Scud-B' missiles), and
six commando groups, the last usually
operating in conjunction with the two
paratroop brigades.

An examination of the *matériel*
available to the Egyptian Army reveals

that much of its current equipment is of
Russian origins, and that most of the
equipment on order or recently
delivered is of western European or
American provenance. This reflects the
rift between Egypt and the Soviet
Union in the mid-1960s, and Egypt's
decision to switch as quickly as possible
to western sources of supply. In the
short term, however, this has left the
Egyptian Army in an unenviable
position so far as serviceability is
concerned, there being few spares for
its Russian equipment. It must be
remembered, therefore, that an
unknown, but sizable, proportion of
Egypt's *matériel* may be unserviceable
for lack of spares. Cannibalisation may
ease the problem, and the Egyptians are

trying to develop locally produced spares as well as bringing in western technicians and spares in an effort to keep their weapons and vehicles serviceable.

This problem with *matériel* is more acute still with the weapons of the Air Defence Command whose missiles, already obsolescent, are made the more vulnerable to unserviceability by their very sophistication. It is debatable, therefore, how efficient the Egyptian SAM defences are. The AA gun defences might prove more successful in combat, but here again modern AA guns are reliant on radar-enhanced fire-control systems, and these too may be at a low rate of serviceability in the Egyptian Army.

It is difficult to assess the combat worth of the Egyptian Army because of the unknown serviceability rate of its Russian weapons and vehicles, and the uncertain morale of its men, large numbers of whom are relatively unwilling conscripts called up for three years. The problem has been made more difficult by the fact that the 1978 'Camp David' accord between Egypt and Israel may lead to a feeling among many soldiers that they have been let down by the country's political leaders after fighting four bloody wars against Israel in the period between 1948 and 1973. The Camp David accord may have exactly the opposite effect, on the other hand. It is interesting to note that the Egyptian Army has improved enormously in ability during the period of the four Arab-Israeli wars. At first it was hopelessly inefficient and unwieldy. The 1973 'Yom Kippur' War showed that the Egyptians were capable of sophisticated military planning, and their soldiers of determined, and at times successful, fighting. The army still has a long way to go in the development of a good officer corps and an NCO force of initiative, but there can be little doubt that with application the Egyptians are capable of producing a first-class army. Whether or not they will do so remains to be seen.

Egypt's para-military forces number about 50,000, including 6,000 National Guard, 6,000 Frontier Corps, 30,000 Defence and Security, and 7,000 Coast Guard.

350,000 men and 500,000 reservists (about).

2 armd divs (each with 1 armd, 2 mech bdes).
3 mech inf divs.
5 inf divs (each with 2 inf bdes).
1 Republican Guard Brigade (div).
3 indep armd bdes.
7 indep inf bdes.
2 airmobile bdes.
2 para bdes, 6 cdo gps.
6 arty, 2 hy mor bdes.
1 ATGW bde.
2 SSM regts (up to 24 'Scud').
850 T-54/-55, 750 T-62 med, 80 PT-76 lt tks; 300 BRDM-1/-2 scout cars; 200 BMP-76PB MICV; 2,500 OT-62/-64, BTR-40/-50/-60/-152, *Walid* APC; 1,300 76mm, 100mm, 122mm, 130mm, 152mm and 180mm guns/how; about 200 SU-100 and JSU-152 SP guns; 300 120mm, 160mm and 240mm mor; 300 122mm, 140mm and 240mm RL; 30 FROG-4/-7, 24 'Scud-B', 'Samlet' SSM; 900 57mm, 85mm and 100mm ATK guns; 900 82mm and 107mm RCL; 1,000 'Sagger', 'Snapper', 'Swatter', *Milan*, 'Beeswing' ATGW; 350 ZSU-23-4, ZSU-57-2 SP AA guns; SA-7/-9 SAM.*

(M-113 APC, Swingfire ATGW on order.)

* (Spares for Russian equipment are in very short supply.)

Air Defence Command (75,000): 360 SA-2, 200 SA-3, 75 SA-6 SAM; 2,500 20mm, 23mm, 37mm, 40mm, 57mm, 85mm and 100mm AA guns; missile radars incl 'Fan Song', 'Low Blow', 'Flat Face', 'Straight Flush' and 'Long Track'; gun radars 'Fire Can', 'Fire Wheel' and 'Whiff'; EW radars 'Knife Rest' and 'Spoon Rest'.
(*Crotale* SAM on order.)

Para-Military Forces: about 50,000; National Guard 6,000, Frontier Corps 6,000, Defence and Security 30,000 Coast Guard 7,000.

T-62

Type: main battle tank
Crew: four
Weights: Empty
 Loaded 82,673 lb (37,500 kg)
Dimensions: Length (hull) 22 ft (6.715 m)
 Width 11 ft (3.352 m)
 Height 7 ft 10½ in (2.4 m)
Ground pressure: 11.38 lb/in² (0.8 kg/cm²)
Performance: road speed 34 mph (55 kph); range 298 miles (480 km); vertical obstacle 31½ in (80.0 cm); trench 9 ft 2¼ in (2.8 m); gradient 60%; ground clearance 16¾ in (42.5 cm); wading 4 ft 7 in (1.6 m) without preparation, and 13 ft (3.96 m) with the aid of a schnorkel
Engine: one 700-hp V-2-62 inline diesel engine
Armament: one 115-mm U-5TS smooth-bore gun with 40 rounds of APFSDS, HE and HEAT, plus one 7.62-mm PKT machine-gun co-axial with the main armament, and one 12.7-mm DShK AA machine-gun on the commander's cupola. Some 2,000 or 3,500 rounds of 7.62-mm ammunition are carried.
Armour: 6¾ in (170 mm) maximum
Used also by: Afghanistan, Algeria, Czechoslovakia, East Germany, Hungary, India, Iraq, Israel, Libya, Malawi, Poland, Romania, Syria, Tanzania, USSR
Notes: Derived from the T-54/T-55 series, the T-62 entered service in 1961. It differs from its predecessors mainly in having a 115-mm smooth-bore gun in place of the 100-mm rifled weapon, the T-62A variant having a 12.7- in place of a 7.62-mm AA weapon on top of the turret. Standard equipment includes an NBC system, night vision equipment, smokelaying capability and long-range fuel tanks on the rear of the hull.

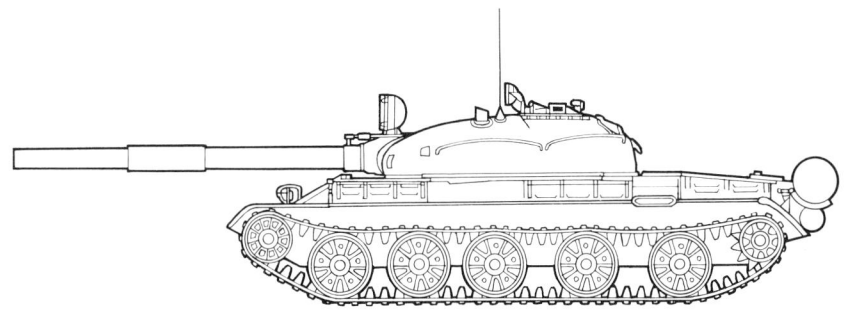

BTR-60

Type: armoured personnel carrier
Crew: two, plus up to 14 infantrymen
Weights: Empty
    Loaded 22,707 lb (10,300 kg)
Dimensions: Length 24 ft 9⅔ in (7.56 m)
    Width 9 ft 3 in (2.82 m)
    Height (to turret top) 7 ft 7 in
    (2.31 m)
Ground pressure:
Performance: road speed 50 mph (80 kph); water speed 6.2 mph (10 kph); range 311 miles (500 km); the BTR-60 is fully amphibious, being driven in the water by a single waterjet; vertical obstacle 15¾ in (40.0 cm); trench 6 ft 6¾ in (2.0 m); gradient 30°; ground clearance 18¾ in (47.5 cm)
Engine: two 90-bhp GAZ-49E inline petrol engines
Armament: One turret-mounted 14.5-mm KPVT machine-gun, plus one 7.62-mm PKT co-axial machine-gun, plus optional fits of a flare/rocket launcher on the right track guard, and an anti-tank rocket-launcher on the left track guard
Armour: ⅗ in (14 mm)
Used also by: Afghanistan, Algeria, Angola, Bulgaria, Cuba, East Germany, Egypt, Ethiopia, Finland, Hungary, Iran, Iraq, Israel, Libya, Mongolia, North Korea, Poland, Romania, Somali Republic, Syria, USSR, Vietnam, Yugoslavia
Notes: The BTR-60 is an 8 × 8 vehicle, and

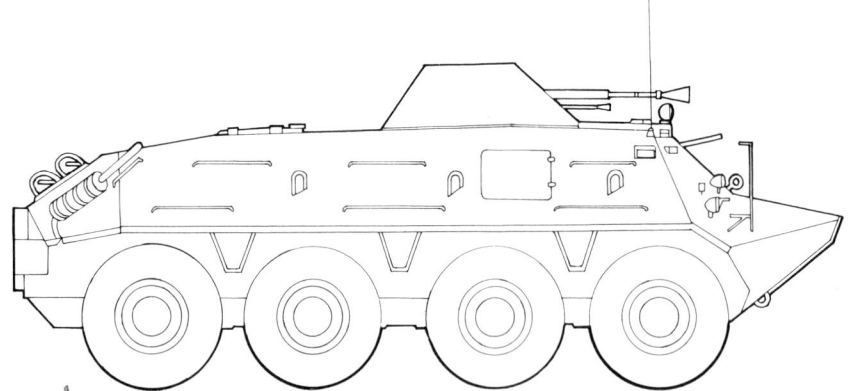

entered service in 1961. There is a central tyre pressure regulation system and limited night vision equipment, but no NBC system. There are several versions:

1. BTR-60P, which has an open top or canvas top, and accommodation for 16 infantrymen. Armament is one 12.7-mm DShK and one to three 7.62-mm SGMB or PK machine-guns
2. BTR-60PK, which has an armoured roof and accommodation for 16 infantrymen, entered service in 1964. This has an armament of one 12.7-mm DShK and one 7.62-mm SGMB or PK machine-gun
3. BTR-60PB, to which the technical

specification above applies, which entered service in 1965. This has cupolas for the driver and co-driver, and a turret for the commander. The turret, with co-axial 14.5- and 7.62-mm machine-guns, is also used on the BTR-40PB
4. BTR-60PU command vehicle, with additional radio equipment
5. BTR-60PB (FAC) forward air controller vehicle, which is the BTR-60PB with the armament removed and an additional generator at the rear of the hull to power extra radio equipment.

SSC-2B 'Samlet'

Type: surface-to-surface coastal defence missile

Guidance: probably semi-active radar homing plus mid-course radio guidance

Dimensions: Span about 16 ft 4 $\frac{9}{10}$ in (5.0 m)
Body diameter
Length about 22 ft 11 $\frac{3}{8}$ in (7.0 m)

Booster: solid-propellant rocket

Sustainer: turbojet

Warhead: HE

Weights: Launch about 6,720 lb (3,050 kg)
Burnt out

Performance: cruising speed about Mach 0.9; range possibly 124 miles (200 km) with mid-course guidance

Used also by: Cuba, Poland, USSR

Notes: The 'Samlet' is a coast defence version of the AS-1 air-to-surface missile.

SM-4-1 gun

Type: coastal defence gun
Calibre: 130 mm
Barrel length:
Muzzle velocity: 3,445 ft (1.050 m) per second
Ranges: Maximum 32,261 yards (29,500 m)
Minimum
Elevation: −5° to +45°
Traverse: 360°
Rate of fire: five rounds per minute
Weights: For travel
In firing position 35,274 lb (16,000 kg)
Dimensions: Length 42 ft (12.8 m)
Width 9 ft 4¼ in (2.85 m)
Height 10 ft (3.05 m)
Ammunition: APHE and HE
Crew:
Used also by: USSR and possibly other Warsaw Pact forces
Notes: The SM-4-1 was developed by the Russians after World War II on the basis of the German 150-mm c/28 coastal gun and the Russian 180-mm naval gun. The gun is mobile on a wheeled carriage, and is used in conjunction with radar for the most part. The HE shell weighs 73.6 lb (33.4 kg), and the APHE 74 lb (33.6 kg).

Goryunov SG43 and SGM machine-guns

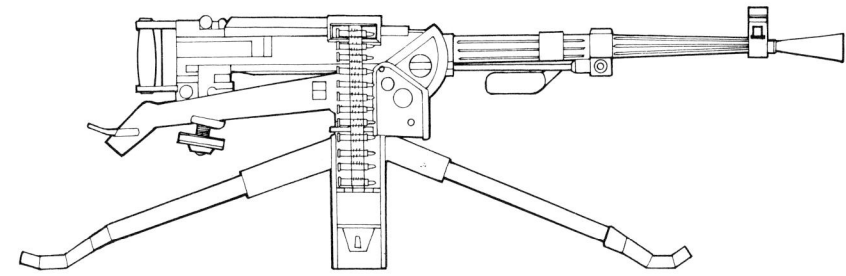

Type: machine-gun
Calibre: 7.62 mm
System of operation: gas
Muzzle velocity: 2,625 ft (800 m) per second
Range: effective 1,094 yards (1,000 m)
Rate of fire: 650 rounds per minute (cyclic); 250 rounds per minute (automatic)
Cooling system: air
Feed system: metal-link belt
Dimensions: Barrel length 28.3 in (719 mm)
Overall length 44.09 in (1.12 m)
Width
Height
Weights: 29.98 lb (13.6 kg) empty
Sights: cylinder (fore) and tangent with U (rear)
Ammunition: 7.62 × 54R

Used also by: China, Middle Eastern 'freedom fighter' groups, and other nations in Africa and south-east Asia
Notes: The SG43 was designed in World War II to increase the firepower of Russian infantry units. There were six models of the basic type made, two of which were the major types:
1. SG43 original model, with no cooling fins on the barrel and the cocking handle between the spade grips
2. SGM improved model, with longitudinal cooling fins along the barrel and the cocking handle on the right of the receiver.
The Chinese have made both types, under the designations Type 53 and Type 57 respectively. The type was also made in Czechoslovakia and Poland.

Eire

13,227 men.

2 inf bdes (1 with 3 inf bns, 1 with 2 inf bns, each with 1 recce sqn, 1 fd arty bty, 1 engr coy).
2 inf bn gps (each with 1 recce sqn, 1 fd arty bty, 1 engr coy).
4 indep inf bns.
1 AA arty bty.
8 AML H90, 24 AML H60 armd cars; 30 Panhard VTT/M3, 10 Unimog APC; 48 25-pdr gun/how; 204 81mm mor; 447 Carl Gustav 84mm, 96 PV-1110 90mm RCL; 26 Bofors 40mm AA guns.
(4 Scorpion lt tks, 5 Timoney APC on order.)

Deployment: Lebanon (UNIFIL): 1 bn (665); Cyprus (UNFICYP): 6.

Reserves (all services): 18,661 (1st line 456, 2nd line 18,205).

Timoney armoured personnel carrier

Type: armoured personnel carrier
Crew: driver and 11 infantrymen
Weights: Empty 14,000 lb (6,350 kg)
Loaded 18,000 lb (8,165 kg)
Dimensions: Length 16 ft 3 in (4.95 m)
Width 7 ft 10¾ in (2.406 m)
Height 8 ft 1 in (2.465 m)
Ground pressure:
Performance: road speed 61 mph (98 kph); road range 300 miles (483 km); water speed 3 mph (4.8 kph); vertical obstacle 30 in (76.2 cm); trench negligible; gradient 60%; ground clearance 15 in (38.1 cm)
Engine: one 200-bhp Chrysler Model 360 8-cylinder petrol
Armament: two 7.62-mm machine-guns
Armour: all-welded
Used also by: Belgium
Notes: Doors and firing-ports in sides and rear of hull. Other armament installations under development include a 76-mm gun. Belgian vehicles have a full NBC system.

El Savador

6,000 men.

3 inf 'bdes'.
1 arty 'bde'.
1 mixed cav bn.
1 engr bn.
1 AD bn.
1 para 'bn' (coy).
2 cdo/ranger coys.
12 AMX-13, 3 M-3 lt tks; 20 UR-416
   APC; 30 105mm how.

Ethiopia

90,000 men. *

8 inf divs with some 12 tk bns.
3 lt divs.
2 para/cdo bdes.
5 arty, 2 engr bns.
24 M-60, 30 M-47, 50 T-34, 400 T-54/-
   55 med, 50 M-41 lt tks; 56 AML-60
   armd cars; BRDM-2 scout cars;
   BMP-1 MICV; about 70 M-113, Commando, 300 BTR-40/-60/-152 APC;
   52 105mm, 150 122mm, 130mm,
   152mm, 12 155mm towed, 12 M-109
   155mm SP how; 82mm, 120mm, 280
   M-2/-30 4.2in mor; BM-21 122mm
   RL; 'Sagger' ATGW; ZU-23, 37mm,
   ZU-57 AA guns.

* Augmented by 100,000 People's Militia, with
a further 50,000 under training. Some
16–17,000 Cubans also serve with the Ethiopian
forces and operate ac and hy equipment.

Type 56 rifle

Type: selective fire assault rifle
Calibre: 7.62 mm
System of operation: gas
Muzzle velocity: 2,329 ft (710 m) per second
Range: effective 328 yards (300 m)
Rate of fire: 600 rounds per minute (cyclic);
100 rounds per minute (automatic); 40
rounds per minute (single shot)
Cooling system: air
Feed system: 30-round box
Dimensions: Barrel length 16.3 in (414 mm)
          Overall length 34.2 in (869
          mm)
          Width
          Height
Weights: 9.48 lb (4.3 kg)
Sights: post (fore) and tangent with notch
(rear)
Ammunition: 7.62 mm × 39
Used also by: China, Pakistan and some
south-east Asian countries
Notes: The Chinese Type 56 is a direct copy
of the later version of the Russian AK-47.
There is only one variant, the Type 56-1
with a folding metal stock.

Finland

34,400 men.

1 armd bde.
6 inf bdes.
8 indep inf bns.
3 fd arty regts.
2 indep fd arty bns.
2 coast arty regts.
3 indep coast arty bns.
1 AA arty regt.
4 indep AA arty bns.
T-54, T-55 med, PT-76 lt tks;
   BTR-50P/-60 APC; 76mm, 105mm,
   122mm, 130mm, 150mm, 152mm,
   155mm guns/how; 60mm, 81mm,
   120mm mor; 55mm, 95mm RCL; SS-
   11 ATGW; 23mm, 30mm, 35mm,
   40mm, 57mm towed, ZSU-57-2 SP
   AA guns.

Deployment: Egypt (UNEF): 654;
Cyprus (UNFICYP): 12.

Para-Military Forces: 4,000 frontier
guards.

Tampella M-60 gun

Type: field gun
Calibre: 122 mm
Barrel length: 53 cal
Muzzle velocity: 3,117 ft (950 m) per second
Ranges: Maximum 27,340 yards (25,000 m)
  Minimum
Elevation: −5° to +50°
Traverse: 90° total (360° with extra equipment)
Rate of fire:
Weights: For travel
  In firing position 18,739 lb (8,500 kg)
Dimensions: Length
  Width
  Height
Ammunition: HE
Crew:
Used only by: Finland
Notes: The M-60 is entirely of Finnish design and manufacture. The wheels are powered by an hydraulic motor. The HE shell weighs 55 lb (25 kg).

M-61/37 and M-37/10 howitzers

Type: light field howitzers
Calibre: 105 mm
Barrel length:
Muzzle velocity: 1,968 ft (600 m) per second
Ranges: Maximum 14,654 yards (13,400 m)
  Minimum
Elevation: +6° to +45°
Traverse: 53° total
Rate of fire: seven rounds per minute
Weights: For travel
  In firing position 3,968 lb (1,800 kg)
Dimensions: Length
  Width
  Height
Ammunition: HE
Crew:
Used only by: Finland
Notes: The M-61/37 is made up of the new Tampella howitzer on the carriage of an elderly Tampella mortar, while the M-37/10 is made up of the Tampella LFH howitzer from the carriage above, mounted on the Russian LFF M-10 122-mm carriage. In each case shell weight is 32.85 lb (13.9 kg).

M-58/M-61 recoilless rifle

Type: anti-tank recoilless rifle
Calibre: 95 mm
Barrel length: 33.7 cal
Muzzle velocity: 2,018 ft (615 m) per second
Ranges: Maximum 1,094 yards (1,000 m)
  Minimum
Elevation:
Traverse:
Rate of fire: six to eight rounds per minute
Weights: For travel
  In firing position 309 lb (140 kg)
Dimensions: Length
  Width
  Height
Ammunition: HEAT
Crew: three
Used only by: Finland

Notes: The M-58/M-61 weapon is an excellent anti-tank RR, with performance only little short of that of the British 120-mm Wombat. Penetration is 11.8 in (300 mm), and maximum effective range 766 yards (700 m).

M-1955 grenade launcher

Type: anti-tank grenade launcher
Calibre: 55 mm
Barrel length: 3 ft 1 in (0.94 m)
Muzzle velocity:
Ranges: Maximum effective 219 yards (200 m)
  Minimum

Elevation:
Traverse:
Rate of fire: three to five rounds per minute
Weights: For travel 18.74 lb (8.5 kg)
  In firing position 24.25 lb (11 kg)
Dimensions: Length (with grenade) 4 ft 0$\frac{4}{8}$ in (1.24 m)
  Width
  Height

Ammunition: HEAT warhead
Crew:
Used only by: Finland
Notes: The M-1955 is a man-portable anti-tank weapon of Finnish design and manufacture. The grenade weighs 5$\frac{1}{2}$ lb (2.5 kg), and its warhead will penetrate 7.87 in (200 mm) of armour.

M-1940 mortar

Type: medium mortar
Calibre: 120.25 mm
Barrel length: 16.63 cal
Muzzle velocity:
Ranges: Maximum 6,999 yards (6,400 m)
  Minimum
Elevation: 45° to 80°
Traverse: 360°

Rate of fire: 12 to 15 rounds per minute
Weights: For travel 1,323 lb (600 kg)
  In firing position about 628 lb (285 kg)
Dimensions: Length
  Width
  Height
Ammunition: HE, and probably other types
Crew: three
Used also by: Eire, Israel, Sweden

Notes: The Tampella M-1940 is a useful but somewhat heavy weapon, firing a 29.3-lb (13.3-kg) bomb. The type is built in Sweden as the M/41C, and in Israel by Soltam. Sweden has produced an improved M-1973 version, with a weight of 520.3 lb (236 kg), capable of firing its 28.2-lb (12.8-kg) bomb to 8,749 yards (8,000 m).

KK62 machine-gun

Type: light machine-gun
Calibre: 7.62 mm
System of operation: gas
Muzzle velocity: 2,395 ft (730 m) per second
Range: effective 492 yards (450 m)
Rate of fire: 1,100 rounds per minute (cyclic); 300 rounds per minute (practical)

Cooling system: air
Feed system: 100-round metal-link belt
Dimensions: Barrel length 18.5 in (470 mm)
  Overall length 42.72 in (1.085 m)
  Width
  Height
Weights: 18.3 lb (8.3 kg) empty; 23.37 lb (10.6 kg) with a loaded belt

Sights: pillar (fore) and aperture (rear)
Ammunition: 7.62 mm × 39
Used only by: Finland
Notes: This Finnish light machine-gun entered service in 1966, and is based on the Czech Zb26.

M-1938/1956 mortar

Type: light mortar
Calibre: 81 mm
Barrel length:
Muzzle velocity:
Ranges: Maximum 3,280 yards (3,000 m)
  Minimum
Elevation:
Traverse:
Rate of fire: 20 rounds per minute
Weights: For travel
  In firing position 132.3 lb (60 kg)
Dimensions: Length
  Width
  Height
Ammunition: HE
Crew: three or four
Used also by: Israel
Notes: There appear to be few differences between the Tampella M-1938 and M-1956, at least externally. However, the M-1956 weapon probably fires a 9.26-lb (4.2-kg) bomb rather than a 7.7-lb (3.5-kg) bomb, and range is 4,921 yards (4,500 m). The type is made in modified form by the Israeli Soltam company.

M/32–33 Maxim machine-gun

Type: medium machine-gun
Calibre: 7.62 mm
System of operation: short recoil
Muzzle velocity: 2,440 ft (744 m) per second
Range: effective 3,030 yards (2,770 m)
Rate of fire: 600 rounds per minute (cyclic); 200 rounds per minute (automatic)
Cooling system: water

Feed system: 250-round canvas belt
Dimensions: Barrel length 28.25 in (718 mm)
  Overall length 46.5 in (1.181 m)
  Width
  Height
Weights: 40 lb (18.2 kg) empty
Sights: blade (fore) and leaf, notch (rear)
Ammunition: 7.62 mm × 39

Used also by: China, Vietnam
Notes: The Finnish M/32–33 is typical of the British Maxim machine-gun type, which entered service in the 1890s. The weapon is totally reliable and has a long effective range, but is heavy by modern standards because of its cooling jacket and water. The 0.303-in (7.7-mm) Maxim is the version used by China and Vietnam as the Type 24.

M-1931 sub-machine gun

Type: sub-machine gun
Calibre: 9 mm
System of operation: blowback
Muzzle velocity: 1,310 ft (399 m) per second
Range: effective 219 yards (200 m)
Rate of fire: 900 rounds per minute (cyclic); 120 rounds per minute (automatic); 40 rounds per minute (single shot)
Cooling system: air

Feed system: 50-round box or 71-round drum
Dimensions: Barrel length 12.52 in (318 mm)
  Overall length 34.25 in (870 mm)
  Width
  Height
Weights: 10.71 lb (4.68 kg) unloaded; 15.63 lb (7.09 kg) with 71-round drum
Sights: blade (fore) and tangent with notch (rear)

Ammunition: 9 mm × 19 Parabellum
Used only by: Finland
Notes: Otherwise known as the Suomi, the M-1931 sub-machine gun was an advanced weapon for its time, although it was very heavy. However, the weapon was very expensive to produce as it was all machined from steel stock. The M-1931 was unusual in two main features: the high magazine capacities, and the provision of a bipod.

M-1944 sub-machine gun

Type: sub-machine gun
Calibre: 9 mm
System of operation: blowback
Muzzle velocity: 1,310 ft (399 m) per second
Range: effective 219 yards (200 m)
Rate of fire: 650 rounds per minute (cyclic); 120 rounds per minute (automatic)

Cooling system: air
Feed system: 36-round box or 71-round drum
Dimensions: Barrel length 9.8 in (249 mm)
  Overall length 32.72 in (831 mm) with stock extended; 24.49 in (622 mm) with stock folded
  Width
  Height

Weights: 6.39 lb (2.9 kg) unloaded; 9.48 lb (4.3 kg) with 71-round drum
Sights: blade (fore) and notch (rear)
Ammunition: 9 mm × 19 Parabellum
Used only by: Finland
Notes: The Finnish M-1944 sub-machine gun is a reworking of the Russian PPS-43 design to use the 9-mm Parabellum cartridge.

M-1960 and M-1962 rifles

Type: selective fire assault rifles
Calibre: 7.62 mm
System of operation: gas
Muzzle velocity: 2,359 ft (719 m) per second
Range: effective 437 yards (400 m)
Rate of fire: 650 rounds per minute (cyclic); 120 rounds per minute (automatic); 40 rounds per minute (single shot)
Cooling system: air
Feed system: 30-round box

Dimensions: Barrel length 16.54 in (420 mm)
  Overall length 35.98 in (914 mm)
  Width
  Height
Weights: 7.72 lb (3.5 kg) empty; 10.36 lb (4.7 kg) loaded
Sights: hooded blade (fore) and tangent aperture (rear)
Ammunition: 7.62 mm × 39
Used only by: Finland

Notes: The Finnish Army adopted the Russian AK-47, with slight modifications, in 1960 as the M-1960, though later modifications resulted in the M-1962, to which the specification above applies. Modifications to the Russian design include the total elimination of wood, the fitting of a tubular stock, the provision of a welded and riveted receiver made up of stampings, and other detail improvements.

France

French Army

The French Army is composed of regular and conscript forces with an officer class drawn from a number of military families and NCOs from both regulars and conscripts. Service is not popular, despite having been reduced to 12 months with a two-week refresher in subsequent years. Pay for a conscript is low, and for men who run small or one-man businesses, call up can be a disaster for their work. The Sandhurst tradition of 'looking after your men' is lacking in an army where the turnover in troops is too quick to allow troop or platoon commanders to get to know their men. Equipment includes some well tried arms which have seen service in Indo-China and Algeria and some futuristic ideas from small arms to missiles.

The French Army has 324,400 men (including an Army Aviation element), with 209,000 conscripts. This is some 64.5 per cent of the total armed forces, which have a budget of about 4.67 per cent of the gross national product. It has two corps HQs, four armoured divisions, three mechanised divisions, two infantry divisions, an alpine division, an air-portable motorised division, and a paratroop division of two brigades. There are seven armoured car regiments and two motorised infantry regiments. The Berlin sector force consists of one light armoured regiment and one regiment of mechanised infantry. The French have five surface to surface missile regiments with a total of 30 Pluton and four surface to air missile regiments with 54 HAWK.

Equipment includes 1,060 AMX-30 MBTs and 1,100 AMX-13 light tanks. The smaller armoured fighting vehicles are a mixture, including 410 Panhard EBR heavy and 450 AML light armoured cars, 500 AMX-10 mechanised infantry combat vehicles, and large numbers of AMX-VCI APCs, with 1,500 AMX-13 VTT and 100 VAB armoured personnel carriers.

Artillery includes 195 Model 56 105-mm pack howitzers, 115 155-mm howitzers, with 168 105-mm guns on AMX chassis and 185 155-mm self-propelled howitzers. There are 265 120-mm mortars, while anti-tank capability includes the 105-mm and 106-mm recoilless guns, the SS-11 and SS-12 missile and Milan, HOT and ENTAC anti-tank guided weapons. Anti-aircraft capacity includes 40-mm towed and 30-mm SP AA guns, plus HAWK and Roland missiles. The French have armed a number of their tanks and armoured cars with HOT and Milan missiles to give them an additional kill capability.

Army aviation (ALAT), with 6,450 men, has a mixture of fixed-wing aircraft and helicopters for troop-carrying and liaison. Among the helicopters are the Anglo-French Puma and Gazelle. The French favour anti-tank attack helicopters armed with ATGW and pioneered these tactics with *Alouettes* armed with SS-11 and SS-12 missiles.

Deployment of the French forces includes small contingents in colonies and ex-colonies like Senegal (1,000), Ivory Coast (400), Gabon (450), Chad (1,500), a United Nations force of 1,244 in the Lebanon, and 4,000 men in Djibouti (including two infantry regiments, an artillery regiment and two squadrons of light tanks). These commitments reflect French foreign policy, which was demonstrated dramatically by an airborne assault on Kolwezi in Zaire in 1978. France is using her regular forces to support governments under attack by Communist-backed insurgents and to show that Africa is not a free battle ground for Cuba, Russia or China.

Other troops are deployed in Germany (34,000 men in two mechanised divisions) and Berlin where there is one light armoured regiment and one mechanised infantry regiment with a total strength of 2,000 men.

Reserves, which are largely ex-conscripts, stand at 300,000. The para-military forces are composed of the *Gendarmerie*, which has AMX-13 light tanks, AML armoured cars and *Alouette* helicopters with 4,800 conscripts and 71,600 regulars, and 6,900 men in the *Service de Santé* which has 230 conscripts. The small numbers in the *Service de Santé* reflect the specialised nature of its work but the *Gendarmerie*, which has a police and counter-insurgency role, is well able to train and use men in their period of service.

324,400 men (incl Army Aviation and 209,000 conscripts)* and about 300,000 reservists.

2 corps HQ.
4 armd divs.
3 mech divs.
2 inf divs.
1 alpine div.
1 air-portable mot div (Marines).
1 para div of 2 bdes.
7 armd car regts.
2 mot inf regts.
Berlin sector force (1 lt armd regt, 1 mech inf regt).
5 SSM regts with 30 Pluton.
4 SAM regts with 54 HAWK.
1,060 AMX-30 med, 1,100 AMX-13 lt tks; some 960 AFV, incl 410 Panhard EBR hy, 450 AML lt armd cars; 500 AMX-10 MICV, AMX-VCI, 1,500 AMX-13 VTT, 100 VAB APC; 195 Model 56 105mm pack, 115 155mm how; 168 AMX 105mm, 185 155mm SP how; *Pluton* SSM; 265 120mm mor; 105/6mm RCL; SS-11/-12, *Milan*, HOT, *Entac* ATGW; 40mm towed, 30mm SP AA guns; HAWK; Roland SAM. (30 AMX-30 med tks; 40 AMX-10 armd cars, 40 AMX-10 MICV, 330 VAB APC; HOT, *Milan* ATGW; 120 Vadar 20mm SP AA guns; 35 Roland I, 70 Roland II SAM on order.)

ARMY AVIATION (ALAT): 6,450.
2 groups, 6 helicopter regts and 5 regional commands.
30 *Broussard*, 91 L-19 lt ac.
190 *Alouette* II, 70 *Alouette* III, 135 SA-330 Puma, 170 SA-341 Gazelle helicopters (20 Gazelle on order).

DEPLOYMENT:
Germany: 34,000; 2 mech divs.
Berlin: 2,000; 1 lt armd regt, 1 mech inf regt.
Djibouti: 4,000; 2 inf regts, 1 arty regt, 2 sqns lt tks.
Senegal: 1,000 (all services).
Ivory Coast: 400.
Gabon: 450.
Lebanon (UNIFIL): 1,244; 1 bn and log units.
Chad: 1,500.
Overseas Commands:
There are four overseas commands (Antilles-Guyana, South Indian Ocean, New Caledonia, Polynesia), and two naval comds (ALINDIEN, ALPACI). Some 19,000 from all services are deployed overseas (numbers can vary according to local circumstances); equipment incl: 130 AFV, 36 helicopters, 9 frigates, 2 FPB, 1 tender ship, 2 lt transport ships, 12 combat and 15 transport ac.

* The army is being restructured; the 4 armd and 2 inf divs now have the new establishment of 8,000 men in 2 tk, 2 mech inf, and 2 arty regts and 6,500 men in 3 mot inf, 1 armd car and 1 arty regt respectively. In 1979 the 3 mech divs will re-organize to form 4 more armd and 2 inf divs. (A fifth inf div is to be formed later.) An additional 14 inf divs will be formed on mobilization.

AMX-30

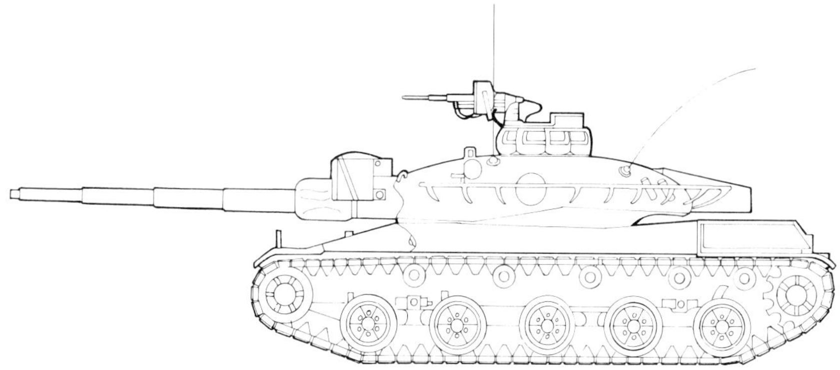

Type: main battle tank
Crew: four
Weights: Empty
Loaded 79,366 lb (36,000 kg)
Dimensions: Length (gun reversed) 31 ft 1 in (9.48 m); (hull) 21 ft 8 in (6.6 m)
Width 10 ft 2 in (3.1 m)
Height (overall) 9 ft 4 in (2.86 m)
Ground pressure: 10.95 lb/in^2 (0.77 kg/cm^2)
Performance: road speed 40 mph (65 kph); range 400 miles (650 km); vertical obstacle $35\frac{2}{5}$ in (90.0 cm); trench 9 ft 6 in (2.9 m); gradient 60%; ground clearance $17\frac{3}{4}$ in (45.0 cm); wading 7 ft $2\frac{2}{3}$ in (2.2 m) without preparation
Engine: one 720-bhp Hispano-Suiza HS 110 supercharged inline multi-fuel engine
Armament: one 105-mm CN-105-F1 gun with 50 rounds of HE, HEAT, Smoke, Illuminating and Practice, plus one 12.7-mm co-axial machine-gun with 600 rounds, and one 7.62-mm machine-gun with 1,600 rounds on the commander's cupola. (The 12.7-mm gun is being replaced by a 20-mm cannon)
Armour: about 2 in (50 mm) maximum
Used also by: Greece, Iraq, Qatar, Saudi Arabia, Spain, Venezuela
Notes: The AMX-30 was introduced into French service in 1967, and is still in production. Of the three main parameters of tank performance (firepower, protection and mobility), the French have chosen the combination of high firepower, only slight protection, and very high mobility. Unusually, the 12.7-mm/20-mm weapon can be elevated independently of the main armament, so allowing helicopters to be engaged. Other tanks are engaged with the HEAT round, which weighs $48\frac{1}{2}$ lb (22 kg) complete, and is fired at a muzzle velocity of 3,281 ft (1,000 m) per second. This will penetrate $14\frac{1}{3}$ in (360 mm) of armour at 0° (ie vertical). An NBC system and night vision equipment are standard on French AMX-30s, which can ford up to a depth of 13 ft 2 in (4.0 m) with a schnorkel. So far, the only AMX-30 MBTs with laser rangefinders are the AMX-30S vehicles for Saudi Arabia, French vehicles having an optical (coincidence) rangefinder. There are several variants:

1. AMX-30 MBT
2. AMX-30S MBT for Saudi Arabia with a laser rangefinder, sand shields and an altered transmission
3. AMX-30 *Char Poseur de Pont* or bridgelayer, which can bridge a 65 ft $7\frac{1}{2}$ in (20.0 m) gap
4. AMX-30D *Char de Depannage* or armoured recovery vehicle, with a dozer blade, a crane capable of lifting 33,069 lb (15,000 kg), and two winches, one with a capacity of 77.161 lb (35,000 kg) and the other of 8,814 lb (4,000 kg)
5. AMX-30-S 401 A AA vehicle fitted with two 30-mm cannon and all-weather radar and fire-control system
6. AMX-30 Javelot, under development for the Javelot multiple-missile AA system
7. AMX-30 155-mm GCT self-propelled 155-mm gun
8. AMX-30 Roland with twin Roland AA missile-launchers, radar and eight reload missiles in the hull
9. AMX-30 Pluton, the launcher for France's tactical nuclear missile.

Panhard EBR-75

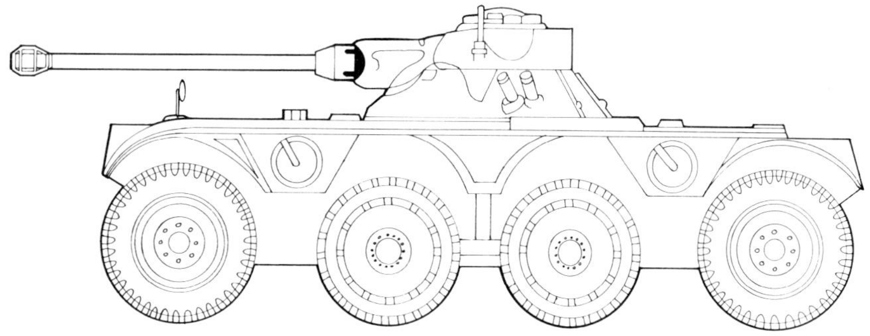

Type: armoured car
Crew: four
Weights: Empty
Loaded 29,760 lb (13,500 kg)
Dimensions: Length (gun forward) 20 ft 2 in (6.15 m); (hull) 18 ft 3 in (5.56 m)
Width 7 ft 11 in (2.42 m)
Height (on eight wheels) 7 ft 7 in (2.32 m)
Ground pressure:
Performance: road speed 65 mph (105 kph); range 404 miles (650 km); vertical obstacle $15\frac{3}{4}$ in (40.0 cm); trench 6 ft 7 in (2.0 m); gradient over 70%
Engine: one 200-hp Panhard inline petrol engine
Armament: one 90-mm gun, plus one 7.5-mm machine-gun co-axial with the main armament, and one 7.5-mm machine-gun in each of the two driver's positions
Armour: $\frac{3}{16}$ in (8 mm) minimum; $\frac{3}{5}$ in (15 mm) maximum
Used also by: Mauritania, Morocco, Tunisia
Notes: The EBR-75 entered French service in 1951 as the standard *Engin Blindé de Reconnaissance* or armoured reconnaissance vehicle, armed with a 75-mm gun in the FL-11 turret, with 56 rounds of ammunition. The vehicles were later rearmed with a 90-mm gun, and some received the FL-10 oscillating turret of the AMX-13 light tank, though this increased height and weight. The EBR-75 is unusual in having four tyreless central wheels. These are raised off the ground on good going, and lowered to provide extra traction on poor going. The EBR also has two drivers, one at the front and one at the rear, the latter normally acting as the radio operator, but able to drive the vehicle backwards at high speed if the situation demands. There is also the VTT armoured personnel carrier variant of the EBR, used only by Portugal.

AMX-10RC

Type: reconnaissance vehicle
Crew: four
Weights: Empty
Loaded 33,069 lb (15,000 kg)
Dimensions: Length (hull) 20 ft $5\frac{3}{4}$ in (6.243 m)
Width 9 ft $3\frac{4}{5}$ in (2.84 m)
Height (overall) 8 ft 5 in (2.565 m)
Ground pressure:
Performance: road speed 53 mph (85 kph); range 497 miles (800 km); vertical obstacle $27\frac{3}{5}$ in (70.0 cm); trench 5 ft 3 in (1.6 m); gradient 60%; ground clearance is variable; the AMX-10RC is fully amphibious
Engine: one 276-hp Hispano-Suiza HS 115-2 inline petrol engine
Armament: one 105-mm gun, plus one 7.62-mm machine-gun co-axial with the main armament
Armour: classified
Used only by: France
Notes: Intended as a replacement for the EBR armoured car, the AMX-10RC entered service in 1977. The suspension is of the infinitely variable hydro-pneumatic type, with its consequent tactical advantages. Water propulsion is by a pair of waterjets. Passive night vision equipment and an NBC system are fitted as standard, and the vehicle has a sophisticated fire-control system for its 105-mm main armament, based on the use of a laser or optical rangefinder and a low-light TV system. Maximum effective range of the 105-mm gun is 1,804 yards (1,650 m).

AMX-10P

Type: mechanised infantry combat vehicle
Crew: two, plus up to nine infantrymen
Weights: Empty 24,912 lb (11,300 kg)
Loaded 30,423 lb (13,800 kg)
Dimensions: Length 19 ft 1 in (5.778 m)
Width 9 ft 1 in (2.78 m)
Height (overall) 8 ft 4 in (2.54 m)
Ground pressure: 7.53 lb/in² (0.53 kg/cm²)
Performance: road speed 40 mph (65 kph); water speed 4.9 mph (7.92 kph); range 373 miles (600 km); vertical obstacle 27⅜ in (70.0 cm); trench 5 ft 3 in (1.6 m); gradient 60%; ground clearance 17¾ in (45.0 cm); the AMX-10P is fully amphibious
Engine: one 276-hp Hispano-Suiza HS 115-2 inline diesel engine
Armament: one 20-mm M693 cannon with 800 rounds, plus one 7.62-mm machine-gun with 2,000 rounds co-axial with the main armament
Armour: about 1⅛ in (30 mm) maximum
Used also by: Greece, Qatar, Saudi Arabia
Notes: The AMX-10P began to replace the AMX-VCI as the French Army's standard APC in 1973, the power-operated turret with a main armament of one 20-mm high-velocity cannon making the vehicle a fairly effective mechanised infantry combat vehicle (MICV). Among the standard fittings are night vision and fighting equipment, and NBC gear. Fully amphibious, the AMX-10P is driven in the water by a pair of waterjets. There are a number of variants:

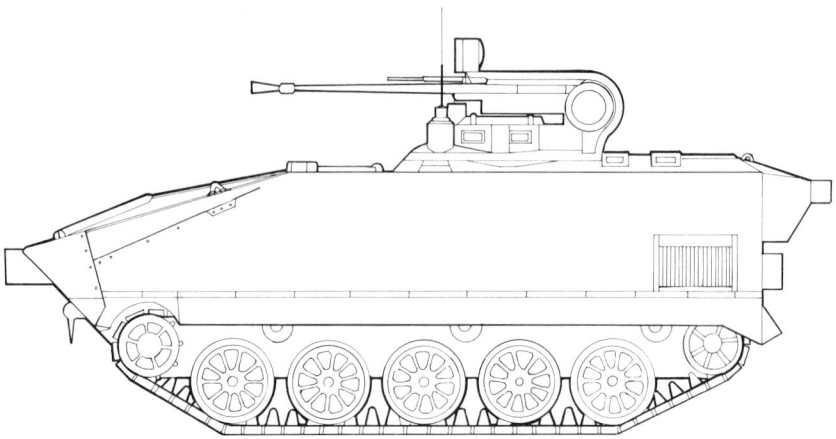

1. AMX-10P mechanised infantry combat vehicle or armoured personnel carrier, to which the specification applies
2. AMX-10P RATAC, with a field artillery fire-control radar
3. AMX-10P HOT, under development as an anti-tank vehicle, with a new turret fitted with a pair of HOT anti-tank missile launchers on each side, and some 15 to 20 missiles stored in the hull
4. AMX-10 TM tow vehicle for the Brandt 120-mm towed mortar, some 60 bombs being carried in the hull
5. AMX-10PC command vehicle with extra radio equipment and a tent for additional room
6. AMX-10P (Training) for driver training, without the turret
7. AMX-10ECH light repair vehicle for the AMX-10P family
8. AMX-10P ambulance, with a capacity of four to nine casualties
9. AMX-10RC 6 × 6 wheeled reconnaissance vehicle developed from the tracked vehicle
10. AMX-10C reconnaissance vehicle, derived from the AMX-10P tracked vehicle, but fitted with the 105-mm gun turret of the AMX-10RC.

Saviem/Creusot-Loire VAB

Type: utility armoured vehicle
Crew: two, plus 10 passengers
Weights: Empty 26,455 lb (12,000 kg)
Loaded 30,864 lb (14,000 kg)
Dimensions: Length 19 ft 7⅖ in (5.98 m)
Width 8 ft 2 in (2.49 m)
Height 6 ft 9 1/10 in (2.06 m)
Ground pressure:
Performance: road speed 62 mph (100 kph); water speed 4.3 mph (7 kph); road range 683 miles (1,100 km); vertical obstacle 23¾ in (60.0 cm); gradient 60%; ground clearance 15¾ in (40.0 cm)
Engine: one 230-hp Saviem HM-71 2356 6-cylinder diesel

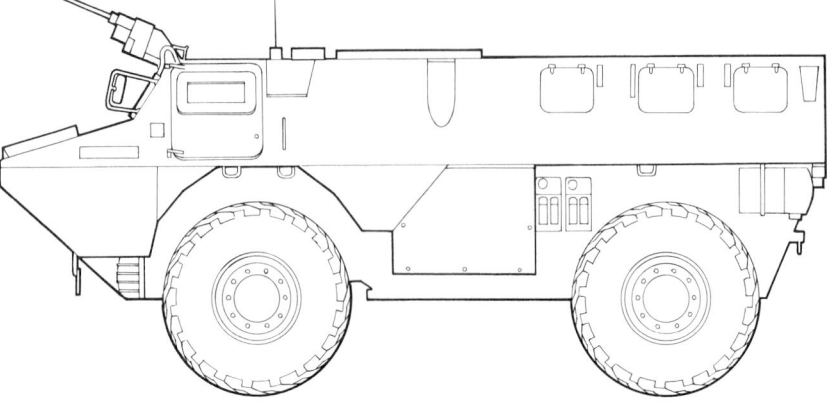

Armament: see notes
Armour:
Used also by: Ecuador
Notes: The *Véhicule de l'Avant Blindé* (VAB) or Front Armoured Vehicle is the result of a French Army requirement of 1969, for which both Panhard and Saviem built 4 × 4 and 6 × 6 prototypes. Saviem was declared the winner, and both 4 × 4 and 6 × 6 vehicles will shortly enter service to complement the AMX-10P. The VAB is fully amphibious, being driven in the water by twin waterjets, has an NBC system, and can be fitted with night vision equipment. The specification applies to the 6 × 6 model. There will be a wide variety of derivatives:

1. VAB-VTT (*Transport de Troupe*) armoured personnel carrier, with accommodation for 10 passengers and an armament of one 7.62-mm turret-mounted machine-gun
2. VAB-Cargo freight carrier with an armament of one 7.62-mm machine-gun
3. VAB-PC (*Poste de Commandement*) command model with extra radio equipment, accommodation for six men and an armament of one 7.62-mm machine-gun
4. VAB-Ambulance, which is unarmed and can carry four stretchers or 10 sitting wounded
5. VAB-*Echelon* repair vehicle, with an armament of one 7.62-mm machine-gun
6. *Véhicule de Combat d'Infanterie* export armoured personnel carrier, with accommodation for 10 infantrymen, and an armament of one turret-mounted 20-mm cannon
7. *Véhicule Portier Mortier de 81mm* export 81-mm mortar carrier
8. *Véhicule Tracteur de Mortier de 120mm* export 120-mm mortar tow vehicle, with 60 mortar rounds carried in the hull and a 7.62-mm machine-gun carried for local defence, as in the 81-mm mortar carrier
9. *Véhicule de Combat Anti-Char* anti-tank export model, to be armed with TOW, HOT or Milan missiles and a 7.62-mm machine-gun
10. *Véhicule Moyens Electroniques* carrier for the RATAC battlefield radar system
11. *Véhicule Maintien d'Ordre* internal security vehicle
12. *Véhicule TS 90* reconnaissance and anti-tank vehicle, fitted with the H-90 or Lynx 90 turret, armed with a 90-mm gun and co-axial 7.62-mm machine-gun
13. *Véhicule TG 120* AA vehicle, fitted with a SAMM TG 120 turret armed with a 20-mm cannon and a co-axial 7.62-mm machine-gun
14. *Véhicule TA 20* AA vehicle with twin turret-mounted 20-mm cannon.

AMX-13 VCA

Type: Mk F3 SP gun support vehicle
Crew: two, plus up to six artillerymen
Weights: Empty
　　　　　 Loaded 30,203 lb (13,700 kg)
Dimensions: Length 19 ft 0⅓ in (5.8 m); (with ARE trailer) 31 ft 4 in (9.55 m)
　　　　　 Width 8 ft 10¼ in (2.7 m); (ARE trailer) 7 ft 1⅘ in (2.18 m)
　　　　　 Height 7 ft 10½ in (2.4 m); (ARE trailer) 4 ft 10¼ in (1.48 m)
Ground pressure:
Performance: (with trailer) road speed 37 mph (60 kph)
Engine: one 270-bhp SOFAM 8 inline petrol engine

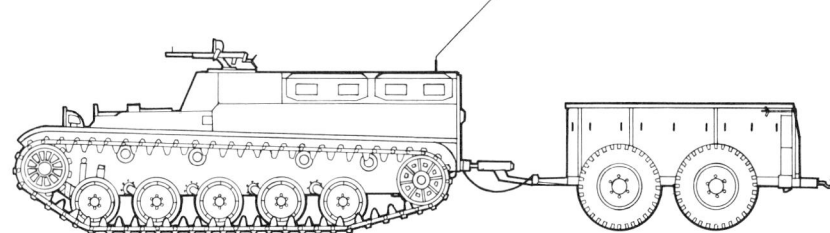

Armament: one 20-mm cannon or 12.7-mm machine-gun on the commander's cupola
Armour:
Used also by: Ecuador, United Arab Emirates
Notes: The AMX-13 VCA is based on the chassis of the AMX-13, with an APC superstructure, as a vehicle to support the Mk F3 self-propelled gun. The VCA can carry eight men and up to 25 rounds of 155-mm ammunition, and can tow the ARE trailer, which is 12 ft 7⅞ in (3.85 m) long and weighs 4,850 lb (2,200 kg) laden.

Panhard ERC

Type: armoured car
Crew: three
Weights: Empty
　　Loaded 15,432 lb (7,000 kg)
Dimensions: Length (with gun) 19 ft 6⅘ in (5.965 m); (hull) 16 ft 9½ in (5.12 m)
　　Width 8 ft (2.45 m)
　　Height 7 ft (2.13 m)
Ground pressure:
Performance: road speed 68 mph (110 kph); range 590 miles (950 km); vertical obstacle 39 in (1.0 m); trench 39⅖ in (1.0 m); gradient 60%; wading 3 ft 11¼ in (1.2 m)
Engine: one 140-hp Peugeot inline petrol engine
Armament: see notes
Armour: classified
Used only by: France
Notes: Developed as a private venture, the *Engin de Reconnaissance Canon* (ERC) is a 6 × 6 vehicle that can be fitted with a number of armament installations:

1. ERC 90 Lynx, with a CNMP-Berthiez turret fitted with a 90-mm gun and co-axial 7.62-mm machine gun, plus a 7.62-mm AA machine-gun on the turret roof. Some 40 rounds of 90-mm and 3,000 rounds of 7.62-mm ammunition are carried, and the turret is equipped with a laser rangefinder
2. ERC 90 *Sagaie*, with a GIAT turret fitted with a 90-mm gun firing a hollow-charge round capable of penetrating 12⅗ in (320 mm) of armour at 0°, or 4¾ in (120 mm) at 65°. There are also 7.62-mm co-axial and AA machine-guns. Ammunition stowage provides for 30 rounds of 90-mm and 3,000 rounds of 7.62-mm
3. ECM 81-mm mortar carrier, with a turret-mounted breech-loading 81-mm mortar with 95 rounds, and a 7.62-mm machine-gun with 1,000 rounds on the turret roof
4. ERC TG 120 *Guepard*, with a SAMM turret fitted with a 20-mm cannon and 7.62-mm machine-gun, with 500 and 2,200 rounds respectively
5. ERC 60–20 *Serval*, with a turret fitted with a 60-mm breech-loading

mortar with 50 rounds, a 20-mm cannon with 350 rounds, and a 7.62-mm machine-gun with 2,200 rounds. The technical specification above refers to the ERC 90 Lynx. The type can also be supplied in either of two amphibious forms, the first being driven in the water by its wheels at 2.8 mph (4.5 kph), the other by a pair of waterjets at 5.6 mph (9 kph). As with other Panhard wheeled AFVs, the centre of the three pairs of wheels can be raised hydraulically for normal running.

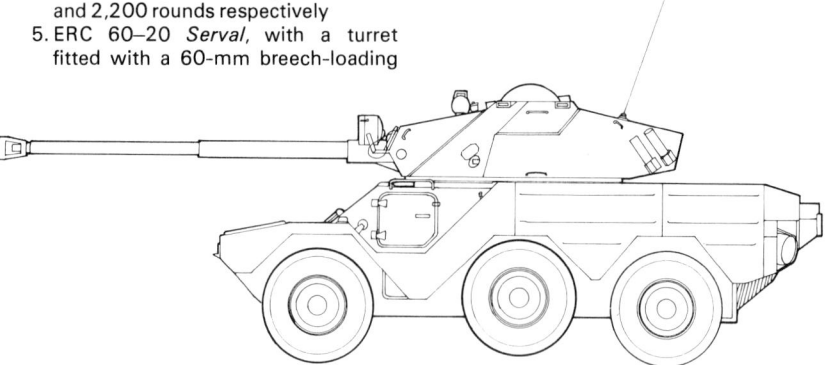

Aérospatiale *Pluton*

Type: tactical nuclear weapon system, vehicle-launched
Guidance: inertial
Dimensions: Span 55½ in (1.41 m)
　　Body diameter 25⅗ in (65.0 cm)
　　Length 25 ft 0¾ in (7.64 m)
Booster: dual-thrust solid-propellant rocket motor with 2,646 lb (1,200 kg) of propellant
Sustainer: see above
Warhead: nuclear, 15 or 25 kilotons
Weights: Launch 5,342 lb (2,423 kg)
　　Burnt out
Performance: range 6.2 to 74.6 miles (10 to 120 km); CEP between 164 and 328 yards (150 and 300 m) depending on range

Used only by: France

Notes: Introduced in 1974, the *Pluton* is now in service with five regiments, each regiment having six launchers and ancillary equipment.

Aérospatiale *Entac*

Type: anti-tank missile, container-launched from a vehicle

Guidance: command to line-of-sight by means of wire

Dimensions: Span
   Body diameter 5 $\frac{9}{16}$ in (15.0 cm)
   Length 2 ft 8 $\frac{3}{16}$ in (82.0 cm)

Booster: solid-propellant rocket

Sustainer: solid-propellant rocket

Warhead: shaped-charge high explosive, 17.64 lb (8.0 kg)

Weights: Launch 26.9 lb (12.2 kg)
   Burnt out

Performance: range 437–2,187 yards (400–2,000 m); speed 190 mph (305 kph); armour penetration 25.6 in (650 mm)

Used also by: Australia, Belgium, Canada, India, Indonesia, Iran, Morocco, Norway, South Africa, Switzerland, USA

Notes: 1st-generation AT missile, designed primarily for infantry use. Introduced in 1957. The whole system comprises a controller, a 4-missile launcher, missiles, a launch vehicle and test equipment (*Entac* = *Engin Téléguidé Anti-Char* or remotely-controlled anti-tank weapon).

Aérospatiale SS.10

Type: surface-to-surface anti-tank missile
Guidance: command to line-of-sight by means of wires
Dimensions: Span $29\frac{1}{2}$ in (75.0 cm)
Body diameter $6\frac{1}{2}$ in (16.5 cm)
Length $33\frac{1}{2}$ in (85.1 cm)
Booster: solid-propellant rocket
Sustainer: solid-propellant rocket
Warhead: HE weighing 12.13 lb (5.5 kg)
Weights: Launch 32.63 lb (14.8 kg)
Burnt out
Performance: speed up to 259 ft (79 m) per second; range from 984 to 1,640 yards (900 to 1,500 m)
Used also by: various nations
Notes: The SS.10 is a simple, first-generation, wire-guided anti-tank missile, now largely replaced by more advanced weapons.

Aérospatiale SS.11B1

Type: surface-to-surface tactical missile, vehicle-launched from a ramp
Guidance: command to line-of-sight by means of wire
Dimensions: Span 19.7 in (50.0 cm)
Body diameter $6\frac{1}{2}$ in (16.4 cm)
Length 3 ft $11\frac{3}{5}$ in (1.21 m)
Booster: solid-propellant rocket
Sustainer: solid-propellant rocket
Warhead: Type 140AC penetrates 23.6 in (600 mm) of armour; Type 140AP02 explosive semi-perforating anti-personnel warhead (5.73 lb/2.6 kg of high explosive) penetrates $\frac{2}{5}$ in (1 cm) of steel plate at 3,280 yards (3,000 m) and explodes some 6 ft $10\frac{3}{4}$ in (2.1 m) beyond it; and Type 140AP59 high-fragmentation anti-personnel
Weights: Launch 65.9 lbs (29.9 kg)
Burnt out
Performance: range 547–3,280 yards (500–3,000 m); speed 425 mph (685 kph); minimum turning radius 1,094 yards (1.0 km)
Used also by: Argentina, Belgium, Canada, Finland, Greece, India, Iran, Iraq, Israel, Italy, Libya, Netherlands, South Africa, Spain, Tunisia, Turkey, Venezuela, USA, West Germany and others
Notes: Designed as a battlefield missile for use from land vehicles, naval vessels and slow aircraft.

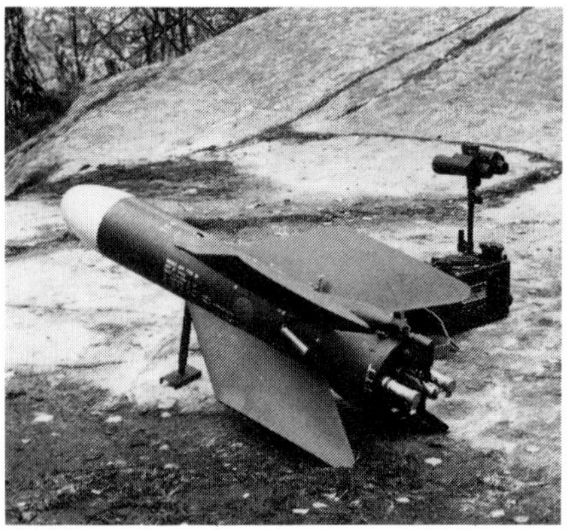

Aérospatiale SS.12

Type: surface-to-surface battlefield missile
Guidance: semi-automatic command to line-of-sight by means of wire
Dimensions: Span 25 $\frac{5}{8}$ in (65.0 cm)
Body diameter 7 $\frac{1}{10}$ in (18.0 cm)
Length 6 ft $1\frac{5}{8}$ in (1.87 m)
Booster: solid-propellant rocket
Sustainer: solid-propellant rocket
Warhead: anti-personnel and HEAT
Weights: Launch 165.35 lb (75.0 kg)
Burnt out
Performance: speed 623 ft (190 m) per second; range from 437 to 6,562 yards (400 to 6,000 m)
Used also by: Argentina, Iran
Notes: The SS.12 is basically a larger and more powerful version of the SS.11.

Euromissile *HOT*

Type: long-range anti-tank missile (with airborne and shipborne possibilities), tube-launched
Guidance: semi-automatic command to line-of-sight by means of wire
Dimensions: Span 1 ft $0\frac{1}{5}$ in (31.0 cm)
Warhead diameter $5\frac{1}{3}$ in (13.6 cm)
Length 4 ft $2\frac{1}{5}$ in (1.275 m)
Booster: solid-propellant rocket
Sustainer: solid-propellant rocket
Warhead: hollow-charge high explosive
Weights: Launch 40.09 lb (20 kg)
Burnt out
Performance: range 82 yards to more than $2\frac{1}{2}$ miles (75 m to more than 4 km); speed 590 mph (950 kph); armour penetration more than 31.5 in (800 mm)
Used also by: Kuwait, Syria
Notes: Introduced in 1977. Developed by Euromissile, a French/German consortium. The *HOT (Haut subsonique Optiquement téléguidé tiré d'un Tube* or High subsonic Optically guided Tube-launched missile) is a versatile missile capable of multiple launch options. Its warhead is extremely powerful.

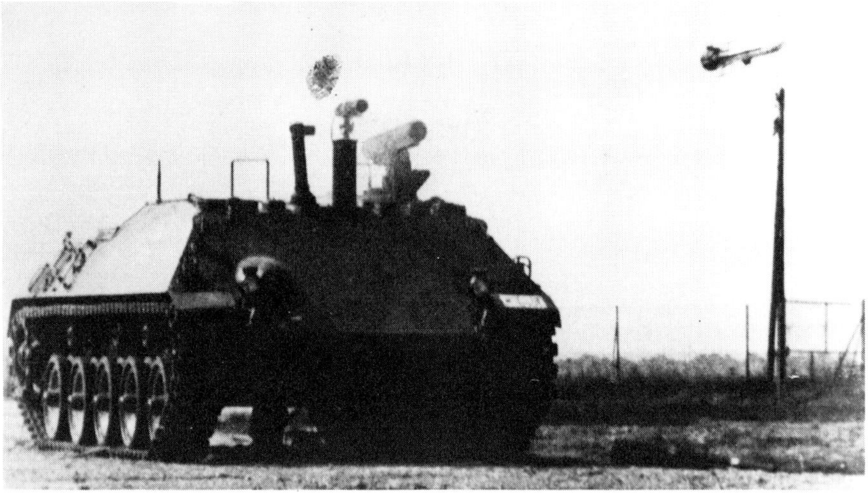

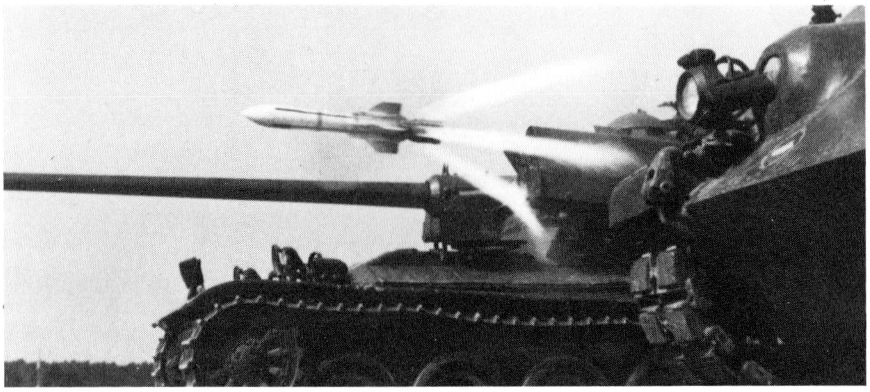

Thomson-CSF *Crotale*

Type: land-mobile all-weather surface-to-air guided missile

Guidance: radio command, based on infra-red and radar information

Dimensions: Span 21¼ in (54.0 cm)
Body diameter 5 9/16 in (15.0 cm)
Length 9 ft 5⅘ in (2.89 m)

Booster: single-stage solid-propellant rocket

Sustainer: see above

Warhead: 33-lb (15-kg) high explosive

Weights: Launch about 176 lb (80 kg)
Burnt out

Performance: speed Mach 2.3

Used also by: Egypt, Morocco, Pakistan, Saudi Arabia (as the *Shahine*), South Africa (as the Cactus), United Arab Emirates

Notes: The *Crotale* is a fast reacting missile system, highly manoeuvrable and capable of engaging targets moving at Mach 1.2 at altitudes up to 9,840 ft (3,000 m) at range of up to 5¼ miles (8.5 km). The time from target detection to missile launch is only 6 seconds, and the hit probability is 90%.

Messerschmitt-Bölkow-Blohm/ Aérospatiale Roland

Type: land-mobile surface-to-air guided missile

Guidance: (Roland I) command to line-of-sight with infra-red tracking; (Roland II) as Roland I but with radar rather than optical aiming

Dimensions: Span 19 7/10 in (50.0 cm)
Body diameter 6 3/10 in (16.0 cm)
Length 7 ft 10¼ in (2.4 m)

Booster: solid-propellant rocket

Sustainer: solid-propellant rocket

Warhead: high explosive

Weights: Launch 139 lb (63 kg)
Burnt out

Performance: speed about Mach 1.6; range 547 yards to 3¾ miles (500 m to 6 km)

Used also by: Brazil, USA, West Germany

Notes: Designed by Aérospatiale of France and Messerschmitt-Bölkow-Blohm of West Germany, the Roland is intended for the defence of armoured formations and the like against low-level air attack in all weathers. The two main launch vehicles are the AMX-30R and SPz *Marder* in France and Germany, and the M109 in the USA. The Roland I is a clear-weather system, used by France, and Roland II an all-weather system, used by France and

West Germany. The US Roland is based on the Roland II, but with different tracking radar.

AMX DCA-30 (AMX-13) vehicle

Type: self-propelled twin AA cannon mounting
Calibre: 30 mm
Barrel length:
Muzzle velocity: 3,280 ft (1,000 m) per second
Ranges: Maximum 10,936 yards (10,000 m); effective 3,828 yards (3,500 m)
Minimum
Elevation: −8° to +85°
Traverse: 360°
Rate of fire: 650 rounds per minute (cyclic) per barrel
Weights: For travel
In firing position
Dimensions: Length 17 ft 8⅗ in (5.4 m)
Width 8 ft 2⅖ in (2.5 m)
Height 9 ft 10 in (3.0 m)
Ammunition: 300 rounds per gun in the turret, plus 300 rounds per gun in the hull
Crew: four
Used only by: France
Notes: The AMX DCA-30 (AMX-13) is the SAMM S40 1A turret, with two 30-mm Hispano-Suiza Type 831L cannon, on the chassis of the AMX-13 light tank. Maximum road speed is 37.3 mph (60 kph). The system has a performance very similar to that of the AMX DCA-30 based on the chassis of the AMX-30 MBT.

AMX GCT

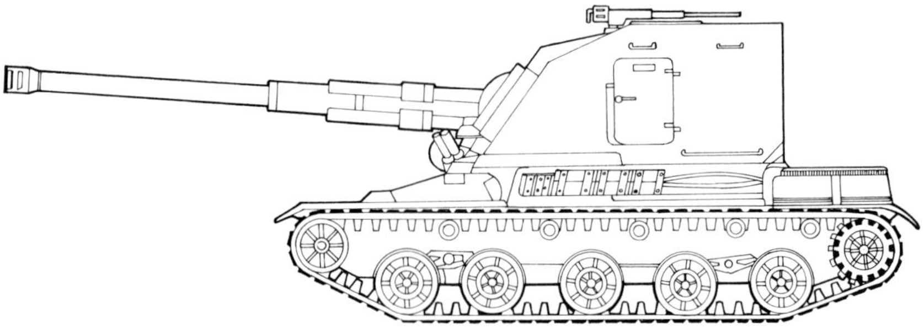

Type: self-propelled gun
Crew: four
Weights: Empty
Loaded 88,185 lb (40,000 kg)
Dimensions: Length (gun forward) 33 ft 3 in (10.4 m); (hull) 21 ft 3 in (6.485 m)
Width 10 ft 4 in (3.15 m)
Height (without AA gun) 10 ft 4⅘ in (3.17 m)
Ground pressure: 12.8 lb/in² (0.9 kg/cm²)
Performance: road speed 37 mph (60 kph); range 280 miles (450 km); vertical obstacle 36⅗ in (93.0 cm); trench 9 ft 6 in (3.9 m); gradient 60%; ground clearance 17 in (43.0 cm); wading 7 ft 2⅗ in (2.2 m) without preparation
Engine: one 720-hp Hispano-Suiza HS 110 supercharged multi-fuel inline engine
Armament: one 155-mm gun with 42 rounds, plus one 7.62-mm machine-gun on the turret roof with 2,000 rounds
Armour: about 2 in (50 mm) maximum
Used only by: France
Notes: The *Grande Cadence de Tir* (GCT) is a highly effective weapon system entering service with the French Army in 1978. NBC protection is standard, and night vision equipment can be installed if necessary. The 155-mm gun is 40 calibres long, and is mounted in a turret capable of 360° traverse. The ammunition is of the separate type, and carried in seven racks of six for projectile and charge, at the rear of the turret. Two men can reload the racks in 10 minutes. Gun loading is achieved by a hydraulically operated automatic system, which allows a rate of fire of up to eight rounds per minute. Maximum range of the *Modèle* 56 ammunition is 23,294 yards (21,300 m), and of the hollow-base shell, which weighs 95¼ lb (43.2 kg), 25,700 yards (23,500 m). The turret of the GCT has also been fitted to the chassis of the German Leopard tank.

Mk F3

Type: self-propelled howitzer
Crew: eight (two for vehicle)
Weights: Empty
Loaded 38,360 lb (17,400 kg)
Dimensions: Length 20 ft 4⅘ in (6.22 m)
Width 8 ft 10¼ in (2.7 m)
Height 7 ft 2⅗ in (2.2 m)
Ground pressure:
Performance: road speed 37 mph (60 kph); range 186 miles (300 km)
Engine: one 270-hp SOFAM Model 8 Gxb inline petrol engine
Armament: one 155-mm L/33 howitzer with HE, Illuminating and Smoke rounds
Armour:
Used also by: Argentina, Chile, Ecuador, Kuwait, Morocco, Qatar, United Arab Emirates, Venezuela
Notes: The Mk F3 is based on the chassis of the AMX-13 light tank, and is not amphibious. No NBC protection is provided. The crew and ammunition are transported in the AMX-13 VCA accompanying vehicle. The howitzer elevates from 0° to +67°, and fires a 95-lb (43-kg) hollow-base shell to a maximum range of 23,512 yards (21,500 m). Maximum rate of fire is some four rounds per minute.

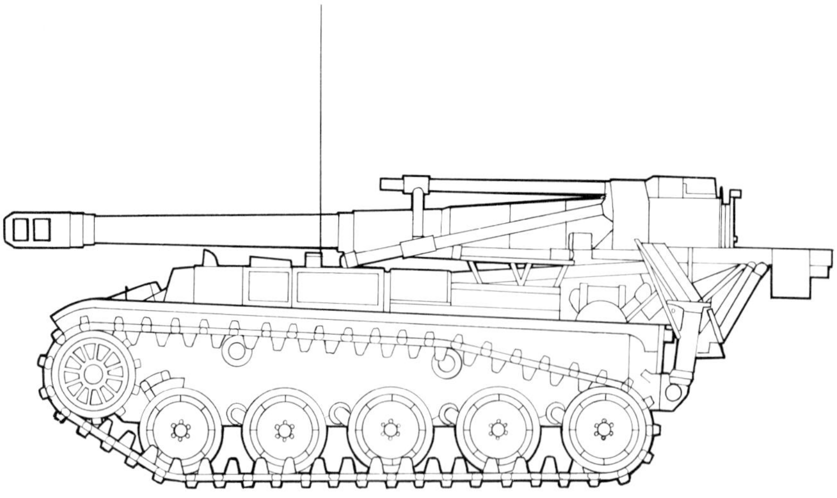

AMX-105 Mark 61

Type: self-propelled howitzer
Crew: five
Weights: Empty
      Loaded 36,376 lb (16,500 kg)
Dimensions: Length (overall) 21 ft (6.4 m)
              Width 8 ft 8 in (2.65 m)
              Height (with cupola) 8 ft 10 in
              (2.7 m)
Ground pressure: 11.38 lb/in² (0.8 kg/cm²)
Performance: road speed $37\frac{1}{4}$ mph (60 kph);
range 218 miles (350 km); vertical obstacle $25\frac{3}{8}$ in (65.0 cm); trench 6 ft 3 in (1.9 m); gradient 60%
Engine: one 250-hp SOFAM 8 Gxb inline petrol engine
Armament: one 105-mm howitzer (23 or 30 calibres in length) with 56 rounds of HE, Illuminating and Smoke, plus one 7.5-mm AA machine-gun
Armour: $\frac{1}{2}$ in (12 mm) minimum; $\frac{4}{5}$ in (20 mm) maximum
Used also by: Morocco, Netherlands
Notes: Based on the chassis of the AMX-13 light tank, the AMX-105 SP howitzer entered French service in 1952 as the *Obusier de 105 Modèle 1950 sur Affût Automoteur* Mk 61. The turret is a fixed unit, the howitzer having a traverse of 20° left and 20° right. The French Army uses the 23-calibre barrel, the Dutch Army the 30-calibre. There are two types of ammunition: US M1, with a range of 12,575 yards (11,500 m), and French Mk 63, with a range of 16,404 yards (15,000 m). A rotating-turret model of the vehicle was tested.

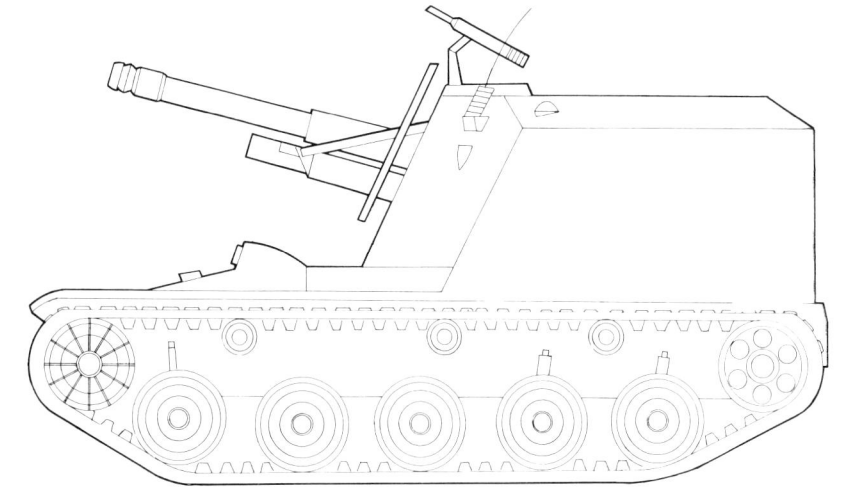

Type 53 T2 cannon mounting

Type: anti-aircraft cannon mounting
Calibre: 20 mm
Barrel length:
Muzzle velocity: 4,265 ft (1,300 m) with APDS; 3,445 ft (1,050 m) per second with HEI
Ranges: Maximum (AA) 4,921 ft (1,500 m)
Minimum

Elevation: −8° to +83°
Traverse: 360°
Rate of fire:
Weights: For travel 1,852 lb (840 kg)
In firing position 1,455 lb (660 kg)
Dimensions: Length
Width 5 ft 3 in (1.9 m)
Height
Ammunition: APDS, HEI and HEI-T
Crew: three

Used by: under development for France
Notes: This French weapon is an F2 M693 cannon on a special mounting. The gun is fitted with two magazines, one holding 40 rounds of APDS, and the other 100 rounds of HEI or HEI-T. The APDS round will penetrate $\frac{4}{8}$ in (20 mm) of armour at 60° at 1,094 yards (1,000 m). One of the best features of the system is that it can be brought into action from travelling in only 15 seconds.

ACL-STRIM launcher

Type: man-portable anti-tank rocket launcher
Calibre: 89 mm
Barrel length:
Muzzle velocity: 984 ft (300 m) per second
Ranges: Maximum effective 437 yards (400 m)
Minimum

Elevation:
Traverse:
Rate of fire:
Weights: For travel 9.92 lb (4.5 kg)
In firing position 16.09 lb (7.3 kg)
Dimensions: Length 5 ft 3 in (1.6 m)
Width
Height
Ammunition: HEAT warhead
Crew: three

Used only by: France
Notes: The French ACL-STRIM, known in service as the *Lance-Roquette Anti-Char de 98mm F1*, is an advanced anti-tank rocket launcher. The missile weighs 4.85 lb (2.2 kg), of which 0.8 lb (0.365 kg) is explosive. The shaped-charge head will penetrate 15$\frac{3}{4}$ in (400 mm) of armour or 4 ft 3 in (1,300 mm) of concrete.

SARPAC launcher

Type: man-portable anti-tank rocket launcher
Calibre: 68 mm
Barrel length:
Muzzle velocity: 492 ft (150 m) per second
Ranges: Maximum effective 219 yards (200 m)
Minimum
Elevation:
Traverse:

Rate of fire:
Weights: For travel 4.19 lb (1.9 kg)
In firing position 6.6 lb (2.99 kg)
Dimensions: Length 3 ft 3$\frac{3}{4}$ in (0.997 m)
Width
Height
Ammunition: Anti-Personnel (ROCAP), HEAT (ROCHAR) and Illuminating (ROCLAIR)
Crew: two or three

Used only by: France
Notes: The SARPAC is a simple weapon of French design and manufacture, intended primarily for the anti-tank role. The figures above refer to this model with the ROCHAR AT round. This weighs 2.4 lb (1.09 kg), and will penetrate 11.8 in (300 mm) of armour. The anti-personnel and illuminating rounds are heavier and longer ranged, but have lower muzzle velocities.

ACL-APX launcher

Type: man-portable anti-tank rocket launcher
Calibre: 80 mm
Barrel length:
Muzzle velocity: 1,312 ft (400 m) per second
Ranges: Maximum effective 634 yards (580 m)
Minimum

Elevation:
Traverse:
Rate of fire:
Weights: For travel 18.96 lb (8.6 kg)
In firing position 28.66 lb (13 kg)
Dimensions: Length 4 ft 7 in (1.4 m)
Width
Height

Ammunition: anti-personnel and anti-tank
Crew: two or three
Used only by: France
Notes: The ACL-APX is a useful battlefield weapon of French design and manufacture. The AT round weighs 7.94 lb (3.6 kg), and its 1.2-lb (0.55-kg) explosive warhead will penetrate any known armour plate.

MO-120-RT-61 mortar

Type: rifled heavy mortar
Calibre: 120 mm
Barrel length: 17.33 cal including breech
Muzzle velocity:
Ranges: Maximum 14,217 yards (14,000 m)
with PRPA; 9,132 yards (8,350 m)
with PR14
Minimum

Elevation: 30° to 85°
Traverse: 14°
Rate of fire: six to ten rounds per minute
Weights: For travel
In firing position 1,283 lb (582 kg)
Dimensions: Length 9 ft 10¾ in (3.015 m)
Width 6 ft 4 in (1.93 m)
Height
Ammunition: HE (PR14), HE (PRPA) and Il-
luminating (PRECLAIR)

Crew: three
Used only by: France
Notes: This Thomson-Brandt rifled mortar is a powerful weapon with good range and lethality performance. The PR14 bomb weighs 34.6 lb (15.7 kg) and is a conventional round. The PRPA (*Projectile Rayé à Propulsion Additionelle*) is a 34.4-lb (15.6-kg) round with additional rocket propulsion to increase range.

MO-120 AM 50 mortar

Type: heavy mortar
Calibre: 120 mm
Barrel length: 13.73 cal including breech
Muzzle velocity:
Ranges: Maximum 9,842 yards (9,000 m)
with PEPA
Minimum 1,312 yards (1,200 m)
Elevation: 45° to 80°
Traverse: 17°

Rate of fire: eight to twelve rounds per
minute
Weights: For travel 886 lb (402 kg)
In firing position 533 lb (242 kg)
Dimensions: Length
Width
Height
Ammunition: HE (M44), HE (PEPA/LP), Il-
luminating, Smoke (Coloured) and Smoke
WP
Crew: four

Used only by: France
Notes: This Thomson-Brandt mortar is designed as a versatile weapon for use on its wheeled carriage or from a bipod. Amongst other rounds, the mortar can fire the PEPA (*Projectile Empenné à Propulsion Additionelle*) long-range finned round, which weighs 29.6 lb (13.42 kg), compared with the 28.7 lb (13 kg) of the other rounds.

MO-120-M65

Type: heavy mortar
Calibre: 120 mm
Barrel length: 13.66 cal including breech
Muzzle velocity:
Ranges: Maximum 9,842 yards (9,000 m)
Minimum 1,312 yards (1,200 m)
Elevation: 40° to 85°
Traverse: 17°
Rate of fire: eight to twelve rounds per
minute

Weights: For travel 317 lb (144 kg)
In firing position 229 lb (104 kg)
Dimensions: Length
Width
Height
Ammunition: HE (M44), HE (PEPA/LP), HE
(Coloured), Illuminating and Smoke WP
Crew: two or three
Used only by: France
Notes: The Thomson-Brandt MO-120-M65
was designed to combine the range per-

formance of the MO-120 AM 50 with the lightness of the MO-120 M60 (light) heavy mortar. To this end the baseplate is only a light unit, and the carriage is a two-wheeled light tubular structure. As with other French 120-mm mortars, the MO-120-M65 can fire the PEPA/LP (*Projectile Empenné à Propulsion Additionelle/Longue Portée*) round weighing 29.6 lb (13.42 kg), as well as the other 28.7 lb (13 kg) bombs.

MO-120 M60 mortar

Type: (light) heavy mortar
Calibre: 120 mm
Barrel length: 13.6 cal including breech
Muzzle velocity:
Ranges: Maximum 7,229 yards (6,610 m)
with PEPA/LP; 6,015 yards (5,500
m) with M44
Minimum 656 yards (600 m)
Elevation: 40° to 80°

Traverse: 17°
Rate of fire: eight to fifteen rounds per minute
Weights: For travel
In firing position 212 lb (96 kg)
Dimensions: Length
Width
Height
Ammunition: HE (M44), HE (PEPA/LP), Il-
luminating, Smoke (Coloured) and Smoke
WP

Crew: three
Used also by: Argentina
Notes: The Thomson-Brandt MO-120 M60 is designed to provide the lightest possible weapon for firing 120-mm mortar bombs. Although standard bombs can be used, only reduced charges can be employed to fire them, so range is reduced. Nevertheless, the weapon is a powerful adjunct for short-range engagements.

MO-81-61C mortar

Type: light mortar
Calibre: 81 mm
Barrel length: 14.2 cal
Muzzle velocity:
Ranges: Maximum 3,718 yards (3,400 m)
with HE; 4,484 yards (4,100 m) with
M57D
Minimum 131 yards (120 m)

Elevation: 30° to 85°
Traverse: 360°
Rate of fire: 15 rounds per minute
Weights: For travel
In firing position 87 lb (39.4 kg)
Dimensions: Length
Width
Height
Ammunition: HE, Illuminating and Smoke

Crew: two or three
Used only by: France
Notes: The MO-81-61C light mortar is designed to give French infantry adequate fire support under all battle conditions. The standard HE bomb weighs 7.28 lb (3.3 kg) and can be fired to 3,718 yards (3,400 m), while the M57D ammunition can be fired to longer ranges.

MO-81-61L mortar

Type: light mortar
Calibre: 81 mm
Barrel length: 17.9 cal
Muzzle velocity:
Ranges: Maximum 5,468 yards (5,000 m)
with Mark 61
Minimum 82 yards (75 m)

Elevation: 30° to 85°
Traverse: 360°
Rate of fire: 15 rounds per minute
Weights: For travel
In firing position 91½ lb (41.5 kg)
Dimensions: Length
Width
Height

Ammunition: HE, Illuminating and Smoke
Crew: two or three
Used only by: France
Notes: The MO-81-61L is the long-barrel version of the MO-81-61C mortar, using Mark 61 ammunition for greater range.

MO-60-63 mortar

Type: light mortar
Calibre: 60 mm
Barrel length: 12.06 cal including breech
Muzzle velocity:
Ranges: Maximum 2,187 yards (2,000 m)
with HE
Minimum less than 55 yards (50 m)

Elevation: 40° to 85°
Traverse: 17°
Rate of fire:
Weights: For travel
In firing position 32.6 lb (14.8 kg)
Dimensions: Length
Width
Height
Ammunition: HE, Illuminating and Smoke

Crew: two or three
Used also by: West Germany
Notes: The MO-60-63 is designed to be carried by mobile infantry, and to provide them with all necessary short-period fire support. The HE bomb weighs 3.8 lb (1.73 kg), and apart from the Mark 61 ammunition designed for the weapon, a number of other 60-mm types can be used.

'Commando' mortar

Type: light mortar
Calibre: 60 mm
Barrel length: 10.8 cal
Muzzle velocity:
Ranges: Maximum 1,148 yards (1,050 m)
Minimum
Elevation:
Traverse:

Rate of fire: 12 to 20 rounds per minute
Weights: For travel
In firing position 22.05 lb (10 kg)
Dimensions: Length 33.46 in (0.85 m)
Width
Height
Ammunition: HE, Illuminating, Marker and Smoke
Crew: one
Used also by: various nations

Notes: The 'Commando' mortar is made in two versions: Type A described above, with controlled firing; and Type V with automatic firing from a fixed firing pin. The latter is only 26.77 in (0.68 m) long and weighs 17.86 lb (8.1 kg). The larger of the two HE bombs weighs 3.8 lb (1.73 kg). Both elevation and line are controlled by the firer's hand.

AA 52 machine-gun

Type: general-purpose machine-gun
Calibre: 7.5 mm
System of operation: delayed blowback
Muzzle velocity: 2,625 ft (800 m) per second
Range: effective 1,312 yards (1,200 m) with heavy barrel; 875 yards (800 m) with light barrel
Rate of fire: 900 rounds per minute (cyclic); 250 to 700 rounds per minute (practical) with heavy barrel; 150 rounds per minute (practical) with light barrel
Cooling system: disintegrating metal-link belt
Dimensions: Barrel length 23.62 in (600 mm) heavy barrel; 19.69 in (500 mm) light barrel (both without flash hider)
Overall length 49 in (1.245 m) with heavy barrel and butt extended
Width
Height

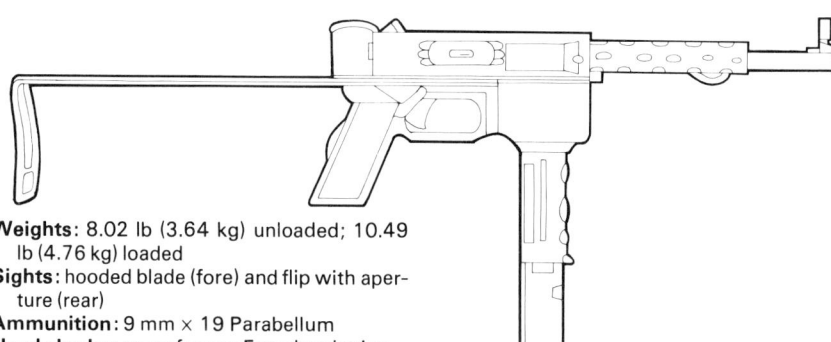

Weights: 21.38 lb (9.7 kg) with light barrel and bipod but no flash hider; 24.58 lb (11.15 kg) with heavy barrel, bipod and flash hider
Sights: slit blade (fore) and leaf (rear)
Ammunition: 7.5 mm × 54
Used only by: France
Notes: The AA 52, or more properly *Arme Automatique Transformable Modèle* 1952, was France's first machine-gun of indigenous design after World War II, and was intended as a general-purpose weapon of useful power, but of light weight and great ease of manufacture, stampings being used as widely as possible. Later it was thought advisable to produce a version for the 7.62 mm standard NATO round, and this is the AA 7.62 NF-1. Both versions can be fitted with heavy or light barrels. For the sustained fire role, the weapons can be mounted on the US M2 tripod.

MAT 49 sub-machine gun

Type: sub-machine gun
Calibre: 9 mm
System of operation: blowback
Muzzle velocity: 1,161 ft (354 m) per second
Range: effective 219 yards (200 m)
Rate of fire: 600 rounds per minute (cyclic); 128 rounds per minute (automatic)
Cooling system: air
Feed system: 32-round box
Dimensions: Barrel length 8.98 in (228 mm)
Overall length 27.95 in (710 mm) with stock extended; 21.97 in (558 mm) with stock retracted
Width
Height

Weights: 8.02 lb (3.64 kg) unloaded; 10.49 lb (4.76 kg) loaded
Sights: hooded blade (fore) and flip with aperture (rear)
Ammunition: 9 mm × 19 Parabellum
Used also by: some former French colonies
Notes: The MAT 49 is an unexceptional weapon, with adequate killing power and accuracy, and simple to make as steel sheet and stampings are widely used. The gun is capable of automatic fire only.

Gevarm et Gevelot sub-machine gun

Type: sub-machine gun
Calibre: 9 mm
System of operation: blowback
Muzzle velocity: 1,197 ft (365 m) per second
Range: effective 109 yards (100 m)
Rate of fire: 600 rounds per minute (cyclic)
Cooling system: air
Feed system: 32-round box
Dimensions: Barrel length 8.66 in (220 mm)
Overall length 19.69 in (500 mm) with stock retracted
Width
Height
Weights: 7.05 lb (3.2 kg) unloaded; 8.63 lb (3.915 kg)
Sights: blade (fore) and flip (rear)
Ammunition: 9 mm × 19 Parabellum
Used only by: France
Notes: The Gevarm et Gevelot sub-machine gun is designed for total simplicity of use and maintenance under all conditions of warfare and climate.

MAS 36 rifle

Type: bolt-action magazine rifle
Calibre: 7.5 mm
System of operation: manually operated bolt
Muzzle velocity: about 2,625 ft (800 m) per second
Range: effective 547 yards (500 m)
Rate of fire:
Cooling system: air
Feed system: 5-round integral box
Dimensions: Barrel length 22.6 in (574 mm)
Overall length 40.08 in (1.018 m)
Width
Height
Weights: 8.38 lb (3.8 kg)
Sights: hooded barleycorn (fore) and aperture (rear)
Ammunition: 7.5 mm M29
Used also by: former French colonies

Notes: This pre-World War II French rifle is now used as an operational weapon only by former French colonies. The action is basically a modified Mauser type. There are several variants:

1. M-1936CR39 paratroop model with a shorter barrel and folding stock
2. M-1936M-51 postwar model with a grenade launcher
3. FR-F1 sniper's derivative.

MAS 49 rifle

Type: self-loading rifle
Calibre: 7.5 mm
System of operation: gas (direct action)
Muzzle velocity: 2,700 ft (823 m) per second
Range: effective 656 yards (600 m)
Rate of fire: 30 rounds per minute
Cooling system: air
Feed system: 10-round box
Dimensions: Barrel length 22.83 in (584 mm)
Overall length 43.31 in (1.1 m)
Width
Height
Weights: 10.36 lb (4.7 kg)
Sights: blade (fore) and ramp, aperture (rear)
Ammunition: 7.5 mm M29
Used also by: several former French colonies
Notes: The MAS 49 is a conventional weapon except in its method of operation, which uses direct gas action rather than the more usual piston and cylinder.

FR-F1 rifle

Type: sniping rifle
Calibre: 7.5 mm
System of operation: manually operated bolt action
Muzzle velocity: 2,795 ft (852 m) per second
Range: effective 875 yards (800 m)
Rate of fire: 10 to 15 rounds per minute
Cooling system: air
Feed system: 10-round box
Dimensions: Barrel length 21.73 in (552 mm)
Overall length 44.8 in (1.138 m)
Width
Height
Weights: 11.46 lb (5.2 kg) unloaded
Sights: pyramid (fore) and square notch (rear), or ×4 telescope
Ammunition: 7.5 mm × 54, or 7.6 mm × 51
Used only by: France

Notes: The FR-F1 (*Fusil à Répétition* F1) is the standard sniping rifle of the French Army, and is based on the MAS M-1936 bolt-action rifle, although few standard parts of the original rifle are interchangeable with those of the FR-R1.

Wooden spacers are provided for the length of the stock to be increased to suit the firer's physique. The weapon is provided with a bipod near the centre of gravity.

Model 1954/57 flamethrower

Type: portable flamethrower
Weights: Empty 28.44 lb (12.9 kg)
Loaded 44.75 lb (20.3 kg)
Ranges: Maximum 66 yards (60 m) with jellified fuel
Effective 44 yards (40 m) with jellified fuel
Fuel capacity: 45.46 pints (10 litres)
Notes: Model 1954/57 is the French Army's standard flamethrower, its fuel being sufficient for one 6-second burst or six 1-second bursts.

Gabon

950 men.

1 inf bn.
2 cdo coys.
1 engr coy.
1 service coy.
AML-90 armd cars; 12 VXB APC; 81mm mor; 106mm RCL (6 Commando APC on order).

Beretta Model 12 sub-machine gun

Type: sub-machine gun
Calibre: 9 mm
System of operation: blowback

Muzzle velocity: 1,250 ft (381 m) per second
Range: effective 219 yards (200 m)
Rate of fire: 550 rounds per minute (cyclic); 120 rounds per minute (automatic)
Cooling system: air
Feed system: 20-, 30- or 40-round box
Dimensions: Barrel length 7.87 in (200 mm) Overall length 25.39 in (645 mm) with stock extended;

16.38 in (416 mm) with stock folded
Width
Height
Weights: 6.61 lb (3 kg) unloaded, with metal stock; 9.22 lb (4.18 kg) loaded, with wooden stock; 8.31 lb (3.77 kg) loaded, with metal stock
Sights: blade (fore) and flip, notch (rear)

Ammunition: 9 mm × 19 Parabellum
Used also by: Brazil, Indonesia, Italy, Libya, Nigeria, Saudi Arabia, Venezuela
Notes: The Beretta Model 12 is of wholly Italian manufacture, and appeared in 1958. The weapon is quite simple, and is relatively cheap to manufacture. It is durable, however, and can be used in adverse geographical locations. The wrap-round bolt makes for great steadiness of firing.

Ghana

15,000 men.

2 bdes (6 inf bns and support units).
1 recce bn.
1 mor bn.
1 fd engr, 1 sigs bn.
1 AB coy.
9 Saladin armd cars; 26 Ferret scout cars; 81mm, 10 120mm mor.

Deployment: Egypt (UNEF): 1 bn, 597 men.

Para-Military Forces: 3,000, 3 Border Guard bns.

Alvis FV601 Saladin

Type: armoured car
Crew: three
Weights: Empty
Loaded 25,550 lb (11,590 kg)
Dimensions: Length (with gun forward) 17 ft 4 in (5.28 m); (hull) 16 ft 2 in (4.93 m)
Width 8 ft 4 in (2.54 m)
Height 9 ft 7 in (2.93 m)
Ground pressure:
Performance: road speed 45 mph (72 kph); range 250 miles (400 km); vertical obstacle 18 in (46.0 cm); trench 5 ft (1.52 m); gradient 60%
Engine: one 160-bhp Rolls-Royce B.80 Mark 6A inline petrol engine

Armament: one 76-mm gun with 42 rounds of HE, HESH and Smoke, plus one 0.3-in (7.62-mm) machine-gun co-axial with main armament, and one 0.3-in (7.62-mm) AA machine-gun on a pintle mount on the turret roof
Armour: $\frac{2}{5}$ in (10 mm) minimum; $1\frac{1}{4}$ in (32 mm) maximum
Used also by: Bahrain, Indonesia, Kenya, Kuwait, Nigeria, North Yemen, Oman, Qatar, South Yemen, Sri Lanka, Sudan, Tunisia, Uganda, United Arab Emirates, UK
Notes: The Saladin entered British service in 1955, and shares many components with the Saracen. The Saladin has proved well able to cope with mine damage, and its protection, mobility and the punch of its 76-mm HESH round make the type a formidable AFV to this day.

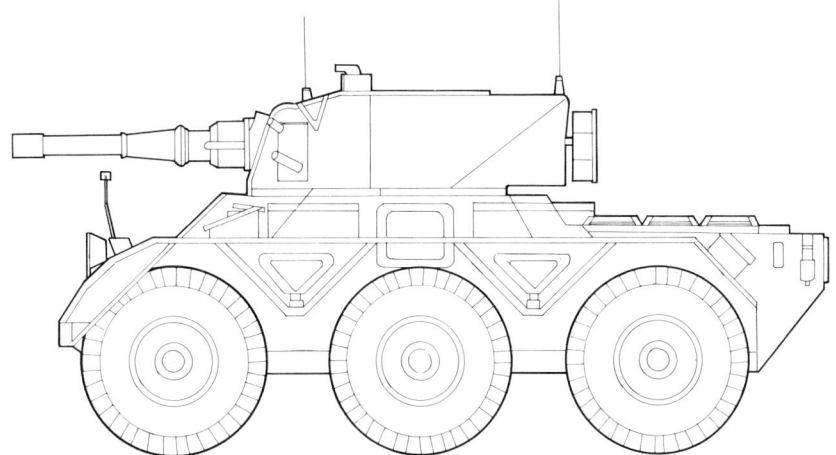

Greece

150,000 men (123,000 conscripts) and about 250,000 reservists.

1 armd div.
11 inf divs (some mech).
1 armd bde.
1 para cdo bde.
1 marine inf bde.
2 SSM bns with 8 Honest John.
1 SAM bn with 12 Improved HAWK.
12 arty bns.
14 army aviation coys.
300 M-47, 750 M-48, 120 AMX-30 med, 170 M-24 lt tks; 180 M-8 armd cars; 460 M-59, 520 M-113, MOWAG APC; AMX-10P MICV; 100 75mm pack, 80 105mm, 240 155mm how; M-52 105mm, M-44 155mm, M-107 175mm, M-110 203mm SP guns/how; 8 Honest John SSM; 550 106mm RCL; SS-11, Cobra, TOW, Milan ATGW; 40mm, 75mm, 90mm AA guns; Improved HAWK, Redeye SAM; 1 Super King Air, 2 Aero Commander, 20 U-17, 15 L-21 ac; 5 Bell 47G, 20 UH-1D, 42 AB-204/-205 helicopters.
(100 AMX-30 med tks, AMX-10P MICV on order.)

Para-Military Forces: 29,000 Gendarmerie, 100,000 National Guard.

M48 Patton

Type: main battle tank
Crew: four
Weights: Empty 98,000 lb (44,453 kg)
Loaded 104,000 lb (47,174 kg)
Dimensions: Length (with gun forward) 28 ft 6 in (8.687 m); (hull) 24 ft 5 in (7.44 m)
Width 11 ft 11 in (3.63 m)
Height (overall) 10 ft 10 in (3.3 m)
Ground pressure: 11.94 lb/in² (0.84 kg/cm²)
Performance: road speed 30 mph (48 kph); range 249 miles (400 km); vertical obstacle 36 in (91.4 cm); trench 8 ft 6 in (2.59 m); gradient 60%; ground clearance 15⅓ in (38.9 cm); wading 48 in (1.22 m) without preparation
Engine: one 750-bhp Continental AVDS-1790-2A turbo-charged inline diesel engine
Armament: one 90-mm M41 L/48 gun with 60 rounds of HE, HEAT, HVAP, White Phosphorus and Canister, plus one 7.62-mm machine-gun with 6,000 rounds, co-axial with the main armament, and one 0.5-in (12.7-mm) Browning M2 machine-gun with 630 rounds for AA defence on the commander's cupola
Armour: 1 in (25.4 mm) minimum; 4⅓ in (110 mm) maximum
Used also by: Iran, Israel, Jordan, Morocco, Norway, Pakistan, Portugal, South Korea, Spain, Taiwan, Turkey, USA, West Germany

Notes: The M48 is essentially an improved M47, the most important distinguishing features of the former being a revised turret shape, with less rear overhang and the addition of a large commander's cupola. The type entered service in 1953, and has since showed itself an adequate MBT, with the great virtues of simplicity and reliability. Many Israeli M48s have been regunned with the L7 105-mm gun, and night vision equipment can be added to all marks. There are several versions and derivatives of the M48:

1. M48 initial production model, with the 810-bhp Continental AV-1790 SRS inline petrol engine, giving a speed of 30 mph (48 kph) but a range of only 100 miles (160 km), and with an M4-type cupola and an exposed remotely controlled machine-gun
2. M48C training tank made of mild steel
3. M48A1, still with the AV-1790 SRS engine, but with an M1 cupola and a larger driver's hatch
4. M48A2, with the 825-hp Continental AVL-1790-8 inline petrol engine
5. M48A2C mild steel training tank
6. M48A2E1 with a multi-fuel engine
7. M48A2/SS.10 with five SS.10 anti-tank missiles, two to the left, two to the right and one over the 90-mm gun
8. M48A3, the production model of the M48A2E1, with the 750-hp Continental AVDS-1790-2A diesel engine. The technical specification above applies to this model

9. M48A4, the M48A3 with the turret of the M60, armed with a 105-mm gun, and the M19 cupola
10. M48A5, the standard up to which all surviving US tanks are to be brought, with 105-mm guns, new machine-guns and other detail improvements
11. M48 with Expendable Roller Mine Clearing device
12. M48 with Heavy Mine Clearing Roller (High Herman), with 25 plain and ser-rated discs
13. M48 with Light Mine Clearing Roller (Larrapin' Lou), with two units each of six serrated discs
14. M48 or M48A2 Armoured Vehicle-Launched Bridge for gaps up to 60 ft (18.29 m) in width, for vehicles in the 60-ton class
15. M67, M67A1 and M67A2 flame tanks, with flame guns in place of the 90-mm gun
16. M88 Medium Armoured Recovery Vehicle.

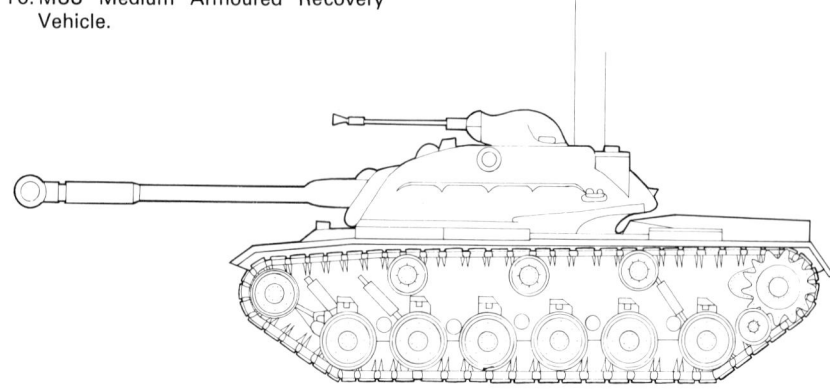

M107

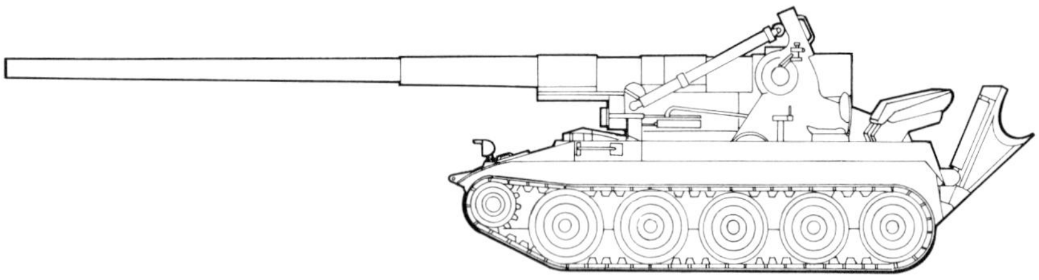

Type: self-propelled gun
Crew: 13
Weights: Empty
Loaded 62,095 lb (28,166 kg)
Dimensions: Length 37 ft 1 in (11.3 m)
Width 10 ft 2$\frac{1}{2}$ in (3.14 m)
Height 11 ft 4$\frac{1}{2}$ in (3.47 m)
Ground pressure: 13.5 lb/in² (0.95 kg/cm²)
Performance: road speed 33.5 mph (54 kph); range 450 miles (724 km); vertical obsta-cle 40 in (1.016 m); trench 7 ft 9 in (2.362 m); gradient 60%; wading 42 in (1.066 m)
Engine: one 405-hp Detroit Diesel Model 8V71T turbo-charged inline diesel engine
Armament: one 175-mm L/60 gun with separate loading HE ammunition
Armour: $\frac{4}{5}$ in (20 mm) maximum
Used also by: Iran, Israel, Italy, Netherlands, South Korea, Spain, UK, USA, Vietnam, West Germany
Notes: The M107 uses the same chassis as the M110, and is in the process of being phased out in favour of the dual-purpose M110A1 and M110A2 self-propelled howitzers. The M107 fires its 147-lb (66.6-kg) shell at a muzzle velocity of 3,028 ft (923 m) per second to a range of 35,750 yards (32,700 m). Elevation is from +2° to +65°, and traverse is 30° left and right. Five of the crew are carried on the M107, and the other eight on the accompanying M548. The M107 entered service in 1962–3.

M44

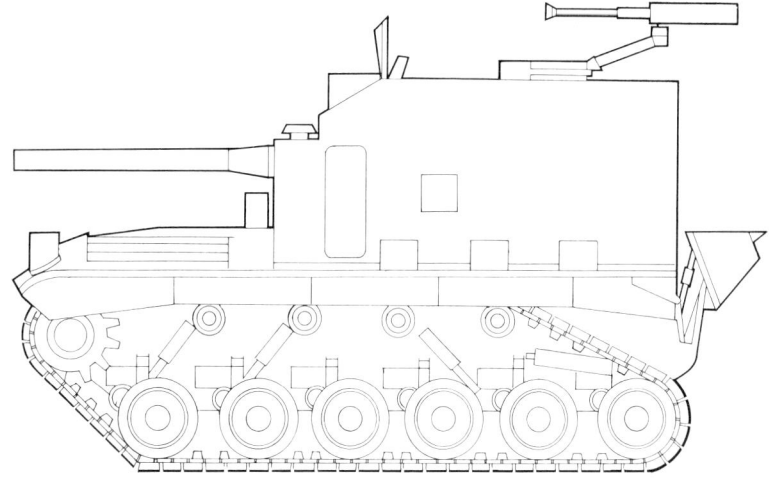

Type: self-propelled howitzer
Crew: six
Weights: Empty
Loaded 62,940 lb (28,549 kg)
Dimensions: Length 20 ft (6.09 m)
Width 10 ft 10 in (3.3 m)
Height 10 ft 2 in (3.1 m)
Ground pressure: 9.24 lb/in² (0.65 kg/cm²)
Performance: road speed 35 mph (56 kph); range 75 miles (120 km); vertical obstacle 30 in (76.2 cm); trench 6 ft (1.83 m); gradient 60%
Engine: one 500-hp Continental AOS-895-3 inline petrol engine
Armament: one 155-mm howitzer with 24 rounds of Chemical, HE and Smoke ammunition, plus one 0.5-in (12.7-mm) Browning M2 machine-gun for AA defence, with 900 rounds
Armour: $\frac{3}{5}$ in (15 mm)
Used also by: Belgium, Italy, Jordan, Spain
Notes: The M44 self-propelled howitzer is very similar to the M52, differing only in the fighting compartment and howitzer. The turret traverses 360°, and the howitzer elevates from −5° to +60°. The howitzer's maximum range is 16,185 yards (14,800 m). The fighting compartment is open-topped.

Rheinmetall Mark 20 Rh.202 gun

Type: twin AA cannon mounting
Calibre: 20 mm
Barrel length: 92 cal excluding muzzle brake
Muzzle velocity: 3,609 ft (1,100 m) per second with API
Ranges: Maximum (horizontal) 7,655 yards (7,000 m)
Minimum
Elevation: −5° to +83°
Traverse: 360°
Rate of fire: 1,000 rounds per minute (cyclic) per barrel
Weights: For travel 4,630 lb (2,100 kg)
In firing position 3,197 lb (1,450 kg)
Dimensions: Length 14 ft 9½ in (4.5 m)
Width 7 ft 9⅓ in (2.37 m)
Height 6 ft 2¾ in (1.9 m)

Ammunition: API, API-T, HEI, HEI-T and APDS-T
Crew: three
Used also by: Norway, West Germany
Notes: The Rh.202 is a versatile AA and light AT weapon, capable of being brought into action quickly. The API round weighs 0.24 lb (0.111 kg), and will penetrate 1.26 in (32 mm) of armour at 1,094 yards (1,000 m).

Guatemala

13,500 men.

3 bde HQ.
10 inf bns.
1 Presidential Guard bn.
1 para bn.
1 engr bn.
1 armd car coy.
9 arty btys.
8 AMX-13 lt tks; 8 M-8 armd cars; 6 M-3A1, 10 M-113, 10 RBY-1, 7 Commando APC; 12 75mm, 12 105mm how; 81mm, 12 4.2in mor, 10 40mm SP AA guns.

Para-Military Forces: 3,000.

M4 Sherman

Type: medium tank
Crew: five
Weights: Empty
Loaded 69,565 lb (31,554 kg)
Dimensions: Length 20 ft 7 in (6.27 m)
Width 8 ft 11 in (2.67 m)
Height 11 ft 1 in (3.37 m)
Ground pressure: 14.3 lb/in² (1.0 kg/cm²)
Performance: road speed 26 mph (42 kph); range 100 miles (160 km); vertical obstacle 24 in (61.0 cm); trench 7 ft 6 in (2.29 m); gradient 60%; wading 36 in (91.0 cm)
Engine: one 500-hp Ford GAA inline petrol engine
Armament: one 75-mm M3 gun with 95 rounds, plus one 0.3-in (7.62-mm) Browning M1919A4 machine-gun co-axial with the main armament, one 0.3-in (7.62-mm) Browning M1919A4 in the hull nose (7,750 rounds), one 0.5-in (12.7-mm) Browning M2 machine-gun on the turret roof
Armour: $\frac{3}{5}$ in (15 mm) minimum; 4 in (100 mm) maximum

Used also by: Argentina, Brazil, Chile, Colombia, Nicaragua, Pakistan, Paraguay, Peru, Uganda, Yugoslavia
Notes: The M4 Sherman was the most successful tank produced by the Western Allies in World War II, and went through a large number of modifications and improvements. The specification above applies to the M4A3 model.

Guinea - Bissau

8,000 men.

1 armd bn.
4 inf bns.
1 engr bn.
30 T-34/-54 med, 10 PT-76 lt tks; 40 BTR-40/-152 APC; 76mm, 85mm, 105mm, 122mm, guns/how; 57mm ATK, 37mm, 57mm, 100mm AA guns.

M-1945 (D-44) gun

Type: field and medium anti-tank gun
Calibre: 85 mm
Barrel length: 55.2 cal
Muzzle velocity: 3,379 ft (1,030 m) per second with HVAP
Ranges: Maximum 17,115 yards (15,650 m)
  Minimum
Elevation: −7° to +35°
Traverse: 54° total
Rate of fire: 15 rounds per minute
Weights: For travel 3,803 lb (1,725 kg)
  In firing position
Dimensions: Length 27 ft 4$\frac{1}{3}$ in (8.34 m)
  Width 5 ft 10 in (1.78 m)
  Height 4 ft 7$\frac{4}{5}$ in (1.42 m)
Ammunition: APHE, HE and HVAP

Crew: eight
Used also by: Albania, Algeria, Bulgaria, China, Cuba, East Germany, Egypt, Hungary, Iran, Iraq, Laos, Mali, Morocco, North Korea, Poland, Romania, Sudan, Syria, USSR, Vietnam
Notes: The M-1945 was developed at the end of World War II, and uses the same basic gun as the T-34/85 medium tank. It is also known as the D-48, especially in the AT role. The HE round weighs 20.94 lb (9.5 kg), and the HVAP round 11 lb (5 kg). The penetration of the APHE round is 4 in (102 mm) at 1,094 yards (1,000 m), that of the HVAP round 5.12 in (130 mm) at the same range. There is also the SD-44 version with an auxiliary power unit for limited independent travel.

Guyana

2,000 total manpower.

2 inf bns.
4 Shorland armd cars; 12 81mm mor.

Haiti

6,000 men.

Pres Guard.
1 inf bn.
garrison dets.
M-113, 6 V-150 Commando APC; 75mm, 105mm how; 81mm mor; 37mm, 57mm ATK guns.

M116 howitzer

Type: pack howitzer
Calibre: 75 mm
Barrel length: 20 cal
Muzzle velocity: 1,250 ft (381 m) per second with HEAT
Ranges: Maximum 9,300 yards (8,504 m) with HEAT
  Minimum
Elevation: −5° to +45°
Traverse: 6° total
Rate of fire: 22 rounds per minute maximum; three to five rounds per minute practical
Weights: For travel 1,440 lb (653 kg)
  In firing position 1,440 lb (653 kg)
Dimensions: Length 12 ft (3.66 m)
  Width 3 ft 11 in (1.19 m)
  Height 3 ft 1 in (0.94 m)

Ammunition: Chemical, HE, HEAT and Smoke
Crew: four
Used also by: Brazil, China, Cuba, Honduras, India, Iran, Japan, Laos, Oman, Pakistan, Taiwan, Thailand, Vietnam
Notes: The American M116 pack howitzer was developed in World War II as the M1A1 on M8 carriage pack howitzer for airborne troops, design work having started in the 1930s. The gun can be broken down into eight loads for mule transport, or nine loads for parachute dropping. To get the gun into action takes three minutes and nine minutes respectively. Shell weight is 13.76 lb (6.25 kg).

Honduras

13,000 men.

10 inf bns.
1 Presidential Guard bn.
3 arty btys.
1 engr, 1 sigs bn.
12 75mm pack, 8 105mm how; 81mm, 120mm mor; 57mm RCL.
(Scorpion lt tks on order.)

Para-Military Forces: 3,000.

Hungary

91,000 men (70,000 conscripts) and 130,000 reservists.

1 tk div.
5 motor rifle divs.
1 SSM bde with 'Scud'.
3 arty regts.
2 AA arty regts.
1 SAM regt with SA-6.
1 AB bn.
Danube Flotilla.
About 1,000 T-54/-55 med, 100 PT-76 lt tks; about 600 FUG-65/-66 scout cars; 1,500 PSZH APC; 250 122mm, 36 152mm guns/how; 300 82mm, 100 120mm mor; 75 BM-21 122mm RL; 24 FROG, 12 'Scud' SSM; 300 57mm and 85mm ATK guns; 75 'Sagger', 'Snapper' ATGW; 200 57mm and 100mm towed, 40 ZSU-23-4 and ZSU-57-2 SP AA guns; 20 SA-6, SA-7, 50 SA-9 SAM; 10 100-ton patrol craft, river MCM, 5 small landing craft.

Para-Military Forces: 15,000 border guards (11,000 conscripts) with lt inf weapons; 60,000 part-time Workers' Militia.

PT-76

Type: light tank
Crew: three
Weights: Empty
    Loaded 30,864 lb (14,000 kg)
Dimensions: Length (with gun) 25 ft (7.625 m); (hull) 22 ft 8 in (6.91 m)
    Width 10 ft 5⅛ in (3.18 m)
    Height 7 ft 2¾ in (2.2 m)
Ground pressure: 6.97 lb/in² (0.49 kg/cm²)
Performance: road speed 27 mph (44 kph); water speed 6.8 mph (11 kph); range 155 miles (250 km); vertical obstacle 41¾ in (1.06 m); trench 9 ft (2.74 m); gradient 28°; ground clearance 13¾ in (35.0 cm); the PT-76 is fully amphibious, being driven in the water by waterjets
Engine: one 240-bhp inline diesel engine
Armament: one 76-mm D-56 gun with 40 rounds of HE, HEAT and HVAP ammunition, plus one 7.62-mm SGMT machine-gun with 1,000 rounds, co-axial with the main armament
Armour: ⅖ in (11 mm) minimum; ⅗ in (14 mm) maximum
Used also by: Afghanistan, Angola, China, Congo, Cuba, East Germany, Egypt, Finland, Guinea-Bissau, Hungary, India, Indonesia, Iraq, Israel, Laos, Mozambique, North Korea, Pakistan, Poland, Syria, Uganda, USSR, Vietnam, Yugoslavia
Notes: The PT-76 light tank is widely used by the Warsaw Pact nations as their primary reconnaissance vehicle, in which capacity the type's excellent cross-country and amphibious performance is a prime asset. There are a number of minor variants of the type, but four main models and several derivatives:
  1. PT-76 Model 1 with a D-56T gun with a multi-baffle muzzle brake and no bore evacuator
  2. PT-76 Model 2 with a D-56TM gun with a double-baffle muzzle brake and a bore evacuator
  3. PT-76 Model 3 with a clean-barrelled D-56 gun
  4. PT-76 Model 4, also known as the PT-76B, with a stabilised D-56TM gun
  5. the chassis of the PT-76 is used as the basis for the following AFVs: ASU-85, SA-6 'Gainful' launcher, BTR-50, FROG-2, 3, 4 and 5 launcher, GSP bridging vehicle, OT-62 and ZSU-23-4.

The PT-76 has no NBC or night vision equipment, and has largely been replaced in Russian service as a reconnaissance vehicle by the BMP.

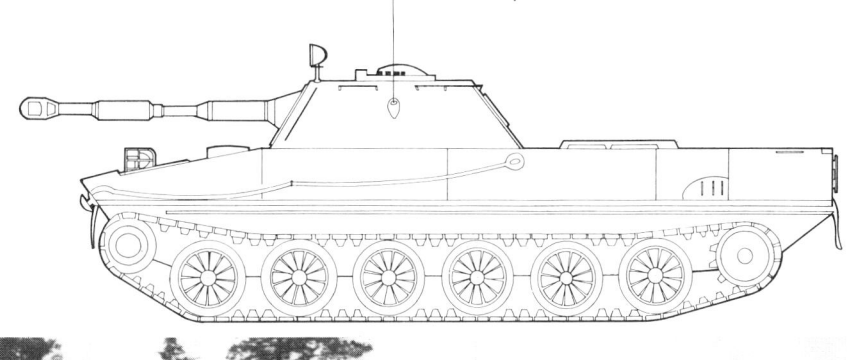

FUG M-1963 (OT-65)

Type: scout car
Crew: five
Weights: Empty
    Loaded 13,448 lb (6,100 kg)
Dimensions: Length 19 ft (5.79 m)
    Width 7 ft 9 in (2.36 m)
    Height (without armament) 6 ft 3 in (1.91 m)

Ground pressure:
Performance: road speed 54 mph (87 kph); water speed 5.6 mph (9 kph); range 310 miles (500 km); vertical obstacle 15¾ in (40.0 cm); trench 4 ft 3 in (1.6 m); gradient 60%; ground clearance 12 in (30.5 cm); the FUG M-1963 is fully amphibious
Engine: one 100-hp Csepel D-414.44 inline diesel engine

Armament: one 7.62-mm SGMB machine-gun with 1,250 rounds
Armour: ⅖ in (10 mm) maximum
Used also by: Czechoslovakia, Poland
Notes: The FUG M-1963 is probably based on the Russian BRDM-1 scout car, and fulfils a similar function. The vehicle is fully amphibious, and propelled in the water by twin waterjets. On land, the FUG M-1963 is a 4 × 4 vehicle, has an NBC system and can be fitted with night vision equipment. The Czechs have developed a derivative designated OT-65A, which has the turret of the OT-62B, and is armed with a 7.62-mm machine-gun and a T-21 82-mm recoilless rifle.

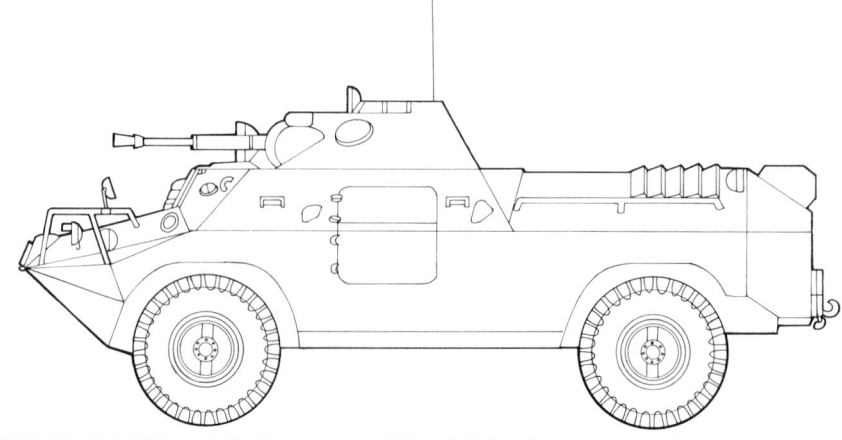

Model 51 flamethrower

Type: portable flamethrower
Notes: The Model 51 is the standard portable flamethrower of the Hungarian Army. The equipment consists of two cylinders on the firer's back, one cylinder containing fuel and the other pressurised propellant. No details of the equipment are known, but it seems likely that maximum range is about 22 yards (20 m).

AMD sub-machine gun

Type: sub-machine gun
Calibre: 7.62 mm
System of operation: gas
Muzzle velocity: 2,297 ft (700 m) per second
Range: 328 yards (300 m)
Rate of fire: 600 rounds per minute (cyclic); 120 rounds per minute (automatic); 40 rounds per minute (single shot)
Cooling system: air
Feed system: 30-round box

Dimensions: Barrel length 14.88 in (378 mm) with muzzle brake
Overall length 33.5 in (851 mm) with stock extended; 25.51 in (648 mm) with stock folded
Width
Height
Weights: 7.21 lb (3.27 kg)
Sights: pillar (fore) and tangent (rear)
Ammunition: 7.62 mm × 39
Used only by: Hungary

Notes: The AMD is a Hungarian modification of the Russian AKM assault rifle, but is used only as a sub-machine gun. The provenance of the weapon is visible in the weapon's sturdiness, size, and excellent performance. The breech action is that of the AKM, but the weapon can be readily distinguished from the AKM by the shorter barrel and the pistol grip, as well as the prominent muzzle brake.

India

The Indian Army

India has a long and impressive military history, although much of it in recent centuries has been under British command. Since 1947, however, India has been independent of the United Kingdom, and has built up her own powerful army, still drawing strongly on the ethnic groups that provided most of the manpower for the British Indian army. Strength is currently 950,000 men, all volunteers, about 86.68 per cent of India's total armed forces. The annual military budget is in the order of 3.53 per cent of the gross national product.

The main strength of the Indian Army's combat strength lies in its two armoured divisions (using some of the T-54/55 and *Vijayanta* MBTs for the

most part, with a sprinkling of Centurion MBTs, and PT-76 and AMX-13 light tanks), 18 infantry divisions (one of which is forming), 10 mountain divisions, five independent armoured brigades, one independent infantry brigade, one paratroop brigade, and 14 independent artillery brigades. These last include some 20 AA artillery regiments, four artillery observation squadrons and various independent flights.

A back-up for the main force is provided by 200,000 regular reservists and 40,000 men of the territorial army.

For the most part, the Indian Army is well provided with AFVs, especially medium tanks. It should be noted, however, that recently the *Vijayanta* as come under much criticism for lack of serviceability, and this may have a

serious effect on India's armoured strength if true. Artillery, much of it towed, is also available in adequate quantities, though it must be noted that much of this equipment is obsolescent, and in the process of replacement by indigenously designed and produced Indian equipment. Where the Indian Army is woefully deficient, though, is in armoured personnel carriers, there being only about 700 such vehicles, all of Russian origins, available. The mass of infantry, therefore, must enter battle on foot even if they have been transported to the theatre of war by rail or lorry. As a mitigating factor, it should be pointed out that India's likely adversaries, notably Pakistan, are no better provided with APCs.

The Indian Army is adequately provided with anti-tank weapons, both missiles and guns, but lacks sufficient AA defences except by short-range battlefield defence AA guns. The small number of Tigercat missiles is sufficient for only a small-scale action. Clearly, therefore, the Indian Army will shortly have to give some considerable thought to the updating and increasing of its missile forces, both anti-tank and anti-aircraft.

Almost isolated in the Indian subcontinent, India faces only three possible adversaries: to the east Bangladesh, which poses no threat; to the north China, the adversary against which the 10 mountain divisions are maintained, for fighting with China would necessarily involve operations in the Himalayas; and to the west Pakistan, the most likely foe, and the one against whom strong armoured and infantry formations are maintained. Sri Lanka poses no threat.

950,000 men and 200,000 reservists.

2 armd divs.
17 inf divs (1 more forming).
10 mountain divs.
5 indep armd bdes.
1 indep inf bde.
1 para bde.
14 indep arty bdes, incl about 20 AA arty regts, 4 arty observation sqns and indep flts.
100 Centurion Mk 5/7, 900 T-54/-55, some 700 *Vijayanta* med, 150 PT-76, AMX-13 lt tks; 700 BTR-50/-152, OT-62/-64(2A) APC; about 2,000 75mm, 25-pdr (mostly towed), about 300 100mm, 105mm (incl pack how) and Abbot 105mm SP, 550 130mm, 5.5-in, 155mm, 203mm guns/how; 500 120mm, 160mm mor; 106mm RCL; SS-11, *Entac* ATGW; 57mm, 100mm ATK guns; ZSU-23-4 SP, 30mm, 40mm AA guns; 40 Tigercat SAM; 40 *Krishak*, 20 Auster AOP9 lt ac; some *Alouette* III, 38 Cheetah helicopters (70 T-72 med tks, 75 Cheetah helicopters on order.)

Para-Military Forces: About 200,000 Border Security Force, 100,000 in other organizations.

Vickers MBT

Type: main battle tank
Crew: four
Weights: Empty
Loaded 83,995 lb (38,100 kg)
Dimensions: Length (with armament) 32 ft 1¾ in (9.79 m); (hull) 24 ft 9¾ in (7.56 m)
Width 10 ft 4½ in (3.16 m)
Height 8 ft 1⅔ in (2.48 m)
Ground pressure: 11.23 lb/in² (0.79 kg/cm²)
Performance: road speed 33 mph (53 kph); range 300 miles (483 km); vertical obstacle 36 in (91.4 cm); trench 8 ft 3 in (2.51 m); gradient 30°; ground clearance 15¾ in (40.0 cm); wading 44 in (1.12 m) without preparation, and 7 ft 4 in (2.23 m) with preparation
Engine: one 750-hp General Motors 12V-71T diesel powerpack
Armament: one 105-mm L7A2 gun with 50 rounds of APDS, HESH and Smoke, plus one 0.5-in (12.7-mm) ranging machine-gun, one 7.62-mm machine-gun co-axial with the main armament, and one 7.62-mm machine-gun on the commander's cupola
Armour: 3 1/10 in (80 mm) maximum
Used also by: Kenya, Kuwait
Notes: The Vickers MBT was developed as a private venture, using many Chieftain components, for countries who wished a simple, yet powerful, MBT at minimum cost. The Mark 1, which weighs 81,350 lb (36,900 kg), has a 600-bhp Leyland L.60 diesel engine and no laser rangefinder, is built in India as the *Vijayanta*. The Mark 3 was produced to improve the battlefield performance of the type by increasing the power available, adding a laser rangefinder, and updating the capabilities of the commander's cupola.

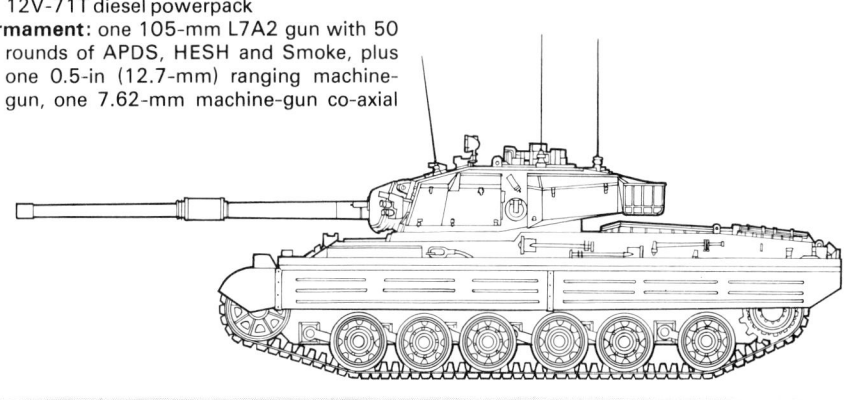

Vickers Abbot

Type: self-propelled howitzer
Crew: four
Weights: Empty
Loaded 37,037 lb (18,600 kg)
Dimensions: Length 18 ft 8½ in (5.7 m)
Width 8 ft 6⅓ in (2.6 m)
Height 8 ft 6⅓ in (2.6 m)
Ground pressure: 11.94 lb/in² (0.84 kg/cm²)
Performance: road speed 30 mph (48 kph); range 230 miles (370 km); vertical obstacle 24 in (61.0 cm); trench 6 ft 9 in (2.06 m); gradient 60%; wading 43⅓ in (1.1 m) without preparation
Engine: one 213-bhp Rolls-Royce K.60 inline diesel engine
Armament: one 105-mm howitzer with 36 rounds of HE and HESH
Armour: ¼ in (6 mm) minimum; ½ in (12 mm) maximum
Used only by: India
Notes: The Vickers Abbot, otherwise known as the Value Engineered Abbot, is basically the same vehicle as the Abbot used by the British Army, but with several items of equipment (flotation screen, NBC system, auxiliary armament and night vision equipment) removed, though these can be reinstated as optional extras.

M-1944 (D-10) gun

Type: field and anti-tank gun
Calibre: 100 mm
Barrel length: 60.7 cal
Muzzle velocity: 3,280 ft (1,000 m) per second with APHE
Ranges: Maximum 22,966 yards (21,000 m) with HE
Minimum
Elevation: −5° to +45°
Traverse: 58° total
Rate of fire: eight to ten rounds per minute
Weights: For travel 8,047 lb (3,650 kg)
In firing position 7,628 lb (3,460 kg)
Dimensions: Length 30 ft 9 in (9.37 m)
Width 7 ft 0⅔ in (2.15 m)
Height 4 ft 11 in (1.5 m)
Ammunition: APHE, HE and HEAT
Crew: six to eight
Used also by: Bulgaria, China, East Germany, Egypt, Hungary, Mongolia, North Korea, Poland, Romania, Somali Republic, Vietnam
Notes: The M-1944 is a dual-purpose gun introduced in 1944 by the Russians. Like many other high-velocity Russian guns of the period, this was developed from a naval gun. In modified form it is used in the T-54 and SU-100 AFVs.

3.7-in gun

Type: anti-aircraft gun
Calibre: 3.7 in (94 mm)
Barrel length: 50 cal
Muzzle velocity: 2,600 ft (793 m) per second
Ranges: Maximum (horizontal) 20,560 yards (18,800 m); (vertical) 39,370 ft (12,000 m)
Minimum
Elevation: −5° to +85°
Traverse: 360°
Rate of fire: eight to 20 rounds per minute
Weights: For travel 20,725 lb (9,401 kg)
In firing position 20,541 lb (9,326 kg)
Dimensions: Length 28 ft 6 in (8.69 m)
Width 8 ft (2.44 m)
Height 8 ft 2½ in (2.5 m)
Ammunition: AP, HE and Shrapnel
Crew:
Used also by: Burma, Egypt, Malaysia
Notes: The 3.7-in AA gun was developed before World War II, and was an excellent gun of its type. Unfortunately, no suitable low mounting for the AT role was developed, and the type was thus not as versatile as the comparable German Flak 36, 37 and 41 88-mm AA/AT guns. The 3.7-in gun's effective ceiling is 32,000 ft (9,760 m), and HE shell weight is 28.56 lb (12.96 kg).

Sexton

Type: self-propelled gun
Crew: six
Weights: Empty
Loaded 57,000 lb (25,855 kg)
Dimensions: Length 20 ft 1 in (6.12 m)
Width 8 ft 11 in (2.72 m)
Height (to top of superstructure) 8 ft (2.44 m)
Ground pressure: 11.5 lb/in² (0.81 kg/cm²)
Performance: road speed 25 mph (40 kph); range 180 miles (290 km); vertical obstacle 2 ft (60.9 cm); trench 8 ft 3 in (2.51 m); gradient 60%
Engine: one 484-bhp Continental R-975-4 radial petrol engine
Armament: one 25-pounder (88-mm) gun with 112 rounds of AP, HE and Smoke, plus two 0.303-in (7.7-mm) Bren guns for AA and local defence purposes
Armour: 1 in (25.4 mm) maximum
Used also by: Italy, Portugal, South Africa
Notes: The Sexton self-propelled 25-pounder gun was the British equivalent to the American M7 Priest 105-mm self-propelled gun. The vehicle consisted of a 25-pounder, with a strengthened saddle and pintle, mounted on the modified chassis of the Grizzly I tank (Canadian-produced M4A1 Sherman). The type entered British service in 1944, and some 2,150 had been built by the end of World War II.

L4 Bren machine-gun

Type: light machine-gun
Calibre: 7.62 mm
System of operation: gas
Muzzle velocity: 2,700 ft (823 m) per second
Range: effective 656 yards (600 m)
Rate of fire: 500 rounds per minute (cyclic)
Cooling system: air
Feed system: 30-round box
Dimensions: Barrel length 21.1 in (536 mm)
Overall length 44.61 in (1.133 m)
Width
Height
Weights: 21 lb (9.53 kg) unloaded; 23.61 lb (10.71 kg) loaded
Sights: blade (fore) and tangent with aperture (rear)
Ammunition: 7.62 mm × 51
Used also by: Australia, China, Lebanon, Pakistan, UK and former UK colonies
Notes: The L4 Bren gun is the series firing the 7.62-mm standard NATO round, and is used by Australia, India and the UK. The original 0.303-in (7.7-mm) models are used by Lebanon and Pakistan, and China probably still uses the 7.92-mm model made during World War II in Canada for the Chinese Nationalists. The Bren gun has its origins in the Czech Zb26 light machine-gun.

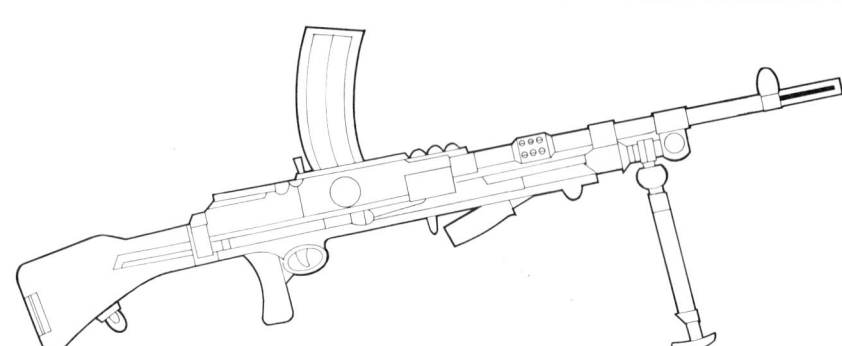

Bofors M-1936 gun

Type: light anti-aircraft gun
Calibre: 40 mm
Barrel length: 56 cal
Muzzle velocity: 2,887 ft (880 m) per second
Ranges: Maximum 9,842 ft (3,000 m) effective
Minimum
Elevation: −5° to +90°
Traverse: 360°
Rate of fire: 140 rounds per minute (cyclic)
Weights: For travel 5,418 lb (2,460 kg)
In firing position 4,740 lb (2,150 kg)
Dimensions: Length 20 ft 11½ in (6.38 m)
Width 5 ft 7¾ in (1.72 m)
Height
Ammunition: AP and HE
Crew: five or six
Used also by: Austria, Burma, Cyprus, Egypt, Eire, Finland, Israel, Ivory Coast, Jordan, Lebanon, Libya, Malaysia, Nigeria, Sudan, Tunisia, Yugoslavia, Zaire
Notes: This Swedish AA gun, perhaps the most celebrated light AA weapon ever produced, is still a formidable item of its type. The AP shot weighs 1.96 lb (0.89 kg).

Indonesia

180,000 men.

1 armd cav bde (1 tk bn, support units).
14 inf bdes (90 inf, 14 arty, 13 AA, 10 engr bns, 1 in strategic reserve).
2 AB bdes (6 bns).
5 fd arty regts.
4 AA arty regts.

Stuart, 150 AMX-13, 75 PT-76 lt tks; 75 Saladin armd, 55 Ferret scout cars; AMX-VCI MICV; Saracen, 130 BTR-40/-152 APC; 50 76mm, 40 105mm, 122mm guns/how; 200 120mm mor; 106mm RCL; *Entac* ATGW; 20mm, 40mm, 200 57mm AA guns; 2 C-47, 2 Aero Commander

680, 1 Beech 18, Cessna 185, 18 *Gelatik* ac; 16 Bell-205, 7 *Alouette* III helicopters.

Deployment: Egypt (UNEF): 1 bn (510).

Para-Military Forces: 12,000 Police Mobile bde; about 100,000 Militia.

Madsen machine-gun

Type: light machine-gun
Calibre: 7.92 mm
System of operation: recoil
Muzzle velocity:
Range: effective 875 yards (800 m)
Rate of fire: 125 rounds per minute
Cooling system: air
Feed system: 30-round box
Dimensions: Barrel length
           Overall length about 39.37 in
           (1.0 m)
           Width
           Height
Weights: about 26 lb (11.8 kg)
Sights: blade (fore) and V (rear)
Ammunition: 7.92 mm Mauser
Used also by: other nations in south-east Asia
Notes: The Madsen uses an action unique among machine-guns, derived from the Martin-Henry (Peabody) rifle action. Madsen machine-guns were made in a wide variety of calibres from 6.5 mm to 8 mm, including the British 0.303 in (7.7 mm) and the US 0.30-06 (7.62 mm). Although expensive, the Madsen guns have the virtue of great reliability. Some models were converted to belt feed by the Germans during World War II.

Madsen-Saetter machine-gun

Type: general-purpose machine-gun
Calibre: 7.62 mm
System of operation: gas
Muzzle velocity: 2,749 ft (838 m) per second
Range: effective 875 yards (800 m)
Rate of fire: 750 rounds per minute (cyclic); 200 rounds per minute (automatic)
Cooling system: air
Feed system: metal-link belt
Dimensions: Barrel length 22.2 in (564 mm)
           Overall length 38.19 in (970 mm)
           Width
           Height
Weights: 22.27 lb (10.1 kg)
Sights: blade (fore) and tangent, notch (rear)
Ammunition: 7.62 mm × 51
Used by: possibly other nations in south-east Asia
Notes: The Madsen-Saetter was the last weapon made by the parent company, and was produced in limited quantities in Indonesia. It is not notable for its reliability.

PM Model VII sub-machine gun

Type: sub-machine gun
Calibre: 9 mm
System of operation: blowback
Muzzle velocity: 1,250 ft (381 m) per second
Range: effective 219 yards (200 m)
Rate of fire: 600 rounds per minute (cyclic); 120 rounds per minute (automatic)
Cooling system: air
Feed system: 33-round box
Dimensions: Barrel length 10.79 in (274 mm) with compensator
           Overall length 33.07 in (840 mm) with stock extended; 21.26 in (540 mm) with stock retracted
           Width
           Height
Weights: 7.25 lb (3.29 kg) unloaded; 8.64 lb (3.92 kg) loaded
Sights:
Ammunition: 9 mm × 19 Parabellum
Used only by: Indonesia
Notes: The PM Model VII is of indigenous Indonesian design and manufacture, although several features are borrowed from the US M3 and Italian Beretta sub-machine guns.

Iran

285,000 men and 300,000 reservists.

3 armd divs.
3 inf divs.
4 indep bdes (1 armd, 1 inf, 1 AB, 1 special force).
4 SAM bns with HAWK.
Army Aviation Command.
760 Chieftain, 400 M-47/-48, 460 M-60A1 med tks; 250 Scorpion lt tks; Fox, Ferret scout cars; about 325 M-113, 500 BTR-40/-50/-60/-152 APC; 710 guns/how, incl 75mm pack, 85mm, 330 105mm, 130mm, 155mm, 203mm towed, 440 M-109 155mm, 38 M-107 175mm, 14 M-110 203mm SP; 72 BM-21 122mm RL; 106mm RCL; *Entac*, SS-11, SS-12, Dragon, TOW ATGW; 1,800 23mm, 35mm, 40mm, 57mm, 85mm towed, 100 ZSU-23-4, ZSU-57-2 SP AA guns; HAWK SAM; ac incl 40 Cessna 185, 6 Cessna 310, 10 Cessna O-2, 2 F-27; 202 AH-1J, 210 Bell 214A, 21 Huskie, 88 AB-205A, 70 AB-206, 30 CH-47C helicopters. (1,297 Chieftain/*Shir* 2 med, 110 Scorpion lt tks, BMP MICV, ASU-85 SP ATK, 100 ZSU-23-4 SP AA guns, Rapier, Improved HAWK, SA-7/-9 SAM, 163 Bell 214A, 350 Bell 214ST helicopters on order.)

Deployment: Oman: 2 coys, 1 helicopter sqn (400). Syria (UNDOF): 385. Lebanon (UNIFIL): 1 bn (524).

Para-Military Forces: 74,000 Gendarmerie with O-2 lt ac and helicopters; 32 patrol boats.

FV4030 *Shir* 2

Type: main battle tank
Crew: four
Weights: Empty
        Loaded about 121,694 lb (55,200 kg)
Dimensions: Length (with gun forward) 35 ft 5 in (10.795 m); (hull) 24 ft 7½ in (7.505 m)
        Width (overall) 12 ft (3.66 m)
        Height (overall) 9 ft 6 in (2.895 m)
Ground pressure: 11.94 lb/in² (0.84 kg/cm²)
Performance: road speed 31 mph (50 kph); range 311 miles (500 km); vertical obstacle 36 in (91.4 cm); trench 10 ft 4 in (3.15 m); gradient 60%; ground clearance 19$\frac{7}{10}$in (50.0 cm); wading 3 ft 6 in (1.06 m) without preparation, and 15 ft (4.57 m) with the aid of a schnorkel
Engine: one 1,200-hp Rolls-Royce CV12TC inline diesel engine
Armament: one 120-mm L11A5 gun with 53 rounds of APDS, APFSDS, HEAT and HESH ammunition, plus one 0.5-in (12.7-mm) L21A2 (Browning M2) ranging machine-gun with 600 rounds, co-axial with the main armament, one 7.62-mm L8A1 machine-gun co-axial with the main armament, and one 7.62-mm L37A1

machine-gun on the turret roof. Some 6,000 rounds of 7.62-mm ammunition are carried
Armour: of the Chobham laminate type
Used only by: Iran
Notes: Developed from the Chieftain Mark 5, the *Shir* 2 differs principally in having Chobham armour, the new 1,200-hp Rolls-Royce engine, the new David Brown TN-37 transmission, Dunlop hydro-pneumatic suspension and a range of new ammunition. Features the *Shir* 2 and Chieftain Mark 5 have in common are the main and secondary armaments, and the Integrated Fire-Control System, which is usable at ranges from 547 to 10,936 yards (500 to 10,000 m). The system co-ordinates the Barr & Stroud laser rangefinder with the GEC-Marconi ballistic computer to produce relevant information for the gunner. The new powerplant will increase the power:weight ratio of the *Shir* 2 to 21.74 hp/tonne from the 15.61 hp/tonne of the Chieftain Mark 5, with a consequent improvement in battlefield mobility. As an interim measure, Iran is receiving modified Chieftain Mark 5 MBTs. These have the new Rolls-Royce engine, the David Brown TN-37 transmission, hydropneumatic suspension and other detail improvements, under the designation *Shir* 1.

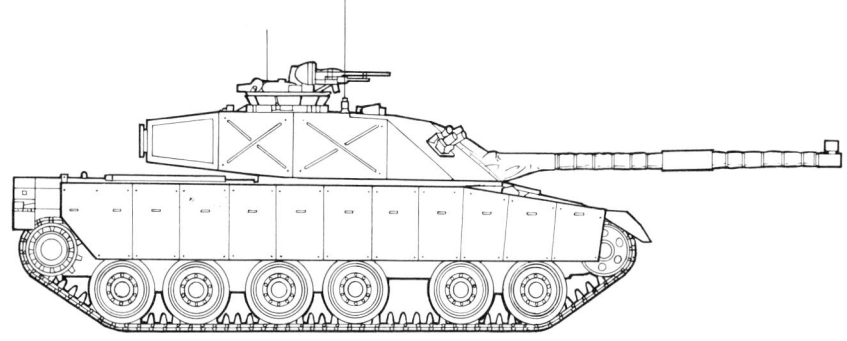

FV721 Fox

Type: armoured car
Crew: three
Weights: Empty
  Loaded 14,079 lb (6,386 kg)
Dimensions: Length (hull) 13 ft 10 in (4.216 m)
  Width 7 ft (2.134 m)
  Height (overall) 7 ft 2½ in (2.2
Ground pressure: 6.5 lb/in² (0.46 kg/cm²)
Performance: road speed 65 mph (104 kph); range 272 miles (438 km); vertical obstacle small; trench 4 ft (1.22 m) with channels; ground clearance 16 in (40.6 cm); wading 30 in (76.0 cm) without preparation
Engine: one 185-bhp Jaguar XK inline petrol engine
Armament: one 30-mm Rarden cannon with 96 rounds, plus one 7.62-mm machine-gun co-axial with the main armament, with 2,600 rounds

Armour:
Used also by: Nigeria, Saudi Arabia, UK
Notes: The Fox is a reconnaissance vehicle with good performance and a high-powered 30-mm cannon capable of destroying any light AFV at ranges of up to 1,094 yards (1,000 m). To keep weight down, Fox has light alloy armour.

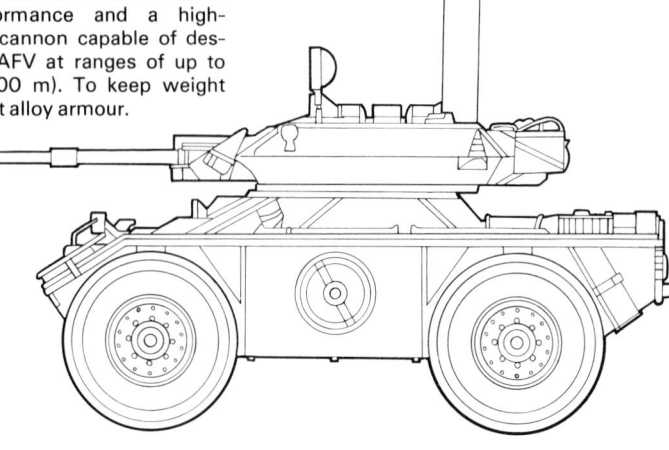

PPSh-41 sub-machine gun

Type: sub-machine gun
Calibre: 7.62 mm
System of operation: blowback
Muzzle velocity: 1,608 ft (490 m) per second
Range: effective 219 yards (200 m)
Rate of fire: 900 rounds per minute (cyclic); 105 rounds per minute (automatic)
Cooling system: air
Feed system: 35-round box, or 71-round drum
Dimensions: Barrel length 10.63 in (270 mm)
  Overall length 33.19 in (843 mm)
  Width
  Height
Weights: 8 lb (3.63 kg) unloaded; 9.5 lb (4.31 kg) loaded with box magazine; 12 lb (5.45 kg) loaded with drum magazine
Sights: post (fore) and flip, notch (rear)
Ammunition: 7.62 mm × 25 Pistol 'P'
Used also by: China, Hungary, North Korea, Vietnam and other nations
Notes: The *Pistolet-Pulomet Shpagina* was designed in 1941 by Georgi Shpagin in an effort to increase the firepower of Russian troops attempting to stem the German drive into Russia. Although simple in design, the PPSh-41 has proved an admirable weapon of great reliability and efficiency even under the most trying conditions. The weapon has been made in China as the Type 50, and has also been produced in Hungary, Iran and North Korea.

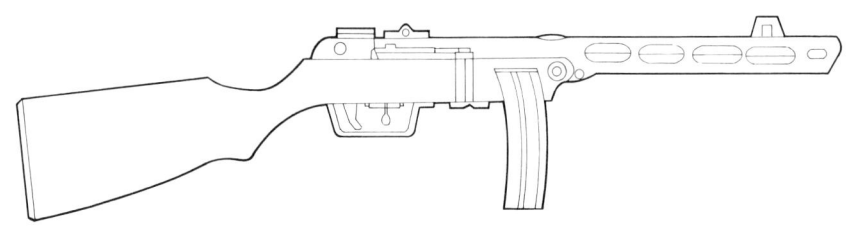

Iraq

180,000 men and 250,000 reservists.

4 armd divs (each with 2 armd, 1 mech bde).
2 mech divs.
4 inf divs.
1 indep armd bde.
1 Republican Guard mech bde.
1 indep inf bde.
1 special forces bde.
1,700 T-54/-55/-62, 100 T-34, AMX-30 med, 100 PT-76 lt tks; 120 BMP MICV; about 1,500 AFV, incl BTR-50/-60/-152, OT-62, VCR APC; 800 75mm, 85mm, 122mm, 130mm, 152mm guns/how; 90 SU-100, 40 JSU-122 SP guns; 120mm, 160mm mor; BM-21 122mm RL; 26 FROG-7, 12 'Scud-B' SSM; 'Sagger', SS-11 ATGW; 1,200 23mm, 37mm, 57mm, 85mm, 100mm towed, ZSU-23-4, ZSU-57-2 SP AA guns; SA-7 SAM. (T-62 med tks, 'Scud' SSM on order.)

Para-Military Forces: 4,800 security troops, 75,000 People's Army.

Panhard M-3

Type: armoured personnel carrier
Crew: two, plus up to 10 infantrymen
Weights: Empty 11,684 lb (5,300 kg)
Loaded 13,448 lb (6,100 kg)
Dimensions: Length 14 ft 7 in (4.45 m)
Width 7 ft 10 in (2.4 m)
Height (hull) 6 ft 6¾ in (2.0 m);
(with turret) 8 ft 1⅓ in (2.48 m)
Ground pressure:
Performance: road speed 62 mph (100 kph);
water speed 2.5 mph (4 kph); range 373
miles (600 km); vertical obstacle 12 in
(30.0 cm); trench 31½ in (using one chan-
nel); gradient 60%; ground clearance 13¾
in (35.0 cm); the M-3 is fully amphibious
Engine: one 90-hp Panhard Model 4 HD
inline petrol engine
Armament: see notes
Armour: ⅓ in (8 mm) minimum; ½ in (12 mm)
maximum
Used also by: Argentina, Cameroon, Dominican Republic, Eire, Guatemala, Kenya,
Malagasy Republic, Malaysia, Morocco,
Saudi Arabia, Togo, United Arab Emirates,
Zaire
Notes: The M-3 was designed as a 4 × 4
wheeled personnel carrier to operate in
conjunction with the Panhard AML
armoured car, and entered service in 1971.
Fully amphibious, the M-3 is driven in the
water by its wheels. The following turrets
and armament installations are possible:
1. turret with twin 7.62-mm machine-
guns
2. turret with one 7.62-mm machine-
gun and three STRIM rocket-
launchers
3. turret with one 7.62-mm machine-
gun and one STRIM rocket-launcher
4. ring mount for one 12.7-mm
machine-gun

5. ring mount for one 7.62-mm
machine-gun
6. turret with one 20-mm cannon
7. VPM, with an 81-mm breech-loaded
mortar
8. VAT repair vehicle
9. VPC command/cargo vehicle
10. VDA anti-aircraft vehicle, with twin
turret-mounted 20-mm cannon and
radar
11. VTS ambulance

12. M-3 HOT, with four HOT anti-tank
missile-launchers, and another 10
missiles stored in the hull
13. turret with a 60-mm mortar.
A single 7.62-mm machine-gun can be
mounted on the rear of most vehicles in addition to the turret-mounted armament.
Intrinsic trench-crossing ability of the four-
wheeled M-3 is poor, but with five special
channels the vehicle can cross a gap of up
to 10 ft 2 in (3.1 m).

Panhard VCR

Type: armoured personnel carrier
Crew: two, plus 10 infantrymen
Weights: Empty
Loaded 15,432 lb (7,000 kg)
Dimensions: Length 14 ft 11¾ in (4.565 m)
Width 8 ft 2 in (2.49 m)
Height 6 ft 8 in (2.03 m)
Ground pressure:
Performance: road speed 68 mph (110 kph);
water speed 2.8 mph (4.5 kph); range 528
miles (850 km); vertical obstacle 39⅖ in
(1.0 m); trench 39⅖ in (1.0 m); gradient

60%; the VCR is fully amphibious, being
driven in the water by its wheels
Engine: one 140-hp Peugeot inline petrol engine
Armament: various options are available, including a single 7.62-mm machine-gun,
twin 7.62-mm machine-guns, a 20-mm
cannon and a 7.62-mm machine-gun, a
60-mm breech-loaded mortar, and a 7.62-
mm machine-gun with a 40-mm grenade-
launcher
Armour:
Used only by: Iraq
Notes: The *Véhicule de Combat à Roues* is a
Panhard private venture, using many com-

ponents of the ERC armoured car. The vehicle has 6 × 6 drive, and a V-shaped floor to
minimise mine damage. There are three
variants:
1. VCR/PC command post vehicle, with
a 7.62-mm machine-gun or 20-mm
cannon, accommodation for seven,
and mapboards and other command
equipment
2. VCR/TH HOT anti-tank vehicle with
four HOT ATGW launchers and 14
missiles
3. VCR/15 ambulance, for four stretchers.

BMP-1

Type: mechanised infantry combat vehicle
Crew: three, plus up to eight infantrymen
Weights: Empty 25,353 lb (11,500 kg)
Loaded 27,558 lb (12,500 kg)
Dimensions: Length 22 ft 1¾ in (6.75 m)
Width 9 ft 10 in (3.0 m)
Height (to top of turret) 6 ft 6¾
in (2.0 m)
Ground pressure: 8.1 lb/in² (0.57 kg/cm²)
Performance: road speed 34 mph (55 kph);
water speed 5 mph (8 kph); range 311
miles (500 km); vertical obstacle 43⅓ in
(1.1 m); trench 6 ft 6¾ in (2.0 m); gradient
60%; ground clearance 15¾ in (40.0 cm);
the BMP-1 is fully amphibious, being
driven in the water by its tracks
Engine: one 280-hp inline diesel engine
Armament: one 73-mm gun with 40 HEAT
rounds, 28 of them in an automatic loader,

plus one 7.62-mm PKT machine-gun with 1,000 rounds co-axial with the main armament, and one AT-3 'Sagger' anti-tank missile on a rail above the main armament, and another three missiles carried inside the vehicle

Armour: ⅝ in (14 mm) maximum

Used also by: Afghanistan, Czechoslovakia, East Germany, Egypt, Ethiopia, Iran, Iraq, Libya, Poland, Syria, USSR

Notes: The BMP-1 is a formidable MICV, perhaps only excelled by the German *Marder*, and has been in service since 1967. It has night vision equipment and an NBC system, and is the first Russian APC to be designed as such from scratch, though components of the PT-76 light tank are

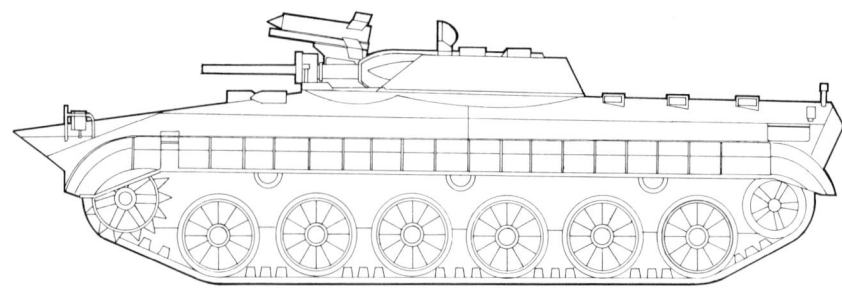

used. The eight infantrymen can use their weapons from inside the vehicle. There appear to be at least two variants of the BMP-1:

1. battlefield radar vehicle, with the radar on a turret replacing the troop compartment
2. command/reconnaissance vehicle, without the ATGW.

Israel

138,000 men (120,000 conscripts), 375,000 on mobilisation.

20 armd bdes.*
9 mech bdes.*
9 inf bdes.*
5 para bdes.*
3,000 med tks, incl 1,000 Centurion, 650 M-48, 810 M-60, 400 T-54/-55, 150 T-62, 40 *Merkava*; 65 PT-76 lt tks; about 4,000 AFV, incl AML-60, 15 AML-90 armd cars; RBY *Ramta*, BRDM recce vehs; M-2/-3/-113, BTR-40/-50P(OT-62)/-60P/-152 APC; 500 105mm how; 450 122mm, 130mm and 155mm guns/how; 24 M-109 155mm, L-33 155mm, 60 M-107 175mm, M-110 203mm SP guns/how; 900 81mm, 120mm and 160mm mor (some SP); 122mm, 135mm, 240mm RL; Lance, *Ze'ev* (Wolf) SSM; 106mm RCL; TOW, Cobra, Dragon, SS-11, 'Sagger' ATGW; about 900 Vulcan/Chaparral 20mm msl/gun systems, 30mm and 40mm AA guns; Redeye SAM.
(125 M-60 med tks, 700 M-113 APC, 94 155mm how, 175mm guns, Lance SSM, TOW ATGW on order.)

*11 bdes (5 armd, 4 inf, 2 para) normally kept near full strength; 6 (1 armd, 4 mech, 1 para) between 50 per cent and full strength; the rest at cadre strength.

Para-Military Forces: 4,500 Border Guards and 5,000 Nahal Militia.

Merkava **Mark 1**

Type: main battle tank
Crew: four
Weights: Empty
Loaded about 132,276 lb (60,000 kg)
Dimensions: Length
Width
Height
Ground pressure:
Performance: road speed about 31 mph (50 kph)
Engine: one 900-hp Teledyne Continental inline diesel engine
Armament: one 105-mm gun with 62 rounds of APFSDS, HEAT and HESH ammunition,

M60

Type: main battle tank
Crew: four
Weights: Empty
Loaded 107,997 lb (48,987 kg)
Dimensions: Length (with gun forward) 30 ft 11½ in (9.44 m); (hull) 22 ft 9½ in (6.93 m)
Width 11 ft 11 in (3.63 m)
Height (overall) 10 ft 8¼ in (3.26 m)
Ground pressure: 11.1 lb/in² (0.78 kg/cm²)
Performance: road speed 30 mph (48 kph); range 311 miles (500 km); vertical obstacle 36 in (91.4 cm); trench 8 ft 6 in (2.59 m); gradient 60%; ground clearance 18 in (45.7 cm); wading 4 ft (1.22 m) without preparation, and 13 ft 6 in (4.11 m) with the aid of a schnorkel
Engine: one 750-bhp Continental AVDS-1790-2A turbo-charged inline diesel engine
Armament: one 105-mm L/51 gun with 63 rounds of APDS, HEAT and HEP, plus one 7.62-mm machine-gun with 5,500 rounds, co-axial with the main armament, and one 0.5-in (12.7-mm) machine-gun with 900 rounds on the commander's cupola

plus one 7.62-mm MAG machine-gun co-axial with the main armament

Armour: steel

Used only by: Israel

Notes: The *Merkava* Mark 1 is a fascinating AFV, reflecting Israel's thirty years of combat experience in the Middle East. The engine is located at the front, to provide the crew with maximum protection from HEAT projectiles, and there is also an explosion-suppressing system. At the rear is a compartment in which up to eight troops can ride into battle, and six casualties ride out of it. Also at the rear are large ammunition loading doors, allowing the vehicle to be restocked very quickly. A laser rangefinder is provided.

Armour: 1 in (25.4 mm) minimum; 4⅓ in (110 mm) maximum

Used also by: Austria, Ethiopia, Iran, Italy, Jordan, Saudi Arabia, South Korea, USA, Zaire

Notes: Developed from the M47/M48 family, the M60 series is the main gun-armed MBT in service with the US forces at present. The M60 differs from its immediate predecessors in having a 105-mm gun, a diesel engine, and additional armour protection, especially to the turret. The M60 entered service in 1959, but the main production variant has been the M60A1, which differs from the M60 only in having a redesigned turret front to eliminate the flat mantlet of the initial model. Although the M60 series was to have been supplemented and then replaced by the XM803 in the 1980s, delays to the XM803 programme have persuaded the US authorities to improve the M60 series to keep it battleworthy until the advent of the next MBT. Current improvements include the incorporation of a gun stabilisation system, a laser rangefinder in place of the coincidence optical system, a

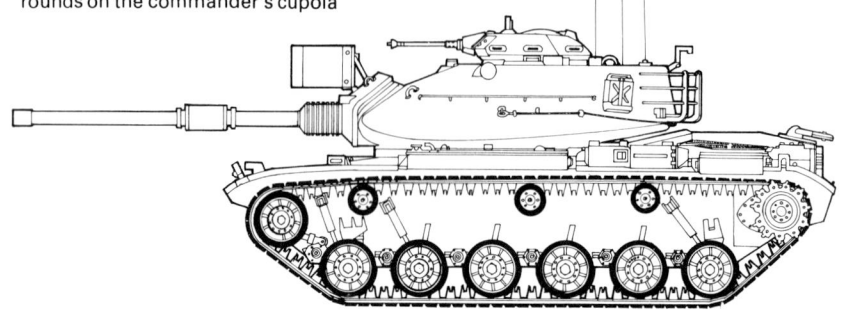

solid-state ballistic computer, improved tracks with long life, and more reliable powerplant and electrical systems. The programme is divided into three parts: Phase 1 for the stabilisation system, new tracks, and improved engine air intakes to increase engine life; Phase 2 for the laser rangefinder, the ballistic computer with sensors for cross-wind, vehicle tilt and barrel wear, a thermal sleeve on the gun, and modifications to the engine and electri-

cal system, the whole resulting in a vehicle designated M60A3; and Phase 3 for a new engine developing some 900-hp, and a new transmission. It is further anticipated that the M60A3 will also have a low-profile commander's cupola, track skirts, improved ammunition stowage, a 7.62-mm machine-gun on the loader's hatch, and smoke generating equipment. As on the M60A1, NBC protection and night vision equipment are standard. There are

three derivatives of the M60A1:
1. M60A2 MBT with the 152-mm XM162 gun/missile-launcher
2. M60 AVLB (Armored Vehicle-Launched Bridge), which can lay a 59-ft (18-m) bridge of 60-ton capacity in less than two minutes
3. M728 CEV (Combat Engineer Vehicle), which has a 165-mm demolition gun, 11-ton winch, 8-ton A-frame crane, and a dozer blade.

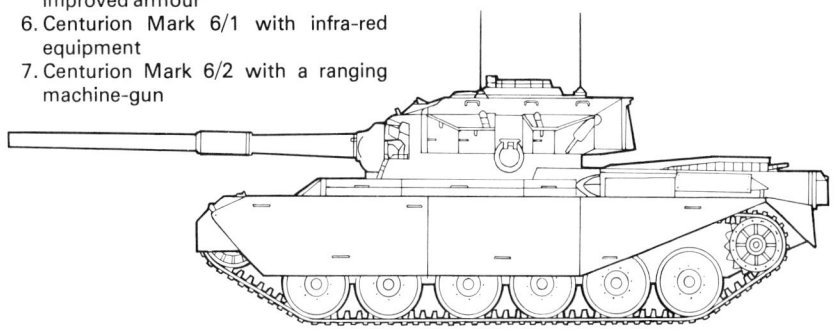

Centurion Mark 13

Type: main battle tank
Crew: four
Weights: Empty
Loaded 114,250 lb (51,820 kg)
Dimensions: Length (gun forward) 32 ft 4 in (9.854 m); (hull) 25 ft 8 in (7.82 m)
Width (including skirts) 11 ft 1½ in (3.39 m)
Height 9 ft 10½ in (3.01 m)
Ground pressure: 13½ lb/in² (0.95 kg/cm²)
Performance: road speed 21½ mph (34.5 kph); range 118 miles (190 km); vertical obstacle 3 ft (91.4 cm); trench 11 ft (3.35 m); gradient 60%; ground clearance 15¾ in (40.0 cm)
Engine: one 650-bhp Rolls-Royce Meteor Mark IVB inline petrol engine
Armament: one 105-mm L7A2 gun with 64 rounds of APDS and HESH, one 0.5-in (12.7-mm) ranging machine-gun, one 7.62-mm machine-gun co-axial with main armament, and one 7.62-mm machine-gun on the commander's cupola
Armour: ⅔ in (17 mm) minimum; 6 in (152 mm) maximum
Used also by: Denmark, India, Israel, Jordan, Kuwait, Netherlands, South Africa, Sweden, Switzerland

Notes: The Centurion was introduced into British service in 1949, and has since proved itself one of the all-time greats amongst AFVs. Many variants of this fine MBT are still in service. The type's chief tactical disadvantage is lack of range. The main variants are:
1. Centurion Mark 3 with a 20-pounder gun
2. Centurion Mark 5 with a 20-pounder gun
3. Centurion Mark 5/1 with improved armour
4. Centurion Mark 5/2 with a 105-mm gun
5. Centurion Mark 6 with a 105-mm gun, additional fuel capacity and improved armour
6. Centurion Mark 6/1 with infra-red equipment
7. Centurion Mark 6/2 with a ranging machine-gun

8. Centurion Mark 7 with a 20-pounder gun but redesigned hull to increase fuel capacity
9. Centurion Mark 7/1 with improved armour
10. Centurion Mark 7/2 with a 105-mm gun
11. Centurion Mark 8 with a 20-pounder gun fitted with a fume extractor
12. Centurion Mark 8/1 with improved armour
13. Centurion Mark 8/2 with a 105-mm gun
14. Centurion Mark 9 is a Mark 7 with a 105-mm gun and improved armour
15. Centurion Mark 9/1 with infra-red equipment

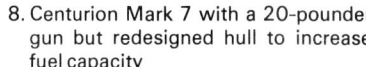

16. Centurion Mark 9/2 with a ranging machine-gun
17. Centurion Mark 10 is a Mark 8 with improved armour and a 105-mm gun
18. Centurion Mark 10/1 with infra-red equipment
19. Centurion Mark 10/2 with a ranging machine-gun
20. Centurion Mark 11 is a Mark 6 with infra-red equipment and a ranging machine-gun
21. Centurion Mark 12 is a Mark 9 with infra-red equipment and a ranging machine-gun
22. Centurion Mark 13 is a Mark 10 with infra-red equipment and a ranging machine-gun

Israeli Patton

Type: main battle tank
Crew: four
Weights: Empty
      Loaded 107,502 lb (48,770 kg)
Dimensions: Length
           Width
           Height

Ground pressure:
Performance: 45 mph (72 kph)
Engine: diesel engine, possibly of Cummins manufacture
Armament: main armament is now one 105-mm L7 series gun
Armour:
Used only by: Israel

Notes: This is an Israeli modification to the standard Patton tank, and has featured mainly the substitution of a 105-mm gun for the original 90-mm weapon, and the fitting of a diesel engine to those vehicles which did not already have one. Ammunition stowage is only about 90% of the original.

Isherman (Modified M4 Sherman)

Type: medium tank
Crew: five
Weights: Empty
      Loaded 87,302 lb (39,600 kg)
Dimensions: Length (hull) 19 ft 5½ in (5.93 m)
      Width 9 ft 9¼ in (2.98 m)
      Height 9 ft 7 in (2.92 m)

Ground pressure: 12.66 lb/in² (0.89 kg/cm²)
Performance: road speed 28 mph (45 kph); range 150 miles (241 km); vertical obstacle 34 in (86.0 cm); trench 7 ft 6 in (2.29 m); gradient 31%; ground clearance 17 in (43.0 cm); wading 36 in (91.4 cm)
Engine: one 460-hp Cummins inline diesel engine
Armament: one 105-mm 1508d gun with 55 rounds of HE, HEAT and Phosphorus, plus one 0.3-in (7.62-mm) Browning machine-gun co-axial with the main armament, one

0.3-in (7.62-mm) Browning machine-gun in the hull, and one 0.5-in (12.7-mm) Browning machine-gun on the commander's hatch
Armour: classified
Used only by: Israel
Notes: The *Isherman* is basically the M4 Sherman fitted with a French 105-mm gun and a Cummins diesel engine, and probably with appliqué armour. The type is still a useful second-line vehicle, but is relatively vulnerable to guns of 100-mm calibre and more.

M3

Type: armoured personnel carrier
Crew: three, plus 10 infantrymen
Weights: Empty
      Loaded 20,000 lb (9,072 kg)
Dimensions: Length 20 ft 3 in (6.17 m)
      Width 7 ft 4 in (2.22 m)
      Height 7 ft 5 in (2.26 m)

Ground pressure: 11.3 lb/in² (0.79 kg/cm²)
Performance: road speed 45 mph (72 kph); range 210 miles (312 km); vertical obstacle 12 in (30.0 cm); trench negligible; gradient 60%; ground clearance 11¼ in (28.6 cm); wading 32 in (80.0 cm)
Engine: one 147-hp White 160AX inline petrol engine
Armament: one 0.5-in (12.7-mm) Browning M2 or 0.3-in (7.62-mm) Browning

M1919A4 machine-gun with 700 and 7,750 rounds respectively
Armour: ¾ in (6.35 mm) minimum; ½ in (12.7 mm) maximum
Used only by: Israel
Notes: The most extensively built US personnel carrier of World War II, the M3 is still in large-scale use in Israel, together with the slightly older M2.

XR311

Type: combat support vehicle
Crew: three
Weights: Empty 4,600 lb (2,087 kg)
      Loaded 6,085 lb (2,760 kg)
Dimensions: Length 14 ft 3 in (4.34 m)
      Width 6 ft 4 in (1.93 m)
      Height 5 ft 3 in (1.6 m)

Ground pressure:
Performance: road speed 80 mph (130 kph); range 300 miles (480 km); vertical obstacle 19¾ in (50.0 cm); gradient 60%; wading 29½ in (75.0 cm)
Engine: one 190-hp Chrysler inline petrol engine

Armament: usual armament comprises one BGM-71 TOW anti-tank missile launcher, one 106-mm recoilless rifle, or one 0.5-in (12.7-mm) Browning machine-gun
Armour: none
Used only by: Israel
Notes: The XR311 was developed by the FMC Corporation as a multi-role utility vehicle.

RBY Mark 1

Type: light reconnaissance vehicle
Crew: eight
Weights: Empty

      Loaded 7,937 lb (3,600 kg)
Dimensions: Length 16 ft 4⅖ in (4.988 m)
      Width 6 ft 8 in (2.03 m)
      Height (without armament) 5 ft 5⅓ in (1.66 m)

Ground pressure:
Performance: road speed 62 mph (100 kph); range 342 miles (550 km); ground clearance 10⅔ in (27.0 cm)

Engine: one 120-hp Dodge Model 225-2
  inline petrol engine
Armament: two 7.62-mm machine-guns, or
  one 12.7-mm machine-gun, or one 20-mm
  cannon, or one 106-mm recoilless rifle
Armour: $\frac{1}{3}$ in (8 mm) sides; $\frac{2}{5}$ in (10 mm) floor
Used only by: Israel

Notes: The RBY Mark 1 is a remarkably fast
vehicle for its type, with good protection
and well thought out measures against
mine damage. The silhouette is very low,
and the 4 × 4 drive offers good cross-
country performance.

Ze'ev missile

Type: surface-to-surface battlefield missile
Guidance:
Dimensions: Span
      Body diameter
      Length

Booster:
Sustainer:
Warhead:
Weights: Launch
      Burnt out
Performance:
Used only by: Israel

Notes: Virtually nothing is known of the *Ze'ev*
missile, and even that little is confusing,
suggesting as it does the existence of two
missiles, the one capable of carrying a warhead of 352.74 lb (160 kg) over 1,094
yards (1,000 m), and the other of carrying a
warhead of 154.3 lb (70 kg) over 4,921
yards (4,500 m).

Soltam M-1971 gun

Type: field gun/howitzer
Calibre: 155 mm
Barrel length: 39 cal
Muzzle velocity:
Ranges: Maximum more than 26,246 yards
      (24,000 m)
      Minimum

Elevation:
Traverse:
Rate of fire:
Weights: For travel
      In firing position
Dimensions: Length
      Width
      Height
Ammunition: all NATO types

Crew:
Used only by: Israel
Notes: Very little is known about this new
Israeli gun/howitzer. It is an impressive
weapon with good performance and accuracy, and clearly has a high rate of fire, a
pneumatic rammer fed from a pressure
bottle on the carriage being provided. An
SP version based on the chassis of the Centurion MBT is also being developed.

L-33

Type: self-propelled gun/howitzer
Crew:
Weights: Empty
      Loaded 91,491 lb (41,500 kg)
Dimensions: Length 27 ft 9$\frac{1}{2}$ in (8.47 m)
      Width 11 ft 5$\frac{3}{4}$ in (3.5 m)
      Height 10 ft 8 in (3.25 m)
Ground pressure:
Performance: road speed 22 mph (36 kph);
      range 161 miles (260 km)
Engine: one 460-bhp Cummins inline diesel
  engine
Armament: one 155-mm M68 L/33 gun/
  howitzer
Armour:

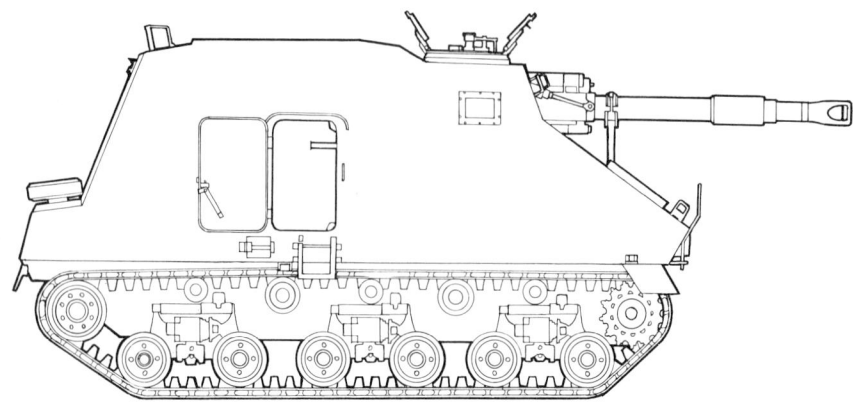

Used only by: Israel

Notes: This weapon combines the Soltam M68 155-mm gun/howitzer with the modified chassis of the M4 Sherman tank. Advanced features include a semi-automatic breech mechanism, and a pneumatic lifting/loading system. The M68 weapon fires a 96.3-lb (43.7-kg) HE shell to a range of 23,512 yards (21,500 m) at a muzzle velocity of 2,379 ft (725 m) per second. The gun can be elevated from −3° to +52°, and traverse is 30° left and 30° right.

M-1966 Tampella mortar

Type: heavy mortar
Calibre: 160 mm
Barrel length: 17.8 cal
Muzzle velocity:
Ranges: Maximum 10,170 yards (9,300 m)
            Minimum
Elevation: 43° to 70°
Traverse: 360°
Rate of fire: five to eight rounds per minute
Weights: For travel 3,197 lb (1,450 kg) without baseplate
            In firing position 3,748 lb (1,700 kg)
Dimensions: Length
                    Width
                    Height
Ammunition: HE and Smoke
Crew: seven
Used also by: Finland
Notes: This Tampella mortar is built by Soltam in Israel, and is an accurate smooth-bore weapon. The HE bomb weighs 88.2 lb (40 kg), of which 6.6 lb (3 kg) is explosive.

Tampella 120-mm mortar

Type: medium mortar
Calibre: 120 mm
Barrel length: 17.95 cal
Muzzle velocity:
Ranges: Maximum 8,968 yards (8,200 m)
    Minimum 492 yards (450 m)
Elevation:
Traverse:
Rate of fire:
Weights: For travel 827 lb (375 kg)
    In firing position 533 lb (242 kg)
Dimensions: Length
    Width
    Height
Ammunition: HE, Illuminating and Smoke
Crew: three
Used only by: Israel
Notes: This Tampella-designed mortar is a relatively new weapon with light weight and good range performance. The HE bomb weighs 31.3 lb (14.2 kg).

M-1965 Tampella mortar

Type: standard mortar
Calibre: 120 mm
Barrel length: 16.17 cal
Muzzle velocity:
Ranges: Maximum 6,780 yards (6,200 m) with M58F; 9,077 yards (8,300 m) with ST
    Minimum 437 yards (400 m)
Elevation: 39° to 87°
Traverse: 13.5°
Rate of fire: 10 rounds per minute
Weights: For travel 805 lb (365 kg)
    In firing position 485 lb (220 kg)
Dimensions: Length 8 ft 8⅓ in (2.65 m)
    Width 5 ft (1.53 m)
    Height 3 ft 5⅓ in (1.05 m)
Ammunition: HE and Smoke
Crew: three
Used only by: Israel
Notes: This is a smooth-bore Tampella mortar designed for towed transport,

although the weapon can be broken down into four basic parts for transport over difficult terrain. The standard M58F HE bomb weighs 28.66 lb (13 kg), of which 5.07 lb (2.3 kg) are HE.

Tampella 120-mm Light mortar

Type: light mortar
Calibre: 120 mm
Barrel length: 14.4 cal including breech
Muzzle velocity:
Ranges: Maximum 6,780 yards (6,200 m)
    Minimum 437 yards (400 m)
Elevation: 45° to 70°
Traverse: 4.7° at 45° elevation; 7.3° at 70° elevation
Rate of fire: five to ten rounds per minute
Weights: For travel
    In firing position 239 lb (108.5 kg)
Dimensions: Length
    Width
    Height
Ammunition: HE and Smoke
Crew: three
Used only by: Israel
Notes: This weapon is a lightened version of the Tampella 120-mm standard mortar, and can fire the same ammunition to the same ranges with equal accuracy.

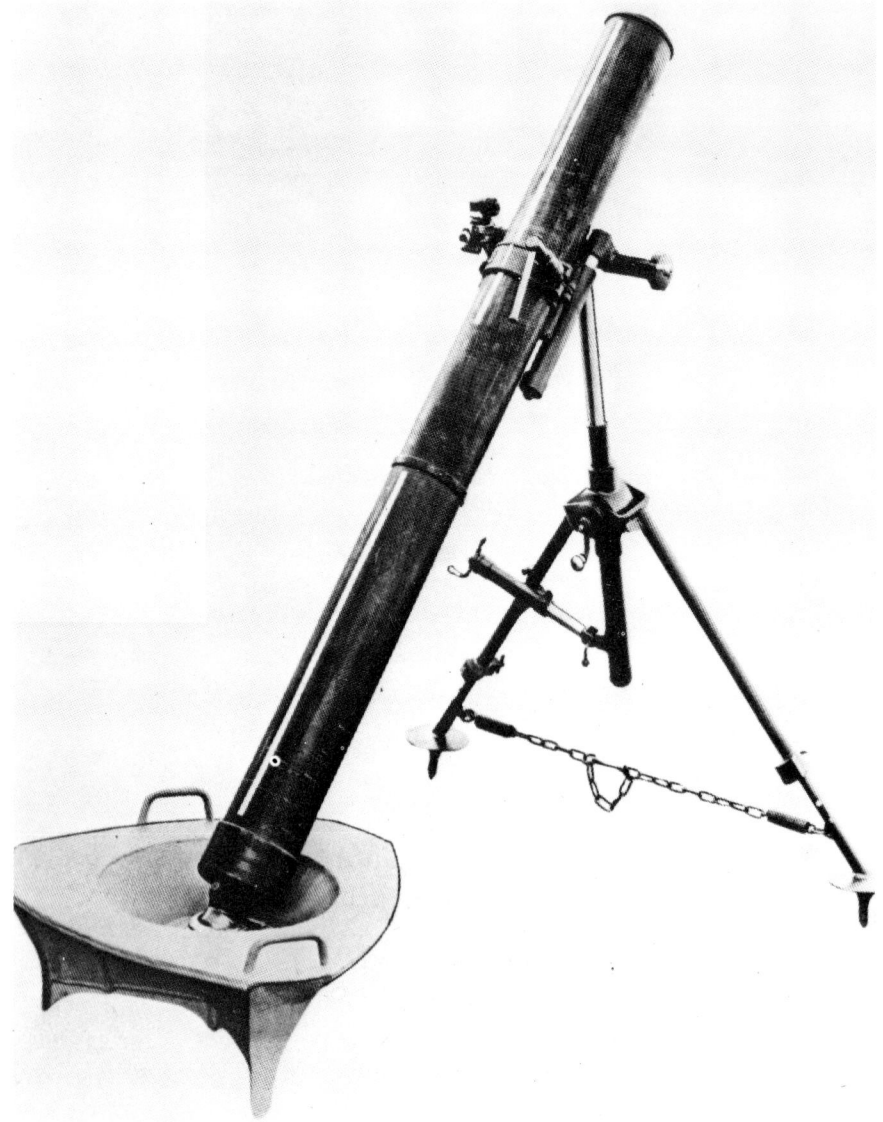

M-1964 Tampella mortar

Type: light mortar
Calibre: 81 mm
Barrel length: 17.96 cal (long barrel); 14.26 cal (short barrel)
Muzzle velocity:
Ranges: Maximum 5,031 yards (4,600 m) with long barrel; 4,374 yards (4,000 m) with short barrel
Minimum 164 yards (150 m) with long barrel; 153 yards (140 m) with short barrel
Elevation: 43° to 80°
Traverse: 5.6° at 45° elevation
Rate of fire: 15 to 20 rounds per minute
Weights: For travel
In firing position 88 lb (40 kg) with long barrel; 81.6 lb (37 kg) with short barrel
Dimensions: Length
Width
Height
Ammunition: HE and Smoke
Crew: three
Used only by: Israel
Notes: This Tampella-designed mortar has been produced in three forms: two of them detailed above, with barrels of different lengths, the third with a barrel of the long type, but made up of two parts of equal length for ease of transport. All three weapons fire an HE round of 8.5-lb (3.86-kg) weight.

Tampella mortar Type A

Type: light mortar
Calibre: 60.75 mm
Barrel length: 15.47 cal
Muzzle velocity: 722 ft (220 m) per second
Ranges: Maximum 4,374 yards (4,000 m)
Minimum 164 yards (150 m)
Elevation: 40° to 79°
Traverse: 6.5° at 50° elevation; 7.7° at 70° elevation
Rate of fire:
Weights: For travel
In firing position 38.6 lb (17.5 kg)
Dimensions: Length
Width
Height
Ammunition: HE and Smoke
Crew: two
Used only by: Israel
Notes: The Tampella Type A is designed to provide mobile infantry with a large quantity of fire support quickly and at minimum weight. The HE bomb weighs 3.5 lb (1.59 kg).

Tampella mortar Type B

Type: light mortar
Calibre: 60.75 mm
Barrel length: 12.18 cal
Muzzle velocity:
Ranges: Maximum 2,794 yards (2,555 m)
Minimum 164 yards (150 m)
Elevation: 40° to 79°
Traverse: 6.5° at 50° elevation; 7.7° to 70°
elevation
Rate of fire:
Weights: For travel
In firing position 34.17 lb (15.5 kg)
Dimensions: Length
Width
Height
Ammunition: HE, Illuminating and Smoke
Crew: one or two
Used only by: Israel
Notes: The Tampella Type B is basically the
same as the Type A, but has a shorter
barrel, is lighter, and has less range.

Tampella mortar Type C

Type: light mortar
Calibre: 60.75 mm
Barrel length:
Muzzle velocity:
Ranges: Maximum 984 yards (900 m)
Minimum 109 yards (100 m)
Elevation:
Traverse:
Rate of fire:
Weights: For travel
In firing position 12.57 lb (5.7 kg)
Dimensions: Length 1 ft 9 in (0.533 m)
Width
Height
Ammunition: HE, Illuminating and Smoke
Crew: one
Used only by: Israel
Notes: The Tampella Type C is based on the
Types A and B, but is shorter still, lighter,
and has only very limited range. The
weapon is used without a bipod, and has
only a small baseplate. The firer controls
the weapon in elevation and line by hand.

IMI mortar

Type: light mortar
Calibre: 52 mm
Barrel length: 9.42 cal
Muzzle velocity:
Ranges: Maximum 459 yards (420 m)
Minimum 142 yards (130 m)

Elevation: 20° to 85°
Traverse:
Rate of fire: 20 to 35 rounds per minute
Weights: For travel
In firing position 16.75 lb (7.9 kg)
Dimensions: Length 2 ft 1 in (0.637 m)
Width
Height

Ammunition: HE, Illuminating and Smoke
Crew: one
Used only by: Israel
Notes: The Israel Military Industries light mortar is intended for one-man use in close-range combat, and fires an HE bomb weighing 2.25 lb (1.02 kg).

UZI sub-machine gun

Type: sub-machine gun
Calibre: 9 mm
System of operation: blowback
Muzzle velocity: 1,312 ft (400 m) per second
Range: effective 219 yards (200 m)
Rate of fire: 550 to 600 rounds per minute (cyclic); 128 rounds per minute (automatic)
Cooling system: air
Feed system: 25-, 32- or 64-round box
Dimensions: Barrel length 10.12 in (259 mm)
Overall length 25.12 in (640 mm) with wooden stock; 18.5 in (470 mm) with metal stock folded
Width
Height
Weights: 7.94 lb (3.6 kg) empty; 9.08 lb (4.12 kg) with 25-round magazine
Sights: post (fore) and flip, aperture (rear)
Ammunition: 9 mm × 19 Parabellum
Used also by: Belgium, Iran, Netherlands, Venezuela, West Germany and other nations
Notes: The UZI was produced in Israel during the late 1940s by Major Uziel Gal, and shows the influence of Czech thinking about sub-machine guns. It is a highly efficient weapon, relatively cheap to produce, but accurate and reliable. Metal pressings are widely used in the construction of the type.

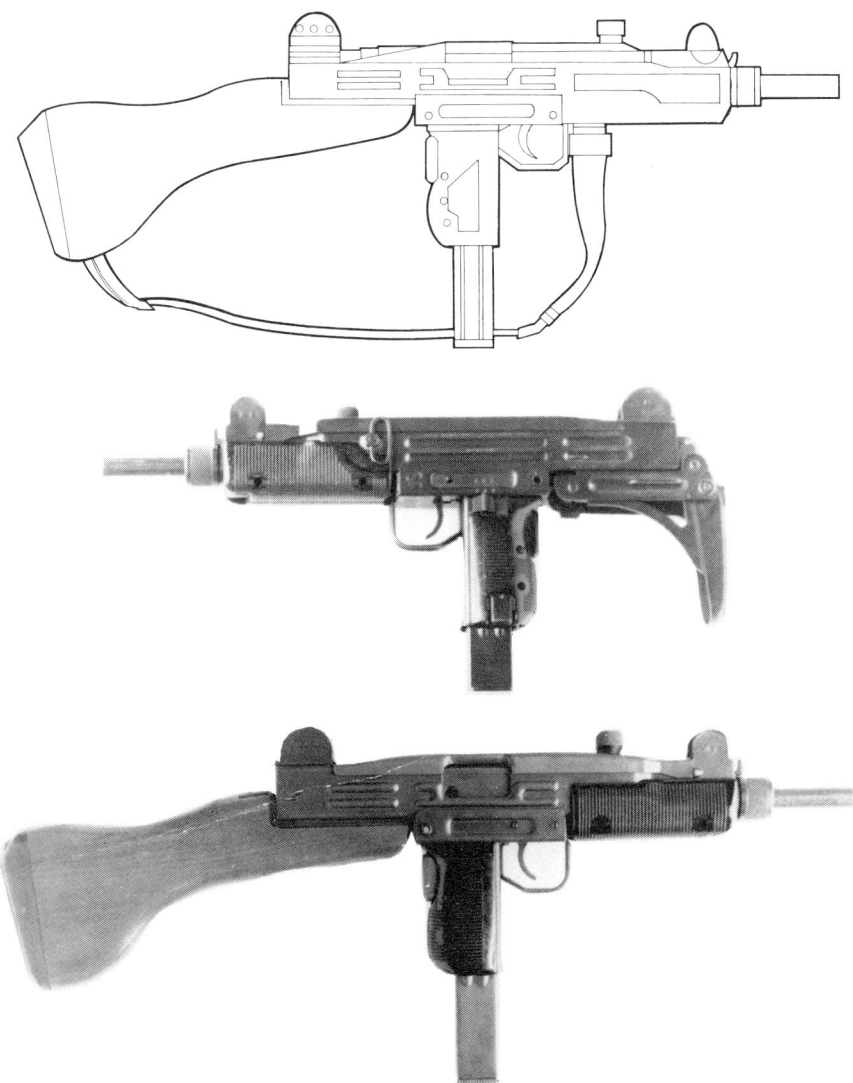

Galil rifle

Type: selective fire assault rifle
Calibre: 5.56 mm
System of operation: gas
Muzzle velocity: 3,018 ft (920 m) per second (ARM); 3,215 ft (980 m) per second (SAR)
Range: 656 yards (600 m) for ARM; 437 yards (400 m) for SAR
Rate of fire: 650 rounds per minute (cyclic); 105 rounds per minute (automatic); 40 rounds per minute (single shot)
Cooling system: air
Feed system: 33- or 50-round box
Dimensions: Barrel length 18.11 in (460 mm) for ARM; 12.99 in (330 mm) for SAR
Overall length 38.19/29.13 in (970/740 mm) with stock extended/folded (ARM); 32.28/23.62 in (820/600 mm) with stock extended/folded (SAR)
Width
Height
Weights: 8.6/7.72 lb (3.9/3.5 kg) empty (ARM/SAR); 9.48 lb (4.3 kg) for ARM

empty with bipod and carrying handle; 1.57 lb (0.71 kg) for 35-round magazine, 2.2 lb (1 kg) for 50-round magazine, loaded
Sights: post (fore) and flip, aperture (rear)
Ammunition: 5.56 mm × 45
Used only by: Israel

Notes: Designed by Yaacov Lior and Israel Galili, the Galil assault rifle was chosen for the Israeli army in 1972 after stringent tests of this and other weapons. The tests placed great emphasis on reliability under desert fighting conditions.

Italy

251,000 men (180,000 conscripts) and 550,000 reservists.

3 corps HQ.
1 armd div (of 1 armd, 2 mech bdes).
3 mech divs (each of 1 armd, 1 mech bde).
1 indep mech bde.
5 indep mot bdes.
5 alpine bdes.
1 AB bde.
2 amph bns.
1 msl bde with 1 Lance SSM, 4 HAWK SAM bns.
650 M-47, 300 M-60A1, 700 Leopard med tks; 4,000 M-106, M-113, M-548, M-577 APC; 1,500 guns/how, incl 334 105mm pack, 155mm, 203mm; 108 M-44, 200 M-109 155mm, 36 M-107 175mm, 150 M-55 203mm SP guns/how; 81mm, 107mm, 120mm mor; Lance SSM; 57mm, 106mm RCL; Mosquito, Cobra, SS-11, TOW ATGW; 300 40mm AA guns; Indigo, 22 HAWK SAM. (180 Leopard tks, 600 M-113 APC, 160 FH-70, SP-70, M-109 SP how, TOW ATGW, CL-89 drones on order.)

Army Aviation: 20 units with 40 O-1E, 39 L-21, 80 SM-1019 lt ac; helicopters incl 70 AB-47G/J, 36 AB-204B, 98 AB-205A, 140 AB-206A/A-1, 26 CH-47C, 5 A-109 (60 A-129 on order).

Para-Military Forces: 83,500 Carabinieri, 1 mech bde with 13 bns, 1 AB bn, 2 cav sqns; 140 M-47 tks, 240 M-6, M-8 armd cars, 96 M-113 APC, 30 AB-47, 11 AB-205, 12 AB-206 helicopters; 70,000 Public Security Guard, with 16 mot bns, 4 rescue bns (30 Fiat 6616 armd cars on order). 13 P-64B ac, 18 AB-47J, 13 AB-206, 2 AB-212 helicopters. 42,000 Finance Guards, with 47 AB-47J, 49 NH-500M helicopters.

Fiat/OTO Melara Type 6614CM

Type: armoured personnel carrier
Crew: two, plus up to eight infantrymen
Weights: Empty 12,897 lb (5,850 kg)
Loaded 15,432 lb (7,000 kg)
Dimensions: Length 18 ft 2$\frac{9}{10}$ in (5.56 m)
Width 7 ft 11$\frac{3}{10}$ in (2.37 m)
Height (without armament) 5 ft 6 in (1.68 m)
Ground pressure:
Performance: road speed 60 mph (96 kph); vertical obstacle 17$\frac{3}{4}$ in (45.0 cm); trench negligible; gradient 60%; ground clearance

Fiat/OTO Melara Type 6616

Type: armoured car
Crew: three
Weights: Empty
Loaded 16,314 lb (7,400 kg)
Dimensions: Length 17 ft 2 in (5.235 m)
Width 8 ft 2 in (2.5 m)
Height (to top of turret) 6 ft 6 in (1.98 m)
Ground pressure:
Performance: road speed 59 mph (95 kph); water speed 2.8 mph (4.5 kph); range 466 miles (750 km); vertical obstacle 17$\frac{3}{4}$ in (45.0 cm); trench none; gradient 60%; ground clearance 14$\frac{2}{3}$ in (37.0 cm)
Engine: one 147-hp Fiat Model 8062.22 turbo-charged inline diesel engine
Armament: one 20-mm Rheinmetall Rh.202 cannon with 400 rounds, plus one 7.62-mm machine-gun co-axial with the main armament with 1,000 rounds

13$\frac{4}{6}$ in (35.0 cm); the Type 6614 is fully amphibious, being driven in the water by its wheels at 2.8 mph (4.5 kph)
Engine: one 128-hp Fiat 8026 diesel engine
Armament: a variety of options are available, usually centred on 12.7-mm (0.5 in) and 7.62-mm machine-guns
Armour: $\frac{1}{4}$ in (6 mm) minimum; $\frac{1}{3}$ in (8 mm) maximum
Used only by: Italy
Notes: The Type 6614 APC is designed principally for internal security duties, and is closely related to the Type 6616 armoured car. The latest 6614M is slightly larger and powered by a 147-hp engine.

Armour: $\frac{1}{4}$ in (6 mm) minimum; $\frac{1}{3}$ in (8 mm) maximum
Used only by: Italy
Notes: The Model 6616 uses many of the components of the Model 6614M armoured personnel carrier made by the same two firms. The vehicle is fully amphibious, being driven in the water by its wheels. An NBC system is fitted as standard, and the vehicle has a winch for self-recovery operations. Provision has been made for the fitting of a TOW or *Milan* anti-tank missile-launcher on the turret roof if necessary.

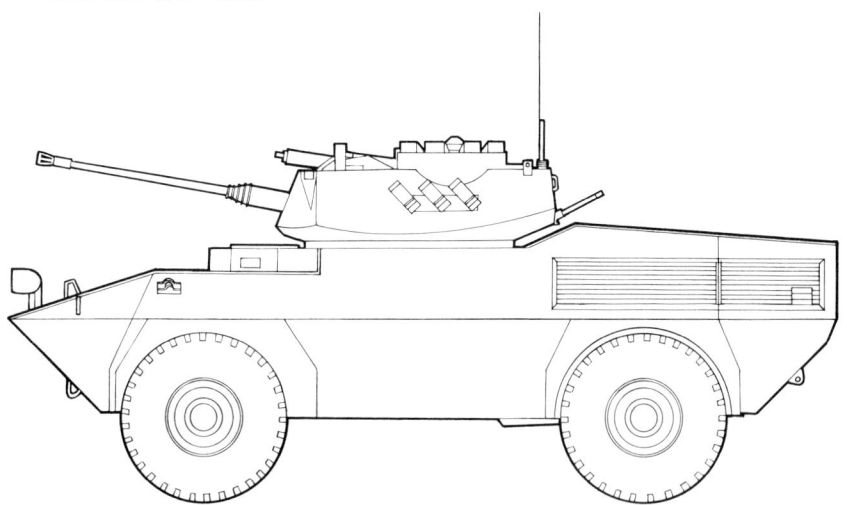

OTO Melara AIFV

Type: armoured infantry fighting vehicle
Crew: two, plus up to seven infantrymen
Weights: Empty
Loaded 25,485 lb (11,560 kg)
Dimensions: Length 16 ft 6$\frac{1}{2}$ in (5.04 m)
Width 8 ft 10 in (2.69 m)
Height 8 ft 10$\frac{1}{4}$ in (2.57 m)
Ground pressure: 8.1 lb/in² (0.57 kg/cm²)
Performance: road speed 40 mph (64.4 kph); range 340 miles (547 km); vertical obstacle 2 ft (61.0 cm); trench 5 ft 6 in (1.68 m); gradient 60%; ground clearance 16 in (41.0 cm)
Engine: one 215-bhp GMC Model 6V53 inline diesel engine

Armament: see notes
Armour:
Used only by: Italy
Notes: The AIFV is derived from the US M113A1 armoured personnel carrier, and has a revised hull with five firing ports each with its own viewing block. There are three versions:
1. AIFV Mark 1, with a 0.5-in (12.7-mm) Browning M2 machine-gun in a cupola at the front of the troop compartment and a 7.62-mm machine-gun on a ring mount at the rear of the troop compartment. Ammunition for the two guns is 1,050 and 1,000 rounds respectively
2. AIFV Mark 2, with a 0.5-in (12.7-mm)

Browning M2 machine-gun in a remotely controlled turret forward, and a ring-mounted 7.62-mm machine-gun at the rear

3. AIFV Mark 3, with a 20-mm cannon in a remotely controlled turret forward, and a ring-mounted 7.62-mm machine-gun at the rear.

Breda *Sparviero*

Type: anti-tank missile, frame-launched
Guidance: automatic infra-red beam-riding
Dimensions: Span 1 ft 8 $\frac{9}{10}$ in (53.0 cm)
    Body diameter 5 $\frac{1}{10}$ in (13.0 cm)
    Length 4 ft 6 $\frac{1}{3}$ in (1.38 m)
Booster: solid-propellant rocket
Sustainer: solid-propellant rocket
Warhead: hollow-charge high explosive, 8.8 lb (4.0 kg)
Weights: Launch 36.38 lb (16.5 kg)
    Burnt out
Performance: range 820–3,281 yards (75–3,000 m); speed 650 mph (1,045 kph)
Used by: under development for the Italian Army
Notes: Being developed for surface-to-surface and air-to-surface use. The *Sparviero* (Hawk) is a 3rd-generation AT missile, and is the first missile of this generation to do away with wire guidance.

Contraves Italiana Mosquito

Type: anti-tank missile, man-portable and container-launched
Guidance: command to line-of-sight by means of wire
Dimensions: Span 1 ft 11 $\frac{4}{5}$ in (60.0 cm)
    Body diameter 4 $\frac{3}{4}$ in (12.0 cm)
    Length 3 ft 7 $\frac{7}{10}$ in (1.11 m)
Booster: solid-propellant rocket
Sustainer: solid-propellant rocket
Warhead: hollow-charge high explosive or fragmentation, 8.8 lb (4.0 kg), capable of penetrating 2 $\frac{3}{5}$ in (66 mm) of armour
Weights: Launch 31.1 lb (14.1 kg)
    Burnt out
Performance: range 394–2,515 yards (360–2,300 m); speed 201 mph (325 kph)
Used only by: Italy
Notes: Typical man-portable anti-tank missile, capable of being operated by a single man.

Selenia *Spada* Air Defence System

Type: surface-to-air short- and medium-range guided missile air defence system
Guidance: semi-active radar homing
Dimensions: Span 31 $\frac{1}{2}$ in (80.0 cm)
    Body diameter 8 in (20.3 cm)
    Length 12 ft 1 $\frac{2}{3}$ in (3.7 m)
Booster: solid-propellant rocket
Sustainer: none
Warhead: high explosive
Weights: Launch 485 lb (220 kg)
    Burnt out
Performance: speed more than Mach 2.5
Used only by: Italy
Notes: The *Spada* air-defence system uses the *Aspide* missile, as does the Albatros naval air defence system. Designed for the short- and medium-range protection of Italian army units from air attack, the *Spada* system comprises:
    1. a search and interrogation radar (SIR)
    2. tracking and illumination radars (TIR)
    3. control units
    4. *Aspide* missile launchers.
The missile launchers are sextuple units. The *Aspide* missile is also used in the Mobile *Spada* system under development for the Italian army.

Sistel CT40 GM Indigo

Type: land-mobile surface-to-air tactical missile system
Guidance: beam-riding and radio command, with optional optical and infra-red tracking combined with radio command
Dimensions: Span 33½ in (85.0 cm)
Body diameter 7⁷⁄₁₆ in (19.5 cm)
Length 10 ft 10¾ in (3.32 m)

Booster: single-stage solid-propellant rocket, delivering 8,377-lb (3,800-kg) static thrust for 2½ seconds
Sustainer: none
Warhead: 46¼-lb (21-kg) high explosive
Weights: Launch 267 lb (121 kg)
Burnt out
Performance: speed Mach 2.5; slant range about 6¼ miles (10 km); ceiling about 16,400 ft (5,000 m)

Used only by: Italy
Notes: Once a target has been acquired by the improved Superfledermaus radar, the missile is fired from a separate trailer within 6 seconds. Single-shot hit probability is 50%. The missile is basically a beam-rider, with optional radio command, and in beam-jamming conditions the missile can be operated by radio command alone, with optical and infra-red tracking.

M55

Type: self-propelled howitzer
Crew: six
Weights: Empty
Loaded 108,025 lb (49,000 kg)
Dimensions: Length 23 ft (7.02 m)
Width 11 ft 9¾ in (3.6 m)
Height 11 ft 6 in (3.5 m)
Ground pressure: 11.23 lb/in² (0.79 kg/cm²)
Performance: road speed 35 mph (56 kph); range 155 miles (250 km); gradient 60%
Engine: one 810-hp inline diesel engine
Armament: one 8-in (203-mm) howitzer with 10 rounds of HE and Nuclear ammunition, plus one 0.5-in (12.7-mm) Browning M2 machine-gun for AA defence
Armour: ⅝ in (15 mm)
Used also by: USA, West Germany
Notes: The M55 is based on the chassis of the M48 tank, with a turret for the 8-in (203-mm) howitzer capable of traversing only 30° left and right. The howitzer fires at a muzzle velocity of 1,950 ft (594 m) per second to a range of 18,480 yards (16,900 m). The weapon is now only in reserve service with the USA and West Germany.

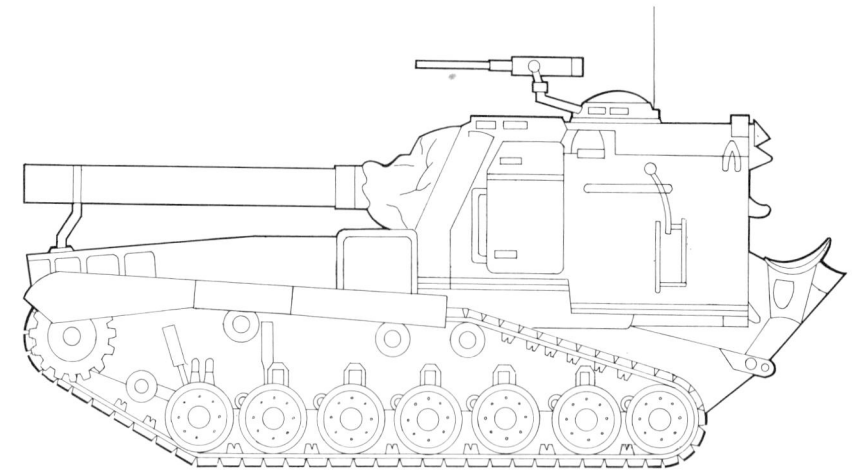

M-1956 105/14 howitzer

Type: pack howitzer
Calibre: 105 mm
Barrel length: 16.34 cal including muzzle brake
Muzzle velocity:
Ranges: Maximum 11,565 yards (10,575 m), or 14,217 yards (13,000 m) with RAP
Minimum
Elevation: −5° to +65°
Traverse: 36° total (56° total in AT role)
Rate of fire: eight rounds per minute
Weights: For travel 2,844 lb (1,290 kg)
In firing position
Dimensions: Length 11 ft 11¾ in (3.65 m)
Width 4 ft 11 in (1.5 m)
Height 6 ft 5 in (1.96 m)
Ammunition: AP, HE, HEAT, Illuminating, Smoke and Target Indicating
Crew: six
Used also by: Argentina, Australia, Belgium, Canada, Chile, France, India, Malaysia, New Zealand, Nigeria, Pakistan, Peru, Philippines, Rhodesia, Saudi Arabia, Spain, United Arab Emirates, UK, Venezuela, West Germany, Zambia
Notes: The OTO Melara M-1956 105/14 pack howitzer has been one of the most successful pieces of ordnance produced since World War II. The shell weighs 32.85 lb (14.9 kg), and the penetration of the HEAT round is 4.57 in (116 mm). For AT use, the gun is lowered on its carriage to reduce the silhouette. The whole piece breaks down into 11 loads, the heaviest weighing 269 lb (122 kg).

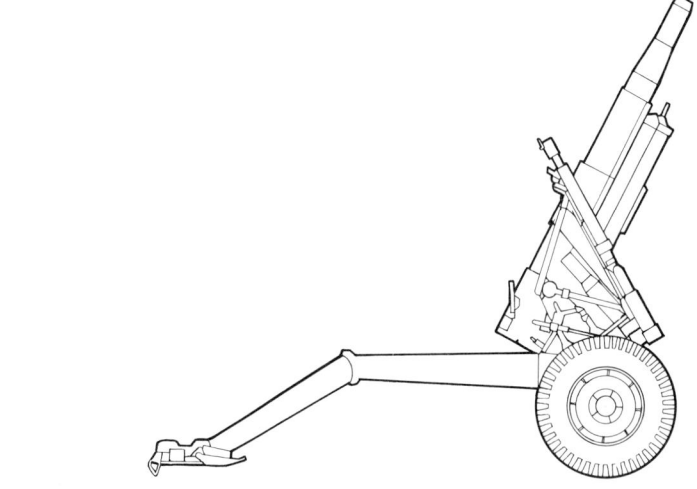

Attila Mark II

Type: artillery rocket
Calibre: 82.5 mm
Barrel length:
Burnt-out velocity:
Ranges: Maximum more than 8,202 yards (7,500 m)
Minimum

Elevation:
Traverse:
Rate of fire:
Weights: For travel
In firing position 23.6 lb (10.7 kg)
Dimensions: Length 4 ft 7 in (1.4 m)
Span 8.86 in (22.5 cm)
Body diameter 3.25 in (8.25 cm)

Ammunition: HE warhead
Crew:
Used only by: Italy
Notes: The Attila Mark II is the successor to the now obsolete Attila Mark I, and carries an HE warhead of 6.6 lb (3 kg). Launch is from a man-portable single launcher, or from a vehicle-borne 40-rail launcher.

Breda *Folgore* launcher

Type: man-portable anti-tank rocket launcher
Calibre: 80 mm
Barrel length:
Muzzle velocity: 2,132 ft (650 m) per second some distance after leaving the tube
Ranges: Maximum 1,094 yards (1,000 m)
Minimum 82 yards (75 m)

Elevation:
Traverse:
Rate of fire:
Weights: For travel 23.8 lb (10.8 kg)
In firing position 33.07 lb (15 kg)
Dimensions: Length 4 ft 11 in (1.5 m)
Width
Height

Ammunition: HEAT warhead
Crew: two
Used only by: Italy
Notes: The *Folgore* is an anti-tank weapon of Italian design and manufacture. The complete round weighs 9.26 lb (4.2 kg), the rocket comprising 6.17 lb (2.8 kg) of this.

Model T-148 flamethrower

Type: portable flamethrower
Weights: Empty 29.98 lb (13.6 kg)
Flamegun 8.05 lb (3.65 kg)
Loaded 63.93 lb (29 kg)
Notes: The T-148 is the standard flamethrower of the Italian Army, and is in many respects a superior weapon of its type, principally because it has a high-power electronic ignition system. This lights the fuel instantly, and does not need to be lit up before the weapon's use, thereby giving away the firer's position and intentions. The napalm fuel weighs 24.8 lb (11.25 kg).

Beretta Model 38/42 sub-machine gun

Type: sub-machine gun
Calibre: 9 mm
System of operation: blowback
Muzzle velocity: 1,250 ft (381 m) per second
Range: effective 219 yards (200 m)
Rate of fire: 550 rounds per minute (cyclic); 120 rounds per minute (automatic)
Cooling system: air
Feed system: 20- or 40-round box
Dimensions: Barrel length 8.39 in (213 mm)
Overall length 31.5 in (800 mm)
Width
Height
Weights: 7.21 lb (3.27 kg) unloaded; 8.88 lb (4.03 kg) loaded
Sights: blade (fore) and flip, notch (rear)
Ammunition: 9 mm × 19 Parabellum
Used by: in small-scale use in a number of countries
Notes: The Model 1938/42 was issued to the Italian Army during World War II, and was a useful weapon, making use of stampings in the receiver.

Franchi Model LF57 sub-machine gun

Type: sub-machine gun
Calibre: 9 mm
System of operation: blowback
Muzzle velocity: 1,296 to 1,378 ft (395 to 420 m) per second
Range: effective 219 yards (200 m)
Rate of fire: 450 to 470 rounds per minute (cyclic)
Cooling system: air
Feed system: 20-, 30- or 40-round box
Dimensions: Barrel length 8.07 in (205 mm)
Overall length 27 in (686 mm) with stock extended; 16.73 in (425 mm) with stock folded
Width
Height
Weights: 7.28 lb (3.3 kg)
Sights: blade (fore) and notch (rear)
Ammunition: 9 mm × 19 Parabellum
Used also by: several African nations
Notes: The LF57 is a compact sub-machine gun which has proved moderately successful as a police as well as military weapon.

Beretta Model 38/49 sub-machine gun

Type: sub-machine gun
Calibre: 9 mm
System of operation: blowback
Muzzle velocity: 1,250 ft (381 m) per second
Range: effective 219 yards (200 m)
Rate of fire: 550 rounds per minute (cyclic); 120 rounds per minute (automatic)
Cooling system: air
Feed system: 20- or 40-round box
Dimensions: Barrel length 8.39 in (213 mm)
Overall length 31.5 in (800 mm)
Width
Height
Weights: 7.21 lb (3.27 kg) unloaded; 8.88 lb (4.03 kg) loaded
Sights: blade (fore) and flip, notch (rear)
Ammunition: 9 mm × 19 Parabellum
Used also by: Costa Rica, Dominican Republic, Egypt, Indonesia, South Yemen, Thailand, Tunisia
Notes: Model 38/49 is a successive improvement of the Model 38/44, itself an updated version of the Model 38/42. The improvements of the Model 38/49 consist mainly of better safety precautions than those of

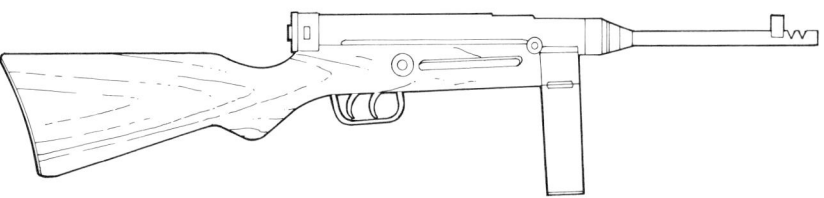

the Model 38/44, which is a simplified model of the Model 38/42. The Model 38/49 is also used by the West German Border Police.

Ivory Coast

4,500 men.

3 inf bns.
1 tk sqn.
1 para coy.
2 arty btys.
1 AA arty bty.
1 engr coy.
5 AMX-13 lt tks; 16 AML-60/-90 armd cars; 4 105mm how; 81mm, 120mm mor; 10 40mm AA guns.

AMX-13

Type: light tank
Crew: three
Weights: Empty
      Loaded 33,069 lb (15,000 kg)
Dimensions: Length (gun forward) 20 ft 10 in (6.36 m); (hull) 15 ft (4.88 m)
      Width 8 ft 2 in (2.5 m)
      Height 7 ft 7 in (2.3 m)
Ground pressure: 10.8 lb/in² (0.76 kg/cm²)
Performance: road speed 37 mph (60 kph); range 218 miles (350 km); vertical obstacle 2 ft 2 in (65.0 cm); trench 5 ft 3 in (1.6 m); gradient 60%; ground clearance $14\frac{1}{2}$ in (37.0 cm); wading 2 ft (60.0 cm) without preparation
Engine: one 250-hp SOFAM Model 8 Gxb inline petrol engine
Armament: one 75-, 90- or 105-mm gun with 12, 34 or 32 rounds, plus one 7.5- or 7.62-mm co-axial machine-gun with 3,600 rounds
Armour: $\frac{2}{5}$ in (10 mm) minimum; $1\frac{3}{5}$ in (40 mm) maximum
Used also by: Algeria, Argentina, Chile, Dominican Republic, Ecuador, El Salvador, France, Guatemala, India, Indonesia, Kampuchea, Kenya, Lebanon, Morocco, Netherlands, Nepal, Peru, Saudi Arabia, Singapore, Switzerland, Tunisia, Venezuela
Notes: The AMX-13 was adopted into French service in 1953, and has since then been built in considerable numbers for French and foreign use, in several models. The first vehicles have a 75-mm gun in the FL-10 oscillating turret, which houses only two crewmen and a 12-round automatic loader for the gun. The gun fires HE or HEAT rounds, the latter penetrating $6\frac{7}{10}$ in (170 mm) of armour at 2,187 yards (2,000 m). Then came the 105-mm gun version, with the FL-12 turret, whose rounds can penetrate $14\frac{1}{5}$ in (360 mm) of armour. The final version, still in production, has a 90-mm gun. Many vehicles have been retrofitted with night vision equipment, and many French AMX-13s have provision for four SS.11 anti-tank missiles, two on each side of the turret, to provide the vehicle with a long-range AT capability. There are 23 variants based on the AMX-13, including:
1. 155-mm self-propelled howitzer
2. 105-mm self-propelled howitzer
3. AA versions with cannon
4. mortar carrier

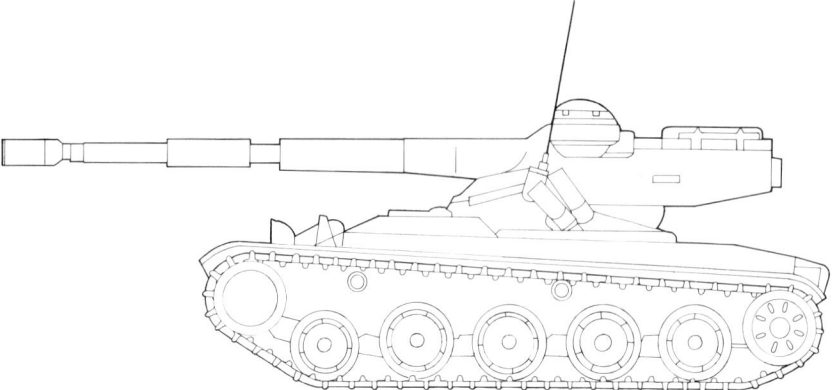

5. armoured personnel carrier (VCI)
6. bridgelayer (*Char Poseur de Pont*)
7. dozer
8. recovery vehicle (*Char de Depannage*) with a $15\frac{3}{4}$-ton (16,000-kg) main winch
9. ammunition carrier
10. ambulance.

Jamaica

1,800 men.

1 inf bn.
1 spt bn.
10 V-150 Commando APC; 6 81mm
   mor.

Japan

155,000 men and 39,000 reservists.

1 mech div.
12 inf divs (7–9,000 men each).
1 tk bde.
1 AB bde.
1 composite bde.
1 arty bde.
5 engr bdes.
1 sigs bde.
8 SAM gps (each of 4 btys) with HAWK.
1 helicopter wing and 34 aviation sqns.
690 Type 61 and Type 74 med, 100 M-
   41 lt tks; 640 Type 60 and Type 73
   APC; 900 75mm, 105mm, 155mm,
   203mm guns/how; 470 105mm,
   155mm SP how; 1,900 81mm and
   107mm mor (some SP); 4 Type 75
   130mm SP RL; 1,100 57mm,
   75mm, 106mm, 106mm SP RCL;
   Type 30 SSM; Type 64, KAM-9
   ATGW; 260 35mm twin, 37mm,
   40mm and 75mm AA guns; HAWK
   SAM; 90 L-19, 20 LM-1/2, 7 LR-1 ac;
   50 KV-107, 40 UH-1H, 80 UH-1B,
   70 OH-6J, 50 H-13 helicopters.
(48 Type 74 tks; Carl Gustav 84mm
   RL; Hawk SAM; 2 LR-1 ac, 3 KV-107,
   13 UH-1H, 10 OH-6D, 1 AH-1S
   helicopters on order.)

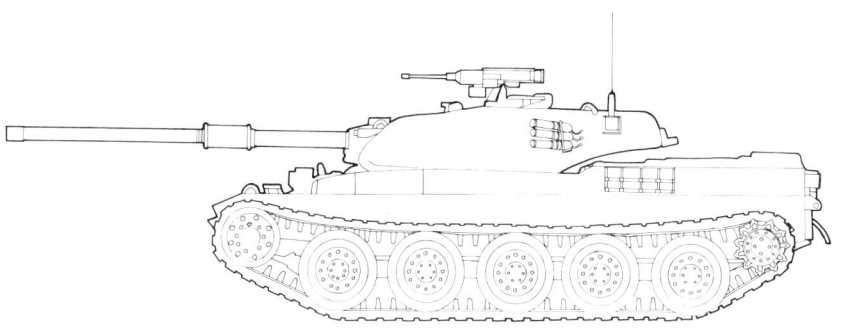

Type 74

Type: main battle tank
Crew: four
Weights: Empty
   Loaded 83,776 lb (38,000 kg)
Dimensions: Length (gun forward) 29 ft 10 in
   (9.09 m); (hull) 22 ft 6 in (6.85
   m)
   Width 10 ft 5 in (3.18 m)
   Height (with AA machine-gun)
   8 ft 10 in (2.675 m)
Ground pressure: 12 lb/in² (0.85 kg/cm²)
Performance: road speed 37 mph (60 kph);
   range 310 miles (500 km); vertical obstacle 3 ft 3⅖ in (1.0 m); trench 8 ft 10 in (2.7
   m); gradient 60%; ground clearance 15¾ in
   (40.0 cm) in normal running conditions;
   wading 3 ft 3⅖ in (1.0 m) without preparation, and 9 ft 10 in with a schnorkel
Engine: one 750-bhp Mitsubishi 10ZF Model
   21 WT inline diesel engine
Armament: one 105-mm L7 gun with 50
   rounds, plus one 7.62-mm machine-gun
   co-axial with the main armament, and one
   0.5-in (12.7-mm) M2 machine-gun on the
   commander's cupola for AA defence

Armour: classified
Used only by: Japan
Notes: The Type 74 MBT entered Japanese
   service in 1973, and has an NBC system
   and night vision equipment fitted as standard. The suspension is of the hydro-
   pneumatic type, allowing the chassis to be
   raised from a ground clearance of just
   under 8 in (20.0 cm) to 2 ft 1½ in (65.0 cm).
   The front and back can be moved independently, the depression of the front and the
   elevation of the back giving the main armament a tactically useful angle of depression. A Nippon Electric laser rangefinder and
   Mitsubishi Electric ballistic computer are
   used with the stabilised main armament.

Type 61

Type: main battle tank
Crew: four
Weights: Empty
Loaded 77,172 lb (35,000 kg)
Dimensions: Length (with armament) 26 ft 10½ in (8.19 m); (hull) 20 ft 8 in (6.3 m)
Width 9 ft 8 in (2.95 m)
Height (to top of cupola) 10 ft 4 in (3.16 m)
Ground pressure: 13.5 lb/in² (0.95 kg/cm²)
Performance: road speed 28 mph (45 kph); range 124 miles (200 km); vertical obstacle 30 in (68.5 cm); trench 8 ft 2 in (2.49 m); gradient 60%; ground clearance 15¾ in (40.0 cm); wading 3 ft 3⅜ in (1.0 m) without preparation
Engine: one 600-hp Mitsubishi Type 12 HM 21WT inline diesel engine
Armament: one 90-mm gun, plus one 0.3-in (7.62-mm) M1919A4 machine-gun co-axial with the main armament, and one 0.5-in (12.7-mm) M2 machine-gun on the cupola
Armour: 2½ in (64 mm) maximum
Used only by: Japan
Notes: Introduced into Japanese service in 1962, the Type 61 tank has a strong resemblance to the US M47 medium tank, but the Japanese vehicle is significantly smaller, to capitalise on the generally smaller size of Japanese crewmen. No NBC system is fitted, but some examples have received night vision equipment. There are four variants:
1. Type 61 MBT
2. Type 67 Armoured Vehicle-Launched Bridge
3. Type 67 Armoured Engineer Vehicle
4. Type 70 Armoured Recovery Vehicle.

Type 60

Type: armoured personnel carrier
Crew: two, plus up to eight infantrymen
Weights: 23,369 lb (10,600 kg)
Loaded 26,455 lb (12,000 kg)
Dimensions: Length 15 ft 11 in (4.85 m)
Width 7 ft 10½ in (2.4 m)
Height 5 ft 6 in (1.7 m)
Ground pressure: 8.1 lb/in² (0.57 kg/cm²)
Performance: road speed 28 mph (45 kph); range 143 miles (230 km); ground clearance 15¾ in (40.0 cm); vertical obstacle 23⅜ in (60.0 cm); trench 5 ft 11¾ in (1.82 m); gradient 60%
Engine: one 220-bhp Mitsubishi 8 HA-21WT inline diesel engine
Armament: one pintle-mounted 0.5-in (12.7-mm) machine-gun, and one hull-mounted 0.3-in (7.62-mm) machine-gun
Armour: ⅝ in (15 mm) maximum
Used only by: Japan
Notes: The Type 60 APC was built by Mitsubishi Heavy Industries, and is very restricted in performance, not being amphibious. The infantry complement is low by modern standards.

Type 73

Type: mechanised infantry combat vehicle
Crew: two, plus up to 10 infantrymen
Weights: Empty
Loaded 30,865 lb (14,000 kg)
Dimensions: Length 18 ft 4 in (5.6 m)
Width 9 ft 2 in (2.8 m)
Height 5 ft 7 in (1.7 m)
Ground pressure:
Performance: road speed 37 mph (60 kph); vertical obstacle 25⅔ in (65.0 cm); trench 5 ft 3 in (1.6 m); gradient 60%; ground clearance 15¾ in (40.0 cm); the Type 73 is fully amphibious
Engine: one 300-hp Mitsubishi Model 4ZF inline diesel engine
Armament: one 0.5-in (12.7-mm) M2 machine-gun on the commander's cupola, and one 0.3-in (7.62-mm) M1919A4 machine-gun in the bow
Armour: classified
Used only by: Japan
Notes: Although designated a mechanised infantry combat vehicle, the Type 73 is really an armoured personnel carrier, though it seems likely that the Japanese may develop the type into a proper MICV in the future by adding a turret-mounted 20-mm cannon and proper facilities for the infantry to use their personal weapons from inside the vehicle. An NBC system and night vision equipment are fitted as standard. The vehicle is fully amphibious, being propelled in the water by its tracks.

Type 75

Type: self-propelled howitzer
Crew: six
Weights: Empty
Loaded 52,910 lb (24,000 kg)
Dimensions: Length 21 ft 9⅝ in (6.64 m)
Width 7 ft 4⅔ in (2.25 m)
Height 10 ft 5⅛ in (3.18 m)
Ground pressure:
Performance:
Engine: one 420-hp Mitsubishi inline diesel engine
Armament: one 155-mm howitzer, plus one 12.7-mm AA machine-gun on the turret roof
Armour:
Used only by: Japan
Notes: This weapon has been produced by Mitsubishi Heavy Industries on the chassis of the Type 74 MBT. The barrel appears to be the same as that used in the US M109A1 SP howitzer. The gun elevates from −5° to +65°, and the turret traverses through 360°. Range of the 155-mm howitzer is probably in the order of 20,232 yards (18,500 m).

Kawasaki KAM-9 (TAN-SSM)

Type: anti-tank and battlefield tactical missile, man-portable and tube-launched
Guidance: semi-automatic command to line-of-sight by means of wire
Dimensions: Span 13 in (33.0 cm)
Body diameter 5⁹⁄₁₀ in (15.0 cm)
Length 4 ft 1 1⁄₁₀ in (1.5 m)
Booster: Daicel solid-propellant rocket
Sustainer: Daicel solid-propellant rocket
Warhead: armour-piercing high explosive
Weights: Launch
Burnt out
Performance: range probably 3,281+ yards (3,000+ m)
Used only by: Japan
Notes: The KAM-9 is a modernisation of the KAM-3, with higher performance and improved range. The booster ejects the missile from the tube-launcher, after which the fins unfold and the sustainer ignites. Sighting is optical and tracking probably infra-red.

Kawasaki KAM-3D

Type: anti-tank missile, man-portable and stand-launched
Guidance: command to line-of-sight by means of wire
Dimensions: Span 1 ft 1 $1\frac{3}{5}$ in (60.0 cm)
Body diameter $4\frac{7}{10}$ in (12.0 cm)
Length 3 ft $3\frac{2}{5}$ in (1.0 m)
Booster: Daicel solid-propellant rocket
Sustainer: Daicel solid-propellant rocket
Warhead: hollow-charge high explosive
Weights: Launch 34.6 lb (15.7 kg)
Burnt out
Performance: range 383-1,968 yards (350-1,800 m); speed 190 mph (305 kph); turning radius 273 yards (250 m)
Used only by: Japan
Notes: Introduced in 1964, and needs a three-man crew. Can be carried in jeeps and helicopters.

Type 60

Type: self-propelled recoilless rifle
Crew: three
Weights: Empty
Loaded 17,681 lb (8,020 kg)
Dimensions: Length 14 ft 1 in (4.3 m)
Width 7 ft 7 in (2.23 m)
Height 4 ft 67 in (1.38 m)
Ground pressure: 8.96 lb/in² (0.63 kg/cm²)
Performance: road speed 30 mph (48 kph); range 80 miles (130 km); vertical obstacle $20\frac{4}{5}$ in (53.0 cm); trench 5 ft 10 in (1.78 m); gradient 67%; ground clearance $13\frac{3}{4}$ in (35.0 cm); wading $31\frac{1}{2}$ in (80.0 cm) without preparation
Engine: one 120-hp Komatsu T120 inline diesel engine
Armament: two 106-mm Type 60 recoilless rifles with 10 rounds of HE or HEAT, plus one 0.5-in (12.7-mm) ranging machine-gun
Armour: $\frac{3}{5}$ in (15 mm) maximum
Used only by: Japan
Notes: Similar in concept to the US Marine Corps M50 Ontos, the Type 60 anti-tank vehicle was introduced into service in 1960. Although it has a very low silhouette and is quite agile, the vehicle has a low ammunition capacity, and all the tactical disadvantages of recoilless rifles, whose back-blast on firing almost inevitably gives away the vehicle's position. The Type 60 has no NBC or night vision equipment.

Type 30 artillery rocket

Type: artillery rocket
Calibre: 300 mm
Barrel length:
Muzzle velocity:
Ranges: Maximum 27,340 yards (25,000 m)
Minimum
Elevation:
Traverse:
Rate of fire:
Weights: For travel
In firing position
Dimensions: Length 14 ft $9\frac{1}{5}$ in (4.5 m)
Span
Body diameter $11\frac{4}{5}$ in (30.0 cm)
Ammunition: HE warhead
Crew:
Used only by: Japan
Notes: The Type 30 is the largest of a family of Japanese artillery rockets. Launch is effected from a twin launcher on the rear of a lorry, and propulsion is by a single-stage solid-propellant rocket motor.

M-1962 machine-gun

Type: machine-gun
Calibre: 7.62 mm
System of operation: gas
Muzzle velocity: 2,805 ft (855 m) per second
Range: effective 656 yards (600 m) with a bipod; 1,203 yards (1,100 m) with a tripod
Rate of fire: 550 rounds per minute (cyclic)
Cooling system: air
Feed system: metal disintegrating link belt
Dimensions: Barrel length 25 in (635 mm)
Overall length 47.25 in (1.2 m)
Width
Height
Weights: 23.59 lb (10.7 kg)
Sights: blade (fore) and leaf, aperture (rear)
Ammunition: 7.62 mm x 51
Used only by: Japan
Notes: The Japanese M-1962 is an effective and reliable weapon despite its complexity. A telescopic sight is standard.

SCK M-1965 sub-machine gun

Type: sub-machine gun
Calibre: 9 mm
System of operation: blowback
Muzzle velocity: 1,181 ft (360 m) per second
Range: effective 219 yards (200 m)
Rate of fire: 550 rounds per minute (cyclic); 120 rounds per minute (automatic)
Cooling system: air
Feed system: 30-round box
Dimensions: Barrel length
Overall length 30 in (762 mm) with stock extended; 19.73 in (501 mm) with stock folded
Width
Height
Weights: 8.99 lb (4.08 kg)
Sights: blade (fore) and flip, aperture (rear)
Ammunition: 9 mm x 19 Parabellum
Used only by: Japan
Notes: The M-1965 is the standard sub-machine gun of the Japanese army, together with the M-1966, which differs only in having a rate of fire of 465 rounds per minute (cyclic).

Type 64 rifle

Type: selective fire rifle
Calibre: 7.62 mm
System of operation: gas
Muzzle velocity: 2,625 ft (800 m) per second
with full load; 2,297 ft (700 m) per second
with reduced load
Range: effective 437 yards (400 m)
Rate of fire: 500 rounds per minute (cyclic);
100 rounds per minute (automatic) for one
minute; 20 rounds per minute (single shot)
Cooling system: air
Feed system: 20-round box
Dimensions: Barrel length 17.72 in (450
          mm)
          Overall length 38.98 in (990
          mm)
          Width
          Height
Weights: 9.7 lb (4.4 kg) empty with bipod;
11.29 lb (5.12 kg) loaded with bipod
Sights: blade (fore) and aperture (rear)
Ammunition: 7.62 mm × 51
Used only by: Japan
Notes: The standard Japanese military rifle,
the Type 64 gets over the problem of the
Japanese infantryman's smaller average
mass by using a reduced charge round, only
90% of that of the standard NATO 7.62-
mm round. With the gas regulator set to a
special position, the NATO round can be
fired, though. Notable design features include the provision of a bipod, and the
straight-through design.

Jordan

61,000 men.

2 armd divs.
2 mech divs.
3 special forces bns.
2 AA bdes incl 6 btys with Improved
HAWK SAM.
320 M-47/-48/-60, 180 Centurion med
tks; 140 Ferret scout cars; 600
M-113 and 120 Saracen APC; 110
25-pdr, 90 105mm, 16 155mm,
203mm how; 35 M-52 105mm, 20
M-44 155mm SP how; 81mm,
107mm, 120mm mor; 106mm,
120mm RCL; TOW, Dragon ATGW;
Vulcan 20mm, 200 M-42 40mm
SP AA guns; Redeye SAM, Improved
HAWK SAM.
(100 M-113 APC, M-110 203mm SP
how, 100 M-163 Vulcan 20mm AA
guns, Improved HAWK SAM on
order.)

Para-Military Forces: 10,000; 3,000
Mobile Police Force, 7,000 Civil
Militia.

M2 gun

Type: field gun
Calibre: 155 mm
Barrel length: 45 cal
Muzzle velocity: 2,740 ft (835 m) per second
Ranges: Maximum 25,700 yards (23,500 m)
Minimum
Elevation: −2° to +63°
Traverse: 60° total
Rate of fire: one round per minute

Weights: For travel 30,600 lb (13,880 kg)
In firing position 27,780 lb (12,601 kg)
Dimensions: Length 34 ft 2¾ in (10.434 m)
Width 9 ft 11 in (3.02 m)
Height 8 ft 6 in (2.59 m)
Ammunition: AP, Chemical, HE and Smoke WP, all separate loading
Crew: 14
Used also by: Austria, Argentina, Greece, Italy, Japan, Netherlands, Pakistan, South Korea, Spain, Turkey, Yugoslavia

Notes: The M2 is the redesignated M1A1 gun introduced to US service in 1938 and soon nicknamed 'Long Tom' for its range and accuracy. The gun was also known after World War II as the M59. An effective and hard hitting weapon, the M2 suffers from a general lack of mobility. The HE shell weighs 95 lb (43.1 kg).

M52

Type: self-propelled howitzer
Crew: five
Weights: Empty
Loaded 53,000 lb (24,041 kg)
Dimensions: Length 19 ft (5.8 m)
Width 10 ft 10 in (3.3 m)
Height 10 ft 2 in (3.1 m)
Ground pressure: 7.96 lb/in² (0.56 kg/cm²)
Performance: road speed 35 mph (56 kph); range 95 miles (153 km); gradient 60%
Engine: one 506-hp inline diesel engine
Armament: one 105-mm howitzer with 102 rounds, plus one 0.5-in (12.7-mm) Browning M2 machine-gun for AA defence
Armour: ⅜ in (15 mm)
Used also by: Belgium, Greece, Japan
Notes: The M52 is based on the chassis of the M41 Walker Bulldog light tank, with a turret capable of traversing only 30° left and right. The gun elevates from −9° to +60°, and fires its shell to a maximum range of 12,250 yards (11,200 m). The M52A1 has a fuel-injection engine.

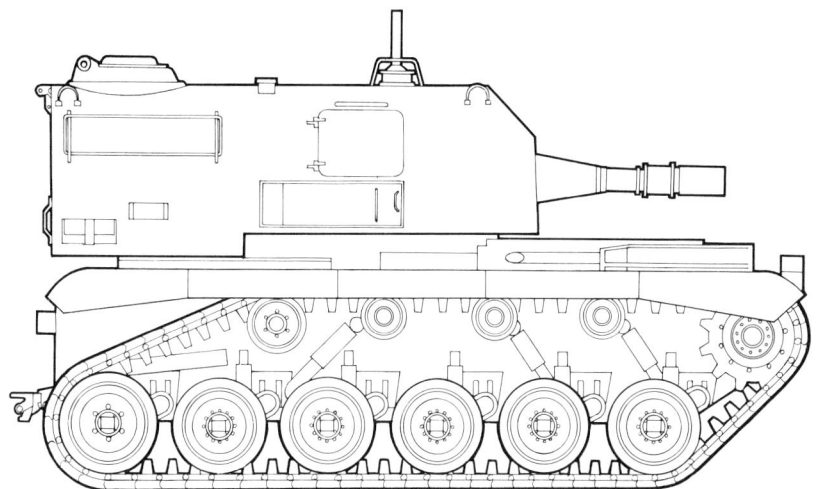

Kampuchea

70,000 total armed forces.

The former Khmer Liberation Army, which was organized into some 4 divs and 3 indep regts, appears still to have the same strength it had at the end of hostilities in 1975, and none of the former regime's troops seem to have been incorporated into the structure. Equipment, a mixture of Soviet, Chinese and American arms, includes AMX-13 lt tks; 10 BTR-152, 200 M-113 APC; 300 105mm, 122mm, 130mm, 20 155mm guns/how; 107mm, 120mm mor; 57mm, 75mm, 82mm, 107mm RCL, 40mm AA guns.

M-1942 (ZIS-3) gun

Type: field anti-tank gun
Calibre: 76.2 mm
Barrel length: 45.34 cal including muzzle brake
Muzzle velocity: 3,166 ft (965 m) per second with HVAP
Ranges: Maximum 14,534 yards (13,290 m) with HE
  Minimum
Elevation: −5° to +37°
Traverse: 54° total

Rate of fire: 15 rounds per minute
Weights: For travel 5,512 lb (2,500 kg)
  In firing position 2,535 lb (1.150 kg)
Dimensions: Length 20 ft (6,095 m)
  Width 5 ft 4¾ in (1.645 m)
  Height 4 ft 6 in (1.375 m)
Ammunition: APHE, HE, HEAT and HVAP
Crew: six or seven
Used also by: Albania, Bulgaria, China, Cuba, Czechoslovakia, East Germany, Egypt, Finland, Ghana, Hungary, Indonesia, Morocco, Nigeria, North Korea, North Yemen, Poland, Romania, Somali Republic, Tanzania, Vietnam, Yugoslavia
Notes: The ZIS-3 entered Russian divisional service in 1942 after development from the M-1936, M-1939 and M-1941 guns. The carriage is based on that of the 57-mm gun carriage. The weapon is built in China as the Type 55 57-mm AT gun. The APHE round weighs 14.33 lb (6.5 kg) and will penetrate 2.72 in (69 mm) of armour at 547 yards (500 m); the HVAP round weighs 6.83 lb (3.1 kg) and will penetrate 3.62 in (92 mm) at 547 yards (500 m); the HEAT round weighs 8.8 lb (4.0 kg) and will penetrate 4.73 in (120 mm) of armour at any range.

Kenya

7,500 men.

4 inf bns.
1 arty bn.
1 spt gp, 1 engr bn.
3 Saladin, 30 AML-60/-90 armd, 14 Ferret scout cars; 15 UR-416, 10 Panhard M3 APC; 8 105mm lt guns; 20 81mm, 8 120mm mor; 56 84mm Carl Gustav and 120mm RCL. (38 Vickers Mk3 med tks on order.)

Para-Military Forces: 1,500 police (General Service Unit), 9 Cessna light aircraft.

Kuwait

10,500 men.

1 armd bde.
2 inf bdes.
24 Chieftain, 50 Vickers, 50 Centurion med tks; 100 Saladin armd, 20 Ferret scout cars; 130 Saracen APC; 10 25-pdr guns; 20 AMX 155mm SP how; SS-11, HOT, TOW, Vigilant, Harpon ATGW. (129 Chieftain med tks; Scorpion lt tks; APC; arty; SA-7 SAM on order.)

Vickers-Armstrong Vigilant

Type: anti-tank missile, man-portable and container-launched
Guidance: command to line-of-sight by means of wire
Dimensions: Span 11 in (27.9 cm)
  Body diameter 5 in (12.7 cm)
  Length 36 in (91.4 cm)
Booster: solid-propellant rocket
Sustainer: solid-propellant rocket
Warhead: hollow-charge high explosive, 11.5 lb (5.22 kg)

Weights: Launch 32.54 lb (14.76 kg)
  Burnt out
Performance: range 219–1,504 yards (200–1,375 m)
Used also by: Finland, Kuwait, Libya, North Yemen, United Arab Emirates, UK
Notes: Introduced in 1963, and manufactured by the British Aircraft Corporation until 1974. Can also be launched from vehicles.

Laos

46,000 men.*

(Lao People's Liberation Army): 100
  inf bns (under Military Regions).
Supporting arms and services.
M-24, PT-76 lt tks; BTR-40, M-113
  APC; 75mm, 85mm, 105mm, 155mm
  how; 81mm, 82mm, 4.2-in mor;
  107mm RCL; 37mm AA guns; 4
  U-17A lt ac.

*The Royal Lao Army has been disbanded;
some men may have been absorbed into the Liberation Army.

Lebanon

7,000 men.

2 armd recce bns.
6 inf bns (some incomplete).
2 arty bns.
Saladin armd cars; Saracen, 80 M-113
  APC; 10 122mm, 155mm guns.

Para-Military Forces: Internal Security
  Force 5,000; small arms, 40 Saladin
  armd cars, 5 Saracen APC.

Liberia

5,250 men.

5 inf bns.
1 Guard bn.
1 arty bn.
1 engr bn.
1 service bn.
1 recce coy.
12 M-3A1 scout cars; 75mm, 105mm
  how; 60mm, 10 81mm mor; 106mm
  RCL.

Libya

30,000 men.

1 armd bde.
2 mech inf bdes.
1 National Guard bde.
1 special forces bde.
3 arty, 2 AA arty bns.
2,000 T-54/-55/-62 med tks; 100 Saladin, Panhard, 200 EE-9 Cascavel
  armd cars; 140 Ferret scout cars;
  BMP MICV; 400 BTR-40/-50/-60,
  140 OT-62/-64, 70 Saracen, 100
  M-113A1 APC; 40 105mm, 80
  130mm how; M-109 155mm SP how;
  300 Vigilant, SS-11, 'Sagger' ATGW;
  25 'Scud-B' SSM; 180 23mm, L/70
  40mm, 57mm, ZSU-23-4 SP AA guns;
  SA-7 SAM; 6 AB-47, 5 AB-206, 4
  Alouette III helicopters; some Cessna
  O-1 lt ac. (16 CH-47C helicopters on
  order.)

EE-9 *Cascavel*

Type: armoured car
Crew: commander, gunner and driver
Weights: Empty 22,046 lb (10,000 kg)
  Loaded 24,251 lb (11,000 kg)
Dimensions: Length 19 ft 5$\frac{7}{10}$ in (5.94 m)
  with gun forward; 17 ft 0$\frac{1}{4}$ in
  (5.19 m) hull only
  Width 8 ft 6 in (2.59 m)
  Height 7 ft 8$\frac{9}{10}$ in (2.36 m)
Ground pressure:
Performance: road speed 59 mph (95 kph);
  road range 497 miles (800 km); step 1 ft
  11$\frac{3}{4}$ in (0.6 m); unprepared wading 3 ft 3$\frac{3}{8}$
  in (1.0 m); ground clearance 1 ft 1$\frac{3}{4}$ in (0.35
  m); gradient 60%
Engine: one 174-hp Mercedes Benz (Brazil)
  Model OM 352 6-cylinder diesel
Armament: one French D-921 90-mm gun
  with 20 rounds of HE and Hollow Charge
  ammunition; one co-axial 7.62-mm
  machine-gun with 2,400 rounds (both in
  AML-90 turret: traverse 360°, elevation
  15°, depression 8°)

Armour: ¼ in (6 mm) minimum; ⅘ in (20 mm) maximum

Used also by: Brazil, Qatar

Notes: Latest production models have a 90-mm gun of Brazilian manufacture.

Luxembourg

660 men.

1 lt inf bn.
1 indep coy.
TOW ATGW.

Para-Military Forces: 430 Gendarmerie.

Sola sub-machine gun

Type: sub-machine gun
Calibre: 9 mm
System of operation: blowback
Muzzle velocity: 1,300 ft (396 m) per second
Range: effective 219 yards (200 m)
Rate of fire: 550 rounds per minute (cyclic); 120 rounds per minute (automatic)
Cooling system: air
Feed system: 32-round box
Dimensions: Barrel length 12 in (305 mm)
Overall length 35 in (889 mm) with stock extended; 24 in (610 mm) with stock retracted
Width
Height
Weights: 6.3 lb (2.86 kg) unloaded; 7.94 lb (3.6 kg) loaded
Sights: blade (fore) and flip, aperture or notch (rear)
Ammunition: 9 mm × 19 Parabellum
Used also by: some North African and South American armies

Notes: The Luxembourgeois Sola sub-machine-gun was designed in 1954, and made in limited numbers before the parent company went out of business. The weapon is designed for simplicity, ease of manufacture and cheapness, having only 38 parts.

Malagasy Republic

9,550 men.

2 inf regts.
1 engr regt.
1 sigs regt.
1 service bn.
M-8 armd, Ferret scout cars; M-3 APC;
81mm mor; 106mm RCL.

Malawi

2,400 men.

2 inf bns.
1 recce coy.
10 Ferret scout cars; 81mm mor.

Malaysia

52,500 men and about 26,000 reservists.

2 div HQ.
9 inf bdes, consisting of:
29 inf bns.
3 recce regts.
3 arty regts.
2 AD btys.
1 special service unit.
5 engr, 4 sigs regts.
Administrative units.
140 Panhard, M-3 armd, 60 Ferret
scout cars; 200 V-150 Commando,
M-3 APC; 80 105mm how; 81mm
mor; 120mm RCL; 35 40mm AA guns.
(AT-105 APC; 12 105mm how on
order.)

Para-Military Forces: Police Field
Force of 13,000: 17 bns, 200 V-150
Commando APC, 40 patrol boats.
People's Volunteer Corps over
200,000.

Cadillac Gage Commando Scout

Type: reconnaissance vehicle
Crew: two
Weights: Empty
Loaded 13,007 lb (5,900 kg)
Dimensions: Length 15 ft 5 in (4.699 m)
Width 7 ft 1 in (2.159 m)
Height 6 ft 9 in (2.057 m)
Ground pressure:
Performance: road speed 62 mph (100 kph);
range 400 miles (644 km); gradient 60%
Engine: one 155-hp inline petrol engine
Armament: one 0.5-in (12.7-mm) machine-
gun and one 0.3-in (7.62-mm) machine-
gun co-axial with the main armament

Armour:
Used by:
Notes: The Commando Scout is undergoing
its final trials before production. The armament installation can comprise two 0.3-in
or 0.62-mm machine-guns, or alternatively
the armament turret can be replaced by a
two-man 'pod'. The tyres are of the run-flat
type.

Mali

4,200 men.

5 inf bns.
1 tk coy.
1 para coy.
1 arty bn.
1 engr coy.
20 T-34, 6 Type 62 lt tks; 20 BRDM-2
armd cars; BTR-152 APC; 85mm,
100mm guns; 81mm, 120mm mor;
37mm, 57mm AA guns.

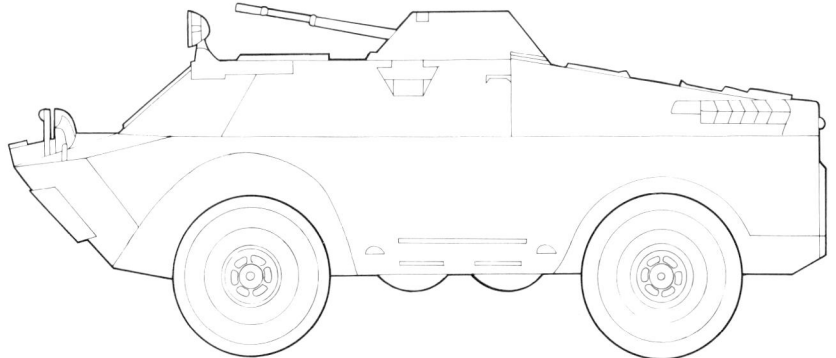

BRDM-2 (or BTR-40PB)

Type: reconnaissance car
Crew: four
Weights: Empty
Loaded 15,432 lb (7,000 kg)

Dimensions: Length 18 ft 10⅝ in (5.75 m)
Width 7 ft 8½ in (2.35 m)
Height 7 ft 7 in (2.31 m)
Ground pressure:
Performance: road speed 62 mph (100 kph);
water speed 6.2 mph (10 kph); range 466

113

miles (750 km); vertical obstacle 29 in (74.0 cm); trench 4 ft 1⅕ in (1.25 m); gradient 60%; ground clearance 12⅖ in (31.5 cm); the BRDM-2 is fully amphibious, being driven in the water by a single water-jet

Engine: one 140-hp GAZ-41 inline petrol engine

Armament: one turret-mounted 14.5-mm KPVT machine-gun with 500 rounds, plus one 7.62-mm PKT with 2,000 rounds, coaxial within the main armament

Armour: ⅖ in (10 mm)

Used also by: Angola, Bulgaria, East Germany, Egypt, Israel, Poland, Romania, Syria, Uganda, USSR, Yugoslavia

Notes: The BRDM-2, otherwise known as the BTR-40PB, is derived from the BRDM-1, but is larger, has a more powerful powerplant, a twin-gun turret and an advanced navigation system. The turret is the same as that fitted to the BTR-60PB and the OT-64 Model 3. The Hungarian FUG M1966 is derived from the BRDM-2. There are several variants:

1. BTR-40PB (Sagger) without a turret but with launching facilities for six AT-3 'Sagger' anti-tank missiles
2. BTR-40PB (SAM) without a turret but with launching facilities for four or eight SA-7 'Grail' surface-to-air missiles
3. BRDM-2U command vehicle without a turret but with additional radio equipment
4. BRDM-2-rkh reconnaissance vehicle to locate and mark areas contaminated by radiological and chemical agents.

Mauritania

12,000 men.

30 mot inf sqns.
3 recce sqns.
1 AB coy.
1 para/cdo coy.
15 EBR-75, AML-60/-90 armd cars; APC; 60mm, 81mm mor; 57mm, 75mm, 106mm RCL.

Mexico

72,000 regular and 250,000 conscripts.

1 mech bde gp (Presidential Guard).
1 inf bde gp.
1 para bde.
Zonal Garrisons incl:
23 indep cav regts, 64 indep inf bns, 1 arty regt.
AA, engr and support units.
M-3, M-5 lt tks; 100 M-3A1, M-8 armd cars; HWK-11 APC; 75mm, 105mm how (incl M-8 75mm, M-7 105mm SP).

HWK 11

Type: armoured personnel carrier
Crew: two, plus 10 infantrymen
Weights: Empty 19,841 lb (9,000 kg)
Loaded 24,251 lb (11,000 kg)
Dimensions: Length 16 ft 6⅘ in (5.05 m)
Width 8 ft 3⅗ in (2.53 m)
Height (without armament) 5 ft 2⅖ in (1.585 m)
Ground pressure: 7.82 lb/in² (0.55 kg/cm²)
Performance: road speed 40 mph (65 kph); range 199 miles (320 km); vertical obstacle 26¾ in (68.0 cm); trench 6 ft 6¾ in (2.0 m); gradient 60%; ground clearance 17¼ in (43.5 cm); wading 3 ft 11 in (1.2 m)
Engine: one 211-hp Chrysler 361 B 75M inline petrol engine
Armament: one 0.3- or 0.5-in (7.62- or 12.7-mm) machine-gun
Armour: ⅓ in (8 mm) minimum; ⅗ in (14.5 mm) maximum
Used only by: Mexico
Notes: The HWK 11 is one of a family of vehicles developed by Henschel Werke of Kassel, of which only this model has entered service. The vehicle is very limited, and has neither NBC nor night vision equipment.

M8

Type: self-propelled howitzer
Crew: four
Weights: Empty
Loaded 33,000 lb (14,969 kg)
Dimensions: Length 14 ft 6¾ in (4.44 m)
Width 7 ft 4¼ in (2.24 m)
Height 7 ft 6½ in (2.3 m)
Ground pressure: 11.83 lb/in² (0.83 kg/cm²)
Performance: road speed 45 mph (72 kph); range 180 miles (290 km); vertical obstacle 24 in (61.0 cm); trench 5 ft 5 in (1.65 m); gradient 30%; ground clearance 6½ in (16.5 cm); wading 30 in (76.2 cm)
Engine: two 110-hp Cadillac Series 42 inline petrol engines
Armament: one 75-mm M3 howitzer with 46 rounds, and one 0.5-in (12.7-mm) Browning M2 machine-gun with 400 rounds
Armour: 1 in (25.4 mm) minimum; 1½ in (38 mm) maximum
Used only by: Mexico
Notes: The M8 had a special turret on the chassis of the M5 light tank. The turret was later fitted with great success to the LVT(A)5. The M8 entered US service in 1942, but was soon found to be undergunned. It was soon replaced by the M7 self-propelled 105-mm howitzer.

RM2 machine-gun

Type: light machine-gun
Calibre: 0.3 in (7.62 mm)
System of operation: gas
Muzzle velocity:
Range: effective 875 yards (800 m)
Rate of fire: 600 rounds per minute (cyclic)
Cooling system: air
Feed system: 20-round box
Dimensions: Barrel length 24 in (610 mm)
Overall length 43.3 in (1.1 m)
Width
Height
Weights: 14.1 lb (6.4 kg)

Sights: hooded barleycorn (fore) and aperture (rear)
Ammunition: 0.3 in–06
Used only by: Mexico
Notes: The Mexican RM2 is a simple weapon, but distinctly limited tactically by the fact that the barrel cannot be changed, which prevents the gun being used for sustained fire. On the other hand, the weapon has the virtue of extreme lightness, even with the fitted bipod.

HM-3 sub-machine gun

Type: sub-machine gun
Calibre: 9 mm
System of operation: blowback
Muzzle velocity:
Range: effective 219 yards (200 m)
Rate of fire: about 600 rounds per minute (cyclic)
Cooling system: air
Feed system: 32-round box
Dimensions: Barrel length 10 in (254 mm)
Overall length 25 in (635 mm)
Width
Height
Weights: 5.93 lb (2.69 kg) unloaded; 7.37 lb (3.35 kg)
Sights:
Ammunition: 9 mm × 19 Parabellum
Used only by: Mexico
Notes: The HM-3 is made by the same firm as the RM2 machine-gun, and is notable, like the machine-gun, for its extreme lightness.

Mongolia

28,000 men and 30,000 reservists.

2 inf bdes.
1 construction bde.
30 T-34, 100 T-54/-55 med tks; 40 BTR-60, 50 BTR-152 APC; 76mm, 100mm, 130mm, 152mm guns/how; 10 SU-100 SP guns; Snapper ATGW; 37mm, 57mm AA guns.

Para-Military Forces: about 18,000 frontier guards and security police.

Morocco

81,000 men.

1 lt security bde.
1 para bde.
5 armd bns.
9 mot inf bns.
18 inf bns.
2 Royal Guard bns.
7 camel corps bns.
2 desert cav bns.
7 arty gps.
2 engr bns.
50 M-48, 40 T-54 med, 80 AMX-13 lt tks; 36 EBR-75, 50 AML and M-8 armd cars; 40 M-3 half-track, 60 OT-62/-64, 30 UR-416, 100 M-113 APC; 150 75mm, 105mm, 34 M-114 155mm how; 20 AMX-105, 36 155mm SP how; 81mm, 82mm, 120mm mor; 75mm, 106mm RCL; *Entac,* Dragon, TOW ATGW; 50 37mm, 57mm, 100mm AA guns; SA-7, 10 Chaparral SAM.
(60 M-48 med tks; 234 M-113 APC; *Crotale* SAM on order.)

Deployment: Mauritania: 6 bns (8,000). Zaire: 1,700.

Para-Military Forces: 30,000, incl 11,000 Sureté Nationale.

BM 59 rifle

Type: selective fire rifle
Calibre: 7.62 mm
System of operation: gas
Muzzle velocity: 2,700 ft (823 m) per second
Range: effective 656 yards (600 m)
Rate of fire: 750 rounds per minute (cyclic); 120 rounds per minute (automatic); 40 rounds per minute (single shot)
Cooling system: air
Feed system: 20-round box
Dimensions: Barrel length 19.29 in (490 mm)
Overall length 43.11 in (1.095 m)
Width
Height
Weights: 10.14 lb (4.6 kg)
Sights: blade (fore) and aperture (rear)
Ammunition: 7.62 mm × 51
Used also by: Indonesia, Italy
Notes: The BM 59 is basically the US Garand M1 semi-automatic rifle made in Italy with considerable improvements by Beretta, as a successor to the M1 made under licence by the firm after World War II. There are a number of marks, indicated by suffixes to the basic designation, for special tasks such as paratroop use etc. The specification above applies specifically to the BM 59 Mark Ital, once Italy's standard army rifle.

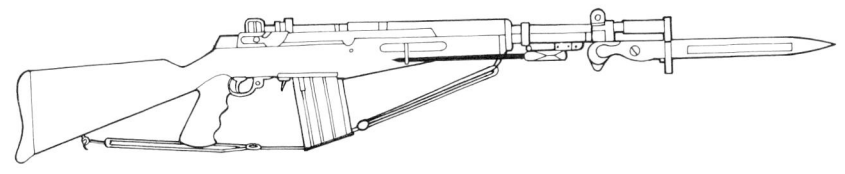

Beretta 70/223 rifle

Type: selective fire assault rifle
Calibre: 5.56 mm (0.223 in)
System of operation: gas
Muzzle velocity: 3,182 ft (970 m) per second
Range: effective 437 yards (400 m)
Rate of fire: 630 rounds per minute (cyclic); 100 rounds per minute (automatic); 40 rounds per minute (single shot)
Cooling system: air
Feed system: 30-round box
Dimensions: Barrel length 17.72 in (450 mm)
Overall length 37 in (940 mm)
Width
Height
Weights: 7.52 lb (3.41 kg) empty; 8.8 lb (3.99 kg) loaded
Sights: post (fore) and flip, aperture (rear)
Ammunition: 5.56 mm × 45
Used also by: Italy
Notes: The AR70 (Automatic Rifle 1970) is

the only one of the three 5.56-mm weapons designed by the Italian firm of Beretta yet to enter production.

Mozambique

20,000 men.

1 tk bn.
28 inf bns.
2–3 arty bns.
150 T-34/-54/-55 med, some PT-76 lt tks; BTR-40, BRDM armd cars; BTR-40/-152 APC; 76mm, 85mm, 100mm, 122mm guns/how; BM-21 multiple RL; 60mm, 82mm, 120mm mor; 82mm, 107mm RCL; Sagger ATGW; 23mm, 37mm, 57mm AA guns; 24 SA-6, SA-7 SAM.

Degtyarev DP machine-gun

Type: light machine-gun
Calibre: 7.62 mm
System of operation: gas
Muzzle velocity: 2,756 ft (840 m) per second
Range: effective 875 yards (800 m)
Rate of fire: 600 rounds per minute (cyclic); 80 to 90 rounds per minute (automatic)
Cooling system: air
Feed system: 47-round drum
Dimensions: Barrel length 23.82 in (605 mm)
              Overall length 50 in (1.27 m)
              Width
              Height
Weights: 20.06 lb (9.1 kg) empty; 28.22 lb (12.8 kg) loaded, with bipod and flash hider
Sights: post (fore) and tangent with V (rear)
Ammunition: 7.62 mm × 54R

Used also by: China, other Asian countries, and many African nations
Notes: The DP (Degtyarev Pekhotnyy) is a Russian design of the mid-1920s. It entered service with the Red Army in 1933 and performed well in the Spanish Civil War and World War II. The only significant improvements resulted in the DPM of 1944: the return spring was moved from under the barrel to a housing at the rear of the receiver, resulting in a cyclindrical projection over the stock, a pistol grip was added, and the grip safety was abandoned in favour of a lever on the right of the receiver. The DT is the heavy-barrel tank version of the DP. The DPM has been made in China as the Type 53.

Nepal

20,000 men.

5 inf bdes (1 Palace Guard).
1 para bn.
1 arty regt.
1 engr regt.
1 sigs regt.
AMX-13 lt tks; 4 3.7-in pack how; 4 4.2-in, 18 120mm mor; 2 40mm AA guns; 3 Skyvan, 1 HS-748 transports; 5 *Alouette* III, 2 Puma helicopters.

Deployment: Lebanon (UNIFIL): 1 bn (642).

Para-Military Forces: 12,000 Police Force.

4.2-in mortar Mark 3

Type: heavy mortar
Calibre: 4.2 in (107 mm)
Barrel length: 18.5 cal
Muzzle velocity: 731 ft (223 m) per second
Ranges: Maximum 4,100 yards (3,750 m)
              Minimum
Elevation: 45° to 80°
Traverse: 7° to 21° depending on elevation
Rate of fire: 12 rounds per minute
Weights: For travel
              In firing position 1,213 lb (550 kg)
Dimensions: Length
              Width
              Height
Ammunition: HE and Smoke
Crew: six

Used also by: Ethiopia, Laos, Malaysia, Turkey
Notes: The 4.2-in mortar is a British weapon of World War II, and proved an effective heavy means of dropping high-angle fire. The HE round weighs 20 lb (9.1 kg).

Netherlands

75,000 men (43,000 conscripts) and 145,000 reservists.

2 armd bdes.
4 mech inf bdes.
2 SSM bns with Honest John (to be replaced by Lance).

3 army aviation sqns (Air Force crews).
340 Centurion, 460 Leopard med, AMX-13 lt tks; 2,000 AMX-VCI, YP-408 and M-113 APC; 105mm, 155mm, 203mm how; AMX 105mm, M-109 155mm, M-107 175mm, M-110 203mm SP guns/how; 107mm,

120mm mor; 8 Honest John SSM; Carl Gustav 84mm, 106mm RCL; LAW, TOW ATGW; L/70 40mm AA guns; 60 *Alouette* III, 30 BO-105 helicopters. (880 YPR-765 APC, 90 35mm *Gepard* SP AA guns, 350 Dragon ATGW, Lance SSM on order.)

Reserves: 145,000; 1 armd, 2 inf bdes and corps troops, incl 1 indep inf bde, would be completed by call-up of reservists. A number of inf bdes could be mobilized for territorial defence.

Para-Military Forces: 3,800 Gendarmerie; 4,446 Home Guard.

FMC Corporation AIFV

Type: armoured infantry fighting vehicle
Crew: three, plus up to seven infantrymen
Weights: Empty 25,536 lb (11,583 kg)
       Loaded 30,688 lb (13,920 kg)
Dimensions: Length 17 ft 3 in (5.26 m)
       Width 9 ft 3 in (2.82 m)
       Height (overall) 9 ft $1\frac{3}{4}$ in (2.79 m)
Ground pressure: 9.53 lb/in² (0.67 kg/cm²)
Performance: road speed 38.5 mph (62 kph); water speed 4 mph (6.4 kph); range 305 miles (491 km); vertical obstacle 25 in (63.5 cm); trench 5 ft 6 in (1.68 m); gradient 60%; ground clearance 17 in (43.1 cm); the AIFV is inherently amphibious, being driven in the water by its tracks

Engine: one 264-bhp Detroit Diesel Model 6V53T turbo-charged inline diesel engine
Armament: one turret-mounted 25-mm cannon with 324 rounds, plus one 7.62-mm machine-gun co-axial with the main armament
Armour: aluminium and steel
Used only by: Netherlands
Notes: The AIFV has been developed by FMC as a private venture, based on the XM765 built for US Army evaluation. Both types incorporate a number of M113 components, but the AIFV has a type of laminate spaced armour, high-capacity shock absorbers, and a turbo-charged diesel engine. There are several variants under development:
  1. ambulance for four stretchers
  2. cargo vehicle for 5,511 lb (2,500 kg) of military stores

  3. command post vehicle, armed like the cargo carrier with a single 0.5-in (12.7-mm) machine-gun, and with extra radio equipment, mapboards and accommodation for a staff of six
  4. mortar tractor for the 120-mm MO-120-RT-61 mortar, with an armament of one 0.5-in (12.7-mm) machine-gun and stowage for 51 mortar rounds
  5. TOW vehicle, with a turret mounting one 7.62-mm machine-gun and two TOW anti-tank missile launchers, with stowage for 10 missiles.

DAF YP-408

Type: armoured personnel carrier
Crew: two, plus up to 10 infantrymen
Weights: Empty 20,944 lb (9,500 kg)
       Loaded 26,456 ln (12,000 kg)
Dimensions: Length 20 ft 6 in (6.23 m)
       Width 7 ft 10 in (2.4 m)
       Height (including machine-gun) 7 ft 9 in (2.37 m)
Ground pressure:
Performance: road speed 50 mph (80 kph); range 311 miles (500 km); vertical obstacle $27\frac{2}{3}$ in (70.0 cm); trench 3 ft 11 in (1.2 m); gradient 60%; ground clearance $20\frac{2}{5}$ in (51.8 cm); wading 3 ft 11 in (1.2 m) without preparation
Engine: one 165-bhp DAF Model DS 575 turbo-charged inline diesel engine
Armament: one 0.5-in (12.7-mm) M2 machine-gun
Armour: $\frac{1}{3}$ in (8 mm) minimum; $\frac{3}{5}$ in (15 mm) maximum
Used only by: Netherlands
Notes: The DAF YP-408 is derived from the same company's 6 × 6 YA-328 lorry, but is an 8 × 6 vehicle. No NBC system or deep wading gear is provided, but night vision equipment can be installed. There are a number of variants:
  1. PWI-S (GR) armoured personnel carrier
  2. PWI-S (PC) platoon commander's vehicle, with additional radio equipment and a crew of nine

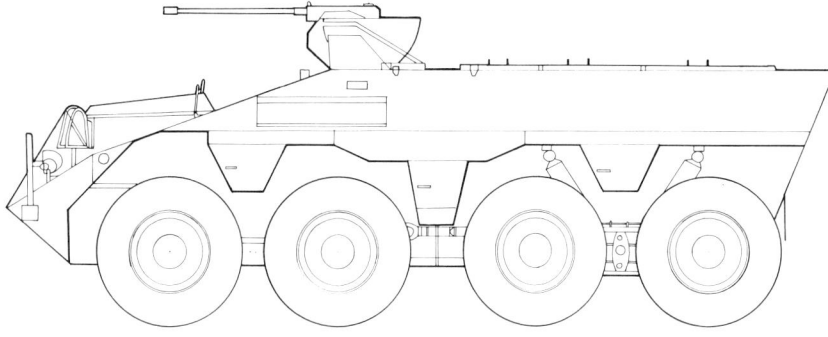

3. PWCO company or battalion commander's vehicle with extra radio equipment, mapboards, a tent and a crew of six
4. PW-GWT ambulance for up to four casualties
5. PW-V cargo carrier with a crew of two and a capacity of 3,307 lb (1,500 kg)
6. PW-MT tractor for the 120-mm Brandt mortar, with 50 bombs carried inside the vehicle.

New Zealand

5,730 men and 1,571 regular reservists, 5,812 territorial.

2 inf bns.
1 arty bty.
Regular troops also form the nucleus of 2 bde gps and a log gp; these would be completed by mobilization of Territorials.

7 M-41 lt tks; 9 Ferret scout cars; 66 M-113 APC; 15 5.5-in guns; 44 105mm how; 24 106mm RCL.

Deployment: Singapore: 1 inf bn with log support.

Nicaragua

5,400 men.

Pres Guard.
1 inf bn.
1 engr bn.
16 inf coys.
1 arty bty.
1 AA arty bty.
Some M-4 med tks; Staghound armd, 3 M-3A1 scout cars; 4 105mm how; 12 20mm, 8 40mm AA guns.

AR-10 rifle

Type: selective fire assault rifle
Calibre: 7.62 mm
System of operation: gas
Muzzle velocity: 2,772 ft (845 m) per second
Range:
Rate of fire: 700 rounds per minute (cyclic); 80 rounds per minute (automatic); 40 rounds per minute (single shot)
Cooling system: air
Feed system: 20-round box
Dimensions: Barrel length 20 in (508 mm)
Overall length 40.5 in (1.029 m)
Width
Height

Weights: 9 lb (4.1 kg) empty; 10.63 lb (4.82 kg) loaded
Sights: blade (fore) and aperture (rear)
Ammunition: 7.62 mm × 51
Used also by: Burma, Portugal, Sudan
Notes: The AR-10 has not been a particularly successful weapon, and is notable largely as the predecessor of the AR-15, the basic model of the M16 rifle widely used by many armies. The AR-10 has also been built in carbine and light machine-gun forms, but only as prototypes.

Niger

2,000 men.

1 recce sqn.
5 inf coys.
1 para coy.
1 engr coy.
10 M-8, M-20 armd cars; 60mm, 81mm mor; 57mm, 75mm RCL.

Nigeria

221,000 men.

4 inf divs.
4 engr bdes.
4 recce regts.
4 arty regts.
50 Scorpion lt tks; 20 Saladin, 15 AML-60/-90 armd cars; 25 Ferret, 20 Fox scout cars; 8 Saracen APC; 105mm, 122mm guns/how; 76mm ATK guns; 20mm, 40mm AA guns.

Deployment: Lebanon (UNIFIL): 1 bn (669).

M-1955 (D-74) howitzer

Type: field howitzer
Calibre: 122 mm
Barrel length: 54 cal including muzzle brake
Muzzle velocity: 3,117 ft (950 m) per second with APHE
Ranges: Maximum 23,950 yards (21,900 m) with HE; 1,312 yards (1,200 m) with APHE
Minimum
Elevation: −2° to +50°
Traverse: 60° total
Rate of fire: six or seven rounds per minute
Weights: For travel
In firing position 14,550 lb (6,600 kg)

Dimensions: Length 32 ft (9.76 m)
Width 6 ft 7¾ in (2.03 m)
Height 9 ft 0⅔ in (2.76 m)
Ammunition: APHE, HE, Illuminating and Smoke
Crew: 10
Used also by: Bulgaria, China, Cuba, East Germany, Egypt, Hungary, Poland, Romania, USSR, Vietnam
Notes: The D-74 122-mm gun/howitzer is older than the D-30 weapon of the same calibre, and was designed to give Russian infantry and mechanised divisions support fire. The type can also be used for the AT role, its 55-lb (25-kg) APHE round being capable of penetrating 9.06 in (230 mm) of armour at 1,094 yards (1,000 m).

VZ53 (Model 37) machine-gun

Type: medium machine-gun
Calibre: 7.92 mm
System of operation: gas
Muzzle velocity: 2,602 ft (793 m) per second
Range: effective 1.094 yards (1,000 m)
Rate of fire: 450 or 700 rounds per minute (cyclic); 200 rounds per minute (automatic)
Cooling system: air
Feed system: belt

Dimensions: Barrel length 26.7 in (678 mm)
Overall length 43.5 in (1.105 m)
Width
Height
Weights: 41.5 lb (18.82 kg)
Sights: blade (fore) and leaf (rear)
Ammunition: 7.92 mm × 57
Used by: Nigeria and possibly other African countries

Notes: This Czech weapon was adopted in Czech Army service in 1937 as Model 37, and sold commercially as the VZ53. The weapon is derived from the VZ26, the gun from which the Bren was derived. The VZ53 was made in Britain during World War II as the 7.92-mm Besa machine-gun for tank use. Two rates of fire are possible by virtue of a buffer system to shorten the recoil distance for high rates of fire.

VZ23 sub-machine gun

Type: sub-machine gun
Calibre: 9 mm
System of operation: blowback
Muzzle velocity: 1,250 ft (381 m) per second
Range: effective 219 yards (200 m)
Rate of fire: 650 rounds per minute (cyclic)
Cooling system: air
Feed system: 24- or 40-round box
Dimensions: Barrel length 11.18 in (284 mm)

Overall length 27 in (686 mm) with stock extended; 17.52 in (445 mm) with stock folded
Width
Height
Weights: 7.2 lb (3.27 kg)
Sights: hooded barleycorn (fore) and V notch (rear)
Ammunition: 9 mm × 19 Parabellum
Used also by: Cuba, Syria
Notes: The design of this gun dates to 1949, when the Czech designer Vaclav Holek pro-

duced a family of four sub-machine guns, the VZ23, 24, 25 and 26. The first and third fire the 9 mm Parabellum round, and the second and fourth the 7.62 mm × 25 Pistol 'P' round. The difference within each pair is that the first has a fixed wooden stock, and the second a folding metal stock.

North Korea

440,000 men.

2 tk divs.
3 mot inf divs.
20 inf divs.
4 inf bdes.
3 recce bdes.
8 lt inf bdes.
3 AA arty divs.
5 indep tk regts.
5 AB bns.
3 SSM bns with FROG.
20 arty regts.
10 AA arty regts.
350 T-34, 1,600 T-54/-55 and Type 59 med, 100 PT-76, 50 T-62 lt tks; 800 BTR-40/-60/-152, M-1967 APC; 3,000 guns and how up to 152mm; 1,300 RL; 9,000 82mm, 120mm and 160mm mor; 1,500 82mm RCL; 57mm to 100mm ATK guns; 9 FROG-5 SSM; 5,000 AA guns, incl 37mm, 57mm, 85mm, 100mm, ZSU-57-2 SP.

T59

Type: main battle tank
Crew: four
Weights: Empty
Loaded 77,162 lb (35,000 kg)
Dimensions: Length (with gun forward) 29 ft 6 in (8.99 m); (hull) 21 ft 2 in (6.45 m)
Width 10 ft 9 in (3.27 m)
Height (overall) 9 ft (2.74 m)
Ground pressure: 10.95 lb/in² (0.77 kg/cm²)
Performance: road speed 31 mph (50 kph); range 249 miles (400 km); vertical obstacle $31\frac{9}{10}$ in (81.0 cm); trench 8 ft $11\frac{1}{2}$ in (2.73 m); gradient 60%; ground clearance 17 in (43.0 cm); wading 4 ft 11 in (1.5 m) without preparation, and 17 ft $8\frac{3}{8}$ in (5.4 m) with the aid of a schnorkel
Engine: one 520-hp inline diesel engine

Armament: one 100-mm gun with 34 rounds, plus one co-axial 7.62-mm machine-gun, one 7.62-mm machine-gun in the hull nose, and one 12.7-mm AA machine-gun on the turret roof
Armour: $\frac{4}{5}$ in (20 mm) minimum; $8\frac{1}{4}$ in (210 mm) maximum
Used also by: Albania, China, Congo, Pakistan, Tanzania, Vietnam
Notes: The T59 is the Chinese-built version of the Russian T-54, and differs from the latter principally in having neither night vision nor NBC equipment, no gun stabilisation system, and only hand traverse for the turret. All these factors must seriously hinder T59 operations against more sophisticated MBTs.

BA-64

Type: armoured car
Crew: two
Weights: Empty
Loaded 5,291 lb (2,400 kg)
Dimensions: Length 12 ft (3.66 m)
Width 5 ft (1.53 m)
Height 6 ft 3 in (1.9 m)
Ground pressure:
Performance: road speed 50 mph (80 kph); range 375 miles (600 km); vertical obstacle small; trench small; gradient 30°; ground clearance $8\frac{1}{4}$ in (21.0 cm); wading 1 ft 8 in (50.8 cm) without preparation
Engine: one 54-hp Model GAZ-MM inline petrol engine
Armament: one 7.62-mm DT machine-gun normally, with 1,260 rounds when a radio

is not fitted, or 1,071 rounds when a radio is fitted
Armour: $\frac{1}{4}$ in (6 mm) minimum; $\frac{2}{5}$ in (10 mm) maximum
Used also by: various nations
Notes: The BA-64 armoured car was introduced into Russian service in 1942, and is still in use by smaller nations up to the present. There are several models, including the following:
1. BA-64 basic production model
2. BA-64B with a wider track and bullet-resistant tyres
3. BA-64ZhD scouting model for armoured trains, with provision to run along the rails on flanged wheels
4. BA-64DShK, with a 12.7-mm DShK machine-gun as armament.
The BA-64 is a 4 × 4 vehicle.

M-1937 (ML-20) howitzer

Type: gun/howitzer
Calibre: 152 mm
Barrel length: 32.4 cal including muzzle brake

Muzzle velocity: 2,149 ft (655 m) per second with HE
Ranges: Maximum 18,919 yards (17,300 m) with HE
Minimum
Elevation: −2° to +65°

Traverse: 58° total
Rate of fire: four rounds per minute
Weights: For travel 17,482 lb (7,930 kg)
In firing position 15,714 lb (7,128 kg)
Dimensions: Length 23 ft 7¾ in (7.21 m)
Width 7 ft 7 in (2.31 m)
Height 7 ft 5 in (2.26 m)
Ammunition: APHE and HE
Crew: 10

Used also by: Albania, Algeria, Bulgaria, China, Cuba, Czechoslovakia, East Germany, Egypt, Hungary, Iraq, Poland, Romania, Syria, Yugoslavia

Notes: Effective still in terms of weight and accuracy of fire, the M-1937 is now a heavy and unwieldy weapon. The HE shell weighs 96 lb (43.6 kg), while the APHE shell weighs 107.6 lb (48.8 kg) and will penetrate 4.88 in (124 mm) of armour at 1,094 yards (1,000 m).

Type 96 machine-gun

Type: light machine-gun
Calibre: 6.5 mm
System of operation: gas
Muzzle velocity: 2,400 ft (732 m) per second
Range: effective 547 yards (500 m)
Rate of fire: 550 rounds per minute (cyclic); 120 rounds per minute (automatic)
Cooling system: air
Feed system: 30-round box
Dimensions: Barrel length 21.69 in (551 mm)
Overall length 41.5 in (1.054 m)
Width
Height
Weights: 20 lb (9.1 kg)
Sights: barleycorn (fore) and tangent, aperture (rear)
Ammunition: 6.5 mm Arisaka (Type 38)
Used only by: North Korea
Notes: This Japanese weapon appeared in 1936 and is a Nambu design. Unusually for a light machine-gun, the weapon has provision for fixing a bayonet, and a ×2½ telescopic sight can also be fitted.

Type 99 machine-gun

Type: light machine-gun
Calibre: 7.7 mm
System of operation: gas
Muzzle velocity: 2,400 ft (731 m) per second
Range: effective 656 yards (600 m)
Rate of fire: 850 rounds per minute (cyclic)
Cooling system: air
Feed system: 30-round box
Dimensions: Barrel length 21.5 in (546 mm)
Overall length 46.73 in (1.187 m)
Width
Height
Weights: 23.15 lb (10.5 kg)
Sights: barleycorn (fore) and tangent, aperture (rear)
Ammunition: 7.7 mm Type 99, or 7.92 mm × 57
Used by: North Korea, and possibly other countries under Japanese rule during World War II
Notes: The Type 99 Japanese light machine-gun is Type 96 modified to fire the 7.7-mm rimless round, and fitted with a flash hider and adjustable monopod under the stock. The weapon was introduced in 1942. It seems that many surviving weapons have been modified to 7.92-mm calibre by the Chinese.

RP-46 machine-gun

Type: company machine-gun
Calibre: 7.62 mm
System of operation: gas
Muzzle velocity: 2,755 ft (840 m) per second
Range: effective 875 yards (800 m)
Rate of fire: 600 rounds per minute (cyclic); 200 rounds per minute (automatic)
Cooling system: air
Feed system: metal-link belt or 47-round drum
Dimensions: Barrel length 23.9 in (607 mm)
Overall length 50.5 in (1.283 m)
Width
Height
Weights: 28.66 lb (13 kg)
Sights: post (fore) and tangent with V (rear)
Ammunition: 7.62 mm × 54R
Used also by: China, and other countries in Asia and Africa
Notes: The RP-46 is a reworking of the DPM by the Russian designers Dibinin, Poliakov and Shilin, the object being to produce a weapon capable of firing from a belt for sustained fire, and from a drum for assault work. The weapon was not widely used by the Russians after its introduction in 1946, but has been made by the Chinese as Type 58 and the North Koreans as Type 64.

North Yemen

36,000 men.

2 inf divs (10 inf bdes, incl 3 reserve).
2 armd bdes.
1 para bde.
2 cdo bdes.
5 arty bns.
2 AA arty bns.
220 T-34, T-54 med tks; 50 Saladin armd, Ferret scout cars; 350 BTR-40/-152, *Walid* APC; 50 76mm, 122mm guns; 50 SU-100 SP guns; 82mm, 120mm mor; 75mm RCL; 20 Vigilant ATGW; 37mm, 57mm AA guns. (How, AA guns on order.)

Deployment: Lebanon (Arab Peacekeeping Force): 1,500.

Para-Military Forces: 20,000 tribal levies.

Norway

20,000 men (17,250 conscripts) and 120,000 reservists.

1 bde gp of 3 inf bns in North Norway. Indep armd sqns, inf bns and arty regts. 78 Leopard, 38 M-48 med, 70 NM-116 lt tks (M-24/90); M-113 APC; 250 105mm, 155mm how, 130 M-109 155mm SP how; 107mm mor; 75mm,

Carl Gustav 84mm, 106mm RCL; *Entac*, TOW ATGW; Rh-202 20mm, L/60 and L/70 40mm AA guns; 40 O-1E, L-18 lt ac.

Deployment: Lebanon (UNIFIL): 1 bn and log units (930).

Reserves: 120,000. 11 Regimental Combat Teams (bdes) of about

5,000 men each, supporting units and territorial forces; 21 days' refresher training each 3rd/4th year. Home Guard (all services) 85,000 (90 days initial service).

Oman

16,200 men.

2 bde HQ.
8 inf bns.
1 Royal Guard regt.
1 arty regt.
1 sigs regt.
1 armd car sqn.
1 para sqn.
1 engr sqn.
36 Saladin armd cars; 36 105mm guns;
    81mm, 120mm mor; TOW ATGW.

Para-Military Forces: 3,300 tribal
    Home Guard (Firqats). Police Air
    Wing: 1 Learjet, 2 Turbo-Porter, 2
    Merlin 1VA, 4 AB-205, 2 AB-206
    helicopters.

British Aerospace Rapier

Type: land-mobile, air-transportable sur-
face-to-air tactical guided missile
Guidance: semi-automatic command to
line-of-sight
Dimensions: Span
          Body diameter 5 in (12.7 mm)
          Length 7 ft 4 in (2.24 m)
Booster: solid-propellant rocket
Sustainer: solid-propellant rocket

Warhead: high explosive
Weights: Launch about 143 lb (65 kg)
          Burnt out
Performance: speed probably about Mach 2;
ceiling about 16,400 ft (5,000 m)
Used also by: Australia, Iran, United Arab
Emirates, UK, Zambia
Notes: Designed as a battlefield defence
system against supersonic aircraft, the
Rapier has proved remarkably accurate, to
the extent that it is at present fitted only
with an impact fuse. The operator acquires

the target visually on receipt of basic data
from a surveillance radar, and thereafter
keeps his sights on the target. A television
camera then follows flares on the tail of the
fired missile, and the launcher's computer
reduces the missile's deviation from the
operator's line-of-sight to nought.

Pakistan

400,000 men (incl 29,000 Azad
Kashmir troops) and 500,000
reservists.

2 armd divs.
16 inf divs.
3 indep armd bdes.
3 indep inf bdes.
6 arty, 2 AD bdes.
5 army aviation sqns.
M-4, 250 M-47/-48, 50 T-54/-55, 700
    T-59 med, 15 PT-76, T-60, 50 M-24
    lt tks; 550 M-113 APC; about 1,000
    75mm pack, 25-pdr, 100mm,
    105mm, 130mm and 155mm guns/
    how; M-7 105mm SP guns; 270
    107mm, 120mm mor; 57mm, M-36
    90mm SP ATK guns; 75mm, 106mm
    RCL; Cobra ATGW; ZU-23, 30mm,
    37mm, 40mm, 57mm, 90mm, 3.7-in
    AA guns; 9 *Crotale* SAM; 40 O-1E lt
    ac; 12 Mi-8, 6 Puma, 20 *Alouette* III,
    12 UH-1, 15 Bell 47G helicopters.
    (TOW ATGW, 29 Puma helicopters
    on order.)

Para-Military Forces: 109,100. 22,000
    National Guard, 65,000 Frontier
    Corps, 15,000 Pakistan Rangers,
    2,000 Coastguard, 5,100 Frontier
    Constabulary.

Messerschmitt-Bölkow-Blohm
BO 810 Cobra 2000

Type: anti-tank missile, man-portable and
jump-launched without frame or container
Guidance: command to line-of-sight by
means of wire
Dimensions: Span 1 ft 6$\frac{9}{10}$ in (48.0 cm)
          Body diameter 3$\frac{9}{10}$ in (10.0 cm)
          Length 3 ft 1$\frac{2}{5}$ in (90.0 cm)
Booster: solid-propellant rocket
Sustainer: solid-propellant rocket
Warhead: hollow-charge high explosive (6
lb/2.7 kg), capable of penetrating 19.7 in
(500 mm) of armour; or anti-tank/shrapnel
high-explosive (6 lb/2.7 kg) penetrating
13.8 in (350 mm) of armour and destruc-

tion within a radius of 32 ft 9$\frac{7}{10}$ in (10.0 m)
Weights: Launch 22.7 lb (10.3 kg)
          Burnt out 17.6 lb (8.0 kg)
Performance: range 437 to 2,187 yards
(400 to 2,000 m); speed 186 mph (300
kph)
Used also by: Argentina, Brazil, Greece,
Israel, Italy, Spain, Turkey
Notes: One infantryman can carry and operate two of these missiles, introduced in
1960. When the missile is launched, the
booster causes the missile to 'jump' clear of
the ground, whereupon the sustainer
ignites. Can also be frame-launched from a
vehicle.

ZU-23 mounting

Type: twin AA cannon mounting
Calibre: 23 mm
Barrel length: 87.4 cal
Muzzle velocity: 3,182 ft (970 m) per second
Ranges: Maximum (horizontal) 7,655 yards (7,000 m); (vertical) 16,404 ft (5,000 m) Minimum
Elevation: −10° to +90°
Traverse: 360°
Rate of fire: 1,000 rounds per minute (cyclic) per barrel
Weights: For travel In firing position 2,094 lb (950 kg)
Dimensions: Length 15 ft 3 in (4.65 m) Width 9 ft 1 $\frac{1}{10}$ in (2.77 m) Height 6 ft 9 $\frac{1}{2}$ in (2.07 m)
Ammunition: API and HEI
Crew: five
Used also by: Cuba, Czechoslovakia, East Germany, Egypt, Ethiopia, Finland, Iran, Iraq, Libya, Poland, Syria, USSR, Vietnam

Notes: The Russian ZU-23 mounting was intended to replace the earlier ZPU-2 and ZPU-4 machine-gun mountings. There is no provision for radar control, so the ZU-23 is a clear-weather system. Ammunition feed is from one 50-round belt in a box on the outside of each barrel. Maximum effective AA range is 4,921 ft (1,500 m). Both rounds weigh 0.42 lb (0.19 kg), and the API round will penetrate 1 in (25 mm) of armour at 547 yards (500 m).

RPD machine-gun

Type: light machine-gun
Calibre: 7.62 mm
System of operation: gas
Muzzle velocity: 2,297 ft (700 m) per second
Range: effective 875 yards (800 m)
Rate of fire: 700 rounds per minute (cyclic); 150 rounds per minute (automatic)
Cooling system: air
Feed system: metal-link belt
Dimensions: Barrel length 20.5 in (521 mm) Overall length 40.79 in (1.036 m) Width Height
Weights: 15.65 lb (7.1 kg)
Sights: post (fore) and tangent with V (rear)
Ammunition: 7.62 mm × 39
Used also by: China, Egypt, North Korea, Vietnam and several African nations

Notes: The RPD was designed in 1943 by Degtyarev as a successor to his DP, using the new 7.62 × 39 mm round. The new weapon entered production soon after the end of World War II, and was soon in very widespread service in communist countries. The RPD has also been manufactured in China, as Type 56 and Type 56-1, and in North Korea, as Type 62. Although obsolescent in all its five versions, the RPD is still extensively used by emergent countries and 'freedom fighter' groups.

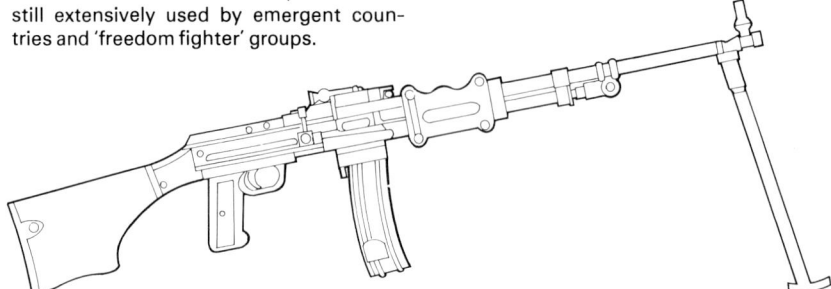

Sten sub-machine gun

Type: sub-machine gun
Calibre: 9 mm
System of operation: blowback
Muzzle velocity: 1,200 ft (366 m) per second
Range: effective 219 yards (200 m)
Rate of fire: 540 rounds per minute (cyclic); 128 rounds per minute (automatic)
Cooling system: air
Feed system: 32-round box
Dimensions: Barrel length 7.8 in (198 mm) Overall length 30 in (762 mm) Width Height
Weights: 8.6 lb (3.9 kg) unloaded; 10 lb (4.54 kg) loaded
Sights: barleycorn (fore) and aperture (rear)
Ammunition: 9 mm × 19 Parabellum
Used by: still widely used in many parts of the world, especially former British territories
Notes: The Sten gun (the name comes from the project manager, R.V. Shepherd, the designer, H.J. Turpin, and the factory at Enfield where the gun was produced initially) first appeared in 1941 as a cheap and easily produced sub-machine gun for the British forces. There have been many versions of the standard weapon.

1. Sten Mark I with an unperforated barrel jacket, flash hider and a hinged vertical fore grip
2. Sten Mark I* without flash hider and wooden fore grip
3. Sten Mark II with a two-groove barrel and a tubular steel T-shaped stock
4. Sten Mark IIS silenced version of the Mark II
5. Sten Mark III with a non-detachable barrel
6. Sten Mark IV trials gun for airborne troops, with a pistol grip and short barrel
7. Sten Mark V, to which the specification above applies, with a wooden stock and a forward pistol grip
8. Sten Mark VI silenced version of the Mark V.

The major criticism of the Sten was its poor magazine design.

Paraguay

12,500 men.

1 cav 'div' (bde) with 2 mech cav regts, 1 inf bn, 1 arty bty.
6 inf 'divs' (bn gps).
2 indep horsed cav regts.
2 indep inf bns.
1 Presidential Guard bn.
1 arty regt.
5 engr, 1 sigs bns.
9 M-4 med, 6 M-3 lt tks; APC; 75mm pack, 105mm how; 2 Bell 47, 3 UH-12E helicopters.

Para-Military Forces: 4,000 security forces.

Madsen Model 50 sub-machine gun

Type: sub-machine gun
Calibre: 9 mm
System of operation: blowback
Muzzle velocity: 1,280 ft (390 m) per second
Range: effective 164 yards (150 m)
Rate of fire: 550 rounds per minute (cyclic); 100 rounds per minute (automatic)
Cooling system: air
Feed system: 32-round box
Dimensions: Barrel length 7.8 in (198.12 mm) Overall length 31.25 in (793.7 mm) with stock extended; 20.8 in (528.3 mm) with stock folded Width Height
Weights: 7.05 lb (3.2 kg) empty
Sights: blade (fore) and aperture (rear)
Ammunition: 9 mm × 19 Parabellum
Used also by: Denmark and several South American countries
Notes: Model 50 (1950) is the second of a family of four Danish sub-machine guns with the same basic design, the others being Model 46, Model 53 and the Mark II.

Peru

65,000 men (49,000 conscripts).

2 armd 'divs' (bdes).
2 armd, 2 horsed regts (cav 'div').
8 inf and mech 'divs' (bdes).
1 para-cdo 'AB div' (bde).
1 jungle 'div' (bde).
3 armd recce sqns.
Arty and engr bns.
250 T-54/-55, 60 M-4 med, 110 AMX-13 lt tks; M-8 armd cars; 50 M-3A1 scout cars; 300 M-113, V-200 *Chaimite*, UR-416, MOWAG APC; 105mm, 122mm, 130mm, 155mm how; 120mm mor; 28 40mm, 76mm towed, ZSU-23-4 SP AA guns; SA-3 SAM; 5 U-10B, 5 Cessna 185 lt ac; 42 Mi-8 (36 in store), 4 *Alouette* III, 5 Lama helicopters.
(200 T-55 tks, 122mm, 130mm guns, SA-3/-7 SAM, 2 Nomad lt transport ac on order.)

Para-Military Forces: 20,000 Guardia Civil.

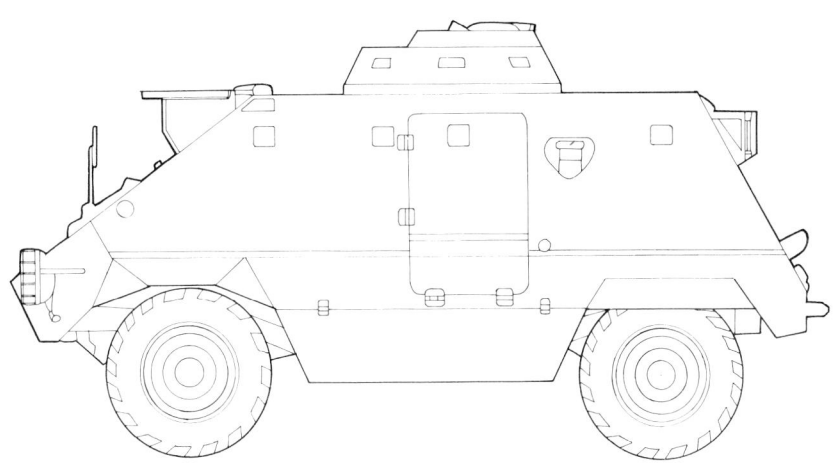

UR-416

Type: armoured personnel carrier
Crew: two, plus up to six infantrymen
Weights: Empty 10,582 lb (4,800 kg)
       Loaded 13,889 lb (6,300 kg)
Dimensions: Length 16 ft $4\frac{1}{2}$ in (4.99 m)
       Width 7 ft 5 in (2.26 m)
       Height 7 ft $1\frac{4}{5}$ in (2.18 m)
Ground pressure:
Performance: road speed 50 mph (80 kph); range 435 miles (700 km); vertical obstacle $21\frac{3}{5}$ in (55.0 cm); trench negligible; gradient 70%; ground clearance $17\frac{1}{3}$ in (44.0 cm); wading $21\frac{2}{3}$ in (55.0 cm) without preparation

Engine: one 110-hp Daimler-Benz OM 352 inline diesel engine
Armament: see notes
Armour: $\frac{1}{3}$ in (9 mm)
Used also by: El Salvador, Greece, Kenya, Morocco, Netherlands, Peru, Togo, Venezuela, West Germany
Notes: Based on a commercial chassis, the UR-416 is designed basically for internal security and border patrol duties. The basic vehicle can be fitted out for a number of roles, including ambulance, cargo carrying and command vehicle. Armament can include TOW or Cobra 2000 anti-tank missiles, or turret-mounted 20-mm cannon, 7.62-mm machine-gun or 90-mm recoilless rifle.

MOWAG Roland

Type: armoured personnel carrier
Crew: three, plus three or four infantrymen
Weights: Empty 8,598 lb (3,900 kg)
       Loaded 10,362 lb (4,700 kg)
Dimensions: Length 14 ft $6\frac{3}{4}$ in (4.44 m)
       Width 6 ft 7 in (2.01 m)
       Height (with turret) 6 ft 8 in (2.03 m)
Ground pressure:
Performance: road speed 68 mph (110 kph); range 342 miles (550 km); vertical obstacle $15\frac{3}{4}$ in (40.0 cm); trench negligible; gradient 60%; wading $39\frac{2}{5}$ in (1.0 m) without preparation
Engine: one 202-hp Chrysler inline petrol engine
Armament: a wide variety of armament options is available, including turret-mounted 7.62- or 12.7-mm machine-guns, or 20- or 25-mm cannon
Armour:
Used also by: Argentina, Bolivia, Canada, Chile, Greece
Notes: A 4 × 4 vehicle, the MOWAG Roland is suitable for internal security duties and a number of other military roles from

123

armoured personnel carrier to ambulance or command vehicle.

Philippines

63,000 men and 17,000 reservists.

4 lt inf divs.
1 indep inf bde.
21 Scorpion, 7 M-41 lt tks; 60 M-113, 20 V-150 Commando APC; 120 105mm, 5 155mm how; 81mm, 40 107mm mor; 75mm, 106mm RCL; HAWK SAM.

Para-Military Forces: 65,000: 40,000 Philippine Constabulary, 25,000 Local Self-Defence Force.

Poland

222,000 men (166,000 conscripts) and 500,000 reservists.

5 tk divs.
8 motor rifle divs.
1 AB div.
1 amph assault div.
4 SSM bdes with 'Scud'.
3 arty bdes, 1 arty regt.
6 AA arty regts.
33 ATK regts.
3,800 T-34/-54/-55 med, 300 PT-76 lt tks; 2,000 OT-65 and BRDM-1/-2 scout cars; BMP MICV; OT-62/-64 APC; 400 76mm, 85mm, 700 122mm, 150 152mm guns/how; 122mm SP guns; 600 82mm, 120mm mor; 250 BM-21 122mm, 140mm RL; 52 FROG-3/-7, 36 'Scud' SSM; 76mm, 85mm towed, ASU-85 SP ATK guns; 73mm, 82mm, 107mm RCL; 'Sagger' ATGW; 400 23mm, 57mm, 85mm, 100mm towed, ZSU-23-4, 24-ZSU-57-2 SP AA guns; SA-6/-7/-9 SAM.

Deployment: Egypt (UNEF): 957; Syria (UNDOF): 90.

Para-Military Forces: 95,000: 18,000 Border Troops (Ministry of Interior); 77,000 Internal Security and Internal Defence Troops (incl 21,000 Construction Troops). Some tks, AFV, ATK guns; 34 small boats operated by coastguard; 350,000 Citizens' Militia.

WP-8 artillery rocket launcher

Type: mobile artillery rocket launcher
Calibre: 140 mm
Number of tubes: eight
Muzzle velocity: 1,312 ft (400 m) per second
Ranges: Maximum 11,592 yards (10,600 m)
　　　　Minimum
Elevation: 0° to +45°
Traverse: 30°
Time to reload: two minutes
Weights: For travel
　　　　In firing position
Dimensions: Length
　　　　　Width
　　　　　Height
Ammunition: HE warhead on rocket
Crew: five
Used only by: Poland
Notes: The Polish WP-8 system is designed for use by airborne forces, and uses the same rocket as that in the Russian BM-14 launcher. The launcher is mounted on a small wheeled trailer towed by a vehicle such as the GAZ 69 lorry.

Portugal

40,000 men.

6 regional commands.
1 inf bde.
1 tk regt.
2 cav regts.
16 inf regts.
4 indep inf bns.
3 arty regts, 2 arty gps.
1 coast arty regt, 2 indep AA arty bns.
2 engr regts.
1 sigs regt.
90 M-47, 23 M-48 med, 10 M-24 lt tks;
100 Panhard EBR armd cars; 86 M-113, 60 *Chaimite* (Commando) APC; 30 5.5-in guns, 50 105mm guns/how; 107mm mor; 80 120mm RCL; 15 TOW ATGW; coast and 40mm AA arty.

Para-Military Forces: 9,500 National Republican Guard, 13,700 Public Security Police, 6,200 Fiscal Guard.

Humber FV1609 'Pig'

Type: armoured personnel carrier
Crew: two, plus up to eight infantrymen
Weights: Empty 10,515 lb (4,770 kg)
Loaded 12,765 lb (5,790 kg)
Dimensions: Length 16 ft 2 in (4.93 m)
Width 6 ft 8½ in (2.04 m)
Height 7 ft (2.13 m)
Ground pressure:
Performance: road speed 40 mph (64 kph); range 260 miles (402 km)
Engine: one 120-hp Rolls-Royce B.60 Mark 5A inline petrol engine

Armament: none
Armour: ⅖ in (10 mm) maximum
Used also by: UK
Notes: The FV1609, nicknamed the 'Pig', entered British service in 1955, and is still used for internal security operations in Northern Ireland.

Heckler und Koch HK21 machine-gun

Type: general-purpose machine-gun
Calibre: 7.62 mm
System of operation: delayed blowback
Muzzle velocity: 2,625 ft (800 m) per second
Range: effective 1,312 yards (1,200 m)
Rate of fire: 900 rounds per minute (cyclic); 200 rounds per minute (automatic)
Cooling system: air
Feed system: metal-link belt or box

Dimensions: Barrel length 17.72 in (450 mm)
Overall length 40.2 in (1.021 m)
Width
Height
Weights: 16.14 lb (7.32 kg) with bipod
Sights. blade (fore) and drum, aperture (rear)
Ammunition: 7.62 mm × 51
Used only by: Portugal
Notes: The HK21 is a Heckler und Koch Group I weapon, using the standard 7.62-mm NATO round (Group II weapons fire the US 5.56 mm × 45 round, and Group III

weapons the 7.62 mm × 39 round). Although the HK21 is primarily a Group I weapon, it can be adapted quite simply to Group II or III. The weapon can be used as a belt-fed, bipod-mounted light machine-gun; magazine-fed, bipod-mounted light machine-gun; belt-fed, tripod-mounted sustained-fire machine-gun; and belt-fed, vehicle-mounted sustained-fire machine-gun. The latest model of the gun, the HK21A1, has improved feed characteristics.

FBP M48 sub-machine gun

Type: sub-machine gun
Calibre: 9 mm
System of operation: blowback
Muzzle velocity: 1,250 ft (381 m) per second
Range: 219 yards (200 m)
Rate of fire: 500 rounds per minute (cyclic); 120 rounds per minute (automatic)
Cooling system: air

Feed system: 32-round box
Dimensions: Barrel length 9.8 in (249 mm)
Overall length 32 in (813 mm) with stock extended; 25 in (635 mm) with stock folded
Width
Height
Weights: 8.27 lb (3.75 kg) unloaded; 9.77 lb (4.43 kg) loaded
Sights: blade (fore) and aperture (rear)

Ammunition: 9 mm × 19 Parabellum
Used also by: Angola, Mozambique
Notes: There is little original in the FBP M48, which is an adequate but unexceptional weapon of Portuguese design and manufacture.

Qatar

2 armd car regts.
1 Guards inf bn.
1 mobile regt.
12 AMX-30 med tks; 30 Saladin, 20 EE-9 *Cascavel* armd, 10 Ferret scout cars; 12 AMX-10P MICV; 8 Saracen APC; 4 25-pdr guns; 81 mm mor. (HAWK SAM on order.)

Short Brothers & Harland Shorland

Type: armoured patrol car
Crew: three
Weights: Empty
Loaded 7,407 lb (3,360 kg)
Dimensions: Length 15 ft 1 in (4.6 m)
Width 5 ft 10 in (1.778 m)
Height 7 ft 6 in (2.29 m)

Ground pressure:
Performance: road speed 55 mph (88 kph); range 320 miles (515 km) with long-range tanks
Engine: one 96-bhp Rover inline petrol engine
Armament: one turret-mounted 7.62-mm machine-gun with 1,500 rounds
Armour: ⅓ in (8 mm)
Used also by: Argentina, Guyana, United Arab Emirates

Notes: The Shorland is designed as a patrol vehicle, and is based on the long-wheelbase Land Rover. The technical specification above relates to the Mark 3, the Marks 1 and 2 having lower powered engines and reduced performance.

Short Brothers Tigercat

Type: land-mobile, air-transportable surface-to-air tactical guided missile
Guidance: radio command to line-of-sight
Dimensions: Span 25½ in (64.77 cm)
Body diameter 7½ in (19.05 cm)
Length 4 ft 10 in (1.48 m)
Booster: solid-propellant rocket
Sustainer: solid-propellant rocket
Warhead: high explosive
Weights: Launch 139 lb (63 kg)
Burnt out
Performance:
Used also by: Argentina, India, Iran, Israel, Rhodesia, South Africa, UK
Notes: Developed from the Seacat, the Tigercat is intended to provide low-level close-range air defence with minimum equipment. Having acquired the target visually, the operator then fires a missile from the triple launcher into his field of vision; he then directs the missile along his line-of-sight to the target by means of a thumb-stick control. There is also a Radar Enhanced Tigercat with Marconi ST850 radar, and optional S860 surveillance radar.

Rhodesia

9,500 men (3,250 conscripts).

1 armd car regt.
6 inf bns.§
4 Special Air Service sqns.
Selous Scouts (Special Forces unit).
Grey's Scouts, mounted inf (250).
1 arty regt.
6 engr sqns.
7 signals sqns.
60 AML-90 Eland armd cars; Ferret scout cars; Hippo, Hyena and Leopard (local-built) lt APC; 25-pdr, 105mm how, 5.5-in guns/how; 105mm RCL; Tigercat SAM.

§ (1 white bn and 4 black bns, with a fifth black bn forming.)

Reserves:
White, Asian and Coloured citizens aged 17–25 undergo 18 months National Service before joining Territorial Army units (8 bns). Thereafter operational duties amount to about 4 months a year in periods of 30 or 56 days at one time. Those aged 26–37 without previous military training usually receive 84 days basic training for the Territorial Army or 56 days for the Police Reserve or Ministry of Internal Affairs. Commitments thereafter are for up to 4 months a year on a periodic basis. Men aged 38–50 undergo 3 weeks basic training before being posted to the Police Reserve, operational duty

consists of up to 70 days a year in periods of 2–4 weeks.
Those over 50 are posted to the Rhodesia Defence Regiment (RDR). The RDR includes all Asians and Coloureds and those not fit for more active duty. Some men over 50 join the Special Reserves with police duties.

Para-Military Forces: British South African Police (BSAP): 8,000 active, 35,000 reservists (the White population provides about a third of the active strength but nearly three-quarters of the reservist strength). Guard Force: establishment 1,000.

Romania

140,000 men (95,000 conscripts) and 300,000 reservists.

2 tk divs.
8 motor rifle divs.
2 mountain bdes.
1 AB regt.
2 SSM bdes with 'Scud'.
2 arty bdes.
3 arty regts.
2 ATK regts.
2 AA arty regts.
200 T-34, 1,500 T-54/-55 med tks;

1,000 BRDM scout cars; BTR-50/-60, TAB-70/-72 (BTR-60) APC; 60 76mm, 50 85mm, 600 122mm, 150 152mm guns/how; 130 SU-100 SP guns; 1,000 82mm, 200 120mm mor; 122mm, 150 130mm RL; 30 FROG, 20 'Scud' SSM; 57mm ATK guns; 260 76mm and 82mm RCL; 120 'Sagger', 'Snapper' ATGW; 300 30mm, 37mm, 250 57mm, 85mm, 100mm AA guns; SA-6/-7 SAM.

Para-Military Forces: 37,000: 17,000

border, 20,000 security troops with AFV, ATK guns. About 700,000 Patriotic Guard.

Orita M-1941 sub-machine gun

Type: sub-machine gun
Calibre: 9 mm
System of operation: blowback
Muzzle velocity: 1,250 ft (381 m) per second
Range: effective 219 yards (200 m)
Rate of fire: 600 rounds per minute (cyclic); 120 rounds per minute (automatic)

Cooling system: air
Feed system: 25-round box
Dimensions: Barrel length 11.3 in (287 mm)
Overall length 35.2 in (894 mm)
Width
Height

Weights: 7.63 lb (3.46 kg) empty; 8.82 lb (4 kg) loaded
Sights: blade (fore) and tangent, notch (rear)
Ammunition: 9 mm × 19 Parabellum
Used only by: Romania
Notes: An unexceptional weapon of Romanian design and manufacture, the M-1941 is now used only as a second-line weapon.

Rwanda

3,750 men.

1 recce sqn.
8 inf coys.
1 cdo coy.
12 AML-60/-90 armd cars; 6 57mm guns; 8 81mm mor.

MAS M-1949/56 rifle

Type: self-loading rifle
Calibre: 7.5 mm
System of operation: gas
Muzzle velocity: 2,680 ft (817 m) per second
Range: effective 656 yards (600 m)
Rate of fire: 30 rounds per minute
Cooling system: air
Feed system: 10-round box
Dimensions: Barrel length 20.51 in (521 mm)
Overall length 39.76 in (1.01 m)
Width
Height

Weights: 8.6 lb (3.9 kg) without magazine; 9.57 lb (4.34 kg) loaded
Sights: blade (fore) and tangent with aperture (rear)
Ammunition: 7.5 mm × 54
Used also by: Cameroon, Chad, Dahomey, Ivory Coast, Malagasy Republic
Notes: The M-1949/56 is a modification of the M-1949, French first indigenously designed rifle after World War II. The M-1949/56 differs from its predecessor in having a shorter wooden fore-end, and a combined grenade launcher/muzzle brake.

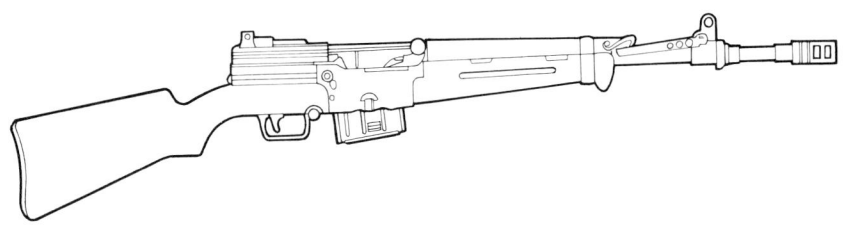

Saudi Arabia

45,000 men.

2 armd bdes.
4 inf bdes.
2 para bns.
1 Royal Guard bn.
3 arty bns.
6 AA arty btys.
10 SAM btys with HAWK.
250 AMX-30, 75 M-60 med tks; 200 AML-60/-90 armd, Ferret, 50 Fox scout cars; 300 AMX-10P MICV; M-113, Panhard M-3, APC; 105mm pack how, 105mm and 155mm SP how; 75mm RCL; TOW ATGW; M-42 40mm SP, AMX-30 SP AA guns; HAWK SAM.
(175 M-60 med tks; 50 Fox scout cars; 200 AMX-10P MICV; Dragon ATGW; M-163 Vulcan 20mm SP AA guns; Redeye, *Shahine (Crotale)*, 6 btys Improved HAWK SAM on order.)

Deployment:
Lebanon (Arab Peace-keeping Force): 700.

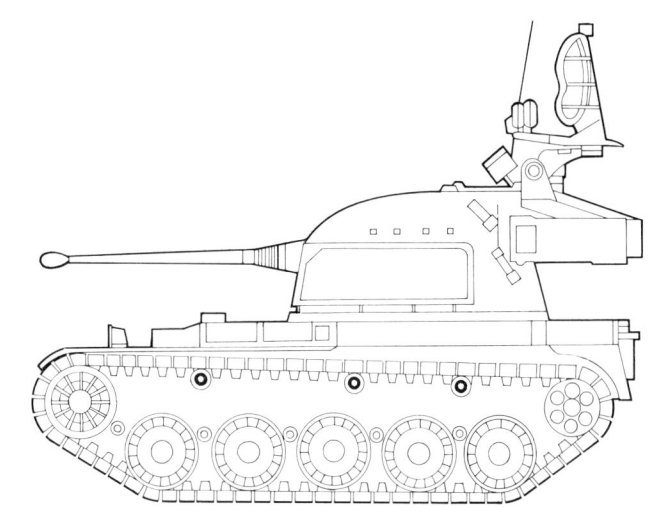

AMX-30-S 401 A

Type: self-propelled twin AA cannon mounting
Calibre: 30 mm
Barrel length:
Muzzle velocity: 3,280 ft (1,000 m) per second
Ranges: Maximum 10,936 yards (10,000 m); effective 3,828 yards (3,500 m)
Minimum
Elevation: −8° to +85°
Traverse: 360°
Rate of fire: 650 rounds per minute (cyclic) per barrel

Weights: For travel
In firing position 79,366 lb (36,000 kg)
Dimensions: Length 22 ft 3¾ in (6.8 m)
Width 10 ft 2 in (3.1 m)
Height 9 ft 10 in (3.0 m)
Ammunition: 300 rounds per gun in the turret, plus 300 rounds per gun in the hull
Crew: four
Used only by: Saudi Arabia
Notes: The AMX-30-S 401 A is based on the chassis of the AMX-30 MBT, and uses the TGA 230A turret fitted with two 30-mm Hispano-Suiza Type 831L cannon. Fire-control is aided by the *Oeil Vert* radar,

which has two main ranges: $9\frac{1}{3}$ miles (15 km) for normal use, and 4 miles (6.5 km) for close operations. Road speed of the system is 40.4 mph (65 kph).

Aérospatiale *Harpon*

Type: anti-tank and battlefield missile, vehicle-launched from a frame
Guidance: automatic command to line-of-sight by means of wire
Dimensions: Span 1 ft $7\frac{7}{10}$ in (50.0 cm)
Body diameter $6\frac{1}{2}$ in (16.4 cm)
Length 3 ft $11\frac{4}{8}$ in (1.215 m)

Booster: solid-propellant rocket
Sustainer: solid-propellant rocket
Warhead: as for SS.11
Weights: Launch 67 lb (30.4 kg)
Burnt out
Performance: range 437–3,280 yards (400–3,000 m); speed 425 mph (685 kph); minimum turning radius 1,094 yards (1.0 km); armour penetration 23.6 in (600 mm) minimum
Used also by: France, Kuwait, West Germany

Notes: Designed as a wire-guided missile for use on land vehicles. The automatic guidance system means that all the operator has to do is keep his sights on the target: the system then spots any deviation from this line by the missile and corrects accordingly.

Senegal

6,000 men.

4 inf bns.
1 engr bn.
1 recce sqn.
2 para coys.
2 cdo coys.
1 arty bty.
AML armd cars; 12 VXB-170 APC; 75mm pack how, 6 105mm how; 8 81mm mor; 30mm, 40mm AA guns.

Deployment: Lebanon (UNIFIL): 1 bn (634).

Berliet VXB

Type: armoured personnel carrier
Crew: one, plus up to 11 infantrymen
Weights: Empty 21,605 lb (9,800 kg)
Loaded 27,998 lb (12,700 kg)
Dimensions: Length 19 ft $7\frac{4}{8}$ in (5.99 m)
Width 8 ft $2\frac{1}{2}$ in (2.5 m)
Height (without armament) 6 ft $8\frac{1}{10}$ in (2.05 m)
Ground pressure:
Performance: road speed 53 mph (85 kph); water speed 2.5 mph (4 kph); range 466 miles (750 km); vertical obstacle small; trench negligible; gradient 60%; ground clearance 19 in (48.0 cm); the VXB is fully amphibious, being driven in the water by its wheels

Engine: one 160-bhp Berliet V800 inline diesel engine
Armament: a wide variety of armament installations is possible, ranging from a one-man turret fitted with a 20-mm cannon or a machine-gun, to one or more machine-guns on simple mounts on top of the hull
Armour: $\frac{3}{10}$ in (7 mm)
Used also by: France and various African nations
Notes: Although used in metropolitan France only by the *Gendarmerie*, the VXB is a useful and versatile vehicle, easy to maintain and with a good cross-country performance. It can readily be used as a cargo carrier, ambulance and in a number of other roles.

M-1924/29 machine-gun

Type: light machine-gun
Calibre: 7.5 mm
System of operation: gas
Muzzle velocity: 2,789 ft (850 m) per second
Range: effective 875 yards (800 m)
Rate of fire: 500 rounds per minute (cyclic); 125 rounds per minute (automatic)
Cooling system: air
Feed system: 26-round box
Dimensions: Barrel length 19.69 in (500 mm)
Overall length 42.6 in (1.082 m)
Width
Height
Weights: 20.82 lb (9.2 kg)
Sights: blade (fore) and tangent (rear)
Ammunition: 7.5 mm × 54
Used by: a number of ex-French colonies
Notes: This weapon, of Chatellerault design, might more properly be described as an automatic rifle, and proved very effective in this role in the hands of the Viet Cong and North Vietnamese Army in the Vietnam War. The weapon has a bipod attached to the barrel just in front of the gas cylinder, and can also be fitted with an adjustable

monopod under the stock. There is also a heavier version, the M-1931A, which is usually tripod-mounted.

Sierra Leone

2,000 men.

2 inf bns.
10 MOWAG armd cars; 60mm, 81mm mor.

Singapore

30,000 men and 45,000 reservists.

1 armd bde (1 tk, 2 APC bns).
4 inf bdes (9 inf, 5 arty, 3 engr, 3 sigs bns).
75 AMX-13 tks; 250 M-113, 30 V-100, 250 V-200 Commando APC; 60 155mm how; 50 120mm mor; 90 106mm RCL. (294 M-113 APC on order.)

Reserves: 45,000, 18 reserve battalions.

Para-Military Forces: 7,500 police/ marine police; Gurkha guard units; 30,000 Home Guard.

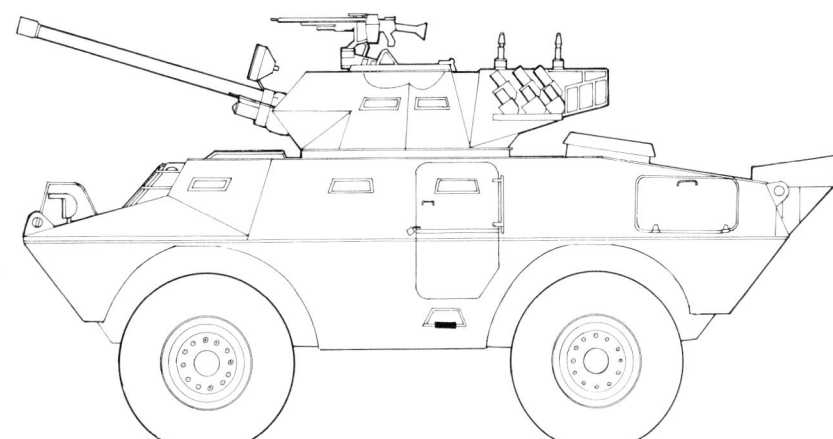

Cadillac Gage V-150 Commando

Type: utility armoured vehicle
Crew: three, plus up to nine infantrymen
Weights: Empty 15,035 lb (6,820 kg)
Loaded 21,055 lb (9,550 kg)
Dimensions: Length 18 ft 8 in (5.689 m)
Width 7 ft 5 in (2.26 m)
Height 6 ft 2 in (1.88 m)
Ground pressure:
Performance: road speed 55 mph (88.5 kph); water speed 3 mph (4.8 kph); range 300 miles (483 km); vertical obstacle 24 in (60.9 cm); trench negligible; gradient 60%; ground clearance 25 in (63.5 cm); the Commando is fully amphibious, being driven in the water by its wheels
Engine: one 210-bhp inline petrol engine
Armament: see notes
Armour: about $\frac{1}{2}$ in (12 mm) maximum
Used also by: Bolivia, Ethiopia, Laos, Lebanon, Malaysia, Oman, Peru, Saudi Arabia, Somali Republic, Sudan, Turkey, USA, Vietnam and several other nations
Notes: The V-150 Commando, introduced in 1971, has replaced the older V-100 and V-200, and can be used as the basis for a number of vehicles. Drive is either 4 × 2 or 4 × 4, and night vision equipment can be fitted if required. All vehicles have 'run-flat' tyres, and a winch with a capacity of 10,060 lb (4,563 kg). The following types are in service:
1. Armoured personnel carrier, with a pintle-mounted 0.3-in or 7.62-mm machine-gun with 3,200 rounds. The technical specification above applies to this model
2. Twin combination machine-gun turret model, with a single-man turret fitted with two 0.3-in or 7.62-mm machine-guns, or a combination of 0.3-in, 7.62-mm and 0.5-in machine-guns. Ammunition stowage naturally varies with the weapons fitted, but a twin 7.62-mm installation would have 3,800 rounds. This model carries only seven infantrymen, weight is 18,600 lb (8,437 kg), and height is 8 ft 4 in (2.54 m)
3. Twin combination machine-gun turret model, with a turret of better ballistic shape than the previous model's turret, but with the same armament capabilities. Ammunition stowage in this model is 700 rounds of 0.5-in and 2,400 rounds of 7.62-mm ammunition. This model carries seven infantrymen, weight is 19,300 lb (8,754 kg), and height is 8 ft 6 in (2.59 m)
4. 20-mm turret model, with a 20-mm Oerlikon cannon and a co-axial 7.62-mm machine-gun, with 400 and 3,200 rounds respectively. Only five infantrymen are carried, weight is 20,100 lb (9,525 kg), height is 8 ft 4 in (2.54 m)
5. 76-mm turret model, with a British 76-mm L23A1 gun and a co-axial 0.3-in or 7.62-mm machine-gun with 41 and 3,600 rounds of ammunition respectively. Six infantrymen are carried, weight is 20,100 lb (9,525 kg), height is 8 ft 1 in (2.463 m)
6. 90-mm turret model, with a 90-mm Mecar gun, a co-axial 7.62-mm machine-gun and a 7.62-mm AA machine-gun on the roof. Some 41 rounds of 90-mm and 2,600 rounds of 7.62-mm ammunition are carried. Infantry accommodation is three, weight is 21,100 lb (9,525 kg), height is 8 ft 4 in (2.54 m)
7. 81-mm mortar model, with an 81-mm M29 mortar with 62 rounds
8. TOW model, with a TOW launcher and seven missiles
9. Command model, with additional radio equipment
10. Base security model, with bi-fold doors
11. Police emergency rescue model, which has a fixed armoured pod on the roof like the two previous models, and 13 gun ports
12. Recovery model, with a 25,000-lb (11,340-kg) winch and a 10,000-lb (4,536-kg) A-frame crane. Like the command and base security models, armament is one 7.62-mm machine-gun.

Soltam M-1968 howitzer

Type: howitzer
Calibre: 155 mm
Barrel length: 33 cal
Muzzle velocity: 2,625 ft (800 m) per second
Ranges: Maximum 25,153 yards (23,000 m)
Minimum
Elevation: −3° to +52°
Traverse: 90° total (360° with extra equipment)
Rate of fire:
Weights: For travel 20,944 lb (9,500 kg)
In firing position
Dimensions: Length
Width
Height
Ammunition: HE
Crew: 10
Used only by: Singapore
Notes: The M-1968 is very similar to the Finnish Tampella M-1960. The HE shell weighs 96.34 lb (43.7 kg), and the ammunition is of the separate loading type.

Somali Republic

50,000 men (and 20,000 militia).

3 div HQ.
20 bde HQ.
7 tk bns.
8 mech inf bns.
14 mot inf bns.
16 inf bns.
2 cdo bns.
13 fd, 10 AA arty bns.
50 T-34, 30 T-54/-55 med tks; BRDM-2 scout cars; 50 BTR-40/-50/-60, 100 BTR-152 APC; about 100 76mm, 85mm, 80 122mm, 130mm guns/how; 81mm mor; 100mm ATK guns; 106mm RCL; Milan ATGW; 150 14.5mm, 37mm, 57mm and 100mm towed, ZSU-23-4 SP AA guns; SA-2/-3 SAM.

Para-Military Forces: 29,500; 8,000 Police; 1,500 border guards; 20,000 People's Militia.

M-1938 (M-30) howitzer

Type: field howitzer
Calibre: 122 mm
Barrel length: 22.7 cal
Muzzle velocity: 1,690 ft (515 m) per second
Ranges: Maximum 12,904 yards (11,800 m)
Minimum
Elevation: −3° to +63.5°
Traverse: 49° total
Rate of fire: five or six rounds per minute
Weights: For travel
In firing position 5,512 lb (2,500 kg)
Dimensions: Length 19 ft 4$\frac{1}{4}$ in (5.9 m)
Width 6 ft 5$\frac{3}{4}$ in (1.975 m)
Height 5 ft 11$\frac{2}{3}$ in (1.82 m)

Ammunition: Chemical, HE, HEAT, Illuminating and Smoke
Crew: eight
Used also by: Albania, Algeria, Bulgaria, China, Cuba, Czechoslovakia, East Germany, Egypt, Finland, Hungary, Iraq, Lebanon, Libya, North Korea, Poland, Romania, USSR, Vietnam, Yugoslavia
Notes: The M-1938 field howitzer was introduced into Russian divisions in 1938. The HE shell weighs 48 lb (21.8 kg), while the HEAT projectile weighs 31 lb (14.1 m). The HEAT round can penetrate 7.87 in (200 mm) of armour at 689 yards (630 m).

South Africa

50,000 men (43,000 conscripts) and 138,000 reservists.

1 corps, 2 div HQ (1 armd, 1 inf).
1 armd bde.*
2 mech bdes.*
4 mot bdes.*
3 para bns.*
11 fd and 1 med arty regts.*

9 lt AA arty regts.*
10 fd engr sqns.*
5 sigs regts.*
Some 150 Centurion, 20 Comet med, 90 M-41 lt tks; 1,400 Eland (AML-60/-90), Mk IV armd cars; 230 scout cars incl Ferret, M-3A1; 280 Saracen, *Ratel* APC; 500 lt APC incl Hippo, Rhino; 125 25-pdr, 5.5-

in towed, 50 Sexton 25-pdr SP guns, 81mm, 120mm mor; 15 17-pdr, 900 90mm ATK guns; SS-11, *Entac* ATGW; 204GK 20mm, 55 K-63 twin 35mm, 25 L/70 40mm, 15 3.7-in AA guns; 18 Cactus (*Crotale*), Tigercat SAM.

* Cadre units, forming 2 divs when brought to full strength on mobilization of Citizen Force.

Ratel 20

Type: armoured personnel carrier
Crew: two, plus up to eight infantry
Weights: Empty 33,069 lb (15,000 kg)
Loaded 37,478 lb (17,000 kg)
Dimensions: Length
Width
Height
Ground pressure:
Performance: road speed 65 mph (105 kph); wading 47¼ in (1.2 m) without preparation

Engine: one inline diesel engine
Armament: one turret-mounted 20-mm cannon with a co-axial 7.62-mm machine-gun, plus one pintle-mounted 7.62-mm machine-gun at the rear of the hull
Armour:
Used only by: South Africa
Notes: The Ratel 20 has a fairly strong resemblance to the French VXB armoured personnel carrier, and has been tested with a 90-mm gun.

M7 'Priest'

Type: self-propelled howitzer
Crew: seven
Weights: Empty
Loaded 50,634 lb (22,967 kg)
Dimensions: Length 19 ft 9 in (6.02 m)
Width 9 ft 5 in (2.87 m)
Height 9 ft 7 in (2.92 m)
Ground pressure: 10.4 lb/in² (0.73 kg/cm²)

Performance: road speed 26 mph (42 kph); range 125 miles (200 km); vertical obstacle 24 in (61.0 cm); trench 7 ft 6 in (2.29 m); gradient 60%; wading 48 in (1.22 m)
Engine: one 340-hp Continental R-975 radial petrol engine
Armament: one 105-mm M2 howitzer with 69 rounds, plus one 0.5-in (12.7-mm) Browning M2 AA machine-gun with 300 rounds

Armour: ½ in (12.7-mm) minimum; 4½ in (114.5 mm) maximum
Used also by: Brazil
Notes: The 'Priest' (so nicknamed for the 'pulpit' for the AA machine-gun) entered service in 1942, and is based on the chassis of the M4 Sherman medium tank. The howitzer has a maximum range of 12,000 yards (10,973 m).

South Korea

560,000 men and 1,100,000 reservists.

1 mech div.
19 inf divs.
2 armd bdes.
5 special forces bdes.
2 AD bdes.
7 tk bns.
30 arty bns.
1 SSM bn with Honest John.
2 SAM bdes with Improved HAWK and Nike Hercules.
M-60, 880 M-47/-48 med tks; 500 M-113/-577, 20 Fiat 6614 APC; 2,000 105mm, 155mm, 203mm towed, M-107 175mm and M-110 203mm SP guns/how; 5,300 81mm and 107mm mor; Honest John SSM; M-18 76mm SP ATK guns; 57mm, 75mm, 106mm RCL; TOW, LAW ATGW; Vulcan 20mm, 40mm AA guns; 80 HAWK, 45 Nike Hercules

SAM; 14 O-2A ac; 44 OH-6A, 5 KH-4 helicopters. (150 Fiat 6614 APC; TOW ATGW, 56 OH-6A helicopters on order.)

Para-Military Forces: A local defence militia, 1,000,000 Homeland Defence Reserve Force.

M18 Hellcat

Type: tank destroyer
Crew: five
Weights: Empty
Loaded 37,557 lb (17,036 kg)
Dimensions: Length 21 ft 10 in (6.65 m)
Width 9 ft 5 in (2.87 m)
Height 8 ft 5 in (2.58 m)
Ground pressure: 11.9 lb/in² (0.84 kg/cm²)
Performance: road speed 55 mph (88 kph); range 105 miles (168 km); vertical obstacle 36 in (91.0 cm); trench 6 ft 2 in (1.88 m); gradient 60%; wading 48 in (1.22 m)
Engine: one 400-hp Continental R-975-C4 radial petrol engine
Armament: one 76-mm M1A1 gun with 45 rounds, plus one 0.5-in (12.7-mm) Browning M2 machine-gun on the turret top for AA defence with 1,000 rounds
Armour: ³⁄₁₆ in (7.9 mm) minimum; 1 in (25.4 mm) maximum
Used also by: Venezuela, Yugoslavia
Notes: The M18 entered US service in 1944.

South Yemen

19,000 men.

10 inf bdes, each of 3 bns.
2 armd bns.
5 arty bns.
1 sigs unit.
1 trg bn.
260 T-34, T-54 med tks; 10 Saladin armd cars; 10 Ferret scout cars; BTR-40/-152 APC; 25-pdr, 105mm pack, 122mm, 130mm how; 120mm mor; 122mm RCL; 37mm, 57mm, 85mm, ZSU-23-4 SP AA guns; SA-7 SAM.

Para-Military Forces: Popular Militia; 15,000 Public Security Force.

M-1950 (S-60) gun

Type: light anti-aircraft gun
Calibre: 57 mm
Barrel length: 77 cal including muzzle brake
Muzzle velocity: 3,280 ft (1,000 m) per second
Ranges: Maximum (horizontal) 13,123 yards (12,000 m); (vertical) 26,246 ft (8,000 m)
Minimum
Elevation: −5° to +85°
Traverse: 360°
Rate of fire: 120 rounds per minute (cyclic)
Weights: For travel 10,273 lb (4,660 kg)
In firing position 9,921 lb (4,500 kg)
Dimensions: Length 27 ft 10⅔ in (8.5 m)
Width 6 ft 8¾ in (2.054 m)
Height 7 ft 9¼ in (2.37 m)
Ammunition: APHE and HE
Crew: seven

Used also by: Albania, Algeria, Bulgaria, China, Congo, Czechoslovakia, East Germany, Egypt, Indonesia, Iran, Iraq, Kampuchea, Libya, Mongolia, North Korea, Pakistan, Poland, Romania, Somali Republic, Syria, Vietnam, Yugoslavia
Notes: The S-60 was introduced to Russian service in 1950, and was developed from the German Type 58 55-mm L/70.7 gun. The weapon is used in the ZSU-57 SP AA gun. Ammunition feed is from four-round clips, the APHE round weighing 6.83 lb (3.1 kg) and the HE round 6.17 lb (2.8 kg). The APHE round will penetrate 4.17 in (106 mm) of armour at 547 yards (500 m). Effective AA ranges are 13,123 feet (4,000 m) with the weapon's own fire-control system, and 19,685 ft (6,000 m) with external fire-control equipment.

Spain

240,000 men (150,000 conscripts) and 700,000 reservists.

About 70 per cent strength: 1 armd div, 1 mech inf div, 1 mot inf div, 2 mountain divs, 1 armd cav bde, 10 indep inf bdes.
1 mountain bde.
1 airportable bde.
1 para bde.
2 arty bdes.
10 mixed AA/coast arty regts.
3 Foreign Legion regts.
3 *Regulares* regts (local forces in Ceuta/Melilla).
1 SAM bn with Nike Hercules and HAWK.
200 AMX-30, 480 M-47/-48 med, 180 M-41 lt tks; 88 AML-60, 100 AML-90 armd cars; 375 M-113 APC; 860 105mm, 200 122mm, 80 155mm, 24 203mm towed, 48 M-108 105mm, 70 M-44, 70 M-109 155mm, 12 M-107 175mm, 4 M-110 203mm SP guns/how; 216mm, 300mm, 381mm multiple RL; 60mm, 800 81mm, 300 120mm mor; 90mm, 106mm RCL; SS-11, Milan, Cobra ATGW; 54 35mm, 280 40mm, 150 90mm AA guns; 200 88mm, 6-in, 12-in, 15-in coast arty guns; Nike Hercules, Improved HAWK SAM; 10 CH-47C, 3 Puma, 65 UH-1B/H, 5 *Alouette* III, 1 AB-206A, 15 OH-13, 15 OH-58A helicopters.
(60 M-60 tks; 102 M-113 APC; Dragon, TOW ATGW; 38 Skyguard AD systems; 18 OH-58A, 8 UH-1H helicopters on order.)

Deployment: Balearics: 6,000. Canaries: 16,000. Ceuta/Melilla: 18,000.

Para-Military Forces: 65,000 Guardia Civil, 38,000 Policía Armada.

LVTP-7

Type: amphibious assault vehicle
Crew: three, plus up to 25 infantrymen
Weights: Empty 40,250 lb (18,257 kg)
Loaded 52,150 lb (23,655 kg)
Dimensions: Length 26 ft 0¾ in (7.94 m)
Width 10 ft 6 in (3.2 m)

Height 10 ft 3 in (3.12 m)
Ground pressure: 7.68 lb/in² (0.54 kg/cm²)
Performance: road speed 40 mph (64 kph); water speed 8.4 mph (13.5 kph); road range 300 miles (483 km); water range 55 miles (88.5 km); vertical obstacle 36 in (91.4 cm); trench 7 ft 10½ in (2.4 m); gradient 60%; the LVTP-7 is inherently am-

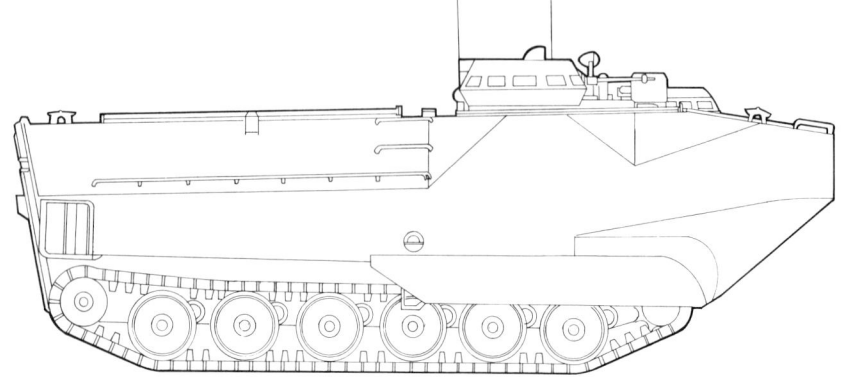

phibious, being driven in the water by
waterjets

Engine: one 406-bhp General Motors Corporation 8V53T turbo-charged inline diesel
engine

Armament: one 12.7-mm M85 machine-gun
in a forward turret, with 1,000 rounds

Armour: aluminium, $\frac{3}{10}$ in (7 mm) minimum;
$1\frac{1}{5}$ in (30 mm) maximum

Used also by: Italy, Thailand, USA

Notes: The Landing Vehicle Tracked Personnel (LVTP) 7 was introduced to service in
1971, and is a formidable amphibious assault craft, with high speed in and out of the
water, the capacity for 25 troops or 9,920
lb (4,500 kg) of cargo, the ability to come
ashore through surf 9 ft 10 in (3.0 m) high,

and sufficient protection and fire-power to
accompany troops in combat. There are
several versions:
1. LVTP-7 basic personnel carrier
2. LVTR-7 recovery vehicle
3. LVTC-7 command and communications vehicle, with extra radio
equipment, mapboards and the like
4. LVTE-7 mine and obstacle clearing
vehicle (not in service).

105-mm/46 howitzer

Type: field howitzer
Calibre: 105 mm
Barrel length: 31.9 cal
Muzzle velocity: 1,654 ft (504 m) per second
with Spanish ammunition

Ranges: Maximum 12,522 yards (11,450 m)
Minimum
Elevation: −5° to +45°
Traverse: 50° total
Rate of fire: four rounds per minute
Weights: For travel
In firing position 4,299 lb (1,950
kg)
Dimensions: Length 19 ft 11$\frac{2}{5}$ in (6.08 m)
Width 6 ft 10$\frac{7}{10}$ in (2.1 m)
Height
Ammunition: HE

Crew:
Used only by: Spain
Notes: The howitzer was developed from the
earlier M-1943 weapon, still used for training. Maximum effective range with Spanish
and American ammunition is 9,296 yards
(8,500 m).

75-mm gun

Type: anti-tank gun
Calibre: 75 mm
Barrel length: 46 cal
Muzzle velocity: 2,526 ft (770 m) per second
with APC
Ranges: Maximum 8,421 yards (7,700 m)
with HE
Minimum

Elevation: −5° to +22°
Traverse: 65° total
Rate of fire:
Weights: For travel
In firing position 3,142 lb (1,425
kg)
Dimensions: Length 19 ft 2 in (5.84 m)
Width
Height
Ammunition: APC, HE and HEAT

Crew:
Used only by: Spain
Notes: This is the standard AT gun used by
Spanish infantry units. The APC round
weighs 26.23 lb (11.9 kg), the HE round
20.06 lb (9.1 kg), and the HEAT round
17.12 lb (7.8 kg).

D-3 artillery rocket

Type: artillery rocket
Calibre: 300 mm
Barrel length:
Muzzle velocity:
Ranges: Maximum 18,591 yards (17,000 m)
Minimum
Elevation:
Traverse:
Rate of fire:
Weights: For travel
In firing position 545.6 lb (247.5
kg)
Dimensions: Length 6 ft 2$\frac{3}{4}$ in (1.898 m)
Span
Body diameter 11$\frac{4}{5}$ in (300
mm)
Ammunition: HE, Incendiary or Smoke war-
heads
Crew:
Used only by: Spain
Notes: The D-3 rocket is used in the Spanish
D-10 system, which has 10 rockets (two
rows of five) mounted on the rear of a 6 × 6
lorry. The rocket has a warhead weighing
197 lb (89.4 kg) in the HE version.

E-3 artillery rocket

Type: artillery rocket
Calibre: 216 mm
Barrel length:
Muzzle velocity:
Ranges: Maximum 15,857 yards (14,500 m)
Minimum
Elevation:
Traverse:
Rate of fire:
Weights: For travel
In firing position 222.66 lb (101 kg)
Dimensions: Length 4 ft 7$\frac{1}{3}$ in (1.406 m)
Span
Body diameter 8$\frac{1}{2}$ in (216 mm)
Ammunition: HE, Incendiary or Smoke war-
heads
Crew:
Used only by: Spain
Notes: The E-3 artillery rocket is used in the
E-21 system, which has a cage with three
rows of seven launchers for the E-3,
mounted at the rear of a 6 × 6 lorry. The E-
3 in its HE form has a warhead of 82.67 lb
(37.5 kg). The cage unit of the E-21 system
can be traversed 90°, and the reloading of
the cage takes 14 minutes.

R6B2 artillery rocket

Type: artillery rocket
Calibre: 108 mm
Barrel length:
Muzzle velocity:
Ranges: Maximum 10,936 yards (10,000 m)
Minimum
Elevation:
Traverse:
Rate of fire:
Weights: For travel
In firing position 42.77 lb (19.4 kg)
Dimensions: Length 3 ft 0 in (0.935 m)
Span
Body diameter 4$\frac{1}{4}$ in (108 mm)
Ammunition: HE, Incendiary or Smoke war-
heads
Crew:
Used only by: Spain
Notes: The R6B2 rocket, which has an HE
warhead weighing 19.4 lb (8.8 kg), is used
in the E-32 system. This has a launcher
cage for 32 rockets in four rows of eight on
the back of a 4 × 4 lorry. The cage unit tra-
verses 45°.

M-1965 launcher

Type: man-portable anti-tank rocket launcher
Calibre: 88.9 mm
Barrel length:
Muzzle velocity: 755 ft (230 m) per second
with CH M66
Ranges: Maximum 2,734 yards (2,500 m)
with CH M66
Minimum
Elevation:
Traverse:
Rate of fire:

Weights: For travel 11.9 lb (5.4 kg)
In firing position 18.74 lb (8.5 kg)
with MB 66
Dimensions: Length 5 ft 3 in (1.6 m)
Width
Height
Ammunition: Anti-personnel (MB 66), Anti-
tank (CH M66) and Incendiary (FI M66),
plus Practice (MI 66)
Crew: two
Used only by: Spain
Notes: The M-1965 is a Spanish designed
and produced rocket launcher of the ba-

zooka' type. The CH M66 AT round weighs
4.4 lb (2 kg), and can penetrate 13 in (330
mm) of armour at a maximum effective
range of 492 yards (450 m). The MB 66
rocket weighs 6.83 lb (3.1 kg), and can
penetrate 9.84 in (250 mm) of armour at
328 yards (300 m).

ECIA Model L mortar (120-mm)

Type: heavy mortar
Calibre: 120 mm
Barrel length: 13.33 cal
Muzzle velocity:
Ranges: Maximum 7,283 yards (6,660 m)
    with L bomb; 6,234 yards (5,700 m)
    with N bomb
    Minimum

Elevation: 45° to 85.5°
Traverse:
Rate of fire: 12 rounds per minute
Weights: For travel 697 lb (316 kg)
    In firing position 470 lb (213 kg)
Dimensions: Length
    Width
    Height
Ammunition: HE and Smoke
Crew: four

Used only by: Spain
Notes: The Model L is a standard mortar, designed for travel on a wheeled carriage. Two HE rounds are used: round L and round N. The former weighs 29.09 lb (13.195 kg) with 5.16 lb (2.34 kg) of explosive, and the latter weighs 36.94 lb (16.754 kg) with 7 lb (3.175 kg) of explosive.

ECIA Model SL mortar (120-mm)

Type: heavy mortar
Calibre: 120 mm
Barrel length: 13.33 cal
Muzzle velocity:
Ranges: Maximum 5,468 yards (5,000 m)
    with N bomb; 6,496 yards (5,940 m)
    with L bomb
    Minimum
Elevation:
Traverse:
Rate of fire: 12 rounds per minute
Weights: For travel 567 lb (257 kg)
    In firing position 271 lb (123 kg)
Dimensions: Length
    Width
    Height
Ammunition: HE and Smoke
Crew: four
Used only by: Spain
Notes: The Model SL is basically a smaller version of the Model L, with a shorter and lighter barrel, and lighter baseplate. It fires the same ammunition as the Model L.

ECIA Model L mortar (105-mm)

Type: medium mortar
Calibre: 105 mm
Barrel length: 14.29 cal
Muzzle velocity:
Ranges: Maximum 7,710 yards (7,050 m)
    Minimum
Elevation:
Traverse:
Rate of fire: 12 rounds per minute
Weights: For travel 476 lb (216 kg)
    In firing position 231 lb (105 kg)
Dimensions: Length
    Width
    Height
Ammunition: HE and Smoke
Crew: three
Used only by: Spain
Notes: The Model L 105-mm mortar is a light, easily transported mortar, firing an HE round weighing 20.3 lb (9.2 kg).

ECIA Model L (81-mm)

Type: light mortar
Calibre: 81.35 mm
Barrel length: 17.82 cal or 14.14 cal
Muzzle velocity:
Ranges: Maximum 5,031 yards (4,600 m)
    with long barrel; 4,511 yards (4,125 m) with short barrel
    Minimum
Elevation:
Traverse:
Rate of fire: 15 rounds per minute
Weights: For travel
    In firing position 99 lb (45 kg) with long barrel; 95 lb (43 kg) with short barrel
Dimensions: Length
    Width
    Height
Ammunition: HE and Smoke
Crew: three
Used only by: Spain
Notes: The 81-mm mortar appears in two models, both having the unusual feature of a tripod to support the barrel. The two models have barrels of different lengths, but are otherwise almost identical. The HE round (NA bomb) weighs 7.05 lb (3.2 kg), but there is available the N bomb, which weighs 9.1 lb (4.13 kg) and increases range of the long-barrelled model to 5,687 yards (5,200 m), and of the short-barrelled model to 4,670 yards (4,270 m).

ECIA Model C Commando mortar

Type: light mortar
Calibre: 60 mm
Barrel length: 10.83 cal
Muzzle velocity:
Ranges: Maximum 1,170 yards (1,070 m)
    Minimum

Elevation:
Traverse:
Rate of fire: 30 rounds per minute
Weights: For travel
    In firing position 13.67 lb (6.2 kg)
Dimensions: Length
    Width
    Height

Ammunition: HE and Smoke
Crew: one
Used only by: Spain
Notes: The Commando is a light, smooth-bore weapon for one-man use, and intended for close-range infantry actions. The HE bomb weighs 3.15 lb (1.43 kg).

ECIA Model L mortar (60-mm)

Type: light mortar
Calibre: 60 mm
Barrel length: 10.83 cal
Muzzle velocity:
Ranges: Maximum 2,160 yards (1,975 m)
　　　　Minimum
Elevation: about 49.5° to 89.5°
Traverse:
Rate of fire: 15 to 30 rounds per minute
Weights: For travel 33 lb (14.96 kg)
　　　　In firing position 25.26 lb (11.46 kg)
Dimensions: Length
　　　　Width
　　　　Height
Ammunition: HE and Smoke
Crew: one
Used only by: Spain
Notes: The 60-mm Model L is a light conventional mortar fired from a tripod barrel support. The HE bomb weighs 3.15 lb (1.43 kg).

Star Model Z62 sub-machine gun

Type: sub-machine gun
Calibre: 9 mm
System of operation: blowback
Muzzle velocity: 1,250 ft (381 m) per second with Parabellum
Range: effective 219 yards (200 m)
Rate of fire: 550 rounds per minute (cyclic); 120 rounds per minute (automatic)
Cooling system: air
Feed system: 20-, 30-, or 40-round box
Dimensions: Barrel length 7.91 in (201 mm)
　　　　Overall length 27.6 in (701 mm) with stock extended; 18.9 in (480 mm) with stock folded
　　　　Width
　　　　Height
Weights: 6.33 lb (2.87 kg) empty; 7.83 lb (3.55 kg) with 30 rounds loaded
Sights: blade (fore) and flip, aperture (rear)
Ammunition: 9 mm × 19 Parabellum, or 9 mm × 23 Bergmann Bayard (Largo)
Used only by: Spain
Notes: The Z62 is of Spanish design and manufacture, and is intended as the replacement for the Z45. The weapon has excellent safety features, and makes considerable use of pressings and plastic components. The Z62 has been supplemented by the Z70/B, which has an improved trigger mechanism but otherwise remains identical with the Z62.

C2 sub-machine gun

Type: sub-machine gun
Calibre: 9 mm
System of operation: blowback
Muzzle velocity: 1,066 ft (325 m) per second with Parabellum: 1,115 ft (340 m) per second with Largo
Range: effective 219 yards (200 m)
Rate of fire: 600 rounds per minute (cyclic)
Cooling system: air
Feed system: 32-round box
Dimensions: Barrel length 8.35 in (212 mm)
　　　　Overall length 28.35 in (720 mm) with stock extended; 19.69 in (500 mm) with stock folded
　　　　Width
　　　　Height
Weights: 5.84 lb (2.65 kg) empty
Sights: blade (fore) and flip (rear)
Ammunition: 9 mm × 19 Parabellum, or 9 mm × 23 Bergmann Bayard (Largo)
Used only by: Spain
Notes: The C2 is of Spanish design, and is intended as a small sub-machine gun in which the balance is good enough for one-hand firing if necessary. Mechanically, the C2 is similar to the Z62.

CETME Model C rifle

Type: selective fire assault rifle
Calibre: 7.62 mm
System of operation: delayed blowback
Muzzle velocity: 2,560 ft (780 m) per second
Range: effective 656 yards (600 m)
Rate of fire: 550 to 650 rounds per minute (cyclic)
Cooling system: air
Feed system: 20-round box
Dimensions: Barrel length 17.72 in (450 mm)
　　　　Overall length 39.96 in (1.015 m)
　　　　Width
　　　　Height
Weights: 9.92 lb (4.5 kg) with bipod and metal handguard
Sights: protected blade (fore) and leaf with V notch (rear)
Ammunition: 7.62 mm × 51
Used only by: Spain
Notes: The CETME Model C assault rifle uses the standard NATO round, and is fitted with a flash eliminator/grenade launcher, with provision for infra-red sights. There are two models, the standard version having no bipod and a wooden handguard, and the other version a fitted bipod and metal handguard.

CETME Model L rifle

Type: selective fire assault rifle
Calibre: 5.56 mm
System of operation: delayed blowback
Muzzle velocity: 3,018 ft (920 m) per second for the standard model; 2,789 ft (850 m) per second for the short-barrel model
Range:
Rate of fire: 700 to 800 rounds per minute (cyclic)
Cooling system: air

Feed system: 10-, 20- or 30-round box
Dimensions: Barrel length 15.75 in (400 mm) for standard model; 12.6 in (320 mm) for short-barrel model
Overall length 36.4 in (925 mm) for standard model; 33.86/26.18 in (860/665 mm) for short-barrel model with stock extended/contracted
Width
Height
Weights: 7.5 lb (3.4 kg) unloaded for standard model

Sights: protected post (fore) and disc with notch or apertures (rear)
Ammunition: 5.56 mm × 45
Used by: under development for Spain
Notes: The CETME Model L is an interesting development in the new 5.56-mm calibre, with automatic, semi-automatic and limited-burst fire capabilities. There are two versions, a standard model with a fixed stock, and a short-barrel model with a telescopic stock. A bipod and telescopic sight can be fitted.

Sri Lanka

8,900 men and 12,000 reservists.

1 bde of 3 bns.
1 recce regt.
1 arty regt.
1 engr regt.
1 sigs regt.
6 Saladin armd cars, 30 Ferret scout cars; 10 BTR-152 APC; 76mm, 85mm guns.

Reserves: 12,000; 7 bns, supporting services and a Pioneer Corps.

Para-Military Forces: 14,500 Police Force, 4,500 Volunteer Force.

Sudan

50,000 men.

2 armd bdes.
7 inf bdes.
1 para bde.
3 arty regts.
3 AD arty regts.
1 engr regt.
70 T-54, 60 T-55 med tks; 30 T-62 lt tks (Chinese); 50 Saladin armd cars; 60 Ferret scout cars; 100 BTR-40/-

50/-152, 60 OT-64, 49 Saracen, 45 Commando APC; 55 25-pdr, 40 100mm, 20 105mm, 18 122mm guns/how; 30 120mm mor; 30 85mm ATK guns; 80 40mm, 80 37mm, 85mm AA guns.
(50 AMX-10 APC on order.)

Deployment: Lebanon (Arab Peace-keeping Force): 1,000.

Para-Military Forces: 3,500: 500 National Guard, 500 Republican Guard, 2,500 Border Guard.

Sweden

40,580 men (34,700 conscripts).*

Peace establishment:
47 non-operational armd, cav, inf, arty, AA, engr and sig trg regts for basic conscript trg.
War establishment:
5 armd bdes.
20 inf bdes.
4 Norrland bdes.
50 indep inf, arty and AA arty bns.
23 Local Defence Districts with 100 indep bns and 400–500 indep coys.
350 Strv 101, 102 (Centurion), 300 103B (S-tank) med, Ikv 91 lt tks; Pbv 302A APC; 105mm, 150mm, 155mm how; Bk 1A (L/50) 155mm SP guns; 81mm, 120mm mor; 90mm ATK guns; Carl Gustav 84mm, Miniman RCL; Bantam ATGW; 20mm, 40mm AA guns; Redeye, RBS-70, HAWK SAM; 20 Sk-61 (Bulldog), 12 Super Cub ac; 15 HKP-3 (AB-204B), 19 HKP-6 (JetRanger) helicopters. (Ikv 91 lt tanks, FH77

155mm how, TOW ATGW, Improved HAWK SAM on order.)

Deployment: Cyprus (UNFICYP): 427; Egypt (UNEF): 687; Lebanon (UNIFIL): 216.

* There are normally some 120,000 more conscripts (105,000 army, 10,000 navy, 5,000 air force) plus 15,000 officer and NCO reservists doing 18–40 days refresher training at some time in the year.

Bofors Strv 103

Type: main battle tank

Crew: three

Weights: Empty 81,570 lb (37,000 kg)
Loaded 85,979 lb (39,000 kg)

Dimensions: Length (overall) 32 ft 1⁴⁄₅ in (9.8 m); (hull) 27 ft 6¾ in (8.4 m); Width 11 ft 9¾ in (3.6 m); Height 7 ft (2.14 m)

Ground pressure: 13.37 lb/in² (0.94 kg/cm²)

Performance: road speed 31 mph (50 kph); water speed 3.7 mph (6 kph); range 242 miles (390 km); trench 7 ft 6½ in (2.3 m); gradient 30°; wading 4 ft 11 in (1.5 m) without preparation; ground clearance 19¾ in (50.0 cm)

Engine: one 240-bhp Rolls-Royce K.60 inline multi-fuel engine, and one 490-bhp Boeing 553 gas turbine

Armament: one 105-mm L7A1 L/62 gun with 50 rounds of APDS, HE and Smoke, plus two 7.62-mm FN machine-guns on a pack on the left track guard, and one 7.62-mm FN AA machine-gun on the commander's cupola

Armour:

Used only by: Sweden

Notes: *Stridsvagn* 103, otherwise known as the S-tank, has been one of the most advanced and interesting AFVs in the world since its introduction to service in 1967. Unique among modern tanks, the Strv 103 has no turret: the gun is located in the hull with an automatic loader. This reduces the crew from four to three, lowers the silhouette of the vehicle, allows a very flat glacis plate of good ballistic performance to be fitted, and reduces the overall weight of the vehicle. The Strv 103 has hydro-

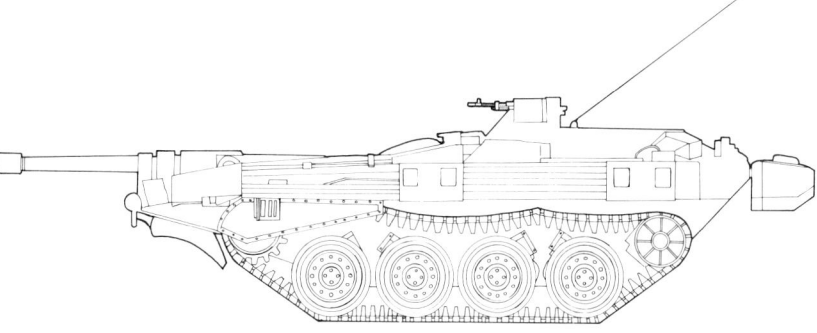

pneumatic suspension, and it is this that allows the extraordinary gun system: for the gun is elevated and depressed between +12° and −10° by altering the relative heights of the vehicle's suspension at front and rear. Traverse of the main armament is effected by slewing the tank on its tracks for fine traverse after the tank has halted in approximately the right direction. Ranging is effected by either an optical or a laser rangefinder. Night vision equipment for the driver is standard, and a flotation screen (that can be erected in 15 minutes) is fitted, but there is no provision for NBC protection. Reloading of the magazine from outside can be carried out in 10 minutes, and with the automatic loader the rate of fire is some 12 rounds per minute. The radio operator faces the rear, and also acts as emergency get-away driver. The commander/gunner can also drive the tank on his own. There have been two versions, the Strv 103A with less power and no flotation screen, and the Strv 103B, with a flotation

screen and the engines quoted in the technical specification above. All Strv 103A vehicles have now been brought up to Strv 103B standard. The diesel engine can be started in cold weather by the gas turbine. The vehicle can move under the power of either engine, but both engines are needed for the fine traverse of the main armament.

Hägglund & Söner Ikv 91

Type: light tank
Crew: four
Weights: Empty
    Loaded 34,171 lb (15,500 kg)
Dimensions: Length (hull) 21 ft (6.41 m)
    Width 9 ft 10 in (3.0 m)
    Height (overall) 7 ft 8¾ in
    (2.355 m)
Ground pressure: 6.4 lb/in² (0.45 kg/cm²)
Performance: road speed 43 mph (69 kph);
    water speed 4.3 mph (7 kph); range 342
    miles (550 km); trench 9 ft 2¼ in (2.8 m);
    gradient 30°
Engine: one 330-bhp Volvo-Penta turbo-
    charged inline diesel engine
Armament: one 90-mm Bofors L/54 gun
    with 59 rounds of HE and HEAT, plus
    one 7.62-mm machine-gun mounted co-
    axial with the main armament, and one
    7.62-mm machine-gun on the loader's
    hatch. Some 4,500 rounds of 7.62-mm
    ammunition are carried
Armour:

Used only by: Sweden
Notes: The *Infanterikanonvagn* (Ikv) 91 is
intended to provide infantry formations
with a mobile anti-tank system, and
combines a vehicle of excellent ballistic
shape with a low-pressure anti-tank gun
firing HEAT ammunition, a sophisticated
fire-control system using a laser rangefinder, and useful performance based on
an extremely low ground pressure. The
vehicle is fully amphibious without any
preparation. An NBC system is standard.

Hägglund & Söner Pbv 302

Type: armoured personnel carrier
Crew: two, plus up to 10 infantrymen
Weights: Empty
    Loaded 29,762 lb (13,500 kg)
Dimensions: Length 17 ft 6⅜ in (5.35 m)
    Width 9 ft 4¾ in (2.86 m)
    Height 8 ft 2⅖ in (2.5 m)
Ground pressure: 8.5 lb/in² (0.6 kg/cm²)
Performance: road speed 40 mph (65 kph);
    water speed 5 mph (8 kph); range 186

miles (300 km); vertical obstacle 23⅝ in
(60.0 cm); trench 4 ft 11 in (1.5 m); ground
clearance 15¾ in (40.0 cm); the Pbv 302 is
fully amphibious, driven in the water by its
tracks
Engine: one 280-bhp Volvo-Penta THD 100
    B turbo-charged inline diesel engine
Armament: one turret-mounted 20-mm
    Hispano-Suiza cannon with 505 rounds
Armour: ⅘ in (20 mm) maximum
Used only by: Sweden
Notes: The *Pansarbandvagn* (Pbv) 302 has

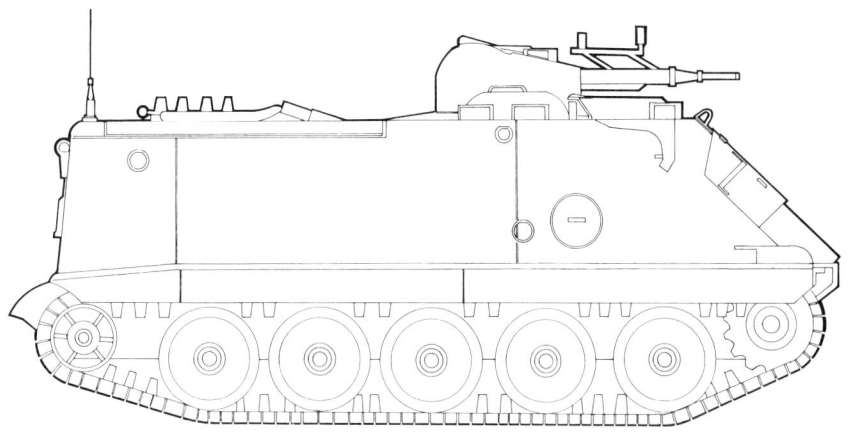

succeeded the intermediate Pbv 301 APC in Swedish Army service, and is one of the best APCs developed in recent years. It was introduced to service in 1967. Although the vehicle's armour is steel, the double-walled nature of this armour helps to make the Pbv 302 an inherent amphibian. With a minimum of alteration, the type can also be produced as an armoured command vehicle (Slpbv), observation post vehicle (Epbv) and fire-direction post vehicle (Bplpbv). There are two major variants:

1. Bgbv 82 armoured recovery vehicle, which weighs 57,320 lb (26,000 kg), is 22 ft 1¾ in (6.75 m) long and 10 ft 6⅘ in (3.21 m) wide. The Bgbv is

intended to recover heavy vehicles, and has a dozer blade, a crane and a 44,092-lb (20,000-kg) winch. A 310-bhp engine is fitted
2. Brobv 941 bridgelayer, which weighs 61,729 lb (28,000 kg) and can lay a 50-ton capacity bridge over gaps 49 ft (15 m) wide.

Bofors RB53 Bantam

Type: anti-tank missile, man-portable and container-launched
Guidance: command by means of wire
Dimensions: Span 15¾ in (40.0 cm)
　　　　　　Body diameter 4⅓ in (11.0 cm)
　　　　　　Length 2 ft 9½ in (85.0 cm)
Booster: Bofors solid-propellant rocket
Sustainer: Bofors solid-propellant rocket
Warhead: hollow-charge high explosive, 4.2 lb (1.9 kg), capable of penetrating more than 19.69 in (500 mm) of armour

Weights: Launch 16.53 lb (7.5 kg)
　　　　Burnt out
Performance: range less than 328 to 2,187 yards (300–2,000 m); speed 190 mph (305 kph)
Used also by: Argentina, Switzerland
Notes: Introduced in 1963, and can be operated by one man. It can also be fired from vehicles and slow aircraft.

Bofors RBS 70

Type: man-portable surface-to-air tactical guided missile
Guidance: laser beam-riding
Dimensions: Span
    Diameter $4\frac{1}{6}$ in (10.6 cm)
    Length 4 ft 4 in (1.32 m)

Booster: solid-propellant rocket
Sustainer: solid-propellant rocket
Warhead: high explosive
Weights: Launch (with container) 51.8 lb
    (23.5 kg)
    Burnt out
Performance: range 3 miles (5 km)
Used only by: Sweden

Notes: The RBS 70 consists of three man-portable loads: the missile in its container, the launch stand, and the sight. The system can be used on its own, or in conjunction with other similar units with the support of a radar system and IFF apparatus. Once he has acquired the target visually, the operator illuminates it with the laser in his sight, and fires the missile in the direction of the target. The missile's onboard computer then keeps the missile in the centre of the beam until detonation of the warhead.

Bofors FH77 howitzer

Type: field howitzer
Calibre: 155 mm
Barrel length:
Muzzle velocity:
Ranges: Maximum 24,059 yards (22,000 m)
Minimum
Elevation: −3° to +50°
Traverse: 60° total
Rate of fire: 15 rounds per minute
Weights: For travel 24,251 lb (11,000 kg)
In firing position
Dimensions: Length 25 ft 7 in (7.8 m)
Width 9 ft 0$\frac{1}{4}$ in (2.75 m)
Height 8 ft 2 in (2.5 m)
Ammunition: HE, Illuminating and Smoke
Crew: nine

Used only by: Sweden
Notes: The FH77 is an advanced howitzer of Swedish design, fitted with an auxiliary power unit to provide limited independent movement (at 5 mph/8 kph), to assist in towed cross-country movement, to assist in laying and traversing, and to provide power for the hydraulic ramming. This last makes possible the high rate of fire. The HE shell weighs 94.8 lb (43 kg), and is filled with a special high-power explosive.

Model F howitzer

Type: field howitzer
Calibre: 155 mm
Barrel length: 23 cal
Muzzle velocity: 2,133 ft (650 m) per second
Ranges: Maximum 19,357 yards (17,700 m)
Minimum
Elevation: −4° to +69°
Traverse: 82° total
Rate of fire: three or four rounds per minute
Weights: For travel 19,841 lb 9,000 kg)
In firing position 17,967 lb (8,150 kg)
Dimensions: Length 25 ft 7 in (7.8 m)
Width 9 ft 0$\frac{1}{4}$ in (2.75 m)
Height 8 ft 2$\frac{2}{3}$ in (2.5 m)

Ammunition: HE
Crew: nine
Used only by: Sweden
Notes: The Model F is the Swedish-built version of the French M-1950 155-mm howitzer, and fires a 96.45-lb (43.75-kg) shell. The weapon is heavy for its fire-power, and is more mobile than the SP version used by Israel, based on the chassis of the Sherman medium tank.

105-mm 4140 howitzer

Type: field howitzer
Calibre: 105 mm
Barrel length: 28 cal
Muzzle velocity: 1,991 ft (607 m) per second
Ranges: Maximum 15,967 yards (14,600 m)
Minimum
Elevation: −5° to +65°
Traverse: 360°
Rate of fire: eight rounds per minute (25 rounds per minute are possible for short periods)
Weights: For travel 6,614 lb (3,000 kg)
In firing position 6,173 lb (2,800 kg)
Dimensions: Length 22 ft 3$\frac{7}{10}$ in (6.8 m)
Width 5 ft 11$\frac{1}{4}$ in (1.81 m)
Height 6 ft 0$\frac{4}{5}$ in (1.85 m)

Ammunition: HE
Crew: six
Used also by: Switzerland
Notes: The model 4140 gun is built by Bofors, and is the standard Swedish medium field howitzer. The use of semi-fixed ammunition, and easy access to the breech, ensures a high rate of fire. The shell weighs 34.17 lb (15.5 kg).

PV-1110 recoilless gun

Type: anti-tank recoilless gun
Calibre: 90 mm
Barrel length: 41 cal
Muzzle velocity: 2,346 ft (715 m) per second
Ranges: Maximum 984 yards (900 m) effective
Minimum
Elevation: −10° to +15°
Traverse: 75° to 110° depending on elevation

Rate of fire: six rounds per minute
Weights: For travel 573 lb (260 kg)
In firing position
Dimensions: Length 13 ft 5$\frac{2}{5}$ in (4.1 m)
Width 4 ft 6 in (1.375 m)
Height 2 ft 10$\frac{1}{4}$ in (0.87 m)
Ammunition: hollow charge
Crew: two or three
Used also by: Eire
Notes: The PV-1110 is a powerful AT weapon of Swedish design. The whole round weighs 21.16 lb (9.6 kg), and the

projectile 6.83 lb (3.1 kg). This hollow-charge warhead is capable of penetrating 15 in (380 mm) of armour at 90° at 766 yards (700 m). Spotting is by a 7.62-mm rifle with a 10-round magazine.

Bofors M54 gun

Type: light AA gun mounting
Calibre: 57 mm
Barrel length: 60 cal
Muzzle velocity: 3,018 ft (920 m) per second
Ranges: Maximum (horizontal) 15,857 yards (14,500 m); (slant) 4,374 yards (4,000 m); (vertical) 6,562 ft (2,000 m)
Minimum
Elevation: −5° to +90°
Traverse: 360°

Rate of fire: 160 rounds per minute (cyclic)
Weights: For travel 17,857 lb (8,100 kg)
In firing position
Dimensions: Length 27 ft 8 in (8.435 m)
Width 7 ft 9 $\frac{7}{10}$ in (2.38 m)
Height 9 ft 2 $\frac{3}{8}$ in (2.81 m)
Ammunition: HE
Crew: six or more
Used also by: Belgium
Notes: The M54 is a Swedish weapon, and is derived from the 40-mm Bofors gun. The

shell weighs 5.73 lb (2.6 kg), and a high
rate of fire is possible for only a short time
because of the difficulty in keeping up an
adequate supply of ammunition.

M40-70 cannon

Type: AA cannon
Calibre: 20 mm
Barrel length: 70 cal
Muzzle velocity: 2,674 ft (815 m) per second
Ranges: Maximum (horizontal) 8,202 yards
(7,500 m); (vertical) 5,250 ft (1,600
m)
Minimum
Elevation: −5° to +35°
Traverse: 360°
Rate of fire: 360 rounds per minute (cyclic)
Weights: For travel
In firing position 1,102 lb (500 kg)
Dimensions: Length
Width
Height

Ammunition: HE
Crew: three
Used only by: Sweden
Notes: This Swedish weapon is used at brigade level, and has a basic design dating
back to the 1930s. This latest model has a
projectile weighing 0.32 lb (0.145 kg).

Bandkanon **1A**

Type: self-propelled gun
Crew: five
Weights: Empty
Loaded 112,435 lb (51,000 kg)
Dimensions: Length 36 ft 1 in (11.0 m)
Width 10 ft 10 in (3.3 m)
Height 10 ft 8 in (3.25 m)
Ground pressure:
Performance: road speed 17.4 mph (28 kph);
range 142 miles (230 km)
Engine: one 240-hp Rolls-Royce K.60 inline
multi-fuel engine, and one 300-hp Boeing
502-10 MA gas turbine engine
Armament: one 155-mm L/50 gun, plus one
7.62-mm machine-gun for local defence
Armour: $\frac{4}{5}$ in (20 mm) maximum
Used only by: Sweden
Notes: The *Bandkanon* 1A is a sophisticated
SP gun, with a fully automatic loading se-
quence from a 14-round magazine. This
allows a maximum rate of fire of 15 rounds
per minute. The L/50 gun fires a 187-lb (85-

kg) fixed round, the range of the 105.8-lb
(45-kg) HE conventional shell being in the
order of 27,340 yards (25,000 m), and that
of the reported rocket-assisted projectile
considerably greater. Muzzle velocity with
the conventional round is between 2,838
and 1,968 ft (865 and 600 m) per second.
The gun is elevated between −3° and +40°
manually, and traversed 15° left and 15°
right manually. Reloading takes only 2 minutes.

Bofors M-1948 gun

Type: light anti-aircraft gun
Calibre: 40 mm
Barrel length: 70 cal
Muzzle velocity: 3,280 ft (1,000 m) per
second with HE

Ranges: Maximum (horizontal) 4,374 yards
(4,000 m); (vertical) 9,842 ft (3,000
m)
Minimum
Elevation: −5° to +90°
Traverse: 360°
Rate of fire: 240 rounds per minute (cyclic)

Weights: For travel 11,354 lb (5,150 kg)
In firing position 10,582 lb (4,800 kg)
Dimensions: Length 20 ft 6¾ in (6.27 m)
Width 7 ft 4½ in (2.25 m)
Height 7 ft 8½ in (2.35 m)
Ammunition: AP-T, APDS-T and HE
Crew: six
Used also by: Austria, Belgium, Denmark, France, Greece, India, Israel, Italy, Netherlands, Norway, Portugal, Spain, Turkey, UK
Notes: The M-1948 Bofors AA gun was developed from the prewar M-1936 40-mm gun, and entered service in 1951. Ammunition weight is 2.12 lb (0.96 kg) per round, and the carriage holds 48 rounds, 16 of them above the breech for ready use. There are four models: the M-1948 basic model, the M-1948D with provision for radar control, and the M-1948R with provision for radar control, and the M-1948C. Some of the carriages have provision for an auxiliary power unit for limited independent travel.

Carl Gustav M2-550 launcher

Type: man-portable anti-tank rocket launcher
Calibre: 84 mm
Barrel length:
Muzzle velocity: 951 ft (290 m) per second
  with HEAT
Ranges: Maximum effective 766 yards (700
  m)
  Minimum
Elevation:
Traverse:
Rate of fire:
Weights: For travel 33 lb (15 kg)
  In firing position 39.7 lb (18 kg)
Dimensions: Length 3 ft 8½ in (1.13 m)
  Width
  Height
Ammunition: HE and HEAT
Crew: two
Used also by: Eire, Japan, Kenya, Netherlands, Norway, UK
Notes: The Carl Gustav M2-550 is an improved version of the Carl Gustav M2 in service with the armies of Austria, Canada, Denmark, Eire, Ghana, Netherlands, Norway, Sweden, United Arab Emirates, UK, West Germany. The M2-550 has

improved sighting arrangements and a better AT round. This weighs 6.6 lb (3 kg), of which 4.85 is the shell. This can penetrate 15¾ in (400 mm) of armour, but at longer range than the 492 yards (450 m) of the M2's HEAT shell.

Miniman launcher

Type: man-portable anti-tank rocket launcher
Calibre: 74 mm
Barrel length:
Muzzle velocity: 525 ft (160 m) per second
Ranges: Maximum 273 yards (250 m) against a stationary target
Minimum
Elevation:
Traverse:
Rate of fire:
Weights: For travel 6.4 lb (2.9 kg)
In firing position as above
Dimensions: Length 2 ft 11⅝ in (90.0 cm)
Width
Height

Ammunition: HEAT warhead
Crew: one
Used only by: Sweden
Notes: The Miniman is a powerful one-shot anti-tank weapon, the remains of which are discarded after the rocket has been fired. The shell weighs 1.94 lb (0.88 kg), of which 0.66 lb (0.3 kg) is explosive. The warhead can penetrate 11.8 in (300 mm) of armour.

M-1941C mortar

Type: heavy mortar
Calibre: 120.25 mm
Barrel length: 16.63 cal
Muzzle velocity: 1,040 ft (317 m) per second
Ranges: Maximum 6,999 yards (6,400 m)
Minimum
Elevation: 45° to 80°
Traverse: 360°
Rate of fire: 12 rounds per minute
Weights: For travel 1,323 lb (600 kg)
In firing position 628 lb (285 kg)
Dimensions: Length
Width
Height

Ammunition: HE, Illuminating and Smoke
Crew: four
Used also by: Eire
Notes: The Swedish M-1941C is a licence-built version of the Finnish Tampella M-1940 mortar, fitted with a new stand of Hotchkiss-Brandt design in 1956, and new sights in 1972. The HE bomb weighs 29.3 lb (13.3 kg).

M-1929 mortar

Type: medium mortar
Calibre: 81.4 mm
Barrel length: 12.29 cal
Muzzle velocity: 623 ft (190 m) per second
Ranges: Maximum 2,843 yards (2,600 m)
Minimum
Elevation: 45° to 80°
Traverse: 90°
Rate of fire: 15 to 18 rounds per minute
Weights: For travel
In firing position 132.3 lb (60 kg)
Dimensions: Length
Width
Height

Ammunition: HE
Crew: two or three
Used also by: Eire
Notes: The Swedish M-1929 is still a useful weapon, despite the fact that it is basically a licence-built version of the French M-1917 Stokes-Brandt mortar. The HE bomb weighs 7.7 lb (3.5 kg).

Model 45 sub-machine gun

Type: sub-machine gun
Calibre: 9 mm
System of operation: blowback
Muzzle velocity: 1,197 ft (365 m) per second
Range: effective 219 yards (200 m)
Rate of fire: 550 to 600 rounds per minute (cyclic)
Cooling system: air
Feed system: 36-round box
Dimensions: Barrel length 8 in (203.2 mm)
Overall length 31.8 in (808 mm) with stock extended; 21.7 in (501 mm) with stock folded
Width
Height
Weights: 9.23 lb (4.2 kg) loaded
Sights: post (fore) and flip (rear)
Ammunition: 9 mm × 19 Parabellum
Used also by: Egypt, Indonesia
Notes: The Carl Gustav Model 45 is the standard sub-machine gun of the Swedish forces.

Ljungman AG42 rifle

Type: self-loading rifle
Calibre: 6.5 mm
System of operation: gas (direct action)
Muzzle velocity: 2,461 ft (750 m) per second
Range: effective 656 yards (600 m)
Rate of fire: 40 rounds per minute
Cooling system: air
Feed system: 10-round box
Dimensions: Barrel length 24.49 in (622 mm)
Overall length 47.8 in (1.214 m)
Width
Height
Weights: 10.38 lb (4.71 kg)
Sights: barleycorn (fore) and leaf, aperture (rear)

Ammunition: 6.5 mm × 55
Used also by: Denmark, Egypt
Notes: The Ljungman was the world's first service rifle using direct gas action, and entered service in 1942. A version with a modified trigger mechanism was named the AG42B, the Danish model the Madsen-Ljungman, and the Egyptian model the Hakim, using the 7.92-mm round.

Switzerland

18,500 men and 621,500 Militia.

War establishment:
3 fd corps, each of 1 armd, 2 inf divs.
1 mountain corps of 3 mountain inf divs.
Some indep inf and fortress bdes.
320 Centurion, 150 Pz-61, 170 Pz-68 med, 200 AMX-13 lt tks; 1,250 M-113 APC; 105mm guns; 105mm, 155mm, 150 M-109U 155mm SP how; 120mm mor; 80mm multiple RL; 75mm, 90mm, 105mm ATK guns; 83mm, 106mm RCL; Bantam, Dragon ATGW; 10 patrol boats. (150 Pz-68 med tks, Dragon ATGW on order.)

Panzer 68

Type: main battle tank
Crew: four
Weights: Empty
Loaded 85,979 lb (39,000 kg)
Dimensions: Length (hull) 22 ft 3¾ in (6.8 m)
Width 10 ft 2 in (3.1 m)
Height 8 ft 11 in (2.72 m)
Ground pressure: 12.1 lb/in² (0.85 kg/cm²)
Performance: road speed 34 mph (55 kph); range 217 miles (350 km); vertical obstacle 29½ in (75.0 cm); trench 8 ft 6⅖ in (2.6 m); gradient 70%; wading 44 in (1.12 m) without preparation
Engine: one 660-bhp Daimler Benz MB 837 inline diesel engine
Armament: one 105-mm L7A2 L/51 gun, plus one 7.5-mm machine-gun co-axial with the main armament, and one 7.5-mm AA machine-gun on the loader's hatch
Armour: 2⅓ in (60 mm) maximum
Used only by: Switzerland
Notes: The Pz 68, which entered service in 1968, is an improved Pz 61, with a 105-mm main gun stabilised in azimuth and elevation, the co-axial 20-mm cannon replaced by a 7.5-mm machine-gun, increased range and speed, and improved tracks. There is an improved version of the Pz 68, designated the Pz 68 AA2, which has a thermal sleeve on the 105-mm gun, an improved stabilisation system, more ammunition, improved disposal for the empty ammunition cases, an updated NBC system and other detail modifications. There are only two derivatives of the Pz 68:

1. *Brückenpanzer* (BrüPz) 68 armoured vehicle-launched bridge, which weighs 99,207 lb (45,000 kg), and can bridge a gap of 59 ft (18 m) for a vehicle of up to 50 tons
2. *Panzerkanone* 68, which has appeared only in prototype form, and has a turret-mounted 155-mm howitzer.

Panzer 61

Type: main battle tank
Crew: four
Weights: Empty
Loaded 83,775 lb (38,000 kg)
Dimensions: Length (hull) 22 ft 3 in (6.78 m)
Width 10 ft (3.05 m)
Height 9 ft 11½ in (2.73 m)
Ground pressure: 12.1 lb/in² (0.85 kg/cm²)
Performance: road speed 31 mph (50 kph); range 186 miles (300 km); vertical obstacle 29½ in (75.0 cm); trench 8 ft 6⅓ in (2.6 m); gradient 70%; wading 44 in (1.12 m) without preparation
Engine: one 630-bhp Daimler-Benz MB 837 inline diesel engine
Armament: one 105-mm L7A2 L/51 gun with APDS and HESH rounds, plus one one 20-mm Oerlikon cannon co-axial with the main armament and one 7.5-mm machine-gun for AA defence on the loader's hatch
Armour: 2⅓ in (60 mm) maximum
Used only by: Switzerland
Notes: The Pz 61 is essentially the chassis of the intermediate Pz 58 tank armed with a 105-mm British gun. An interesting design feature results from the Swiss decision that firepower and protection should have precedence over mobility: light alloys are used

wherever possible to allow the steel armouring of key areas in greater thicknesses than would otherwise have been possible. The Pz 61 entered service in 1964, and in service has proved very reliable, with a good cross-country performance. Limited NBC protection is provided. There is only one derivative of the Pz 61, the *Entpannungspanzer* (EntpPz) 65 armoured recovery vehicle.

MOWAG Grenadier

Type: multi-purpose military vehicle
Crew: two, plus up to six infantrymen when in use as an armoured personnel carrier
Weights: Empty 10,362 lb (4,700 kg)
Loaded 14,109 lb (6,400 kg)
Dimensions: Length 15 ft 10¼ in (4.84 m)
Width 7 ft 11¾ in (2.43 m)
Height (to turret top) 7 ft 6½ in (2.3 m)
Ground pressure:
Performance: road speed 62 mph (100 kph); range 342 miles (550 km); vertical obstacle 15¾ in (40.0 cm); trench negligible; gradient 60%; ground clearance 15¾ in (40.0 cm); the Grenadier is fully amphibious
Engine: one 202-hp Chrysler inline petrol engine
Armament: see notes
Armour:

Used also by: several nations
Notes: The Grenadier can be used as an APC, reconnaissance vehicle, ambulance, cargo carrier, mortar carrier and in a number of other roles. Fully amphibious, the Grenadier is driven in the water by one propeller; on land the vehicle uses 4 × 2 or 4 × 4 drive. Among the armament installations possible are a turret-mounted 20-mm cannon, a remotely controlled 7.62-mm machine-gun, and an Oerlikon multiple rocket-launcher.

British Aerospace Bloodhound Mark 2

Type: mobile surface-to-air tactical guided missile
Guidance: semi-active radar homing
Dimensions: Span 9 ft 3½ in (2.83 m)
Body diameter 21½ in (54.6 cm)
Length 25 ft (7.62 m)

Booster: four solid-propellant rockets
Sustainer: two Rolls-Royce (Bristol Siddeley) Thor ramjets
Warhead: high explosive
Weights: Launch 5,410 lb (2,454 kg)
Burnt out
Performance: range more than 50 miles (80 km); effective ceiling about 98,425 ft (30,000 m)

Used also by: Singapore, Sweden, UK

Notes: Developed from the Bristol Aircraft Bloodhound Mark 1, the Mark 2 version of the weapon has improved capabilities in an ECM environment by virtue of having continuous-wave doppler radar instead of pulse radar. Once a target has been found by a surveillance radar, the Bloodhound site's Firelight (mobile) or Scorpion (static) target-illuminating radar (TIR) 'lights up' the target for the missile's seeker. The missile is then fired by the launch control post, which supervises the activities of a four-missile section.

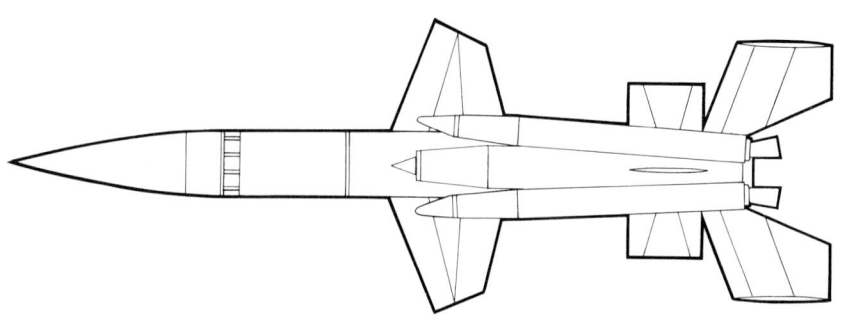

M109U (*Panzerhaubitze* 66)

Type: self-propelled howitzer
Crew: eight
Weights: Empty
Loaded 51,808 lb (21,500 kg)

Dimensions: Length (overall) 21 ft 8½ in (6.61 m); (hull) 20 ft 0½ in (6.11 m)
Width 10 ft 9¾ in (3.26 m)
Height (to turret top) 10 ft (3.05 m)

Ground pressure:
Performance: road speed 35 mph (56 kph); range 240 miles (386 km)
Engine: one 405-bhp Detroit Diesel 8V71T turbo-charged inline diesel engine
Armament: one 155-mm L/23 howitzer with 28 rounds, plus one 0.5-in (12.7-mm) AA machine-gun on the turret roof
Armour: $1\frac{1}{2}$ in (38 mm) maximum
Used only by: Switzerland

Notes: This *Panzerhaubitze* 66 is the Swiss version of the US M109 self-propelled howitzer, and differs from the US model mainly in its electrical systems. Rate of fire is up to eight rounds per minute, and maximum range of the HE shell is 19,685 yards (18,000 m).

M-42 howitzer

Type: medium howitzer
Calibre: 150 mm
Barrel length: 28 cal
Muzzle velocity: 1,903 ft (580 m) per second
Ranges: Maximum 16,404 yards (15,000 m)
          Minimum
Elevation: −5° to +65°
Traverse: 45° total
Rate of fire: five rounds per minute
Weights: For travel
          In firing position 14,330 lb (6,500 kg)
Dimensions: Length
              Width
              Height

Ammunition: HE
Crew:
Used only by: Switzerland
Notes: The M-42 is a Swedish design, by Bofors, and now used only by Switzerland. Shell weight is 92.6 lb (42 kg).

M-46 howitzer

Type: light howitzer
Calibre: 105 mm
Barrel length: 22 cal
Muzzle velocity: 1,608 ft (490 m) per second
Ranges: Maximum 10,939 yards (10,000 m)
          Minimum
Elevation: 0° to +65°
Traverse: 60° total
Rate of fire:
Weights: For travel
          In firing position 4,079 lb (1,850 kg)
Dimensions: Length
              Width
              Height
Ammunition: HE
Crew: six
Used only by: Switzerland

Notes: The M-46 is a Swedish design, by Bofors, and is now used only by Switzerland. The shell weight is 33.4 lb (15.15 kg).

M-35 gun

Type: light field gun
Calibre: 105 mm
Barrel length: 42 cal
Muzzle velocity: 2,625 ft (800 m) per second
Ranges: Maximum 22,966 yards (21,000 m)
      Minimum
Elevation: −3° to +45°
Traverse: 60° total
Rate of fire: five rounds per minute
Weights: For travel
      In firing position 8,466 lb (3,840 kg)

Dimensions: Length
      Width
      Height
Ammunition: HE
Crew: six
Used only by: Switzerland
Notes: The M-35 gun is of Swedish design, by Bofors, and now used only by Switzerland. Shell weight is 33.73 lb (15.3 kg).

PaK 57 gun

Type: anti-tank gun
Calibre: 90 mm
Barrel length:
Muzzle velocity: 1,968 ft (600 m) per second
Ranges: Maximum up to 1,094 yards (1,000 m) effective
      Minimum
Elevation:
Traverse:
Rate of fire: eight to ten rounds per minute
Weights: For travel 1,213 lb (550 kg)
      In firing position
Dimensions: Length
      Width
      Height
Ammunition: HEAT

Crew:
Used only by: Switzerland
Notes: The PaK 57 is a companion to the other main Swiss AT gun, the PaK 50, and seems to have a similar performance. The shell weight is 6.94 lb (3.15 kg), and this is capable of penetrating 9.84 in (250 mm) of armour.

PaK 50 gun

Type: anti-tank gun
Calibre: 90 mm

Barrel length:
Muzzle velocity: 1,968 ft (600 m) per second
Ranges: Maximum 547 yards (500 m) effective

Minimum
Elevation:
Traverse:
Rate of fire: eight to ten rounds per minute
Weights: For travel 1,213 lb (550 kg)
In firing position
Dimensions: Length
Width
Height
Ammunition: HEAT (?)

Crew:
Used only by: Switzerland
Notes: Despite its age, this AT gun is little known, and performance figures are not available.

Type 661 cannon mounting

Type: AA cannon mounting
Calibre: 30 mm
Barrel length:
Muzzle velocity: 3,543 ft (1,080 m) per second
Ranges: Maximum (slant) 3,280 yards (3,000 m); (vertical) 3,280 ft (1,000 m)
Minimum
Elevation:
Traverse: 360°
Rate of fire: 650 rounds per minute (cyclic)
Weights: For travel 3,417 lb (1,550 kg)
In firing position
Dimensions: Length
Width
Height

Ammunition: HE
Crew: one
Used only by: Switzerland
Notes: This is a powerful AA weapon, which can be used optically or with a fire-control computer. Elevation and traverse are hydraulically powered. Ammunition feed is from a 40-round box, and shell weight is 0.79 lb (0.36 kg). The cannon itself is an Oerlikon Type 831-SLM.

DIRA artillery rocket

Type: artillery rocket
Calibre: 81 mm
Barrel length:
Muzzle velocity: 1,607 ft (490 m) per second
Ranges: Maximum 9,514 yards (8,700 m)
Minimum
Elevation:
Traverse:
Rate of fire:
Weights: For travel
In firing position 34.4 lb (15.6 kg)
Dimensions: Length 4 ft 3 in (1.3 m)
Span
Body diameter 3.19 in (81 mm)
Ammunition: HE warhead
Crew:

Used only by: Switzerland
Notes: The DIRA rocket can be used in a number of ways, including a standard ground launch method from two 15-round launcher groups on an M113 APC chassis, with a traverse of 360°. The 34.4-lb (15.6-kg) rocket has a warhead of 15.4 lb (7 kg); alternatively, there is a 25.6-lb (11.6-kg) rocket with a warhead of 6.6 lb (3 kg).

M-1958 launcher

Type: man-portable anti-tank rocket launcher
Calibre: 83 mm
Barrel length:
Muzzle velocity: 328 ft (100 m) per second
Ranges: Maximum effective 328 yards (300 m)
Minimum
Elevation:
Traverse:
Rate of fire:
Weights: For travel 16.53 lb (7.5 kg)
In firing position 20.55 lb (9.32 kg)
Dimensions: Length 4 ft 3⅛ in (1.3 m)
Width
Height
Ammunition: HEAT warhead
Crew: two
Used only by: Switzerland
Notes: The M-1958 is a lightened version of the Swiss M-1950 launcher, itself a derivative of the Belgian 83-mm *Blindicide* weapon. The M-1958 has itself been developed into the M-1975, which has improvements such as an effective range of 547 yards (500 m).

Minenwerfer 72 mortar

Type: medium mortar
Calibre: 81 mm
Barrel length: 15.84 cal
Muzzle velocity: 853 ft (260 m) per second
Ranges: Maximum 4,484 yards (4,100 m)
          Minimum
Elevation: 45° to 90°
Traverse: 360° (10° top traverse)
Rate of fire:
Weights: For travel
          In firing position 100.3 lb (45.5 kg)
Dimensions: Length
             Width
             Height
Ammunition: Fragmentation, HE and Smoke
Crew: three
Used only by: Switzerland
Notes: The Mw 72 is a much updated model
of the Mw 33, with considerable savings in
weight. Originally intended for Swiss
mountain forces, the weapon is now in
general service. The Mw 72 fires the same
ammunition as the Mw 33.

Minenwerfer 64 mortar

Type: heavy mortar
Calibre: 120 mm
Barrel length: 12.7 cal
Muzzle velocity: 1,378 ft (420 m) per second
Ranges: Maximum 8,749 yards (8,000 m)
      Minimum
Elevation: 45° to 85°
Traverse: 60° (10° top traverse)
Rate of fire: 10 rounds per minute
Weights: For travel 1,367 lb (620 kg)
      In firing position 527 lb (239 kg)
Dimensions: Length 7 ft 8½ in (2.35 m)
      Width 4 ft 11⅔ in (1.51 m)
      Height 3 ft 8½ in (1.13 m)
Ammunition: HE, Incendiary and Smoke
Crew: six
Used only by: Switzerland
Notes: The Mw 64 is found in two forms, the
    first transportable on a two-wheeled trailer,
    and the second mounted in the back of an
    M106 mortar carrier. The round weighs
    31.6 lb (14.33 kg).

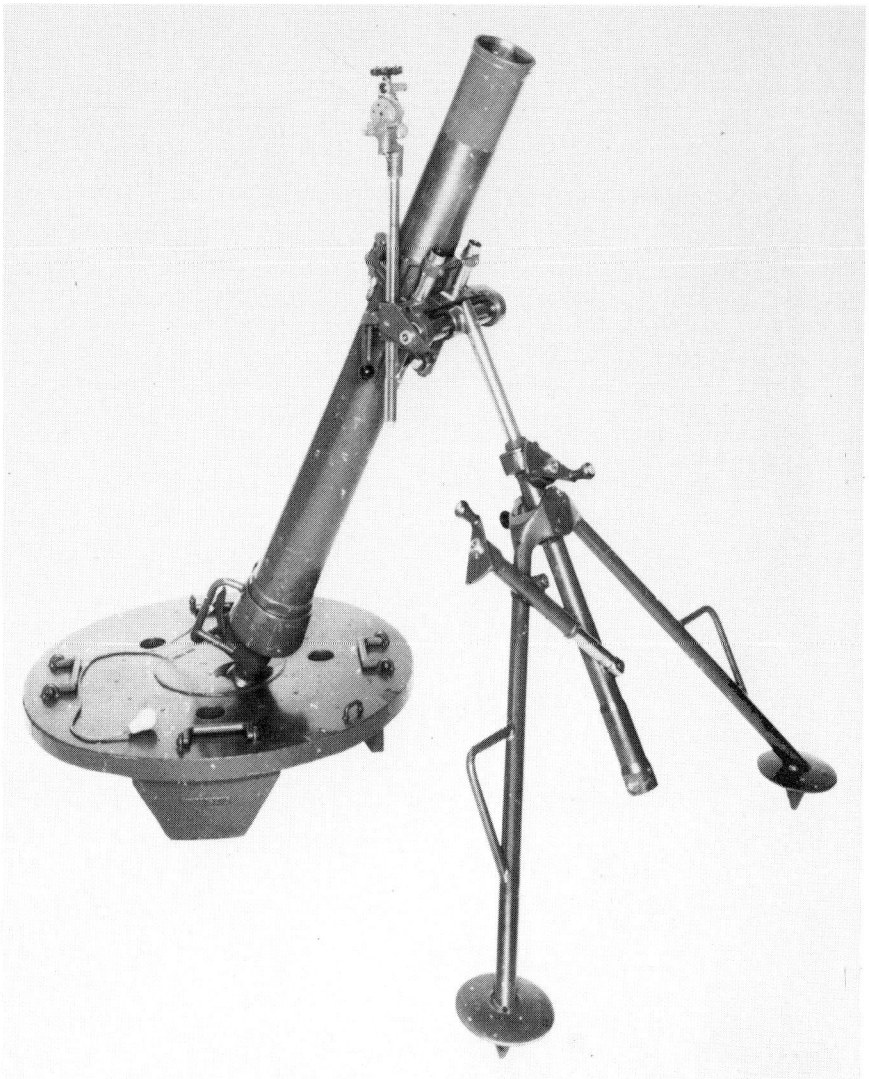

Minenwerfer 33 mortar

Type: medium mortar
Calibre: 81 mm
Barrel length: 15.6 cal
Muzzle velocity: 853 ft (260 m) per second
Ranges: Maximum 4,484 yards (4,100 m)
      Minimum
Elevation: 45° to 90°
Traverse: 45° to 56° (8° top traverse)
Rate of fire:
Weights: For travel
      In firing position 136.7 lb (62 kg)
Dimensions: Length
      Width
      Height
Ammunition: Fragmentation, HE and Smoke
Crew: three
Used only by: Switzerland
Notes: There is little of note in this weapon,
    which is of standard 1930s design. The HE
    bomb weighs 6.99 lb (3.17 kg).

M-1951 machine gun

Type: light machine-gun
Calibre: 7.5 mm
System of operation: gas-assisted recoil
Muzzle velocity: 2,460 ft (750 m) per second
Range: effective 875 yards (800 m) with a bipod
Rate of fire: 1,000 rounds per minute (cyclic)
Cooling system: air
Feed system: metal-link belt
Dimensions: Barrel length 22.05 in (560 mm)
Overall length 50 in (1.27 m)
Width
Height
Weights: 35.3 lb (16 kg) with bipod
Sights: folding blade (fore) and tangent (rear)

Ammunition: 7.5 mm M11
Used only by: Switzerland
Notes: The Swiss M-1951 is derived from the German MG42 of World War II, and is an exceptionally fine weapon. However, the fact that parts of the MG42 were stamped, and in the M-1951 are machined, makes the weapon both expensive and heavy. The latter factor makes it sensible that the main users of the weapon are motorised units. The M-1951 can also be used on a tripod.

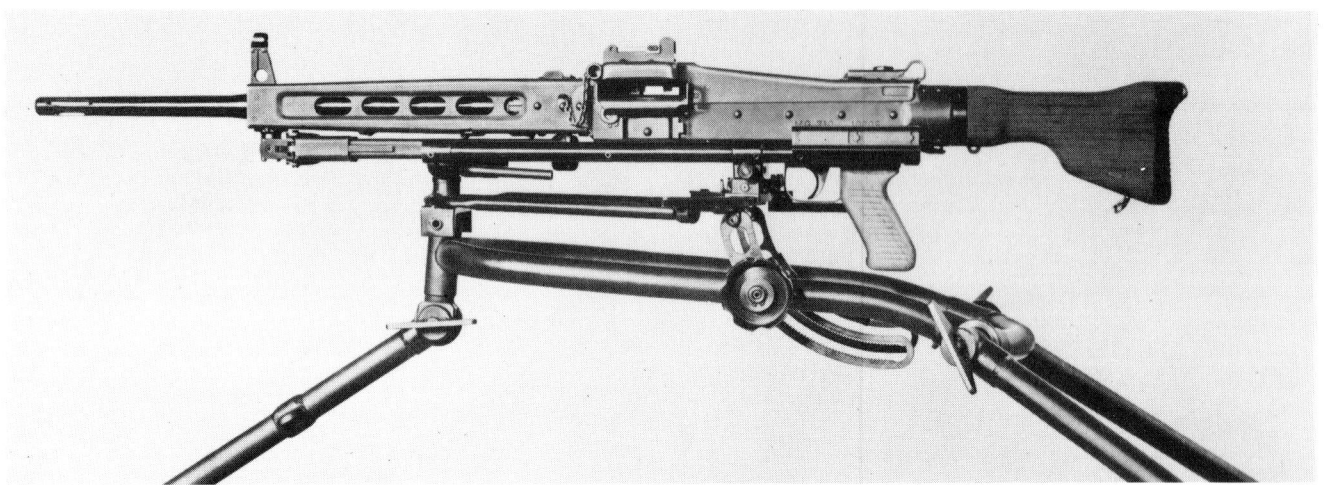

SIG 710-3 machine-gun

Type: general-purpose machine-gun
Calibre: 7.62 mm
System of operation: delayed blowback
Muzzle velocity: 2,592 ft (790 m) per second
Range: effective 875 yards (800 m) with a bipod; 2,406 yards (2,200 m) with a tripod
Rate of fire: 600 rounds per minute (cyclic); 200 rounds per minute (automatic)
Cooling system: air
Feed system: metal-link belt
Dimensions: Barrel length 22 in (559 mm)
Overall length 45 in (1.143 m)
Width
Height
Weights: 20.4 lb (9.25 kg)
Sights: blade (fore) and leaf, notch (rear)
Ammunition: 7.62 mm × 51
Used by:

Notes: The SIG 710-3 is one of the most advanced general-purpose machine-guns in the world today, and is derived from the MG45 on which the Germans were working at the end of World War II. The gun can be fitted with heavy or light barrels, and fired from a bipod or a tripod.

M-1925 machine-gun

Type: light machine-gun
Calibre: 7.5 mm
System of operation: recoil
Muzzle velocity: 2,460 ft (750 m) per second
Range: effective 875 yards (800 m) with a bipod
Rate of fire: 450 rounds per minute (cyclic)
Cooling system: air
Feed system: 30-round box
Dimensions: Barrel length 23 in (585 mm)
Overall length 45.67 in (1.16 m)
Width
Height
Weights: 23.81 lb (10.8 kg) with bipod

Sights: blade (fore) and tangent (rear)
Ammunition: 7.5 mm M11
Used only by: Switzerland
Notes: Although an elderly weapon, and technically obsolete, the M-1925 has the virtue of reliability and lightness.

SG510-4 rifle

Type: selective fire rifle
Calibre: 7.62 mm
System of operation: delayed blowback
Muzzle velocity: 2,592 ft (790 m) per second
Range: effective 656 yards (600 m)
Rate of fire: 600 rounds per minute (cyclic); 80 rounds per minute (automatic); 40 rounds per minute (single shot)
Cooling system: air
Feed system: 20-round box
Dimensions: Barrel length 19.88 in (505 mm)
Overall length 40 in (1.016 m)
Width
Height
Weights: 9.37 lb (4.25 kg) empty; 9.8 lb (4.45 kg) with bipod
Sights: post (fore) and aperture (rear)
Ammunition: 7.62 mm × 51
Used also by: Bolivia, Chile
Notes: The SG510 series of rifles is based on the Stgw 57, itself developed from the German *Sturmgewehr* 45 of World War II. The two main members of the SG510 family have been the SG510-3 and SG510-4, the former firing the Russian 7.62 mm × 39 round, and the latter the NATO 7.62 mm × 51 round. Apart from some internal dimensional changes and different weights, the rifles are virtually indistinguishable. Both can be used with a bipod and infra-red sights, and are well made, effective weapons.

SG542 rifle

Type: selective fire assault rifle
Calibre: 7.62 mm
System of operation: gas
Muzzle velocity: 2,690 ft (820 m) per second
Range: effective 437 yards (400 m)
Rate of fire: 650 to 800 rounds per minute (cyclic)
Cooling system: air
Feed system: 20-round box
Dimensions: Barrel length 18.3 in (465 mm)
Overall length 39.45 in (1.005 m) with fixed stock; 29.69 in (754 mm) with folding stock
Width
Height
Weights: 7.83 lb (3.55 kg) empty; 10.05 lb (4.56 kg) loaded, with bipod
Sights: post (fore) and aperture (rear)
Ammunition: 7.62 mm × 51
Used by:
Notes: The SG542 is the 7.62-mm model of the SG540 series assault rifle, the other two being the SG540 and 543, each firing the 5.56 mm × 45 round, loaded in 20- or 30-round magazines. Each model can be provided with a fixed or a folding stock, and although the basic design of the three weapons is the same, externally the three differ considerably, the SG540 being 37.4 in (950 mm) long, the SG542 39.45 in (1.005 m) long, and the SG543 31.7 in (805 mm) long (fixed stock). The muzzle velocity of the 5.56-mm weapons is higher than that of the 7.62-mm rifle.

Syria

200,000 (incl 15,000 AD Comd) and 100,000 reservists.

2 armd divs (each 2 armd, 1 mech bde).
3 mech divs (each 1 armd, 2 mech bdes).
3 armd bdes.
1 mech bde.
3 inf bdes.
2 arty bdes.
6 cdo bns.
4 para bns.
1 SSM bn with 'Scud', 2 btys with FROG.
48 SAM btys with SA-2/-3/-6.
200 T-34, 1,500 T-54/-55, 800 T-62 med, 100 PT-76 lt tks; BRDM recce vehs; BMP MICV; 1,600 BTR-40/-50/-60/-152, OT-64 APC; 800 122mm 130mm, 152mm and 180mm guns/how; JSU-122/-152, 75 SU-100 SP guns; 122mm, 140mm, 240mm RL; 30 FROG-7, 36 'Scud' SSM; 82mm, 120mm, 160mm mor; 57mm, 85mm, 100mm ATK guns; 'Snapper', 'Sagger', 'Swatter' ATGW; 23mm, 37mm, 57mm, 85mm, 100mm towed, ZSU-23-4, ZSU-57-2 SP AA guns; SA-7/-9 SAM; 25 Gazelle helicopters.

(60 T-62 tks, Milan, HOT ATGW, SA-6/-8/-9 SAM; 24 Gazelle helicopters on order.)

Deployment: Lebanon: (Arab Peacekeeping Force): 30,000.

Air Defence Command:*
24 SAM btys with SA-2/-3, 14 with SA-6, AA arty interceptor ac and radar.

* Under Army Command, with Army and Air Force manpower.

Para-Military Forces: 9,500. 8,000 Gendarmerie; 1,500 Desert Guard (Frontier Force).

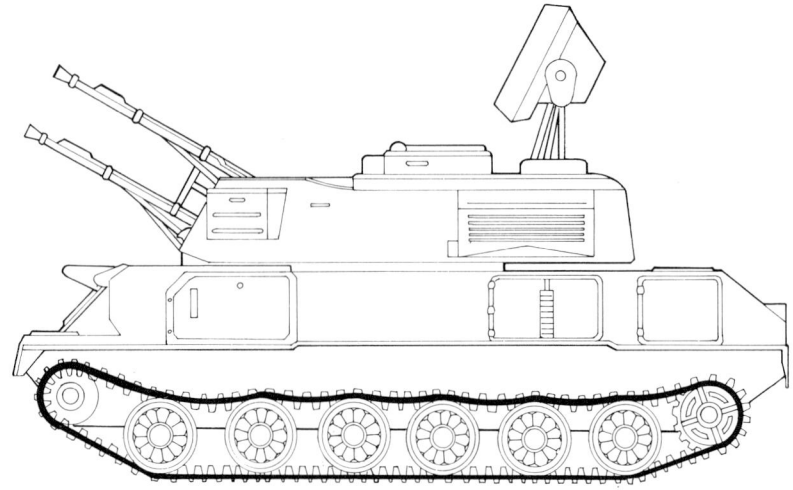

ZSU-23-4

Type: self-propelled AA gun mounting
Crew: four
Weights: Empty
Loaded 30,864 lb (14,000 kg)
Dimensions: Length 20 ft 8 in (6.3 m)
Width 9 ft 8 in (2.95 m)
Height (with radar stowed) 7 ft 4$\frac{3}{8}$ in (2.25 m)
Ground pressure:
Performance: road speed 27 mph (44 kph); range 162 miles (260 km); vertical obstacle 43$\frac{3}{10}$ in (1.1 m); trench 9 ft 2$\frac{1}{4}$ in (2.8 m); gradient 60%; ground clearance 15$\frac{3}{4}$ in (40.0 cm); wading 42 in (1.07 m) without preparation
Engine: one 240-hp Model V-6 inline diesel engine
Armament: four 23-mm ZU-23 cannon with 2,000 rounds of API and HEI ammunition

Armour: $\frac{2}{5}$ in (10 mm)
Used also by: Bulgaria, Czechoslovakia, East Germany, Egypt, Finland, Hungary, India, Iran, Iraq, Poland, South Yemen, USSR
Notes: The ZSU-23-4 is a formidable AA weapons system. Based on a PT-76 light tank chassis, the vehicle has a turret capable of 360° traverse, and fitted with four ZU-23 cannon. These have an effective ceiling of 8,202 ft (2,500 m), and an effective ground range of 2,187 yards (2,000 m). The guns can be elevated from −7° to +80°, and have a rate of fire of 200 rounds per barrel per minute in combat. The guns operate with a fire-control computer and 'Gun Dish' radar, mounted at the rear of the turret. This can acquire targets at a range of 12.4 miles (20 km).

ZSU-57-2

Type: self-propelled AA gun mounting
Crew: six
Weights: Empty
Loaded 61,949 lb (28,100 kg)
Dimensions: Length (with guns forward) 27 ft 10 in (8.48 m); (with guns up) 20 ft 6 in (6.22 m)
Width 10 ft 9 in (3.27 m)
Height (with guns forward) 9 ft (2.75 m)
Ground pressure:
Performance: road speed 30 mph (48 kph); range 249 miles (400 km)
Engine: one 520-hp V-54 inline diesel engine
Armament: two 57-mm S-68 L/71 AA guns with 316 or 360 rounds
Armour: $\frac{3}{5}$ in (15 mm) maximum
Used also by: Bulgaria, Czechoslovakia, East Germany, Egypt, Finland, Hungary, Iran, Iraq, North Korea, Poland, Romania, USSR, Vietnam, Yugoslavia

Notes: The ZSU-57-2 was introduced in 1957, and is based on the shortened chassis of the T-54 tank, with four instead of five road wheels. Potentially a formidable AA vehicle, the ZSU-57-2 is hampered tactically by lack of deep wading facility and of any system of radar control for the guns, which are derived from the German 5.7-cm *Flakgerät* 58 designs captured at the end of World War II. Elevation (from −5° to +85°) and traverse (360°) are hydraulic. The HE shell weighs 6.15 lb (2.79 kg), and is effective against aircraft up to altitudes of 15,994 ft (4,875 m). Rate of fire is 120 rounds per gun per minute.

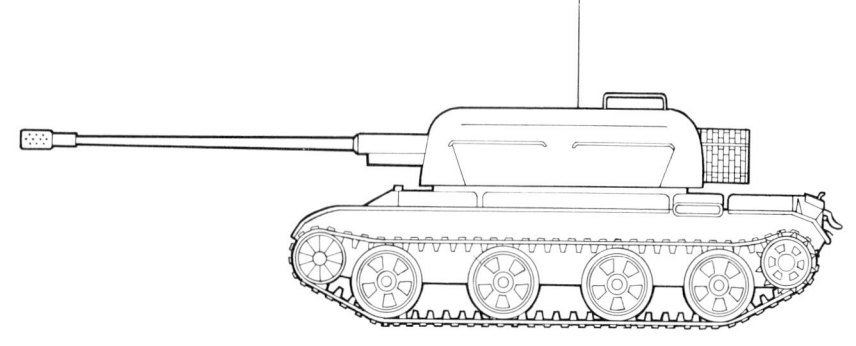

M-1943 (D-1) howitzer

Type: field howitzer
Calibre: 152 mm
Barrel length: 25 cal
Muzzle velocity: 1,667 ft (508 m) per second
with HE
Ranges: Maximum 13,561 yards (12,400 m)
with HE
Minimum
Elevation: −3° to +63.5°
Traverse: 35° total
Rate of fire: three or four rounds per minute
Weights: For travel
In firing position 7,937 lb (3,600 kg)
Dimensions: Length 24 ft 9½ in (7.56 m)
Width 6 ft 6½ in (1.99 m)
Height 6 ft 0⅘ in (1.85 m)
Ammunition: HE and SAP
Crew: seven
Used also by: Albania, China, East Germany, Hungary, Poland, Vietnam
Notes: The D-1 howitzer consists of a new barrel on the carriage of the M-30 122-mm howitzer, and was introduced to Russian service in 1943. The HE projectile weighs 87.96 lb (39.9 kg), while the SAP projectile weighs 112.66 lb (51.1 kg) and can penetrate 3.23 in (82 mm) of armour at 1,094 yards (1,000 m).

Taiwan

330,000 men and 1,000,000 reservists.

2 armd divs.
12 hy inf divs.
6 lt inf divs.
2 armd cav regts.
2 AB bdes.
4 special forces gps.
1 SSM bn with Honest John.
3 SAM bns: 2 with 80 Nike Hercules, 1 with 24 HAWK.
150 M-47/-48 med, 625 M-41 lt tks; 300 M-113 APC; 550 105mm, 300 155mm guns/how; 350 75mm M-116 pack, 90 203mm, 10 240mm how; 225 105mm SP how; 81mm mor; Honest John SSM; 150 M-18 76mm SP ATK guns; 500 106mm RCL; 300 40mm AA guns (some SP); Nike Hercules, 20 Chaparral SAM; 80 UH-1H, 2 KH-4, 7 CH-34 helicopters. (TOW ATGW, 24 Improved HAWK SAM, 118 UH-1H helicopters on order.)

Deployment: Quemoy: 60,000; Matsu: 20,000.

Para-Military Forces: 100,000 militia.

M115 howitzer

Type: heavy field howitzer
Calibre: 8 in (203 mm)
Barrel length: 25 cal
Muzzle velocity: 1,950 ft (594 m) per second
Ranges: Maximum 18,375 yards (16,802 m)
Minimum
Elevation: −2° to +65°
Traverse: 60° total
Rate of fire: one round every two minutes
Weights: For travel 32,000 lb (14,505 kg)
In firing position 29,700 lb (13,471 kg)
Dimensions: Length 36 ft (10.97 m)
Width 9 ft 4 in (2.84 m)
Height 9 ft (2.74 m)
Ammunition: Atomic, HE, HE Spotting, Gas and RAP
Crew: 14
Used also by: Belgium, Denmark, Greece, India, Iran, Italy, Japan, South Korea, West Germany
Notes: The US M115 howitzer is the largest piece of conventional ordnance in service today, but was designed during World War II as the M1. The HE projectile weighs 200 lb (90.7 kg).

Tanzania

25,000 men.

4 bde HQ.
1 tk regt.
13 inf bns.
3 arty bns.
1 engr regt.
20 T-59 med, T-60, 14 T-62 lt tks; BTR-40/-152, K-63 APC; 24 76mm guns, 30 122mm how; 82mm, 50 120mm mor; 14.5mm, 37mm AA guns; SA-3 SAM.

Deployment: Mozambique: 1 inf bn.

Para-Military Forces: 1,400 Police Field Force and a police marine unit; 35,000 Citizen's Militia.

Thailand

141,000 men and 500,000 reservists.

1 cav div.
6 inf divs (incl 4 tk bns).
3 indep regimental combat teams.
4 AB and special forces bns.
1 SAM bn with 40 HAWK.
5 aviation coys and some flts.
150 M-41 lt tks; 20 Saracen armd cars; 32 Shorland Mk 3 recce; 250 M-113, LVTP-7 APC; 300 105mm, 50 155mm how; 81mm mor; 57mm RCL; 40mm AA guns; 90 O-1 lt ac; 90 UH-1B/D, 4 CH-47, 24 OH-13, 16 FH-1100, 3 Bell 206, 2 Bell 212, 6 OH-23F, 28 KH-4 helicopters. (Scorpion lt tks; 80 APC and armd cars, 24 how, 3 Merlin IVA transport ac, 2 Bell 214B helicopters on order.)

Para-Military Forces: 52,000 Volunteer Defence Corps, 14,000 Border Police, 20 V-150 Commando APC, 16 lt ac, 27 helicopters.

Heckler und Koch HK33 rifle

Type: selective fire rifle
Calibre: 5.56 mm
System of operation: delayed blowback
Muzzle velocity: 3,018 ft (920 m) per second
Range: effective 437 yards (400 m)
Rate of fire: 750 rounds per minute (cyclic); 100 rounds per minute (automatic); 40 rounds per minute (single shot)
Cooling system: air
Feed system: 20- or 40-round box
Dimensions: Barrel length
  Overall length 33.98 in (863 mm) with stock extended; 26.77 in (680 mm) with stock retracted (HK33KA1 rifle)
  Width
  Height

Weights: 8.77 lb (3.98 kg) unloaded; 10.09 lb (4.58 kg) loaded with 40 rounds
Sights: post (fore) and V or aperture (rear)
Ammunition: 5.56 mm × 45
Used also by: Brazil, Malaysia, and other nations
Notes: The HK33 is a Heckler und Koch Group II weapon (5.56 mm × 45 cartridge), Group I weapons firing the 7.62 mm × 51 NATO round, and Group III weapons the 7.62 mm × 39 Russian round. There are three versions of the HK33:
  1. HK33A2 with a fixed plastic stock
  2. HK33A3 with a twin-strut telescopic stock
  3. HK33KA1 short model.
Essentially, each of the three models is a scaled-down G3 rifle. There is also a version with a ×4 telescopic sight, known by the designation HK33ZF.

6-pounder gun

Type: anti-tank gun
Calibre: 57 mm
Barrel length: 45 cal
Muzzle velocity: 2,700 ft (900 m) per second
Ranges: Maximum 9,830 yards (8,990 m)
  Minimum
Elevation: −5° to +15°
Traverse: 90°
Rate of fire: 20 rounds per minute
Weights: For travel 2,700 lb (1,225 kg)
  In firing position 2,471 lb (1,112 kg)

Dimensions: Length 15 ft 6 in (4.72 m)
  Width 6 ft 2½ in (1.89 m)
  Height 4 ft 2½ in (1.28 m)
Ammunition: APDS
Crew: three to six
Used also by: Bangladesh, Brazil, Burma, Cameroon, Egypt, India, Israel, Malaysia, Pakistan, Spain
Notes: The 6-pounder AT gun was introduced into British service in 1940, and was also built by the Americans as the M1. Both versions are still in service, and have respectable performances against light AFVs, having a penetration of 5¾ in (146 mm) at 1,094 yards (1,000 m).

Togo

2,950 men.

1 mot inf bn.
2 inf bns.
2 para/cdo bns.
5 M-8 armd cars; 5 M-3, 30 UR-416 APC.

Tunisia

18,000 men (12,000 conscripts).

2 combined arms regts.
1 Sahara regt.
1 para-cdo bn.
1 arty bn.
1 engr bn.
30 AMX-13, 20 M-41 lt tks; 20 Saladin, 15 EBR-75 armd cars; 40 105mm, 10 155mm how, SS-11 ATGW; 40mm AA guns.

(Chaparral SAM, 45 *Kürassier* SP ATK guns on order.)

Para-Military Forces: 2,500; 1,500 Gendarmerie (3 bns), 1,000 National Guard.

Panzerjäger 'K'

Type: self-propelled anti-tank gun
Crew: three
Weights: Empty
    Loaded 39,683 lb (18,000 kg)
Dimensions: Length 25 ft 6¼ in (7.78 m) with
    gun forward
    Width 8 ft 2½ in (2.5 m)
    Height 7 ft 8 in (2.335 m)
Ground pressure: 9.67 lb/in² (0.68 kg/cm²)
Performance: road speed 42 mph (67 kph);
road range 329 miles (530 km); step 2 ft
7½ in (0.8 m); trench 7 ft 10¼ in (2.4 m);
unprepared wading 3 ft 3⅔ in (1.0 m);
ground clearance 1 ft 3¾ in (0.4 m); gradient 70%
Engine: one 300-bhp Steyr 6FA 6-cylinder
diesel
Armament: one French D-1504 105-mm QF
gun with 43 rounds of HEAT, HE and
Smoke ammunition (traverse 360°, elevation 13° and depression 6°), one co-axial
7.62-mm machine-gun
Armour: ⅓ in (8mm) minimum; ½ in (12mm)

maximum
Used by: Austria and Tunisia
Notes: Based on the chassis of the 4K4FA

APC, with a French FL-12 turret of the oscillating type. An ARV based on the
Panzerjäger 'K' is in production.

Turkey

390,000 men (300,000 conscripts) and
500,000 reservists.

About half below strength: 1 armd
div. 2 mech inf divs. 14 inf divs. 5
armd bdes. 4 mech inf bdes. 5 inf
bdes. 1 para, 1 cdo bde.
4 SSM bns with Honest John.
2,800 M-47 and M-48 med tks; 1,650
M-113, M-59 and Commando APC;
1,500 75mm, 105mm, 155mm and
203mm how; 265 105mm, 190
155mm, 36 175mm SP guns; 1,750
60mm, 81mm, 4.2-in mor; 18 Honest
John SSM; 1,200 57mm, 390 75mm,
800 106mm RCL; 85 Cobra, SS-11,
TOW ATGW; 900 40mm AA guns; 2
DHC-2, 18 U-17, 3 Cessna 421, 7
Do-27, 9 Do-28, 20 Beech Baron ac;
100 AB-205/-206, 20 Bell 47G, 48
UH-1D helicopters. (193 Leopard
tks; TOW, *Milan* ATGW; 56 AB-205
helicopters on order.)

Deployment: Cyprus: 2 inf divs
(25,000).

Para-Military Forces: 110,000 Gendarmerie (incl 3 mobile bdes).

Mauser *Gewehr* 1898 rifle

Type: bolt-action rifle
Calibre: 7.92 mm
System of operation: manually operated bolt
Muzzle velocity: 2,475 ft (754 m) per second
Range: effective 656 yards (600 m)
Rate of fire: 10 to 15 rounds per minute
Cooling system: air
Feed system: 5-round box
Dimensions: Barrel length 23.5 in (597 mm)
    Overall length 43.6 in (1.107 m)
    Width
    Height
Weights: 8.58 lb (3.89 kg)
Sights: blade (fore) and tangent, notch (rear)
Ammunition: 7.92 mm × 57
Used also by: Indonesia and several African
and South American countries
Notes: Mauser's *Gewehr* 98 and its deriva-
tives is the most numerous and popular
military rifle ever made, and of seminal importance in the development of military
bolt-action rifles. The data above refer to
the *Gewehr* 98k, the short model introduced during the 1920s to produce a han-
dier weapon for the shorter ranges that
became common in World War I.

Uganda

20,000 men.

2 bdes, each of 4 bns.
1 recce bn.
1 mech inf bn.
1 para/cdo, 1 marine/cdo bn.
1 trg bn.
1 arty regt.
10 T-34, 15 T-54/-55, 10 M-4 med, PT-
76 lt tks; BRDM-2, Saladin armd, 15
Ferret scout cars; 120 BTR-40/-152,
OT-64, Saracen APC; 76mm, 122mm
guns; 82mm, 120mm mor; 'Sagger'
ATGW; 50 40mm AA guns; SA-7 SAM.

Alvis FV603 Saracen

Type: armoured personnel carrier
Crew: two, plus up to 10 infantrymen
Weights: Empty 17,725 lb (8,040 kg)
    Loaded 22,420 lb (10,170 kg)
Dimensions: Length 17 ft 2 in (5.23 m)
    Width 8 ft 4 in (2.54 m)
    Height 8 ft 1 in (2.46 m)
Ground pressure: 13.93 lb/in² (0.98 kg/cm²)
Performance: road speed 45 mph (72 kph);
range 250 miles (400 km); vertical obsta-
cle 18 in (46.0 cm); trench 5 ft (1.52 m);
gradient 42%
Engine: one 160-hp Rolls-Royce B.80 Mark
6A inline petrol engine
Armament: one 0.3-in (7.62-mm) machine-
gun in the turret with 3,000 rounds, plus

the machine-gun of the infantry squad carried

Armour: $\frac{1}{3}$ in (8 mm) minimum; $\frac{7}{10}$ in (18 mm) maximum

Used also by: Indonesia, Jordan, Kuwait, Lebanon, Libya, Nigeria, Qatar, South Africa, Sudan, Uganda, United Arab Emirates, UK

Notes: The Saracen entered British service in 1953, and has since proved an excellent vehicle, especially on internal security operations, as a result of its versatility, ruggedness, speed, relative quietness and good cross-country performance.

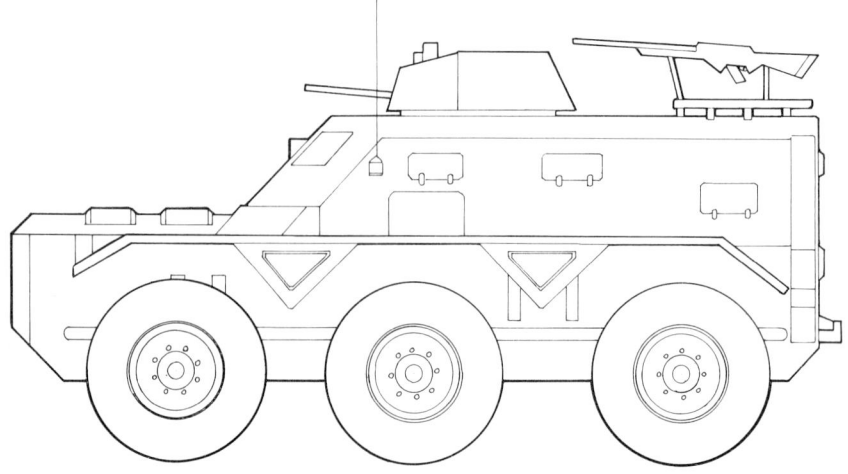

Union of Soviet Socialist Republics

The Russian Army

The Soviet Union has an army of 1,825,000, second in size only to China. This manpower strength is some 50.16 per cent of the armed forces, whose annual budget amounts to about 14 per cent of the gross national product according to most estimates. She deploys 31 divisions in central and eastern Europe, 20 in East Germany, two in Poland, four in Hungary and five in Czechoslovakia. Together, these field 10,500 medium and heavy tanks.

On her eastern border with China she has 44 divisions, of which six are armoured. However, while units in Europe are in a Category 1 state of readiness with three-quarters to full strength and complete equipment, some of those in the Far East are also in Category 2. They are therefore at between half and three-quarters strength, but with all their fighting vehicles. Units in central and southern USSR are in Category 3 as reserves, with about quarter strength but all vehicles, though some of these may be obsolescent.

Service in the army is for two years. Men are drafted into mixed ethnic units and drawn from across the whole Soviet Union. The armed forces are therefore a useful way of breaking down many of the traditional and national loyalties which are still a powerful force outside European Russia.

In addition to her standing land forces, the Soviet Union can call on a considerable reserve force. Conscripts have a Reserve obligation to the age of 50, and reserves may be as high as 25,000,000, of whom 6,800,000 have served in the last five years.

Russia also possesses 450,000 paramilitary forces, including; 200,000 KGB border guards and 250,000 MVD security troops. Border guards are armed and equipped with tanks, self-propelled guns, armoured fighting vehicles and even ships and aircraft. The MVD have tanks and AFVs. Soviet children are also prepared for their military training by DOSAAF, a part-time military training organisation which controls athletics, shooting and parachuting.

The army is made up of 46 tank divisions, 115 motor rifle divisions and eight airborne divisions. Though a considerable transport fleet exists within the Soviet Air Force, the 1,300 civil airliners of *Aeroflot* can be used for troop lifting.

Russia has 50,000 tanks. These include the older JS-2 and JS-3, and the T-10 and T-10M heavy tanks. Her medium armour includes the T-54, T-55, T-62, T-64 and T-72, while there are large numbers of the light PT-76. Most tanks are fitted for deep wading and require very little preparation. Russia also holds 55,000 BRDM scout cars; BMP mechanised infantry combat vehicles; and BTR-40, BTR-50, BTR-60, BTR-152, MT-LB and BMD armoured personnel carriers. Both tracked and wheeled armoured vehicles have NBC protection.

Though the bulk of her artillery is still towed 122-mm and 152-mm equipment, some SP mounts have been seen at parades, and the airportable ASU-57 and newer ASU-85 have been in service for some years. The ZSU-23-4 and ZSU-57-2 SP AA guns are excellent tracked protection for tanks and APCs. Russia's AA guns are complemented by the SA-4 'Ganef', SA-6 'Gainful', SA-7 'Grail', SA-8 'Gecko' and SA-9 'Gaskin' mobile/ portable surface to air missile systems.

Russian field artillery stands at 20,000 100-mm, 122-mm, 130-mm, 152-mm, 180-mm and 203-mm guns. These are backed up by 7,200 82-mm, 120-mm, 160-mm and 240-mm mortars, plus 2,700 122-mm, 140-mm and 240-mm multiple rocket-launchers. In addition to the 'Sagger' and 'Swatter' anti-tank guided weapons, she has 76-mm, 85-mm and 100-mm anti-tank guns. Battlefield tactical nuclear missiles stand at 1,300 launchers, and include FROG, SS-21 'Scud B', and SS-12 'Scaleboard'.

At the far end of the scale Soviet infantry are equipped with small arms derived from designs by Mikhail Kalashnikov, which allows for some interchangeing of parts and a standardised ammunition. Warsaw Pact armies use their own versions of these arms which differ in a few small details.

The Soviet Union, like the United States, has vast stocks of obsolescent weaponry which is not scrapped but passed on to friendly or allied countries. With her arms she lends technicians and so she has been able to participate in a number of African and Middle East wars by proxy. However, this has only tested a small élite. For the bulk of her armed forces there are vast exercises held to test air mobility, river crossing and the deployment of massed armour and artillery.

The Soviet Army is designed for assault and with its considerable conventional superiority it could afford to adopt 'steamroller' tactics in Europe. Under nuclear conditions Soviet armoured forces are expected to advance at 31 miles (50 km) per day, while in conventional warfare this is reduced to 18.6 miles (30 km). Successful attacks require a superiority of three to one, while in critical areas they aim to have a superiority of four or five to one.

They are assisted by versatile engineer equipment and by the design of their formations, which are almost independent of supplies and communications. A unit has its own 'tail' which, like a tadpole, is consumed as it moves. When the supply train has been expended another can be added or the unit withdrawn. Extra supply trains can be added to beef up a force assigned an important task.

The main arm of Soviet tank forces is the T-62, but this is being replaced by the T-72. The T-72 has a 125-mm gun with a range of over 2,500 metres and carries 40 rounds of HE, APFSDS and HEAT ammunition. The T-62 which saw action during the Arab-Israeli war of 1973 has a smooth-bore 115-mm gun, which was not ideal in the long-range actions fought in the desert. The

T-72 has a three-man crew which confirms that it is equipped with an automatic loading mechanism, thereby much reducing crew fatigue, previously a bad feature of Soviet tank design.

One vehicle deployed with Soviet motor rifle regiments which is unique in the armoury of either superpower is the BMP-1. This tracked armoured infantry combat vehicle combines the features of a light tank, APC and anti-tank missile carrier. It has a crew of three, with eight passengers who can

fire their weapons from ports in the hull. The BMP is amphibious and can fire its 73-mm gun while on the move in the water.

Soviet artillery includes some pieces which at the time they were introduced represented advanced tactical design. The D-30 122-mm howitzer has a triple trail which allows the gun to be traversed through 360° when it is in a firing position. Even heavy pieces like the D-30 have an anti-tank capability, and this feature is found in most Soviet

guns which makes their SP versions useful in a direct fire role.

The 85-mm SD-44 and 57-mm M-1955 each have a small auxiliary motor which allow these anti-tank guns to be brought in and out of a firing position without using a large and obvious towing vehicle.

More recent additions to the artillery arm are the SP 152-mm howitzer and SP 122-mm howitzer. The 122-mm has an amphibious capability and carries HEAT as well as HE.

However, it is an axiom that equipment is only as good as the men who use it. The Soviet soldier, like his Western counterpart, has been denigrated as 'soft' by military commentators within Russia. It is true that many of the young men in Russia have a reluctance to do their military service, which is an interference in their careers. The government has therefore reduced the entry age to 18–18½, and service time to two years. It has also linked academic grades to military standards so that military inefficiency equates to academic examination results.

Officers and senior NCOs are regulars, and military traditions run in families. The occupation is highly regarded in the Soviet Union and there has been a gradual improvement in uniforms to give recognition to its status.

The Soviet soldier remains however a tough and patient, if unimaginative, enemy with a military system which is designed to keep him obedient and uncritical.

1,825,000 men and total reserves (all services) could be 25,000,000 of which some 6,800,000 have served in last five years.

46 tk divs.
115 motor rifle divs.
8 AB divs.
Tanks: 50,000 JS-2/-3, T-10, T-10M hy, T-54/-55/-62/-64/-72 med and PT-76 lt (most tks fitted for deep wading).
AFV: 55,000 BRDM scout cars; BMP MICV; BTR-40/-50/-60/-152, MT-LB, BMD APC.
Artillery: 20,000 100mm, 122mm, 130mm, 152mm, 180mm and 203mm fd guns/how, 122mm, 152mm SP guns; 7,200 82mm, 120mm, 160mm and 240mm mor; 2,700 122mm, 140mm and 240mm multiple RL; 10,800 ASU-57 and ASU-85 SP, 76mm, 85mm and 100mm ATK guns; 'Swatter', 'Sagger' ATGW.
AA Artillery: 9,000 23mm and 57mm towed, ZSU-23-4 and ZSU-57-2 SP guns.
SAM (mobile systems): SA-4 'Ganef', SA-6 'Gainful', SA-7 'Grail', SA-8 'Gecko', SA-9 'Gaskin'.
SSM (nuclear capable): about 1,300 launchers (units organic to formations), incl FROG, SS-21 'Scud-B', SS-12 'Scaleboard'.

DEPLOYMENT AND STRENGTH:
Central and Eastern Europe: 31 divs: 20 (10 tk) in East Germany, 2 tk in Poland, 4 (2 tk) in Hungary, 5 (2 tk) in Czechoslovakia; 10,500 med and hy tks.*
European USSR (Baltic, Byelorussian, Carpathian, Kiev, Leningrad, Moscow and Odessa Military Districts (MD)): 64 divs (about 22 tk).
Central USSR (Volga, Ural MD): 6 divs (1 tk).
Southern USSR (North Caucasus, Trans-Caucasus, Turkestan MD): 24 divs (1 tk).
Sino-Soviet border (Central Asian, Siberian, Transbaikal and Far East MD): 44 divs (about 6 tk), incl 3 in Mongolia.

* (Excluding tks in reserve.)

Soviet divs have three degrees of combat readiness: Category 1, between three-quarters and full strength, with complete eqpt; Category 2, between half and three-quarters strength, complete with fighting vehicles; Category 3, about one-quarter strength, possibly complete with fighting vehicles (some obsolescent).

The 31 divs in Eastern Europe are Category 1, about half those in European USSR and the Far East are in Category 1 or 2. Most of the divs in Central and Southern USSR are likely to be Category 3. Tk divs in Eastern Europe have 325 med tks, motor rifle divs up to 266, but elsewhere holdings may be lower.

NAVAL INFANTRY (Marines):
5 naval inf regts, each of 3 inf, 1 tk bn, one assigned to each of Northern, Baltic and Black Sea fleets, two to Pacific fleet. T-54/-55 med, PT-76 lt tks, BTR-60P, BMP-76 APC; BM-21 122mm RL; ZSU-23-4 SP AA guns; SA-9 SAM.

PARA-MILITARY FORCES: 450,000.
200,000 KGB border troops, 250,000 MVD security troops. Border troops equipped with tks, SP guns, AFV, ac and ships; MVD with tks and AFV. Part-time military training organization (DOSAAF) conducts such activi-

ties as athletics, shooting, parachuting and pre-military training given to those of 15 and over in schools, colleges and workers' centres. Claimed active membership 80 million, with 5 million instructors and activists; effectives likely to be much fewer.

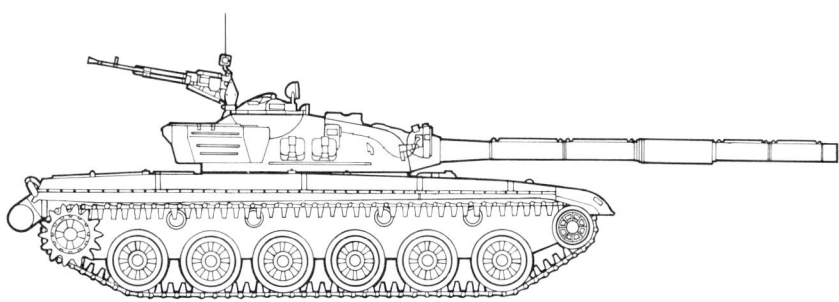

T-64 (or T-72)

Type: main battle tank
Crew: three
Weights: Empty
　　　　Loaded 90,389 lb (41,000 kg)
Dimensions: Length (overall) 29 ft 7 in (9.02 m); (hull) 21 ft (6.4 m)
　　　　Width 11 ft 0 $\frac{9}{10}$ in (3.375 m)
　　　　Height (to top of cupola) 7 ft 5 $\frac{1}{5}$ in (2,265 m)
Ground pressure:
Performance: road speed 62 mph (100 kph); range 311 miles (500 km) without the fuel in optional rear hull tanks; vertical obstacle 32 in (81.0 cm); trench 9 ft 2 $\frac{1}{4}$ in (2.8 m); gradient 60%; wading 4 ft 7 $\frac{1}{10}$ in (1.4 m) without preparation, and 18 ft (5.486 m) with the aid of a schnorkel
Engine: one 700-hp inline diesel engine
Armament: one 125-mm gun with 12 rounds of APFSDS, 22 of HE and 6 of HEAT, plus one 7.62-mm PKT machine-gun co-axial with the main armament, and one 12.7-mm DShK machine-gun for AA defence on the commander's hatch
Armour:
Used only by: USSR
Notes: The T-64 (sometimes referred to as the T-72) entered service with the Russian Army in 1976. For its capabilities the T-64 is a small vehicle, as a result of the 28-round automatic loader, and the use of only small men in the crew. The 125-mm main armament is an unusual weapon, the section nearer the breech being smooth bored, and the section nearer the muzzle rifled. An NBC system and night vision equipment are fitted as standard. The Russian claim for a top speed of 62 mph (100 kph) seems too high in view of the tank's weight and admitted horsepower, and a figure of up to 43 mph (70 kph) seems more realistic. Some commentators have claimed that the engine produces 1,000 hp, however, so it is conceivable that the T-64 could make its claimed speed on good roads. The cartridge cases are semi-combustible, leaving the crew to deal only with the stubs, and it appears likely that the gunner can use either a stereoscopic optical rangefinder or a laser rangefinder.

T-10

Type: heavy tank
Crew: four
Weights: Empty
　　　　Loaded 108,025 lb (49,000 kg)
Dimensions: Length (with gun) 33 ft 9 in (10.29 m); (hull) 24 ft 3 $\frac{1}{3}$ in (7.4 m)
　　　　Width 11 ft 3 $\frac{1}{2}$ in (3.44 m)
　　　　Height (to top of cupola) 7 ft 5 in (2.26 m)
Ground pressure: 10.1 lb/in² (0.71 kg/cm²)

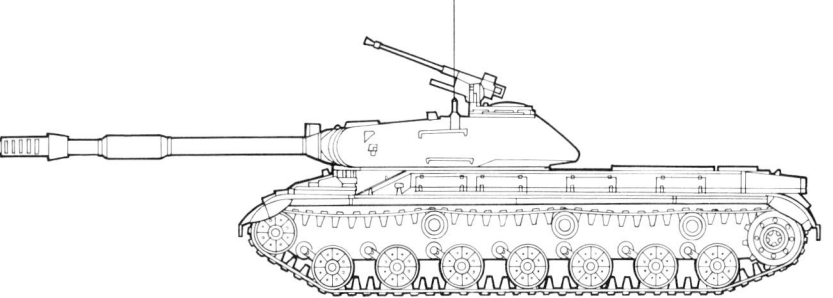

Performance: road speed 22 mph (35 kph); range 217 miles (350 km); vertical obstacle 35½ in (90.0 cm); trench 9 ft 10 in (3.0 m); gradient 60%; ground clearance 18 in (45.6 cm); wading 47¼ in (1.2 m) without preparation

Engine: one 690-hp V-2-JS inline diesel engine

Armament: one 122-mm gun with 30 rounds of APHE, HE and HEAT ammunition, plus one 14.5-mm KPV machine-gun co-axial with the main armament, and one 14.5-mm KPV AA machine-gun on the turret roof. Some 1,000 rounds of 14.5-mm ammunition are carried

Armour: 8¼ in (210 mm) maximum

Used also by: Czechoslovakia, East Germany, Egypt, Hungary, Poland, Romania, Syria, Vietnam

Notes: The T-10 succeeded the JS-3 heavy tank in service during the 1950s, and is still in limited use today. Although slightly lighter than modern MBTs such as the Chieftain and M60, the T-10 has a gun of comparable firepower, and thick armour. Mobility is considerably less than that of western MBTs of about the same weight, however. The T-10 was later succeeded by the T-10M, which has 14.5- instead of 12.7-mm machine-guns, night vision equipment, an NBC system, a main armament stabiliser, a stowage bin on the turret bustle and a schnorkel.

BMD

Type: light tank/armoured personnel carrier

Crew: three, plus up to six infantrymen

Weights: Empty
Loaded 19,841 lb (9,000 kg)

Dimensions: Length 17 ft 4⅔ in (5.3 m)
Width 8 ft 8⅓ in (2.65 m)
Height 6 ft 0⅖ in (1.85 m)

Ground pressure:

Performance: road speed more than 40 mph (65 kph); water speed 6 mph (10 kph); range 249 miles (400 km); the BMD is fully amphibious, being driven in the water by waterjets

Engine: one 280-hp inline diesel engine

Armament: one turret-mounted 73-mm smooth-bore gun fed from a 3-round automatic loader, plus one 7.62-mm PKT machine-gun co-axial with the main armament, one 7.62-mm PKT machine-gun on each side of the forward hull, and one AT-3

'Sagger' anti-tank missile on a rail above the main armament

Armour: probably $\frac{4}{5}$ in (20 mm)

Used only by: USSR

Notes: The BMD was at first designated the M1970 light tank, and is now known to be an airportable light tank/armoured personnel carrier (or infantry combat vehicle) for the Russian airborne forces. The turret of the *Boyevaya Machine Desantnaya* (BMD) is the same as that fitted to the BMP-1 MICV, and the vehicle is fitted with night vision equipment and an NBC system. The infantry are carried on open seats at the back of the vehicle.

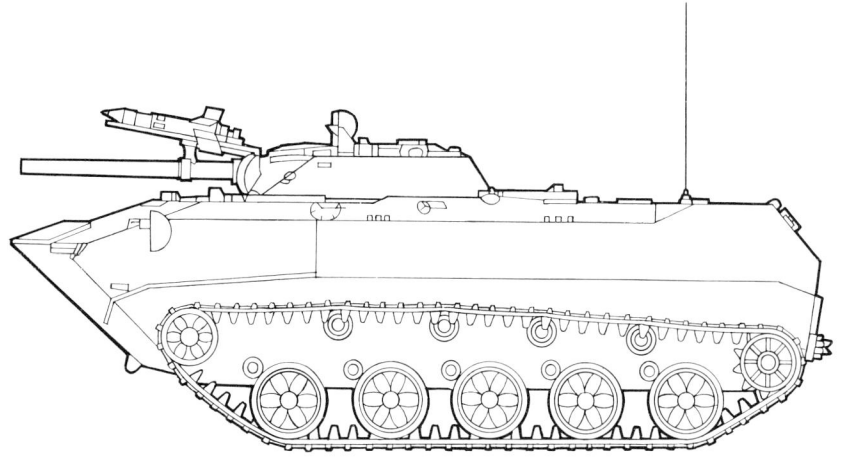

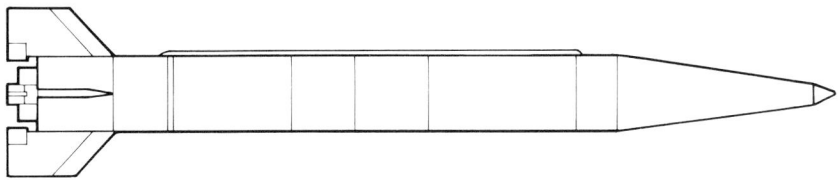

SS-1 'Scud'

Type: surface-to-surface artillery missile, vehicle-launched

Guidance: inertial, with possible radio command assistance at lift-off

Dimensions: Span
Body diameter $33\frac{1}{2}$ in (85 cm)
Length 36 ft 11 in (11.25 m)

Booster: liquid-propellant rocket

Sustainer: none

Warhead: nuclear or high explosive

Weights: Launch about 13,889 lb (6,300 kg)
Burnt out

Performance: range 100 to 168 miles (160 to 270 km)

Used also by: Bulgaria, Czechoslovakia, East Germany, Egypt, Hungary, Iraq, Libya, Poland, Romania, Syria

Notes: The basic artillery missile used by the forces of the Warsaw Pact and allied nations, the 'Scud' family has two members:
1. 'Scud A', probably no longer in front-line service
2. 'Scud B', launched from MAZ-543 transporters, instead of the converted JS-3 chassis often used earlier.

Only Russian 'Scuds' have nuclear warheads. 'Scud A' entered service in 1957, 'Scud B' in 1965.

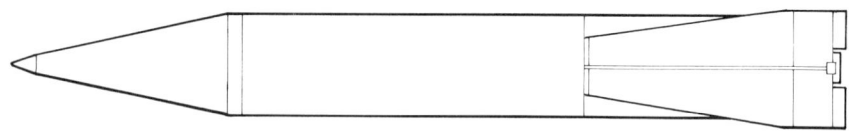

SS-12 'Scaleboard'

Type: surface-to-surface tactical missile.
vehicle-launched
Guidance: presumed inertial
Dimensions: Span
Body diameter $39\frac{2}{5}$ in (100 cm)
Length 36 ft 11 in (11.25 m)
Booster: liquid-propellant rocket
Sustainer: none
Warhead: nuclear
Weights: Launch 14,992 lb (6,800 kg) or
more
Burnt out
Performance: range about 500 miles (800
km)
Used only by: USSR

Notes: Transported on the MAZ-543 eight-
wheeled transporter, the SS-12 is believed
to have a warhead in the megaton range.

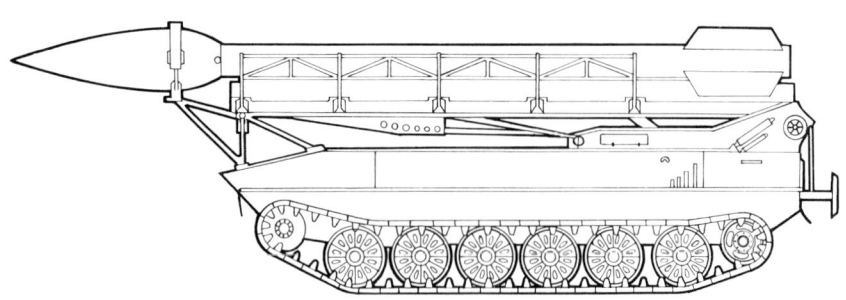

FROG-2 missile

Type: land-mobile artillery rocket
Guidance: none

Dimensions: Span 3 ft 6 in (1.05 m)
Body diameter 12 in (30.5 cm);
Warhead diameter 23.62 in
(60.0 cm)
Length 31 ft 2 in (9.5 m)

Booster: solid-propellant rocket
Sustainer: none
Warhead: Chemical, HE or Nuclear
Weights: Launch 5,400 lb (2,450 kg)
  Burnt out
Performance: range 12 to 15.5 miles (19 to 25 km)
Used only by: USSR
Notes: The FROG-2 is probably now used only for training purposes, but is typical of the early missiles of this series. The launch vehicle is a modified PT-76 chassis, which gives the whole system fairly good cross-country mobility. It seems that the system may be inherently amphibious as the whole weighs only 33,069 lb (15,000 kg). Road speed is 21.75 mph (35 kph), and road range 155 miles (250 km). The FROG-3 is mounted on a chassis that differs only in having two track return rollers.

FROG-3 missile

Type: battlefield missile
Guidance: none
Dimensions: Span
  Body diameter 15¾ in (40.0 cm)
  Length 34 ft 5⅝ in (10.5 m)
Booster: solid-propellent rocket
Sustainer: solid-propellant rocket
Warhead: chemical, HE or nuclear
Weights: Launch 4,960 lb (2,250 kg)
  Burnt out
Performance: range 22 to 28 miles (36 to 45 km)
Used also by: Egypt, Poland
Notes: The FROG-3 is the oldest of the FROG (Free Rocket Over Ground) family still in service. This was the first two-stage FROG missile, and has an HE warhead of 992 lb (450 kg) The launcher vehicle is based on the PT-76, which gives the system a road speed of 22 mph (35 kph) and a range of 149 miles (240 km). The weapon was introduced in 1960.

FROG-4 missile

Type: battlefield missile
Guidance: none
Dimensions: Span
Body diameter 15¾ in (40.0 cm)
Length 33 ft 5⅗ in (10.2 m)
Booster: solid-propellant rocket
Sustainer: solid-propellant rocket
Warhead: HE or nuclear
Weights: Launch about 4,409 lb (2,000 kg)
Burnt out
Performance: range about 28 miles (45 km)
Used also by: Algeria, Cuba, Cechoslovakia, Egypt
Notes: The FROG-4 differs in major aspects from the FROG-3 only in having a warhead of the same diameter as the rest of the body, rather than bulged as on the FROG-3.

FROG-5 missile

Type: battlefield missile
Guidance: none
Dimensions: Span
Body diameter 15¾ in (40.0 cm)
Length 29 ft 10¼ in (9.1 m)
Booster: solid-propellant rocket
Sustainer: solid-propellant rocket
Warhead: HE or nuclear
Weights: Launch about 6,614 lb (3,000 kg)
Burnt out
Performance: range about 34 miles (55 km)
Used also by: North Korea
Notes: The FROG-5 is derived from the FROG-4, but has a different warhead. The HE warhead weighs about 992 lb (450 kg).

FROG-7 missile

Type: battlefield missile
Guidance: none
Dimensions: Span
Body diameter 21⅔ in (55.0 cm)
Length about 29 ft 6⅓ in (9.0 m)
Booster: solid-propellant rocket
Sustainer: none
Warhead: HE or nuclear
Weights: Launch about 5,071 lb (2,300 kg)
Burnt out
Performance: range about 37¼ miles (60 km)
Used also by: Bulgaria, Czechoslovakia, East Germany, Egypt, Hungary, Iraq, North Korea, Poland, Romania, Syria
Notes: The FROG-7 reverts to the original single-stage layout, and is shorter and beamier than the intermediate FROGs. At the same time a new launch vehicle, the ZIL-135, has been introduced. The HE warhead weighs about 992 lb (450 kg). The FROG-6 and FROG-8 are training missiles, and the FROG-9 is about to enter service.

SSC-1 'Shaddock'

Type: surface-to-surface coastal defence missile
Guidance: infra-red or active radar homing, plus mid-course correction by radio
Dimensions: Span 6 ft 10$\frac{3}{10}$ in (2.1 m)
Body diameter 3 ft 3⅖ in (1.0 m)
Length about 32 ft 9$\frac{7}{10}$ in (10.0 m)
Booster: two solid-propellant rockets
Sustainer: ramjet or turbojet
Warhead: HE or nuclear
Weights: Launch 25,992 lb (11,790 kg)
Burnt out
Performance: speed Mach 1.5; range 280 miles (450 km) with mid-course guidance
Used only by: USSR
Notes: The 'Shaddock' coastal defence cruise missile is probably based on the naval SS-N-3 missile.

SSC-2A 'Salish'

Type: surface-to-surface coastal defence missile
Guidance: probably semi-active radar homing
Dimensions: Span about 16 ft 4$\frac{9}{10}$ in (5.0 m)
Body diameter
Length about 22 ft 11⅗ in (7.0 m)
Booster: solid-propellant rocket
Sustainer: turbojet
Warhead: HE
Weights: Launch
Burnt out
Performance: speed high subsonic; range about 62 miles (100 km)
Used only by: USSR
Notes: The 'Salish' appears to be derived from the AS-1 'Kennel'.

M-1965 RPU-14 artillery rocket launcher

Type: mobile artillery rocket launcher
Calibre: 140 mm
Number of barrels: 16
Muzzle velocity: 1,312 ft (400 m) per second
Ranges: Maximum 10,728 yards (9,810 m)
Minimum
Elevation: 0° to +45°
Traverse: 30° total
Reloading time: four minutes
Weights: For travel
In firing position 2,646 lb (1,200 kg)
Dimensions: Length 13 ft 3 in (4.04 m)
Width 5 ft 10⅘ in (1.8 m)
Height 4 ft 9 in (1.45 m)
Ammunition: HE warhead on each rocket
Crew: five
Used only by: USSR
Notes: The RPU-14 launcher is used by the Russian airborne arm, and fires a rocket with the following principal characteristics: length 3 ft 8¾ in (1.085 m); diameter 5½ in (140 mm); weight 87.3 lb (39.6 kg). The 16-tube launcher is mounted on a two-wheel carriage.

BM-21 artillery rocket launcher

Type: mobile artillery rocket launcher
Calibre: 122 mm
Number of barrels: 40
Muzzle velocity:
Ranges: Maximum 22,419 yards (20,500 m)
Minimum
Elevation: 0° to +50°
Traverse: 240°

Time to reload: 10 minutes
Weights: For travel
  In firing position 25,353 lb (11,500 kg)
Dimensions: Length 24 ft 1$\frac{2}{8}$ in (7.35 m)
  Width 8 ft 10 in (2.69 m)
  Height 9 ft 4$\frac{1}{8}$ in (2.85 m)
Ammunition: HE warhead on rockets
Crew: six
Used also by: Afghanistan, Angola, Czechoslovakia, East Germany, Egypt, Hungary, Iran, Poland, Syria, Vietnam
Notes: The BM-21 launcher is mounted on a Ural 375 lorry, which has a maximum road speed of 46.6 mph (75 kph) and range of 252 miles (405 km). The rocket used has the following primary characteristics: length 10 ft 7 in (3.23 m); diameter 4.8 in (122 mm); weight 101 lb (45.8 kg).

BM-24 artillery rocket launcher

Type: mobile artillery rocket launcher
Calibre: 240 mm
Number of cages: 12
Muzzle velocity: 1,526 ft (465 m) per second
Ranges: Maximum 11,155 yards (10,200 m)
  Minimum
Elevation: 0° to +65°
Traverse: 140°

Time to reload: four minutes
Weights: For travel
  In firing position 19,026 lb (8,630 kg)
Dimensions: Length 22 ft (6.705 m)
  Width 7 ft 7$\frac{1}{10}$ in (2.315 m)
  Height 9 ft 6$\frac{1}{2}$ in (2.91 m)
Ammunition: HE warhead on rockets
Crew: six

Used also by: Algeria, East Germany, Egypt, Israel, Poland, Syria
Notes: The BM-24 is a mobile artillery rocket system of Russian origin, based on the chassis of the ZIL 157 lorry, which gives the system a road speed of 40.4 mph (65 kph) and a range of 267 miles (430 km). The rocket used has the following principal characteristics: length 4 ft 2$\frac{4}{8}$ in (1.29 m); diameter 9.45 in (240 mm); weight 240.3 lb (109 kg).

BM-25 artillery rocket launcher

Type: mobile artillery rocket launcher
Calibre: 250 mm
Number of cages: six
Muzzle velocity:
Ranges: Maximum 32,800 yards (30,000 m)
  Minimum
Elevation: 0° to +55°
Traverse: 6°

Time to reload: three to four minutes
Weights: For travel
  In firing position 40,002 lb (18,145 kg)
Dimensions: Length 32 ft 2$\frac{1}{3}$ in (9.915 m)
  Width 8 ft 10$\frac{1}{4}$ in (2.7 m)
  Height 11 ft 5$\frac{4}{8}$ in (3.5 m)
Ammunition: HE warhead on rockets
Crew: six
Used only by: USSR

Notes: The BM-25 is the largest multiple rocket launcher produced by the USSR, and is based on the chassis of the KrAZ 214 lorry, which gives the system a road speed of 34 mph (55 kph) and a range of 329 miles (530 km). The rocket used has the following principal characteristics: length 19 ft 1$\frac{1}{10}$in (5.82 m); diameter 9.84 in (250 mm); weight 1,003 lb (455 kg).

AT-1 'Snapper'

Type: anti-tank missile, rail-launched from vehicles (sometimes from ground)
Guidance: command to line-of-sight by means of wire
Dimensions: Span 2 ft 5$\frac{1}{10}$ in (74.0 cm)
  Body diameter 5$\frac{1}{2}$ in (14.0 cm)
  Length 3 ft 8$\frac{1}{2}$ in (1.13 m)

Booster: none
Sustainer: solid-propellant rocket
Warhead: hollow-charge explosive, 11.57 lb (5.25 kg), capable of penetrating 13.78 in (350 mm) of armour
Weights: Launch 49 lb (22.25 kg)
  Burnt out
Performance: range 547-2,515 yards (500-2,300 m); speed 199 mph (320 kph)
Used also by: Afghanistan, Bulgaria, Cuba,

Czechoslovakia, East Germany, Egypt, Hungary, Mongolia, Poland, Romania, Syria, Yugoslavia, Zaire
Notes: Obsolescent and in the process of being replaced by the AT-3 'Sagger'.

AT-2 'Swatter'

Type: anti-tank missile, ramp-launched from vehicles and slow aircraft
Guidance: command to line-of-sight by means of radio
Dimensions: Span 2 ft 2 in (66.0 cm)
  Body diameter 5$\frac{9}{10}$ in (15.0 cm)
  Length 3 ft 8$\frac{1}{10}$ in (1.12 m)
Booster: none
Sustainer: solid-propellant rocket
Warhead: armour-piercing high explosive, capable of penetrating 15.75 in (400 mm) of armour
Weights: Launch 58.4 lb (26.5 kg)
  Burnt out
Performance: range 656–2,734 yards (600–2,500 m)
Used also by: Bulgaria, Czechoslovakia, East Germany, Egypt, Hungary, Poland, Romania, Syria
Notes: Usually carried on BRDM vehicle. The 'Swatter' may employ infra-red final homing.

AT-3 'Sagger'

Type: anti-tank missile, ramp-launched from vehicles

Guidance: command to line-of-sight by means of wire

Dimensions: Span 1 ft $6\frac{1}{10}$ in (46.0 cm) approximately
Body diameter $4\frac{7}{10}$ in (12.0 cm) approximately
Length 2 ft $9\frac{9}{10}$ in (86.0 cm)

Booster: none

Sustainer: solid-propellant rocket

Warhead: hollow-charge high explosive, 5.95 lb (2.7 kg), capable of penetrating 15.75 in (400 mm) of armour

Weights: Launch 24.9 lb (11.3 kg)
Burnt out

Performance: range 547–3,281 yards (500–3,000 m); speed 268 mph (432 kph)

Used also by: Afghanistan, Algeria, Angola, Bulgaria, Czecholsovakia, East Germany, Egypt, Ethiopia, Hungary, Iraq, Israel, Libya, Mozambique, Poland, Romania, Syria, Uganda, Vietnam, Yugoslavia

Notes: The 'Sagger' is a powerful and compact weapon. The type can be fired from a number of vehicle types, and there is a ground-launch pack available. The 'Sagger' is also used as part of the 'Hind' attack helicopter's armament.

SA-1 'Guild'

Type: land-mobile surface-to-air strategic defence missile

Guidance: radio command

Dimensions: Span about 9 ft $2\frac{1}{4}$ in (2.8 m)
Body diameter about $27\frac{3}{5}$ in (70.0 cm)

Length about 39 ft $4\frac{2}{5}$ in (12.0 m)

Booster: solid-propellant rocket

Sustainer: solid-propellant rocket

Warhead: high explosive

Weights: Launch
Burnt out

Performance: slant range perhaps 20 miles (32 km)

Used only by: USSR

Notes: Although seen on a transporter, the 'Guild' is thought to be a strategic defence weapon. The type entered service in 1954, and is now obsolete.

SA-2 'Guideline'

Type: surface-to-air tactical guided missile

Guidance: radio command

Dimensions: Span 5 ft $6\frac{9}{10}$ in (1.7 m)
Body diameter (booster) $27\frac{3}{5}$ in (70.0 cm); (second stage) $19\frac{7}{10}$ in (50.0 cm)
Length 35 ft $1\frac{1}{4}$ in (10.7 m)

Booster: solid-propellant rocket

Sustainer: liquid-propellant rocket

Warhead: 287-lb (130-kg) high explosive

Weights: Launch about 5,071 lb (2,300 kg)
Burnt out

Performance: speed Mach 3.5; slant range about 25 miles (40 km) or more; ceiling 59,055 ft (18,000 m)

Used also by: Albania, Czechoslovakia, Cuba, East Germany, Egypt, Indonesia, Iraq,

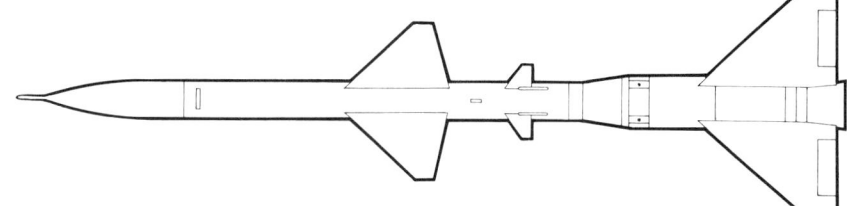

Poland, Romania, Somali Republic, Syria, Vietnam, Yugoslavia

Notes: The SA-2 system is land-mobile, the missile being carried on a Zil 157 semi-trailer transporter and erector. The tracking radar used with the system is the 'Fan Song'. During the 1967 and 1973 Arab-

Israeli wars, 'Guidelines' were dealt with by US-supplied ECM equipment, even after the Russians had provided the Arab nations with improved homing heads using radar. There are suggestions that a nuclear warhead is available.

SA-3 'Goa'

Type: shipborne or land-based surface-to-air tactical guided missile

Guidance: radio command, plus (probably) radar terminal homing

Dimensions: Span 3 ft $11\frac{1}{4}$ in (1.2 m)
Body diameter (booster) $23\frac{3}{5}$ in (60.0 cm); (second stage) $17\frac{7}{10}$ in (45.0 cm)
Length 22 ft (6.7 m)

Booster: solid-propellant rocket

Sustainer: solid-propellant rocket

Warhead: high explosive

Weights: Launch 882 lb (400 kg)
Burnt out

Performance: speed Mach 2; slant range about $18\frac{1}{2}$ miles (30 km); ceiling 39,370+ ft (12,000+ m)

Used also by: Bulgaria, Czechoslovakia, Cuba, East Germany, Egypt, Iraq, Libya,

Peru, Poland, Romania, Somali Republic, Syria, Tanzania, Uganda, Vietnam, Yugoslavia

Notes: The SA-3, whose naval counterpart is designated SA-N-1, is smaller than previous Russian anti-aircraft missiles, and can be carried in pairs on wheeled transporters. The 'Goa' is usually found with 'Low Blow' command radar and 'Flat Face' acquisition radar.

SA-4 'Ganef'

Type: land-mobile surface-to-air tactical guided missile

Guidance: radio command, plus semi-active term radar terminal homing

Dimensions: Span (wings) 7 ft 6½ in (2.3 m); (tail) 8 ft 6⅖ in (2.6 m)
Body diameter 35⅖ in (90.0 cm)
Length 28 ft 10½ in (8.8 m)

Booster: four solid-propellant rockets

Sustainer: ramjet

Warhead: high explosive

Weights: Launch about 3,968 lb (1,800 kg)
Burnt out

Performance: slant range about 43 miles (70 km); ceiling about 59,055+ ft (18,000+ m)

Used also by: Czechoslovakia, East Germany

Notes: The 'Ganef' first appeared in 1964, and is probably intended for the primary role of long-range high-altitude interception. Two 'Ganef' missiles are carried on an armoured tracked launcher. The radars normally associated with the 'Ganef' are 'Pat Hand' target acquisition and fire-control, and 'Long Track' surveillance.

SA-6 'Gainful'

Type: land-mobile surface-to-air tactical guided missile

Guidance: radio command, plus semi-active radar terminal homing

Dimensions: Span 4 ft 0⅘ in (1.24 m)
Body diameter 13⅛ in (33.5 cm)
Length 29 ft 4 1/10 in (6.2 m) with tail cone

Booster: solid-propellant rocket

Sustainer: ramjet, using the same combustion chamber as the booster

Warhead: 88-lb (40-kg) high explosive

Weights: Launch about 1,213 lb (550 kg)
Burnt out

Performance: speed Mach 2.8; range about 37 miles (60 km) at high altitude, 18½ miles (30 km) at low altitude; minimum range about 2½ miles (4 km); ceiling 59,055 ft (18,000 m)

Used also by: Bulgaria, Czechoslovakia, Egypt, Libya, Mozambique, Poland, Romania, Vietnam, Yugoslavia

Notes: Intended as a mobile battlefield defence system, the SA-6 was first revealed in 1967, and proved very effective in the 1973 Arab-Israeli war. Three SA-6 missiles are mounted on a modified PT-76 light tank chassis, and the radar usually associated with the system is the 'Straight Flush' fire-control radar, though 'Long Flush' surveillance radar is often used to acquire the target.

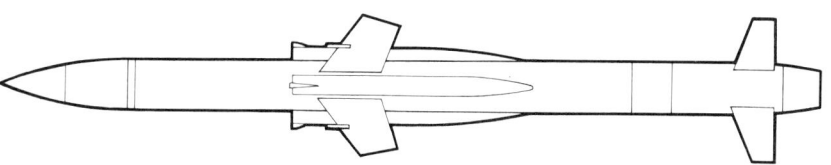

173

SA-8 'Gecko'

Type: land-mobile surface-to-air tactical guided missile
Guidance: radio command
Dimensions: Span about 23⅜ in (60.0 cm)
Body diameter 8¼ in (21.0 cm)
Length 10 ft 6 in (3.2 m)
Booster: probably solid-propellant rocket
Sustainer: probably solid-propellant rocket
Warhead: high explosive
Weights: Launch
Burnt out
Performance: speed possibly Mach 2; range 5 to 10 miles (8 to 16 km); operating altitude between 164 and 19,685 ft (50 and 6,000 m)

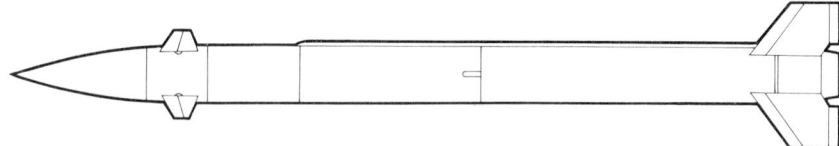

Used also by: Syria
Notes: Intended as a short-range all-weather battlefield defence system, the SA-8 is quadruple-mounted on the turret of an amphibious carrier, the turret also mounting a search and tracking radar, two tracking radars and two command guidance transmitting horns. Outright performance has clearly not been aimed at, the SA-8 system being notable for its mobility, and the manoeuvrability and acceleration of the missile itself. Two missiles, operating on different command frequencies to frustrate ECM, can attack the same target.

SA-9 'Gaskin'

Type: land-mobile surface-to-air tactical guided missile
Guidance: infra-red homing
Dimensions: Span
Body diameter
Length
Booster: solid-propellant rocket

Sustainer: none
Warhead: high explosive
Weights: Launch
Burnt out
Performance: slant range perhaps 5 miles (8 km)
Used also by: Bulgaria, Czechoslovakia, East Germany, Egypt, Hungary, Iran, Poland, Romania, Syria

Notes: The SA-9 system is designed to give Warsaw Pact forces a low-level battlefield air defence capability. The SA-9 missile, derived from the SA-7 'Grail' but with a larger warhead, a more powerful motor and improved controls, is carried in two double mounts on an adapted BRDM-2 vehicle, and launched by an operator located in the rotating base of the launcher system after he has acquired the target optically. Several 'Gaskin'-armed vehicles may operate together with the aid of an acquisition radar.

SU-100

Type: self-propelled gun
Crew: four
Weights: Empty
Loaded 69,665 lb (31,600 kg)
Dimensions: Length (including gun) 31 ft (9.45 m); (hull) 19 ft 5½ in (5.93 m)
Width 9 ft 10 in (3.0 m)
Height 8 ft (2.45 m)
Ground pressure: 11.6 lb/in² (0.82 kg/cm²)
Performance: road speed 33 mph (53 kph); range 186 miles (300 km); vertical obsta-

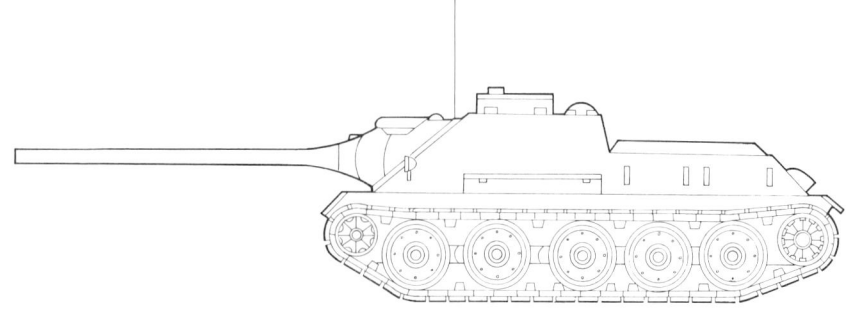

cle 25 in (64.0 cm); trench 9 ft 10 in (3.0 m); gradient 30°; ground clearance 14¾ in (45.0 cm); wading 35⅝ in (90.0 cm)

Engine: one 540-bhp inline diesel engine (originally 500-hp Model V-2-34 inline petrol engine)

Armament: one 100-mm Model 1944 (D-10S) L/54 gun with 52 rounds, plus one 7.62-mm machine-gun

Armour: ⅘ in (20 mm) minimum; 3 in (75 mm) maximum

Used also by: Albania, Algeria, Bulgaria, China, Cuba, Czechoslovakia, East Germany, Egypt, Iraq, Mongolia, Morocco, North Korea, North Yemen, Romania, Syria, Yugoslavia

Notes: The SU-100 was intended to partner the T-34/85 medium tank, in the role of

heavy tank destroyer. Accordingly, a high-velocity gun derived from a prewar naval piece of ordnance was installed in a fixed barbette built up on the chassis of a T-34 tank, and the new SU-100 entered service in 1944, proving well able to master contemporary German tanks. The type's chief tactical disadvantage was that fact that the gun could be depressed to only −2°, a factor partially rectified after the war, when depression was increased to −4°.

SA-7 'Grail'

Type: man-portable surface-to-air tactical guided missile
Guidance: infra-red homing
Dimensions: Span
    Body diameter 2¾ in (7.0 cm)
    Length 4 ft 11 in (1.5 m)
Booster: solid-propellant rocket
Sustainer: solid-propellant rocket
Warhead: high explosive, 5½ lb (2.5 kg)
Weights: Launch about 33 lb (15 kg)
    Burnt out
Performance: speed Mach 1.5; range about 6¼ miles (10 km)
Used also by: Afghanistan, Angola, Bulgaria, China, Czechoslovakia, Cuba, East Germany, Egypt, Hungary, Iran, Iraq, Kuwait, Libya, Morocco, Mozambique, Peru, Poland, Romania, South Yemen, Syria, Vietnam, Yugoslavia
Notes: The 'Grail' is designed to provide infantry with a means of countering aircraft, and particularly helicopters, over the battlefield. The weapon is shoulder-launched once a light indicating target acquisition has been illuminated. The weapon's chief tactical disadvantage is that it is a tail pursuit interception missile. There is apparently a Mark 2 version with improved propellant for greater speed and range, and an improved version with better guidance.

S-23 gun

Type: gun/howitzer
Calibre: 180 mm
Barrel length: 48.88 cal including muzzle brake
Muzzle velocity: 2,592 lb (790 m) per second
Ranges: Maximum 34,995 yards (32,000 m)
    Minimum
Elevation: −2° to +50°
Traverse: 44° total
Rate of fire: one round per minute
Weights: For travel 44,974 lb (20,400 kg)
    In firing position
Dimensions: Length 34 ft 4⅘ in (10.485 m)
    Width 9 ft 10 in (3.0 m)
    Height 8 ft 7⅛ in (2.62 m)
Ammunition: Concrete-piercing, HE and Nuclear
Crew: 14
Used also by: Bulgaria, China, East Germany, Egypt, Poland, Syria
Notes: This weapon was for some time known as the M-1955 203-in field howitzer, and it was not until some examples were captured by the Israelis in 1973 that the true calibre and designation of the piece became known. In Russian service the weapon is deployed at army (equivalent to the western corps) level. The HE projectile weighs 300 lb (136 kg).

M-1975 self-propelled gun

Type: self-propelled gun
Calibre: 152 mm
Barrel length:
Muzzle velocity:
Ranges: Maximum
    Minimum
Elevation:
Traverse:
Rate of fire:
Weights: For travel
    In firing position
Dimensions: Length
    Width
    Height
Ammunition:
Crew:
Used only by: USSR
Notes: Little is known of this new Russian weapon, and even the designation is conjectural. The system appears to be the M-1975 (D-30) howitzer mounted on the tracked chassis usually associated with the SA-4 'Ganef' SAM. For details of the howitzer's performance, see the M-1975 (D-30) entry.

M-1955 (KS-30) gun

Type: heavy anti-aircraft gun
Calibre: 130 mm
Barrel length: 54 cal
Muzzle velocity: 3,117 ft (950 m) per second
Ranges: Maximum (horizontal) 31,714 yards (29,000 m); effective slant 10,936 yards (10,000 m); (vertical) 19,685 ft (6,000 m)
    Mininum
Elevation: −5° to +80°
Traverse: 360°
Rate of fire: 12 rounds per minute
Weights: For travel 65,036 lb (29,500 kg)
    In firing position 54,895 lb (24,900 kg)
Dimensions: Length 37 ft 9½ in (11.52 m)
    Width 9 ft 11½ in (3.033 m)
    Height 10 ft (3.048 m)
Ammunition: HE
Crew: eight
Used also by: Vietnam
Notes: The M-1955 gun entered service with the Russian forces in 1955, but has since been phased out. Designed principally as a static defence weapon, the gun is nonetheless mounted on a wheeled carriage. It is designed for use in conjunction with radar fire-control. The HE projectile weighs 73.6 lb (33.4 kg).

M-1974 (SP.74) self-propelled gun

Type: self-propelled field gun
Calibre: 122 mm
Barrel length: 47 cal
Muzzle velocity:
Ranges: Maximum
　　　　Minimum
Elevation: −5° to +45°
Traverse: 360°

Rate of fire: about six rounds per minute
Weights: For travel 44,092 lb (20,000 kg)
　　　　In firing position
Dimensions: Length 23 ft 11⅝ in (7.3 m)
　　　　Width 9 ft 10¼ in (3.004 m)
　　　　Height 7 ft 11¼ in (2.42 m)
Ammunition:
Crew:
Used also by: Poland
Notes: It is expected that this Russian 122 SP field gun will have replaced all towed 122-

mm guns by the mid-1980s. The mounting is the first such example of the Russians using a field gun for the purpose. The chassis is based on that of the PT-76, and is powered by a 480-bhp diesel engine, giving the vehicle a speed of 31 mph (50 kph). The gun is the M-1955 (D-74) field gun in all probability, and for details of the weapon's performance see the entry on that gun. Ammunition capacity is thought to be about 40 rounds.

T-12 gun

Type: anti-tank gun
Calibre: 100 mm
Barrel length: 84.84 cal
Muzzle velocity: 4,921 ft (1,500 m) per second with APDS
Ranges: Maximum 9,295 yards (8,500 m)
　　　　Minimum
Elevation: −10° to +20°

Traverse: 27° total
Rate of fire: 10 rounds per minute
Weights: For travel 6,614 lb (3,000 kg)
　　　　In firing position
Dimensions: Length 30 ft 0⅜ in (9.16 m)
　　　　Width 5 ft 6⁹⁄₁₀ in (1.7 m)
　　　　Height 4 ft 9 in (1.45 m)

Ammunition: APDS and HEAT
Crew: six
Used also by: Bulgaria, Czechoslovakia, East Germany, Hungary, Poland, Romania
Notes: The Russian T-12 is a high-performance AT gun, and fires a fin-stabilised projectile from a smooth-bore barrel. The weapon is the standard gun of the anti-tank battalions of Warsaw Pact infantry divisions.

M-1955 gun

Type: anti-tank and field gun
Calibre: 100 mm
Barrel length: 54 cal
Muzzle velocity: 3,280 ft (1,000 m) per second with APHE
Ranges: Maximum 22,966 yards (21,000 m) with HE
　　　　Minimum
Elevation: −5° to +45°
Traverse: 55° total
Rate of fire: 10 rounds per minute
Weights: For travel 7,275 lb (3,300 kg)
　　　　In firing position 6,614 lb (3,000 kg)

Dimensions: Length 28 ft 7⁷⁄₁₀ in (8.72 m)
　　　　Width 5 ft 2⅖ in (1.585 m)
　　　　Height 6 ft 2⅖ in (1.89 m)
Ammunition: APHE, HE, HEAT and HVAP
Crew: eight
Used also by: Bulgaria, China, Czechoslovakia, East Germany, Egypt, Hungary, India, Mongolia, North Korea, Poland, Romania, Somali Republic, Vietnam, Yugoslavia

Notes: The M-1955 is apparently the gun on which the T-12 is based, and is itself an effective AT and field gun. The weapon is also used in the T-54A and T-55 tanks. It is large and heavy, but the 22.49-lb (10.2-kg) HEAT round can penetrate 15¾ in (380 mm) of armour at 1,094 yards (1,000 m), while the 35-lb (15.9-kg) APHE round will penetrate 7.28 in (185 mm) at the same range. The HE projectile weighs 34.6 lb (15.7 kg), and is an effective anti-personnel round.

M-1949 (KS-19) gun

Type: anti-aircraft gun
Calibre: 100 mm
Barrel length: 54 cal
Muzzle velocity: 3,280 ft (1,000 m) per second with APHE
Ranges: Maximum (horizontal) 22,966 yards (21,000 m); (effective slant) 7,655 yards (7,000 m); (vertical) 11,483 ft (3,500 m)
　　　　Minimum
Elevation: −3° to +85°
Traverse: 360°
Rate of fire: 15 to 20 rounds per minute

Weights: For travel 42,879 lb (19,450 kg)
　　　　In firing position 24,251 lb (11,000 kg)
Dimensions: Length 30 ft 3¾ in (9.24 m)
　　　　Width 7 ft 6 in (2.29 m)
　　　　Height 7 ft 2⅝ in (2.2 m)
Ammunition: APHE and HE
Crew: seven
Used also by: Afghanistan, Algeria, Bulgaria, China, Cuba, East Germany, Egypt, Hungary, Iraq, Kampuchea, Morocco, Poland, Romania, Vietnam
Notes: The M-1949 was introduced into Russian service in 1949, but is no longer in front line service with any Warsaw Pact forces. The weapon is mobile, but designed

for use with a radar fire-control system. The HE projectile weighs 34.6 lb (15.7 kg), while the APHE projectile weighs 35 lb (15.9 kg), and will penetrate 7.28 in (185 mm) of armour at 1,094 yards (1,000 m).

M-1944 (KS-18) gun

Type: medium anti-aircraft gun
Calibre: 85 mm
Barrel length: 50 cal
Muzzle velocity: 3,379 ft (1,030 m) per second with HVAP
Ranges: Maximum (horizontal) 16,951 yards (15,500 m); (effective slant) 6,562 yards (6,000 m); (vertical) 9,842 ft (3,000 m)
Minimum
Elevation: $-3°$ to $+82°$
Traverse: 360°
Rate of fire: 15 to 20 rounds per minute
Weights: For travel
In firing position 9,480 lb (4,300 kg)
Dimensions: Length 23 ft 1$\frac{1}{2}$ in (7.05 m)
Width 7 ft 0$\frac{2}{3}$ in (2.15 m)
Height 7 ft 4$\frac{3}{5}$ in (2.25 m)
Ammunition: APHE, HE and HVAP
Crew: seven
Used also by: Afghanistan, Albania, Bulgaria, China, Cuba, Czechoslovakia, East Germany, Egypt, Hungary, Iran, Iraq, Kampuchea, North Korea, Poland, South Yemen, Sudan, Syria, Vietnam, Yugoslavia
Notes: The M-1944 was developed from the KS-12 of 1939, and introduced into Russian service during 1944. The type is now used with radar fire-control. The HE projectile weighs 20.94 lb (9.5 kg), while the HVAP projectile weighs 11 lb (5 kg) and can penetrate 5.12 in (130 mm) of armour at 1,094 yards (1,000 m).

M-1945 (SD-44) gun

Type: anti-tank and field gun
Calibre: 85 mm
Barrel length: 53 cal
Muzzle velocity: 3,379 ft (1,030 m) per second with HVAP
Ranges: Maximum 17,115 yards (15,650 m) with HE; 1,750 yards (1,600 m) with HVAP
Minimum
Elevation: $-7°$ to $+35°$
Traverse: 54° total
Rate of fire: 15 rounds per minute
Weights: For travel 4,975 lb (2,257 kg)
In firing position
Dimensions: Length 26 ft 11$\frac{3}{5}$ in (8.22 m)
Width 5 ft 10 in (1.78 m)
Height 4 ft 7$\frac{3}{4}$ in (1.42 m)
Ammunition: APHE, HE and HVAP
Crew: five to seven
Used also by: Albania, Bulgaria, Cuba, Czechoslovakia, East Germany, Hungary, Poland, Romania
Notes: The SD-44 is the auxiliary-powered version of the M-1945 (D-44) AT gun, which differs only in having reduced overall weight as it has no power unit and a higher rate of fire. The HVAP projectile weighs 11 lb (5 kg), and will penetrate 5.12 in (130 mm) of armour at 1,094 yards (1,000 m). The motor provides 14 bhp, giving the SD-44 a speed of 4.66 mph (7.5 kph).

B-11 recoilless gun

Type: anti-tank recoilless gun
Calibre: 107 mm
Barrel length: 33 cal
Muzzle velocity: 1,345 ft (410 m) per second
Ranges: Maximum 7,272 yards (6,650 m)
Minimum
Elevation: $-10°$ to $+45°$
Traverse: 35° total
Rate of fire: five to six rounds per minute
Weights: For travel
In firing position 529 lb (240 kg)
Dimensions: Length 11 ft 8$\frac{1}{5}$ in (3.56 m)
Width 4 ft 9 in (1.45 m)
Height 2 ft 11$\frac{2}{5}$ in (0.9 m)
Ammunition: HE and HEAT
Crew: five
Used also by: Bulgaria, China, East Germany, Egypt, Hungary, Kampuchea, Laos, North Korea, Vietnam
Notes: The B-11 was introduced into Russian service during the 1950s, and is now an obsolescent weapon. The HE projectile weighs 46.96 lb (21.3 kg), while the HEAT projectile weighs 37 lb (16.8 kg), has an effective range of 492 yards (450 m) and can penetrate 15 in (380 mm) of armour at that range.

B-10 recoilless rifle

Type: anti-tank recoilless rifle
Calibre: 82 mm
Barrel length: 20 cal
Muzzle velocity: 1,056 ft (322 m) per second
Ranges: Maximum 4,812 yards (4,400 m)
Minimum
Elevation: $-2°$ to $+35°$
Traverse: 360°
Rate of fire: five to six rounds per minute
Weights: For travel 187 lb (85 kg)
In firing position 159 lb (72 kg)
Dimensions: Length 6 ft 3$\frac{1}{5}$ in (1.91 m)
Width 2 ft 4$\frac{1}{10}$ in (0.714 m)
Height 2 ft 2$\frac{1}{2}$ in (0.673 m)
Ammunition: HE and HEAT
Crew: four
Used also by: Bulgaria, China, East Germany, Egypt, Hungary, North Korea, Pakistan, Poland, Syria, Vietnam
Notes: The Russian B-10 recoilless rifle was introduced in 1950, and is generally an obsolete weapon. The HE projectile weighs 9.92 lb (4.5 kg), while the HEAT projectile weighs 7.94 lb (3.6 kg). The latter can penetrate 11.9 in (300 mm) of armour at 437 yards (400 m).

SPG-9 recoilless gun

Type: portable anti-tank recoilless gun
Calibre: 73 mm
Barrel length:
Muzzle velocity: 1,427 ft (435 m) per second, rising to 2,297 ft (700 m) per second with rocket assistance
Ranges: Maximum 1,422 yards (1,300 m)
Minimum
Elevation:
Traverse:
Rate of fire:
Weights: For travel 131 lb (59.5 kg) with bipod
In firing position
Dimensions: length 6 ft 11 in (2.11 m)
Width
Height 2 ft 7$\frac{1}{2}$ in (0.8 m) with bipod
Ammunition: HEAT warhead
Crew: three
Used also by: Bulgaria, Czechoslovakia, East Germany, Hungary, Poland, Romania
Notes: The Russian 73-mm SPG-9 is an extremely potent AT weapon, its HEAT warhead being able to penetrate more than 15$\frac{1}{3}$ in (390 mm) of armour, despite its small calibre. This is partially the result of the rocket-boosted flight of the missile.

RPG-7 launcher

Type: man-portable anti-tank rocket launcher
Calibre: 40 mm (launcher); 85 mm (projectile)
Barrel length:
Muzzle velocity: 984 ft (300 m) per second
Ranges: Maximum 547 yards (500 m) against a static target
Minimum
Elevation:
Traverse:
Rate of fire:

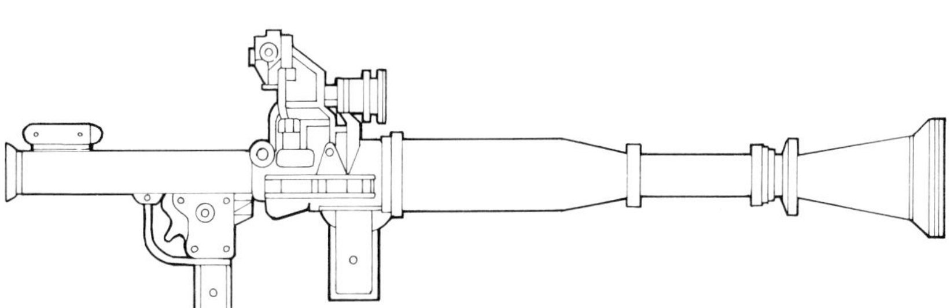

Weights: For travel 15.43 lb (7 kg)
In firing position 20.4 lb (9.25 kg)
Dimensions: Length (launcher) 39 in (0.9 m);
(overall) 3 ft 11¾ in (1.212 m)
Width
Height
Ammunition: HEAT warhead
Crew: two
Used also by: all Warsaw Pact forces, Vietnam, a number of African nations, and a variety of 'freedom' forces

Notes: The RPG-7 was first seen in 1962, and is basically a much improved version of the RPG-2 in concept. The HEAT warhead will penetrate 12⅝ in (320 mm) of armour. The current version is the RPG-7V, which is smaller than the original model but fires a larger rocket projectile. The RPG-7D is derived from the RPG-7V, but has a folding launch tube for use by airborne forces and clandestine operators.

RPG-2 launcher

Type: man-portable anti-tank rocket launcher
Calibre: 40 mm (tube); 82 mm (warhead)
Barrel length:
Muzzle velocity:
Ranges: Maximum effective 164 yards (150 m)
Minimum
Elevation:

Traverse:
Rate of fire: four to six rounds per minute
Weights: For travel 6.24 lb (2.83 kg)
In firing position 10.3 lb (4.67 kg)
Dimensions: Length (launcher) 4 ft 10⅘ in (1.494 m)
Width
Height
Ammunition: HEAT
Crew: two
Used also by: China, Egypt, Iraq, Libya, North Korea, Syria, Vietnam and other nations

Notes: The RPG-2 is basically a Russian development of the German World War II *Panzerfaust*, and is no longer used as a front-line weapon by Warsaw Pact forces. The type has also been manufactured in China as the Type 56, which uses the Type 50 projectile, with an armour penetration of 10.43 in (265 mm) compared with the Russian RPG-2's 7.09 in (180 mm).

M-1953 mortar

Type: heavy mortar
Calibre: 160 mm
Barrel length: 28 cal
Muzzle velocity: 1,132 ft (345 m) per second with HE
Ranges: Maximum 8,793 yards (8,040 m)
Minimum 820 yards (750 m)
Elevation: 50° to 80°
Traverse: 24° total
Rate of fire: two or three rounds per minute
Weights: For travel 3,241 lb (1,470 kg)
In firing position 2,866 lb (1,300 kg)
Dimensions: Length 15 ft 11⅓ in (4.86 m)
Width 6 ft 8 in (2.03 m)
Height 5 ft 6½ in (1.69 m)
Ammunition: HE and Nuclear
Crew: seven to nine
Used also by: Bulgaria, China, Czechoslovakia, East Germany, Egypt, Hungary, Iraq, Poland, Romania, Syria, USSR
Notes: The M-1953 mortar is basically an improvement of the M-1943 mortar of the same calibre, with a stronger and longer barrel. Both weapons are breech-loaded. The M-1953 is issued on the scale of 12 weapons to a motorised infantry (rifle) division. The HE round weighs 89.9 lb (40.8 kg), while the nuclear round weighs 91.5 lb (41.5 kg). The weapon is also built in China as the Type 60 mortar.

M-1953 (M-240) mortar

Type: heavy mortar
Calibre: 240 mm
Barrel length: 22.25 cal
Muzzle velocity: 1,188 ft (362 m) per second with HE
Ranges: Maximum 10,936 yards (10,000 m)
Minimum 1,640 yards (1,500 m)
Elevation: 45° to 65°
Traverse: 17° total
Rate of fire: one round per minute
Weights: For travel
In firing position 7,959 lb (3,610 kg)
Dimensions: Length 21 ft 4³⁄₁₀ in (6.51 m)
Width 8 ft 2 in (2.49 m)
Height 7 ft 3 in (2.21 m)
Ammunition: HE and Nuclear
Crew: eight
Used also by: Bulgaria, China, Romania

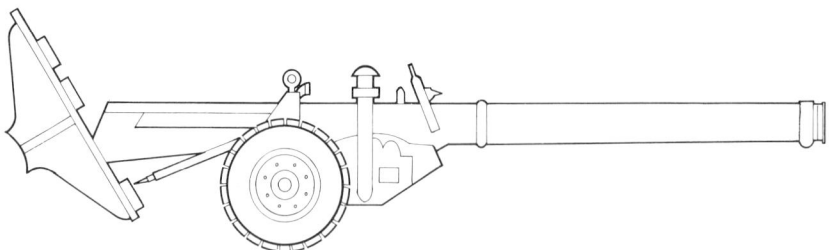

Notes: The M-1953 is the largest mortar in service, and is mounted on a substantial two-wheeled chassis. The weapon is breech-loading, and the types of ammunition are limited to two, an HE round weighing 220.5 lb (100 kg), and a nuclear round weighing 286.6 lb (130 kg). The weapon is deployed at motorised infantry division level (six mortars per division), but may be obsolete in Russian service.

M-1938/1943 mortar

Type: heavy mortar
Calibre: 120 mm
Barrel length: 15.42 cal
Muzzle velocity: 892 ft (272 m) per second
Ranges: Maximum 6,234 yards (5,700 m)
Minimum 503 yards (460 m)
Elevation: 45° to 80°
Traverse: 8° total
Rate of fire: 12 to 15 rounds per minute
Weights: For travel
In firing position 600 lb (272 kg)
Dimensions: Length
Width
Height
Ammunition: HE, Incendiary and Smoke
Crew: five to six
Used also by: Afghanistan, Albania, Algeria, Austria, Bulgaria, China, Congo, Czechoslovakia, East Germany, Egypt, Iraq, Lebanon, Morocco, North Korea, North Yemen, Pakistan, Romania, South Yemen, Syria, Tanzania, Vietnam, Yugoslavia
Notes: This Russian weapon is the standard mortar of motorised rifle regiments' mortar companies, six weapons being allocated to each such company. The M-1938 and M-1943 weapons differ only in the greater length of the latter's recoil cylinders. The HE bomb weighs 33.95 lb (15.4 kg).

M-1937, M-1941 and M-1943 mortars

Type: medium mortars
Calibre: 82 mm
Barrel length: 14.88 cal
Muzzle velocity:
Ranges: Maximum 3,280 yards (3,000 m)
Minimum 109 yards (100 m)
Elevation: 45° to 85°
Traverse: 6°
Rate of fire: 15 to 25 rounds per minute
Weights: For travel
In firing position 123 lb (56 kg)
Dimensions: Length
Width
Height
Ammunition: HE and Smoke
Crew: four or five
Used also by: Albania, Bulgaria, China, Congo, Cuba, Cyprus, Czechoslovakia, East Germany, Egypt, Ghana, Indonesia, Iraq, Kampuchea, North Korea, North Yemen, Syria, Yugoslavia
Notes: This family of useful Russian mortars is no longer in front line service with the forces of the USSR, but is widely used within the Warsaw Pact forces and Soviet client states. The M-1937, to which the data above apply, was derived from the M-1936, itself a copy of the French M-1917/31 Stokes-Brandt mortar. The M-1941 could be broken down for transport or towed on a wheeled carriage, and the M-1943 has wheels which are not removed before the weapon is brought into action. The HE bomb weighs 7.3 lb (3.315 kg). It seems that Russia is currently using a weapon very similar to the M-1937, but probably of lighter weight and fitted with improved sights.

M-1938 (M-107) mortar

Type: heavy mortar
Calibre: 107 mm
Barrel length: 15.6 cal
Muzzle velocity:
Ranges: Maximum 6,890 yards (6,300 m) with light bomb; 5,632 yards (5,150 m) with heavy bomb
Minimum
Elevation: 45° to 80°
Traverse: 6° total
Rate of fire: 10 to 15 rounds per minute
Weights: For travel
In firing position 375 lb (170 kg)
Dimensions: Length
Width
Height
Ammunition: HE
Crew: five or six
Used also by: China, East Germany, Ethiopia, India, Jordan, North Korea, Poland, Vietnam
Notes: The M-1938 is basically a scaled-down version of the 120-mm M-1938, designed principally for mountain warfare. The weapon can be broken down into pack animal loads, or transported on a two-wheeled carriage. The M-107 is an improved version used only by the USSR. There are two HE bombs available, one weighing 19.84 lb (9 kg) and the other 17.4 lb (7.9 kg).

ROKS-2 flamethrower

Type: portable flamethrower
Range: 38 yards (35 m)
Fuel capacity: 45.46 pints (10 litres)
Used also by: several Warsaw Pact armies
Notes: The ROKS-2 is an obsolescent Russian portable flamethrower. The fuel is carried in a large rectangular tank on the operator's back, and the compressed air propellant gas is stored in a small cylinder attached to the tank. The fuel is sufficient for about eight 1-second bursts.

ROKS-3 flamethrower

Type: portable flamethrower
Weights: Empty
Loaded 51.8 lb (23.5 kg)
Ranges: Maximum 37 yards (35 m) with thickened fuel
Maximum 16 yards (15 m) with unthickened fuel
Fuel capacity: 36.37 pints (8 litres)
Used also by: most Warsaw Pact armies
Notes: Although obsolescent, the ROKS-3 is still in limited service. The fuel is stored in a cylinder on the operator's back, with the compressed air propellant tank beside it. Ignition is effected by 10 7.62-mm ignition charges, and the fuel is sufficient for 10 5-second bursts.

LPO-50 flamethrower

Type: portable flamethrower
Weights: Empty 33.07 lb (15 kg)
Loaded 50.7 lb (23 kg)
Ranges: Maximum 77 yards (70 m) with thickened fuel
Maximum 22 yards (20 m) with unthickened fuel
Fuel capacity: 45 pints (9.9 litres)
Used also by: Warsaw Pact armies
Notes: The LPO-50 flamethrower is of Russian design, and consists of three fuel tanks, each topped by a pressurising cartridge, a hose and a flamegun, together with a selector lever and electrical pack. Each tank holds enough fuel for one burst of about two to three seconds.

TPO-50 flamethrower

Type: cart-mounted flamethrower
Weights: Empty 286.6 lb (130 kg)
Loaded 374.8 lb (170 kg)
Ranges: Maximum 197 yards (180 m) with thickened fuel
Maximum 71 yards (65 m) with unthickened fuel
Fuel capacity: 286.4 pints (63 litres)

Used only by: USSR
Notes: The TPO-50 consists of a two-wheeled cart fitted with three flamethrowers, each holding 95.5 pints (21 litres) of fuel. The propellant gas for each fuel cylinder is provided by a pressurisation cartridge on each tank. A two-man crew is necessary.

RPK machine-gun

Type: light machine-gun
Calibre: 7.62 mm
System of operation: gas
Muzzle velocity: 2,400 ft (732 m) per second
Range: effective 875 yards (800 m)
Rate of fire: 660 rounds per minute (cyclic); 80 rounds per minute (automatic)
Cooling system: air
Feed system: 40-round box or 75-round drum (30-round box can also be used)
Dimensions: Barrel length 23.27 in (591 mm)
Overall length 40.75 in (1.035 m)
Width
Height
Weights: 11 lb (5 kg) empty; 13.5 lb (6.13 kg) loaded with 40-round box; 15.65 lb (7.1 kg) loaded with 75-round drum
Sights: post (fore) and leaf, notch (rear)
Ammunition: 7.62 mm × 39

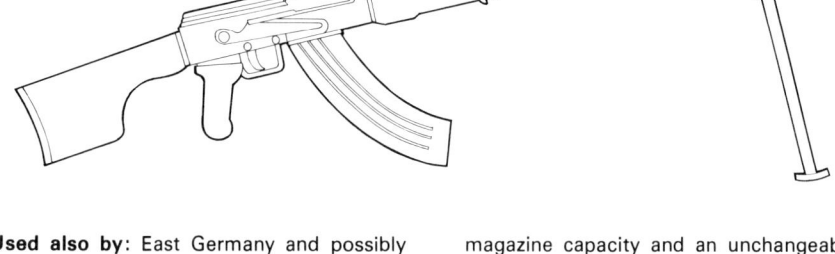

Used also by: East Germany and possibly other Warsaw Pact countries
Notes: The RPK is the standard light machine-gun used at squad level, and its similarities to the AK-47 and AKM reveal it as a Kalashnikov design. A useful weapon, the fact that it has only limited magazine capacity and an unchangeable barrel means that sustained fire is impossible, so the weapon should be considered a heavy-barrel rifle more than as a true light machine-gun. The RPKS variant has a folding stock.

PK machine-gun

Type: machine-gun
Calibre: 7.62 mm
System of operation: gas
Muzzle velocity: 2,705 ft (825 m) per second
Range: effective 1,094 yards (1,000 m)
rate of fire: 650 rounds per minute (cyclic); 250 rounds per minute (automatic)
Cooling system: air
Feed system: metal-link belt
Dimensions: Barrel length 25.9 in (658 mm)
Overall length 45.67 in (1.16 m)
Width
Height
Weights: 19.84 lb (9 kg) empty; 36.38 lb (16.5 kg) with tripod
Sights: post (fore) and leaf (rear)
Ammunition: 7.62 mm × 54R
Used also by: Bulgaria, Czechoslovakia, East Germany, Hungary, Poland, Romania and Russian client nations
Notes: The PK designation covers a family of machine-guns in service with the Russian and other armies. The basic weapon is of

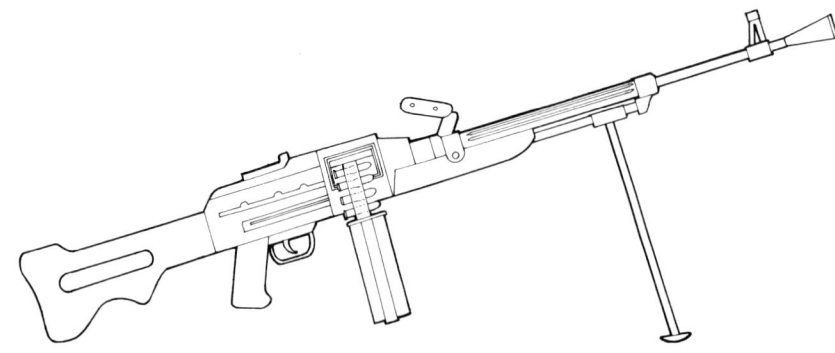

Kalashnikov design, and was first noticed by the west in 1964. The members of the family are:
1. PK basic medium machine-gun with a heavy fluted barrel
2. PKS, the PK mounted on a tripod, and the weapon to which the specification above applies

3. PKT, the PK adapted for use as a co-axial machine-gun in tanks
4. PKM, an improved PK of lighter weight and with an unfluted barrel
5. PKMS, the tripod-mounted PKM
6. PKB, the PKM with spade grips and a butterfly trigger.

Degtyarev DShK-38 and M-1938/46 machine-gun

Type: heavy machine-gun
Calibre: 12.7 mm
System of operation: gas
Muzzle velocity: 2,821 ft (860 m) per second
Range: effective 2,187 yards (2,000 m)
Rate of fire: 575 rounds per minute (cyclic); 80 rounds per minute (practical)
Cooling system: air
Feed system: metal-link belt
Dimensions: Barrel length 42.13 in (1.07 m)
Overall length 62.52 in (1.588 m)
Width
Height
Weights: 78.7 lb (35.7 kg); 259 lb (117.5 kg) for tripod
Sights: post (fore) and leaf with U notch (rear)
Ammunition: 12.7 mm × 108
Used also by: Bulgaria, China, Czechoslovakia, East Germany, Egypt, Hungary, Iraq, Poland, Romania, Syria, Vietnam and other Russian client states
Notes: The DShK-38 is a Russian weapon dating from just before World War II, and is based on the not very successful DK heavy machine-gun of 1934. The DShK-38 is in no way remarkable, but a workmanlike and effective weapon. In 1946 the Model 1938/46 was produced by replacing the earlier weapon's rotary feed mechanism with the more usual shuttle type of mechanism, and the two weapons can be distinguished by the DShK-38's humpred feed cover, and the Model 1938/46's flat feed cover.

KPV machine-gun

Type: heavy machine-gun
Calibre: 14.5 mm
System of operation: recoil
Muzzle velocity: 3,280 ft (1,000 m) per second
Range:
Rate of fire: 600 rounds per minute (cyclic)
Cooling system: air
Feed system: metal-link belt
Dimensions: Barrel length 53 in (1.346 m)
Overall length 78.98 in (2.006 m)
Width
Height
Weights: 108.25 lb (49.1 kg)
Sights: post (fore) and tangent with U notch (rear)
Ammunition: 14.5 mm B32
Used also by: client states of USSR
Notes: The KPV was designed after World War II to use the high-velocity anti-tank round designed by Degtyarev. The weapon is heavy but powerful, and found on the ZPU-1, ZPU-2 and ZPU-3 single, double or triple towed carriages. As such the weapon has proved a potent AA device against low-flying aircraft.

Mosin-Nagant M-1891/30 rifle

Type: bolt-action rifle
Calibre: 7.62 mm
System of operation: manually operated bolt
Muzzle velocity: 2,660 ft (811 m) per second
Range: effective 875 yards (800 m)
Rate of fire: 10 rounds per minute
Cooling system: air
Feed system: 5-round box
Dimensions: Barrel length 28.7 in (729 mm)
Overall length 48.5 in (1.232 m)
Width
Height
Weights: 8.7 lb (3.95 kg)
Sights: post (fore) and tangent, notch (rear)
Ammunition: 7.62 mm × 54R
Used also by: various countries
Notes: The M-1891 rifle uses the action designed by the Russian Colonel Sergei Mosin, and the magazine designed by the Belgian brothers Emile and Leon Nagant, to produce a well made and effective rifle, although it is on the long side.

Simonov SKS rifle

Type: self-loading rifle
Calibre: 7.62 mm
System of operation: gas
Muzzle velocity: 2,411 ft (735 m) per second
Range: effective 437 yards (400 m)
Rate of fire: 20 rounds per minute
Cooling system: air
Feed system: 10-round box
Dimensions: Barrel length 20.47 in (520 mm)
Overall length 40.2 in (1.021 m)
Width
Height
Weights: 8.49 lb (3.85 kg) empty
Sights: post (fore) and tangent with notch (rear)
Ammunition: 7.62 mm × 39
Used also by: some Asian countries
Notes: The Simonov rifle is a self-loading weapon of conventional design, and now obsolete, being used in the USSR only for ceremonial purposes.

AK-47 rifle

Type: selective fire assault rifle
Calibre: 7.62 mm
System of operation: gas
Muzzle velocity: 2,330 ft (710 m) per second
Range: effective 328 yards (300 m)
Rate of fire: 600 rounds per minute (cyclic); 100 rounds per minute (automatic); 40 rounds per minute (single shot)
Cooling system: air
Feed system: 30-round box

Dimensions: Barrel length 16.3 in (414 mm)
Overall length 34.2 in (869 mm) with stock extended; 27.52 in (699 mm) with stock folded
Width
Height

Weights: 9.48 lb (4.3 kg) empty; 11.3 lb (5.13 kg) loaded

Sights: pillar (fore) and tangent (rear)

Ammunition: 7.62 mm × 39

Used also by: Egypt, Syria, Yugoslavia and numerous Asian countries

Notes: The AK-47 is undoubtedly the most successful individual small arm produced since World War II, and is the work of the prolific designer Mikhail Kalashnikov. The design was completed in 1947, and the weapon entered Russian service in 1951. Kalashnikov's machine-guns all use the AK action, modified as necessary. The AK-47 is notable for its ruggedness and high rate of fire, combined with considerable accuracy.

AKM rifle

Type: selective fire assault rifle
Calibre: 7.62 mm
System of operation: gas
Muzzle velocity: 2,345 ft (715 m) per second
Range: effective 328 yards (300 m)
Rate of fire: 600 rounds per minute (cyclic); 100 rounds per minute (automatic); 40 rounds per minute (single shot)
Cooling system: air
Feed system: 30-round box
Dimensions: Barrel length 16.34 in (415 mm)
Overall length 34.5 in (876 mm)
Width
Height

Weights: 6.94 lb (3.15 kg)

Sights: pillar (fore) and tangent with U notch (rear)

Ammunition: 7.62 mm × 39

Used also by: Bulgaria, Cuba, Czechoslovakia, East Germany, Egypt, Hungary, Poland, Romania, Syria and other Russian client nations

Notes: The AKM is the updated model of the AK-47, the principal difference between the two weapons lying in the receiver, which is of machined construction in the

earlier weapon, and riveted pressings in the latter. The basic weapon has a fixed wooden stock, the variant with a folding metal stock being designated AKM-S. The principal distinguishing features of the AKM compared with the AK-47 are the grooved forward handguard, no gas escape holes on the gas tap off, and a small compensator on the muzzle.

Dragunov SVD rifle

Type: sniper rifle
Calibre: 7.62 mm
System of operation: short-stroke gas
Muzzle velocity: 2,723 ft (830 m) per second
Range: effective 1,422 yards (1,300 m)
Rate of fire: 20 rounds per minute
Cooling system: air
Feed system: 10-round box
Dimensions: Barrel length 21.54 in (547 mm)
Overall length 48.23 in (1.225 m)
Width
Height

Weights: 9.48 lb (4.3 kg) with telescopic sight

Sights: ×4 PSO-1 telescopic sight

Ammunition: 7.62 mm × 54R

Used only by: USSR

Notes: The SVD replaced the Mosin-Nagant M-1891/30 as Russia's chief sniping rifle in the late 1960s. The design of the weapon's action is based on that of the AK-

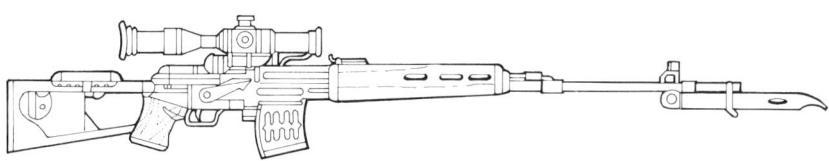

47 and AKM, but firing the 7.62 mm × 54R round rather than the lower-powered 7.62 mm × 39 intermediate round.

United Arab Emirates

23,500 men.*
1 Royal Guard 'bde'.
3 armd/armd car bns.
7 inf bns.
3 arty bns.
3 AD bns.
30 Scorpion lt tks; 80 Saladin, 6 Shorland, Panhard armd cars; 60 Ferret scout cars; AMX VCI, Panhard M-3, 12 Saracen APC; 22 25-pdr, 105mm guns; 16 AMX 155mm SP how; 81mm mor; 120mm RCL; Vigilant ATGW; Rapier, *Crotale* SAM.
(Scorpion lt tks on order.)

Deployment:
Lebanon (Arab Peace-keeping Force): 700.

*The Union Defence Force and the armed forces of Abu Dhabi, Dubai, Ras Al Khaimah and Sharjah were formally merged in May 1976.

AMX-VTP M56

Type: armoured personnel carrier
Crew: two, plus up to 11 infantrymen
Weights: Empty
    Loaded 30,864 lb (14,000 kg)
Dimensions: Length 18 ft 8⅔ in (5.7 m)
    Width 8 ft 10¼ in (2.7 m)
    Height 7 ft 10½ in (2.4 m)
Ground pressure: 9.95 lb/in² (0.7 kg/cm²)
Performance: road speed 37 mph (60 kph); range 230 miles (370 km); vertical obstacle 25⅝ in (65.0 cm); trench 5 ft 3 in (1.6 m); gradient 60%; ground clearance 19 in (48.0 cm)
Engine: one 270-bhp SOFAM 8 inline petrol engine
Armament: one 12.7- or 7.62-mm machine-gun
Armour:
Used also by: Argentina, Belgium, Ecuador, France, Indonesia, Italy, Netherlands, United Arab Emirates, Venezuela

Notes: The AMX-VTP was designed in the mid-1950s on the basis of the AMX-13 chassis. There are several variants:
1. command vehicle
2. dozer vehicle
3. ambulance
4. artillery command vehicle
5. 81-mm mortar carrier
6. 120-mm mortar carrier
7. pioneer vehicle
8. artillery support vehicle
9. cargo carrier
10. missile vehicle with twin *Entac* launchers.

Vickers Mark 1 machine-gun

Type: machine-gun
Calibre: 0.303 in (7.7 mm)
System of operation: short recoil
Muzzle velocity: 2,440 ft (744 m) per second
Range: effective 4,500 yards (4,115 m)
Rate of fire: 450 to 500 rounds per minute
Cooling system: water
Feed system: 250-round fabric belt
Dimensions: Barrel length 28.5 in (724 mm)
    Overall length 45.5 in (1.156 m)
    Width
    Height
Weights: 33 lb (15 kg) without water; 40 lb (18.2 kg) with water; 90 lb (40.9 kg) with water and tripod
Sights: blade (fore) and leaf, aperture (rear)
Ammunition: 0.303 in Ball Mark 8Z

Used also by: Tonga, United Arab Emirates and possibly other ex-British territories
Notes: The Vickers Mark 1 was introduced in 1912, and is one of the most successful machine-guns ever made, so successful, in fact, that no further marks were necessary. The gun is basically an improved and lightened version of the Maxim, and is notable for its accuracy and extreme reliability, its two main drawbacks being its weight and difficulties with the ammunition feed.

United Kingdom

British Army

The British Army is a modest 160,837 strong, with 5,740 women and 7,400 men enlisted outside Britain. This is 51.34 per cent of the total armed forces, whose annual budget is some 4.95 per cent of gross national product. However, it should be explained that quantity does not reflect quality, and that as a long standing volunteer army it has many advantages over conscript forces that sometimes have less than a year to turn a reluctant civilian into a soldier.

The army is composed of 10 armoured regiments, nine armoured reconnaissance regiments, 47 infantry battalions, three parachute battalions (of which only one is in a parachute role), five Gurkha battalions and the Special Air Service Regiment. The Royal Artillery deploys a missile regiment with Lance surface to surface missiles, and three air defence regiments with Rapier surface to air missiles. In addition it has one heavy, 13 field, one commando, one anti-tank and one locating regiment. There are 10 engineer regiments and six army aviation regiments.

The army is in the course of re-equipping with new artillery and AFVs, and discussions for the development of a new main battle tank have begun. Some of the equipment listed is either being phased out or introduced into service: 900 Chieftain MBTs, 271 FV 101 Scorpion light tanks, 243 Saladin armoured cars, 290 Scimitar, 178 FV438 and FV712 armoured fighting vehicles, and 1,429 Ferret and 200 Fox armoured scout cars. The British have 2,338 FV432 armoured personnel carriers with 600 Saracen and 60 Spartan APCs.

A number of the guns, vehicles and helicopters are joint ventures with NATO partners which has the advantage of standardisation and saves costs. The FH 70 155-mm gun has been developed with Germany and Italy. The Royal Artillery still use Italian 105-mm pack howitzers, but these are being replaced by the 105-mm Light Gun, about 100 of both weapons being in service. The Abbot 105-mm SP gun is still in use, and there are 155 of these available. Fifty American M109 155-mm guns, 31 M107 175-mm and 16 M110 203-mm SP gun/howitzers are deployed with the Royal Artillery. The Lance surface to surface missile and Blowpipe and Rapier anti-aircraft missiles are artillery responsibility, while the L/70 Bofors 40-mm AA guns are manned by the Royal Air Force Regiment and Royal Artillery.

The Army Air Corps operates 100 Scout, 7 *Alouette* II, 20 Sioux, 150 Gazelle and 20 Lynx helicopters.

American TOW anti-tank missiles are on order, while infantry anti-tank weapons include the 84-mm Carl Gustav and 120-mm recoilless gun, with the 66-mm LAW for individual close-range attacks.

The main commitment for the British Army is as part of the NATO forces in Germany, and here there is a force of 55,000 composed of one Corps HQ, four armoured divisions, the 5th Field Force, an artillery division and the Berlin Field Force of 3,000 men.

The United Kingdom has the 6th Field Force composed of three regular and two TAVR infantry battalions and logistic support group, the 7th Field Force with three regular and two TAVR battalions, the 8th Field Force with three regular and two TAVR battalions for home defence, a battalion group for the ACE Mobile Force (Land), one SAS regiment and a Gurkha infantry battalion. In Northern Ireland is the 3rd Infantry Brigade HQ with one armoured reconnaissance regiment and a variable number of battalions (generally about nine) on four-month internal security tours. They are supported by three Royal Engineer squadrons, two Army Aviation squadrons and an unknown number of SAS.

Other commitments include Brunei with one Gurkha battalion, Hong Kong where the Gurkha Field Force is composed of one British and three Gurkha battalions, a helicopter flight, an engineer squadron and support elements. In Cyprus British forces are divided between the garrison of the Sovereign Base Areas – an infantry battalion plus two companies with an armoured reconnaissance squadron and a helicopter flight, and the United Nations Force – an infantry battalion less two companies, a helicopter flight, an armoured reconnaissance squadron and logistic support.

Gibraltar has an infantry battalion and an engineer troop, while Belize has an infantry battalion and an armoured reconnaissance troop, an artillery battery, an engineer squadron and a helicopter flight.

The reserves stand at 116,800 Regulars, and 60,700 Territorial and Army Volunteer Reserve which make up two armoured reconnaissance regiments, 38 infantry battalions, two SAS regiments, two medium artillery and three light air defence and seven engineer regiments. As a separate force, the Ulster Defence Regiment deploys 7,800 men in 11 battalions.

Despite the high standards and enthusiasm of many of the men in the Regular and Reserve forces, the British Army has suffered from a starvation of funds and equipment which, with the regular round of Northern Ireland tours for BAOR units, have had a deleterious effect on morale. It is depressing for soldiers to see exported military equipment of a higher standard than that with which they are expected to operate in Germany, or NATO Allies using weapons which are yet to be issued.

160,837 men and 116,800 regular reservists. 60,700 TAVR.

10 armd regts.
9 armd recce regts.
47 inf bns.
3 para bns (1 in para role).
5 Gurkha bns.
1 special air service (SAS) regt.
1 msl regt with Lance SSM.
3 AD regts with Rapier SAM.
1 hy, 13 field, 1 GW, 1 cdo, 1 ATK, 1 locating arty regts.
10 engr regts.
6 army aviation regts.
900 Chieftain med, 271 FV101 Scorpion lt tks; 243 Saladin armd cars; 290 Scimitar, 178 FV438/FV712 AFV; 1,429 Ferret, 200 Fox scout cars; 2,338 FV432, 600 Saracen, 60 Spartan APC; 100 105mm pack how and lt guns; 155 Abbot 105mm, FH70 155mm, 50 M-109 155mm, 31 M-107 175mm, 16 M-110 203mm SP guns/how; 12 Lance SSM; 84mm Carl Gustav, 120mm RCL; *Milan*, Swingfire ATGW; FV102 Striker with ATGW; L/70 40mm AA guns; Blowpipe, Rapier/Blindfire SAM; 100 Scout, 7 *Alouette* II, 20 Sioux, 150 Gazelle, 20 Lynx helicopters. (FH70 155mm guns, TOW ATGW on order.)

DEPLOYMENT AND ORGANIZATION:
United Kingdom: United Kingdom Land Forces (UKLF): United Kingdom Mobile Force (UKMF) – 6th Field Force with 5 (3 regular, 2 TAVR) inf bns and logistal support group; 7th Field Force with 3 Regular, 2 TAVR bns; 8th Field Force with 3 Regular, 2 TAVR bns for home defence; 1 bn group (for ACE Mobile Force (Land)), 1 SAS regt (reduced), 1 Gurkha inf bn. HQ Northern Ireland: 3 inf bde HQ, 1 armd recce regt, variable number of major units in inf role,* 3 engr, 2 army aviation sqns and elements of SAS.
Germany: British Army of the Rhine (BAOR): 55,000: 1 corps HQ, 4 armd divs, 5th field force, 1 arty div. Berlin: 3,000 (Berlin Field Force).
Brunei: 1 Gurkha bn.
Hong Kong: Gurkha Field Force with 1 British, 3 Gurkha inf bns, 1 helicopter flt, 1 engr sqn, spt units.
Cyprus: 1 inf bn less 2 coys, 1 armd recce sqn, 1 helicopter flt and log support with UNFICYP; 1 inf bn plus 2 inf coys, 1 armd recce sqn, 1 helicopter flt in garrison at Sovereign Base Areas.
Gibraltar: 1 inf bn, 1 engr tp.

Belize: 1 inf bn, 1 inf bn (reduced), 1 armd recce tp, 1 arty bty, 1 engr sqn, 1 helicopter flt.

* Some nine drawn from BAOR on short tours.

Reserves: 116,800 Regular reserves. 60,700 Territorial and Army Volunteer Reserve (TAVR): 2 armd recce regts, 38 inf bns, 2 SAS, 2 med, 3 lt AD, 7 engr regts. 7,800 Ulster Defence Regiment: 11 bns.

FV4201 Chieftain

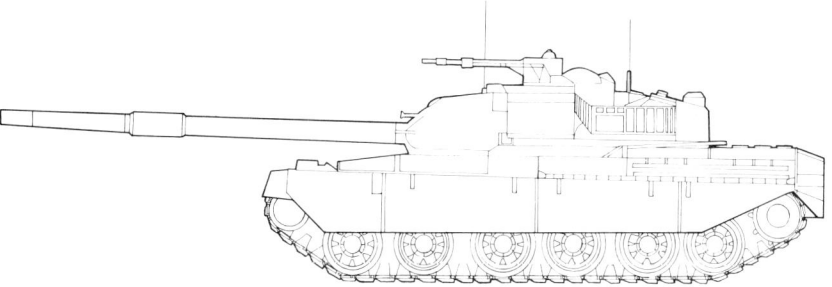

Type: main battle tank
Crew: four
Weights: Empty
    Loaded 121,250 lb (55,000 kg)
Dimensions: Length (gun forward) 35 ft 5 in (10.795 m); (hull) 24 ft 8 in (7.52 m)
    Width (overall, including searchlight) 12 ft (3.66 m)
    Height (overall) 9 ft 6 in (2.895 m)
Ground pressure: 14.22 lb/in² (0.9 kg/cm²)
Performance: road speed 30 mph (48 kph); road range 280 miles (450 km); vertical obstacle 3 ft (91.4 cm); trench 10 ft 4 in (3.15 m); gradient 60%; ground clearance 19⅔ in (50.0 cm)
Engine: one 840-bhp Leyland L.60 No 4 Mark 7A turbo-charged inline multi-fuel engine
Armament: one 120-mm L11A2 gun with 53 rounds of APDS, HESH and Smoke, plus one L21A1 (Brownng M2) 0.5-in (12.7-mm) ranging machine-gun with 300 rounds, one 0.3-in (7.62-mm) Browning machine-gun co-axial with the main armament, and one 0.3-in (7.62-mm) Browning machine-gun for AA defence on the commander's cupola. Some 6,000 rounds of 0.3-in (7.62-mm) ammunition are carried
Armour: 5 9⁄16 in (150 mm) maximum
Used also by: Iran, Kuwait
Notes: The Chieftain is one of the most powerfully armed tanks in the world, and also has good protection. Criticism of the type, which entered British service in 1967, has centred on the tank's weight, lack of power and general lack of agility. Laser range-finding is now used, and coupled with the stabilised gun, this means that targets can be engaged with a high probability of a hit at ranges of up to 3,280 yards (3,000 m) with APDS and 8,750 yards (8,000 m) with HESH ammunition. Night vision and NBC equipment are standard. There have been several marks of Chieftain, and other vehicles have been developed from the type:

1. Chieftain Mark 1 initial production model, used only for training
2. Chieftain Mark 2 operational model with a 650-bhp engine
3. Chieftain Mark 3 with an improved engine, a new cupola, and a better auxiliary generator
4. Chieftain Mark 3/G prototype
5. Chieftain Mark 3/2 with better turret air breathing
6. Chieftain Mark 3/S with yet better turret air breathing
7. Chieftain Mark 3/3 with an improved engine, longer-ranged ranging machine-gun, and a new air cleaning system
8. Chieftain Mark 4 trials model
9. Chieftain Mark 5 production model based on the Mark 3/3 with an up-rated engine and greater ammunition capacity
10. Chieftain Mark 6 will be Mark 2s uprated to Mark 5 standard
11. Chieftain Mark 7 will be Mark 3s and Mark 3/3s uprated to Mark 5 standard
12. FV4204 Armoured Recovery Vehicle
13. FV4205 Armoured Vehicle-Launched Bridge.

GKN Sankey FV432

Type: armoured personnel carrier
Crew: two, plus up to 10 infantrymen
Weights: Empty 30,290 lb (13,739 kg)
    Loaded 33,130 lb (15,280 kg)
Dimensions: Length 17 ft 3 in (5.25 m)
    Width 9 ft 2 in (2.8 m)
    Height (with machine-gun) 7 ft 6 in (2.286 m); (hull) 6 ft 2 in (1.88 m)
Ground pressure: 11.09 lb/in² (0.78 kg/cm²)
Performance: road speed 32 mph (52 kph); water speed 4.1 mph (6.6 kph); range 360 miles (580 km); vertical obstacle 2 ft (60.9 cm); trench 6 ft 9 in (2.05 m); gradient 60%; ground clearance 15¾ in (40.0 cm); wading 3 ft 7½ in (1.1 m) without preparation

Engine: one 240-bhp Rolls-Royce K.60 No 4
Mark 4F inline petrol engine
Armament: one pintle-mounted 7.62-mm
GPMG with 2,000 rounds
Armour: $\frac{1}{4}$ in (6.35 mm) minimum; $\frac{1}{2}$ in (12.7
mm) maximum
Used only by: UK
Notes: The FV432 entered British service in
1963, and is fitted with night-vision equipment and NBC gear as standard. The type
has been developed in a number of forms,
including:
1. carriage for the Wombat anti-tank
weapon and its crew
2. command post
3. fuel and ammunition carrier
4. 81-mm mortar carrier
5. ambulance
6. recovery vehicle with an 8-ton winch
7. artillery observation post
8. carriage for Cymbeline mortar-
locating radar
9. Field Artillery Computer Equipment
(FACE) carrier
10. minelaying vehicle
11. navigation vehicle
12. 84-mm Carl Gustav carrier
13. No 14 Battlefield Radar carrier
14. APC with a turret-mounted GPMG.
Other vehicles using the same chassis as the
FV432 are the Abbot SP gun, the FV434
recovery vehicle, the FV436 with Green
Archer mortar-locating radar, and the

FV438 with Swingfire anti-tank missiles. A
versatile vehicle, the FV432 suffers from
one major tactical disadvantage: the fact
that it has steel rather than aluminium
armour means that the vehicle is not inherently buoyant, so flotation screens have to
be erected before the vehicle can enter
deep water.

Short Brothers & Harland SB.301

Type: armoured personnel carrier
Crew: two, plus up to six infantrymen
Weights: Empty
Loaded 7,815 lb (3,545 kg)
Dimensions: Length 14 ft 1 in (4.29 m)
Width 5 ft 9$\frac{1}{2}$ in (1.77 m)
Height 7 ft 1 in (2.16 m)
Ground pressure:
Performance: road speed 60 mph (96 kph);
range 230 miles (370 km)
Engine: one 91-bhp Rover inline petrol en-
gine
Armament: none
Armour: $\frac{1}{3}$ in (8 mm)
Used by: six countries
Notes: The SB.301 is based on the chassis of
the long-wheelbase Land Rover, and is
intended for internal security operations.
Special protection is provided against
petrol and nail bombs.

GKN Sankey AT 105

Type: armoured personnel carrier
Crew: two, plus up to eight infantrymen
Weights: Empty 18,145 lb (8,230 kg)
Loaded 20,160 lb (9,145 kg)
Dimensions: Length 17 ft (5.18 m)
Width 8 ft 2 in (2.49 m)
Height 8 ft 7$\frac{1}{2}$ in (2.63 m)
Ground pressure:
Performance: road speed 60 mph (96 kph);
wading 44 in (1.12 m) without preparation
Engine: one 147-bhp General Motors Bed-
ford 500 inline diesel engine, or 164-bhp
Rolls-Royce B.81 inline petrol engine
Armament: a variety of installations are pos-
sible to the user's requirements, most
installations being of a turret-mounted

7.62- or 12.7-mm machine gun or 20-mm cannon

Armour: $\frac{1}{4}$ in (6 mm) minimum; $\frac{1}{2}$ in (12.7 mm) maximum

Used also by: Malaysia

Notes: The AT 105 is an improved version of the AT 104, with better cross-country performance and a greater versatility in the armament and other equipment fits possible. The AT105 is a 4 × 4 vehicle.

British Aerospace Swingfire

Type: anti-tank guided missile, container-launched from vehicles or from the ground

Guidance: command to line-of-sight by means of wire

Dimensions: Span 1 ft 2 $\frac{7}{10}$ in (37.3 cm)
Body diameter 6 $\frac{7}{10}$ in (17.0 cm)
Length 3 ft 5 $\frac{3}{4}$ in (1.06 m)

Booster: none

Sustainer: solid-propellant rocket

Warhead: hollow-charge high explosive, capable of penetrating all known armour

Weights: Launch
Burnt out

Performance: range 164–4,374 yards (150–4,000 m)

Used also by: Belgium, Egypt

Notes: Very powerful weapon. Introduced in 1969. The Swingfire can be launched from a number of vehicle types, by infantry and from helicopters in its Hawkswing model. Manufactured by British Aerospace.

187

Short Brothers Blowpipe

Type: man-portable surface-to-air tactical guided missile
Guidance: radio command with optical tracking
Dimensions: Span 10 in (25.4 cm)
            Body diameter 3 in (7.62 cm)
            Length 4 ft 7 in (1.4 m)
Booster: solid-propellant rocket
Sustainer: solid-propellant rocket
Warhead: high explosive
Weights: Launch (with IFF) $47\frac{1}{3}$ lb (21.46 kg)
         Burnt out
Performance:
Used also by: Canada
Notes: Capable of one-man operation, the Blowpipe is designed for close-range battlefield defence against low-flying aircraft and helicopters, both head and tail on. Once he has acquired the target visually, the operator has merely to aim along the sight, fire, and control the flight of the missile by means of a thumb control. The launcher is then discarded, the aiming/control unit then being attached to a fresh round. IFF facility is available with the aiming unit.

FH70 howitzer

Type: field howitzer
Calibre: 155 mm
Barrel length: 39 cal
Muzzle velocity: 2,713 ft (827 m) per second
Ranges: Maximum 26,250 yards (24,003 m) with normal ammunition; 32,808 yards (30,000 m) plus with extended range ammunition
        Minimum
Elevation: −5° to +70°
Traverse: 56° total
Rate of fire: six rounds per minute
Weights: For travel 20,723 lb (9,400 kg)
        In firing position 19,400 lb (8,800 kg)
Dimensions: Length 31 ft (9.45 m)
            Width
            Height 8 ft $4\frac{3}{4}$ in (2.56 m)
Ammunition: AT, HE, Illuminating and Smoke
Crew: eight to ten
Used also by: Italy, West Germany
Notes: The FH70 is a collaborative venture by the three user countries, design being the

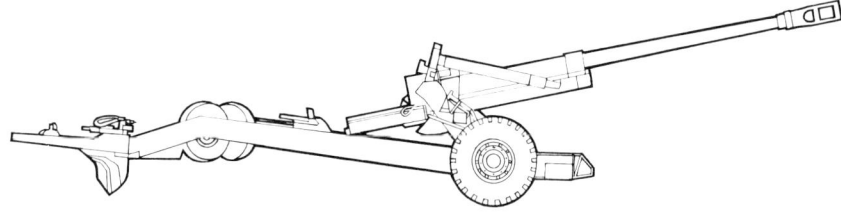

responsibility primarily of the UK and West Germany. The piece is provided with an auxiliary power unit capable of providing the gun with a 12.43-mile (20-km) independent travel capability. The HE projectile weighs 96.12 lb (43.6 m), and the gun is designed to use the US M549 rocket-assisted projectile (RAP), which increases range by about one-fifth.

Vickers FV433 Abbot

Type: self-propelled gun
Crew: four
Weights: Empty
　　　　Loaded 38,640 lb (17,527 kg)
Dimensions: Length (overall) 19 ft 2 in (5.84
　　　　m)
　　　　Width 8 ft 8 in (2.64 m)
　　　　Height 8 ft 2 in (2.49 m)
Ground pressure: 12.65 lb/in² (0.89 kg/cm²)
Performance: road speed 30 mph (48 kph);
　　water speed 3.1 mph (5 kph); range 242
　　miles (390 km); vertical obstacle 2 ft (60.9
　　cm); trench 6 ft 9 in (2.06 m); gradient
　　60%; wading 3 ft 11¼ in (1.2 m)
Engine: one 213-bhp Rolls-Royce K.60 Mark
　　4G inline multi-fuel turbo-charged engine
Armament: one 105-mm gun with 40 rounds
　　of HE and HESH, and one 7.62-mm GPMG
　　with 1,200 rounds
Armour: ¼ in (6.35 mm) minimum; ½ in (12.7
　　mm) maximum
Used also by: India (Value Engineered Abbot)
Notes: Introduced into service with the
　　British Army in 1964, the FV433 Abbot
　　105-mm SP gun is a highly efficient and
　　mobile weapon system. The range of the
　　gun is some 18,600 yards (17 km), and the
　　barrel life of the piece is at least 10,000
　　rounds. Although calibre is somewhat
　　small for an SP gun, the Abbot is an effec-
　　tive system because of its mobility, high
　　rate of fire, and lethal ammunition. Vickers
　　have also produced the Value Engineered
　　Abbot by eliminating some of the more
　　sophisticated equipment.

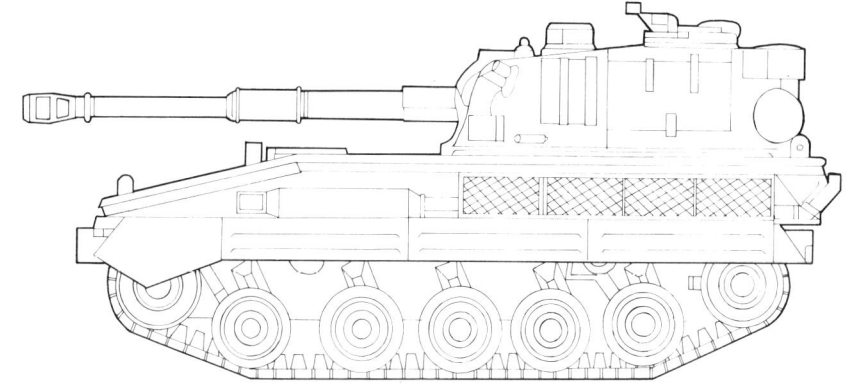

105-mm Light Gun

Type: light field gun
Calibre: 105 mm
Barrel length: 30.2 cal
Muzzle velocity: 2,325 ft (709 m) per second
Ranges: Maximum 19,140 yards (17,501 m)
　　　　Minimum 2,735 yards (2,501 m)
Elevation: −5° to +70°
Traverse: 11° total (360° platform)
Rate of fire: three rounds per minute (sus-
　　tained); six rounds per minute (maximum)
Weights: For travel 3,900 lb (1,769 kg)
　　　　In firing position as above
Dimensions: Length 28 ft 10¼ in (8.8 m) with
　　　　gun forward; 13 ft 4⅔ in (4.08
　　　　m) folded
　　　　Width 5 ft 10 in (1.78 m)
　　　　Height 7 ft (2.13 m) with gun
　　　　forward; 4 ft (1.23 m) folded
Ammunition: Anti-Personnel (Canister), HE;
　　HEAT, Illuminating, Smoke, Target Mark-
　　ing and WP
Crew: six
Used also by: some Middle Eastern countries
Notes: The 105-mm Light Gun has been
　　designed as an all-purpose weapon for all
　　climates, its low silhouette, light weight
　　and fast traverse making it a useful anti-
　　tank weapon. Shell weight is 33 lb (15 kg).

Wombat L6 recoilless rifle

Type: anti-tank recoilless rifle
Calibre: 120 mm
Barrel length: 33.33 cal
Muzzle velocity: 1,515 ft (462 m) per second
Ranges: Maximum 1,094 yards (1,000 m) against a static target; 820 yards (750 m) against a moving target
Minimum
Elevation:
Traverse: 360°
Rate of fire: four rounds per minute
Weights: For travel (portee version) 650 lb (295 kg)
In firing position as above
Dimensions: Length 12 ft 8 in (3.86 m)
Width 2 ft 10 in (0.86 m)
Height 3 ft 7 in (1.09 m)
Ammunition: HESH
Crew: three
Used also by: Australia
Notes: The Wombat was developed as a light successor to the Mobat, and entered British service during the 1960s. Spotting is by a 0.5-in (12.7-mm) rifle. Weight of the whole round is 60 lb (27.2 kg), and of the projectile 28.3 lb (12.84 kg). No details of armour penetration are available, but the round will probably penetrate more than 15¾ in (400 mm) of armour.

Mobat L4 recoilless rifle

Type: anti-tank recoilless rifle
Calibre: 120 mm
Barrel length: 33.33 cal
Muzzle velocity: 1,515 ft (462 m) per second
Ranges: Maximum 875 yards (800 m)
Minimum
Elevation:
Traverse: 360°
Rate of fire:
Weights: For travel 1,685 lb (764 kg)
In firing position as above
Dimensions: Length 11 ft 3¾ in (3.45 m)
Width 5 ft (1.525 m)
Height 3 ft 10¾ in (1.19 m)
Ammunition: HESH
Crew: three
Used only by: UK
Notes: The Mobat is the Wombat's predecessor, and has much the same performance, as it uses exactly the same round. However, weight is considerably greater than that of the Wombat, and tactical mobility considerably less. Spotting is by a modified 7.62-mm Bren gun attached to the Mobat barrel.

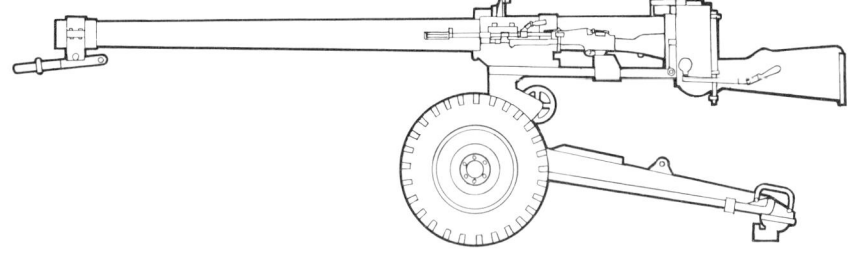

L1A1 mortar

Type: light mortar
Calibre: 81 mm
Barrel length: 15.68 cal
Muzzle velocity:
Ranges: Maximum 4,920 yards (4,500 m)
    with standard charge; 6,190 yards
    (5,660 m) with special charge
    Minimum 220 yards (201 m)
Elevation: 45° to 80°
Traverse: 360° (10° at 45° elevation)
Rate of fire: 15 rounds per minute
Weights: For travel 89.6 lb (40.62 kg)
    In firing position 79 lb (35.9 kg)
Dimensions: Length
            Width
            Height
Ammunition: HE, Illuminating, Marking and
    Smoke WP
Crew: three
Used also by: Canada, Guyana, India, Kenya,
    Malaysia, New Zealand, Nigeria, South
    Yemen, United Arab Emirates
Notes: The L1A1 mortar was designed jointly
    by Canada and the UK. The HE bomb
    weighs 9.7 lb (4.4 kg). The mortar is also
    used in the FV 432 mortar carrier.

51-mm mortar

Type: light mortar
Calibre: 51.25 mm
Barrel length: 10.05 cal
Muzzle velocity: 350 ft (107 m) per second
Ranges: Maximum 875 yards (800 m)
    Minimum 165 yards (150 m)
Elevation:
Traverse:

Rate of fire:
Weights: For travel
    In firing position 10 lb (4.6 kg)
Dimensions: Length
            Width
            Height
Ammunition: HE, Illuminating and Smoke
Crew: one

Used only by: UK
Notes: The 51-mm mortar is a weapon of
    great simplicity, but nevertheless effective
    for short-range engagements. It is
    designed for infantry use, and the HE bomb
    weighs 1.75 lb (0.79 kg).

2-in mortar

Type: light mortar
Calibre: 2 in (51.2 mm)
Barrel length: 10.83 cal
Muzzle velocity:
Ranges: Maximum about 55 yards (503 m)
    Minimum
Elevation:
Traverse:
Rate of fire: 25 rounds per minute
Weights: For travel
    In firing position 23 lb (10.5 kg)
Dimensions: Length
            Width
            Height
Ammunition: HE, Illuminating, Signal and
    Smoke
Crew: one or two
Used only by: UK
Notes: The 2-in mortar is now obsolete and
    about to be replaced by the 51-mm mortar.
    The HE bomb weighs 2.25 lb (1.022 kg).
    The weapon is controlled directly in line
    and elevation by the firer's hand.

L7 machine-gun

Type: general-purpose machine-gun
Calibre: 7.62 mm
System of operation: gas
Muzzle velocity: 2,750 ft (838 m) per second
Range:
Rate of fire: 750 to 1,000 rounds per minute (cyclic); 100 rounds per minute (rapid fire as LMG); 200 rounds per minute (rapid fire as a sustained-fire weapon)
Cooling system: air
Feed system: metal-link belt
Dimensions: Barrel length 21.54 in (547 mm) without flash hider
Overall length 48.5 in (1.232 m) as a light machine-gun; 41.25 in (1.048 m) as a sustained-fire machine-gun
Width
Height
Weights: 24 lb (10.9 kg) as a light machine-gun; 54 lb (24.51 kg) with L4A1 tripod
Sights: blade (fore) and aperture (rear)
Ammunition: 7.62 mm × 51
Used only by: UK
Notes: The L7 is basically the British version of the Belgian FN MAG. The L7A1 initial model entered service in 1961, and the

modified L7A2 shortly after this. None of the changes was of a major nature.

Light Support Weapon

Type: light support weapon (light machine-gun)
Calibre: 4.85 mm
System of operation: gas
Muzzle velocity: 3,050 ft (930 m) per second
Range:
Rate of fire: 700 to 850 rounds per minute (cyclic)
Cooling system: air
Feed system: 20- or 30-round box
Dimensions: Barrel length 25.4 in (646 mm)
Overall length 35.4 in (900 mm)
Width
Height
Weights: 10.32 lb (4.68 kg) unloaded; 11.6 lb (5.26 kg) loaded
Sights:

Ammunition: 4.85 mm Ball
Used by: under development for trials purposes
Notes: The Light Support Weapon has been produced as the British contender for a NATO competition to find a new calibre and weapon to replace current light machine-guns in the 1980s, and has about 80% commonality of parts with the Individual Weapon produced for the same purpose. The LSW is about 2.2 lb (1 kg) heavier than the IW, is longer and has a higher muzzle velocity. The weapon has a straight-through design, and can be fired from the shoulder as well as from its bipod. However, it seems unlikely that the 4.85-mm round will find NATO favour against the established 5.56-mm rounds, and so production of this interesting weapon is unlikely.

L2A3 Sterling sub-machine gun

Type: sub-machine gun
Calibre: 9 mm
System of operation: blowback
Muzzle velocity: 1,280 ft (390 m) per second
Range: effective 219 yards (200 m)
Rate of fire: 550 rounds per minute (cyclic); 102 rounds per minute (automatic)
Cooling system: air
Feed system: 34-round box
Dimensions: Barrel length 7.8 in (198 mm)
Overall length 27.95 in (710 mm) with stock extended; 19 in (483 mm) with stock folded
Width
Height
Weights: 6 lb (2.72 kg) unloaded; 7.65 lb (3.47 kg) loaded
Sights: blade (fore) and flip, aperture (rear)
Ammunition: 9 mm × 19 Parabellum
Used also by: Ghana, India, Libya, Malaysia, Nigeria, Tunisia and 72 other nations
Notes: The Sterling sub-machine gun is the successor to the Sten gun, and was designed initially in 1942, entering production in 1944. The type in service today is the L2A3, which is sold commercially as the Sterling Mark 4.

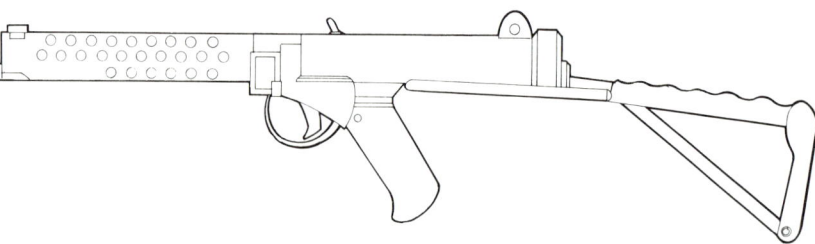

L34A1 Sterling sub-machine gun

Type: silenced sub-machine gun
Calibre: 9 mm
System of operation: blowback
Muzzle velocity: 960 to 1,017 ft (293 to 310 m) per second
Range: effective 164 yards (150 m)
Rate of fire: 515 to 565 rounds per minute (cyclic); 102 rounds per minute (automatic); 45 rounds per minute (single shot)
Cooling system: air
Feed system: 34-round box
Dimensions: Barrel length 7.8 in (198 mm)
Overall length 34 in (864 mm) with stock extended; 26 in (660 mm) with stock folded
Width
Height
Weights: 7.94 lb (3.6 kg) unloaded; 9.5 lb (4.31 kg) loaded
Sights: blade (fore) and flip, aperture (rear)
Ammunition: 9 mm × 19 Parabellum
Used only by: UK
Notes: The L34A1 is the silenced version of the L2A3, and is sold commercially as the Patchett/Sterling Mark 5. The silencing works by allowing much of the propellant gas to escape through the barrel wall through 72 radial holes and move through a diffuser before returning to the barrel to escape through a spiral diffuser extending forward of the muzzle.

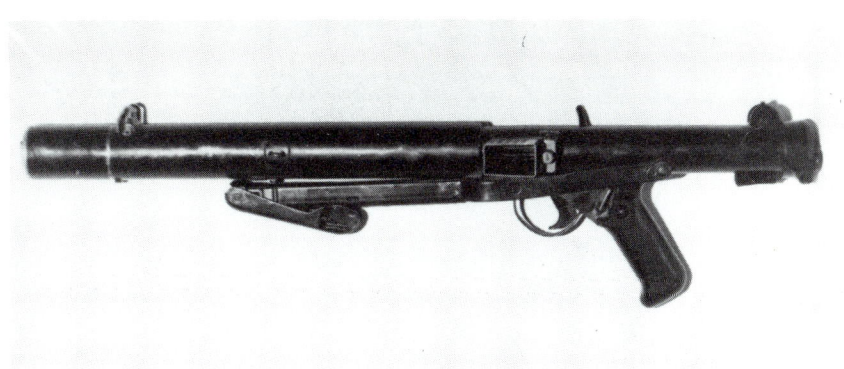

Lee-Enfield SMLE No 4 rifle

Type: bolt-action rifle
Calibre: 0.303 in (7.7 mm)
System of operation: manually operated bolt
Muzzle velocity: 2,465 ft (751 m) per second
Range: effective 547 yards (500 m)
Rate of fire: 20 rounds per minute
Cooling system: air
Feed system: 10-round box
Dimensions: Barrel length 25.2 in (640 mm)
Overall length 44.43 in (1.129 m)
Width
Height
Weights: 9.125 lb (4.14 kg) loaded

Sights: protected blade (fore) and adjustable aperture (rear)
Ammunition: 0.303 in Ball Mark VII
Used by: still widely used in former British territories
Notes: The Rifle No 4 Mark 2 was the last production variant of the celebrated SMLE series, and was developed during the late 1920s and early 1930s as successor to the No 1 Mark III. Rugged and accurate, the weapon is capable of a high rate of fire by bolt-action standards, and is still a moderately effective weapon.

L1A1 rifle

Type: self-loading rifle
Calibre: 7.62 mm
System of operation: gas
Muzzle velocity: 2,750 ft (838 m) per second
Range: effective 656 yards (600 m)
Rate of fire: 40 rounds per minute
Cooling system: air
Feed system: 20-round box
Dimensions: Barrel length 21.8 in (554 mm)
Overall length 45 in (1.143 m)
Width
Height
Weights: 9.5 lb (4.3 kg) empty; 11 lb (5 kg) loaded
Sights: trilux (fore) and aperture (rear)
Ammunition: 7.62 mm × 51
Used only by: UK
Notes: The L7 is the FN FAL weapon built under licence, with modifications, in the UK. The most important difference is that the British weapon is capable of firing only single shots, whereas the Belgian weapon is capable of selective fire.

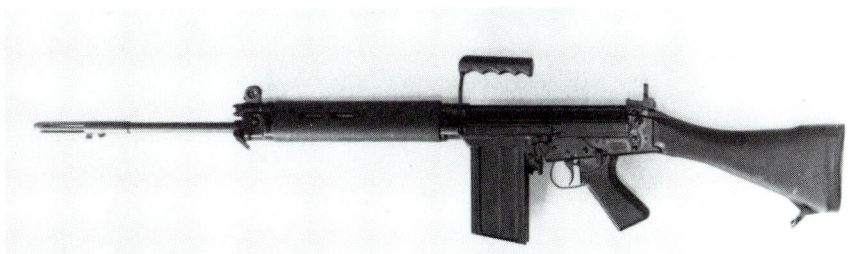

L42A1 rifle

Type: sniper's rifle
Calibre: 7.62 mm
System of operation: manually operated bolt
Muzzle velocity: 2,750 ft (838 m) per second
Range:
Rate of fire:
Cooling system: air
Feed system: 10-round box
Dimensions: Barrel length 27.5 in (699 mm)
Overall length 46.5 in (1.181 m)
Width
Height
Weights: 9.75 lb (4.43 kg)
Sights: L1A1 telescope
Ammunition: 7.62 mm × 51
Used only by: UK
Notes: The L42A1 is a specialist sniper rifle made by adapting No 4 SMLE rifles to fire the 7.62-mm NATO round, and adding provision for a telescopic sight.

Individual Weapon

Type: selective fire assault rifle
Calibre: 4.85 mm
System of operation: gas
Muzzle velocity: 2,953 ft (900 m) per second
Range:
Rate of fire: 700 to 850 rounds per minute (cyclic)
Cooling system: air
Feed system: 20- or 30-round box
Dimensions: Barrel length 20.4 in (518.5 mm) including flash hider
Overall length 30.3 in (770 mm)
Width
Height
Weights: 8.2 lb (3.72 kg) empty; 9.08 lb (4.12 kg)
Sights: × 4 SUSAT telescopic sight
Ammunition: 4.85 mm Ball
Used by: under development for trials purposes
Notes: The Individual Weapon is being developed in parallel with the Light Support Weapon, with which it shares some 80% of components. The IW differs from the LSW mainly in being shorter, and therefore having a lower muzzle velocity, and not being fitted with a bipod. There seems to be little chance that the British 4.85 mm round will be adopted as a standard NATO round, and so the production chances of the IW are slim, despite the manifest capabilities of the weapon.

United States of America

United States Army

Despite being the most powerful army in NATO, the United States Army is caught up in the complex business of changing from a conscript force to a volunteer army. Whereas a conscript army has unsuitable and reluctant men drafted into its ranks, it will also receive men who are quick witted enough to grasp the workings of modern weapons systems and who make excellent soldiers if well led and motivated. A volunteer army, during periods of high employment, is forced to accept low standards if it is to keep its forces up to strength. The US Army is not only faced with this problem of manning, but also with a programme of Equal Opportunities which though conceived with the highest intentions has produced some rather bizarre situations. Women who have always been a vital part of any army are now being moved from their traditional roles to more front line employment. Out of an army of 774,200 some 50,700 are women.

One officer recalls a sergeant who had seen action in Korea and Vietnam reduced to confusion when the female clerk he had vociferously rebuked collapsed in floods of tears.

The peace time army has a career structure for officers which makes the politics of big business look simple. An officer relies on his confidential report for promotion, which puts him at the mercy of his superior. The system, unlike that of the British Army, is not as closely linked with exams and the phrasing of reports would delight the creators of Newspeak in 1984. If an officer has the slightest hint of imperfection in his report, like 'an excellent planner, he has trouble relating to his peers' a reader in the know will see the man as a high brow academic, 'stand offish' and possibly snobbish. To be normal the report must be good and to be good it must be excellent.

The Vietnam War, which nearly split the army apart and which produced the change to a voluntary system, has been forgotten as quickly as possible. The men who commanded platoons are now company commanders; and as one remarked, in the event of a war in Europe the platoon commanders would have to learn from their mistakes as they did in South-East Asia.

Unlike many European reserve forces the United States can boast a reserve arm which has very effective 'teeth'. The National Guard, which was once an alternative to the draft, receives modern equipment, including armour, APCs and vehicles. With a strength of 366,000 it is capable of manning two armoured, one mechanised and five infantry divisions, and 22 independent brigades. The last consist of three armoured, nine mechanised and 10 infantry. Four of the independent brigades and 11 of the battalions would be incorporated into active army divisions in the event of mobilisation. The National Guard also includes four armoured cavalry regiments and reinforcements to flesh out support units in regular formations.

A separate reserve capacity consists of the Army Reserves, with 190,000 men in 12 training divisions and three independent combat brigades. Of these, 49,000 do a short period of active duty annually, usually about two weeks.

The US Army has four armoured divisions, five mechanised divisions, five infantry divisions (one of which will be uprated to mechanised in 1979), an airmobile division, an airborne brigade, an infantry brigade, three armoured cavalry regiments, a brigade on duty in Berlin, and two special mission brigades. Army Aviation consists of an air cavalry combat brigade and independent battalions assigned for tactical transport and casualty evacuation. The vast number of helicopters available to the US Army during the Vietnam War were a source of some discord with the US Air Force who felt that they should be their responsibility. The army also deploys one Honest John, three Pershing and eight Lance SSM battalions.

Deployment is spread between the continental United States, Europe and the Pacific. In the United States there is a strategic reserve consisting of one armoured, one mechanised, three infantry, one airmobile and one airborne division, of which the 7th Army in Europe would receive one armoured and two mechanised divisions, and an armoured cavalry regiment (their equipment is stockpiled in Germany) in the event of hostilities. The United States have a brigade in Alaska and one in Panama.

The total forces in Europe stand at 198,000 men, of whom 189,000 are in Germany. The 7th Army consists of two corps, made up of two armoured and two mechanised divisions, one armoured and two mechanised brigades, and two armoured cavalry regiments, with 3,000 medium tanks, including those held for reinforcements from the United States. In West Berlin there are 4,400 men in an infantry brigade and various headquarters. Greece has a contingent of 800, Italy 3,000 and Turkey 1,200.

The Pacific theatre used to feature prominently in US Army deployment at the expense of Europe. Critics said that priority in equipment went to Vietnam and that stockpiles of vehicles and armour were rusting in Germany. Now the situation has been almost completely reversed. President Carter has suggested that troops be withdrawn from South Korea, but he is at some pains to emphasise America's commitment to the defence of Europe.

South Korea has 30,000 men in one infantry brigade and an air defence artillery brigade, but these forces will be reduced to one brigade in 1978. Hawaii has an infantry division less one brigade.

The armoury of the US Army includes some well tested weapons that have seen action with the US Army or its allies, and also in conflicts in the Middle East and India. America has 10,500 medium tanks, including 3,300 M48, 7,150 M60 (540 have been armed with Shillelagh ATGW and classified

M60A2) and 1,600 M551 Sheridan light tanks with Shillelagh.

The US Army has 22,000 M577, M114 and M113 APCs. Her artillery and missiles include about 2,500 105-mm and 155-mm towed guns and howitzers, 3,000 175-mm SP guns, and 105-mm, 155-mm and 203-mm guns and howitzers on SP mounts. Medium and heavy mortars include 3,000 81-mm and 3,000 107-mm, while there are 6,000 90-mm and 106-mm recoilless guns. Anti-tank guided weapons include the widely deployed TOW and also Dragon, while surface-to-surface missiles are covered by Honest John, which is being replaced by Lance and Pershing.

The US Army has a considerable AA artillery and SAM capacity: 600 20-mm and 40-mm towed and SP AA guns, 20,000 Chaparral SP SAM and Vulcan 20-mm AA gun systems, and Redeye and Stinger man-portable SAMs. The heavier Nike Hercules and Improved HAWK SAMs are due to be replaced by Patriot and Roland, which are currently on order.

The US Army has about 500 aircraft and 9,000 helicopters. Aircraft include 300 OV-1/-10, 200 U-8/-21 and 40 C-12, while helicopters include 1,000 AH-1G/Q/S, 4,000 UH-1/-19, 15 UH-60A, 700 CH-47/-54, 3,600 OH-6A/-58A, and H-13 (148 AH-1S are on order). Though this considerable helicopter strength reflects the lessons of airmobility learned in Vietnam, their role in Europe is more one of attack and tank hunting than massed troop lifts. In this capacity the smaller helicopters armed with TOW have an ability to 'shoot and scoot', hugging the terrain and contour flying until they appear over the skyline to engage a target, and then drop out of sight.

American arms and tactics have been employed with success in the Middle East and after a protracted war with failure in South-East Asia. As an Israeli officer said of Soviet arms and equipment, it is not only the equipment but the men who use it that count. If the United States becomes involved in a war in Europe it will be the motivation of her volunteer army that will count as much as the capacity of their weapons to destroy tanks, aircraft and infantry.

774,200 men and 556,000 reservists.

4 armd divs.
5 mech divs.*
5 inf divs (1 inf div to be mech in 1979).*
1 airmobile div.
1 AB div.
1 armd bde.
1 inf bde.
3 armd cav regts.
1 bde in Berlin.
2 special mission bdes.
Army Aviation: 1 air cav combat bde, indep bns assigned to HQ for tac tpt and medical duties.

1 Honest John, 3 Pershing, 8 Lance SSM bns.

Tanks: some 10,500 med, incl 3,300 M-48, 7,150 M-60 (540 M-60A2 with Shillelagh ATGW); 1,600 M-551 Sheridan lt tks with Shillelagh.

AFV: some 22,000 M-577, M-114, M-113 APC.

Arty and Msls: about 2,500 105mm, 155mm towed guns/how; 3,000 175mm SP guns and 105mm, 155mm and 203mm SP how; 3,000 81mm, 3,000 107mm mor; 6,000 90mm and 106mm RCL; TOW, Dragon ATGW; Honest John, Pershing, Lance SSM.

AA arty and SAM: some 600 20mm, 40mm towed and SP AA guns; some 20,000 Chaparral/Vulcan 20mm AA msl/gun systems, Redeye, Stinger SAM; Nike Hercules and Improved HAWK SAM (to be replaced by Patriot). (Roland SAM on order.)

Aircraft/Helicopters: about 500 ac, incl 300 OV-1/-10, 200 U-8/-21, 40 C-12; 9,000 helicopters, incl 1,000 AH-1G/Q/S, 4,000 UH-1/-19, 15 UH-60A, 700 CH-47/-54, 3,600 OH-6A/-58A, H-13 (148 AH-1S helicopters on order). Trainers incl 310 T-41/-42 ac; 700 TH-55A helicopters.

DEPLOYMENT:
Continental United States:
Strategic Reserve: (i) 1 armd, 1 mech, 3 inf, 1 airmobile, 1 AB divs. (ii) To reinforce 7th Army in Europe: 1 armd, 2 mech divs, 1 armd cav regt.† (iii) Alaska 1 bde. (iv) Panama 1 bde.
Europe: 198,400.
(i) Germany: 189,000. 7th Army: 2 corps, incl 2 armd, 2 mech divs, 1 armd, 2 mech bdes plus 2 armd cav regts; 3,000 med tks.‡
(ii) West Berlin: 4,400. HQ elements and 1 inf bde.
(iii) Greece: 800.
(iv) Italy: 3,000.
(v) Turkey: 1,200.
Pacific:
(i) South Korea: 30,000. 1 inf div, 1 AD arty bde (to be reduced by 1 bde in 1978).
(ii) Hawaii: 1 inf div less 1 bde.

RESERVES: 556,000.
(i) Army National Guard: 366,000: capable after mobilization of manning 2 armd, 1 mech, 5 inf divs, 22 indep bdes§ (3 armd, 9 mech, 10 inf) and 4 armd cav regts, plus reinforcements and support units to fill regular formations.
(ii) Army Reserves: 190,000 in 12 trg divs, 3 indep combat bdes; 49,000 a year do short active duty.

* One National Guard bde is incorporated in 1 mech and 3 inf divs.
† One armd div, 1 mech div, 1 armd cav regt have hy eqpt stockpiled in W. Germany.
‡ Includes those stockpiled for the strategic reserve formations.
§ Including 4 indep bdes and 11 bns incorporated in active army divs.

Marine Corps: 191,500 (3,700 women).

3 divs.

2 SAM bns with Improved HAWK.

575 M-60 med tks; 950 LVTP-7 APC; 175mm SP guns; 105mm, 155mm how; 155mm, 203mm SP how; 230 81mm and 107mm mor; 106mm RCL; TOW, Dragon ATGW; Redeye SAM.

3 Air Wings: 364 combat aircraft.

12 FGA sqns with 144 F-4N/S with Sparrow and Sidewinder AAM.

13 FGA sqns: 3 with 80 AV-8A Harrier, 5 with 60 A-4F/M, 5 with 60 A-6A/E.

1 recce sqn with 10 RF-4B, 1 ECM sqn with 10 EA-6B.

2 observation sqns with 36 OV-10A.

3 assault tpt/tanker sqns with 36 KC-130F.

3 attack helicopter sqns with 54 AH-1J.

4 lt helicopter sqns with 96 UH-1E/N.

9 med helicopter sqns with 162 CH-46F.

6 hy helicopter sqns with 126 CH-53D.

DEPLOYMENT:

(i) *Continental United States*: 2 divs, 2 air wings.

(ii) *Pacific*: 1 div, 1 air wing.

RESERVES: 29,700.

1 div and 1 air wing: 2 fighter sqns with 24 F-4N, 5 attack sqns with 60 A-4E/F, 1 observation sqn with 18 OV-10A, 1 tpt/tanker sqn with 12 KC-130, 7 helicopter sqns (1 attack with 18 AH-1G, 2 hy with 24 CH-53, 3 med with 54 CH-46, 1 lt with 21 UH-1E), 2 tk bns, 1 amph assault bn, 1 SAM bn with HAWK, 1 fd arty gp.

XM-1 Abrams

Type: main battle tank
Crew: four
Weights: Empty
Loaded 119,048 lb (54,000 kg)
Dimensions: Length (including gun) 32 ft 7 in (9.93 m); (hull) 25 ft 6 in (7.767 m)
Width 12 ft (3.657 m)
Height 7 ft 9½ in (2.374 m)
Ground pressure: 13.08 lb/in² (0.92 kg/cm²)
Performance: road speed 43½ mph (70 kph); range 275 miles (442 km); vertical obstacle 4 ft 1 in (1.244 m); trench 9 ft 2 in (2.794 m); gradient 60%; ground clearance 19 in (48.2 cm)
Engine: one 1,500-hp Avco-Lycoming AGT 1500 gas turbine

Armament: one 120-mm smooth-bore gun, plus one 7.62-mm MAG 58 co-axial with the main armament, one 7.62-mm MAG 58 on the loader's hatch, and one 0.5-in (12.7-mm) Browning M2 on the commander's cupola
Armour: Chobham type
Used by: under development for the USA
Notes: The XM-1 has had a troublesome development period, bedevilled by problems stemming as much from politicians as from the army staff. However, it has been decided to fit the tank in its definitive form with a German smooth-bore 120-mm gun, and the XM-1 should soon be in service as a powerful and versatile AFV, with a new type of powerplant and armour, and sophisticated electronics of all types.

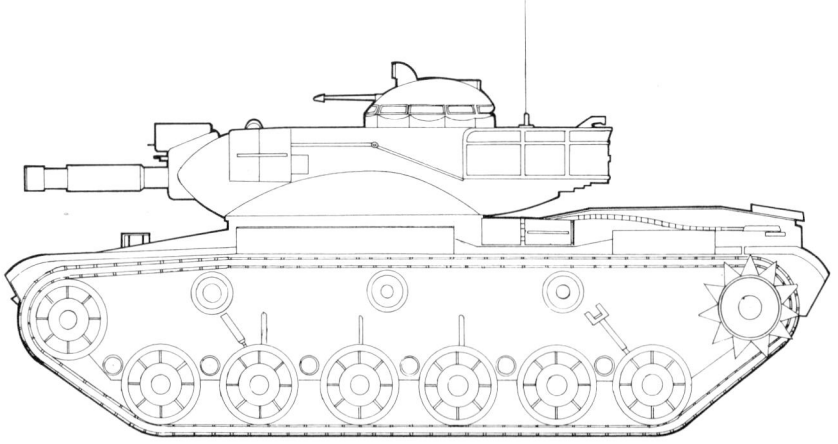

M60A2

Type: main battle tank
Crew: four
Weights: Empty
Loaded 129,920 lb (58,931 lb))
Dimensions: Length (with gun forward) 24 ft 0¾ in (7.33 mm); (hull) 22 ft 11½ in (7.0 m)
Width 11 ft 11 in (3.63 m)
Height 10 ft 6 in (3.2 m)

Ground pressure: 10.8 lb/in² (0.76 kg/cm²)
Performance: road speed 30 mph (48 kph); range 280 miles (450 km); vertical obstacle 36 in (91.4 cm); trench 8 ft 6 in (2.59 m); gradient 60%; ground clearance 16 in (41.0 cm); wading 4 ft (1.22 m) without preparation, and 13 ft 6 in (4.11 m) with the aid of a schnorkel
Engine: one 750-bhp Continental AVDS-1790-2A turbo-charged inline diesel engine
Armament: one 152-mm XM162 gun/

launcher with 13 Shillelagh missiles and 33 HEAT and HE rounds, plus one 7.62-mm machine-gun with 5,500 rounds, co-axial with the main armament, and one 0.5-in (12.7-mm) machine gun on the commander's cupola, with 900 rounds

Armour: 1 in (25.4 mm) minimum; 4⅓ in (110 mm) maximum

Used only by: USA

Notes: The M60A2, formerly designated the M60A1E2, is based on the M60 MBT, but has an entirely new turret to house the XM162 gun/launcher weapon. This 152-mm system can launch Shillelagh missiles, which use infra-red command to gunner's line of sight as the guidance principle, or conventional 152-mm ammunition. The turret is fully stabilised to allow weapon operation on the move, and the commander's cupola is independently stabilised. The fire-control system uses a laser rangefinder allied with a full-solution ballistic computer. Full NBC protection and night vision equipment are standard, and the type entered service in 1972.

M551 Sheridan

Type: light tank
Crew: four
Weights: Empty
　　　　Loaded 33,600 lb (15,241 kg)
Dimensions: Length 20 ft 8 in (6.3 m)
　　　　Width 9 ft 2¼ in (2.8 m)
　　　　Height (overall) 9 ft 10 in (3.0 m)
Ground pressure: 6.83 lb/in² (0.48 kg/cm²)
Performance: road speed 43 mph (70 kph); water speed 3.1 mph (5 kph); range 373 miles (600 km); vertical obstacle 33 in (84.0 cm); trench 8 ft 4 in (3.54 m); gradient 60%; ground clearance 19 in (48.3 cm); the M551 is amphibious with the aid of a permanently carried flotation screen
Engine: one 300-bhp General Motors Corporation turbo-charged inline diesel engine
Armament: one 152-mm M81 gun/launcher

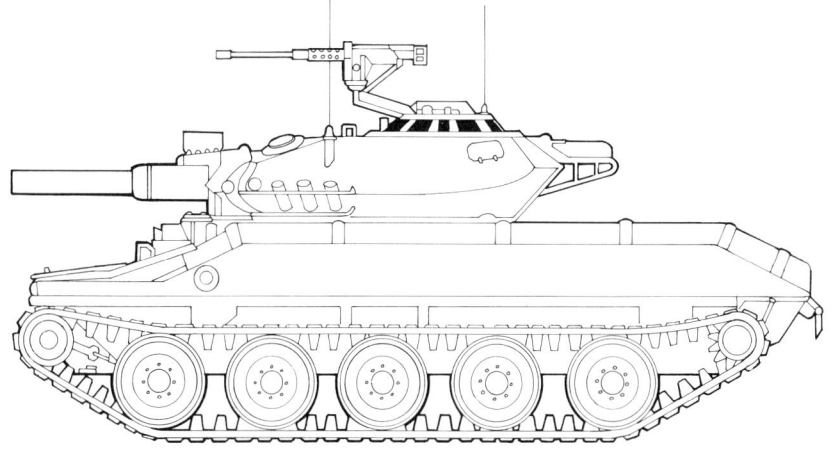

with 10 Shillelagh infra-red command to line of sight anti-tank missiles and 20 Canister and HEAT rounds, plus one 7.62-mm machine-gun co-axial with the main armament, and one 0.5-in (12.7-mm) machine-gun on the turret roof

Armour: classified

Used only by: USA

Notes: The M551 Sheridan light tank is an interesting vehicle, used by the US Army as its ARAAV (Armored Reconnaissance Airborne Assault Vehicle), with reconnaissance taking precedence over the airborne assault role. The most important feature of the vehicle is the dual-function gun/launcher, whose conventional ammunition uses a wholly combustible cartridge case. Unfortunately, the M551 was placed in production before its automotive system was fully ready and this, combined with the need to upgrade the tank's protection against mines, has obscured the M551's better points, such as the fact that it has excellent cross-country performance, making it a first-class reconnaissance tank. Night vision equipment is fitted as standard, and an NBC system can be fitted if required.

M114

Type: command and reconnaissance vehicle

Crew: three or four

Weights: Empty
  Loaded 15,344 lb (6,960 kg)

Dimensions: Length 14 ft 8 in (4.47 m)
  Width 7 ft 8 in (2.34 m)
  Height 7 ft 8 in (2.34 m)

Ground pressure: 4.98 lb/in² (0.35 kg/cm²)

Performance: road speed 35 mph (57 kph); water speed 3 mph (4.8 kph); range 300 miles (482 km); vertical obstacle 18 in (45.7 cm); trench 5 ft (1.52 m); gradient 44%; ground clearance 16 in (40.6 cm); the M114 is inherently amphibious, being driven in the water by its tracks

Engine: one 160-bhp Chevrolet inline petrol engine

Armament: one turret-mounted 0.5-in (12.7-mm) Browning M2 machine-gun with 1,000 rounds, plus one pintle-mounted 7.62-mm machine-gun

Armour:

Used only by: USA

Notes: The M114 was designed to replace the Jeep 4 × 4 vehicle as a light reconnaissance vehicle, and entered service

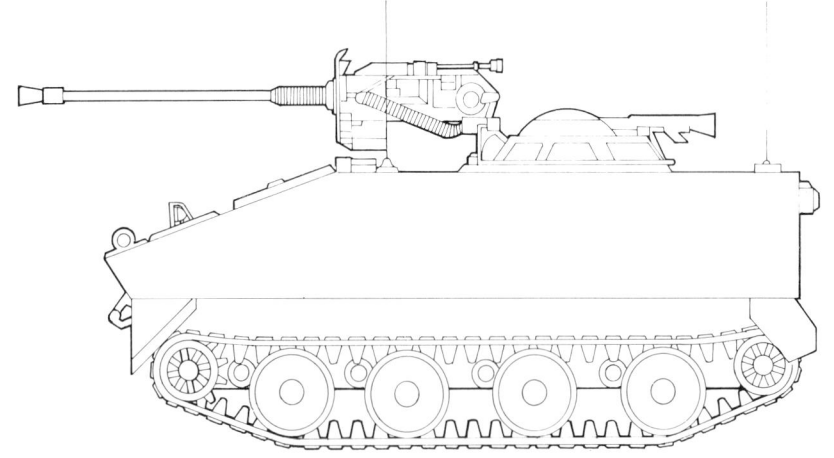

in 1962. There is also a variant armed with a 20-mm Hispano-Suiza cannon in place of the 0.5-in weapon. The M114 has a fixed cupola, meaning that the commander has to expose himself to fire the 0.5-in machine-gun; but on the M114A1 the cupola revolves, and the commander can aim and fire his weapon without exposing himself.

XM723

Type: mechanised infantry combat vehicle
Crew: 12
Weights: Empty 38,911 lb (17,650 kg)
       Loaded 42,990 lb (19,500 kg)
Dimensions: Length 20 ft (6.12 m)
          Width 10 ft 6 in (3.2 m)
          Height 9 ft 1 in (2.77 m)
Ground pressure: 6.1 lb/in² (0.43 kg/cm²)
Performance: road speed 45 mph (72 kph); water speed 5 mph (8 kph); range 300 miles (482 km); vertical obstacle 36 in (91.4 cm); trench 8 ft 4 in (2.54 m); gradient 60%; ground clearance 19 in (48.3 cm); the XM723 is fully amphibious, being driven in the water by its tracks
Engine: one 500-hp Cummins VTA-903 inline diesel engine
Armament: one turret-mounted 25-mm Bushmaster cannon, one co-axial 7.62-mm machine-gun, and one TOW launcher with two rounds
Armour: classified
Used by: under development for the USA
Notes: Known also as the Infantry Fighting Vehicle/Cavalry Fighting Vehicle or Fighting Vehicle System, the XM723 has been under development since 1972. In the opening months of 1978, however, it was decided by the US Army not to go ahead with procurement of the type pending a decision on the vehicle's role and cost effectiveness, already brought into question by the Congress in 1977. It may yet be decided to press on with definitive development of the XM723, or build a new MICV using the chassis of the XM-1 MBT.

Vought MGM-52C Lance

Type: surface-to-surface tactical guided missile, vehicle-launched
Guidance: inertial
Dimensions: Span
          Body diameter 22 in (56.0 cm)
          Length 20 ft 2 in (6.146 m)
Booster: Rocketdyne P8E–9 liquid-propellant two-part rocket
Sustainer: see above
Warhead: M234 nuclear (10-kiloton) or XM251 HE cluster
Weights: Launch between 2,833 and 3,366 lb (1,285 and 1,527 kg)
         Burnt out
Performance: speed Mach 3; range 75 miles (120 km)
Used also by: Belgium, Israel, Italy, Netherlands, UK, West Germany

Notes: The Lance entered service in 1972. Highly mobile, the missile requires a launch crew of eight, and only two vehicles of the M113 family. The Lance can also be delivered to forward sites by aircraft and helicopter.

Martin Marietta MGM-31A Pershing 1A

Type: surface-to-surface tactical missile, air-transportable and vehicle-launched
Guidance: inertial
Dimensions: Span about 80 in (2.02 m)
Body diameter 40 (1.01 m)
Length about 34 ft 6in (10.52 m)
Booster: Thiokol XM105 solid-propellant rocket
Sustainer: Thiokol XM106 solid-propellant rocket
Warhead: nuclear, in the region of 400 kilotons in most missiles, though some have warheads of about 60 kilotons
Weights: Launch about 10,141 lb (4,600 kg)
Burnt out
Performance: speed Mach 8; range between 100 and 520 miles (160 and 840 km)
Used also by: West Germany
Notes: Derived from the Pershing 1, the Pershing 1A entered service in 1969. Improvements over the earlier version include wheeled rather than tracked launch vehicles, quicker launch procedure, and improved launch navigation. There is also a Pershing II, derived from the Pershing 1A, and using the same launch vehicles and propulsive stages. The Pershing II has a new terminal guidance system, however, which works by correlating a current radar image of the impact area with a preset radar image provided by reconnaissance.

Univac MGM-29A Sergeant

Type: surface-to-surface tactical guided missile, vehicle-launched
Guidance: inertial
Dimensions: Span
Body diameter $31\frac{1}{4}$ in (79.0 cm)
Length 34 ft $5\frac{2}{3}$ in (10.5 m)
Booster: Thiokol single-stage solid-propellant rocket
Sustainer: none
Warhead: nuclear or high explosive
Weights: Launch 10,000 lb (4,536 kg)
Burnt out

Performance: speed supersonic; range between 28 and 87 miles (45 and 140 km)
Used also by: West Germany
Notes: Successor to the Corporal tactical missile, the Sergeant field artillery ballistic missile has the advantage of a solid-propellant rocket motor, and quite short reaction time thanks to updated electronics.

MGR-1 Honest John rocket

Type: surface-to-surface artillery rocket, vehicle launched
Guidance: none
Dimensions: Span
Body diameter 30 in (76.2 cm)
Length 24 ft 8 in (7.52 m)
Booster: solid-propellant rocket
Sustainer: none

Warhead: nuclear (20-kiloton) or HE
Weights: Launch 4,500 lb (2,041 kg)
Burnt out
Performance: speed supersonic; range between 8,200 and 40,500 yards (7,498 and 37,034 m)
Used also by: Belgium, Denmark, Greece, Netherlands, South Korea, Taiwan, Turkey, West Germany

Notes: The Honest John missile is an unguided battlefield support weapon of great reliability, accuracy and mobility. It requires only a four-man firing crew.

M91 artillery rocket launcher

Type: mobile artillery rocket launcher
Calibre: 115 mm
Number of barrels: 45
Muzzle velocity:
Ranges: Maximum 13,125 yards (12,001 m)
Minimum 3,300 yards (3,017 m)
Elevation: +1° to +60°
Traverse: 20° total
Time to emplace: 30 minutes
Weights: For travel 1,200 lb (545 kg)
In firing position 4,220 lb (1,914 kg)
Dimensions: Length 12 ft 8 in (3.86 m)
Width 9 ft 9 in (2.97 m)
Height 5 ft 7 in (1.7 m)

Ammunition: Chemical warhead on rocket
Crew:
Used only by: USA
Notes: The M91 system is designed for the delivery of chemical loads only, and is probably obsolete in US service. The launcher is transported on a 6 × 6 lorry, the carriage's small wheels being intended only for manoeuvring.

McDonnell Douglas FGM-77A (M47) Dragon

Type: anti-tank and assault missile, man-portable and tube-launched

Guidance: command to line-of-sight by means of wire

Dimensions: Span 13 in (33.02 cm)
　　　　　　Body diameter 5 in (12.7 cm)
　　　　　　Length 2 ft 5⅓ in (74.4 cm)

Booster: none

Sustainer: solid-propellant rockets, in 30 side-thrusting pairs

Warhead: 5.4-lb (2.45-kg) linear shaped-charge high explosive, capable of penetrating 36 in (914.4 mm) of reinforced concrete

Weights: Launch 13.67 lbs (6.2 kg)
　　　　Burnt out

Performance: range 1,094 yards (1,000 m); speed 225 mph (360 kph)

Used also by: Iran, Israel, Jordan, Morocco, Netherlands, Saudi Arabia, Spain, Switzerland

Notes: Extremely powerful weapon, introduced in 1975. A laser beam-riding development is under consideration.

Hughes BGM-71A TOW (M151E2)

Type: heavy anti-tank missile, tube-launched from a vehicle or the ground

Guidance: automatic command to line-of-sight by means of wire

Dimensions: Span 13.4 in (34.04 cm)
　　　　　　Body diameter 6 in (15.2 cm)
　　　　　　Length 4 ft 2⅜ in (1.285 m)

Booster: solid-propellant rocket

Sustainer: solid-propellant rocket

Warhead: 5.3-lb (2.4-kg) shaped-charge high explosive

Weights: Launch 54 lb (24.5 kg)
　　　　Burnt out

Performance: range 71–4,100 yards (65–3,750 m); speed 447 mph (720 kph) upwards

Used also by: Canada, Denmark, Greece, Iran, Israel, Italy, Jordan, Kuwait, Lebanon, Luxembourg, Morocco, Netherlands, Norway, Oman, Pakistan, Portugal, Sweden, Taiwan, Turkey, Saudi Arabia, South Korea, Spain, West Germany

Notes: Very powerful anti-tank weapon system introduced in 1972. TOW = Tube-launched Optically-tracked Wire-command link guided missile.

Martin Marietta Copperhead (M712)

Type: cannon-launched guided projectile (CLGP)
Guidance: nose-mounted seeker to laser-illuminated target
Dimensions: Span
Body diameter $6\frac{1}{10}$ in (155 mm)
Length 54 in (1.372 m)
Booster: none
Sustainer: none
Warhead: 14 lb (6.4 kg) of high explosive
Weights: Launch 49.6 lb (22.5 kg)
Burnt out
Performance: minimum range 1.86 miles (3 km); maximum range 12.4 miles (20 km)
Used only by: USA
Notes: After conventional launch from a 155-mm howitzer, the seeker in the nose of the shell looks for a target marked by a laser designator, and then homes the winged shell onto the target.

Ford Aerospace MGM–51C Shillelagh

Type: lightweight close-support missile, gun-launched from a vehicle
Guidance: infra-red command to line-of-sight
Dimensions: Span $11\frac{2}{8}$ in (29.0 cm)
Body diameter 6 in (15.2 cm)
Length 3 ft 9 in (1.14 m)
Booster: gun-launch
Sustainer: Amoco Chemicals solid-propellant rocket
Warhead: 15-lb (6.8-kg) shaped-charge high explosive (Octol)
Weights: Launch 59.5 lb (27.0 kg)
Burnt out
Performance: speed high subsonic; range up to 3 miles (4.8 km)
Used only by: USA
Notes: A powerful weapons system. The launch method is from the barrel of a 152-mm gun. A proposed development uses laser beam-riding.

Raytheon MIM-23 HAWK

Type: mobile surface-to-air tactical guided missile system
Guidance: semi-active radar homing
Dimensions: Span 4 ft (1.22 m)
Body diameter 14 in (35.6 cm)
Length 16 ft $9\frac{1}{2}$ in (5.12 m)
Booster: Aerojet XM22E–8 dual-thrust solid-propellant rocket (MIM–23A); Aerojet XM112 dual-thrust solid-propellant rocket (MIM–23B)
Sustainer: as above
Warhead: 100-lb (45.4-kg) blast/preformed-splinter fragmentation type (MIM–23A); 120-lb (54-kg) warhead of the same type (MIM–23B)
Weights: Launch 1,295 lb (587 kg) for MIM–23A; 2,835 lb (625 kg) for MIM–23B
Performance: speed more than Mach 2; engagement altitude from less than 98 to

more than 36,100 ft (33 to 11,000 m); range 18 miles (30 km) for MIM–23A and 25 miles (40 km) for MIM–23B

Used also by: Belgium, Denmark, France, Greece, Iran, Israel, Italy, Japan, Jordan, Kuwait, Netherlands, Saudi Arabia, South Korea, Spain, Sweden, Taiwan, Thailand, West Germany

Notes: The HAWK (Homing All the Way Killer) was designed primarily for the interception of low-level supersonic targets, but has proved remarkably flexible in operation, and has an anti-missile capability. The HAWK became operational in 1959. HAWKs are operated by Battery Control Centers, each Center having one Tactical Control Officer and a number of Fire Control Operators, with the aid of a pulse volume radar, a carrier-wave acquisition radar, and range-only radar. Once the Fire Control Operator has been allocated a target by the Tactical Control Operator, he illuminates the target and launches a missile from the triple launcher. There is an Improved Hawk (MIM–23B) with improved rocket, larger warhead, and updated guidance.

Aeronutronic MIM-72 (M48) Chaparral

Type: land-mobile surface-to-air tactical guided missile system

Guidance: optical aiming and infra-red homing

Dimensions: Span 25 in (63.5 cm)
Body diameter 5 in (12.7 cm)
Length 9 ft 6½ in (2.91 m)

Booster: Rocketdyne Mk 36 Model 5 single-stage solid-propellant rocket

Sustainer: none

Warhead: 11-lb (5-kg) HE preformed-splinter fragmentation type (MIM–72A); Picatinny Arsenal M250 blast fragmentation type (MIM–72C)

Weights: Launch about 185 lb (84 kg)
Burnt out

Performance: speed Mach 2.5; range 2½ miles (4 km)

Used also by: Morocco, Taiwan, Tunisia

Notes: The Chaparral system uses a missile (MIM-72A and MIM-72C) developed from the US Navy's Sidewinder 1C ground-launched AA missile, plus an M730 tracked carrier, to provide the US Army with a fully mobile low-altitude clear-weather air defence system. Four missiles are carried on the launch vehicle's turret. Current development is aimed at producing an all-weather version to fill the gap before the Roland is introduced to US service.

M163

Type: self-propelled AA gun system
Crew: four
Weights: Empty
        Loaded 26,455 lb (12,000 kg)
Dimensions: Length 15 ft 11 in (4.86 m)
              Width 8 ft 10 in (2.69 m)
              Height 8 ft 6$\frac{1}{4}$ in (2.6 m)
Ground pressure:
Performance: road speed 42 mph (68 kph); range 300 miles (483 km); gradient 60%
Engine: one 215-bhp General Motors Corporation Model 6V53 inline diesel engine
Armament: one 20-mm M168 Vulcan 6-barrel cannon with 2,000 rounds
Armour: 1$\frac{1}{2}$ in (38 mm) aluminium
Used only by: USA
Notes: The M163 AVADS (Auto-track Vulcan Air Defense System) comprises an M168 Vulcan rotary cannon, an M741 (modified M113 APC) Vulcan Weapon Carrier, and a sophisticated radar- and computer-controlled fire-control system.

M167 cannon mounting

Type: light AA cannon mounting
Calibre: 20 mm
Barrel length: 76.2 cal
Muzzle velocity: 3,380 ft (1,030 m) per second
Ranges: Maximum (radar) 5,475 yards (5,006 m)
         Minimum
Elevation: −5° to +80°
Traverse: 360°

Rate of fire: 1,000 rounds per minute minimum; 3,000 rounds per minute maximum
Weights: For travel 3,500 lb (1,588 kg)
        In firing position as above
Dimensions: Length 15 ft 5 in (4.7 m)
              Width 6 ft 6 in (1.98 m)
              Height 6 ft 8 in (2.03 m)
Ammunition: API, API-T, HEI and HEI-T, plus others
Crew: one (on weapon), plus three others
Used also by: Belgium, Israel
Notes: The M167 Vulcan Air Defense System, Towed, uses the M61A1 Vulcan 20-mm rotary six-barrel cannon on a wheeled carriage with a special fire-control system, based on an X-band pulse-doppler radar.

205

General Dynamics FIM-43A Redeye

Type: man-portable surface-to-air tactical guided missile
Guidance: optical aiming, plus infra-red homing
Dimensions: Span 5½ in (14.0 cm)
　　　　　　　Body diameter 2¾ in (7.0 cm)
　　　　　　　Length 4 ft (1.22 m)
Booster: Atlantic Research dual-thrust solid-propellant rocket
Sustainer: as above
Warhead: smooth-case fragmentation
Weights: Launch 28½ lb (13 kg)
　　　　　　Burnt out

Performance: speed low supersonic; range up to 2 miles (3.3 km)
Used also by: Australia, Denmark, Greece, Israel, Jordan, Saudi Arabia, Sweden, West Germany
Notes: The Redeye is carried and launched from a sealed container tube, and is designed for protection against low-flying attack aircraft. The missile can only be fired on a pursuit course, and no provision is made for IFF. On spotting a target, the operator raises the weapon system to his shoulder and energises the guidance package. Once this has been energised, a buzzer informs the operator, who has been tracking the target and can now fire.

M110

Type: self-propelled howitzer
Crew: 13
Weights: Empty
　　　　　　Loaded 58,000 lb (26,309 kg)
Dimensions: Length 24 ft 6½ in (7.48 m)
　　　　　　　Width 10 ft 3½ in (3.14 m)
　　　　　　　Height (firing) 21 ft (6.4 m)
Ground pressure:
Performance: road speed 33.5 mph (54 kph); range 450 miles (724 km); vertical obstacle 40 in (1.016 m); trench 7 ft 9 in (2.362 m); gradient 60%; wading 42 in (1.066 m)
Engine: one 405-hp Detroit Diesel Model 8V71T turbo-charged inline diesel engine
Armament: one 8-in (203-mm) M2A1E1 howitzer with separate loading HE and Nuclear ammunition
Armour: ⅘ in (20 mm) maximum
Used also by: Belgium, Greece, Iran, Israel, Jordan, Netherlands, South Korea, Spain, UK, West Germany
Notes: The M110 was introduced in 1962, and is a useful weapon system. The howitzer fires to a maximum range of 18,375 yards (16,800 m) at a muzzle velocity of 1,950 ft (594 m) per second. The barrel elevates from +2° to +65°, and total traverse is 30°. The M110 is in the process of being supplemented by the M110E2, which has the new XM201 barrel, which is 8 ft (2.44 m) longer than the M2A1E1, and can deliver its M106 HE shell to a range of

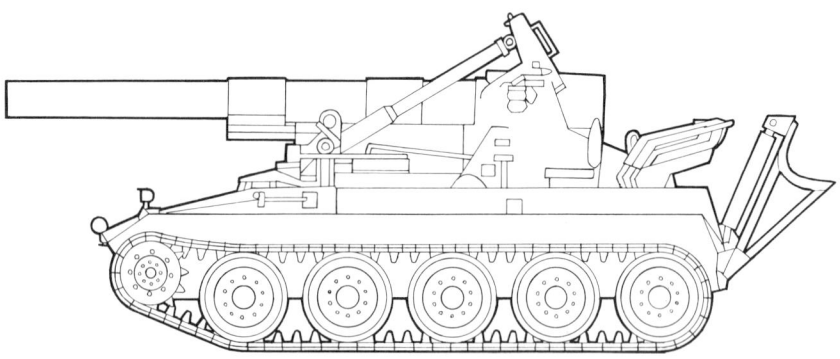

22,965 yards (21,000 m). The howitzer will also have a new ammunition, including rocket-assisted projectiles, incendiary rounds, HE and nuclear. The weight of the M110E2, which will enter service as the M110A1, is 62,100 lb (28,168 kg). The M110A2 will be the M110A1 fitted with a muzzle brake.

M109

Type: self-propelled howitzer
Crew: six
Weights: Empty
        Loaded 52,460 lb (23,796 kg)
Dimensions: Length 20 ft (6.09 m)
        Width 10 ft 3½ in (3.14 m)
        Height 10 ft (3.04 m)
Ground pressure: 11.4 lb/in² (0.8 kg/cm²)
Performance: road speed 34 mph (55 kph); range 75 miles (120 km); vertical obstacle 21 in (53.3 cm); trench 6 ft (1.83 m); gradient 60%; wading 5 ft (1.524 m)
Engine: one 405-hp Detroit Diesel Model 8V71T turbo-charged inline diesel engine
Armament: one 155-mm L/23 howitzer with 28 rounds of Canister, Chemical, HE or Nuclear ammunition, plus one 0.5-in (12.7-mm) Browning M2 AA machine-gun with 500 rounds
Armour: 1½ in (38 mm) maximum
Used also by: Austria, Belgium, Canada, Denmark, Iran, Israel, Italy, Libya, Netherlands, Norway, Spain, Switzerland, UK, West Germany
Notes: The M109 self-propelled howitzer entered service in 1961, and in most respects other than gun calibre is identical with the M108. The 155-mm howitzer is capable of a rate of fire of 45 rounds per hour, and fires its 95-lb (43-kg) shell to a range of 15,975 yards (14,608 m). The turret has a traverse of 360°. The M109A1 has an improved howitzer, with barrel length increased from 12 ft 1¾ in (3.7 m) to 20 ft (6.1 m), and weight to 53,060 lb (24,068 kg). Maximum range of the longer barrel is 19,685 yards (18,000 m). All M109s are to be brought up to M109A1 standard.

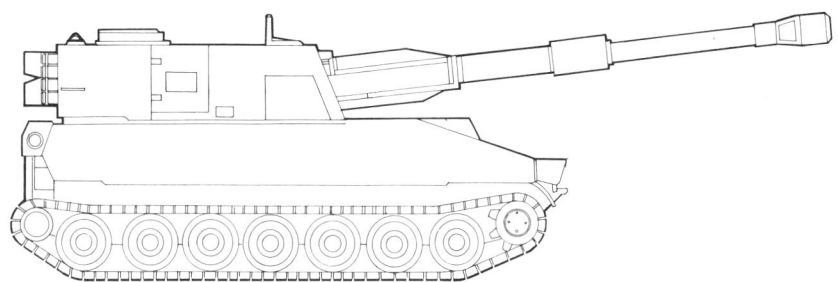

M198 howitzer

Type: field howitzer
Calibre: 155 mm
Barrel length:
Muzzle velocity:
Ranges: Maximum 32,808 yards (30,000 m) with RAP
Minimum
Elevation: −5° to +72°
Traverse: 45° total (360° with turntable)
Rate of fire: four rounds per minute
Weights: For travel 15,255 lb (6,920 kg)
In firing position 14,600 lb (6,623 kg)
Dimensions: Length 24 ft 6 in (7.47 m)
Width 9 ft 2 in (2.79 m)
Height 6 ft 11½ in (2.12 m)
Ammunition: CLGP, HE, Nuclear and RAP
Crew: 11
Used only by: USA
Notes: The M198 howitzer is currently entering US service as a replacement for the M114A1 weapon. Ammunition is interchangeable with that of the FH70 and the M109A1 and M109A2. Standard range is 26,245 yards (24,000 m), and that with CLGP 17,500 yards (16,000 m).

M102 howitzer

Type: light howitzer
Calibre: 105 mm
Barrel length: 31.7 cal
Muzzle velocity:
Ranges: Maximum 15,310 yards (14,000 m)
Minimum 1,094 yards (1,000 m)
Elevation: −5° to +75°
Traverse: 360°
Rate of fire: three rounds per minute
Weights: For travel 3,240 lb (1,470 kg)
In firing position as above
Dimensions: Length 17 ft (5.18 m)
Width 6 ft 5⅓ in (1.96 m)
Height 5 ft 2¾ in (1.59 m)
Ammunition: Chemical, Flechette, HE, HEAT, Illuminating and Smoke WP
Crew: eight
Used also by: Brazil
Notes: The M-102 was produced as a replacement for the M101 in service with US airborne and airmobile forces. The two HE rounds available have projectile weights of 32.85 lb (14.9 kg) and 28 lb (12.7 kg), and the HEAT round can penetrate 4 in (102 mm) of armour at 1,640 yards (1,500 m).

XM204 howitzer

Type: field artillery direct support weapon system
Calibre: 105 mm
Barrel length:
Muzzle velocity:
Ranges: Maximum 13,013 yards (11,900 m) with standard charge; 16,075 yards (14,700 m) with XM200 charge; 17,060 yards (15,600 m) with RAP
Minimum
Elevation: −5° to +75°
Traverse: 360°
Rate of fire: 20 rounds per minute maximum; three to five rounds per minute sustained
Weights: For travel 4,810 lb (2,182 kg)
In firing position as above
Dimensions: Length 16 ft 8 in (5.08 m)
Width 6 ft 5 in (1.955 m)
Height 5 ft 10 in (1.78 m)
Ammunition: HE, HEAT and HE-RAP
Crew:
Used only by: USA
Notes: The XM204 is under final development as a US replacement for the M101A1 and M102 105-mm howitzers. The system is based on the concept of soft recoil, this making the gun more compact, allowing higher rates of fire, reducing complexity, and reducing weight by obviating the need for trail spades.

M72 launcher

Type: man-portable anti-tank rocket launcher
Calibre: 66 mm
Barrel length:
Muzzle velocity: 475 ft (145 m) per second
Ranges: Maximum effective 328 yards (300 m) against stationary targets
Minimum
Elevation:
Traverse:
Rate of fire:
Weights: For travel
In firing position 5.2 lb (2.36 kg)
Dimensions: Length 2 ft 11 in (0.893 m)
Width
Height
Ammunition: HEAT warhead
Crew: one
Used only by: USA
Notes: The M72 is also known as the LAW (Light Anti-tank Weapon), and is generally obsolete in the US armed forces in its original form, though the M72A1 and M72A2 are still in service. The rocket weighs 2.2 lb (1 kg), and its warhead can penetrate 12 in (305 mm) of steel plate with its 0.75 lb (0.34 kg) of explosive.

M67 recoilless rifle

Type: man-portable anti-tank recoilless rifle
Calibre: 90 mm
Barrel length:
Muzzle velocity:
Ranges: Maximum 2,300 yards (2,103 m); effective 437 yards (400 m)
Minimum

Elevation:
Traverse:
Rate of fire: one round per minute, with periods of five rounds per 30 seconds
Weights: For travel 35.25 lb (16 kg)
In firing position

Dimensions: Length 4 ft 4 in (1.32 m)
Width
Height (ground-mounted) 17 in (0.43 m)
Ammunition: HEAT warhead
Crew: two
Used by: various nations
Notes: Although generally obsolescent, the M67 recoilless rifle is still used by some reserve US formations.

M20 launcher

Type: man-portable anti-tank rocket launcher
Calibre: 3.5 in (89 mm)
Barrel length:
Muzzle velocity:
Ranges: Maximum 1,300 yards (1,188 m); effective 120 yards (110 m)
Minimum
Elevation:
Traverse:
Rate of fire:
Weights: For travel 12 lb (5.5 kg)
In firing position 20.9 lb (9.5 kg)
Dimensions: Length 5 ft 1 in (1.55 m)
Width
Height
Ammunition: HEAT warhead
Crew: two
Used by: various nations
Notes: The US M20 rocket launcher is obsolescent, but still in service with a number of countries. The rocket weighs 8.9 lb (4.04 kg), of which 1.9 lb (0.87 kg) are the explosive.

M18 launcher

Type: man-portable anti-tank rocket launcher
Calibre: 2.25 in (57 mm)
Barrel length:
Muzzle velocity: 1,180 ft (360 m) per second
Ranges: Maximum effective 492 yards (450 m)
Minimum
Elevation:
Traverse:
Rate of fire:
Weights: For travel 44.5 lb (20.2 kg)
In firing position
Dimensions: Length 5 ft 1⅝ in (1.57 m)
Width
Height
Ammunition: HE and HEAT
Crew: two
Used also by: Austria, Brazil, China, Cuba, Cyprus, France, Greece, Honduras, India, Italy, Japan, Laos, Netherlands, Norway, South Korea, Taiwan, Thailand, Turkey, Vietnam, Yugoslavia, Zaire
Notes: Despite its obsolescence, the US M20 is widely used, though it is a cumbersome weapon.

M29 mortar

Type: medium mortar
Calibre: 81 mm
Barrel length: 16.05 cal
Muzzle velocity: 863 ft (263 m) per second
Ranges: Maximum 5,180 yards (4,737 m)
Minimum
Elevation: 40° to 85°
Traverse: 10°
Rate of fire: 30 rounds per minute for 1 minute; 4 rounds per minute sustained
Weights: For travel
In firing position 107 lb (48.5 kg)
Dimensions: Length
Width
Height
Ammunition: HE, Illuminating and Smoke
Crew: five
Used also by: Australia, Austria, Belgium, Brazil, Cuba, Denmark, Greece, India, Israel, Italy, Japan, Kampuchea, Liberia, Luxembourg, Netherlands, North Yemen, Norway, Pakistan, Philippines, South Korea, Spain, Switzerland, Taiwan, Thailand, Trinidad, Turkey, Vietnam, Yugoslavia
Notes: The M29 mortar succeeded the M1 of the same calibre. It differs from its predecessor principally in having a longer barrel and hence better performance, but still weighs less than the earlier weapon. The HE bomb is filled with 2.1 lb (0.95 kg) of explosive.

M30 mortar

Type: heavy mortar
Calibre: 4.2 in (107 mm)
Barrel length: 14.25 cal
Muzzle velocity: 960 ft (293 m) per second
Ranges: Maximum 6,180 yards (5,651 m) with M329A1
Minimum 950 yards (869 m) with M3
Elevation: 45° to 85°
Traverse: 16°
Rate of fire: 20 to 25 rounds per minute
Weights: For travel
In firing position 672 lb (305 kg)
Dimensions: Length
Width
Height
Ammunition: Chemical, HE (M3), HE (M329), Illuminating and Smoke
Crew: five or six
Used also by: Austria, Canada, Zaire
Notes: The M30 was introduced into US service in 1951. The HE (M329) bomb weighs 27 lb (12.28 kg).

XM224 mortar

Type: light mortar
Calibre: 60 mm
Barrel length:
Muzzle velocity:
Ranges: Maximum
Minimum
Elevation:
Traverse:
Rate of fire: probably 25 to 30 rounds per minute
Weights: For travel
In firing position 45 lb (20.4 kg)
Dimensions: Length
Width
Height
Ammunition: HE, Illuminating and Smoke
Crew: three
Used by: under final development for USA
Notes: The XM224 lightweight company mortar is soon to enter service. So far, however, very few details of the weapon have been released. The weapon will be used with a forward observation officer equipped with a laser rangefinder, this obviating the need for ranging rounds to be fired. Keynotes of the XM224 are simplicity, light weight and versatility.

M1 mortar

Type: medium mortar
Calibre: 81 mm
Barrel length: 14.26 cal
Muzzle velocity: 768 ft (234 m) per second with M362
Ranges: Maximum 3,300 yards (3,016 m) with M43
Minimum
Elevation: 40° to 85°
Traverse: 10°
Rate of fire: 18 to 30 rounds per minute
Weights: For travel
In firing position 132 lb (59.87 kg)

Dimensions: Length
Width
Height
Ammunition: HE (M43), HE (M56), HE (M362), Illuminating and Smoke
Crew: two or three
Used also by: Austria, Belgium, Brazil, Cuba, Denmark, Greece, India, Indonesia, Italy, Japan, Kampuchea, Liberia, Luxembourg, Netherlands, North Yemen, Norway, Pakistan, Philippines, South Korea, Spain, Taiwan, Thailand, Trinidad, Turkey, Vietnam, Yugoslavia
Notes: The M1 fires a variety of ammunition, and is still a useful weapon.

ABC-M9-7 flamethrower

Type: portable flamethrower
Weights: Empty 26 lb (11.8 kg)
Loaded 50 lb (22.7 kg)
Range: 45 to 60 yards (41 to 55 m)
Fuel capacity: 68.8 pints (15.14 litres)
Used only by: USA
Notes: The American ABC-M9-7 portable flamethrower is now obsolescent. The fuel is carried in two aluminium tanks, and the compressed propellant gas in a steel sphere. The fuel is sufficient for one 8-second burst, or five shorter bursts.

M2A1-7 flamethrower

Type: portable flamethrower
Range: 45 to 60 yards (41 to 55 m)
Fuel capacity: 68.2 pints (15 litres)
Used only by: USA
Notes: The M2A1-7 portable flamethrower is an obsolete weapon, consisting of a pressure cylinder with a cylindrical fuel tank on each side, and the associated hose and flamegun equipment. The fuel is sufficient for one 10-second burst, or five 2-second bursts.

M9A1-7 flamethrower

Type: portable flamethrower
Weights: Empty 25 lb (11.3 kg)
Loaded 50 lb (22.7 kg)
Range: about 55 yards (50 m)
Fuel capacity: about 68.2 pints (15 litres)
Used only by: USA
Notes: The M9A1-7 is currently replacing the ABC-M9-7 and M2A1-7 portable flamethrowers. The operator carries on his back a steel pressurised air propellant tank and two fuel tanks, sufficient for several short bursts. The equipment also includes a carrier group, containing four spare fuel tanks and two spare compressed air propellant tanks.

Browning M1917A1 machine-gun

Type: medium machine-gun
Calibre: 0.3 in (7.62 mm)
System of operation: short recoil
Muzzle velocity: 2,800 ft (854 m) per second
Range: 5,500 yards (5,029 m) with M1 ball
Rate of fire: 450 to 600 rounds per minute (cyclic); 250 rounds per minute (automatic)
Cooling system: water
Feed system: 250-round fabric belt
Dimensions: Barrel length 23.9 in (607 mm)
Overall length 38.6 in (981 mm)
Width
Height

Weights: 32.63 lb (14.8 kg) without water; 41 lb (18.6 kg) with water; 94.15 lb (42.7 kg) with M1917A1 tripod
Sights: blade (fore) and leaf, aperture (rear)
Ammunition: 0.3 in M1, or 0.3 in M2
Used also by: numbers of South American armies
Notes: The basic design of this American weapon dates back to the 1890s, and it is indicative of the type's virtues, principally its reliability and weight of fire over long ranges, that the weapon served as the US Army's main support machine-gun throughout World War II. The M1917A1 differs from the original M1917 only in details of the feed mechanism, sights and tripod mounting.

Browning M1919A6 machine-gun

Type: medium machine-gun
Calibre: 0.3 in (7.62 mm)
System of operation: short recoil
Muzzle velocity: 2,800 ft (854 m) per second
Range: effective 1,094 yards (1,000 m)
Rate of fire: 400 to 500 rounds per minute (cyclic); 120 rounds per minute (automatic)
Cooling system: air
Feed system: 250-round fabric or metal-link belt
Dimensions: Barrel length 24 in (610 mm)
Overall length 53 in (1.346 m)
Width
Height
Weights: 32.5 lb (14.74 kg) with metal stock and bipod
Sights: blade (fore) and leaf, aperture (rear)
Ammunition: 0.3 in M1, or 0.3 in M2
Used also by: most countries allied in any way with the USA
Notes: The M1919A6 is basically an air-cooled version of the M1917A1, usually fitted with a bipod for use as a squad light automatic weapon. The M1919A4 is

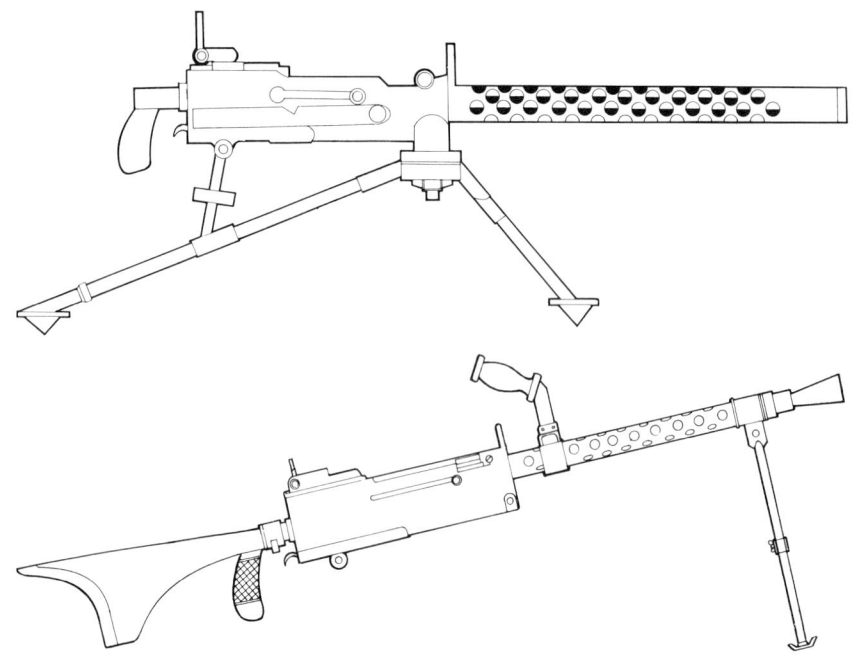

basically similar, but designed for use in AFVs as well as on the ground. It is usually found on a tripod mounting, and can be distinguished from the M1919A6 by its lack of a carrying handle, and its pistol grip at the rear of the receiver, where the M1919A6 has a pistol grip and shoulder stock. Both weapons are notable for their reliability.

Browning M2 machine-gun

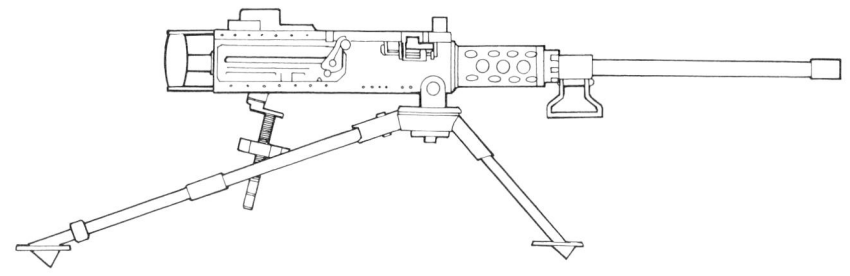

Type: heavy machine-gun
Calibre: 0.5 in (12.7 mm)
System of operation: short recoil
Muzzle velocity: 2,930 ft (893 m) per second
Range:
Rate of fire: 500 to 650 rounds per minute (cyclic) for M2AA; 450 to 550 rounds per minute (cyclic) for M2HB
Cooling system: water (M2AA) or air (M2HB)
Feed system: 110-round disintegrating metal-link belt
Dimensions: Barrel length 45 in (1.143 m)
Overall length 66 in (1.676 m) for M2AA; 65 in (1.653 m) for M2HB
Width
Height
Weights: 121 lb (54.9 kg) including water for M2AA; 84 lb (38.1 kg) for M2HB
Sights: blade (fore) and leaf, aperture (rear)

Ammunition: 0.5 in M2
Used also by: many other nations
Notes: The M2 heavy machine-gun was an improved model of the M1921A1 0.5-in (12.7-mm) machine-gun, and entered service in 1933. In its water-cooled version (M2AA) it was used as a heavy AA machine-gun, but the air-cooled model with a heavy barrel (M2HB) became the US Army's standard sustained fire heavy machine-gun for ground forces, acquiring a great reputation for lethality and reliability. The type was also used as aircraft armament.

M60 machine-gun

Type: general-purpose machine-gun
Calibre: 7.62 mm
System of operation: gas
Muzzle velocity: 2,820 ft (860 m) per second
Range: effective 875 yards (800 m) with a bipod; 1,968 yards (1,800 m) with a tripod
Rate of fire: 550 rounds per minute (cyclic); 200 rounds per minute (automatic)
Cooling system: air
Feed system: disintegrating metal-link belt
Dimensions: Barrel length 22 in (560 mm) without flash hider
Overall length 43.3 in (1.1 m)
Width
Height
Weights: 23.1 lb (10.48 kg) with bipod; 38 lb (17.28 kg) with M122 tripod
Sights: blade (fore) and leaf with U notch (rear)
Ammunition: 7.62 mm × 51
Used also by: Australia, Taiwan, Vietnam
Notes: The M60 is the US Army's current general-purpose machine-gun, and makes extensive use of stampings, with rubber and plastic replacing many wood and steel components.

M134 Minigun machine-gun

Type: 6-barrel rotary machine-gun
Calibre: 7.62 mm
System of operation: external power source
Muzzle velocity: 2,850 ft (869 m) per second
Range:
Rate of fire: up to 6,000 rounds per minute
Cooling system: air
Feed system: metal-link belt or linkless
Dimensions: Barrel length 22 in (559 mm)
Overall length 31.5 in (800 mm)
Width
Height
Weights: 70.54 lb (32 kg)
Sights: optional
Ammunition: 7.62 mm × 51
Used only by: USA
Notes: The Minigun is a weapon designed to deliver a high volume of fire, and was designed by General Electric during the Vietnam War as the principal gun armament of helicopter gunships. The principle used is that of the Gatling gun, with six barrels rotating around a common axis, firing when each barrel reaches the 12 o'clock position. An external power source has to be used to rotate the barrels, the loading, firing and extracting process being mechanical.

Stoner Mark 23 Commando machine-gun

Type: light machine-gun
Calibre: 5.56 mm
System of operation: gas
Muzzle velocity: 3,280 ft (1,000 m) per second
Range: effective 875 yards (800 m)
Rate of fire: 750 rounds per minute (cyclic); 60 rounds per minute (automatic)
Cooling system: air
Feed system: disintegrating metal-link belt
Dimensions: Barrel length 20 in (508 mm)
Overall length 40.25 in (1.022 m)
Width
Height
Weights: 11 lb (5 kg); 15.5 lb (7.03 kg) with sling and 150-round belt in box
Sights: post (fore) and tangent leaf (rear)
Ammunition: 5.56 mm × 45
Used only by: USA
Notes: The Mark 23 Commando is the modified Stoner 63 System light machine-gun used by the US Marine Corps to provide offensive patrols with high firepower. The weapon was tested as the XM207, and proved popular as the gun and 800 rounds of ammunition weigh only 35 lb (18 kg).

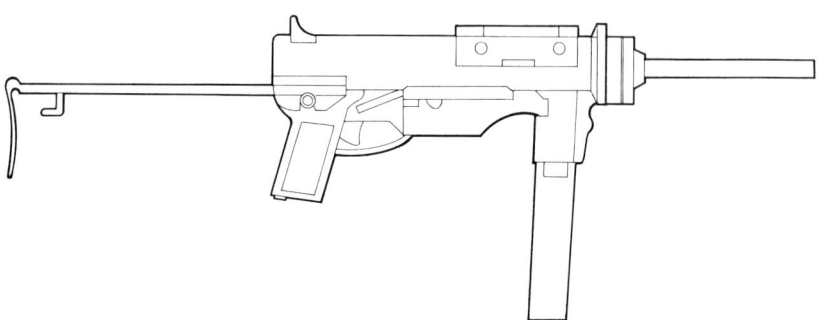

M3A1 sub-machine gun

Type: sub-machine gun
Calibre: 0.45 in (11.43 mm)
System of operation: blowback
Muzzle velocity: 920 ft (280 m) per second
Range: effective 219 yards (200 m)
Rate of fire: 450 rounds per minute (cyclic); 120 rounds per minute (automatic)
Cooling system: air
Feed system: 30-round box
Dimensions: Barrel length 8 in (203 mm)
Overall length 29.8 in (757 mm) with stock extended; 22.8 in (579 mm) with stock retracted
Width
Height

Weights: 7.65 lb (3.47 kg) empty; 9.96 lb (4.52 kg) loaded
Sights: blade (fore) and aperture (rear)
Ammunition: 0.45 in ACP
Used also by: Taiwan and several South American countries
Notes: The original M3 was accepted for US service in late 1942 as an eventual replacement for the Thompson sub-machine gun, which was expensive to produce, heavy and mechanically unreliable. The M3 proved adequate, but trouble was encountered with the cocking mechanism, which was removed and replaced by a finger hole in the bolt on the improved M3A1 introduced in 1944.

Springfield M1903 rifle

Type: bolt-action rifle
Calibre: 0.3 in (7.62 mm)
System of operation: manually operated bolt
Muzzle velocity: 2,295 to 2,790 ft (700 to 850 m) per second depending on ammunition
Range: effective 875 yards (800 m)
Rate of fire: 10 rounds per minute
Cooling system: air
Feed system: 5-round box
Dimensions: Barrel length 24 in (610 mm)
Overall length 43.3 in (1.1 m)
Width
Height

Weights: 8.8 lb (4 kg)
Sights: blade (fore) and leaf or ramp, aperture (rear), or telescope
Ammunition: 0.3 in-06, or 0.3 in M1, or 0.3 in M2
Used also by: many countries in Africa, Asia and South America
Notes: The Springfield M1903 is the most celebrated bolt-action military rifle produced by the United States, and is based on the excellent Mauser action. There were several models, but the data above are typical of the basic type.

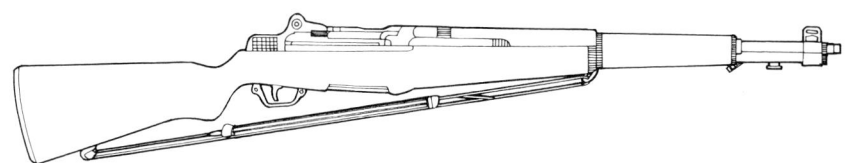

Garand M1 rifle

Type: self-loading rifle
Calibre: 0.3 in (7.62 mm)
System of operation: gas
Muzzle velocity: 2,838 ft (865 m) per second
Range: effective 656 yards (600 m)
Rate of fire: 30 rounds per minute
Cooling system: air
Feed system: 8-round clip
Dimensions: Barrel length 24 in (610 mm)
Overall length 43.5 in (1.106 m)
Width
Height

Weights: 9.5 lb (4.3 kg) empty
Sights: blade (fore) and aperture (rear)
Ammunition: 0.3 in M2
Used also by: Italy
Notes: The Garand M1 entered production in 1937, and during World War II replaced the M1903 bolt-action rifle as the US Army's main infantry rifle. The weapon is still used by the US National Guard, and by the Italian Army in 7.62-mm calibre.

M1 carbine

Type: self-loading carbine
Calibre: 0.3 in (7.62 mm)
System of operation: gas
Muzzle velocity: 1,990 ft (607 m) per second
Range: effective 328 yards (300 m)
Rate of fire: 750 rounds per minute (cyclic) for M2 and M3; 75 rounds per minute (automatic) for M2 and M3; 40 rounds per minute (single shot)
Cooling system: air
Feed system: 15- or 30-round box
Dimensions: Barrel length 18 in (458 mm)
Overall length 35.6 in (904 mm)
Width
Height
Weights: 5.2 lb (2.36 kg) unloaded; 5.8 lb (2.63 kg) with sling and loaded magazine
Sights: blade (fore) and flip, aperture (rear)
Ammunition: 0.3 in M2
Used also by: various countries in Africa and South America
Notes: The M1 carbine started life as a light rifle, called for in 1940 as a replacement for pistols and sub-machine guns in arms other than the infantry. The Winchester weapon was accepted for production in 1941, and thereafter saw widespread service in World War II. There were several variants:
  1. M1 self-loading production model
  2. M1A1 with a folding metal stock
  3. M1A2 project with a different rear sight
  4. M1A3 project with a pantograph stock
  5. M2 selective fire carbine
  6. M3 selective fire sniper carbine without sights but with provision for infrared 'Sniperscope'. A flash hider was fitted.

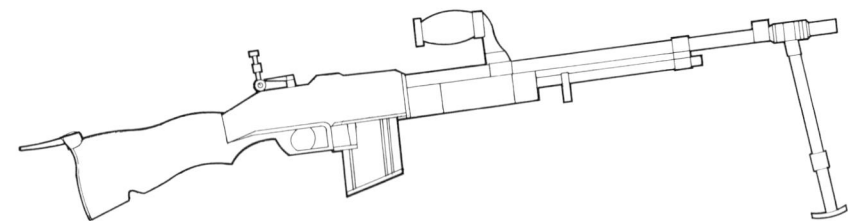

Browning M1918A2 Automatic Rifle

Type: automatic rifle (light machine-gun)
Calibre: 0.3 in (7.62 mm)
System of operation: gas
Muzzle velocity: 2,820 ft (860 m) per second
Range: effective 656 yards (600 m)
Rate of fire: 550 rounds per minute (cyclic); 300 to 450 rounds per minute (slow automatic) and 500 to 600 rounds per minute (fast automatic) for M1918A2 only; 40 rounds per minute (single shot) for all except M1918A2
Cooling system: air
Feed system: 20-round box
Dimensions: Barrel length 24 in (610 mm)
Overall length 47.8 in (1.215 m) for M1918A2 only
Width
Height
Weights: 19.44 lb (8.82 kg) for M1918A2
Sights: blade (fore) and tangent, aperture (rear)

Ammunition: 0.3 in M1, or 0.3 in M2
Used also by: Greece and other countries in South America and Africa
Notes: Although designated the Browning Automatic Rifle (BAR), this weapon should more accurately be known as a light machine-gun, and was one of the most important weapons designed by the brilliant John M. Browning. The BAR in its various models remained in service with the US Army from 1918 to 1957:
1. M1918 with a smooth barrel and no bipod
2. M1918A1, introduced in 1937, with a bipod
3. M1918A2, introduced in 1941, with skid feet on the bipod, and two rates of automatic fire
4. Machine Rifle Model 1922 with a finned barrel, for cavalry use and not very successful
5. T34 Automatic Rifle for the NATO 7.62-mm round, but not adopted for service.

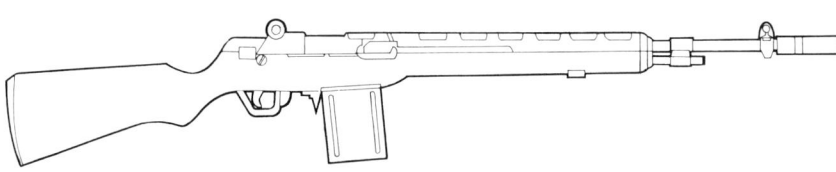

M14 rifle

Type: self-loading rifle
Calibre: 7.62 mm
System of operation: gas
Muzzle velocity: 2,800 ft (853 m) per second
Range: effective 765 yards (700 m) with a bipod
Rate of fire: 40 rounds per minute
Cooling system: air
Feed system: 20-round box
Dimensions: Barrel length 22 in (559 mm)
Overall length 44 in (1.12 m) with flash suppressor
Width
Height
Weights: 13 lb (5.9 kg) loaded, with bipod

Sights: post (fore) and tangent, aperture (rear)
Ammunition: 7.62 mm × 51
Used only by: USA
Notes: The M14 is the standard US Army rifle firing the NATO 7.62-mm round. The weapon has been produced as the self-loading M14, and the selective fire M14A1, the latter having a cyclic rate of 700 to 750 rounds per minute, and an automatic rate of 60 rounds per minute for the first minute, reducing to 40 rounds per minute for five minutes, 30 rounds per minute for 10 minutes, and 20 rounds per minute for 30 minutes or more. The standard US sniper rifle, the M21, is basically the M14 fitted with a special telescopic sight.

AR-15 (M16) rifle

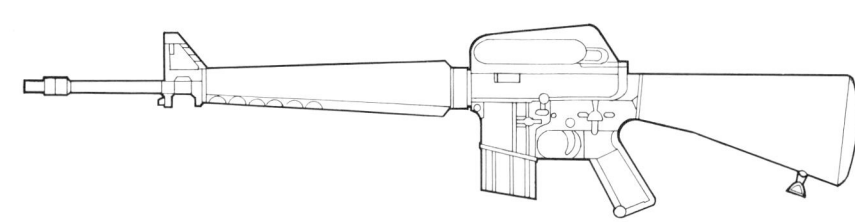

Type: selective fire rifle
Calibre: 5.56 mm
System of operation: gas (direct action)
Muzzle velocity: 3,280 ft (1,000 m) per second
Range: effective 437 yards (400 m)

Rate of fire: 700 to 950 rounds per minute (cyclic); 150 to 200 rounds per minute (automatic); 45 to 65 rounds per minute (single shot)
Cooling system: air
Feed system: 20- or 30-round box
Dimensions: Barrel length 20 in (508 mm)
　　　　　Overall length 39 in (990 mm) with flash suppressor
　　　　　Width
　　　　　Height
Weights: 6.83 lb (3.1 kg) empty for M16; 7 lb (3.18 kg) empty for M16A1; 8.22 lb (3.73 kg) with 30 rounds and sling for M16; 8.42 lb (3.82 kg) with 30 rounds and sling for M16A1
Sights: cylinder (fore) and flip, aperture (rear)
Ammunition: 5.56 mm × 45
Used also by: Australia, Philippines, Singapore, Taiwan, UK and other American allies

Notes: The AR-15, in service as the M16 and M16A1, was designed by the eminent Eugene Stoner to make full use of the new 5.56-mm round. The weapon is derived in essence from the Armalite AR-10, also designed by Stoner. The M16 is used principally by the US Air Force, and the M16A1 by the US Army. The latter is distinguishable by the plunger on the right rear of the receiver. This is used to push the bolt forward when it gets clogged with dirt and sticks at the rear.

AR-18 rifle

Type: selective fire rifle
Calibre: 5.56 mm
System of operation: gas
Muzzle velocity: 3,280 ft (1,000 m) per second
Range: effective 500 yards (457 m)
Rate of fire: 800 rounds per minute (cyclic); 80 rounds per minute (automatic); 40 rounds per minute (single shot)
Cooling system: air
Feed system: 20-round box
Dimensions: Barrel length 18.25 in (464 mm)
　　　　　Overall length 37 in (940 mm) with stock extended; 29 in (736 mm) with stock folded
　　　　　Width
　　　　　Height

Weights: 7 lb (3.17 kg) empty; 7.9 lb (3.58 kg) loaded
Sights: post (fore) and flip, aperture (rear)
Ammunition: 5.56 mm × 45
Used by:
Notes: The AR-18 was developed by Arthur Miller of the Armalite company in an effort to produce a weapon with superior performance to the M16 (AR-15), but at a unit cost cheap enough to interest emergent countries, it being unlikely that the US forces, already committed to the M16, would buy the AR-18. There are three models:
　　1. AR-18 standard model
　　2. AR-18S sub-machine gun model with a short barrel
　　3. AR-180 self-loading rifle.

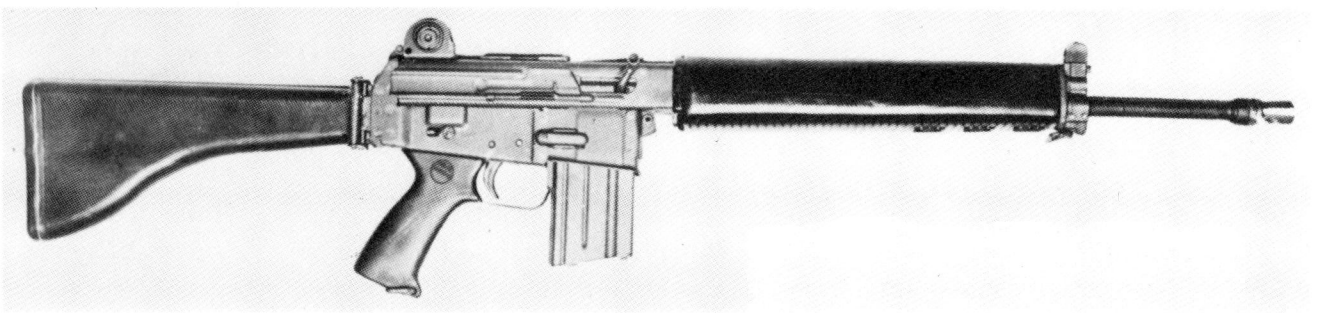

Upper Volta

8,070 men.

11 inf bns.
1 armd sqn.
1 para coy.
1 arty bty.
AML-60/-90, M-8 armd, Ferret scout
cars; 105mm how; 60mm, 81mm
mor; 75mm RCL.

Uruguay

20,000 men.

4 regional 'Armies' (divs) comprising:
3 armd regts, 13 inf bns, 6 cav regts,
4 arty 'bns' (btys), 1 AD bn, 5 engr
bns.
17 M-24, 18 M-3A1 lt tks; 10 M-3A1
scout cars; 15 M-113 APC; 25 105mm
how.

Para-Military Forces: 2,200.

M24 Chaffee

Type: light tank
Crew: four or five
Weights: Empty
     Loaded 40,500 lb (18,370 kg)
Dimensions: Length 18 ft (5.49 m)
     Width 9 ft 8 in (2.95 m)
     Height 8 ft 2 in (2.77 m)
Ground pressure: 11.3 lb/in² (0.79 kg/cm²)
Performance: road speed 34 mph (54 kph);
range 100 miles (160 km); vertical obstacle 36 in (91.0 cm); trench 8 ft (2.44 m);
gradient 60%; wading 40 in (1.02 m) without preparation, and 6 ft 6 in (1.98 m) with
preparation
Engine: two 110-hp Cadillac 44T24 inline
petrol engines
Armament: one 75-mm M6 gun, plus one
0.3-in (7.62-mm) Browning M1919A4
machine-gun co-axial with the main armament, one 0.3-in (7.62-mm) Browning
M1919A4 machine-gun in the hull nose,
and one 0.5-in (12.7-mm) Browning M2
machine-gun on the turret roof for AA
defence
Armour: ⅜ in (10 mm) minimum; 1½ in (38
mm) maximum
Used also by: various nations
Notes: The M24 entered US service in 1944,
and is still in wide use throughout the
world.

Venezuela

28,000 men.

2 med, 1 lt tk bns.
2 mech, 11 inf bns.
13 ranger bns.
1 horsed cav bn.
7 arty gps.
5 AA arty and engr bns.
142 AMX-30 med, 40 AMX-13 lt tks; 12 M-8 armd cars; AMX-VCI, 20 UR-416 APC; 75mm pack, 105mm how; 20 AMX 155mm SP guns; 81mm, 120mm mor; 35 M-18 76mm SP ATK guns; 106mm RCL; SS-11 ATGW; 40mm AA guns; some 20 *Alouette* III and Bell 47G helicopters.

Para-Military Forces: 10,000 National Guard.

Vietnam

600,000 men.*

25 inf divs,† 2 trg divs.
1 arty comd (of 10 regts).
1 engr comd.
About 15 indep inf regts.
35 arty regts.
40 AA arty regts.
20 SAM regts (each with 18 SA-2 launchers).
15 indep engr regts.
900 T-34, T-54 and T-59 med, PT-76, Type 60 lt tks; BTR-40/-50/-60 APC; 75mm, 76mm, 85mm, 100mm, 105mm, 122mm, 130mm, 152mm, 155mm guns/how; SU-76, JSU-122 SP guns; 82mm, 100mm, 107mm, 120mm, 160mm mor; 107mm, 122mm, 140mm RL; Sagger ATGW; 23mm, 37mm, 57mm, 85mm, 100mm, 130mm towed, ZSU-57-2 SP AA guns; SA-2/-3/-6/-7 SAM.

Deployment: 40,000 in Laos (numbers fluctuate).

Para-Military Forces: 70,000 Frontier, Coast Security and People's Armed Security Forces; Armed Militia of about 1,500,000.

* Equipment of the former forces of South Vietnam are not included here. It is estimated to have included up to 550 M-48 med and M-41 lt tks; 1,200 M-113 APC; 1,330 105mm and 155mm guns/how (some SP); 2 frigates; 2 patrol vessels; 42 patrol gunboats; 13 landing ships; 17 landing craft; 800 riverine craft; 11 support vessels; 1,000 ac of all types, incl 75 F-5A, 113 A-37B, 10 C-130, 25 A-1H/J, 37 AC-119C/K, 10 AC-47, 114 O-1, 33 DHC-2, 13 C-47; 36 CH-47, 430 UH-1 helicopters.
† Inf divs, normally totalling 8–10,000 men, include 1 tk bn, 3 inf, 1 arty regts and support elements.

M-1955 (D-20) howitzer

Type: howitzer
Calibre: 152 mm
Barrel length: 37 cal
Muzzle velocity: 2,149 ft (650 m) per second
Ranges: Maximum 18,919 yards (17,300 m) Minimum
Elevation: −5° to +63°
Traverse: 90° total
Rate of fire: four rounds per minute
Weights: For travel
 In firing position 12,456 lb (5,650 kg)
Dimensions: Length 26 ft 8½ in (8.14 m)
 Width 6 ft 7$\frac{9}{10}$ in (2.03 m)
 Height 9 ft 0$\frac{2}{3}$ in (2.76 m)
Ammunition: APHE, Chemical and HE
Crew: eight
Used also by: Bulgaria, Czechoslovakia, East Germany, Hungary, India, Poland, Romania, USSR

Notes: The M-1955 field howitzer was introduced to Russian service in 1955, and is still a powerful weapon. The ammunition is separate loading, the HE projectile weighing 96.12 lb (43.6 kg) and the APHE projectile 107.6 lb (48.8 kg). The APHE round will penetrate 4.88 in (124 mm) of armour at 1,094 yards (1,000 m). The weapon is very similar to the D-74, though the latter has a longer barrel.

ZPU-2 gun

Type: twin AA gun mounting
Calibre: 14.5 mm
Barrel length: 93.7 cal
Muzzle velocity: 3,280 ft (1,000 m) per second with API
Ranges: Maximum (horizontal) 7,655 yards (7,000 m); (vertical) 16,404 ft (5,000 m); (effective vertical) 4,593 ft (1,400 m) Minimum
Elevation: −15° to +85°
Traverse: 360°
Rate of fire: 600 rounds per minute (cyclic) per barrel
Weights: For travel
In firing position 1,400 lb (635 kg)
Dimensions: Length 12 ft 8⅓ in (3.87 m)
Width 4 ft 6 in (1.37 m)
Height 3 ft 9¼ in (1.1 m)
Ammunition: API

Crew: four
Used also by: Bulgaria, China, Cuba, East Germany, Egypt, Hungary, North Korea, Poland, Romania
Notes: The ZPU-2 AA mounting has two KPV machine-guns, each provided with a magazine holding a belt of 150 rounds. The API round will penetrate 1.26 in (32 mm) of armour at 547 yards (500 m).

TUL-1 machine-gun

Type: light machine-gun
Calibre: 7.62 mm
System of operation: gas
Muzzle velocity:
Range:
Rate of fire:
Cooling system: air
Feed system: 75-round drum
Dimensions: Barrel length
Overall length
Width
Height

Weights:
Sights:
Ammunition: 7.62 mm × 39
Used only by: Vietnam
Notes: Although similar to the Russian RPK in appearance, this Vietnamese weapon is based on the Chinese Type 56 assault rifle, itself derived in essence from the AK-47.

MAS M38 sub-machine gun

Type: sub-machine gun
Calibre: 7.65 mm
System of operation: blowback
Muzzle velocity: 1,152 ft (351 m) per second
Range: effective 164 yards (150 m)
Rate of fire: 600 rounds per minute (cyclic); 120 rounds per minute (automatic)
Cooling system: air
Feed system: 32-round box
Dimensions: Barrel length 8.82 in (224 mm)
Overall length 28.9 in (734 mm)
Width
Height
Weights: 6.33 lb (2.87 kg) unloaded; 7.5 lb (3.4 kg) loaded
Sights: blade (fore) and notch (rear)

Ammunition: 7.65-mm Long
Used by: Vietnam and possibly other ex-French territories
Notes: The MAS M38 is unique among current sub-machine guns in using the 7.65 mm Long cartridge. The weapon is extremely rugged, being made of machined parts.

K-50 M sub-machine gun

Type: sub-machine gun
Calibre: 7.62 mm
System of operation: blowback
Muzzle velocity: 1,600 ft (488 m) per second
Range: effective 219 yards (200 m)
Rate of fire: 700 rounds per minute (cyclic); 105 rounds per minute (automatic)
Cooling system: air
Feed system: 35-round box
Dimensions: Barrel length 10.6 in (269 mm)
Overall length 29.76 in (756 mm) with stock extended; 22.48 in (571 mm) with stock retracted
Width
Height
Weights: 7.5 lb (3.4 kg) empty; 9 lb (4.09 kg) loaded
Sights: post (fore) and flip, notch (rear)
Ammunition: 7.62 mm × 39

Used only by: Vietnam
Notes: The K-50 M is the Vietcong-modified Chinese K-50 sub-machine gun, itself a copy of the Russian PPSh-41 sub-machine gun. The Vietcong modifications consist of a sliding rather than a folding stock, a shorter barrel jacket, the addition of a pistol grip, and the elimination of the compensator/muzzle brake.

West Germany

Federal German Army

West Germany, like other 'front line' NATO nations, has a greater interest in her national security than some of her slightly more secure partners who can envisage fighting in North-West Europe ending before Warsaw Pact forces cross their frontiers. Not only has West Germany developed some very successful arms, but has an army almost twice the size of Great Britain's, and a tank force of impressive proportions. Military service is 15 months and there is a strong professional element in the officer and NCO group.

The West German army is divided into a Field and Territorial element, the latter not unlike the British territorial and reserve forces since their role is home defence and the formation of communications, police and service units on mobilisation. The *Bundesheer* consists of three Territorial Commands of six Military Districts with six Home Defence groups. These have 28 motorised infantry battalions with 300 infantry companies. In support are four service support commands, a signal brigade, and two signal and two engineer regiments. Like similar forces in Scandanavia, their role is to keep the rear areas and communications secure, and so allow regular forces to be fully deployed in the battle area.

The regular forces consist of 336,200 men, of whom 187,000 are conscripts. There are 5,000 reserve duty training positions for former conscripts. The army has 16 armoured brigades, each of which contains two tank, one armoured infantry, and one armoured artillery battalion. Twelve armoured infantry brigades each have one tank, two armoured infantry and one armoured artillery battalion. These mobile armoured forces are backed by three light infantry brigades, two mountain brigades and three airborne brigades. There are 15 surface-to-surface missile battalions, 11 with Honest John missiles and the other four with Lance. There are also three army aviation commands.

The Federal German army has 1,342 M48A2 tanks and 2,437 Leopard 1 medium tanks; 408 *Spähpanzerwagen* Pz-2 *Luchs*, 1,100 SPz 11-2 and 460 SPz 12-3 (HS-30) armoured cars; 2,136 *Marder* MICV; and 4,020 M-113 APCs. This armour is backed by 275 105-mm and 71 155-mm towed howitzers, and by 586 M109 155-mm, 149 M107 175-mm and 77 M110 203-mm SP guns. The Germans also include in their inventory 956 120-mm mortars and 209 LARS 110-mm multiple rocket-launchers – weapons that reflect experience on the Eastern Front during World War II. Her missile armoury consists of 65 Honest John

and 26 Lance SSM, while anti-tank arms include 770 KJPz-4 and 5 SP AT guns, 106-mm recoilless guns, 316 SS.11, 561 Milan and 170 TOW guided missiles, while her 316 RJPz-2 SP anti-tank guided missile mounts give greater mobility to her considerable tank-killing capability. With this anti-tank capacity West Germany also deploys an effective anti-aircraft arm ranging from 1,731 20-mm guns, via 710 40-mm guns to 70 *Gepard* 35-mm SP AA guns, plus 911 Redeye SAMs.

The helicopter support for the army consists of 190 UH-1D, 225 *Alouette* II/III, 109 CH-53G. Germany is updating this equipment with orders for 1,800 Leopard II tanks, 214 FH-70 SP guns, 114 RJPz-3 SP ATGW systems, and 177 TOW and 1,939 Milan anti-tank guided weapons. The anti-aircraft defence will receive 362 *Gepard* AA guns, while 140 Roland II SAMs and 227 German-designed BO 105M helicopters are also on order.

336,200 (187,000 conscripts).*

Field Army:
16 armd bdes (each with 2 tk, 1 armd inf, 1 armd arty bns).
12 armd inf bdes (each with 1 tk, 2 armd inf, 1 armd arty bns).
3 lt inf bdes.
2 mountain bdes.
3 AB bdes.
(Organized in 3 corps: 12 divs (4 armd, 4 armd inf, 2 Jäger, 1 mountain, 1 AB)).
15 SSM bns: 11 with Honest John, 4 with Lance.
3 army aviation comds (each with 1 lt, 1 med tpt regt).

Territorial Army:
3 Territorial Commands, 6 Military Districts, 6 Home Defence groups, 28 mot inf bns, 300 inf coys. In support are 4 service support comds, 1 sig bde, 2 sig, 2 engr regts. The Territorial Army provides defensive, comms, police and service units on mobilization.
1,342 M-48A2, 2,437 Leopard 1 med tks; 408 Spä Pz-2 *Luchs*, 1,100 SPz 11–2, 460 SPz 12–3 (HS-30) armd cars; 2,136 *Marder* MICV; 4,020 M-113 APC; 275 105mm, 71 155mm how; 586 M-109 155mm, 149 M-107 175mm, 77 M-110 203mm SP guns/ how; 956 120mm mor; 209 LARS 110mm multiple RL; 65 Honest John, 26 Lance SSM; 770 KJPz 4–5 SP ATK guns; 106mm RCL; 316 SS-11, 561 *Milan*, 170 TOW ATGW; 316 RJPz-2 SP ATGW; 1,731 20mm, 710 40mm, 70 *Gepard* 35mm SP AA guns; 911 Redeye SAM; 190 UH-1D, 225 *Alouette* II/III, 109 CH-53G helicopters; 5 CL-89 drones. (1,800 Leopard 2 tks, 214 FH-70, 114 RJPz-3 SP ATGW, 177 TOW, 1,939 *Milan* ATGW, 362 *Gepard* AA guns, 140 Roland II SAM, 212 PAH-1, 227 BO-105M helicopters on order.)

Para-Military Forces: 20,000 Federal Border Guard with armd cars, APC, mor, ATK weapons, *Alouette* II, UH-1D and CH-53G helicopters.

*The army is being reorganized to form 15 armd bdes (each with 3 tk, 1 armd inf, 1 armd arty bns), 17 armd inf bdes (each with 2 tk, 2 armd inf, 1 armd arty bns) and 3 AB bdes.

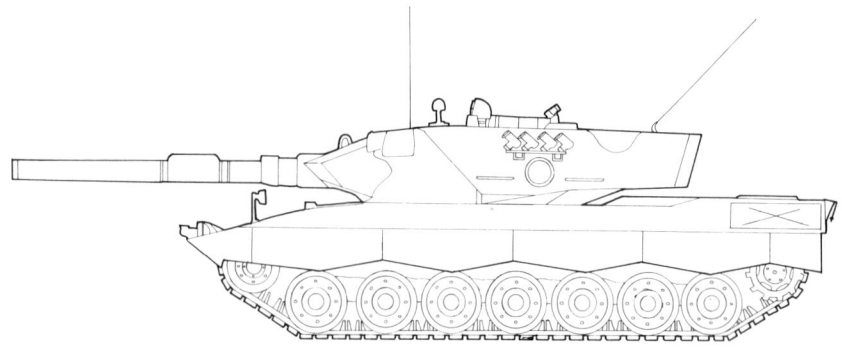

Leopard 2

Type: main battle tank
Crew: four
Weights: Empty
    Loaded 124,780 lb (56,600 kg)
Dimensions: Length (including main armament) 32 ft 1 in (9.78 m); (hull) 25 ft 4 in (7.73 m)
    Width (with skirts) 11 ft 7 in (3.54 m)
    Height 8 ft (2.45 m)
Ground pressure: 12.23 lb/in² (0.86 kg/cm²)
Performance: road speed 42 mph (68 kph); range classified; vertical obstacle 3 ft 9¼ in (1.15 m); trench 10 ft 2 in (3.1 m); gradient 60%; ground clearance 19¾ in (50.0 cm); wading 3 ft 7¼ in (1.1 m) without preparation, 7 ft 4½ in (2.25 m) with preparation, and 13 ft 1½ in (4.0 m) with a schnorkel
Engine: one 1,500-hp MTU MB 873 Ka-500 inline multi-fuel engine
Armament: one 120-mm Rheinmetall smooth-bore gun with 40 rounds of APDS and one other fin-stabilised ammunition, plus one 7.62-mm MG3 machine-gun co-axial with the main armament, and one 7.62-mm MG3 machine-gun for AA defence on the loader's hatch. Some 3,000 rounds of 7.62-mm ammunition are carried
Armour: classified, but of the Chobham type
Used only by: West Germany
Notes: The Leopard 2 will shortly enter service with the German Army, and is a highly advanced MBT. An NBC system and night vision equipment are standard, the gun is fully stabilised, there is a hydraulically assisted loading mechanism, the propellant cases are semi-combustible and so take up less room, and the gunner has both optical and laser rangefinders.

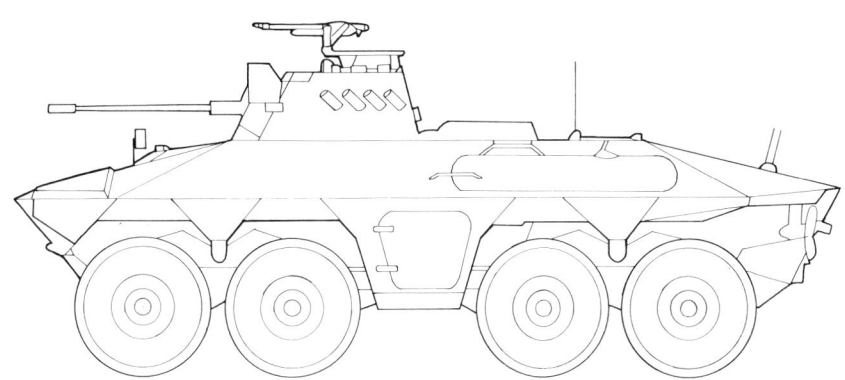

Spähpanzer 2 Luchs

Type: reconnaissance vehicle
Crew: four
Weights: Empty
      Loaded 43,122 lb (19,560 kg)
Dimensions: Length 25 ft 5 in (7.743 m)
      Width 9 ft 9 in (2.98 m)
      Height 9 ft 3⅜ in (2.84 m)
Ground pressure:
Performance: road speed 56 mph (90 kph); water speed 5.6 mph (9 kph); range 497 miles (800 km); vertical obstacle 23⅝ in (60.0 cm); trench 6 ft 6 in (1.9 m); gradient 60%; ground clearance 16 in (40.5 cm); the *Luchs* is fully amphibious
Engine: one 390-hp Mercedes-Benz Model OM 403 VA multi-fuel inline engine
Armament: one 20-mm Rheinmetall Rh.202 cannon, plus one 7.62-mm MG3 machine-gun on the turret roof for AA defence
Armour: classified

Used only by: West Germany
Notes: The *Spähpanzer* 2 is an 8 × 8 reconnaissance vehicle, and entered German service in 1976. The type is one of a new series of wheeled vehicles for the German Army, all making use wherever possible of the same components in their automotive systems. The vehicle is fully amphibious, being driven in the water by a pair of propellers. The *Luchs* also has twin driving positions, one at the front and the other at the rear. In emergencies the rear driver can drive the vehicle off at full speed without delay. An NBC system and night vision equipment are standard.

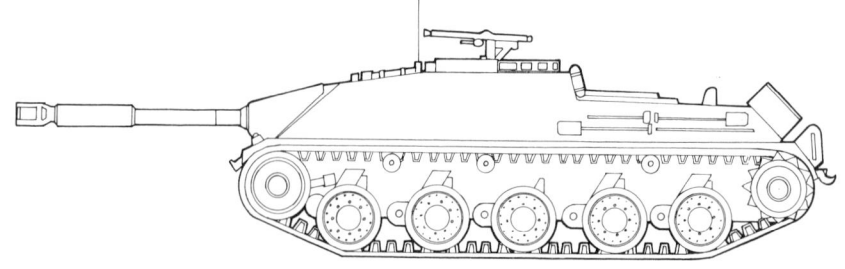

Jagdpanzer 4-5 Kanone

Type: tank destroyer
Crew: four
Weights: Empty
  Loaded 60,627 lb (27,500 kg)
Dimensions: Length (including armament)
  28 ft 9 in (8.75 m); (hull) 20 ft 6
  in (6.238 m)
  Width 9 ft 9 in (2.98 m)
  Height (without AA machine-
  gun) 6 ft 10 in (2.085 m)
Ground pressure: 10.67 lb/in² (0.75 kg/cm²)
Performance: road speed 43½ mph (70 kph);
  range 250 miles (400 km); vertical obsta-
  cle 29½ in (75.0 cm); trench 6 ft 7 in (2.0

m); gradient 60%; ground clearance 17¾ in
(45.0 cm); wading 4 ft 7 in (1.4 m) without
preparation
Engine: one 500-hp Daimler-Benz Model MB
837 Aa inline diesel engine
Armament: one 90-mm Rheinmetall *Bord-
kanone* L/40.8 gun with 51 rounds of HEP
and HEAT, plus one 7.62-mm machine-
gun co-axial with the main armament, and
one 7.62-mm machine-gun on a pintle
mount on the commander's cupola. Some
4,000 rounds of 7.62-mm ammunition are
carried
Armour: ⅖ in (10 mm) minimum; 2 in (50
mm) maximum
Used also by: Belgium
Notes: The Jpz 4-5 tank destroyer entered
service with the German Army in 1965.
Armour is only moderate for such a vehicle,
and the Jpz 4-5 relies for survival on its
high speed and low silhouette. The 90-mm
gun has an effective range of 2,187 yards
(2,000 m), and a rate of fire of 12 rounds
per minute. Belgian vehicles, which
entered service in 1975, have an improved
transmission and suspension, plus updated
fire control characteristics, based on the
use of a laser rangefinder.

Jagdpanzer Rakete **M1966**

Type: tank destroyer
Crew: four
Weights: Empty
        Loaded 50,706 lb (23,000 kg)
Dimensions: Length 21 ft 1 in (6.43 m)
              Width 9 ft 9 in (2.98 m)
              Height 6 ft 6 in (1.98 m)
Ground pressure: 8.96 lb/in² (0.63 kg/cm²)
Performance: road speed $43\frac{1}{2}$ mph (70 kph); range 217 miles (350 km); vertical obstacle $29\frac{1}{2}$ in (75.0 cm); trench 6 ft 7 in (2.0 m); gradient 60%; ground clearance $17\frac{3}{4}$ in (45.0 cm); wading 4 ft 7 in (1.4 m) without preparation
Engine: one 500-bhp Daimler-Benz Model 837 Aa inline diesel engine
Armament: two launchers for SS.11 anti-tank missiles with 14 missiles, plus one 7.62-mm MG3 machine-gun firing through the front plate, and one 7.62-mm MG3 in front of the commander's hatch
Armour: $\frac{2}{5}$ in (10 mm) minimum; 2 in (50 mm) maximum
Used only by: West Germany
Notes: The *Jagdpanzer Rakete* is based on the same chassis as the Jpz 4-5, and entered service in 1967. Reloading of the

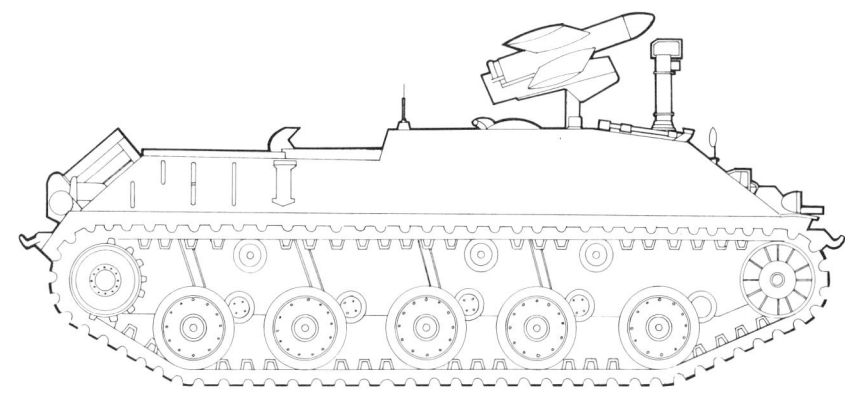

missile-launchers is automatic, and a rate of fire of one missile per minute is possible. The Jpz *Rakete* was designed to enhance the long-range tank-killing chances of German *Panzergrenadier* units, the SS.11 having a maximum effective range of 3,280 yards (3,000 m). In the near future, all vehicles are to be refitted to use the superior HOT anti-tank missile.

Schützenpanzer Neu M1966 Marder

Type: mechanised infantry combat vehicle
Crew: three, plus up to seven infantrymen
Weights: Empty
Loaded 62,169 lb (28,200 kg)
Dimensions: Length 22 ft 3 in (6.79 m)
Width 10 ft 8 in (3.25 m)
Height 9 ft 8 in (2.95 m)
Ground pressure: 11.3 lb/in² (0.8 kg/cm²)
Performance: road speed 46.6 mph (75 kph); range 323 miles (520 km); vertical obstacle 3 ft 3⅝ in (1.0 m); trench 8 ft 2 in (2.5 m); gradient 60%; ground clearance 17¾ in (45.0 cm); wading 4 ft 11 in (1.5 m) without preparation and 8 ft 2½ in (2.5 m) with a schnorkel
Engine: one 600-bhp MTU MB 833 Ea-500 turbo-charged inline diesel engine
Armament: one 20-mm Rheinmetall Rh.202 cannon with 1,250 rounds, plus one 7.62-mm MG3 machine-gun co-axial with the main armament, and one 7.62-mm MG3 machine-gun in a remotely-controlled mount on the roof of the troop compartment. Some 5,000 rounds of 7.62-mm ammunition are carried
Armour: classified
Used only by: West Germany

Notes: The *Marder* is probably the most advanced MICV in service today. An NBC system and night vision equipment are standard. The crew compartment has firing ports for the infantry to use their weapons from inside the vehicle. There are several versions in service or under development:

1. *Marder* MICV production model
2. *Marder* Roland, equipped with radar and twin Euromissile Roland surface-to-air missile-launchers, for which there are 10 missiles
3. *Marder* armed with a 120-mm mortar, developed but not put into production
4. *Marder* artillery fire-control vehicle, developed but not put into production
5. *Marder* tank destroyer, with a 105-mm gun, under development
6. *Marder* radar vehicle, developed but not put into production
7. *Marder* with an LWT-3 fully stabilised turret, under development.

Other variants under development include an AA vehicle, an ambulance, a reconnaissance vehicle and a rocket-launching model.

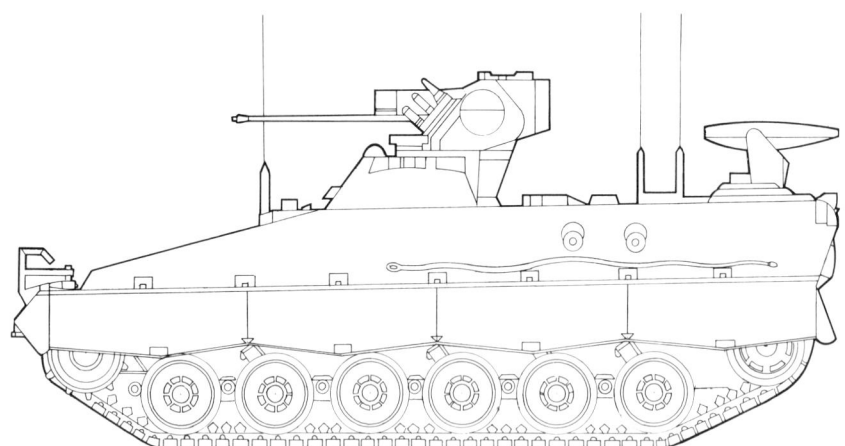

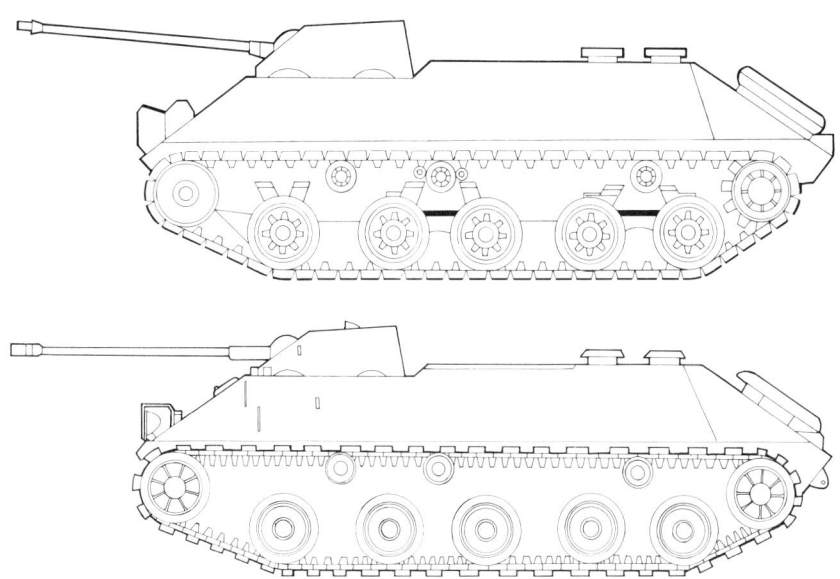

Hotchkiss HS-30
Schützenpanzer 12-3

Type: armoured personnel carrier
Crew: two, plus up to six infantrymen
Weights: Empty 25,794 lb (11,700 kg)
Loaded 31,967 lb (14,600 kg)
Dimensions: Length (including armament) 20 ft 8 in (6.31 m); (hull) 18 ft 3 in (5.56 m)
Width 8 ft 4 in (2.54 m)
Height (with armament) 6 ft 1 in (1.85 m)
Ground pressure: 10.66 lb/in² (0.75 kg/cm²)
Performance: road speed 36 mph (58 kph); range 174 miles (270 km); vertical obstacle 23⅜ in (60.0 cm); trench 5 ft 3 in (1.6 m); gradient 60%; ground clearance 15¾ in (40.0 cm); wading 27½ in (70.0 cm)
Engine: one 235-hp Rolls-Royce B.81 Mark 80F inline petrol engine
Armament: one 20-mm Hispano-Suiza 820 cannon with 2,000 rounds, plus one 7.62-mm MG3 machine-gun on the commander's station
Armour: ⅓ in (8 mm) minimum; 1⅕ in (30 mm) maximum
Used only by: West Germany

Notes: The HS-30 was derived from a Swiss self-propelled AA gun, and was built in Germany and Great Britain, entering service with the German Army in 1959. The HS-30 enjoys certain tactical advantages as a result of its low silhouette and fairly thick armour, but has only limited water-crossing capability and no NBC protection. There are several variants:
1. HS-30 (Spz 12-3) armoured personnel carrier
2. *Panzermörser* Spz 52-3, with a 120-mm mortar in the troop compartment
3. *Jagdpanzer Rakete* Jpz 3-3, with no turret but launchers for two SS.11 anti-tank missiles
4. Spz 21-3 command and radio vehicle
5. Spz 81-3 *Feuerleitpanzer* artillery fire-control and command vehicle
6. Spz 12-3 AT, armed with an M40A1 106-mm anti-tank recoilless rifle.

Hotchkiss *Schützenpanzer* 11-2

Type: reconnaissance vehicle
Crew: five
Weights: Empty
Loaded 18,078 lb (8,200 kg)
Dimensions: Length 14 ft 10 in (4.51 m)
Width 7 ft 6 in (2.28 m)
Height 6 ft 6 in (1.97 m)
Ground pressure: 8.24 lb/in² (0.58 kg/cm²)
Performance: road speed 36 mph (58 kph); range 242 miles (390 km); vertical obstacle 23⅔ in (60.0 cm); trench 4 ft 11 in (1.5 m); gradient 60%
Engine: one 164-hp Hotchkiss inline petrol engine
Armament: one 20-mm Hispano-Suiza cannon with 500 rounds
Armour: ⅓ in (8 mm) minimum; ⅗ in (15 mm) maximum
Used only by: West Germany
Notes: The Hotchkiss reconnaissance vehicle was adopted by the German Army in 1958, and is in the process of being phased out in the late 1970s. There are several members of the family:
1. Spz 11-2 reconnaissance vehicle, to

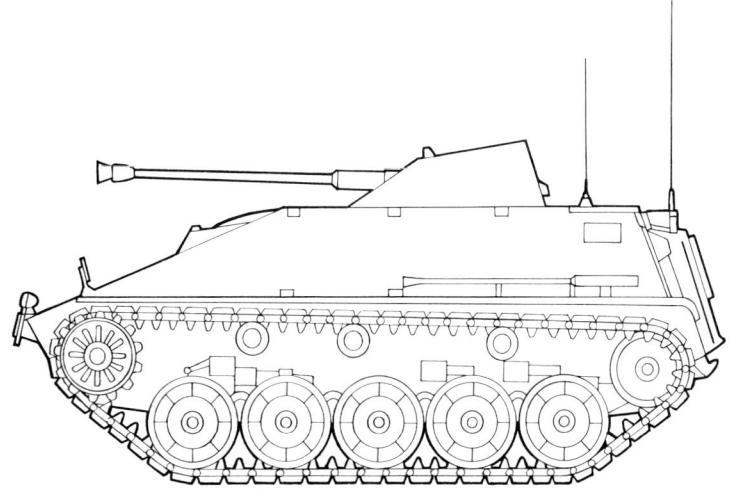

which the technical specification above applies

2. Spz 51-2 *Panzermörser* 81-mm mortar carrier, with 50 mortar rounds and a 7.62-mm MG3 machine-gun
3. Spz 22-2 *Artilleriebeobachter* command vehicle, with a crew of five, three radio sets and an MG3
4. Spz 2-2 *Krankenwagen* ambulance for up to four stretchers
5. Spz *Kurz Nachschubpanzer* cargo carrier.

M109G

Type: self-propelled howitzer
Crew: six
Weights: Empty
      Loaded 54,233 lb (24,600 kg)
Dimensions: Length 22 ft 9¾ in (6.95 m)
      Width 16 ft 7⅙ in (5.06 m)
      Height 9 ft 10 in (3.0 m)
Ground pressure:
Performance: road speed 35 mph (56 kph); range 217 miles (350 km)
Engine: one 420-bhp Otto diesel
Armament: one 155-mm L/23 howitzer
Armour: 1½ in (38 mm) maximum

Used only by: West Germany
Notes: The M109G is a German modification to the US M109 SP howitzer, with a German engine and an improved howitzer, with a vertical sliding breech, better sights and semi-fixed ammunition. The howitzer can be elevated from −5° to +75°, and the turret traverses 360°. The 95.2-lb (43.18-kg) HE shell is fired at 2,250 ft (686 m) per second to a range of 20,013 yards (18,100 m).

Messerschmitt-Bölkow-Blohm BO Mamba

Type: anti-tank missile, man-portable and jump-launched without frame or container

Guidance: command to line-of-sight by means of wire

Dimensions: Span 1 ft 3¾ in (40.0 cm)
Body diameter 4 $\frac{7}{10}$ in (12.0 cm)
Length 3 ft 1⅝ in (95.5 cm)

Booster: none

Sustainer: solid-propellant rocket

Warhead: hollow-charge high explosive (6 lb/2.7 kg), capable of penetrating 18.7 in (475 mm) of armour; anti-tank/shrapnel (6 lb/2.7 kg) capable of penetrating 9.84 in (250 mm) of armour and throwing shrapnel over a radius of 32 ft 9 $\frac{7}{10}$ in (10.0 m); dummy for training

Weights: Launch 24.7 lb (11.2 kg)
Burnt out

Performance: range 328-2,187 yards (300-2,000 m); speed 313 mph (505 kph)

Used by:

Notes: Of the same general design as the Cobra 2000, with a launcher stand included on the missile. Will accept Cobra warheads. Intended for ground launch, but can be set off from vehicles with the aid of a special five-missile launcher.

FH 155(L) howitzer

Type: field howitzer
Calibre: 155 mm
Barrel length:
Muzzle velocity:
Ranges: Maximum
         Minimum
Elevation:
Traverse:
Rate of fire:
Weights: For travel
         In firing position
Dimensions: Length
           Width
           Height
Ammunition:

Crew:
Used by:
Notes: The FH 155(L) is a West German modernisation of the US 155-mm howitzer. The performance and dimensions of the West German weapon are identical with those of the American weapon, the differences between the two weapons lying in a new barrel, breech and muzzle brake, combined with improved sighting and fire-control arrangements.

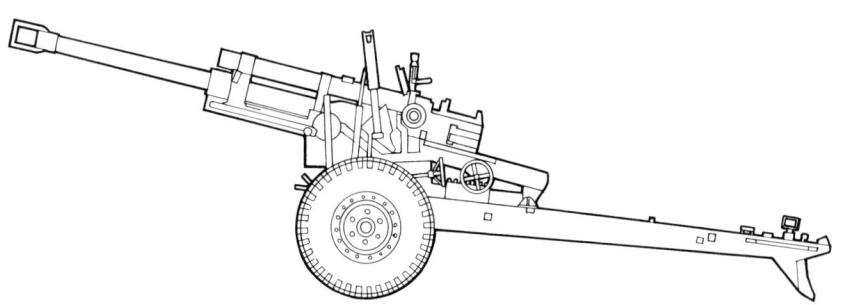

le FH 105(L) howitzer

Type: light field howitzer
Calibre: 105 mm
Barrel length: 35.5 cal
Muzzle velocity: 1,968 ft (600 m) per second
Ranges: Maximum 15,420 yards (14,100 m)
         Minimum
Elevation:
Traverse:
Rate of fire:
Weights: For travel
         In firing position 5,512 lb (2,500 kg)
Dimensions: Length
           Width
           Height
Ammunition:

Crew:
Used only by: West Germany
Notes: The le FH 105(L) is a reworking of the US M101 howitzer by the West Germans to update the weapon. Improvements include a longer barrel with a muzzle brake and improved sighting arrangements. Apart from those above, the principal dimensions and performance figures are the same as those of the basic US weapon.

LARS artillery rocket launcher

Type: mobile artillery rocket launcher
Calibre: 110 mm
Number of barrels: two groups of 18
Muzzle velocity: 2,083 ft (635 m) per second
Ranges: Maximum 16,404 yards (15,000 m)
Minimum 7,108 yards (6,500 m)
Elevation: 0° to +55°
Traverse: 105°
Time to reload: 15 minutes
Weights: For travel 28,660 lb (13,000 kg)
In firing position 33,069 lb (15,000 kg)
Dimensions: Length
Width
Height
Ammunition: HE, Incendiary or Smoke warheads on the rocket
Crew: five

Used only by: West Germany
Notes: The LARS system is based on the rear of a 6 × 6 Magirus Jupiter lorry. The principal characteristics of the rocket used are: length 7 ft 5 in (2.26 m); diameter 4⅓ in (110 mm); weight 55.1 lb (25 kg). The whole group of 36 rockets can be fired in 18 seconds.

Armbrust launcher

Type: man-portable one-shot anti-tank rocket launcher
Calibre: 67 mm
Barrel length:
Muzzle velocity: about 722 ft (220 m) per second
Ranges: Maximum 1,640 yards (1,500 m); effective 328 yards (300 m)
Minimum
Elevation:
Traverse:
Rate of fire:
Weights: For travel 13.88 lb (6.3 kg)
In firing position
Dimensions: Length 2 ft 9½ in (0.85 m)
Width 3.07 in (0.078 m)

Height
Ammunition: HEAT warhead
Crew: one
Used by: under development for West Germany and possibly USA
Notes: The West German *Armbrust* is designed as a one-shot short-range AT weapon, its 2.2-lb (0.99-kg) warhead being able to penetrate more than 11.8 in (300 mm) of armour. Unlike other such weapons, which attain their recoilless effect by jetting back large volumes of hot gas, the *Armbrust* releases an equal mass (5,000 small plastic flakes) of solid material, this making it possible to use the weapon inside rooms and in other confined spaces. The system also helps keep the firer concealed.

Pzf.44 *Lanze* launcher

Type: man-portable anti-tank rocket launcher
Calibre: 44 mm (launcher); 67 mm (grenade)
Barrel length:
Muzzle velocity: 551 ft (168 m) per second, rising to 689 ft (210 m) per second
Ranges: Maximum effective 437 yards (400 m) against stationary targets
Minimum
Elevation:
Traverse:
Rate of fire:
Weights: For travel 17.2 lb (7.8 kg)
In firing position 22.7 lb (10.3 kg)
Dimensions: Length 3 ft 9¾ in (1.162 m)
Width
Height
Ammunition: HEAT warhead

Crew: one
Used only by: West Germany
Notes: The West German Pzf.44 is designed as a close-range anti-tank weapon. The projectile weighs 3.3 lb (1.5 kg), and is capable of penetrating 14.57 in (370 mm) of armour.

Heckler und Koch HK11 machine-gun

Type: light machine-gun
Calibre: 7.62 mm
System of operation: delayed blowback
Muzzle velocity: 2,625 ft (800 m) per second
Range: effective 875 yards (800 m)
Rate of fire: 850 rounds per minute
Cooling system: air
Feed system: 20-round box or 80-round drum

Dimensions: Barrel length 17.72 in (450 mm)
Overall length 40.16 in (1.02 m)
Width
Height
Weights: 13.69 lb (6.2 kg); 15 lb (6.8 kg) with bipod
Sights: blade (fore) and aperture (rear)
Ammunition: 7.62 mm × 51

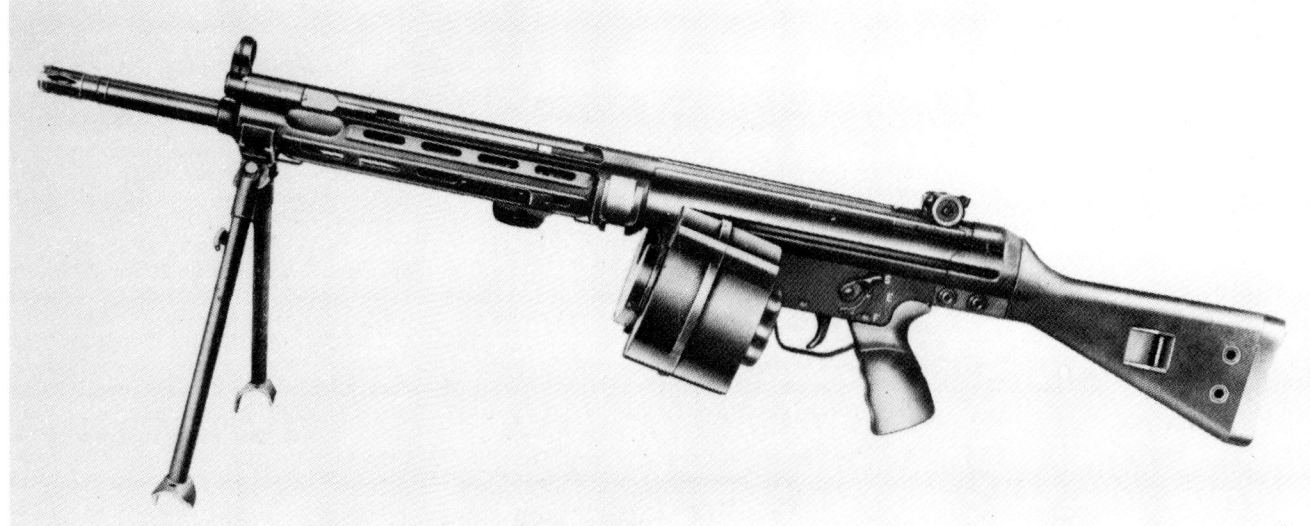

Used also by: several countries in Africa and
South America
Notes: The HK11 is a light machine-gun
using the NATO 7.62-mm standard round,
and based loosely on the design of the G3
rifle.

Heckler und Koch HK13 machine-gun

Type: light machine-gun
Calibre: 5.56 mm
System of operation: delayed blowback
Muzzle velocity: 3,117 ft (950 m) per second
Range: effective 437 yards (400 m)
Rate of fire: 750 rounds per minute (cyclic);
100 rounds per minute (automatic)
Cooling system: air
Feed system: 20-, 30- or 40-round box, or
100-round drum
Dimensions: Barrel length 17.72 in (450
mm)
Overall length 38.58 in (980
mm)
Width
Height

Weights: 11.9 lb (5.4 kg) empty; 13.23 lb (6
kg) with bipod; 18.63 lb (8.45 kg) with
100-round drum and bipod
Sights: blade (fore) and V (rear)
Ammunition: 5.56 mm × 45
Used by: various countries in south-east Asia
Notes: The HK13 is a Heckler und Koch
Group II weapon, ie one firing the 5.56
mm × 45 round. Operation of the weapon is
very similar to that of the G3 rifle.

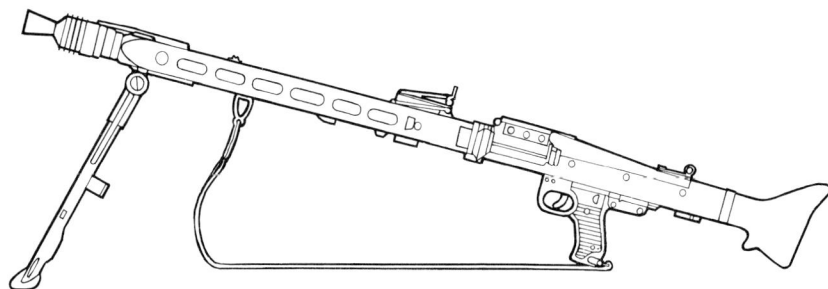

MG3 machine-gun

Type: general-purpose machine-gun
Calibre: 7.62 mm
System of operation: short recoil
Muzzle velocity: 2,690 ft (820 m) per second
Range: effective 875 yards (800 m) with a
bipod; 1,334 yards (1,220 m) with a tripod
Rate of fire: 700 to 1,300 rounds per minute
(cyclic); 250 rounds per minute (automatic)
Cooling system: air
Feed system: metal-link belt

Dimensions: Barrel length 20.9 in (531 mm)
Overall length 48.23 in (1.225
m)
Width
Height
Weights: 23.15 lb (10.5 kg) empty; 24.36 lb
(10.05 kg) with bipod
Sights: barleycorn (fore) and tangent with V
notch (rear)
Ammunition: 7.62 mm × 51
Used also by: Austria, Denmark, Chile, Iran,
Italy, Norway, Pakistan, Portugal, Spain,

Sudan, Turkey, Yugoslavia

Notes: The MG3 is basically the MG42 of World War II reworked to take the NATO 7.62-mm round, eloquent testimony of the virtues of the MG42. The original weapon used by the re-formed *Bundeswehr* was the MG1, manufactured as the MG42/59. In service these weapons were supplemented by the MG2, World War II MG42 guns rebarrelled and rechambered to take the 7.62-mm round. The MG3 was introduced in 1968, and differs from the MG1 only in its ability to take a variety of modern ammunition belts. Yugoslavia uses a 7.92-mm version, the SARAC M-1953.

MP40 sub-machine gun

Type: sub-machine gun
Calibre: 9 mm
System of operation: blowback
Muzzle velocity: 1,250 ft (381 m) per second
Range: effective 219 yards (200 m)
Rate of fire: 500 rounds per minute (cyclic); 120 rounds per minute (automatic)
Cooling system: air
Feed system: 32-round box
Dimensions: Barrel length 9.88 in (251 mm)
Overall length 32.8 in (833 mm) with stock extended; 24.8 in (630 mm) with stock retracted
Width
Height
Weights: 8.88 lb (4.03 kg) empty; 10.36 lb (4.7 kg) loaded
Sights: blade (fore) and flip, notch (rear)

Ammunition: 9mm × 19 Parabellum
Used also by: various countries, especially in Asia
Notes: The MP40 was introduced to German service in 1940 as the mass production version of the MP38, with a receiver of welded sheet steel stampings. The MP40/2 variant features a revised magazine housing allowing two magazines, welded together, to be accommodated. When one magazine is exhausted, the other can be pushed sideways into position.

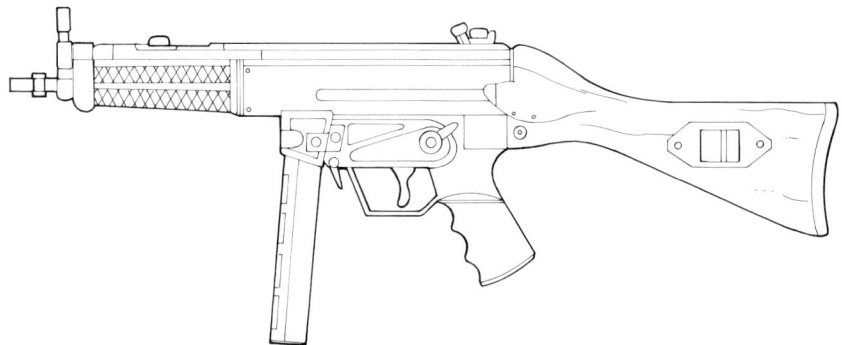

Heckler und Koch MP5 sub-machine gun

Type: sub-machine gun
Calibre: 9 mm
System of operation: delayed blowback
Muzzle velocity: 1,312 ft (400 m) per second
Range: effective 219 yards (200 m)
Rate of fire: 750 rounds per minute (cyclic); 100 rounds per minute (automatic)
Cooling system: air
Feed system: 10-, 15- or 30-round box

Dimensions: Barrel length 8.86 in (225 mm)
Overall length 26.77 in (680 mm) or 25.98 in (660 mm) with stock open; 19.29 in (490 mm) with stock folded
Width
Height
Weights: 5.4 lb (2.45 kg) or 5.62 lb (2.55 kg) empty; 6.48 lb (2.94 kg) or 6.68 lb (3.03 kg) loaded
Sights: post (fore) and apertures (rear)

Ammunition: 9mm × 19 Parabellum
Used also by: various countries
Notes: The MP5 was developed by Heckler und Koch using many components of their G3 rifle. The basic model is the MP5A2, with a rigid plastic stock, while the MP5A3 has a monopole telescopic metal stock, this making the weapon slightly heavier than the MP5A2.

Heckler und Koch MP5 SD sub-machine gun

Type: silenced sub-machine gun
Calibre: 9 mm
System of operation: delayed blowback
Muzzle velocity: 935 ft (285 m) per second
Range: effective 148 yards (135 m)
Rate of fire: 650 rounds per minute (cyclic); 100 rounds per minute (automatic); 40 rounds per minute (single shot)
Cooling system: air
Feed system: 10-, 15- or 30-round box
Dimensions: Barrel length 8.86 in (225 mm) Overall length 30.71 in (780 mm) with a rigid stock; 24.02 in (610 mm) with stock retracted; 21.65 in (550 mm) with receiver cap
Width
Height
Weights: 5.84 lb (2.65 kg) empty, with rigid stock; 6.5 lb (2.95 kg) with retractable stock; 5.29 lb (2.4 kg) with receiver cap; 1.08 lb (0.492 kg) for full 30-round magazine
Sights: post (fore) and apertures (rear), or ×4 telescope, or light projector, or image intensifier

Ammunition: 9 mm × 19 Parabellum
Used by: various countries
Notes: The MP5 SD is the silenced version of the MP5, the silencing being effected by the addition of a jacket round the barrel. Propellant gases from the barrel escape into this via radial holes, and lose velocity moving through a series of helical traps before emerging at a speed below that of sound. There are three models of the MP5 SD, the first having a fixed plastic stock, the second having a retractable metal tubular stock, and the third having no stock at all, the receiver being capped.

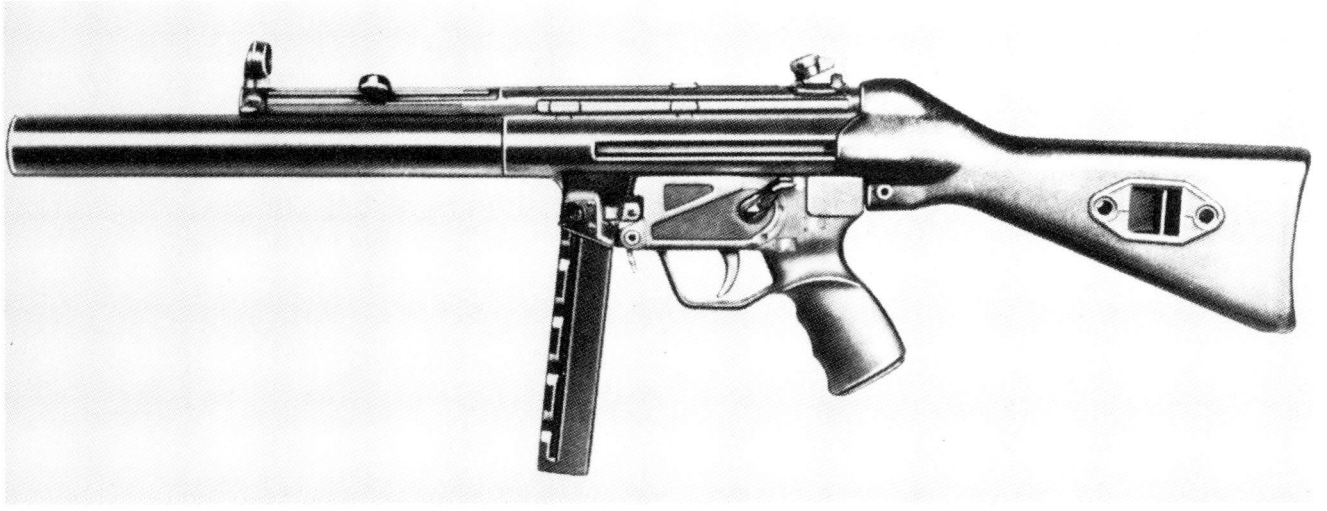

Heckler und Koch G3 rifle

Type: selective fire rifle
Calibre: 7.62 mm
System of operation: delayed blowback
Muzzle velocity: 2,625 ft (800 m) per second
Range: effective 437 yards (400 m)
Rate of fire: 500 to 600 rounds per minute (cyclic); 100 rounds per minute (automatic); 40 rounds per minute (single shot)
Cooling system: air
Feed system: 20-round box
Dimensions: Barrel length 17.72 in (450 mm)
Overall length 40.16 in (1.02 m) with stock extended; 31.5 in (800 mm) with stock retracted

Width
Height
Weights: 9.37 lb (4.25 kg) with fixed stock, empty; 9.92 lb (4.5 kg) with retractable stock, empty; 1.66 lb (0.753 kg) for full steel magazine
Sights: post (fore) and U notch or apertures (rear)
Ammunition: 7.62 mm × 51
Used also by: Bangladesh, Bolivia, Brazil, Brunei, Burma, Chad, Chile, Colombia, Denmark, Dominican Republic, El Salvador, France, Ghana, Guyana, Haiti, Indonesia, Iran, Italy, Jordan, Kenya, Malawi, Malaysia, Morocco, Netherlands, Niger, Nigeria, Norway, Pakistan, Peru, Portugal, Qatar, Saudi Arabia, Senegal,

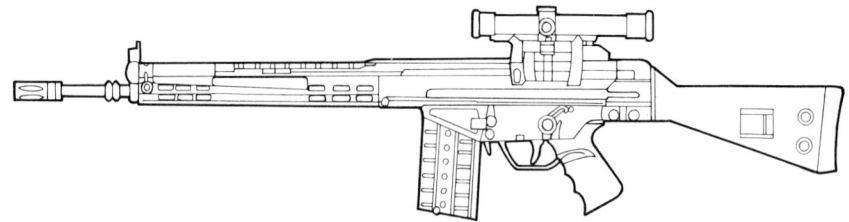

Sudan, Sweden, Switzerland, Tanzania, Thailand, Togo, Turkey, Uganda, United Arab Emirates, Upper Volta, Zambia

Notes: The G3 rifle is after the AK-47 the most successful rifle to be developed since World War II, and has its origins in German small arms thinking during World War II. After the end of that war, several designers moved to Spain, where they acquired experience of delayed blowback weapons in the design of the CETME rifle, in 7.92-mm calibre. Further work on the basic design was undertaken in Holland, and in the late 1950s development of a 7.62-mm version was undertaken by Heckler und Koch, the result being the excellent G3, which entered German service in 1959.

Yugoslavia

200,000 men (130,000 conscripts).

9 inf divs.
7 indep tk bdes.
11 indep inf bdes.
3 mountain bdes.
1 AB bn.
12 arty regts.
6 ATK regts.
12 AA arty regts.
1,500 T-34/-54/-55, M-47, about 650 M-4 med, some PT-76 lt tks; M-3, M-8, BRDM-2 scout cars; M-980 MICV; BTR-50/-60P/-152, M-60 APC; 76mm, 105mm, 122mm, 130mm, 152mm, 155mm guns/how; SU-76, SU-100, 105mm SP how; 81mm, 120mm mor; 128mm multiple RL; FROG-7 SSM; 57mm, 75mm, 100mm towed, M-18 76mm, M-36 90mm, ASU-57 SP ATK guns; 57mm, 75mm, 82mm, 105mm RCL; 'Snapper', 'Sagger' ATGW; 20mm, 30mm, 37mm, 40mm, 57mm, 85mm, 88mm, 90mm, 94mm towed, ZSU-57-2 SP AA guns; SA-6 SAM.

Para-Military Forces and Reserves: 500,000 Reservists, 16,000 Frontier Guards, 1,000,000 Territorial Defence Force.

M980

Type: mechanised infantry combat vehicle
Crew: three, plus up to eight infantrymen
Weights: Empty 24,251 lb (11,000 kg)
Loaded 26,455 lb (12,000 kg)
Dimensions: Length 20 ft 6 in (6.25 m)
Width 9 ft 4$\frac{1}{8}$ in (2.85 m)
Height 8 ft 2$\frac{2}{8}$ in (2.5 m)
Ground pressure:
Performance: road speed 43 mph (70 kph); water speed 5 mph (8 kph); range 311 miles (500 km); vertical obstacle 39$\frac{2}{8}$ in (1.0 m); trench 7 ft 10$\frac{1}{4}$ in (2.4 m); gradient 60%; ground clearance 11$\frac{4}{8}$ in (30.0 cm); the M980 is fully amphibious, being driven in the water by its tracks
Engine: one 276-hp Hispano-Suiza HS 115-2 turbo-charged inline diesel engine
Armament: one turret-mounted 20-mm Hispano-Suiza HSS 804 cannon, plus one co-axial 7.92-mm M-53 machine-gun, and two launcher rails for AT-3 'Sagger' anti-tank missiles at the rear of the turret
Armour:
Used only by: Yugoslavia
Notes: The M980 entered service in the early 1970s, and uses some of the components of the French AMX-10P, as well as the same engine. Night vision equipment is fitted as standard.

M60

Type: armoured personnel carrier
Crew: three, plus up to 10 infantrymen
Weights: Empty
Loaded 20,944 lb (9,500 kg)
Dimensions: Length 16 ft 6⅘ in (5.05 m)
Width 9 ft 0¼ in (2.75 m)
Height 5 ft 10⁹⁄₁₀ in (1.8 m)
Ground pressure: 8.53 lb/in² (0.6 kg/cm²)
Performance: road speed 28 mph (45 kph); water speed 3.7 mph (6 kph); range 249 miles (400 km); vertical obstacle 23⅗ in (60.0 cm); trench 6 ft 6¾ in (2.0 m); gradient 60%; ground clearance 13¾ in (35.0 cm); the M60 is fully amphibious, being driven in the water by its tracks
Engine: one 140-hp FAMOS inline diesel engine
Armament: one 12.7-mm machine-gun on the roof, plus one 7.92-mm machine-gun in the hull nose
Armour: ⅖ in (10 mm) minimum; 1 in (25 mm) maximum
Used also by: Cyprus
Notes: The M60 armoured personnel carrier entered service in the early 1950s, and is based on the chassis of the Russian SU-76 assault gun.

M-1931/37 (A-19) gun

Type: field gun
Calibre: 122 mm
Barrel length: 46 cal
Muzzle velocity: 2,625 ft (800 m) per second
Ranges: Maximum 22,747 yards (20,800 m)
Minimum
Elevation: −2° to +65°
Traverse: 58° total
Rate of fire: five or six rounds per minute
Weights For travel 17,432 lb (7,907 kg)
In firing position 15,690 lb (7,117 kg)
Dimensions: Length 25 ft 9⅘ in (7.87 m)
Width 13 ft 11¾ in (2.46 m)
Height 7 ft 5⅓ in (2.27 m)
Ammunition: APHE, HE and Smoke
Crew: nine
Used also by: Albania, Algeria, Bulgaria, China, Cuba, Egypt, Guinea Bissau, Hungary, Indonesia, Kampuchea, North Korea, North Yemen, Poland, Romania, Somali Republic, South Yemen, Spain, Syria, Tanzania, Vietnam, Zaire
Notes: The M-1937 was widely used by the Soviet forces in World War II, and is a useful, if heavy, weapon to this day. The HE projectile weighs 65.2 lb (25.5 kg), while the APHE projectile weighs 55 lb (25 kg), and will penetrate 7.48 in (190 mm) of armour at 1,094 yards (1,000 m).

M-1956 howitzer

Type: field howitzer
Calibre: 105 mm
Barrel length: 27.9 cal
Muzzle velocity: 1,870 ft (570 m) per second
Ranges: Maximum 14,217 yards (13,000 m)
Minimum
Elevation: −12° to +68°
Traverse: 52° total
Rate of fire: six or seven rounds per minute
Weights: For travel
In firing position 4,806 lb (2,180 kg)
Dimensions: Length
Width
Height
Ammunition: HE, HEAT, Illuminating and Smoke
Crew: six
Used only by: Yugoslavia
Notes: The Yugoslav M-1956 is a licence-built US M101 barrel on a Yugoslav carriage. Range is excellent, so the Yugoslavs must have developed new ammunition for the type. Projectile weight is 33 lb (15 kg).

M-1948 B1 howitzer

Type: mountain howitzer
Calibre: 76.2 mm
Barrel length: 15.5 cal
Muzzle velocity: 1,306 ft (398 m) per second
Ranges: Maximum 9,405 yards (8,600 m)
Minimum
Elevation: −15° to +45°
Traverse: 50° total
Rate of fire: six to seven rounds per minute
Weights: For travel
In firing position 1,554 lb (705 kg)
Dimensions: Length 8 ft (2.44 m)
Width 6 ft (1.83 m)
Height 5 ft (1.52 m)
Ammunition: HE, HEAT and Smoke
Crew: six
Used also by: Burma, Sri Lanka
Notes: The M-1948 is a mountain howitzer of moderate performance and Yugoslav origins. The projectile weight is 13.67 lb (6.2 kg), and the HEAT round will penetrate 4 in (102 mm) of armour. The gun is capable of 25 rounds per minute for short periods.

M-1955 cannon mounting

Type: triple AA cannon mounting
Calibre: 20 mm
Barrel length: 70 cal
Muzzle velocity:
Ranges: Maximum (effective) 1,640 yards (1,500 m)
   Minimum
Elevation: −5° to +83°
Traverse: 360°
Rate of fire: 700 rounds per minute (cyclic) per barrel
Weights: For travel
   In firing position 2,582 lb (1,171 kg)
Dimensions: Length 13 ft 3 in (4.04 m)
   Width 4 ft 2 in (1.27 m)
   Height 6 ft 4 in (1.93 m)
Ammunition: AP and HE
Crew: six
Used only by: Yugoslavia
Notes: The M-1955 comprises three Hispano-Suiza HSS 804 cannon on an HSS 630-3 carriage. Each barrel has its own magazine, holding 50 rounds.

M-1965 recoilless rifle

Type: anti-tank recoilless rifle
Calibre: 105 mm
Barrel length:
Muzzle velocity: 1,493 ft (455 m) per second with HEAT
Ranges: Maximum (direct fire) 6,562 yards (6,000 m); (anti-tank) 1,640 yards (1,500 m)
   Minimum
Elevation: −10° to +30°
Traverse: 360°
Rate of fire: six rounds per minute
Weights: For travel
   In firing position 617 lb (280 kg)
Dimensions: Length 14 ft 10½ in (4.55 m)
   Width 4 ft 8⅓ in (1.43 m)
   Height 3 ft 9 in (1.14 m)
Ammunition: HE and HEAT
Crew: five
Used only by: Yugoslavia
Notes: The Yugoslav M-1965 recoilless rifle is a powerful AT and general support weapon tailored for use in mountainous terrain. Spotting is effected by a 12.7-mm machine-gun. The HEAT round will penetrate 13 in (330 mm) of armour at more than 1,094 yards (1,000 m).

M-1960 recoilless rifle

Type: anti-tank recoilless rifle
Calibre: 82 mm
Barrel length:
Muzzle velocity: 1,273 ft (388 m) per second
Ranges: Maximum (indirect fire) 4,921 yards (4,500 m); (AT) 1,640 yards (1,500 m)
   Minimum
Elevation: −20° to +35°
Traverse: 360°
Rate of fire: four or five rounds per minute
Weights: For travel 269 lb (122 kg)
   In firing position as above
Dimensions: Length 7 ft 2⅜ in (2.2 m)
   Width
   Height
Ammunition: HE and HEAT
Crew: two to five
Used only by: Yugoslavia
Notes: The Yugoslav M-1960 is a remarkably light weapon, and is very manoeuvrable. The HEAT projectile weighs 15.87 lb (7.2 kg), and will penetrate 8.66 in (220 mm) of armour at 547 yards (500 m).

M-1963 artillery rocket launcher

Type: mobile artillery rocket launcher
Calibre: 128 mm
Number of barrels: 32
Muzzle velocity: 1,378 ft (420 m) per second
Ranges: Maximum 10,499 yards (9,600 m)
   Minimum
Elevation: 0° to +48°
Traverse: 30°
Time to reload: three minutes
Weights: For travel
   In firing position about 5,512 lb (2,500 kg)
Dimensions: Length
   Width
   Height
Ammunition: HE warhead on rocket
Crew: three to five
Used only by: Yugoslavia
Notes: The Yugoslav M-1963 system is based on the Czech RM-130 rocket, which is 31½ in (0.8 m) long, 5.04 in (12.8 cm) in diameter, and weighs 50.7 lb (23 kg). The launcher is mounted on a small two-wheeled carriage, towed by a lorry. Maximum rate of fire is 160 rounds per minute.

YRML 32 artillery rocket launcher

Type: mobile artillery rocket launcher
Calibre: 128 mm
Number of barrels: 32
Muzzle velocity: 1,378 ft (420 m) per second
Ranges: Maximum 10,499 yards (9,600 m)
　　　　Minimum
Elevation:
Traverse:
Time to reload: two minutes
Weights: For travel
　　　　In firing position
Dimensions: Length
　　　　　　Width
　　　　　　Height
Ammunition: HE warhead on rocket
Crew:
Used only by: Yugoslavia

Notes: The YMRL 32 system is located on the back of a FAP 2222 BDS 6 × 6 lorry, with 32 rockets in the tubes, and another 32 rockets ready for reloading. This Yugoslav system uses either the Czech RM-130 rocket, as does the other Yugoslav launcher, the M-1963, or a new model, which is provided with a more powerful motor increasing maximum speed and improving range to 19,685 yards (18,000 m).

M-1957 launcher

Type: man-portable anti-tank grenade launcher
Calibre: (tube) 44 mm
Barrel length:
Muzzle velocity:
Ranges: Maximum
　　　　Minimum
Elevation:
Traverse:
Rate of fire:
Weights: For travel
　　　　In firing position
Dimensions: Length
　　　　　　Width
　　　　　　Height
Ammunition:
Crew: two
Used only by: Yugoslavia
Notes: The Yugoslav M-1957, or RB57, is derived from the German World War II *Panzerfaust*, and has dimensions and a performance almost identical with those of the Czech P-27.

UBM-52 mortar

Type: heavy mortar
Calibre: 120 mm
Barrel length: 10.75 cal
Muzzle velocity:
Ranges: Maximum 6,573 yards (6,010 m) with light bomb; 5,206 yards (4,760 m) with heavy bomb
　　　　Minimum
Elevation: 45° to 85°
Traverse: 60° at 45° elevation
Rate of fire: 25 rounds per minute
Weights: For travel 1,036 lb (470 kg)
　　　　In firing position 926 lb (420 kg)
Dimensions: Length
　　　　　　Width
　　　　　　Height
Ammunition: HE and Smoke
Crew: five

Used also by: Burma
Notes: The design of this Yugoslav weapon is based on that of the French MO-120 AM 50, adapted to fire Russian ammunition. The design has distinctive solid-tyred spoked wheels. The UBM-52 was conceived for mortar operations in mountainous terrain, and is quite handy for its weight. There are two HE bombs, the heavier weighing 35 lb (15.9 kg) and the lighter 27 lb (12.25 kg).

M-1968 mortar

Type: medium mortar
Calibre: 81 mm
Barrel length: 17.9 cal
Muzzle velocity:
Ranges: Maximum 5,468 yards (5,000 m)
　　　　Minimum 82 yards (75 m)
Elevation: 30° to 85°
Traverse:
Rate of fire: 15 to 25 rounds per minute
Weights: For travel
　　　　In firing position 91.5 lb (41.5 kg)
Dimensions: Length
　　　　　　Width
　　　　　　Height
Ammunition: HE, Illuminating and Smoke
Crew: three
Used only by: Yugoslavia
Notes: This useful Yugoslav mortar has very marked similarities with the French

MO-81-61L, and can fire two types of HE bomb, one weighing 9.26 lb (4.2 kg) and the other 7.05 lb (3.2 kg).

M-1957 mortar

Type: light mortar
Calibre: 60.75 mm
Barrel length:
Muzzle velocity: 522 ft (159 m) per second
Ranges: Maximum 1,859 yards (1,700 m)
Minimum 82 yards (75 m)
Elevation:
Traverse:
Rate of fire: 25 to 30 rounds per minute
Weights: For travel
In firing position 43.4 lb (19.7 kg)
Dimensions: Length
Width
Height
Ammunition: HE, Illuminating and Smoke
Crew: two
Used only by: Yugoslavia
Notes: The Yugoslav M-1957 mortar is an improved version of the US M2 60-mm weapon. The bomb weighs 2.98 lb (1.25 kg).

M-8 mortar

Type: light mortar
Calibre: 50 mm
Barrel length: 11.2 cal
Muzzle velocity: 262 ft (80 m) per second
Ranges: Maximum 525 yards (480 m)
Minimum 148 yards (135 m)
Elevation:
Traverse:
Rate of fire: 25 to 30 rounds per minute
Weights: For travel
In firing position 16.1 lb (7.3 kg)
kg)
Dimensions: Length
Width
Height
Ammunition: HE, Illuminating and Smoke
Crew: one
Used only by: Yugoslavia
Notes: The Yugoslav M-8 light mortar is basically the British 2-in light mortar, with the addition of a carrying handle on the barrel. The firer controls line and elevation directly by hand. The HE bomb weighs 2.2 lb (1 kg).

M65A and M65B machine-guns

Type: light machine-guns
Calibre: 7.62 mm
System of operation: gas
Muzzle velocity: 2,400 ft (732 m) per second
Range: effective 656 yards (600 m)
Rate of fire: 600 rounds per minute (cyclic); 80 rounds per minute (automatic) for M65A; 120 rounds per minute (automatic) for M65B
Cooling system: air
Feed system: 30-round box
Dimensions: Barrel length 18.5 in (470 mm)
Overall length 43.1 in (1.095 m)
Width
Height
Weights: 12 lb (5.45 kg)
Sights: post (fore) and leaf, notch (rear)
Ammunition: 7.62 mm × 39
Used only by: Yugoslavia
Notes: The M65A and M65B are light machine-gun versions of the Yugoslav M64 assault rifle, otherwise the Russian AK-47. The difference between the two weapons is that the M65A has a fixed barrel, and the M65B a quick-change barrel, making it a more effective sustained fire weapon.

M53 machine-gun

Type: general-purpose machine gun
Calibre: 7.92 mm
System of operation: gas-assisted short recoil
Muzzle velocity: 2,480 ft (756 ft) per second
Range: effective 875 yards (800 m) for direct fire; 3,280 yards (3,000 m) for indirect fire
Rate of fire: 1,200 rounds per minute
Cooling system: air
Feed system: metal-link belt
Dimensions: Barrel length 20.98 in (533 mm)
Overall length 48 in (1.219 m)
Width
Height
Weights: 25.57 lb (11.6 kg) with bipod; 42.33 lb (19.2 kg) for tripod
Sights: barleycorn (fore) and tangent, notch (rear)
Ammunition: 7.92 mm × 57
Used only by: Yugoslavia
Notes: The M1953 is the Yugoslav copy of the German MG42 of World War II.

M49 sub-machine gun

Type: sub-machine gun
Calibre: 7.62 mm
System of operation: blowback
Muzzle velocity: 1,640 ft (500 m) per second
Range: effective 219 yards (200 m)
Rate of fire: 700 rounds per minute (cyclic); 120 rounds per minute (automatic)
Cooling system: air
Feed system: 35-round box
Dimensions: Barrel length 10.75 in (273 mm)
Overall length 34.25 in (870 mm)
Width
Height
Weights: 8.71 lb (3.95 kg) unloaded; 10 lb (4.54 kg) loaded
Sights: blade (fore) and flip, notch (rear)
Ammunition: 7.62 mm × 25 Pistol 'P', or 7.63 mm Mauser
Used only by: Yugoslavia
Notes: The Yugoslav M49 is basically the Russian PPSh-41, although the gun is made of machined or drawn parts where the Russian original uses stampings. The M49/57 differs only in details.

M56 sub-machine gun

Type: sub-machine gun
Calibre: 7.62 mm
System of operation: blowback
Muzzle velocity: 1,640 ft (500 m) per second
Range: effective 219 yards (200 m)
Rate of fire: 600 rounds per minute (cyclic);
120 rounds per minute (automatic)
Cooling system: air
Feed system: 35-round box
Dimensions: Barrel length 9.84 in (250 mm)
Overall length 34.25 in (870 mm) with stock extended; 23.27 in (591 mm) with stock folded
Width
Height
Weights: 6.6 lb (3 kg)
Sights: hooded blade (fore) and U notch (rear)

Ammunition: 7.62 mm × 25 Pistol 'P', or 7.63 mm Mauser
Used only by: Yugoslavia
Notes: The M56 appears to have been derived from the German MP40 of World War II, and appears a fragile weapon.

Zaire

30,000 men.

2 tk bns.
2 armd bns.
1 mech bn.
14 inf bns.
5 para, 2 cdo bns.
4 'Guard' bns.
60 Type-62 lt tks (ex-Chinese); 44 AML-90, 122 AML-60 armd cars; 60 M-3 APC; 75mm pack, 122mm, 130mm guns/how; 82mm, 120mm mor; 107mm RL; 57mm ATK guns; 75mm, 106mm RCL; 'Snapper' ATGW; 20mm, 37mm, 40mm AA guns.
(10 M-60 tks, 10 M-113 APC on order.)

Para-Military Forces: 35,000: 8 National Guard, 6 Gendarmerie bns.

Zambia

12,800 men.

1 armd car regt.
8 inf bns.
1 arty bty.
1 AA arty regt.
1 engr sqn.
1 sigs sqn.
10 T-54 tks; 28 Ferret scout cars; 8 M-56 105mm pack how; 24 20mm AA guns.

Para-Military Forces: 1,200; Police Mobile Unit (PMU) 700 (1 bn of 4 coys); Para-Military Police Unit (PMPU) 500 (1 bn of 3 coys). 2 helicopters.

List of Abbreviations

AA	anti-aircraft
AB	airborne
ac	aircraft
AD	air defence
amph	amphibious
AP	armour-piercing
APC	(i) armoured personnel carrier
	(ii) armour-piercing capped
AP-T	armour-piercing tracer
APDS	armour-piercing discarding sabot
APDS-T	armour-piercing discarding sabot tracer
APFSDS	armour-piercing fin-stabilised discarding sabot
APHE	armour-piercing high explosive
API	armour-piercing incendiary
API-T	armour-piercing incendiary tracer
armd	armoured
arty	artillery
AT	anti-tank
ATGW	anti-tank guided weapon
Atk	anti-tank
bde	brigade
bn	battalion
bty	battery
cav	cavalry
cdo	commando
CEP	circular error probable
CLGP	cannon-launched guided projectile
comd	command
comms	communications
coy	company
det	detachment
div	division
engr	engineer
eqpt	equipment
fd	field
GP	general-purpose
GW	guided weapon
HE	high explosive
HEAT	high explosive anti-tank
HEAT-T	high explosive anti-tank tracer
HEI	high explosive incendiary
HEI-T	high explosive incendiary tracer
hel	helicopter
HEP	high explosive phosphorus
HEP-T	high explosive phosphorus tracer
HESH	high explosive squash head
how	howitzer

HVAP	hyper-velocity armour-piercing
HVAP-DS-T	hyper-velocity armour-piercing discarding sabot tracer
hy	heavy
indep	independent
inf	infantry
IT	incendiary tracer
KT	kiloton
lt	light
mech	mechanised
med	medium
mg	machine-gun
MICV	mechanised infantry combat vehicle
mor	mortar
mot	motorised
msl	missile
MT	megaton
para	parachute
pdr	pounder
RAP	rocket-assisted projectile
RCL	recoilless rifle
recce	reconnaissance
regt	regiment
RL	rocket launcher
SAM	surface-to-air missile
SAP	semi-armour-piercing
SAPHEI	semi-armour-piercing high explosive incendiary
SAPHEI-T	semi-armour-piercing high explosive incendiary tracer
SAR	semi-automatic rifle
sig	signal
smg	sub-machine gun
SP	self-propelled
spt	support
sqn	squadron
SSM	surface-to-surface missile
tac	tactical
tk	tank
tp	troop
tpt	transport
trg	training
UNDOF	United Nations Disengagement Observation Force
UNEF	United Nations Emergency Force
UNFICYP	United Nations Force In Cyprus
UNIFIL	United Nations Interim Force In Lebanon
UNTSO	United Nations Truce Supervisory Organisation
veh	vehicle
WP	white phosphorus

Index

Illustration Credits

Picture Editor: Jonathan Moore

Many organisations and archives kindly helped with photographic material during the preparation of this volume. We would particularly like to thank the following for their invaluable assistance:

Australian Department of Defence, Canberra; Bundeswehr Photos, Bonn; Colonel Boulet of the Canadian National Defence Headquarters, Ottawa; Geoff Cornish Esq., London; FMC Corporation, California; E Speakman & S Reed of the Press Photographs Department, Ministry of Defence, London; Mowag Motorwagenfabrik AG, Switzerland; Oy Tampella AB, Tampere; Mrs Sadie Alford of Novosti Press Agency, London; Service d'Information et des Relations Publiques d'Armée, Paris; Thyssen Industrie AG Henschel, Kassel; and the US Army Audio-Visual Activity, Washington DC.

All artworks in this volume were produced by the County Studio, Leicestershire

Unless otherwise indicated, all photographs were supplied through Military Archive & Research Services (MARS) London.

Key to picture positions: (T) = top, (C) = centre, (B) = bottom, (UC) = upper centre, (LC) = lower centre.

12(T)   T-54/T-55 main battle tanks. An air landing unit at rest (Novosti Press Agency)
(B)   T-54/T-55 main battle tanks move up onto the beach (Novosti Press Agency)
15(T)   MG42 machine-gun, mounted on a weapons carrier (Associated Press Photo)
(B)   TAM medium tank developed by Thyssen Henschel of West Germany for the Argentine Army (Thyssen Henschel, Kassel)
16(T)   AMX-VCI of the Netherlands Army – a version of the AMX-VTP M-56 (Netherlands Army, Amsterdam)
(BL)   35-mm GDF-001 Oerlikon anti-aircraft gun of the Austrian Army (Heerefilm, Vienna)
(BR)   Oerlikon 35-mm twin anti-aircraft gun type GDF-001 of the Swiss Air Force deployed for action (Swiss Air Force, Berne)
17   Australian M113 armoured personnel carriers on the move; 1976 (Defence PR, Canberra)
18(T)   M113A1 with Gun Armour Kit (FMC, San Jose, California)
(C)   Australian gunners firing 5.5-in artillery (Defence PR, Canberra)
(B)   5.5-in guns of 'C' Battery, 3 Royal Horse Artillery during CO's test exercise at Sai Kung, Hong Kong New Territories; 1973 (Crown Copyright (MOD-Army), London)
19   Australian soldier carrying a 9-mm F1 sub-machine gun; 1974 (Defence PR, Canberra)
20(T)   M47 main battle tank of the Bundeswehr (Federal German Army, Bonn)
(C)   4KH7FA-B Greif recovery tank (Steyr-Daimler-Puch, Austria)
(B)   Saurer Schützenpanzer 4K4FA armoured personnel carrier (Steyr-Daimler-Puch, Austria)
21(T)   M42 self-propelled, 40-mm twin anti-aircraft gun (US Army Photograph)
(C)   Steyr 9-mm sub-machine gun (Steyr-Daimler-Puch, Austria)
(B)   Oerlikon Type GAI-BO1 20-mm cannon (Oerlikon-Bührle Ltd. Zurich)
22   Ferret scout car of the Canadian Armed Forces; 1971 (Canadian Armed Forces, Ottawa)
23   Scorpion light tank (Alvis Ltd. Warwickshire)
24(T)   5PFZ-CA1 self-propelled 35-mm anti-aircraft armoured fighting vehicle in service with the Netherlands Army (Netherlands Army, Holland)
(B)   Spartan CVR(T) armoured personnel carrier (Crown Copyright (MOD-Army), London)
25   Milan man-portable anti-tank guided missile, showing both the launch tube/container and sight (Euromissile, France)
26   MAG light machine-gun team of the Netherlands Army (Netherlands Army, Amsterdam)
27(T)   FAL 7.62-mm rifle (heavy barrel) (Associated Press Photo)
(B)   M3 A1 Stuart tank of the Brazilian Army (Brazilian Army, Brazilia)
28   EE-17 Sucuri tank destroyer of the Brazilian Army (Brazilian Army Photo, Brazilia)
29(T)   EE-11 Urutu armoured personnel carrier of the Brazilian Army fitted with 90-mm gun turret (Brazilian Army, Brazilia)
(B)   EE-11 Urutu armoured personnel carrier of the Brazilian Army (Brazilian Army, Brazilia)
30   M59 armoured personnel carrier (Greek Army, Athens)
31   AT 104 armoured personnel carrier (Short Brothers Ltd., Belfast)
32   Comet light tank of the South African Army (South African Army)
34(T)   Panhard AML-245 with H-90 turret (South African Army)
(B)   AML 245 60 HB.127 with 60-mm Brandt mortar (Panhard-Lavassor, Paris)
35(T)   M40A2 recoilless rifle of the US Army (US Army Photograph)
(B)   Deploying a 106-mm recoilless rifle of the Swiss Army (Swiss Army, Berne)
37(T)   Leopard A2 main battle tank (Krauss-Maffei AG, FGR)
(B)   Leopard A main battle tank of the Canadian Armed Forces (Canadian Armed Forces, Ottawa)
38(T)   Leopard armoured recovery vehicle with two MTU MB 838 Ca. M500 10-cylinder multi fuel engines (Krauss-Maffei AG, FGR)
(B)   Cougar fire support vehicle of the Canadian Armed Forces; 1977 (Canadian Armed Forces, Ottawa)
39(T)   Lynx command and reconnaissance vehicle as supplied to the Canadian Armed Forces (FMC, California)
(B)   Canadian soldiers carrying the C1 7.62-mm rifle (Canadian Armed Forces, Ottawa)
40   105-mm (towed) howitzer (Canadian Armed Forces, Ottawa)
42   M-46 130-mm field gun (Novosti Press Agency)

96(T)	M-1965 Tampella mortar (Soltam Ltd., Haifa)
(B)	Tampella 120-mm light mortar (Soltam Ltd., Haifa)
97(T)	M-1964 Tampella mortar (81-mm, long barrel) (Soltam Ltd., Haifa)
(B)	Tampella mortar Type A (Soltam Ltd., Haifa)
98(T)	Tampella mortar Type B (Soltam Ltd., Haifa)
(B)	Tampella mortar Type C (Soltam Ltd., Haifa)
99(T)	UZI sub-machine gun (Israel Military Industries)
(B)	Galil ARM assault rifle manufactured by Israel Military Industries (Israel Military Industries)
101	Italian Infantry Armoured Fighting Vehicle based on the M113 family of vehicles (OTO-Melara, Italy)
102	M-1956 105/14 howitzer (Canadian Armed Forces, Ottawa)
104(T)	Pz 51 (AMX-13) light tanks of the Swiss Army (Swiss Army, Berne)
(B)	Pz 51 (AMX-13) light tank of the Swiss Army (Swiss Army, Berne)
105	Type 74 tank of the Japanese Army (Keystone Press Agency)
106	KAM-9 battlefield anti-tank missile of the Japanese Self-Defence Force (Kawasaki Heavy Industries, Tokyo)
107	KAM-3D battlefield anti-tank missile ready for firing with the Japanese Self-Defence Force (Kawasaki Heavy Industries, Tokyo)
108	Type 64 rifle of the Japanese Self-Defence Force (Associated Press, London)
109	M52 self-propelled howitzer (US Army Photograph)
110	Vigilant wire-guided anti-tank guided missile deployed with members of the Parachute Regiment of the British Army (Crown Copyright (MOD-Army), London)
112(T)	EE-9 Cascavel armoured car of the Brazilian Army (Brazilian Army, Brasilia)
(B)	EE-9 Cascavel armoured car of the Brazilian Army fitted with 90-mm cannon (Brazilian Army, Brasilia)
116	Beretta Model 70/223/5.56-mm rifle (Beretta Spa, Brescia)
117(T)	Armoured Infantry Fighting Vehicle as delivered to the Netherlands Army (FMC, California)
(B)	YP-408 PW-MT mortar tractor towing 120-mm Brandt mortar (DAF, The Netherlands)
121(T)	Launch of a Rapier missile during trials by the British services at a Ministry of Defence range in the United Kingdom (British Aircraft Corporation, London, GB)
(B)	Cobra 2000 anti-tank missile system here deployed on a West German army field car. At launch the Cobra 'jumps' thanks to downward-directed nozzles (Messerschmitt-Bölkow-Blohm, GFR)
123	UR-416 armoured personnel carrier (Thyssen Henschel, Kassel)
124	MOWAG Roland armoured personnel carrier fitted with bullet-proof cross-country wheels (Mowag, Switzerland)
125	HK 21 being used in conjunction with column mount 2400 (Heckler & Koch Gmbh, Oberndorf)
126	Tigercat is a surface-to-air missile system (the land-based version of the Seacat) and is capable of being moved in two Land Rovers in its basic form. Tigercat is in service with the RAF Regiment in Britain and in several overseas armies (Shorts Ltd, Northern Ireland, GB)
128	AMX-30 S401A self-propelled 30-mm twin-gun anti-aircraft system (Thomson-CSF/Roger Violet, France)
130(T)	M-1968 155-mm howitzer being fired (Soltam Ltd., Haifa)
(B)	M-1938 122-mm howitzer battery (Novosti Press Agency)
131	Ratel 20 armoured personnel carrier of the South African Army (South African Army)
132	LVTP-7 amphibious assault vehicle of the US Marine Corps (FMC Corporation, USA)
134(L)	120-mm ECIA Model SL mortar (Esperanza y Cia SA, Spain)
(C)	105-mm ECIA Model L mortar (Esperanza y Cia SA, Spain)
(R)	81-mm ECIA Model L1 mortar (Esperanza y Cia SA, Spain)
135(T)	60-mm ECIA Commando Model C mortar (Esperanza y Cia SA, Spain)
(B)	60-mm ECIA Model L mortar (Esperanza y Cia SA, Spain)
137	Strv 103(S tanks) and Pbv 302 armoured personnel carriers of the Swedish Army during manoeuvres (Swedish Army, Stockholm)
138	Ikv 91 light tank infantry support vehicles during firing practice on the Swedish Army ranges (AB Hägglund & Söner, Sweden)
139	Bgbv 82 armoured recovery vehicle of the Swedish Army. The forward turret is fitted with a 20-mm cannon and the front of the vehicle can withstand 20-mm ammunition (AB Hägglund & Söner, Sweden)
140(TL)	Bantam RB 53 wire-guided anti-tank guided missile of the Swedish Army in its transport and firing container (Swedish Army, Stockholm)
(TR)	Bantam RB 53 wire-guided anti-tank guided missile of the Swedish Army being test fired (Swedish Army, Stockholm)
(B)	Eight Bantam anti-tank guided missiles on a Swiss Army vehicle (Swiss Army, Berne)
142(T)	Swedish 90-mm PY-1110 anti-tank rifle of the Irish Army (Irish Army Photo, Dublin)
(B)	Bofors M54 57-mm anti-aircraft gun of the Swedish Army (Swedish Army Photo, Stockholm)
143	40-mm towed light anti-aircraft gun M-1948 of the Finnish Army (Finnish Army, Helsinki)
144(T)	Bofors M-1948 40-mm light anti-aircraft gun of the Norwegian Army (Norwegian Army Photo, Oslo)
(B)	Carl Gustaf M2 84-mm recoilless rifle deployed ready for action (FFV Ordnance Division, Sweden)
145(T)	Carl Gustaf M2 84-mm recoilless rifle deployed ready for action. The loader kneels with a reload round ready (FFV Ordnance Div., Sweden)
(C)	Carl Gustaf 84-mm recoilless rifle M2 deployed ready for action (FFV Ordnance Div., Sweden)
(B)	Miniman expendable short-range anti-tank weapon of the Swedish Army shortly after being fired. (Swedish Army, Stockholm)

147	Pz 68 GT main battle tank of the Swiss Army (Swiss Federal Construction Works, Thun)
148	Pz 61 main battle tank of the Swiss Army (Swiss Federal Construction Works, Thun)
149	MOWAG Grenadier armoured personnel carrier (Mowag, Switzerland)
150(T)	Bloodhound medium/high altitude missile immediately after launch (B.A.C. Guided Weapons Div., Herts, G.B.)
(B)	Bloodhound Mk 2 surface-to-air missile system (Swiss Air Force, Berne)
151	M-109U 155-mm self-propelled howitzer of the Swiss Army (Swiss Army, Berne)
152(T)	Swiss Army 105-mm anti-tank gun deployed for action (Swiss Army, Berne)
(B)	Swiss Army 90-mm anti-tank gun deployed for action (Swiss Army, Berne)
153	Swiss infantryman with an 83-mm M-1958 recoilless anti-tank rifle (Swiss Army, Berne)
154(T)	Loading an 83-mm M-1958 recoilless anti-tank rifle of the Swiss Army (Swiss Army, Berne)
(B)	Mw 72 81-mm medium mortar of the Swiss Army (Eidgenössische Waffenfabrik, Berne)
155(TL)	Mw 64 120-mm heavy mortar of the Swiss Army (Eidgenössische Waffenfabrik, Berne)
(TR)	Mw 64 120-mm mortar of the Swiss Army (Eidgenössische Waffenfabrik, Berne)
(B)	Mw 33 81-mm mortar of the Swiss Army (Eidgenössische Waffenfabrik, Berne)
156	SIG MG 710-3 machine-gun (SIG, Neuhausen Rheine Falls)
158	ZSU-57-2 self-propelled 57-mm anti-aircraft weapon system of the Finnish Army (Finnish Army, Helsinki)
159	M-1943 152-mm howitzer of the Soviet Army (Novosti Press Agency)
160	HK 33 cal 5.56-mm combat rifle (Heckler & Koch Gmbh, Oberndorf)
161	*Panzerjäger* 'K' Kürassier self-propelled anti-tank gun of the Austrian Army (Heeresfilm, Vienna)
163(T)	BTR-60PB eight-wheeled amphibious personnel carrier of the Soviet Army (Camera Press Ltd, photo by Novosti)
(B)	T-54/55 tanks of the Soviet Army (Novosti Press Agency)
164	T-62 tanks of the Soviet Army (Novosti Press Agency)
166	BMD light tank of the Soviet airborne forces. Over the 73-mm main gun is mounted a Sagger anti-tank missile (Crown Copyright (MOD), London)
167	Soviet SS-1B 'Scud' tactical battlefield missile of the Soviet Army on its transporter (Crown Copyright (MOD), London)
168	Soviet SS-12 'Scaleboard' tactical battlefield missile of the Soviet Army on its transporter (Crown Copyright (MOD), London)
169	FROG-3 battlefield missile of the Soviet Army (Camera Press Ltd, photograph by Novosti)
171(T)	BM-21 artillery rocket launcher of the Soviet Army (Novosti Press Agency)
(B)	AT-2 'Swatter' anti-tank rocket on a BRDM-1 vehicle of the Soviet Army (Camera Press Ltd)
172	AT-3 'Sagger' wire-guided anti-tank missile of the Soviet Army. The missile and carrying case, which also forms part of the launch pad, can be carried and brought into action by a single infantryman (Crown Copyright (MOD), London)
173(T)	SA-4 'Ganef' surface-to-air tactical guided missile of the Soviet Army (Novosti Press Agency)
(B)	SA-6 'Gainful' surface-to-air missile of the Soviet Army on its tracked carrier (Crown Copyright (MOD), London)
174	SA-9 'Gaskin' surface-to-air missiles mounted on a BRDM afv of the Soviet Army (Crown Copyright (MOD), London)
175	SA-7 'Grail' portable anti-aircraft missile launchers of the Soviet Army (Crown Copyright (MOD), London)
176	100-mm M-1955 gun, during Soviet Army exercises (Novosti Press Agency)
178	M-1953 mortar of the Soviet Army (Novosti Press Agency)
179	120-mm mortar of the Austrian Army (Heeresfilm, Vienna)
181	SKS 7.62-mm rifle of the Soviet Army (Associated Press Photo)
182(T)	AK-47 7.62-mm rifle of the Soviet Army (Novosti Press Agency)
(B)	AKM assault rifle (Novosti Press Agency)
185	Chieftain main battle tank of B Sqdn, Queen's Royal Irish Hussars on exercise in the Polle area of West Germany; January 1973 (Crown Copyright (MOD-Army), London)
186(T)	Three FV432s of the 2nd Royal Irish Rangers awaiting orders to attack during exercise Swordthrust; October 1975 (Crown Copyright (MOD-Army), London)
(C)	Shorland SB.301 armoured personnel carrier (Short Brothers Ltd., Belfast)
(B)	GKN Sankey AT105 armoured personnel carrier seen here in standard escort configuration; July 1978 (Crown Copyright (MOD-Army), London)
187(T)	AT105 armoured personnel carriers (Short Brothers Ltd., Belfast)
(B)	Swingfire long-range anti-tank missile being launched from a Ferret scout car of the Parachute Squadron of the Royal Armoured Corps (British Aerospace Corp. London)
188(T)	Blowpipe is mainly a man-portable anti-aircraft missile and shoulder-fired launch tube. It is capable of dealing with lightly armoured vehicles and small surface craft and has been fitted in both ships and aircraft (Shorts Ltd, Belfast)
(B)	FH-70 155-mm gun-howitzer during firing exercises at Larkhill, Wiltshire for the British Army (Crown Copyright (MOD-Army), London)
189(T)	Abbot self-propelled guns firing on Salisbury Plain; February 1978 (Crown Copyright (MOD-Army), London)
(B)	105-mm Light Gun being fired on Salisbury Plain by 13 Light Battery, RA; October 1975 (Crown Copyright (MOD-Army), London)
190(T)	Wombat anti-tank team from 'A' Company, 2 Parachute Regiment in NBC protective clothing fires practice rounds on the Sennelager Ranges, W. Germany; 1976 (Crown Copyright (MOD-Army), London)
(B)	Men of the 1st Bn. The Gordon Highlanders receive instructions on a Mobat anti-tank gun; October 1972 (Crown Copyright (MOD-Army), London)
191(T)	81-mm light mortar being prepared for firing by the British Army (Crown Copyright

230(T) *Armbrust* 300 (Crossbow) is a lightweight man-portable anti-tank missile weighing 4.8 kg (10.6 lb) (Messerschmitt-Bölkow-Blohm, Munich, W. Germany)

(B) HK11 light machine-gun with dual drum fitting (Heckler & Koch GmbH, Oberndorf)

231 HK13 light machine-gun with drum magazine (Heckler & Koch GmbH, Oberndorf)

232 MG3 machine-gun (Federal German Army, Bonn)

233 MP5 SD2 sub-machine gun (Heckler & Koch GmbH, Oberndorf)